THE
SCOTS WORTHIES

BY

JOHN HOWIE
OF LOCHGOIN

REVISED BY

W. H. CARSLAW, D.D.

EDINBURGH
THE BANNER OF TRUTH TRUST

THE BANNER OF TRUTH TRUST
3 Murrayfield Road, Edinburgh EH12 6EL
P.O. Box 621, Carlisle, Pennsylvania 17013, USA

*

This edition first published 1870
Reprinted Banner of Truth Trust 1995
ISBN 0 85151 686 6

*

Printed in Finland by WSOY

CONTENTS.

Contents.

Contents.

Contents.

Preface by the Editor

CCORDING to a family tradition, the accuracy of which
we have no reason to question, three brothers of the
name of Howie (Huet?), belonging to the Albigenses
in the south of France, were obliged, towards the close
of the 12th century, to seek refuge in this land from
the storm of Romish persecution. One of them settled
in the parish of Mearns; another in the parish of
Craigie; while the third took up his abode at Lochgoin, a lonely farm-house in the parish of Fenwick, between Glasgow
and Kilmarnock, still occupied by his descendants after the lapse of
about 700 years.

From its situation in the very heart of a wild moorland waste, as
well as from the religious character of its inmates, this humble dwelling became a favourite resort of the Covenanters during the period
of persecution; and, indeed, there are few places in the West of
Scotland, the bare mention of whose name recalls so many associa-
tions of covenanting interest. Here were often assembled many of
those faithful witnesses of Christ, whose lives are briefly recorded in
this volume; and many an incident of thrilling interest happened at
this lonely spot in the moors of Fenwick. Once when Captain Paton
and four others were met to spend the night in prayer and fellowship,
they were surprised by a company of dragoons; and had it not been

for the presence of mind and courage of Isabel Howie, the mistress of the house (*see* p. 488), they would probably all have been taken. This brave woman was often obliged to seek shelter on the moor; and many a cold night she spent in the moss-hags with a baby at her breast. Her husband and son, too, were subjected to much suffering, frequently having had to run for their lives. Twelve times was their house plundered; and on one occasion their cattle were all driven away, but, through the kindness of Sir William Muir of Rowallan, were afterwards recovered. Still, notwithstanding the frequent and imminent· danger to which they were exposed, James Howie and his son John were both permitted to survive the Revolution, and to share in the joy with which the nation welcomed that event. In a pamphlet, which first appeared about fifty years ago, one of the Howies has the honour assigned him of announcing the tidings to the neighbourhood around. "What do I see?" said the laird of Torfoot, alarmed at the approach of a horseman, and making ready for any danger that might be at hand—"What do I see? But one trooper? And that motley crowd is a rabble—not a troop. That trooper is not of Claverse's band: nor does he belong to Douglas, nor to Inglis, nor to Strachan's dragoons. He waves a small flag. I can discover the scarlet and blue colour of the Covenanter's flag. Ha! welcome you, John Howie of Lochgoin. But what news? Lives our country? Lives the good old cause?" "Glorious news!" exclaimed Howie; "Scotland for ever! She is free. The tyrant James has abdicated. The Stuarts are banished by an indignant nation. Orange triumphs. Our wounds are binding up. Huzza! Scotland and King William and the Covenant for ever!" This Howie, who was the grandfather of our author, lived to the advanced age of 90, and died on the 29th day of June 1755.

John Howie, the author of the "Scots Worthies," was born at Lochgoin on the 14th November 1735. When but a child he was removed to the farm of Blackshill, in the parish of Kilmarnock, occupied by his maternal grandparents, to whose care he was entrusted, and with whom he lived till he reached the age of manhood. When old enough for the purpose, he was sent first to a school at Whirlhall, taught by an uncle, and afterwards to another at Horsehill, where he obtained only a very ordinary education, but where he probably acquired those studious habits, which he retained through life, and turned to such good account. He had other advantages, moreover, which should not be overlooked or undervalued. The friends with whom he lived were pious and intelligent, and would do all in their power to promote his mental and moral improvement; and his grandfather at Lochgoin could not fail to take an interest in the boy, and to encourage the desire which he early manifested to acquaint himself with the sufferings and exploits of the Covenanters. We can easily, without much stretch of imagination, picture to ourselves the old man in his chair, with the boy standing before him, while the former related to his eager listener some of those incidents in which he himself had taken a part, and which are recorded in the following pages. And yet, taking all these circumstances into account, it cannot cease to be a matter of surprise and admiration, that one in his position, and with his imperfect education, should have been able to attain that literary eminence which he afterwards reached, and which he still holds in the estimation of the pious peasantry of Scotland.

The events of his life were few, and of little or no general interest. He was married twice—first to Jean Lindsay, who died soon after, leaving behind her an infant son; and then to his cousin, Janet Howie, a woman of eminent piety, by whom he had five sons and three daughters. It is from the time of this second marriage that he dates his thorough consecration to God in the account he has left us of his religious experience; and from this time, also, he became more assiduous in prosecuting those literary labours, which have given distinction to his name, and have done so much to keep alive the memory of our persecuted forefathers. The first edition of the "Worthies" was published in the year 1775; but, besides it, he prepared and sent to the press, at different periods, the following treatises: (1.) A "Collection of Lectures and Sermons," by some of the most eminent and faithful ministers during the persecution; (2.) An "Alarm to a Secure Generation;" (3.) "Faithful Contendings Displayed," or an account of the state of the Church of Scotland from 1681 till 1691; (4.) "Faithful Witness-bearing Exemplified," consisting of several small treatises, which he collected and prefaced; (5.) "Patronage Anatomised," prepared in connection with the forced settlement of a minister at Fenwick, and published at the request of the parishioners; (6.) "A Vindication of the mode of taking the Elements in the Lord's Supper before giving Thanks;" (7.) "Clarkson's Plain Reasons for Dissenting," with a preface and notes, and an abstract of the principles of the Reformed Presbytery regarding civil government; (8.) "The Looking-glass of the Law of the Gospel," by Mr Brown of Wamphray, with a preface. These works are of varying merit, and some of them demanded much less time and thought than others. But they are a striking testimony to his zeal and diligence, and afford a remarkable illustration of what even a humble and comparatively illiterate man can accomplish by patient and persevering application. When we take into account his position, his education, the time he was obliged to devote to his farm, and the state of his health, which was never robust, but became very infirm towards the close of his life; and when we add to these his seclusion, which, though favourable to study, deprived him of the advantage accruing from the contact of one mind with another, we may well feel surprised at the number and character of his writings; and we need not hesitate to assign to him a prominent place among the peasant writers either of this or of any other land. Many testimonies could easily be adduced to his character and usefulness, both as a Christian and an author; but for the present I must refrain.

It may be interesting to some of my readers to know the terms in which he is referred to by the author of " Old Mortality." When that novel appeared, it was thought by many that the strange being, the repairer of the tombs of the martyrs, whose character the novelist has attempted to delineate, was no other than old John Howie of Lochgoin. This impression, indeed, was so general, that I find the identity of the two is distinctly affirmed both in M'Gavin's and Blackie's edition of the " Scots Worthies." In a letter, however, addressed to my father, which is now in my possession, and which is dated " Abbotsford, 2d May 1827," Sir Walter Scott says : " In reply to your inquiry, I beg to assure you that I did not think of John Howie of Lochgoin, the fine old chronicler of the Cameronians, when the sketch of ' Old Mortality' was drawn. In fact, that character is one of the few I have ever attempted to delineate which had a real identical existence. The real name of Old Mortality was Paterson : his Christian name I have forgotten, but believe it was John," etc.

Besides a library, consisting of several hundred volumes, our author succeeded in collecting many interesting relics of the Covenanting times, to see which, and to visit the abode of the author of the " Scots Worthies," large numbers of people annually come from a distance. Among the curiosities at Lochgoin, are Captain Paton's sword and Bible—the sword which he used so well in so many conflicts, and the Bible, also well used, which he handed to his wife from the scaffold immediately before his execution. There are also a flag and drum—the flag bearing the following inscription : PHINICK

COVENANTING RELICS AT LOCHGOIN.

FOR GOD C^OUNTRY AND COVENANTED WORK **OF** REFORMATION

John Howie had also succeeded in collecting several valuable MSS. of Covenanting interest, but many of these are either in the hands of friends, or lost altogether. I have in my possession a volume, in Howie's own handwriting, containing the notes of seventy-five lectures and sermons, delivered by the most eminent of the field preachers, and hitherto unpublished.

The present edition of the " Scots Worthies " claims to be a reprint of the original work as it passed, revised and enlarged, from the hands of the author in 1781. Nothing has been omitted except a few of the notes, with which the pages were overloaded, and the appendix, containing an account of the wicked lives and miserable deaths of some of the most notable apostates and persecutors. This did not really form an integral part of the work ; and besides, it is regarded by many as proceeding on an unsafe and erroneous principle. Nothing new has been inserted without being carefully marked ; and even these insertions have been made as few and brief as possible, their principal object being to supply important historical links for the reader's information and guidance. A few of Howie's notes have also been put into the text where this could easily be done, and several verbal corrections have been made : but this is absolutely all the change which the book has undergone. Uniformly I have endeavoured to proceed upon the principle of allowing the author to tell his story in his own homely way, and of refraining from any interference with the narrative, even when I may have happened to differ from it.

Whether the plan which has been followed, will commend itself to my readers or not, remains to be seen : but I have been gratified, since the completion of the work, to observe that a similar plan was suggested to my father, while planning a new edition of the " Scots Worthies," by the late Dr M'Crie. In a letter written in 1834, after referring to the remarks in his Life of Knox on the gift of prophecy ascribed to some of the Covenanters, he says :

"If I were to treat the subject afresh, I would perhaps be disposed to interpose more cautions against the danger of mistaking the impressions of a heated imagination for supernatural communications. The extravagant pretensions of the Rowites, in our own day, shows the danger of this extreme, and the tendency of the human mind, in certain circumstances, to fall into it. I have observed generally in good men, that when the imagination was under the control of the judgment, there was little of the marvellous in their biography ; when the imagination predominated, something like miracle ran through their experiences of the events of their life. Calvin is an example of the former, and Luther of the latter. Allowance also must be made, I think, for the scenes and excitement in which individuals were placed and acted. When our fathers were driven from their homes, obliged to live in dens and caves, to traverse mountains and morasses, and when they often made hairbreadth escapes, it was not unnatural for them to yield to extraordinary impressions, produced on their minds by the singular circumstances in which they found themselves. I may add, that in several instances I have been able to trace what have been called prophetical intimations to very simple declarations, which the persons who uttered them never intended to ascribe to supernatural communications. On these grounds I do not give much faith to such prophecies as have been ascribed to Mr Peden and others, and think the interests of religion and the credit of our Worthies would have been much better consulted had they been suppressed. I mention these things as a specimen of the cautions to which I refer. Of course I do not suppose that, in giving a new edition of the ' Scots Worthies,' you would think of altering or expunging any part of the volume; *for I am a great enemy to garbling the works of deceased authors.* . . . I should like that the appendix consisting of an account of the judgments executed on persecutors, were omitted; which, in my opinion, adds neither to the value nor the credibility of the work."

It only remains for me to add, regarding the author of the volume, that after much domestic affliction, and after a painful and protracted illness, induced, as was generally thought, by the damp and unhealthy character of the apartment in which he prosecuted his studies, he died on the 5th of January 1793, and was buried beside his ancestors in the churchyard of Fenwick, where a simple gravestone marks the place where his ashes repose. "Blessed are the dead which die in the Lord from henceforth; yea, saith the Spirit, that they may rest from their labours; and their works do follow them."

W. H. CARSLAW.

HELENSBURGH, *December* 1870.

JOHN HOWIE'S FARM AT LOCHGOIN.

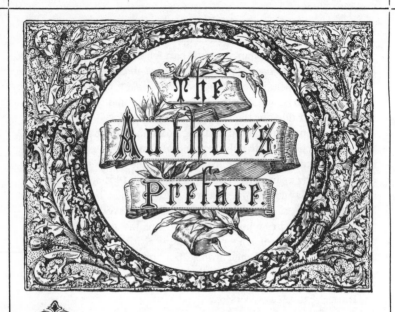

THE design of the following Work was to collect, from the best authorities, a summary account of the lives, characters, and contendings, of a certain number of our most renowned SCOTS WORTHIES, who, for their faithful services, ardent zeal, constancy in sufferings, and other Christian graces and virtues, deserve honourable memorial in the Church of Christ; and for which their names have been, and will be, savoury to all the true lovers of our Zion, while Reformation principles are regarded in Scotland.

Perhaps at first view, some may be surprised to find one so obscure appearing in a work of this nature, especially when there are so many fit hands for such an employment. But if the respect I have for the memories of these Worthies, the familiar acquaintance and sweet fellowship that once subsisted betwixt some of them and some of my ancestors, but, above all, the love and regard which I have for the same cause which they owned and maintained, be not sufficient to apologize for me in this, then I must crave thy patience to hear me in a few particulars; which I hope will plead my excuse for this undertaking.

First, Having for some time had a desire to see something of this kind published, but finding nothing thereof (except a few broken accounts interspersed throughout different publications), at last I took up a resolution to publish a second edition of the life of one of these Worthies already published at large (Renwick's Life by Shields, published 1724). Yet, upon farther reflection, I considered it would be better to collect into one volume the most material relations of as many of our Scots Worthies as could be obtained, from such of the historical records, biographical accounts, and other authenticated manuscripts, as I could have access unto, together with the substance of those lives already in print; which, being all put together, I thought would not only prove useful in giving the reader the pleasure of viewing all at once that which before was scattered up and down in so many corners, but also, at the same time, might be free of the inconveniences that little pamphlets often fall under.

And yet, at the same time, I am aware that some may expect to find a more full account of these Worthies, both as to their number, and matters of fact, than what is here to be met with. But in this publication it is not pretended to give an account either of all our Scots Worthies, or all their transactions: for that were a task now altogether impracticable, and that upon several accounts.

1. There have been many, of different ranks and degrees of men, famous in the Church of Scotland, of whom little more is mentioned in history than their names, places of abode, and the age wherein they existed, and scarcely so much. Again, there are many others, of whom the most that can be stated is only a few faint hints, which, of necessity, must render their lives very imperfect, from what they might and would have been, had they been collected and written nearly a century ago, when their actions and memories were more fresh and recent; several persons being then alive who were well acquainted with their lives and proceedings, whereby they might have been confirmed by many incontestible evidences that cannot now possibly be brought in; yea, and more so, seeing there is a chasm in our history during the time of the Usurper; not to mention how many of our national records were about that time altogether lost.*

* Of these records belonging to the State, carried away by Cromwell to secure our dependence on England, there were 85 hogsheads lost, December 18, 1660, in a ship belonging to Kirkaldy, as she was bringing them back from London. And as for the Church records and registers, a great many of them (either through the confusion of the civil wars, or falling into the hands of the prelates, while prelacy prevailed in Scotland) are also amissing.—*Preface to Stevenson's History.*

2. There were several others, both in the reforming and suffering periods, of whom somewhat is now recorded, and yet not sufficient to form a narrative; so that, excepting by short relations, or marginal notes, their lives cannot be otherwise supplied. For it is with regret that the publishers have it to declare, that, upon application unto several places for farther information concerning some of these worthy men, they could find little or nothing in the most part of their registers (excepting a few things by the way of oral tradition), the information sought being, through course of time, either designedly, or by negligence, lost.

3. Some few of these lives already in print being somewhat prolix, it seemed proper to abridge them; which is done in a manner as comprehensive as possible, so that nothing material is omitted; which, it is hoped, will be thought to be no way injurious to their memory.

Secondly, As to the utility of this subject. Biography in general, as Wodrow has observed, must be one of the most entertaining parts of history; and how much more the lives and transactions of our noble SCOTS WORTHIES, wherein is contained not only a short compend of the testimony and wrestlings of the Church of Scotland for nearly the space of two hundred years—yea, from the earliest period of Christianity in Scotland, the Introduction included—but also a great variety of other things, both instructive and entertaining, which must at once both edify and refresh the serious and understanding reader.

1. In these lives we have a short view of the actions, achievements, and some of the failings of our ancestors, set forth before us as examples for our caution and imitation; wherein, by the experience, and at the expense of former ages, we may learn, by a train of prudent reflections, important lessons for our conduct in life, both in faith and manners; for the furnishing ourselves with the like Christian armour of zeal, faithfulness, holiness, steadfastness, meekness, patience, humility, and other graces.

2. In them we behold what the wisest of men could not think on without astonishment, that "God doth in very deed dwell with men upon earth" (men a little too low for heaven and much too high for earth); nay more, dealeth so familiarly with them, as to make them previously acquainted with His secret designs, both of judgment and mercy, displaying His Divine power and the efficacy of His grace through their infirmities, subduing the most hardened sinners to Himself, while He, as it were, resigns Himself to their prayers, and makes them the subject of His divine care and superintendence.

3. In them we have as it were a mirror, exemplifying and setting forth all the virtues and duties of a religious and a domestic life. Here is the example of a virtuous nobleman, an active statesman, a religious gentleman, a faithful and painful minister in the exercise of his office, "instant in season and out of season," a wise and diligent magistrate, "one fearing God and hating covetousness," a courageous soldier, a good christian, a loving husband, an indulgent parent, a faithful friend in every exigency; and in a word, almost every character worthy of our imitation.

4. In them we have the various changes of soul exercise, experiences, savoury expressions, and last words, of those once living, now glorified witnesses of Christ. And as the last speeches of men are remarkable, how remarkable then must the last words and dying expressions of these noble witnesses and martyrs of Christ be! For the nearer the dying saint is to heaven, and the more of the presence of Christ that he has in his last moments, when death looks him in the face, the more interesting will his conversation be to survivors, and particularly acceptable to real Christians; because all that he says is supported by example, which commonly has considerable influence upon the human mind.

> Sure 'tis a serious thing to die! my soul,
> What a strange moment must it be, when neai
> Thy journey's end, thou hast the gulph in view!
> That awful gulph no mortal e'er repass'd
> To tell what's doing on the other side.—*The Grave, by Blair.*

It is true, there is an innate and latent evil in man's nature, that makes him more prone and obsequious to follow bad rather than good examples; yet sometimes, yea often, there is a kind of compulsive energy arising from the good examples of such as are eminent either in place or godliness, leading forth others to imitate them in the like graces and virtues. We find that the children of Israel followed the Lord all the days of Joshua, and of the elders that outlived him; and Christ's harbinger, John the Baptist, gained as much by his practice and example as by his doctrine: his apparel, his diet, his conversation, and all, did preach forth his holiness. Nazianzen said of him, "that he cried louder by the holiness of his life, than by the sincerity of his doctrine." And were it not so, the apostle Paul would not have exhorted the Philippians unto this, saying, "brethren, be followers together of me, and mark them which walk so as ye have us for an ensample" (Phil. iii. 17). And so says the apostle James, "Take, my brethren, the prophets who have spoken in the name of the Lord, for an example" (Jas. v. 10). And there is no question, that, next to the down-pouring of the Spirit from on high, the rapid and admirable success of the Gospel, both in the primitive times, and in the beginning of our Reformations from Popery and Prelacy, must have been, in a great measure, owing to the simplicity, and holy and exemplary lives, of the preachers and professors thereof. A learned expositor observes, that " Ministers are likely to preach most to the purpose, when they can press their hearers to follow their example." For it is very observable, that without this the Church of Christ is so far from gaining ground, that it loses what it hath already gained in the world ; of which the Church of Scotland is a most glaring example ; yea, truth itself suffers by their means, and can gain no credit from their mouths ; and how despicable must that man's character be, whose authority is lost, and whose example goes for nothing ! So that, upon the whole, I flatter myself, that no small advantage, through the Divine blessing, may accrue to the public from this subject in general, and from the lives of our Scots Worthies in particular, providing these or the like cautions following be observed :

1. That we are not to sit down or rest ourselves upon the person, principle, or practice of any man, yea, the best saint we have ever read or heard of, but only to seek those gifts and graces that most eminently shone forth in them. *Preceptis, non exemplis, standum; i.e.,* "we must not stand by examples, but precepts." For it is the peculiar honour and dignity of Jesus Christ alone, to be worthy of being imitated by all men absolutely ; and for any person or persons to idolise any man or men, in making them a pattern in every particular, were nothing else than to pin an implicit faith upon other men's sleeves. The apostle, in the fore-cited text, gives a very good caveat against this, when he says, " Be ye followers " (or as the Dutch annotators translate it, " Be ye imitators ") " of me, even as I also am of Christ."

2. Neither are we, on the other hand, to dwell too much upon the faults or failings that have sometimes been discovered in some of God's own dear children ; but at the same time to consider with ourselves, that, although they were eminent men of God, yet at the same time they were sons of Adam also. For it is possible, yea, many times has been the case, for good men not only to make foul falls them-

selves, but also, when striking against the errors and enormities of others, to overreach the mark, and go beyond the bounds of truth in some degree ; perfection being no inherent plant in this life. So says the apostle, they are "earthen vessels," "men of like passions with you" (2 Cor. iv. 7 ; Acts xiv. 15).

Thirdly, As to the motives leading to this publication. Can it be supposed that there was ever an age, since the Reformation commenced in Scotland, that stood in more need of useful, holy, and exemplary lives being set before it, and that both with respect to the actions and memories of these Worthies, and with regard to our present circumstances. With respect to the former, it is now a long time since Bishops Spottiswoode, Guthrie, and Burnet (not to mention some English historians), in their writings, clothed the actions and proceedings of these our ancestors, both as to the reforming and suffering periods, in a most grotesque and frantic dress, whereby their names and noble attainments have been loaded with reproach, sarcasm, and scurrility. But as if this had not been enough, some modern writers, under the character of monthly reviewers (*see* the *Edinburgh Monthly Review* for Feb. 1774), have set their engines at work to misrepresent some of them, to render them and their most faithful contendings odious, and set them in a dishonourable light, by giving them a character such as even the above mentioned historians, yea, the most avowed enemies of their own day, would have scarcely subscribed. To such a length is poor degenerate Scotland arrived ! Is it not high time to follow the wise man's advice, "Open thy mouth for the dumb, in the cause of all such as are appointed to destruction" (Prov. xxxi. 8).

Again, with regard to our present circumstances, there needs little more to prove the necessity of this present collection, than to show how many degrees we have descended from the worthy deeds or merit of our renowned forefathers, by running a parallel betwixt their contendings and attainments, and our present national defections and backsliding courses.

Our venerable reformers were not only highly instrumental, in the Lord's hand, in bringing a people out of the abyss of gross Popish darkness, under which they had for a long time continued, but they also brought themselves under most solemn and sacred vows and engagements to the Most High ; and whenever they were to set about any further piece of Reformation, in their advancing state, they always set about the renovation of these Covenants. They strenuously asserted the Divine right of Presbytery, the headship of Christ, and the intrinsic rights of His Church, in the reign of James VI., and suffered much on that account; and they lifted arms once and again in the reign of Charles I., and never ceased until they got a uniformity in doctrine, worship, discipline, and church government, brought out and established in the three kingdoms for that purpose, whereby both Church and State were enabled to exert themselves in rooting out every error and heresy whatever, until they obtained a complete settlement according to the Word of God, and our Covenants established thereon ; which Covenants were then, by several excellent acts, both civil and ecclesiastic, made the MAGNA CHARTA of these nations, with respect to every civil and religious privilege, none being admitted into any office or employment in Church or State, without Scriptural or Covenant qualifications. Then was that part of the ancient prophecy further fulfilled, " In the wilderness shall waters break out, and streams in the desert" (Isa. xxxv. 6) ; "and the isles shall wait for His law" (Isa. xlii. 4). Christ then reigned gloriously in Scotland. His Church appeared "beautiful as Tirzah, comely as Jerusalem" (Cant. vi. 4). For, "from the uttermost part of the earth have we heard songs, even glory to the righteous" (Isa. xxiv. 16).

And although Charles II., and a set of wicked counsellors, overturned the whole fabric of that once glorious structure of Reformation, openly divested the Son of God of His headship in and over His own Church, as far as human laws could do, and burned these solemn Covenants by the hands of the hangman, the owning of which was, by act of Parliament, made high treason afterwards, yet, even then, the seed of the Church produced a remnant, who kept the word of Christ's patience, stood in defence of the whole of His persecuted truths in face of all opposition, and that to the effusion of the last drop of their blood. These two prime truths, Christ's headship and our Covenants, were in the mouths of all our Martyrs, when they mounted the bloody scaffold ; and in the comfort of suffering on such clear grounds, and for such valuable truths, they went triumphing off the stage of time into eternity.

But, alas ! how have we, their degenerate and apostate posterity, followed their example or traced their steps ? Yea, we have rather served ourselves heirs to them who persecuted and killed them, by our long accession to their perjury and apostacy, in a general and avowed denial of our most solemn vows and oaths of allegiance to Jesus Christ.

To mention nothing more of the total extermination of our ancient and laudable constitution, during the reigns of the two tyrants, with the many gravestones cast thereon by the Acts Recissory, etc. (which acts seem by no act in particular yet to be repealed), and Claim of Right at the Revolution ; whereby we have, in a national capacity (whatever be the pretences), declared ourselves to be on another footing than the footing of the once famous Covenanted Church of Scotland, how many are the defections and encroachments annually and daily made upon our most valuable rights and privileges ! For since the Revolution, the duty of national covenanting has not only been slighted and neglected, yea, ridiculed by some, but even some leading churchmen, in their writings, have had the effrontery to impugn (though in a very sly way) the very obligation of these Covenants, asserting that there is little or no warrant for national covenanting under the New Testament dispensation. And what awful attacks since that time have been made upon the crown rights of our Redeemer, notwithstanding some faint Acts then made to the contrary ; as witness the civil magistrate's still retaining his old usurped power, in calling and dissolving the supreme judicatories of the Church ; yea, sometimes to an indefinite time : likewise his appointing diets of fasting and thanksgiving to be observed, under fines, and other civil pains annexed ; imposing oaths, acts, and statutes, upon churchmen, under pain of ecclesiastic censure, or other Erastian penalties. And instead of our Covenants, an unhallowed Union is gone into with England, whereby our rights and liberties are infringed not a little. " Bow down thy body as the ground, that we may pass over." Lordly patronage, which was cast out of the Church in her purest times, is now restored and practised to an extremity. A Toleration Bill is granted, whereby all, and almost every error, heresy, and delusion, appear now rampant and triumphant. Prelacy is now become fashionable and epidemical, and of Popery we are in as much danger as ever. Socinian and deistical tenets only are in vogue with the wits of the age ; *soli rationi cedo*, the old Porphyrian maxim, having so far gained the ascendant at present, that reason (at least pretenders to it, who must needs hear with their eyes, and see with their ears, and understand with their elbows, till the order of nature be inverted) threatens not a little to banish revealed religion, and its most important doctrines, out of the professing world. A latitudinarian scheme prevails among the majority ; the greater part, with the Athenians, spending their time only to hear and see something new, gadding about to change their ways, going in the ways of Egypt and Assyria, to drink the water of Sihor and the river ; unstable souls, like so many light combustibles wrapt up by the eddies of a whirl-wind, tossed hither and thither till utterly dissipated. The doctrine of original sin is by several denied ; others are pulling down the very hedges of Church government, refusing all Church standards, Cove-nants, Creeds, and Confessions, whether of our own or of other Churches ; yea, and national Churches also ; as being all of them carnal, human, or anti-Christian inventions, contrary to many texts of Scripture, particularly 2 Tim. i. 13, "hold fast the form of sound words." And further, the old Pelagian and Arminian errors appear again upon the stage, the merit of the creature, free-will, and good works, being taught from press and pulpit almost everywhere, to the utter discarding of free grace, Christ's imputed righteousness, and the power of true godliness. These pernicious errors were all expunged, and cast over the hedge, by our reforming forefathers : and is it not highly requisite, that their faithful contendings, orthodoxy, and exem-plary lives, should be copied out before us, when we are so far from acknowledging the God of our fathers, and walking before Him with a perfect heart?

Again, if we can run a comparison betwixt the practice of those who are the subject matter of this collection, and our present pre-vailing temper and disposition, we shall find how far these correspond with one another. How courageous and zealous were *they* for the cause and honour of Christ ! How cold and lukewarm are *we*, of whatever sect or denomination ! How willing were *they* to part with all for Him, and what honour did many of them count it, to suffer for His name ! How unwilling are *we* to part with anything for Him, much less to suffer such hardships for His sake ! Of that *we* are ashamed, which *they* counted their ornament ; accounting that *our* glory which *they* looked on as a disgrace. How easy was it for *them* to choose the greatest sufferings, rather than the least sin ! How hard is it for *us* to refuse the greatest sin, before the least suffering ! How active were *they* for the glory of God and the good of souls, and diligent to have their own evidence clear for heaven ! How little concern have *we* for the cause of Christ, His work and interest, and how dark are the most part with respect to their spiritual state and duty ! *They* were sympathising Christians ; but, alas ! how little fellow-feeling is to be found among *us :* it is rather, "stand by, for I am holier than thou." Oh ! that their Christian virtues, constant fidelity, unfeigned love, and unbiassed loyalty to Zion's King and Lord, could awaken us from our neutrality and supine security, wherein, instead of imitating the goodness and virtuous dispositions of these our ancestors, we have, by our defections and vicious courses, invited neglect and contempt on ourselves, being (as a philosopher once observed of passionate people) like men standing on their heads, who see all things the wrong way ; giving up, with the greater part of these our most valuable rights and liberties, all which were most esteemed by our renowned progenitors. " The treacherous dealers have dealt very treacherously."

And if we shall add unto all these, in our progressive and increasing apostacy, our other heinous land-crying sins and enormities, which prevail and increase among all ranks and denominations of men (few mourning over the low state of our Zion, and the daily decay of the interest of Christ and religion), then we not only may say, as the poet once said of the men of Thebes and Athens, that we live only in fable, and nothing remains of ancient Scotland but the name, but also may take up this bitter complaint and lamentation :

" Ah ! Scotland, Scotland ! ' How is the gold become dim ; how is the most fine gold changed ?' Ah ! where is the God of Elijah, and where is His glory ? Where is that Scottish zeal that once flamed in the breasts of thy nobility, barons, ministers, and commoners of all sorts ? Ah ! where is that true courage and heroic resolution for religion and the liberties of the nation, that did once animate all ranks in the land ! Alas ! alas ! true Scots blood now runs cool in our veins ! The cloud is now gone up in a great measure from off our assemblies ; because we have deserted and relinquished the Lord's most noble cause and testimony, by a plain, palpable, and perpetual course of backsliding—' The crown is fallen from our head ; woe unto us, for we have sinned.'"

For surely we may say of these our times, and with as much propriety, what some of these Worthies said of theirs. Thus Mr Davidson, in a letter to the General Assembly, 1601, said, *Quam graviter ingemiscerent illi fortes viri qui ecclesiæ Scoticanæ pro libertate in acie decertarunt, si nostram nunc ignaviam (ne quid gravius dicam) conspicerent,* i.e., " How grievously would these worthy men bewail our stupendous slothfulness (that I should call it no worse), could they but behold it, who of old contended for the liberty of the Scottish Church." Or, to use the words of another in the persecuting period (Mr John Dickson, in a letter, while prisoner in the Bass),

"Were it possible that our reformers (and, we may add our late martyrs), who are entered in among the glorious choristers in the kingdom of heaven, singing their melodious songs on harps about the throne of the Lamb, might have a furlough for a short time, to take a view of their apostatising children, what may we judge would be their conceptions of these courses of defection, so far repugnant to the platform laid down in that glorious work of Reformation!" For if innocent Hamilton, godly and patient Wishart, apostolic Knox, eloquent Rollock, worthy Davidson, courageous Melville, prophetic Welch, majestic Bruce, great Henderson, renowned Gillespie, learned Binning, pious Gray, laborious Durham, heavenly-minded Rutherford, the faithful Guthries, diligent Blair, heart-melting Livingstone, religious Welwood, orthodox and practical Brown, zealous and steadfast Cameron, honest-hearted Cargill, sympathising M'Ward, persevering Blackader, the evangelical Traills, constant and pious Renwick, etc., "were filed off from the assembly of the first-born, and sent as commissioners to haste down from the mount of God, to behold how quickly their offspring are gone out of the way, piping and dancing after a golden calf,—ah! with what vehemency would their spirits be affected, to see their laborious structure almost razed to the foundation, by those to whom they committed the custody of the word of their great Lord's patience; they in the meantime sheltering themselves under the shadow of a rotten lump of fig-tree-leaf distinctions, which will not sconce against the wrath of an angry God in the cool of the day!"

And, *finally*, What can have a more gloomy aspect in the midst of these evils (with many more that might be noticed) when our pleasant things are laid waste, than to see such a scene of strife and division carried on, and maintained, among Christ's professing witnesses in these lands, whereby true love and sympathy are eradicated, the very vitals of religion pulled out, and the ways of God and godliness lampooned and ridiculed, "giving Jacob to the curse, and Israel to the reproaches." And it is most lamentable, that while malignants (now as well as formerly) from without, are cutting down the carved work of the Sanctuary, Christ's professed friends and followers from within, are busied in contention and animosities among themselves, by which means the enemy still advances and gains ground, similar to the case of the once famous and flourishing city and temple of Jerusalem, when it was by Titus Vespasian utterly demolished. All which seem to prelude or indicate, that the Lord is about to inflict His long-threatened, impending, but protracted judgments, upon such a sinning land, Church, and people.

> Well may we tremble now ! what manners reign ?
> But wherefore ask we ? when a true reply
> Would shock too much. Kind Heaven ! avert events,
> Whose fatal nature might reply too plain !
> ——Vengeance delay'd but gathers and ferments ;
> More formidably blackens in the wing,
> Brews deeper draughts of unrelenting wrath,
> And higher charges the suspended storm.— *Young's Night Thoughts.*

And as many of these Worthies have assured us, that judgments are abiding this Church and nation ; so our present condition and circumstances seem to say, that we are the generation ripening for them apace. How much need have we, then, of the Christian armour that made them proof against Satan, his emissaries, and every trial and tribulation to which they were subjected? "Wherefore take unto you the whole armour of God, that ye may be able to withstand in the evil day" (Eph. vi. 13).

Somewhat might have been said concerning the Testimony of the Church of Scotland, as it was carried on and handed down to posterity, by these witnesses of Christ in its different parts and periods. But as this has been somewhat (I may say needlessly) controverted in these our times, it were too large a subject, for the narrow limits of a preface, to enter upon at present, any further than to observe :

1. That the testimony of the Church of Scotland is not only a free, full, and faithful testimony, yea, more extensive than the testimony of any one particular Church since Christianity commenced in the world, but also a sure and costly testimony, confirmed and sealed with blood, and that of the best of our nobles, ministers, gentry, burgesses, and commons of all sorts, "who loved not their lives unto the death, but overcame by the blood of the Lamb, and by the word of their testimony ;" " Bind up the testimony; seal the law" (Rev. xii. 11; Isa. viii. 16).

2. Although there is no truth whatsoever, when once controverted, but becomes the word of Christ's patience, and so ought to be the word of our testimony (Rev. iii. 10, xii. 11), truth and duty being always the same in all ages and periods of time, so that what injures one truth, in some sense, injures and affects all, "for whosoever shall keep the whole law, and yet offend in one point, he is guilty of all " (James ii. 10) ; yet, at the same time, it is pretty evi-

dent, that the Church of Christ in this world is a passing church, still circulating through ages and periods of time, so that she seldom or never turns back under the same point, there being scarcely a century of years elapsed without an alteration of circumstances; yea, and more, I suppose, that there is no certain book that has been or can be written, which will suit the case of one particular Church at all times, and in all circumstances. This pre-eminence the Holy Scriptures alone can claim as a complete rule of faith and manners, principle and practice, in all places, ages and times.

3. These things premised, let it be observed, that the primitive witnesses had the divinity of the Son of God, and an open confession of Him, for their testimony. Our reformers from Popery had Antichrist to struggle with, in asserting the doctrines of the Gospel, and the right way of salvation in and through Jesus Christ. Again, in the reigns of James VI. and Charles I. Christ's REGALIA, and the divine right of Presbytery, became the subject-matter of their testimony. Then, in the beginning of the reign of Charles II. (until he got the whole of our ancient and laudable constitution effaced and overturned), our Worthies only saw it their duty to hold and contend for what they had already attained unto. But, in the end of this and the subsequent tyrant's reign, they found it their duty (a duty which they had too long neglected) to advance one step higher, by casting off their authority altogether, and that as well on account of their manifest usurpation of Christ's crown and dignity, as on account of their treachery, bloodshed, and tyranny. And yet, as all these faithful witnesses of Christ did harmoniously agree in promoting the kingdom and interests of the Messiah, in all His threefold offices, and stood in defence of religion and liberty (and that not only in opposition to the more gross errors of Popery, but even to the more refined errors of English hierarchy), we must take their testimony to be materially all and the same testimony, only under different circumstances; which may be summed up thus: The primitive martyrs sealed the *prophetic* office of Christ in opposition to Pagan idolatry. The reforming martyrs sealed His *priestly* office with their blood, in opposition to Popish idolatry. And last of all, our late martyrs have sealed His *kingly* office with their best blood, in despite of supremacy and bold Erastianism. They indeed have cemented it upon His royal head, so that to the world's end it shall never drop off again.

But, candid reader, to detain thee no longer upon these or the like considerations—I have put the following sheets into thy hands, wherein, if thou findest anything amiss, either as to the matter or method, let it be ascribed unto anything else, rather than unto want of honesty or integrity of intention—considering, that all mankind are liable to err, and that there is more difficulty in digesting such a great mass of materials into such a small composition, than in writing many volumes. Indeed, there is but little probability that a thing of this nature can altogether escape or evade the critical eye of some carping Momus, particularly such as are either altogether ignorant of reformation-principles, or of what the Lord hath done for covenanted Scotland, and those who can bear with nothing but what comes from those men who are of an uniform stature or persuasion with themselves. And yet were it possible to anticipate anything arising here, by way of objection, these few things following might be observed.

Some may object that many things more useful for the present generation might have been published, than the deeds and public actings of those men who have stood so long condemned by the laws of the nation ; being thought to be exploded by some, and accounted by others such a reproach, as unfit to be any longer on record.

In answer to this I shall only notice :

1. That there have been some hundreds of volumes published of things fabulous, fictitious, and romantic, fit for little else than to amuse the credulous reader; while this subject has been in a great measure neglected.

2. We find that it has been the constant practice of the Lord's people in all ages, to hand down and keep on record what the Lord had done by and for their forefathers in former times. We find the royal Psalmist, in name of the Church, oftener than once at this work. "We have heard with our ears, O God, our fathers have told us, what work thou didst in their days, in the times of old." " We will not hide them from their children, shewing to the generation to come the praises of the Lord, and His strength, and His wonderful works that He hath done (Ps. xliv. 1 ; lxxviii. 4).

3. It has been the practice of almost all nations, yea, and our own also, to publish the warlike exploits and martial achievements of their most illustrious heroes, who distinguished themselves in defence of their native country for a little worldly honour or a little temporary subsistence ; and shall we be behind in publishing the lives, characters, and most memorable actions of these noble champions of Christ, who not only stood in defence of religion and liberty, but also fought the battles of the Lord against His and their avowed enemies, till, in

imitation of their princely Master, their garments were all stained with blood, for which their names shall be held in everlasting remembrance ?

4. As to the last part of the objection, it must be granted, that, in *foro hominis,* their actions and attainments cannot now be pled upon ; but, *in foro Dei,* that which was lawful from the beginning cannot afterwards be made sinful or void ; and the longer they have been buried under the ashes of neglect and apostacy, the more need have they to be raised up and revived. It is usual for men to keep that well which was left them by their fathers ; and for us either to oppose or industriously conceal any part of these their contendings, were not only an addition to the contempt already thrown upon the memories of these renowned sires, but also an injury done to posterity. "Your honourable ancestors, with the hazard of their lives, brought Christ into our lands ; and it shall be cruelty to posterity, if ye lose Him to them," said Samuel Rutherford in a letter to the Earl of Cassillis.

Again, some sceptical nullifidian or other may be ready to object farther, that many things related in this collection smell too much of enthusiasm, and that several other things narrated therein are beyond all credit. But such we must suppose to be either quite ignorant of what the Lord did for our forefathers in former times, or else to be in a great measure destitute of the like gracious influences of the Holy Spirit, by which they were actuated and animated. For :

1. These Worthies did and suffered much for Christ and His cause in their day and generation, and therefore, in a peculiar and singular manner, were honoured and beloved of Him ; and although there are some things here narrated of an extraordinary nature, yet, as they imply nothing contrary to reason, they do not forfeit a title to any man's belief, since they are otherwise well attested, nay, obviously referred to a Cause whose ways and thoughts surmount the ways and thoughts of men, as far as the heavens are above our heads. The Sacred History affords us a store of instances and examples of a more transcendent nature than anything here related ; the truth of which we are at as little liberty to question as the divinity of the book in which they are related.

2. As to the soul-exercise and pious devotion of the lives herein related, they are so far supported by the authority of Scripture, that there is mentioned by them (as a ground of their hope) some text or passage thereof carried in upon their minds, suited and adapted to their cases and circumstances ; by which faith they were enabled to

lay claim to some particular promise, "as a lamp unto their feet, a light unto their path," and this neither hypocrite nor enthusiast can do. "For other foundation can no man lay than that is laid, which is Jesus Christ" (1 Cor. iii. 11).

But then, it may be alleged by those who have a high esteem for this subject, that nothing is here given as a commendation suitable or adequate to the merit of these Worthies, considering their zeal, diligence, and activity in the discharge of duty, in that office or station which they filled. This, indeed, comes nearest the truth; for it is very common for biographers to pass eulogiums of a very high strain in praise of those whom they affect. But in these panegyrical orations, they oftentimes rather exceed than excel. It was an ancient, but true saying of the Jews, "That great men (and we may say good men) commonly find stones for their own monuments;" and laudable actions always support themselves. And a thing (as Fuller observes), "if right, will defend itself; if wrong, none can defend it: truth *needs* not, falsehood *deserves* not a supporter."

Indeed, it must be regretted, that this collection is not drawn out with more advantage to the cause of Christ, and the interest of religion, in commending the mighty acts of the Lord done for and by these worthy servants of His, in a way suitable to the merit and dignity of such a subject. But in this case it is the greater pity, that those who have a good-will to such a piece of service cannot do it, while those who should and can do it, will not do it. But I shall make no other apology, than what our Saviour in another case said to the woman, "She hath done what she could."

All that I shall observe anent the form or method used in the following Lives is this: they are all, except one, ranged in order, according to the time of their death, and not according to their birth; and, in general, the historical account of their birth, parentage, and memorable transactions, is first inserted, with as few repetitions as possible; yea, sometimes to save a repetition, a fact is related of one Worthy in the life of another, which is not in his own life: then follows their characteristic part, which oftentimes is just one's testimony successively of another; and, last of all, mention of their works as far as possible. That which is given in their own words mostly stands within inverted commas.

*   *   *   *   *   *

But to conclude: May the Lord arise and plead His own cause, in putting a final stop to all manner of prevailing wickedness, and

hasten that day when the glorious light of the Gospel shall shine forth
in purity, and with such power and success as in former times, that His
large and great dominion may be extended " from the river to the ends
of the earth ;" when all these heats, animosities, and breaking divisions
that now prevail and increase among Christ's professed friends and
followers shall be healed, so that, being cemented and knit to one
another, they may join heart and hand together in the matters of the
Lord, and the concerns of His glory; when " Ephraim shall not
envy Judah, and Judah shall not vex Ephraim; but they shall
fly upon the shoulders of the Philistines" (Isa. xi. 13); with a further
accomplishment of these, and other gracious promises,—" I will also
make thy officers peace, and thine exactors righteousness," and " they
shall see eye to eye, when the Lord shall bring again Zion" (Isa. lx.
17 ; Isa. lii. 8).

Thus, when we are endeavouring to perpetuate the memory of
these Worthies, and commemorate what the Lord did by and for
our forefathers, in the days of old, may we be so happy as to have
somewhat to declare of His goodness and wonderful works done for
us in our day and generation also.

And if the following sheets shall in the least, through Divine
grace, and under the management of an overruling Providence, which
claims the care of directing every mean to its proper end, prove
useful to the reclaiming of neutrals from backsliding courses, the
confirming of halters, and the encouraging of others to the like fortitude and vigorous zeal to contend for our most valuable privileges,
whether of a civil or a religious nature, then I shall think all my
pains recompensed, and my object gained.   For, that many may be
found " standing in the way, to see and ask for the good old paths,
and walk therein, cleaving to the law and to the testimony," would
be the joy, and is the earnest desire, impartial reader, of one who
remains thy friend and well-wisher in the truth,

JOHN HOWIE.

Lochgoin, *July* 21, 1775.

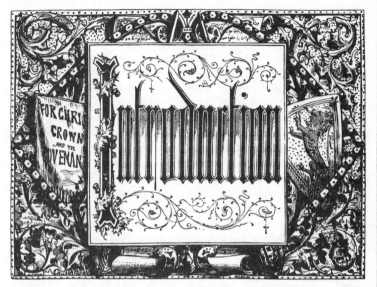

HRISTIANITY seems to have made its appearance in Scotland at a very early period, having been, according to some writers, propagated by the apostles themselves; some saying, that Simon Zelotes, others that Paul, were for some time in this part of the world: but as their opinion is not supported by proper vouchers, it merits only the regard due to conjecture —not the attention which an undoubted narrative calls for. Another and more probable account is, that during the persecution raised by Domitian, the twelfth and last Cæsar, about A.D. 96, some of the disciples of the Apostle John fled into our island, and there taught the religion of Jesus.

It does not seem that Christianity made any very rapid progress for a considerable time. The first account of the success of the Gospel that can be depended on is, that about A.D. 203, King Donald I., with his Queen, and several courtiers, were baptized, and continued afterwards to promote the interests of Christianity, in opposition to Pagan idolatry. But the invasion of the Emperor Severus soon disturbed this king's measures; so that, for the space of more than seventy years after, religion was on the decline, and the ancient idolatry of the Druids prevailed. These were an order of heathen priests who performed their rites in groves of oak trees;

a species of Paganism of great antiquity, being that kind of idolatry to which the Jews often reverted, and of which mention is made
in the lives of Ahab, Manasseh, and others, in the Books of the
Kings of Judah and Israel. The Druids likewise possessed a considerable share of civil power, being the ordinary arbitrators in almost
all controversies, and were highly esteemed by the people. This
made it a very difficult task to establish a religion so opposite to,
and subversive of Druidism; but the difficulties which Christianity
has had to encounter in every age and country, have served its
interests, and illustrated the power and grace of its divine Author.

The Druids were expelled by King Cratilinth, about the year
277, who took special care to obliterate every memorial of them;
and from this period we may date the true era of Christianity in
Scotland; because, henceforward, until the persecution under the
Emperor Diocletian, in the beginning of the fourth century, there
was a gradual increase of the true knowledge of God and religion. That persecution became so hot in the south parts of Britain
as to drive many, both preachers and professors, into Scotland,
where they were kindly received, and had the Isle of Man, then in
possession of the Scots, given them for their residence, and a sufficient maintenance assigned them. King Cratilinth also built a
church for them (called the church of our Saviour, in the Greek,
sotér, and now, by corruption, Sodor), in Icolmkill, or Iona, one of
the western isles. They were not employed, like the Druidical
priests, into whose places they had come, in settling the worldly
affairs of men, but gave themselves wholly to divine services, in
instructing the ignorant, comforting the weak, administering the
sacraments, and training up disciples for the same services.

Whether these refugees were the ancient Culdees, or a different
set of men, is not easily determined; nor is it very material. The
Culdees (from *cultores Dei*, or worshippers of God) flourished at this
time; they were called *monachoi*, or Monks, from the retired religious lives which they led. The cells unto which they retired were,
after their deaths, mostly converted into churches, and to this day
retain their names, as Cell, or Kell, or church, of Marnock; Kil-
Patrick, Kil-Malcolm, etc. The Culdees chose superintendents
from among themselves, whose office obliged them to travel the
country, in order to see that every one discharged his duty properly: but they were utter strangers to the lordly power of the
modern prelate; having no proper diocese, and only a temporary

superintendency, with which they were vested by their brethren, and to whom they were accountable. It was an institution, in the spirit of it the same with the privy censure of ministers among Presbyterians.

During the reigns of Cratilinth, and Fincormac his successor, the Culdees were in a flourishing state; but after the death of the latter, both the church and state of Scotland went into disorder. Maximus, the Roman Prefect, stirred up the Picts to aid him against the Scots, who were totally defeated; their king, Ewing, with most part of the nobility, being slain. This overthrow was immediately succeeded by an edict, commanding all the Scots, without exception, to depart out of the kingdom against a certain day, under pain of death. This drove them entirely into Ireland, and the western isles of Denmark and Norway, excepting a few ecclesiastics, who wandered about from place to place. This bloody battle was fought about the year 380, at the water of Doon in Carrick.

After an exile of forty-four, or according to Buchanan twenty-seven years, which the Scots endured, the Picts became sensible of their mistake in assisting the Romans against them; accordingly they strengthened the hands of the few who remained, and invited the fugitives back into their own land. These were joined by some foreigners, and returned, with Fergus II., then in Denmark, at their head. Their enterprise was the more successful, that at this time many of the Roman forces were called home. Their king was crowned with the usual rites in his own country, and the news of his success drew great numbers to him, insomuch that he recovered all the country out of which the Scots had been expelled. Most of the foreign forces returned home, except the Irish, who received the country of Galloway for their reward. This successful undertaking happened about the year 404, or, as others would have it, 420.

The Culdees were now recalled out of all their lurking places, restored to their livings, and had their churches repaired. At this time they possessed the people's esteem to a higher degree than ever; but tranquillity was again interrupted by a more formidable enemy than before. The Pelagian heresy had now gained considerable ground in Britain; it is so called from Pelagius, a Monk at Rome: its chief articles are—(1.) That original sin is not inherent; (2.) That faith is a thing natural; (3.) That good works done by our own strength, of our own free-will, are agreeable to the law of God, and worthy of heaven. Whether all, or only part of these errors, then infected the Scottish church, is uncertain; but Celestine, then Bishop of Rome, embraced this opportunity to send Palladius among them, who, joining with the orthodox of South Britain, restored peace to .that part of the church, by suppressing the heresy. King Eugenius the Second, being desirous that this church should likewise be purged of the impure leaven, invited Palladius hither, who obtained liberty from Celestine, and being enjoined to introduce the hierarchy as opportunity should offer, came into Scotland, and succeeded so effectually in his commission, as both to confute Pelagianism and new-model the government of the church.

The church of Scotland as yet knew no officers vested with pre-eminence above their brethren, nor had anything to do with the Roman Pontiff, until the year 450. Bede says, that "Palladius was sent unto the Scots, who believed in Christ as their first bishop." (Bede's Eccles. His. lib. i. ch. 13. Buchanan His. book v.). Boetius likewise says, "that Palladius was the first of all who did bear holy magistracy among the Scots, being made bishop by the great Pope." Fordun, in his Chronicle, tells us— "that before the coming of Palladius, the Scots had, for teachers of the faith, and ministers of the sacraments, Presbyters only, or monks, following the customs of the primitive church (Book iii. cap. 8).

But we are not to fix the era of diocesan bishops even so early as this, for there were no such office-bearers in the church of Scotland, until the reign of Malcolm II. in the eleventh century. During the first thousand years after Christ, there were no divided dioceses, nor superiorities over others, but they governed in the church in common with Presbyters; so that they were no more than nominal bishops, possessing little or nothing of that lordly dignity which they now do, and for a long time past have enjoyed. Spottiswoode himself testifies (His History, page 29), that the Scottish bishops, before the eleventh century, exercised their functions indifferently in every place to which they came. Palladius may be said to have rather laid the foundation of the after degeneracy of the church of Scotland, than to have built that superstructure of corruption and idolatry which afterwards prevailed, because she continued for nearly two hundred years in a state comparatively pure and unspotted, when we cast our eyes on the following times.

About the end of the sixth and beginning of the seventh century, a number of pious and wise men flourished in the country, among whom was Kentigern, commonly called Mungo. Some of these persons were employed by Oswald, a Northumbrian King, to instruct his people: they are represented by Bede as eminent for their love to God, and their knowledge of the Holy Scriptures. The light of the Gospel, by their means, broke into other parts of the Saxon dominions, and long maintained an opposition to the growing usurpation of the church of Rome, which, after the middle of this century, was strenuously supported by Augustine and his disciples. Besides these men, the church of Scotland at this time sent many other worthy and successful missionaries into foreign parts, particularly into France and Germany.

Thus was Scotland early privileged, and thus were her privileges improved; but soon "the gold became dim, and the most fine gold was changed."

Popery came now by degrees to show her horrid head. The assiduity of Augustine and his disciples in England was attended with melancholy consequences to Scotland; and by fomenting divisions, corrupting her princes with Romish principles and inattention to the lives of her clergy, the Papal power soon came to be universally acknowledged. In the seventh century, a hot contest arose betwixt Augustine and his disciples on the one side, and the Scots and the northern Saxons on the other, respecting the time of keeping of Easter, immersing three times in baptism, shaving of priests, etc.; which the latter would neither receive, nor submit to the authority that imposed them. Each party refused ministerial communion with the other, until an arbitral decision was given by Oswald, king of the Northumbrians, at Whitby in Yorkshire, in favour of the Romanists; when the opinions of the Scots were condemned, and the modish fooleries of the Papal hierarchy established. This decision, however, was far from putting an end to the confusion which the dissension had occasioned. The Romanists urged their rites with vigour — the others rather chose to yield their places than conform. Their discouragements daily increased as the clerical power was augmented. In the year 886 the priests obtained an act, exempting them from taxes and all civil prosecutions before temporal judges, and ordaining that all matters concerning them should be tried by their bishops, who were at this time vested with those powers which are now in the hands of commissaries, respecting matrimonial causes, testaments, and other civil matters. They were likewise, by the same statute, empowered to make canons, try heretics, etc.; and all future kings were ordained to take an oath at their coronation, for maintaining these privileges to the church. The Convention of Estates which passed this Act was held at Forfar, in the reign of that too-indulgent prince, Gregory.

Malcolm III., Alexander, David, etc., successively supported this dignity, by erecting particular bishoprics, abbeys, and monasteries. The same superstitious zeal seized the nobility of both sexes—some giving a third, some more, and others their whole estates for the support of pontifical pride and spiritual tyranny, which soon became insupportable, and opened the eyes of the nation, so that they discovered their mistake in raising the clerical authority to such a height. Accordingly, we find the nobles complaining of it to Alexander III., who reigned after the middle of the thirteenth century; but he was so far from being able to afford them redress, that, when they were excommunicated by the church on account of this complaint, to prevent greater evils, he was obliged to cause the nobility to satisfy both the avarice and arrogance of the clergy, who had now resolved upon a journey to Rome, with a view to raise as great commotions in Scotland, as Thomas à Becket had lately caused in England.

The Pope's power was now generally acknowledged over Christendom, particularly in Scotland; for which, in return, the church of Scotland was declared free from all foreign spiritual jurisdiction—that of the "apostolic see only excepted." This bull was occasioned by an attempt of Roger, bishop of York, in the year 1159, to raise himself to the dignity of Metropolitan of Scotland, and who found means to be legate of this kingdom; but he lost that office upon the remonstrance of the Scottish clergy, who procured the above bull in their favour, with many other favours of a like nature at this time conferred upon them, by which they were exempted from any other jurisdiction than that of Rome; insomuch, that we find Pope Boniface VIII. commanding King Edward I. of England to cease hostilities against the Scots, alleging that "the Sovereignty of Scotland belonged to the church." This claim seems to have been founded on the Papal appointment for the unction of the Scots kings, which was first used on King Edgar, A.D. 1098, and was at that time regarded by the people as a new mark of royalty; but which, as it was the appointment of the Pope, was really the mark of the beast.

There were now in Scotland all orders of Monks and Friars, Templars, or Red Monks, Trinity Monks of Aberdeen, Cistertian Monks, Carmelite, Black, and Grey Friars, Carthusians, Dominicans, Franciscans, Jacobines, Benedictines; shewing to what a height Antichrist had raised his head in our land, and how readily his oppressive measures were complied with by all ranks.

But the reader must not think, during the period we have now reviewed, that there were none to oppose this torrent of superstition and idolatry; for, from the first appearance of the Romish Antichrist in this kingdom, God wanted not witnesses for the truth, who boldly stood forth for the defence of the blessed and pure Gospel of Christ. Mention is first made of Clemens and Samson, two famous Culdees, who in the seventh century supported the authority of Christ, as the only king and head of His church, against the usurped power of Rome, and who rejected the superstitious rites of Antichrist, as contrary to the simplicity of Gospel institutions. The succeeding age was no less remarkable for learned and pious men, to whom Scotland gave birth, and whose praise was in the churches abroad; particularly Joannes Scotus, who wrote a book upon the eucharist, condemned by Leo IX. in the year 1030, long after his death.

In the ninth century a Convention of Estates was held at Scone for the reformation of the clergy, their lives and conversation being at that time a reproach to common decency and good manners, not to say piety and religion. The remedies provided at this Convention discover the nature of the disease. It was ordained that churchmen should reside upon their charges; that they should not intermeddle with secular affairs, but instruct the people, and be good examples in their conversation; that they should not keep hawks, hounds, nor horses, for their pleasure, etc. And if they failed in the observance of these injunctions, they were to be fined for the first, and deposed for the second transgression. These laws were made under King Constantine II., but his successor Gregory rendered them abortive by his indulgence.

The age following this is not remarkable for witnesses to the truth; but historians are agreed that there were still some of the

Culdees who lived and ministered apart from the Romanists, and taught the people that Christ was the only propitiation for sin, and that His blood alone could wash them from the guilt of it, in opposition to the indulgences and pardons of the Pope. Mr Alexander Shields says ("Hind let Loose," period II. p. 11, first edition), that the Culdees transmitted their testimony to the Lollards, and Pope John XXII., in his bull for anointing King Robert Bruce, complains that there were many heretics in Scotland; so that we may safely affirm, there never was any very great period of time without witnesses for the truth, and against the gross corruptions of the church of Rome. Some of our kings themselves opposed the Pope's supremacy, and prohibited his legates from entering their dominions; the most remarkable instance of this kind being that of King Robert Bruce.

After Robert Bruce had defeated the English at Bannockburn, they became suppliants to the Pope for his mediation, who accordingly sent a legate into Scotland, proposing a cessation of arms, till the Pope should hear and decide the quarrel betwixt the two crowns, and be informed of the right which Edward II. had to the crown of Scotland. To this King Robert replied, " That the Pope could not be ignorant of that business, because it had been often explained to his predecessors, in the hearing of many cardinals then alive, who could tell him, if they pleased, what insolent answers Pope Boniface received from the English, while they were desired to desist from oppressing the Scots;—and now (said he) when it hath pleased God to give us the better by some victories, by which we have not only recovered our own, but can make them live as good neighbours, they have recourse to such treaties, seeking to gain time, in order to fall upon us again with greater force. But in this his Holiness must excuse me, for I will not be so unwise as to let the advantage I have slip out of my hands." The legate regarding this answer as contemptuous, interdicted the kingdom, and departed. But King Robert paying little regard to such proceedings, followed hard after the legate, and, entering England, wasted all the adjacent countries with fire and sword.

In the beginning of the fifteenth century, the reformation from Popery began to dawn in Scotland. At this time there was Pope against Pope—nay, sometimes three of them at once, all excommunicating one another; which schism lasted about thirty years, and by an over-ruling Providence contributed much to the downfall of Antichrist, and to the revival of real religion and learning in Scotland, and many parts in Europe; for many, embracing the opportunity now afforded to them, began to speak openly against the heresy, tyranny, and immorality of the clergy. Amongst those who preached publicly against these evils, were John Huss, and Jerome of Prague, in Bohemia; John Wickliffe, in England; and James Resby, an Englishman and scholar of Wickliffe, in Scotland, who came thither about the year 1407, and was called in question for some doctrines which he taught against the Pope's supremacy; he was condemned to the fire, which he endured with great constancy. About ten years after, Paul Craw, a Bohemian, and follower of Huss, was accused in Scotland of heresy before such as were then called doctors of theology. The articles of charge were, that, in the opinion of the sacrament of the supper, he followed Huss and Wickliffe, who denied that the substance of bread and wine was changed by virtue of any words, or that auricular confession to priests, or praying to saints departed, was lawful. He was committed to the secular judge, who condemned him to the fire at St Andrews, where he suffered, being gagged when led to the stake, that he might not have the opportunity of making his confession. Both the above-mentioned martyrs suffered under Henry Wardlaw, Bishop of St Andrews, who founded that university, in 1412; which might have done him honour had he not imbrued his hands in innocent blood.

These returnings of the Gospel light were not confined to St Andrews; Kyle, Carrick, Cunningham, and other districts in the west of Scotland, were also favoured about the same time; for we find that Robert Blackatter, the first archbishop of Glasgow, *anno* 1494, caused George Campbell of Cessnock, Adam Reid of Barskimming, and a great many others, mostly persons of distinction (opprobriously called the Lollards of Kyle, from one Lollard, an eminent preacher among the ancient Waldenses), to be summoned before King James IV. and his great council at Glasgow, for maintaining that images ought not to be worshipped; that the relics of saints should not be adorned, etc. But they answered their accusers with such constancy and boldness, that it was judged most prudent to dismiss them, with an admonition to content themselves with the faith of the church, and to beware of new doctrines.

Thus have we brought this summary of church-affairs in Scotland down to the time of Patrick Hamilton, whose life stands at the head of this collection; for he was the next sufferer on account of opposition to Romish tyranny and superstition in our country.

CHURCH OF SODOR, IONA.

ST SALVATOR COLLEGE, ST ANDREWS.

Patrick Hamilton.

PATRICK HAMILTON was born about the year of our Lord 1503, and was nephew to the Earl of Arran by his father, and to the Duke of Albany by his mother; he was also related to King James V. of Scotland. He was early educated with a design for future high preferment, and had the abbacy of Ferne, in Ross-shire, given him, for the purpose of prosecuting his studies, which he did with great assiduity.

In order to complete this laudable design, he resolved to travel into Germany. The fame of the university of Wittenberg was then very great, and drew many to it from distant places, among whom our Hamilton was one. He was the first who introduced public disputations upon faith and works, and such theological questions, into the university of Marpurg, in which he was assisted by Francis Lambert, by whose conversation he profited not a little. Here he became acquainted with these eminent reformers, Martin Luther and Philip Melancthon, besides other learned men of their society. By these distinguished masters he was instructed in the knowledge of the true religion, which he had little opportunity to become acquainted with in his own country, because the small remains of it in Scotland at this time were under the yoke of oppression, as we have already shown at the close of the Introduction. He made an amazing proficiency in this most important study, and became soon as zealous in the profession of the true faith, as he had been diligent to attain the knowledge of it.

This drew the eyes of many upon him ; and while they were waiting with impatience to see what part he would act, he came to the resolution of returning to his own country, and there, in the face of all dangers, of communicating the light which he had received. Accordingly, being as yet a youth, not being much past twenty-three years of age, he began sowing the seed of God's word wherever he came, exposing the corruptions of the Romish church, and pointing out the errors which had crept into the Christian religion as professed in Scotland. He was favourably received and followed by many, unto whom he readily "shewed the way of God more perfectly." His reputation as a scholar, and his courteous demeanour, contributed not a little to his usefulness in the good work.

The city of St Andrews was at this time the grand rendezvous of the Romish clergy, and might with no impropriety be called the metropolis of the kingdom of darkness. James Beaton was archbishop, Hugh Spence dean of divinity, John Waddel rector, James Simson official, Thomas Ramsay canon and dean of the abbey, with the several superiors of the different orders of monks and friars. It could not be expected that Patrick Hamilton's conduct would be long concealed from such a body as this. Their resentment against him soon rose to the utmost height of persecuting rage ; the Archbishop particularly, who was Chancellor of the kingdom, and otherwise very powerful, became his inveterate enemy ; but being not less politic than cruel, he concealed his wicked design against Patrick Hamilton, until he had drawn him into the ambush prepared for him, which he effected by prevailing on him to attend a conference at St Andrews.

Being come thither, Alexander Campbell, prior of the Black Friars, who had been appointed to exert his faculties in reclaiming him, had several private interviews with Patrick Hamilton, in which he seemed to acknowledge the force of his objections against the prevailing conduct of the clergy, and the errors of the Romish church. Such persuasions as Campbell used to bring him back to Popery, had rather the tendency to confirm him in the truth. The Archbishop and inferior clergy appeared to make concessions, allowing that many things stood in need of reformation, which they could wish had been brought about. Whether they were sincere in these acknowledgments, or only intended to conceal their bloody designs, and render the innocent and unsuspecting victim of their rage more secure, is a question to which this answer may be returned,—that had they been sincere, the consciousness that Patrick Hamilton spoke truth would, perhaps, have warded off the blow, for at least some longer time, or would have divided their councils and measures against him. That neither of these was the case will now appear.

Patrick Hamilton was apprehended under night, and committed prisoner to the castle ; and at the same time the young king James V., at the earnest solicitation of the clergy, was prevailed upon to undertake a pilgrimage to St Duthach in Ross-shire, that he might be out of the way of any applications that might be made to him for Hamilton's life, which there was reason to believe would be granted. This measure affords full proof, that notwithstanding the friendly conferences which they kept up with him for some time, they had from the beginning resolved on his ruin ; but such instances of Popish dissembling were not new even in Patrick Hamilton's time.

The next day after his imprisonment, he was brought before the Archbishop and his convention, and there charged with maintaining and propagating sundry heretical opinions : and though articles of the utmost importance had been debated betwixt him and them, they restricted their charges to such trifles as pilgrimage, purgatory, praying to saints and for the dead ; perhaps because these were the grand pillars upon which Antichrist built his empire, being the most lucrative doctrines ever invented by men. We must, however, take notice that Spottiswoode, afterwards archbishop of that See, assigns the following as grounds for his suffering : 1. That the corruption of sin remains in children after their baptism. 2. That no man by the mere power of his free will can do any good. 3. That no man is without sin so long as he liveth. 4. That every true Christian may know himself to be in a state of grace. 5. That a man is not justified by works, but by faith only. 6. That good works make not a man good, but that a good man doth good works, and that an ill man doth ill works ; yet the same ill works, truly repented of, make not an ill man. 7. That faith, hope, and charity, are so linked together, that he who hath one of them hath all, and he that lacketh one lacketh all. 8. That God is the cause of sin in this sense, that he withdraweth his grace from man; and, grace withdrawn, he cannot but sin. These articles make up the whole charge along with the following: (1.) That auricular confession is not necessary to salvation. (2.) That actual penance cannot purchase the remission of sin. (3.) That there is no purgatory, and that the holy patriarchs were in heaven before Christ's passion. (4.) That the Pope is Antichrist, and that every priest hath as much power as he.

For holding these articles, and because he refused to abjure them, he was condemned as an obstinate heretic, and delivered to the secular power by the archbishops of St Andrews and Glasgow, the bishops of Dunkeld, Brechin, and Dunblane, and fourteen underlings, who all set their hands to the sentence; which, that it might have the greater authority, was likewise subscribed by every person of note in the university, among whom the Earl of Casillis was one, then not exceeding thirteen years of age. The sentence follows as given by Mr Foxe in his Acts and Monuments, vol. ii. folio edition, 1661, p. 227.

" *CHRISTI nomine invocato:* We, James, by the mercy of God, Archbishop of St Andrews, Primate of Scotland, with the counsel, decree, and authority, of the most reverend fathers in God, and lords, abbots, doctors of theology, professors of the holy Scripture, and masters of the university, assisting us for the time, sitting in judgment, within our metropolitan church of St Andrews, in the cause of heretical pravity, against Patrick Hamilton, abbot or pensionary of Ferne, being summoned to appear before us, to answer to certain articles affirmed, taught, and preached by him; and so appearing before us, and accused, the merits of the cause being ripely weighed, discussed, and understood by faithful inquisition made in Lent last passed, we have found the same Patrick Hamilton, many ways infamed with heresy, disputing, holding, and maintaining divers heresies of Martin Luther and his followers, repugnant to our faith, and which are already condemned by general councils and most famous universities. And he being under the same infamy, we decerning before him, to be summoned and accused upon the premises, he of evil mind (as may be presumed) passed to other parts, forth of the realm, suspected and noted for heresy. And being lately returned, not being admitted, but of his own head, without licence or privilege, hath presumed to preach wicked heresy.

"We have found, also, that he hath affirmed, published, and taught divers opinions of Luther, and wicked heretics, after that he was summoned to appear before us and our council : that man hath no free will—that man is in sin so long as he liveth—that children, incontinent after their baptism, are sinners — all Christians that be worthy to be called Christians, do know that they are in grace—no man is justified by works, but by faith only —good works make not a man good, but a good man doth make good works—that faith, hope, and charity, are so knit, that he that hath one hath the rest, and that he that wants one of them wants the rest, etc., with divers other heresies and detestable opinions; and hath persisted so obstinate in the same, that by no counsel or persuasion he may be drawn therefrom, to the way of our right faith.

"All these premises being considered, we, having the fear of God and the integrity of our faith before our eyes, and following the counsel and advice of the professors of the holy Scripture, men of law, and others assisting us for the time being, do pronounce, determine, and declare the said Patrick Hamilton, for his affirming, confessing, and maintaining of the foresaid heresies, and his pertinacity (they being condemned already by the church, general councils, and most famous universities) to be an heretic, and to have an evil opinion of the faith, and therefore to be condemned and punished, like as we condemn and punish, and define him to be punished, by this our sentence definitive, depriving and sentencing him to be deprived of all dignities, honours, orders, offices, and benefices of the church : and therefore do judge and pronounce him to be delivered over to the secular power, to be punished, and his goods to be confiscated.

"This our sentence definitive, was given and read at our metropolitan church of St Andrews, this last day of the month of February, *anno* 1527, being present, the most reverend fathers in Christ, and lords, Gawand Archbishop of Glasgow, George bishop of Dunkeld, John bishop of Brechin, James bishop of Dunblane, Patrick prior of St Andrews, David abbot of Aberbrothwick (afterwards Cardinal Beaton), George abbot of Dunfermline, Alexander abbot of Cambuskenneth, Henry abbot of Lindores, John prior of Pittenweeme, the dean and subdean of Glasgow, Mr Hugh Spence, Thomas Ramsay, Allan Meldrum, etc. In presence of the clergy and people."

The same day that this doom was pronounced, he was also condemned by the secular power, and on the afternoon of that same day (for they were afraid of an application to the king on his behalf), he was hurried to the stake immediately after dinner, the fire being prepared before the old College.

Being come to the place of martyrdom, he put off his clothes and gave them to a servant who had been with him of a long time, saying : "This stuff will not help me in the fire, yet will do thee some good. I have no more to leave thee but the ensample of my death—which, I pray thee, keep in mind ; for albeit the same be bitter and painful in man's judgment, yet it is the entrance to everlasting life, which none can inherit who deny Christ before this wicked generation." Having so said, he commended his soul into the hands of God, with his eyes fixed towards heaven, and being bound to the stake in the midst of some coals, timber, and other combustibles, a train of powder was made, with a design to kindle the fire, but did not succeed, the explosion scorching only one of his hands and his face. In this situation he remained until more powder was brought from the castle ; during which time his comfortable and godly speeches were often interrupted, particularly by Friar Campbell calling upon him "to recant, pray to our Lady, and say, *Salve regina.*" Upon being repeatedly disturbed in this manner by Campbell, Patrick Hamilton said : "Thou wicked man, thou knowest that I am not an heretic, and that it is the truth of God for which I now suffer ; so much didst thou confess unto me in private, and thereupon I appeal thee to answer before the judgment-seat of Christ." By this time the fire was kindled, and the noble martyr yielded his soul to God, crying out, "How long, O Lord, shall darkness overwhelm this realm ? How long wilt thou suffer this tyranny of men ?" And then ended his speech with Stephen, saying, "Lord Jesus, receive my spirit !"

Thus died this noble martyr of Jesus, on the last day of February 1527, in the twenty-fourth year of his age. His death excited very considerable interest, and was overruled by the Sovereign Disposer of all events, in greatly promoting the interests of the Reformation. Says Pinkerton : "The flames in which he expired were in the course of one generation to enlighten all Scotland, and to consume with avenging fury the Catholic superstition, the papal power, and the prelacy itself."

Friar Campbell soon after became distracted, and died within a

year after Hamilton's martyrdom, under the most awful apprehensions of the Lord's indignation against him. The Popish clergy
abroad congratulated their friends in Scotland upon their zeal for
the Romish faith, discovered in the above tragedy; but it rather
served the cause of reformation than retarded it; especially when
the people began deliberately to compare the behaviour of Patrick
Hamilton and Friar Campbell; they were induced to inquire more
narrowly into the truth than before. The reader will find a very
particular account of the doctrines maintained by Hamilton, in
Knox's "History of the Reformation in Scotland," nigh the beginning.

RUINS OF THE CATHEDRAL, ST ANDREWS.

PORTRAIT OF GEORGE WISHART.

George Wishart.

THIS gentleman was a brother of the Laird of Pit-arrow, in the county of Mearns, and was educated at the university of Cambridge, where his diligence and progress in useful learning soon made him to be respected. From an ardent desire to promote the truth in his own country, he returned to it in the summer of 1544, and began teaching a school in the town of Montrose, which he kept for some time with great applause. He was particularly celebrated for his uncommon eloquence, and agreeable manner of communication. The sequel of this narrative will inform the reader that he possessed the spirit of prophecy to an extraordinary degree, and was at the same time humble, modest, charitable, and patient, even to admiration. One of his own scholars gives the following picture of him: "He was a man of a tall stature, black-haired, long-bearded, of a graceful per-sonage, eloquent, courteous, ready to teach, and desirous to learn. He ordinarily wore a French cap, a frieze gown, plain black hose, and white bands, and hand-cuffs. He frequently gave away several parts of his apparel to the poor. In his diet he was very moderate, eating only twice a-day, and fasting every fourth day ; his lodgings, bedding, and such other circumstances, were correspondent to the things already mentioned." But as these particulars are rather curious than instructive, we shall say no more of them.

After he left Montrose, he came to Dundee, where he acquired still greater fame in public lectures on the Epistle to the Romans; insomuch that the Romish clergy began to think seriously on the consequences which they saw would inevitably ensue, if he were suffered to go on pulling down that fabric of superstition and idolatry, which they with so much pains had reared. They were particularly disgusted at the reception which he met with in Dundee, and immediately set about projecting his ruin.

From the time that Mr Patrick Hamilton suffered, until this period, papal tyranny reigned by fire and faggot, without control. In the year 1539, Cardinal David Beaton succeeded his uncle in the See of St Andrews, and carefully trod the path his uncle had marked out. To show his own greatness, and to recommend himself to his superior at Rome, he accused Sir John Borthwick of heresy, whose goods were confiscated, and himself burnt in effigy —for, being forewarned of his danger, he had escaped out of the country. After this, he suborned a priest to forge a will of King James V., who died about this time, declaring himself, with the Earls of Huntly, Argyle, and Moray, to be regents of the kingdom. The cheat being discovered, the Earl of Arran was elected Governor, and the Cardinal was committed prisoner to the Castle of Dalkeith; but he soon found means to escape from his confinement, and prevailed with the Regent to break all his promises to the party who had elected him to that office, and to join with him in embruing his hands in the blood of the saints. Accordingly, several professors of the Reformed religion in the town of Perth were arraigned, condemned, hanged, and drowned, others were sent into banishment, and some were strangled in private. We have departed thus far from the course of our narrative, to show the reader that the vacancies betwixt the respective lives in this collection were as remarkable for persecution, as the particular instances which are here set before him.

It was this Cardinal who, incensed at Mr Wishart's success in Dundee, prevailed with Robert Mill (formerly a professor of the truth, and who had been a sufferer on that account, but who was now a man of considerable influence in Dundee), to give Mr Wishart a charge in the Queen's and Governor's name, to trouble them no more with his preaching in that place. This commission was executed by Mill one day in public, just as Mr Wishart had ended his sermon. Upon hearing it, he kept silence for a little with his eyes turned towards heaven, and then casting them on the speaker with a sorrowful countenance, he said, " God is my witness that I never minded your trouble, but your comfort ; yea, your trouble is more grievous unto me than it is unto yourselves ; but sure I am, to reject the Word of God, and drive away His messengers, is not the way to save you from trouble, but to bring you into it. When I am gone, God will send you messengers who will not be afraid either for burning or banishment. I have, at the hazard of my life, remained among you preaching the word of salvation ; and now, since you yourselves refuse me, I must leave my innocence to be declared by God. If it be long well with you, I am not led by the Spirit of Truth; and if unexpected trouble come upon you, remember this is the cause, and turn to God by repentance, for He is merciful." These words being pronounced, he came down from the pulpit or preaching-place. The Earl Marischal, and some other noblemen who were present at the sermon, entreated him earnestly to go to the North with them ; but he excused himself, and took journey for the West country, where he was gladly received by many.

Being come to the town of Ayr, he began to preach the Gospel with great freedom and faithfulness. But Dunbar, Archbishop of Glasgow, being informed of the great concourse of people who crowded to his sermons, at the instigation of Cardinal Beaton went to Ayr with the resolution to apprehend him, and took possession of the church to prevent him from preaching in it. The news of this brought Alexander, Earl of Glencairn, and some gentlemen of the neighbourhood, immediately to the town. They offered to put Mr Wishart into the church, but he would not consent, saying, " The Bishop's sermon would not do much hurt, and that, if they pleased, he would go to the market-cross," which he did, and preached with such success that several of his hearers, formerly enemies to the truth, were converted on that occasion. During the time Mr Wishart was thus employed, the Archbishop was haranguing some of his underlings and parasites in the church ; having no sermon to give them, he promised to be better provided against a future occasion, and speedily left the town.

Mr Wishart continued with the gentlemen of Kyle after the

Archbishop's departure, and being desired to preach next Lord's day, in the church of Mauchline, he went thither with that design; but the Sheriff of Ayr had, in the night-time, put a garrison of soldiers in the church to keep him out. Hugh Campbell of Kinzeancleugh, and others of the parish, were exceedingly offended at such impiety, and would have entered the church by force, but Mr Wishart would not suffer it, saying, " Brethren, it is the word of peace which I preach unto you; the blood of no man shall be shed for it this day. Jesus Christ is as mighty in the fields as in the church; and He Himself, while He lived in the flesh, preached oftener in the desert and upon the seaside, than in the Temple of Jerusalem." Upon this, the people were appeased, and went with him to the edge of a muir on the south-west side of Mauchline; where, having placed himself upon a ditch-dyke, he preached to a great multitude who resorted to him. He continued speaking for more than three hours, God working wondrously by him, insomuch that Laurence Rankin, the laird of Shield, a very profane person, was converted by his means. The tears ran from his eyes, to the astonishment of all present, and the whole of his after-life witnessed that his profession was without hypocrisy. While in this country, Mr Wishart often preached with most remarkable success at the church of Galston and other places. At this time and in this part of the country, it might be truly said, that " The harvest was great, but the labourers were few."

After he had been about a month thus employed in Kyle, he was informed that the plague had broken out in Dundee the fourth day after he had left it, and that it still continued to rage in such a manner that great numbers were swept off every day. This affected him so much, that he resolved to return unto them. Accordingly he took leave of his friends in the West, who were filled with sorrow at his departure. The next day after his arrival at Dundee, he caused intimation to be made that he would preach; and for that purpose chose his station upon the head of the Eastgate, the infected persons standing without, and those that were whole within. His text was Psalm cvii. 20 : " He sent his Word, and healed them, and delivered them from their destructions." By this discourse he so comforted the people, that they thought themselves happy in having such a preacher, and entreated him to remain with them while the plague continued, which he complied with, preaching often, and taking care that the poor should not want necessaries more than the rich; in doing which, he exposed himself to the infection, even where it was most malignant, without reserve.

During all this time, his sworn adversary, the Cardinal, had his eye upon him, and bribed a priest called Sir John Wightman to assassinate him. He was to make the attempt as Wishart came down from the preaching place, with the expectation of escaping among the crowd after the deed was done. To effect this, he posted himself at the foot of the steps with his gown loose, and a dagger under it in his hand. Upon Mr Wishart's approach, he looked sternly upon the priest, asking him what he intended to do; and instantly clapped his hand upon the hand of the priest that held the dagger, and took it from him. Upon this, having openly confessed his design, a tumult immediately ensued, and the sick without the gate rushed in, crying to have the assassin delivered to them; but Wishart interposed, and defended him from their violence, telling them that he had done him no harm, and that such as injured the one injured the other likewise. So the priest escaped without any harm.

The plague being now considerably abated, he determined to pay a visit to the town of Montrose, intending to go from thence to Edinburgh, to meet the gentlemen of the West. While he was at Montrose, he administered the sacrament of our Lord's Supper in both elements, and preached with success. Here he received a letter directed to him from his intimate friend the laird of Kinnear, acquainting him that he had taken a sudden sickness, and requesting him to come to him with all diligence. Upon this he immediately set out on his journey, attended by some honest friends in Montrose, who, out of affection, would accompany him part of the way. They had not travelled above a quarter of a mile, when all of a sudden he stopped, saying to the company, " I am forbidden by God to go this journey. Will some of you be pleased to ride to yonder place (pointing with his finger to a little hill), and see what you find, for I apprehend there is a plot against my life; " whereupon he returned to the town, and they, who went forward to the place, found about sixty horsemen ready to intercept him. By this the whole plot came to light; they found that the letter had been forged; and, upon their telling Mr Wishart what they had seen, he replied, " I know that I shall end my life by the hands of that wicked man (meaning the Cardinal), but it will not be after this manner."

The time he had appointed for meeting the West-country gentlemen at Edinburgh drawing near, he undertook that journey, much against the inclination and advice of John Erskine, laird of Dun. The first night after leaving Montrose he lodged at Invergowrie, about two miles from Dundee, with James Watson, a faithful friend; where, being laid in bed, he was observed to rise a little after midnight, and to go out into an adjacent garden, that he might give vent to his sighs and groans without being observed; but being followed by two men, William Spalding and John Watson, at a distance, in order that they might observe his motions, they saw him prostrate himself upon the ground, weeping and making supplication for nearly an hour, and then return to his rest. As they lay in the same apartment with him, they took care to return before him; and upon his coming into the room, they asked him (as if ignorant of all that had passed) where he had been. But he made no answer, and they ceased their interrogations. In the morning they asked him again, why he rose in the night, and what was the cause of such sorrow, (for they told him all that they had seen him do,) when he answered with a dejected countenance, "I wish you had been in your beds, which had been more for your ease, for I was scarcely well occupied." But they praying him to satisfy their minds further, and communicate some comfort unto them, he said, "I will tell you: I assuredly know my travail is nigh an end, therefore pray to God for me, that I may not shrink when the battle waxeth most hot." Hearing these words, they burst into tears, saying, "That was but small comfort to them." He replied, "God will send you comfort after me; this realm shall be illuminated with the light of Christ's Gospel, as clearly as any realm ever was since the days of the apostles; the house of God shall be built in it; yea, it shall not lack (whatsoever the enemies shall devise to the contrary) the very cope-stone; neither shall this be long in doing, for there shall not many suffer after me. The glory of God shall appear, and truth shall once more triumph in despite of the devil; but, alas! if the people become unthankful, the plagues and punishments which shall follow will be fearful and terrible."

After this prediction, which was accomplished in such a remarkable manner afterwards, he proceeded on his journey, and arrived at Leith about the 10th of December, where, being disappointed of a meeting with the West-country gentlemen, he kept himself retired for some days, and then, becoming very uneasy and discouraged, and being asked the reason, he replied, " I have laboured to bring people out of darkness, but now I lurk as a man ashamed to show himself before men." By this they understood that he desired to preach, and told him that they would gladly hear him, but the danger into which he would throw himself thereby prevented them from advising him to it. He answered, " If you and others will hear me next Sabbath, I will preach in Leith, let God provide for me as best pleaseth Him," which he did upon the parable of the sower (Matt. xiii.). After sermon his friends advised him to leave Leith, because the Regent and Cardinal were soon to be in Edinburgh, and his situation would be dangerous on that account. He complied with this advice, and resided with the lairds of Brunston, Longniddry, and Ormiston, by turns.

The following Sabbath he preached at Inveresk, both fore and after noon, to a crowded audience, among whom was Sir George Douglas, who, after the sermon, publicly said, " I know that the Governor and Cardinal shall hear that I have been at this preaching (for they were now come to Edinburgh) ; say unto them, that I will avow it, and will not only maintain the doctrine which I have heard, but also the person of the teacher, to the uttermost of my power ; " which open and candid declaration was very grateful to the whole congregation. During the time of this sermon, Wishart perceived two grey friars standing in the entry of the church, and whispering to every person that entered the door. He called out to the people to make room for them, because, said he, " perhaps they come to learn ; " and then addressed them, requesting them to come forward and hear the word of truth. When they still continued to trouble the people, he reproved them in the following manner : " O ! ye servants of Satan, and deceivers of the souls of men, will ye neither hear God's truth, nor suffer others to hear it ? Depart, and take this for your portion, God shall shortly confound and disclose your hypocrisy within this realm ; ye shall be abominable unto men, and your places and habitations shall be desolate."

The two Sabbaths following he preached at Tranent ; and in all his sermons, after leaving Montrose, he more or less hinted that his ministry was near an end. The next place he preached at was Haddington, where his congregation was at first very large, but the following day very few attended him, which was thought to be owing to the influence of the Earl of Bothwell, who, at the instigation of the Cardinal, had inhibited the people from attending ; for his authority was very considerable in that part of the country. At this time he received a letter from the gentlemen of the West, declaring that they could not keep the diet appointed at Edinburgh. This, with the reflection that so few attended his ministrations at Haddington, grieved him exceedingly. He called upon John Knox, who then attended him, and told him that he was weary of the world, since he perceived that men were become weary of God. Notwithstanding the anxiety and discouragement which he laboured under, he went immediately to the pulpit, and sharply rebuking the people for their neglect of the Gospel, he warned them, "That sore and fearful would be the plagues that should ensue ; that fire and sword should waste them ; that strangers should possess their houses, and chase them from their habitations." This prediction was soon after verified, when the English took and possessed the town, and while the French and Scots besieged it in the year 1548. This was the last sermon which he preached ; in it, as had for some time been usual with him, he spoke of his death as near at hand ; and after it was over, he bade his acquaintances farewell, as if it had been for ever. He went to Ormiston, accompanied by the Lairds of Brunston and Ormiston, and Sir John Sandilands, the younger of Calder. John Knox was also desirous to have gone with him ; but Wishart desired him to return, saying, " One is enough for a sacrifice at this time."

Being come to Ormiston, he entered into some spiritual conversation in the family, particularly concerning the happy state of God's children ; appointed the 51st psalm, according to an old version then in use, to be sung ; and then recommended the company to God, going to bed some time sooner than ordinary. About midnight the Earl of Bothwell beset the house, so as none could escape, and then called upon the laird, declaring the design to him, and entreating him not to hold out, for it would be to no purpose, because the Cardinal and Governor were coming with all their train ; but if he would deliver Mr Wishart up, Bothwell promised upon his honour that no evil should befall him. Being inveigled with this, and consulting with Mr Wishart, who requested that the gates should be opened, saying, " God's will be done," the laird complied. The Earl of Bothwell entered with some gentlemen, who solemnly protested that Mr Wishart should receive no harm, but that he would either carry him to his own house, or return him again to Ormiston in safety. Upon this promise hands were stricken, and Mr Wishart went along with him to Elphinstone, where the Cardinal was ; after which he was first carried to Edinburgh, then to the house of Hailes, the Earl of Bothwell's principle residence in East Lothian,—perhaps upon pretence of fulfilling the engagement which Bothwell had come under to him,—after which he was reconducted to Edinburgh, where the Cardinal had now assembled a convocation of prelates, for reforming some abuses, but without effect. Buchanan says, that he was apprehended by a party of horse, detached by the Cardinal for that purpose ; that at first the laird of Ormiston refused to deliver him up ; upon which the Cardinal and Regent both posted thither, but could not prevail, until the Earl of Bothwell was sent for, who succeeded by flattery and fair promises, not one of which was fulfilled.

Wishart remained at Edinburgh only a few days, until the blood-thirsty Cardinal prevailed· with the Governor to deliver up this faithful servant of Jesus Christ to his tyranny. He was accordingly sent to St Andrews ; and, being advised to it by the Archbishop of Glasgow, he would have got a civil judge appointed to try him, if David Hamilton of Preston, a kinsman to the Regent, had not remonstrated against it, and represented the danger of attacking the servants of God, who had no other crime laid to their charge, but that of preaching the gospel of Jesus Christ. This speech, which Buchanan gives at large, affected the Governor in such a manner, that he absolutely refused the Cardinal's request ; upon which he replied in anger, " That he had only sent to him out of mere civility without any need for it ; for that he, with his clergy, had power sufficient to bring Mr Wishart to condign punishment." Thus was this servant of God left in the hands of that proud and merciless tyrant, the religious part of the nation loudly complaining of the Governor's weakness.

Wishart being now in St Andrews, the Cardinal without delay summoned the bishops and superior clergy to meet at that place on the 27th of February 1546, to deliberate upon a question about which he was already resolved. The next day after this convocation, Mr Wishart received a summons in prison, by the dean of the town, to answer on the morrow for his heretical doctrine before the judges. The next day the Cardinal went to the place of judgment in the Abbey church, with a train of armed men, marching in warlike order ; immediately Mr Wishart was sent for from the sea-tower, which was his prison, and being about to enter the door of the church, a poor man asked alms of him, to whom he threw his purse.

When he came before the Cardinal, John Winram, the sub-prior, went up into the pulpit by appointment, and made a discourse upon the nature of heresy, from Matthew xiii. ; which he did with great caution, and yet in such a way as applied more justly to the accusers than the accused, for he was a secret favourer of the truth. After him rose up one John Lauder, a most virulent enemy of religion, who acted the part of Mr Wishart's accuser. He pulled out a long roll of maledictory charges against Mr Wishart, and dealt out the Romish thunder so liberally, as terrified the ignorant bystanders, but did not in the least discompose this meek servant of Christ. He was accused of disobedience to the Governor's authority, for teaching that man had no free will, and for contemning fasting (all which charges he absolutely refused) ; for denying that there are seven sacraments, and that auricular confession, extreme unction, and the sacrament of the altar, so called, are sacraments, and that we should pray to saints ; for saying that it was necessary for every man to know and understand his baptism ; that the Pope had no more power than another man ; that it is as lawful to eat flesh upon Friday as upon Sunday ; that there is no purgatory ; and that it is in vain to build costly churches to the honour of God ; also for condemning conjuration, the vows of single life, the cursings of the Holy Church, etc.

While Lauder was reading these accusations, he had put himself into a most violent sweat—frothing at the mouth, calling Mr Wishart a runagate traitor, and demanding an answer. This Wishart gave in a short and modest oration, at which they cried out with one consent in a most tumultuous manner. Perceiving that they were resolved to proceed against him to the utmost extremity, he appealed to a more equitable and impartial judge : upon which Lauder, repeating the several titles of the Cardinal, asked him, "If my Lord Cardinal was not an equitable judge?" Mr Wishart replied, "I do not refuse him, but I desire the Word of God to be my judge, the Temporal Estates, with some of your Lordships, because I am my Lord Governor's prisoner." After some scornful language thrown out both against him and the Governor, they proceeded to read the articles against him a second time, and hear his answers, which he made with great solidity of judgment ; after which they condemned him to be burned as a heretic, paying

no regard to his defences, nor to the emotions of their own
consciences, but thinking that by killing him they should do God
good service.   Upon this resolution (for their final sentence was
not yet pronounced), Mr Wishart kneeled down and prayed in the
following manner :

"O Immortal God, how long wilt Thou suffer the rage of the
ungodly? how long shall they exercise their fury upon Thy servants
who further Thy Word in this world, seeing they desire to choke
and destroy Thy true doctrine and verity, by which Thou hast
showed Thyself unto the world, which was drowned in blindness
and ignorance of Thy name?   O Lord, we know surely that Thy
true servants must suffer, for Thy name's sake, both persecution,
affliction, and troubles in this present life, which is but a shadow,
as Thy prophets and apostles have shown us; but yet we desire Thee,
merciful Father, that Thou wouldst preserve, defend, and help Thy
congregation, which Thou hast chosen from before the foundation of
the world, and give them Thy grace to hear Thy word, and to be
Thy true servants in this present life."

After this, the common people were removed until the definitive
sentence should be pronounced, which, being so similar to Mr
Hamilton's, need not here be inserted.   This being done, he was
re-committed to the castle for that night.   In his way thither, two
friars came to him, requesting him to make his confession to
them, which he refused, but desired them to bring Mr Winram, who
had preached that day ; who being come, after some discourse with
Mr Wishart, he asked him if he would receive the sacrament of the
Lord's Supper.   Mr Wishart answered, " Most willingly, if I may
have it administered according to Christ's institution, under both
kinds of bread and wine."   Hereupon the sub-prior went to the
bishops, and asked if they would permit the sacrament to be given
to the prisoner.   But the Cardinal, in all their names, answered,
" That it was not reasonable to give any spiritual benefit to an
obstinate heretic, condemned by the Church."

All this night Mr Wishart spent in prayer, and next morning the
captain of the castle gave him notice that they had denied him the
sacrament, and at the same time invited him to breakfast with him ;
which Mr Wishart accepted, saying, " I will do that very willingly,
and so much the rather, because I perceive you to be a good
Christian, and a man fearing God."   All things being ready, and
the family assembled to breakfast, Mr Wishart, turning himself to the

captain, said, "I beseech you, in the name of God, and for the love you bear to our Saviour Jesus Christ, to be silent a little while, till I have made a short exhortation, and blessed this bread which we are to eat, so that I may bid you farewell." The table being covered, and bread being set upon it, he spake about the space of half-an-hour, of the institution of the Supper, and of our Saviour's death and passion, exhorting those who were present to mutual love and holiness of life. Then, giving thanks, he break the bread, distributing a part to those about him who were disposed to communicate, entreating them to remember that Christ died for them, and to feed on it spiritually; then, taking the cup, he bade them remember that Christ's blood was shed for them, and having tasted it himself, he delivered it unto them, and then, concluding with thanksgiving and prayer, he told them "that he would neither eat nor drink more in this life," and retired to his chamber.

Soon after, by the appointment of the Cardinal, two executioners came to him, and, arraying him in a black linen coat, they fastened some bags of gunpowder about him, put a rope about his neck, a chain about his waist, and bound his hands behind his back, and in this dress they led him to the stake, near the Cardinal's palace. Opposite to the stake they had placed the great guns of the castle, lest any should attempt to rescue him. The fore-tower, which was immediately opposite to the fire, was hung with tapestry, and rich cushions were laid in the windows, for the ease of the Cardinal and prelates, while they beheld the sad spectacle. As he was going to the stake, it is said that two beggars asked alms of him, and that he replied : " I want my hands wherewith I used to give you alms; but the merciful Lord vouchsafe to give you all necessaries, both for soul and body." After this the friars came about him, urging him to pray to our Lady, to whom he answered, " Cease; tempt me not, I entreat you."

Having mounted a scaffold prepared on purpose, he turned towards the people and declared, that he felt much joy within himself in offering up his life for the name of Christ, and told them, that they ought not to be offended with the good Word of God, because of the afflictions he had endured, or the torments which they now saw prepared for him; " but I entreat you," said he, " that you love the Word of God for your salvation, and suffer patiently and with a comfortable heart for the Word's sake, which is your everlasting comfort; but for the true Gospel, which was given me by the Grace of God, I suffer this day with a glad heart. Behold and consider my visage; ye shall not see me change my colour. I fear not this fire, and I pray that you may not fear them that slay the body, but have no power to slay the soul. Some have said that I taught, that the soul shall sleep till the last day; but I know surely, and my faith is such, that my soul shall sup with my Saviour this night." Then he prayed for his accusers, that they might be forgiven, if, through ignorance or evil design, they had forged lies upon him. After this, the executioner asked his forgiveness, to whom he replied, "Come hither to me;" and when he came, he kissed his cheek, and said, "Lo, here is a token that I forgive thee; do thine office." Being raised up from his knees, he was bound to the stake, crying with a loud voice, "O Saviour of the world, have mercy upon me! Father of heaven, I commend my spirit into Thy holy hands!" The executioner having kindled the fire, the powder fastened to his body blew up. The captain of the castle, perceiving that he was still alive, drew near, and bid him be of good courage; whereupon Mr Wishart said, "This flame hath scorched my body, yet it hath not daunted my spirit; but he who, from yonder place, beholdeth us with such pride, shall within a few days lie in the same, as ignominiously as he is now seen proudly to rest himself." As he was thus speaking, the executioner drew the cord that was about his neck so strait that he spoke no more; and thus, like another Elijah, he took his flight by a fiery chariot into heaven, and obtained the martyr's crown on the 1st of March 1546.

Thus lived, and thus died, this faithful witness of Jesus Christ. He was early marked out as a sacrifice to Papal tyranny. Being delated to the Bishop of Brechin for an heretic, because he taught the Greek New Testament to his scholars, while he kept school at Montrose, he was summoned by him, to appear before him, but escaped into England, and at the University of Cambridge completed his education, and was himself an instructor of others. During the whole time he was in his own country, he was hunted as a partridge on the mountains, until the Cardinal got him brought to the stake. Through the whole of his sufferings, his meekness and patience were very remarkable, as was that uncommon measure of the spirit of prophecy which he possessed. Witness the circumstances relative to Dundee, Haddington, the reformation from

Popery, and the Cardinal's death—all of which were foretold by him, and soon after accomplished.*

The Popish clergy rejoiced at his death, and extolled the Cardinal's courage, for proceeding in it against the Governor's order; but the people very justly looked upon Wishart as both a prophet and a martyr. It was also said that, abstractly from the grounds of his suffering, his death was no less than murder, in regard no writ was obtained for it, and the clergy could not burn any without a warrant from the secular power.

This stirred up Norman and John Leslie, of the family of Rothes, William Kircaldy of Grange, James Melvill of the family of Carnbee, Peter Carmichael, and others, to avenge Mr Wishart's death. Accordingly, upon the 28th of May 1546, (not three months after Mr Wishart suffered,) they surprised the castle early in the morning, and either secured or turned out the persons that were lodged in it. On coming to the Cardinal's door, he was by this time alarmed, and had secured it; but upon their threatening to force the door, he opened it (relying partly upon the sanctity of his office, and partly on his acquaintance with some of them), crying, "I am a priest, I am a priest." But this had no effect upon them; for James Melvill having exhorted him in a solemn manner to repentance, and having apprised him that he was now to avenge Mr Wishart's death, stabbed

---

* [The following judicious remarks by Dr M'Crie, in his Biography of Knox and Henderson, may here be quoted with advantage. They will be found to apply to several other incidents recorded in this book: "The canon of our faith, as Christians, is contained in the scriptures of the Old and New Testament; we must not look to impressions or new revelations as the rule of our duty; but that God may, on particular occasions, forewarn persons of some things which shall happen to testify His approbation of them, to encourage them to confide in Him in circumstances of peculiar difficulty, or to serve other important purposes, is not, I think, inconsistent with the principles of either natural or revealed religion. If to believe this be enthusiasm, it is an enthusiasm into which some of the most enlightened and sober men in modern as well as ancient times have fallen. Some of the Reformers were men of singular piety; they "walked with God;" they "were instant in prayer;" they were exposed to uncommon opposition, and had uncommon service to perform; they were endued with extraordinary gifts, and I am inclined to believe, were occasionally favoured with extraordinary premonitions with respect to certain events which concerned themselves, other individuals, or the church in general. But whatever intimations of this kind they enjoyed, they did not rest the authority of their mission upon these, nor appeal to them as constituting any part of the evidence of those doctrines which they preached to the world."—ED.]

him twice or thrice, which ended his wretched days. These persons, with some others who came in to them, held the castle for nearly two years, being assisted by England. They had the Governor's eldest son with them, for he had been put under the Cardinal's care, and was in the castle at the time they surprised it. The castle was at length besieged by the French, and surrendered upon having the lives of all that were in it secured.

Between this and the time of Mr Walter Mill's sufferings, whose life follows, Adam Wallace, *alias* Fean, a simple but very zealous man, was taken at Winton, and was brought to his trial in the Black-friar's church in Edinburgh, where he was charged with articles of heresy, similar to those with which others before him had been charged. He was condemned and burnt on the Castlehill, suffering with great patience and resolution.

There were others condemned before that time ; among whom were Robert Forrester, gentleman ; Sir Duncan Simson, priest; Friar Killore, Friar Beveridge, and Dean Thomas Forrest, a canon regular and Vicar of Dollar, who were all burnt at one stake, upon the Castlehill of Edinburgh, February 28, 1538.

RUINS OF THE CASTLE OF ST ANDREWS.

ABBEY CHURCH OF DUNFERMLINE.

Walter Mill.

WALTER MILL was born about the year 1476. He was educated in the Popish religion, and made priest of Lunan, in the shire of Angus, where he remained, until he was accused by the Archbishop of St Andrews of having left off saying mass, which he had done long before that time. On that account he was condemned in the year 1538; but escaped into Germany, where he married a wife, and was more perfectly instructed in the true religion.

He returned to Scotland about 1556, but kept himself as retired as possible, going about the land reproving vice, and instructing the people in the grounds of religion. This coming at length to the ears of the ecclesiastics, in 1558, he was, by order of the Bishops, apprehended at Dysart, in the shire of Fife, by two priests, and imprisoned in the castle of St Andrews; where the papists, both by threatening and flattery, laboured with him to recant, offering him a place in the abbey of Dunfermline all the days of his life, if he would deny what he had already taught. But continuing constant in his opinions, he was brought to a trial before the Archbishop of St Andrews, the Bishops of Moray, Brechin, Caithness, and others, who were assembled in the cathedral of St Andrews.

When he came to make his defence, he was so old, feeble, and lame, that it was feared none would hear him; but as soon as he began to speak he surprised them all; his voice made the church to ring, and his quickness and courage amazed his very enemies. At first he kneeled and prayed for some time; after which, Sir Andrew Oliphant, a priest, called upon him to arise and answer to the articles of charge, saying, " You keep my Lord of St Andrews too long here;" nevertheless, he continued some time in prayer; and when he arose, said, " I ought to obey God rather than man. I serve a mightier Lord than your lord is; and, whereas, ye call me *Sir Walter*—call me now *Walter :* I have been too long one of the Pope's Knights (for in those days all priests, after their ordination, had the title of *Sir*.) Now, say what you have to say."

Oliphant began his interrogations as follows :

Oliph. Thou sayest there are not seven sacraments?

Mill. Give me the Lord's Supper and Baptism, and take you all the rest?

Oliph. What think you of a priest's marriage?

Mill. I think it a blessed bond ordained by God, and approved of by Christ, and free to all sorts of men : but ye abhor it, and in the meanwhile take other men's wives and daughters. Ye vow chastity and keep it not.

Oliph. How sayest thou that the mass is idolatry?

Mill. A lord or king calleth many to dinner, they come and sit down, but the lord himself turneth his back, and eateth up all; and so do you.

Oliph. Thou deniest the sacrament of the altar to be the real body of Christ in flesh and blood?

Mill. The Scriptures are to be understood spiritually, and not carnally, and so your mass is wrong, for Christ was once offered on the cross for sin, and will never be offered again, for then He put an end to all sacrifice.

Oliph. Thou deniest the office of a bishop?

Mill. I affirm that those you call bishops do no bishop's work, but live after sensual pleasure, taking no care of Christ's flock, nor regarding His word.

Oliph. Thou speakest against pilgrimage, and sayest, it is a pilgrimage to whoredom?

Mill. I say pilgrimage is not commanded in Scripture; and that there is no greater whoredom in any place, except in brothel-houses.

Oliph. You preach privately in houses, and sometimes in the field?

Mill. Yea, and on the sea also, when sailing in a ship.

Oliph. If you will not recant, I will pronounce sentence against you.

Mill. I know I must die once; and therefore, as Christ said to Judas, "What thou doest, do quickly." You shall know that I will not recant the truth; for I am corn, and not chaff; I will neither be blown away by the wind nor burst with the flail, but will abide both.

Then Oliphant, as the mouth of the court, was ordered to pronounce sentence against him, ordaining him to be delivered to the temporal judge, and burnt as an heretic. But they could not procure one as a temporal judge to condemn him. Learmont, provost of the town, and bailie of the Archbishop's regality, refused, and went out of town; and the people of the place were so moved at Walter Mill's constancy, and offended at the wrong done to him, that they refused to supply ropes to bind him, and other materials for his execution, whereby his death was retarded for one day. At last Somerville, a domestic of the Archbishop, undertook to act the part of temporal judge, and the ropes of the Archbishop's pavilion were taken to serve the purpose.

All things being thus prepared, he was led forth by Somerville, with a guard of armed men, to his execution. Being come to the place, some cried out to him to recant, to whom he answered, " I marvel at your rage, ye hypocrites, who do so cruelly pursue the servants of God; as for me, I am now eighty-two years old, and cannot live long by course of nature; but an hundred shall rise out of my ashes, who shall scatter you, ye hypocrites, and persecutors of God's people; and such of you as now think yourselves the best, shall not die such an honest death as I now do. I trust in God, I shall be the last who shall suffer death, in this fashion, for this cause, in the land." Thus his constancy increased as his end drew near. Being ordered by Oliphant to go up to the stake, he refused, and said, " No, I will not go, except thou put me up with thy hand, for by the law of God I am forbidden to put hands to myself; but if thou wilt put to thy hand, and take part of my death, thou shalt see me go up gladly." Then Oliphant putting him forward, he went up with a cheerful countenance saying, *Introibo ad altare Dei* ("I will go unto the altar of God"), and desired that he might be permitted to speak to the people. He was answered by Oliphant, that he had spoken too much already, and that the bishops were exceedingly displeased with what he had said. But some youths took his part, and bade him say on what he pleased.

He first bowed his knees and prayed, then arose, and standing upon the coals, addressed the people to this effect : " Dear friends, the cause why I suffer this day, is not for any crime laid to my charge, though I acknowledge myself a miserable sinner before God, but only for the defence of the truth of Jesus Christ, set forth in the Old and New Testaments. I praise God that He hath called me, among the rest of His servants, to seal up His truth with my life ; as I have received it of Him, so I willingly offer it up for His glory ; therefore, as ye would escape eternal death, be no longer seduced with the lies of bishops, abbots, friars, monks, and the rest of that sect of Antichrist, but depend only upon Jesus Christ and His mercy, that so ye may be delivered from condemnation."

During this speech, loud murmurs and lamentations were heard among the multitude, some admiring the patience, boldness, and constancy, of this martyr ; others complaining of the hard measures and cruelty of his persecutors. After having spoken as above, he prayed a little while, and then was drawn up, and bound to the stake ; and the fire being kindled, he cried, " Lord, have mercy on me. Pray, pray, good people, while there is time." And so he cheerfully yielded up his soul into the hands of his God, on the 28th of April, anno 1558, being then about the eighty-second year of his age.

MARTYRS' MONUMENT, ST ANDREWS.

The fortitude and constancy of this martyr affected the people so much, that they heaped up a great pile of stones on the place where he had been burned, that the memory of his death might be preserved; but the priests gave orders to have it taken down, and carried away, denouncing a curse on any who should lay stones there again; but their anathema was so little regarded, that what was thrown down in the day time was raised again in the night, until at last the papists carried away the stones to build houses in or about the town, which they did in the night with all possible secrecy.

The death of this martyr brought about the downfall of Popery in Scotland; for the people in general were so much inflamed, that, resolving openly to profess the truth, they bound themselves by promises and subscriptions of oaths, that before they would be thus abused any longer, they would take arms and resist the Papal tyranny; which they at last did.

James Stuart, Earl of Moray.

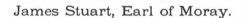

AMES STUART, Earl of Moray, was a natural son of King James V., and brother by the father's side to Mary Queen of Scots. In his infancy he was placed under the care of the celebrated George Buchanan, who instilled such principles into his mind in early life, as, by the Divine blessing, made him an honour to the Scottish nation.

The reader cannot here expect a very minute detail of all the heroic and patriotic deeds of this worthy nobleman, considering the station which he filled, and his activity in the discharge of the duties belonging to it.

He was the principal agent in promoting the work of Reformation from Popery. On the first dawning of it, in the year 1555, he attended the preaching of John Knox at Calder, where he often wished that his doctrine had been more public: which was an open profession of his love and zeal for the true religion.

He went over to France, with some other Scottish noblemen, at the time of his sister's marriage with the Dauphin, where his companions were supposed to have been poisoned, for they died in France. He escaped by the interposition of a kind Providence, but retained a weak and disordered stomach all his life. This did not, however, unfit him for those services, which after this he performed to religion and his country.

In the year 1556, he, and Argyle, wrote to John Knox at Geneva, to return to Scotland, and further the Reformation. Upon this, after having been detained some time at Dieppe, Knox returned in the year 1559, and went to St Johnston (or Perth), where the Reforming Congregation resorted to him; which fact coming to the ears of the Queen Regent, Mary of Guise, she sent the Earl of Argyle and Lord James (for that was the Earl of Moray's title at this time), to know the intent of so great an assembly. Knox returned this answer, " That her enterprise would not prosper in the end, seeing that she intended to fight against God." Upon receiving this reply, she summoned them to depart from the town of St Johnston; but afterwards, hearing of the daily increase of their numbers, she gave them leave to depart peaceably, with many fair promises that they should meet with no further danger; on which they obeyed, and left the town; but they had no sooner done so, than she, with her French guards, entered it in a most outrageous manner, telling the inhabitants, that no faith should be kept with heretics. This flagrant breach of promise so provoked Lord James that he left the Queen Regent, and joined the Lords of the Congregation, for so were the nobles called who favoured the work of Reformation. As soon as the Queen Regent got intelligence of this, she sent a threatening letter to him and Argyle (for they agreed on almost all occasions), commanding them to return, but to no purpose; for they went to Fife, and there began to throw down and remove the Popish images. Here they continued for some time; but being informed that the Queen Regent intended to go to Stirling, they went off from Perth late in the night, and entered Stirling with their associates, where they immediately demolished the monasteries, and purged the churches of idolatry. Such was the zeal of these worthy noblemen for the interest of the Reformed religion in Scotland.

From Stirling they marched for Edinburgh, purging all the superstitious relics of idolatry out of Linlithgow in their way. These summary proceedings alarmed the Queen Regent, insomuch that her zeal for Popery gave way to fears about her civil authority. To make the conduct of these Reformers the more odious to the unthinking part of the nation, she gave out, that they were in open rebellion against her, and that while making a pretence of religion, their real design was to set Lord James on the throne, there being now no male heir to the Crown. These insinuations she found means to transmit to Lord James himself, in a letter, said to be forged, in the names of Francis and Mary, the King and Queen of France, wherein he was further upbraided with ingratitude on account of the favours they pretended to have shown him, was commanded to lay down his arms, and return to his allegiance. To this letter (notwithstanding there were strong reasons to suspect it to be a forgery), he nevertheless returned a resolute answer, declaring, that he was not conscious to himself, in word or deed, of any offence either against the Regent or the laws ; but seeing that the nobility had undertaken the reformation of religion, which was delayed, and that they aimed at nothing but the glory of God, he was willing to bear the reproach which the enemies of religion would load him with ; neither was it just for him to desert that cause, which had Christ himself for its head and defender, whom unless they would voluntarily deny, they could not give up the enterprise in which they were embarked.

While these things were transacting, the Lords of the Congregation being then in and about Edinburgh, French troops to the number of 3000 were landed at Leith, at different times, to support the Queen Regent, between whom, and the Lords of the Congregation, there were several skirmishes, with little success on either side ; yet the Lords retired to Stirling, leaving the French for a time masters of the field, but not without apprehensions of danger from the arrival of an English fleet which was then expected. In the meantime they went over to Fife, spreading devastation everywhere around them, without resistance : whereupon the Queen Regent thus expressed herself: "Where is John Knox's God now? my God is stronger even now in Fife." This impious boast lasted not long, for Argyle and Lord James went to the town of Dysart immediately, to

PORTRAIT OF JAMES STUART, EARL OF MORAY.

stop their career along the coast. The French were 4000 strong, besides the Scots who adhered to them. The army of the Congregation were not above 600 men, yet they behaved with such courage and resolution, that for twenty days successively they faced this army ; and for each man they lost in skirmishes the French lost four. As an evidence of the uncommon attention which these two noblemen bestowed on this business, they never put off their clothes during the whole time, and slept but little.

In the month of June 1560 the Queen Regent died, and, a little after her, Francis King of France died likewise, by which events Scotland was delivered from this foreign army. Lord James went to France, to visit his sister Mary, now left a widow, after settling matters in Scotland as well as he could. He was attended by a splendid retinue, and appears to have met with a cold reception, but after several conversations with Queen Mary, she agreed to return to Scotland. During his stay at Paris he met with many insults on account of his known attachment to the Reformed religion. A box containing some valuable things was stolen from him ; several persons were likewise hired to assassinate him in the street ; but being apprised of his danger by an old friend of his own—not, however, before he was

THE REGENT MORAY'S HOUSE, EDINBURGH.

almost involved in it, being instantly surrounded by a rabble calling out *Huguenot! Huguenot!* and throwing stones—he made his way through them on horseback. Soon after this he left Paris, and returned home in May 1561, with a commission from the Queen, appointing him Regent until her return, which was in August following, when, as Knox expresses it, " Dolour and darkness came along with her." For though justice and equity were yet administered, and crimes were punished (because the administration of civil affairs was yet in the hands of Lord James, who for his management of public concerns was beloved by all), yet, upon the Queen's arrival, French levity and dissipation soon corrupted the Court to a very high degree.

About this time a banditti, called the moss troopers, broke in upon the borders of Scotland, committing very alarming depredations, by robbing and murdering all that came in their way. The Queen sent Lord James with a small force to oppose them; not with the intention that he might have the opportunity of acquiring military reputation, but to expose him to danger, that, if possible, she might get rid of him; for his popularity made her very uneasy, and his fidelity and boldness in reproving her faults, and withstanding her tyrannical measures, made him still more the object of her hatred and disgust. But, contrary to the expectations of many, God so prospered him in this expedition, that in a short time he brought twenty-eight ringleaders of the band to public execution, and obliged the rest to give hostages for their better behaviour in time coming. Thus he returned crowned with laurels, and was immediately created Earl of Mar, and in the February following he was made Earl of Moray, with the universal approbation of all good men. Some thought this act of the Queen was intended by her to conciliate his affections, and make him of her party.

About this time he married a daughter of the Earl Marischal, according to Knox, (Buchanan says, the Earl of March). The marriage took place publicly in the Church of Edinburgh, and after the ceremony was over, the preacher (probably John Knox) said to him, "Sir, the church of God hath received comfort by you, and by your labours unto this day; if you prove more faint therein afterwards, it will be said that your wife hath changed your nature."

It may be observed, that hitherto the nobility appeared very much united in their measures for promoting the interests of religion. This was soon at an end, for the noblemen at Court broke out into factions; among whom the Earl of Bothwell, envying the prosperity of Moray, stirred up some feuds between him and the Hamiltons, which increased so much, that they laid a plot for his life, which Bothwell took in hand to execute, while Moray was with the Queen, his sister, at Falkland; but the Earl of Arran, detesting such an action, sent a letter privately to him discovering the whole conspiracy, by which he escaped that danger. Bothwell fled from justice into France: but his emissaries were not less active in his absence, than they had been while he headed them in person; for another design was formed against the Earl's life by one of the Gordons, while he was with the Queen at Dumbarton. But this proved ineffectual also.

Soon after, the Queen received letters from the Pope, and her uncles, the Guises of France, requesting her to put the Earl of Moray out of the way, because they found by experience that their interest in Scotland could not prosper while he was alive. Upon this the faction against him became more insolent, and appeared in arms under the Earl of Huntly. They were at first suppressed, but soon assembled again, to the number of eight hundred men. This body he was obliged to fight, with little more strength in which he could confide than a hundred horse; but notwithstanding this disparity, by the Divine blessing, he obtained a complete victory, killing of them a hundred and twenty, and taking a hundred prisoners, among whom were Huntly himself and his two sons; and it is said that he did not lose a single man. He returned to Aberdeen with the prisoners, late in the night, where he had appointed a minister of the Gospel to meet him, with whom he returned thanks to God for such a deliverance, exceeding the expectations of all men.

The Earl of Bothwell was soon after this recalled by the Queen from France, and upon his arrival, Moray accused him of his former treasonable practices, and commenced a process at law against him. Bothwell knew that he could not stand an open scrutiny, but relied upon the Queen's favour, which he knew he possessed in a very high degree, and which increased so much the more as her enmity to Moray, on account of his popularity, was augmented. This led her to join more warmly in the conspiracy with Bothwell against his life; a new plot was the result of their joint deliberations, which was to be executed in the following manner. Moray was to be sent for with only a few attendants, to speak with the Queen at Perth, where Lord Darnley (then in suit to her for marriage) was. They knew that Moray would speak his mind freely, upon which they were to quarrel with him, and in the heat of it David Rizzio was to strike the first blow, and all the rest were to follow. But of this design also he got previous intelligence by a friend at the Court; nevertheless he resolved to go, until, advised by Patrick Ruthven, he turned aside to his mother's house, and there staid till the storm was over.

The Earl of Moray, foreseeing what would be the consequence of the Queen's marriage with Lord Darnley, set himself to oppose it; but finding little attention paid to anything he said on that subject in the Convention of Estates, he chose rather to absent himself for some time; and accordingly retired to England, where he staid until the Queen's marriage with Darnley was over.

The tragical events which succeeded, disgusted Moray more and more at the Court. With these the public are well acquainted. The murder of Darnley, and Mary's after-marriage with the assassin of her husband, have occasioned too much speculation of late years, not to be known to every one in the least acquainted with Scottish history. Moray now found it impossible to live at a Court where his implacable enemy was so highly honoured. Bothwell insulted him openly; whereupon he asked leave of the Queen to travel abroad;

and she being willing to get rid of him at all events, granted his desire, upon his promise not to make any stay in England. He went over to France, where he remained till he heard that the Queen was in custody in Lochleven, and that Bothwell had fled to Denmark ; he then returned home.

Upon his arrival, by the joint consent of the Queen and nobles, in the year 1567, he was made Regent during the young King's minority, and entered on the exercise of his office in the spring following. He resolved to make a tour through the whole kingdom, to settle the courts of justice, and repair what was wrong ; but his adversaries, the Hamiltons, perceived that, by the prudence and diligence of this worthy nobleman, the interests of religion would be revived, than which nothing could be more disagreeable to them who, being dissipated and licentious to an extreme degree, could not endure to be regulated by law. They never ceased, therefore, crying out against his administration, and fixed up libels in different places full of dark insinuations, by which it was understood that his destruction was being meditated. Some astrologers told him that he would not live beyond such a day ; by which it appeared they were not ignorant of the designs formed against him. All this had no effect upon his resolution ; his common reply was, that he knew well enough he must die one time or other, and that he could not part with his life more nobly, than by procuring the public tranquillity of his native country.

He summoned a Convention of Estates to meet at Glasgow, for the redress of some grievances, which that part of the country particularly laboured under ; but while thus engaged, he received intelligence that the Queen had escaped from Lochleven Castle, and was come to Hamilton, where those of her faction were assembling with the utmost haste. A hot dispute arose in council, whether the Regent and his attendants should repair to the young King at Stirling, or stay and observe the motions of the Queen and her party ; but, in the very time of these deliberations, a hundred chosen men arrived from Lothian, and many more from the adjacent country were approaching. This made them resolve to stay where they were, and refresh themselves for one day ; after which they determined to march out and face the enemy. The Queen's army, being 6500 strong, resolved to make their way past Glasgow, to lodge the Queen in Dumbarton Castle, and afterwards either to fight the Regent or protract the war at pleasure.

The Regent being informed of this design of the enemy, drew his army out of the town, to observe which way they intended to pass : he had not above 4000 men. The Queen's army was discovered passing along the south side of the river Clyde. Moray commanded the foot to pass the bridge, and the horse to ford the river, marched out to a small village, called Langside, upon the river Cart, and, taking possession of a rising ground, before the enemy could well discover his intention, drew up in order of battle. The Earls of Morton, Semple, Hume, and Patrick Lindsay, were on the right; the Earls of Mar, Glencairn, Monteith, with the citizens of Glasgow on the left; and the musqueteers were placed in the valley below. The Queen's army approaching, a very brisk but short engagement ensued. The Earl of Argyle, who was Commander-in-Chief of the Queen's troops, falling from his horse, they gave way, so that the Regent obtained a complete victory; but by his clement conduct, there was very little blood spilt in the pursuit. The Queen, who all the time remained with some horse, at about the distance of a mile from the place of action, seeing the rout, escaped and fled for England ; and the Regent with his troops returned to Glasgow, where they gave thanks to God for their deliverance from Popery and Papists, who threatened to overturn the work of God among them. This battle was fought upon the 13th of May 1568.

After this the Regent summoned a Parliament to meet at Edinburgh, which the Queen's party laboured to hinder with all their power. In the meantime, letters were received from the Queen of England, requiring them to put off the meeting of Parliament, until she was made acquainted with the whole matter; for she declared she could not bear with the affront which her kinswoman said she had received from her subjects. The Parliament, however, assembled ; and, after much reasoning, it was resolved to send commissioners to England to vindicate their conduct. But none consenting to undertake this business, the Regent resolved upon going himself ; and accordingly chose three gentlemen, two ministers, two lawyers, and Mr George Buchanan, to accompany him ; and, with a guard of a hundred horse, they set out and arrived at York, the appointed place of conference, on the 4th of October. After several meetings with the English commissioners to little purpose, the Queen called the Regent up to London, that she might be better satisfied, by personal conversation with him, about the state of these affairs. But the same difficulties stood in his way here as at York ; he refused to enter upon the accusation of his sister, the Queen of Scots, unless Elizabeth would engage to protect the young King's party, provided the Queen was found guilty.

But while matters were thus remaining in suspense at London, Mary had stirred up a new commotion in Scotland, by means of Sir James Balfour ; so that the Regent found himself exceedingly embarrassed, and resolved to bring the matter to a conclusion as soon as possible. After several interviews with the Queen and Council, in which the Regent and his party supported the ancient rights of their country, and wiped off the aspersions many had thrown on them, a decision was given in their favour ; and the Regent returned home loaded with honours by Elizabeth, attended by the most illustrious of the English Court, and escorted by a strong guard to Berwick. He arrived at Edinburgh on the 2d of February, where he was received with acclamations of joy, particularly by the friends of the true religion.

During his administration, many salutary laws in favour of civil and religious liberty were made, which rendered him more and more the object of Popish malice. At last they resolved at all events to take his life ; the many unsuccessful attempts formerly made having only served to render them more bold and daring. Though the Queen was now at a distance, yet she found means to encourage her party ; and perhaps the hope of delivering her gave strength to their resolution. James Hamilton of Bothwell Haugh, nephew to the Archbishop of St Andrews, incited by his uncle and others, undertook to make away with the Regent, when a convenient opportunity offered itself. He first lay in wait for him at Glasgow, and then at Stirling, but both failed him ; after which he thought Linlithgow the most proper place for perpetrating that execrable deed. His uncle had a house near the Regent's, in which he concealed himself, that he might be in readiness for the assassination. Of this design the Regent got intelligence likewise, but paid not that regard to the danger he was exposed to which he should, and would go no other way than that in which it was suspected the ambush was laid. He trusted to the fleetness of his horse in riding swiftly by the suspected place ; but the great concourse of people, who crowded together to see him, stopped up the way. Accordingly, he was shot from a wooden balcony ; the bullet, entering a little below the navel, killed the horse of George Douglas behind him : the assassin escaped by a back door. The Regent told his attendants that he was wounded, and returned to his lodgings. It was at first thought the wound was not mortal ; but his pain increasing, he began to think of death. Some about him remarked that this was the fruit of his lenity, in sparing so many notorious offenders, and among the rest his own murderer ; but he replied, "Your importunity shall not make me repent of my clemency." Having settled his private affairs, he committed the care of the young King to the nobles there present : and, without speaking a reproachful word of any, he departed this life on the 23d of January 1570.

Thus fell the Earl of Moray (whom historians ordinarily call, The good Regent), after he had escaped so many dangers. He was certainly a worthy governor. " His death," says Buchanan, " was lamented by all good men, who loved him as the public father of his country ; even his enemies confessed his merit when dead, they admired his valour in war, his ready disposition for peace, his activity in business, in which he was commonly very successful ; the Divine favour seemed to shine on all his actions ; he was very merciful to offenders, and equitable in all his decisions. When the field did not call for his presence, he was busied in the administration of justice, by which means the poor were not oppressed, and the terms of law-suits were shortened. His house was like a holy temple ; after meals he caused a chapter of the Bible to be read, and asked the opinions of such learned men as were present upon it, not out of a vain curiosity, but from a desire to learn, and reduce to practice what it contained" (Buchanan's History, vol. ii. 392).

In a word, he was, both in his public and private life, a pattern worthy of imitation ; and happy would it be for us that our nobles were more disposed to walk in the paths which he trod. For Spottiswoode says : " Above all his virtues, which were not few, he shined in piety towards God, ordering himself and his family in such a sort, as did more resemble a church than a court ; for therein, besides the exercise of devotion, which he never omitted, there was no wickedness to be seen, nay, not an unseemly or wanton word to be heard. A man truly good, and worthy to be ranked amongst the best governors that this kingdom hath enjoyed, and therefore to this day honoured with the title of *The good Regent*" (Spottiswoode's History, p. 234).

John Knox.

OHN KNOX was born at Gifford, near Haddington in East Lothian, in the year 1505. His father was related to the ancient house of Ranferlie. When he left the grammar-school, he was sent to the university of St Andrews to study under Mr John Mair, a man of considerable learning at that time, and had the degree of Master of Arts conferred upon him while very young. He excelled in philosophy and polemical divinity, and was admitted into church orders before the usual time appointed by the canons. Then laying aside all unnecessary branches of learning, he betook himself to the reading of the ancients, particularly Augustine's and Jerome's works, with which he was exceedingly pleased. He profited considerably by the preaching of Thomas Guillaume, or Williams, a Black Friar of sound judgment and doctrine, whose discourses led him to study the Holy Scriptures more closely, by which means his spiritual knowledge was increased, and such a zeal for the interest of religion begotten in him, that he became the chief instrument in accomplishing the primitive reformation.

He was a disciple of George Wishart, (as the reader has already seen in the account of his life), which procured him the hatred of the Popish clergy, who could not endure that light which discovered their idolatrous darkness.

After the death of Cardinal Beaton, he retired into the castle of St Andrews, where he preached to the garrison for some time ; but the castle being obliged to surrender to the French, he became their prisoner, and was sent aboard the galleys. Having made his escape about the year 1550, he went to England, where he preached for several years in Berwick, Newcastle, and London, with great applause. His fame at last reached the ears of King Edward VI., who offered him a bishoprick, which he rejected, as contrary to his principles.

During his stay in England he was called before the Council, and required to answer the following questions:

1. Why he refused the benefice provided for him at London ?

2. Whether he thought that no Christian might serve in the ecclesiastical ministration, according to the laws and rights of the realm of England ?

3. If kneeling at the Lord's table was not indifferent.

To the first he said that his conscience witnessed to him that he might profit more in some other place than in London. To the second, that many things needed reformation in the ministry of England, without which no minister did or could discharge his duty before God; for no minister there had authority to separate the leprous from the whole, which was a chief part of his office; and that he refused no office which might in the least promote God's glory and the preaching of Christ's Gospel. And to the third he replied, that Christ's action was most perfect ; that it was most safe to follow His example ; and that kneeling was a human invention. The answer which he gave to this question occasioned a considerable deal of altercation betwixt the Council and him. There were present the Archbishop of Canterbury, the Bishop of Ely, the Lord Treasurer, the Earls of Northampton, Shrewsbury, etc., the Lord Chamberlain, and the Secretaries. After long reasoning, he was desired to take the matter into further consideration, and so was dismissed.

After the death of King Edward VI., he retired to Geneva ; but soon left that place, and went to Frankfort, upon the solicitation of the English congregation there, whose call to him was dated 24th September 1554. While in this city, he wrote his Admonition to England, and was soon involved in troubles, because he opposed the English liturgy, and refused to communicate after the manner it enjoined. Messrs Isaac and Parry, supported by the English doctors, not only got him discharged from preaching, but accused him before the magistrates of high treason against the Emperor's son Philip, and his wife, Queen Mary of England; and to prove the charge, they had recourse to the above-mentioned Admonition, in which they alleged he had called the one little inferior to Nero, and the other more cruel than Jezebel. But the magistrates, perceiving the design of his accusers, and fearing lest he should some way or other fall into their hands, gave him secret information of his danger, and requested him to leave the city, for they could not save him if he should be demanded by the Queen of England in the Emperor's name; and having taken the hint, he returned to Geneva.

Here he wrote an Admonition to London, Newcastle, and Berwick; a letter to Mary of Guise, Dowager of Scotland; an Appeal to the nobility; an Admonition to the Commons of his own country; his First Blast of the Trumpet against the Monstrous Regiment of Women, and other works. He intended to have blown this trumpet three times, if the death of Mary, the Queen Regent, had not prevented him; understanding that an answer was to be given to his first blast, he deferred the publication of the second, till he saw what answer was necessary for the vindication of the first.

While he was at Geneva, he contracted a close intimacy with John Calvin, with whom he consulted on every emergency. Towards the end of harvest 1554, he returned home, upon the solicitation of some of the Scots nobility, and began privately to instruct such as resorted to him in the true religion: among whom were John Erskine of Dun, David Forrest, and Elizabeth Adamson, spouse to James Baron, burgess of Edinburgh. The idolatry of the mass particularly occupied his attention, as he saw some men remarkable for zeal and godliness drawn aside by it. Both in public and private, he exposed its impiety and danger; and his labours succeeded so far, as to draw off some, and alarm many others. In a conversation upon this subject, at the laird of Dun's house, in Forfarshire, in presence of David Forrest, Robert Lockhart, John Willock, and William Maitland, junior of Lethington, he gave such satisfactory answers to all the objections which were started by the company that Maitland ended the conversation, saying, "I see very well that all our shifts will serve nothing before God, seeing they stand us in so small stead before men." From this time forward the mass was very little respected.

John Knox continued a month at the laird of Dun's, preaching every day; the principal gentlemen of that country resorting to his ministry. From thence he went to Calder House, the residence of Sir James Sandilands, where the Earl of Argyle, then Lord Lorn, and Lord James, afterwards Earl of Moray, heard his doctrine, and highly approved of it. During the winter he taught in Edinburgh, and in the beginning of spring went to Kyle, where he preached in different places. The Earl of Glencairn sent for him to Finlayston, where, after sermon, he administered the Lord's Supper, and then returned to Calder.

The people being thus instructed, began to refuse all superstition and idolatry, and set themselves, to the utmost of their power, to support the true preaching of the Gospel. This alarmed the inferior Popish clergy so much, that they came from all quarters complaining to the bishops; whereupon Knox was summoned to appear in the Black Friars' Church of Edinburgh, on the 15th of May following. This appointment he resolved to observe, and accordingly came to Edinburgh, in company with the laird of Dun, and several other gentlemen; but the diet did not hold, because the bishops were afraid to proceed further against him; so that, on the same day that he should have appeared before them, he preached to a greater audience in Edinburgh than ever he had done before. The Earl Marischal, being desired by Lord Glencairn to hear Mr Knox preach, complied, and was so delighted with his doctrine, that he immediately proposed that something should be done to draw the Queen Regent to hear him likewise. He made this proposal in a letter, which was delivered into her own hand by Glencairn. When she had read it, she gave it to Beaton, Archbishop of Glasgow, saying in ridicule, " Please you, my Lord, to read a pasquil."

About this time, 1555, he received a letter from the English congregation at Geneva, who were not in communion with the congregation of that name at Frankfort, in which they besought him, in the name of God, that, as he was their chosen pastor, he would speedily come to them. In obedience to this call, he sent his wife and mother-in-law before him to Dieppe, but by the importunity of some gentlemen he was prevailed on to stay some time behind them in Scotland, which he spent in going about, exhorting the several congregations in which he had preached to be fervent in prayer, frequent in reading the Scriptures, and in mutual conferences, till God should give them greater liberty. The Earl of Argyle was solicited to press John Knox's stay in this country, but he could not succeed. Knox told them, that, if they continued earnest in the profession of the faith, God would bless these small beginnings, but that he must for once go and visit that little flock which the wickedness of men had compelled him to leave ; and being thus resolved, he went immediately to Geneva. As soon as he was gone the bishops summoned him to their tribunal, and for non-compearance, they burned him in effigy at the cross of Edinburgh ; from which unjust sentence, when he heard of it, he appealed to the nobility and commons of Scotland.

Upon the receipt of a letter, dated March 10, 1556, subscribed by the Earls of Glencairn, Erskine, Argyle, and Moray, Knox resolved to return to Scotland. Committing the care of his flock at Geneva to John Calvin, and coming to Dieppe, he wrote from thence to Mrs Anne Locke a declaration of his opinion of the English service-book, expressing himself thus: " Our Captain, Christ Jesus, and Satan His adversary, are now at open defiance, their banners are displayed, and the trumpet is blown on both sides for assembling their armies ; our Master calleth upon His own, and that with vehemency, that they may depart from Babylon ; yea, He threatened death and damnation to such as, either in their forehead or right hand, have the mark of the beast ; and a portion of this mark are all those dregs of papistry, which are left in your great book of England (viz., crossing in baptism, kneeling at the Lord's table, mumbling or singing of the litany, etc., etc.) ; any one jot of which diabolical inventions will I never counsel any man to use."

He was detained in Dieppe much longer than was expected, which obliged the Scots nobility to renew their solicitations ; which he complied with, and arrived in Scotland on the 2d of May 1559, being then fifty-four years old. He preached first at Dundee, and afterwards at Perth, with great success. About this time the Queen Regent put some preachers to the horn, prohibiting all, upon pain of rebellion, to comfort, relieve, or assist them ; which enraged the multitude so, that they would be restrained neither by the preachers nor magistrates, from pulling down the images and other monuments of idolatry in Perth : which being told to the Queen Regent, it so enraged her that she vowed to destroy man, woman, and child in that town, and burn it to the ground. To execute this threat, she caused her French army to march towards the place; but being informed that multitudes from the neighbouring country were assembling in the town for the defence of its inhabitants, her impetuosity was checked, and she resolved to use stratagem where force could not avail her. Accordingly she sent the Earls of Argyle and Moray to learn what was their design in such commotions.

Mr Knox, in the name of the rest, made answer: "The present troubles ought to move the hearts of all the true servants of God and lovers of their country, to consider what the end of such tyrannical measures will be, by which the emissaries of Satan seek the destruction of all friends of religion in the country. Therefore I most humbly require of you, my Lords, to tell the Queen, in my name, that we, whom she in her blind rage doth thus persecute, are the servants of God, faithful and obedient subjects of this realm; and that the religion which she would maintain by fire and sword, is not the true religion of Jesus Christ, but expressly contrary to the same; a superstitious device of men, which I offer myself to prove, against all who in Scotland maintain the contrary, freedom of debate being allowed, and the word of God being the judge. Tell her from me, that her enterprise shall not succeed in the end; for she fights not against man only, but against the eternal God." Argyle and Moray promised to deliver this message; and Knox preached a sermon, exhorting them to constancy; adding, "I am persuaded that this promise (meaning the promise she had made to do them no harm if they would leave the town peaceably), shall be no longer kept than the Queen and her Frenchmen can get the upper hand;" which accordingly happened, for she took possession of the town, and put a garrison of French in it. This breach of promise so displeased the Earls of Argyle and Moray, that they forsook her, and joined the Congregation. Having assembled with Erskine of Dun and others, they sent for John Knox; who, in his way to them, preached in Crail and Anstruther, intending to preach next day at St Andrews.

This design coming to the ears of the Bishop, he raised a hundred spearmen, and sent a message to the Lords of the Congregation, That if John Knox offered to preach there, he should have a warm reception. They, in their turn, forewarned Knox of his danger, and dissuaded him from going. He made answer, "God is my witness that I never preached Jesus Christ in contempt of any man; neither am I concerned about going thither; though I would not willingly injure the worldly interest of any creature, I cannot, in conscience, delay preaching to-morrow, if I am not detained by violence. As for fear of danger to my person, let no man be solicitous about that, for my life is in the hand of Him whose glory I seek, and therefore I fear not their threats, so as to cease from doing my duty, when of His mercy God offereth the occasion. I desire the hand and weapon of no man to defend me ; only I crave audience, which if denied to me here, at this time, I must seek further where I may have it." The Lords were thus satisfied that he would fulfil his intention, which he did with such boldness and success, and without interruption, that the magistrates and people of the town, immediately after sermon, agreed to remove the monuments of idolatry ; which they did with great expedition.

After this, several skirmishes ensued between the Queen Regent and the Lords of the Congregation. But at last the Queen sickened and died, and a general peace, which lasted for some time, was procured ; during which the commissioners of the Scots nobility, were employed in settling ministers in different places. John Knox was appointed to Edinburgh, where he continued until the day of his death.

The same year, 1560, the Scots Confession was compiled and agreed upon ; and that the Church might be established upon a good foundation, a commission and charge were given to John Knox, and five others, to draw up a form of government and discipline. When they had finished it, they presented it to the nobility, by whom it was afterwards ratified and approved of.

But the progress which was daily making in the Reformation soon met with a severe check, by the arrival of the young Queen Mary from France, in August 1561. With her came Popery, and all manner of profanity ; the mass was again publicly set up ; at which the religious part of the nation were highly offended, and none more than John Knox, who ceased not to expose the evil and danger of it on every occasion. On this account the Queen and Court were much exasperated ; they called him before them, and charged him as guilty of high treason. The Queen, being present, produced a letter, written by him, wherein it was alleged, that he had convocated her Majesty's lieges against law ; whereupon a long reasoning ensued between him and Secretary Lethington upon the contents of said letter ; in which Mr Knox gave such solid and bold answers, in defence of himself and doctrine, that at last he was acquitted by the

Lords of the Council, to the no small displeasure of the Queen and those of the Popish party.

John Knox, in a conference with the Queen about this time, said, " If princes exceed their bounds, they may be resisted even by power, for there is no greater honour and obedience to be paid to princes, than God hath commanded to be given to father and mother. If children join together against their father stricken with a frenzy and seeking to slay his own children, apprehend him, take his sword and other weapons from him, bind his hands, and put him in prison till his frenzy overpass, do they any wrong, or will God be offended with them for hindering their father from committing horrible murder? Even so, madam, if princes will murder the children of God, their subjects, their blind zeal is but a mad frenzy. To take the sword from them, to bind them, and to cast them into prison, till they be brought to a sober mind, is not disobedience, but just obedience, because it agreeth with the Word of God." The Queen hearing this, stood for some time as one amazed, and changed countenance. No appearance was at this time of her imprisonment.

After the Queen's marriage with Henry, Earl of Darnley, a proclamation was made, in 1565, signifying that, forasmuch as certain rebels, under the colour of religion (meaning those who opposed the measures of the Court), intended nothing but the subversion of the Commonwealth, therefore it charged all manner of men, under pain of life, lands, and goods, to resort and meet their Majesties at Linlithgow, on the 24th of August. Upon Sabbath the 19th, Darnley came to the High Church of Edinburgh, where John Knox preached from these words : " O Lord our Lord, other lords beside thee have had dominion over us." In his sermon, he took occasion to speak of wicked princes, who, for the sins of a people, were sent as scourges upon them ; and also said, " That God set in that room, boys and women, and that God justly punished Ahab and his posterity, because he would not take order with the harlot, Jezebel." These things enraged Darnley to a very high degree. Knox was immediately ordered before the Council, and went thither, attended by some of the most respectable citizens. When called in, Lethington signified that Darnley was much offended with some words in his sermon, and ordered him to abstain from preaching for fifteen or twenty days; to which Knox answered that he had spoken nothing but according to his text, and if the Church would command him either to speak or refrain from speak-

JOHN KNOX IN ST GILES, EDINBURGH.

ing, he would obey, so far as the Word of God would permit him. Nevertheless, for this and another sermon which he preached before the Lords, in which he showed the bad consequences that would follow upon the Queen's being married to a Papist, he was, by the Queen's order, prohibited from preaching for a considerable time.

It cannot be expected that we should enumerate all the indefatigable labours, and pertinent speeches, which, on sundry occasions, he made to the Queen, nor the opposition which he met with, in promoting the work of Reformation. These will be found at large in the histories of these times.

The Popish faction now found, that it would be impossible to get their idolatry re-established, while the Reformation was making such progress, and while John Knox and his associates had such credit with the people. They therefore set other engines to work than those they had hitherto used, sparing no pains to blast his reputation by malicious calumnies, and even making attempts upon his life. One night as he was sitting at the head of a table in his own house, with his back to the window, as was his custom, he was shot at from the other side of the street, on purpose to kill him. The shot entered at the window, but he being near the other side of the table, the assassin missed his mark. The bullet struck the candlestick before him, and made a hole in the foot of it. Thus was He that was with him stronger than they that were against him.

John Knox was an eminent wrestler with God in prayer, and like a prince prevailed. The Queen Regent herself had given him this testimony, when upon a particular occasion she said that she was more afraid of his prayers than of an army of ten thousand men. He was likewise warm and pathetic in his preaching, in which such prophetical expressions as dropped from him had the most remarkable accomplishment. As an instance of this, when he was confined in the castle of St Andrews, he foretold both the manner of their surrender, and their deliverance from the French galleys; and when the Lords of the Congregation were twice discomfited by the French army, he assured them that the Lord would ultimately prosper the work of Reformation. Again, when Queen Mary refused to come and hear sermon, he bade them tell her that she would yet be obliged to hear the Word of God whether she would or not; which came to pass at her arraignment in England. At another time, he thus addressed himself to her husband, Henry, Lord Darnley, while in the king's seat in the High Church of Edinburgh: " Have you, for the pleasure of that dainty dame, cast the psalm-book into the fire? The Lord shall strike both head and tail." Both King and Queen died violent deaths. He likewise said, when the Castle of Edinburgh held out for the Queen against the Regent, that "the Castle should spue out the captain (meaning Sir William Kircaldy of Grange) with shame, that he should not come out at the gate, but over the wall, and that the tower called Davis Tower, should run like a sand-glass; which was fulfilled a few years after—Kircaldy being obliged to come over the wall on a ladder, with a staff in his hand, and the said fore-work of the Castle running down like a sand-brae.

On the 24th of January 1570, John Knox being in the pulpit, a paper was put into his hands, among others containing the names of the sick people to be prayed for; the paper contained these words, " Take up the man whom you accounted another God," alluding to the Earl of Moray, who was slain the day before. Having read it, he put it into his pocket, without showing the least discomposure. After sermon, he lamented the loss which both Church and State had met with in the death of that worthy nobleman, showing that God takes away good and wise rulers from a people in His wrath; and at last said, " There is one in the company who maketh that horrible murder, at which all good men have occasion to be sorrowful, the subject of his mirth. I tell him, he shall die in a strange land, where he shall not have a friend near him to hold up his head." Thomas Maitland, the author of that insulting paper, hearing what Knox said, confessed the whole to his sister, the Lady Trabrown, but said, that John Knox was raving, to speak of he knew not whom; she replied with tears, that none of John Knox's threatenings fell to the ground. This gentleman afterwards went abroad and died in Italy, on his way to Rome, having no man to comfort him.

John Knox's popularity was now so well established, that the Popish party, finding it impossible to alienate the hearts of the people from him, began now openly to work his destruction, fortifying the town and castle with their garrisons. They vented their malice against him by many furious threatenings; upon which he was urged by his friends to leave Edinburgh for his own safety, which at last he did, in May 1571, and went to St Andrews, where the Earl of Morton (who was afterwards Regent) urged him to inaugurate the Archbishop of that See. This he declined, with solemn protestation against it, and denounced an anathema on the giver and receiver. Though he was then very weak in body, he would not refrain from preaching, and was obliged to be supported by his servant Richard Bannatyne, in going to church; when in the pulpit, he was obliged to rest some time before he could proceed to preach, but before he ended his sermon he became so vigorous and active, that he was like to have broken the pulpit to pieces.

Here he continued till the end of August 1572, when the civil broils were a little abated, upon which, receiving a letter from Edinburgh, he returned to his flock. He was now much oppressed with the infirmities of old age, and the extraordinary fatigues he had undergone; the death of the good Regent, the Earl of Moray, had made deep impression on him; and when he heard of the massacre of St Bartholomew at Paris, and the murder of the good Admiral Coligny, these melancholy news almost deprived him of his life. Finding his dissolution approaching, he prevailed with the Council and Kirk Session of Edinburgh to concur with him in admitting Mr James Lawson as his successor, who was at that time Professor of Philosophy in the College of Aberdeen. He wrote a letter to Mr Lawson, entreating him to accept of this charge; adding this postscript, *Accelera, mi frater, alioqui sero venies* (Make haste, my brother, otherwise you will come too late); meaning that if he did not come speedily, he would find him dead; which words had this effect on Mr Lawson, that he set out immediately, making all possible haste to Edinburgh; where, after he had preached twice to the full satisfaction of the people, the 9th of November was appointed for his admission unto that congregation. Knox, though still weaker, preached upon that occasion with much power, and with the greatest comfort to the hearers. In the close of his sermon he called God to witness, that he had walked in a good conscience among them, not seeking to please men, nor serving his own or other men's inclinations, but in all sincerity and truth preaching the Gospel of Christ. Then praising God, who had given them one in his room, he exhorted them to stand fast in the faith they had received ; and having prayed fervently for the Divine blessing upon them, and the increase of the Spirit upon their new pastor, he gave them his last farewell; with which the congregation were much affected.

Being carried home that same day, he was confined to his bed, and on the 13th of the month was so enfeebled, that he was obliged to lay aside his ordinary reading of the Scriptures. The next day he would rise out of bed. Being asked what he intended by getting out of bed, he replied, he would go to church, thinking it had been the Lord's Day, and told them that he had been all the night meditating upon the resurrection of Christ, which he should have preached ôn in order, after the death of Christ, which he had finished the Sabbath before. He had often desired of God, that he would end his days in teaching and meditating upon that doctrine ; which desire seems to have been granted to him. Upon Monday the 17th, the elders and deacons being come to him, he said, " The time is approaching for which I have long thirsted, wherein I shall be relieved and be free from all cares, and be with my Saviour for ever; and now, God is my witness, whom I have served with my spirit in the Gospel of His Son, that I have taught nothing but the true and solid doctrines of the Gospel, and that the end which I purposed in all my doctrine was to instruct the ignorant, to confirm the weak, to comfort the consciences of those who were humbled under the sense of their sins, and to denounce the threatenings of God's word against such as were rebellious. I am not ignorant that many have blamed me, and yet do blame my too great rigour and severity ; but God knoweth, that in my heart I never hated the persons of those against whom I thundered God's judgments; I did only hate their sins, and laboured, according to my power, to gain them to Christ; that I did forbear none of whatsoever condition, I did it out of the fear of my God, who placed me in this function of the ministry, and I know will bring me to an account." Then he exhorted them to constancy and entreated them never to join with the wicked, but rather to choose with David to flee to the mountains, than to remain with such company.

After this exhortation to the elders and deacons, he charged Mr David Lindsay and Mr James Lawson, to take heed to feed the flock over which the Holy Ghost had made them overseers. To Lawson in particular he said, " Fight the good fight, do the work of the Lord with courage and with a willing mind ; and God from above bless you, and the church whereof you have the charge, against which the gates of hell shall not prevail." Then by prayer he recommended the whole company present to the grace of God, and afterwards desired his wife, or Richard Bannatyne, to read the 17th chapter of John, a chapter of the Ephesians, and the 33d chapter of Isaiah daily, since he was unable to read himself, and sometimes he desired part of John Calvin's sermons, in French, to be read to him. One time when reading these sermons, they supposed him to be sleeping, and asked him if he heard what was read? He replied, " I hear, I praise God, and understand far better."

One day after this, Mr David Lindsay coming to see him, he said, " Well, brother, I thank God I have desired all this day to have had you, that I might send you to that man in the Castle, the Laird of Grange, whom you know I have loved dearly. Go, I pray you, and tell him from me, in the name of God, that unless he leave that evil course wherein he has entered, neither shall that rock (meaning the Castle of Edinburgh, which he then kept out against the King) afford him any help, nor the carnal wisdom of that man, whom he counteth half a god (meaning Maitland of Lethington); but he shall be pulled out of that nest, and brought down over the wall with shame, and his carcase shall be hung before the sun ; so God hath assured me." When Lindsay delivered this message, Kircaldy seemed to be much moved ; but after conference with Lethington, he returned, and dismissed him with a disdainful countenance and answer. On reporting this to Knox, he said, " Well, I have been earnest with my God anent that man ; I am sorry that it should so befall his body, yet God assureth me there is mercy for his soul. But for the other (meaning Lethington), I have no warrant to say that it shall be well with him." The truth of this seemed to appear in a short time thereafter; for it was thought that Lethington poisoned himself, to escape public punishment. He lay unburied in the steeple of Leith, until his body was quite corrupted; but Sir William Kircaldy of Grange was, on the 3d of August next, executed at the Cross of Edinburgh. He caused Lindsay to repeat Knox's words concerning him a little before his execution, and was much comforted by them, and said to him on his way to the scaffold, "I hope, when men shall think I am gone, that I shall give a token of the assurance of God's mercy to my soul, according to the speech of that man of God." Accordingly, when he was cast over the ladder, with his face towards the east, and when all present thought he was dead, he lifted up his hands, which were bound, and let them fall softly down again, as if praising God for His great mercy towards him.

Another of John Knox's visitors desired him to praise God for the good he had done. He answered, "Flesh of itself is too proud, and needs nothing to puff it up;" and protested, that he only laid claim to the free mercy of God in Christ among others. To the Earl of Morton, who was then about to receive the Regency (the Earl of Moray being dead), he was heard to say, "My lord, God hath given you many blessings; He hath given you high honour, birth, great riches, many good friends, and is now to prefer you to the government of this realm. In His name, I charge you that you will use these blessings better in time to come, than you have done in time past. In all your actions seek first the glory of God, the furtherance of His Gospel, the maintenance of His church and ministry; and then be careful of the King, to procure his good, and the welfare of the kingdom. If you act thus, God will be with you; if otherwise, He shall deprive you of all these benefits, and your end shall be shameful and ignominious." This threatening, as Morton to his melancholy experience confessed, was literally accomplished. At his execution, in June 1581, he called to mind John Knox's words, and acknowledged, that in what he had said to him he had been a true prophet.

Upon the Lord's day, November 23, after he had lain for some time very quiet, he said, "If any man be present, let him come and see the work of God;" for he thought (as was supposed) then to have expired. His servant having sent for Mr Johnston of Elphinstone, he burst forth into these words, "I have been in meditation these two last nights upon the troubled kirk of God, despised in the world, but precious in His sight. I have called to God for her, and commended her to Christ, her head; I have been fighting against Satan, who is ever ready for the assault; I have fought against spiritual wickedness, and have prevailed; I have been as it were in heaven, and have tasted of its joys." After sermon several persons came to visit him; one asked him (upon perceiving his breathing shortened), if he had any pain? He answered, "I have no more pain than he that is now in heaven, and am content, if it please God, to lie here seven years." Many times, when he was lying as if asleep, he was in meditation, and was heard to say, "Lord, grant true pastors to Thy church, that purity of doctrine may be retained. Restore peace again to this commonwealth, with godly rulers and magistrates. O serve the Lord in fear, and death shall not be troublesome to you. Blessed is the death of those that have part in the death of Jesus. Come, Lord Jesus, sweet Jesus; into Thy hand I commend my spirit."

That night, Dr Preston having come to him, and being told by some of his constant attendants that he was often very uneasy in his sleep, the doctor asked him after he awoke how he did, and what made him mourn so heavily in his sleep. He answered: "In my life-time I have been often assaulted by Satan, and many times he hath cast my sins in my teeth, to bring me to despair; yet God gave me strength to overcome his temptations; and now that subtle serpent, who never ceaseth to tempt, hath taken another course, and seeks to persuade me that all my labours in the ministry, and the fidelity I have showed in that service, have merited heaven and immortality. But blessed be God that He hath brought to my mind that Scripture, 'What hast thou that thou has not received?' and, 'Not I, but the grace of God, which is in me,' with which he hath gone away ashamed, and shall no more return. And now, I am sure my battle is at an end, and that I shall shortly, without pain of body or trouble of spirit, change this mortal and miserable life for that happy and immortal life that shall never have an end."

Having some time before given orders for making his coffin, he rose out of bed (November 24) about ten o'clock, put on his hose and doublet, sat up about the space of half-an-hour, and then returned to bed again. Being asked by Campbell of Kinzean-cleugh if he had any pain, he answered, "No pain but such as I trust will soon put an end to this battle—yea, I do not esteem that pain to me, which is the beginning of eternal joy." In the afternoon, he caused his wife to read the 15th chapter of 1st Corinthians. When it was ended, he said, " Is not that a comfortable chapter ? " A little after, " I commend my soul, spirit, and body, into Thy hands, O Lord." About five o'clock in the evening, he said to his wife, " Go, read where I cast my first anchor." This was the 17th chapter of John, which she read, together with part of Calvin's sermons on the Ephesians. They then went to prayer, after which Dr Preston asked him if he heard the prayer. He answered, " Would to God that you and all men had heard it as I have done ; I praise God for that heavenly sound ; " adding, " Lord Jesus, receive my spirit." His servant, Richard Bannatyne, hearing him give a long sigh, said, "Now, sir, the time you have long called to God for doth instantly come ; and, seeing all natural power fail, give us some sign that you live upon the comfortable promises which you have so often showed to us." At this speech, he lifted up one of his hands ; and immediately after, without any struggle, as one falling asleep, he departed this life, about eleven o'clock at night. Finishing his Christian warfare, he entered into the joy of his Lord, to receive a crown of righteousness, prepared for him and such as him, from before the foundation of the world.

He was buried in the churchyard of St Giles, now that square called the Parliament Close, upon Wednesday the 26th of November 1572. His funeral was attended by the Regent Earl of Morton, other lords, and a great multitude of people of all ranks. When he was laid in the grave, the Earl of Morton said, "There lies one who in his life never feared the face of man, who hath been often threatened with dag and dagger, but hath ended his days in peace and honour."

John Knox was low in stature, and of a weakly constitution ; which made Mr Thomas Smeaton, one of his contemporaries, say, " I know not if God ever placed a more godly and great spirit in a body so little and frail. I am certain, that there can scarcely be found another in whom more gifts of the Holy Ghost, for the comfort of the Church of Scotland, did shine. No one spared himself less, no one was more diligent in the charge committed to him, and yet no one was more the object of the hatred of wicked men, and more vexed with the reproach of evil speakers ; but this was so far from abating, that it rather strengthened his courage and resolution in the ways of God." Beza calls him the " great apostle of the Scots."

JOHN KNOX'S HOUSE, HIGH STREET, EDINBURGH.

His faithfulness in reproving sin, in a manner that showed he was not awed by the fear of man, made up the most remarkable part of his character, and the success wherewith the Lord blessed his labours was very singular, and is enough to stop the mouth of every enemy against him.

[The following remarks by Froude in his admirable work, the " History of England," will be read with pleasure by those who desire to see the character of two of Scotland's greatest worthies relieved from the aspersions which have too long been cast upon them.   Of Regent Moray he says, " In all Europe there was not a man more profoundly true to the principles of the Reformation, or more consistently, in the best sense of the word, a servant of God;"—and to Knox he bears the following noble testimony : " No grander figure can be found, in the entire history of the Reformation in this island, than that of Knox.   Cromwell and Burghley rank beside him for the work which they effected, but, as politicians and statesmen, they had to labour with instruments which they soiled their hands in touching. In purity, in uprightness, in courage, truth, and stainless honour, the Regent Moray and our English Latimer were perhaps his equals ; but Moray was intellectually far below him, and the sphere of Latimer's

PORTRAIT OF WILLIAM MAITLAND OF LETHINGTON.

influence was on a smaller scale. The time has come when English history may do justice to one but for whom the Reformation would have been overthrown among ourselves ; for the spirit which Knox created saved Scotland ; and if Scotland had been Catholic again, neither the wisdom of Elizabeth's Ministers, nor the teaching of her Bishops, nor her own chicaneries, would have preserved England from revolution. His was the voice which taught the peasant of the Lothians that he was a free man, the equal in the sight of God with the proudest peer or prelate that had trampled on his forefathers. He was the one antagonist whom Mary Stuart could not soften nor Maitland deceive ; he it was that raised the poor Commons of his country into a stern and rugged people, who might be hard, narrow, superstitious, and fanatical, but who, nevertheless, were men whom neither king, noble, nor priest could force again to submit to tyranny." . . . . . . "The reaction when the work was done, a romantic sympathy with the Stuarts, and the shallow liberalism which calls itself historical philosophy, has painted over the true Knox with the figure of a maniac. Even his very bones have been flung out of their resting-place, or none can tell where they are laid ; and yet but for him Mary Stuart would have bent Scotland to her purpose, and Scotland would have been the lever with which France and Spain would have worked on England. But for Knox and Burghley—those two, but not one without the other—Elizabeth would have been flung from off her throne, or have gone back into the Egypt to which she was too often casting wistful eyes."—ED.]

His works are, " An Admonition to England ; " " An Application to the Scots Nobility, etc. ; " " A Letter to Mary the Queen Regent ; " " A History of the Reformation ; " " A Treatise on Predestination ; " " The First and Second Blasts of the Trumpet ; " a Sermon, delivered August 1565, on account of which he was for some time prohibited from preaching.   He left also sundry sermons, tracts, and other unprinted manuscripts.

George Buchanan.

GEORGE BUCHANAN was born in the parish of Kill-earn, Stirlingshire, in the year 1506, and belonged to a family, as he himself characterised it, more remark-able for its antiquity than its opulence.   His father died in the flower of his age, while his grandfather was yet alive, by whose extravagance, the family, which was but low before, was now almost reduced to the ex-tremity of want.   Yet such was the frugal care of his mother, Agnes Heriot, that she brought up five sons and three daughters to men's and women's estate.   Of the five sons, George was the third.   His uncle, James Heriot, perceiving his promising ingenuity in their own country schools (those of Killearn and Dumbarton), took him from thence, and sent him to Paris.   There he applied himself to his studies, and especially to poetry—having partly a natural genius that way, and partly out of necessity, it being the only method of study propounded to him in his youth.

Before he had been there two years, his uncle died, and he himself fell dangerously sick ; and being in extreme want, he was forced to go home to his friends.   After his return to Scotland, he

PORTRAIT OF GEORGE BUCHANAN.

spent almost a year in taking care of his health, and then went into the army, with some French auxiliaries newly arrived in Scotland, to learn the military art. Their expedition into England having proved fruitless, and the troops having suffered much from the severity of the winter, he relapsed into such an illness as confined him all that season to his bed. Early in the spring, he was sent to St Andrews, to hear the lectures of John Major, or Mair, who, though very old, read logic, or rather sophistry, in that university. The summer after, he accompanied him into France, and there he fell into the troubles of the Lutheran sect, which then began to increase. He struggled with the difficulties of fortune almost two years, and at last was admitted into the college of St Barbe, where he was grammar-professor almost three years. During that time, Gilbert Kennedy, Earl of Cassilis, one of the young Scottish nobles, being in that country, was much taken with his ingenuity and abilities, so that he entertained him for five years, and brought him back with him to Scotland.

Afterwards, having a mind to return to Paris to his old studies, he was detained by King James V., and made tutor to James, his natural son. In the meantime, a poem made by him, at leisure times, came into the hands of the Franciscans; wherein he writes, that he was solicited in a dream by St Francis to enter into his order. In this poem there were one or two passages that reflected on them very severely; which those ghostly fathers, notwithstanding their profession of meekness and humility, took more heinously than men having obtained such a vogue for piety among the vulgar ought to have done, upon so small an occasion of offence. But finding no just grounds for their unbounded fury, they attacked him upon the score of religion ; which was their common way of terrifying those they did not wish well to. Thus, whilst they indulged their impotent malice, they made him, who was not well affected to them before, a greater enemy to their licentiousness, and rendered him more inclinable to the Lutheran cause. In the meantime, the King, with Magdalene his wife, came from France, not without the resentment of the priesthood; who were afraid that the royal lady, having been bred up under her aunt, the Queen of Navarre, should attempt some innovation in religion. But this fear soon vanished upon her death, which followed shortly after.

Next, there arose jealousies at Court about some of the nobility, who were thought to have conspired against the King, and in that matter, James V. being persuaded that the Franciscans dealt insincerely, commanded Buchanan, who was then at court, though he was ignorant of the feud between him and that order, to write a satire upon them. He was loath to offend either of them ; and therefore, though he made a poem, it was but short, and such as might admit of a doubtful interpretation, whereby he satisfied neither party ; not the King, who would have a sharp and stinging invective ; nor yet the fathers, who looked on it as a capital offence to have anything said of them but what was honourable. So that, receiving a second command to write more pungently against them, he began that miscellany, which now bears the title of " The Franciscan," and gave it to the King. Shortly after, he was arrested, and committed to custody, but being made acquainted by his friends at court that Cardinal Beaton sought his life, and had offered the King a sum of money as a price for his head, he escaped out of prison, and fled to England. There also, things were at such an uncertainty, that the very same day, and almost in one and the same fire, the men of both factions, Protestants and Papists, were burned ; Henry VIII. in his old age being more intent on his own security, than the purity or reformation of religion. This uncertainty of affairs in England, seconded by his former acquaintance with the French, and their natural courtesy, drew him again into that kingdom.

As soon as he came to Paris, he found Cardinal Beaton, his utter enemy, ambassador there : so that, to withdraw himself from his fury he went to Bordeaux, at the invitation of Andrew Govean. There he taught three years in the schools, which were erected at the public cost. In that time he composed four tragedies, which were afterwards occasionally published. But that which he wrote first, called Baptistes, or the Baptist, was printed last, and next the Medea of Euripides. He wrote them in compliance with the custom of the school, which was to have a play written once a-year, that the acting of them might wean the French youth from allegories, to which they had taken a false taste, and bring them back, as much as possible, to a just imitation of the ancients. This affair succeeding even almost beyond his hopes, he took more pains in compiling the other two tragedies, called Jephthes and Alcestes ; because he thought they would fall under a severer scrutiny of the learned. And yet, during this time, he was not wholly free from trouble, being harassed with the menaces of the Cardinal on the one side, and of the Franciscans on the other ; for the Cardinal had written letters to the Archbishop of Bordeaux, to apprehend him. Providentially, those letters fell into the hands of Buchanan's best friends, and besides, the death of the King of Scots, and the plague, which then raged over all Aquitaine, dispelled all fear of further persecution.

In the interim an express came to Govean from the King of Portugal, commanding him to return to that country, and bring with him some men, learned both in the Greek and Latin tongues ; that they might read the liberal arts, and especially the principles of the Aristotelian philosophy, in those schools which he was then building at a great expense. Buchanan being asked, readily consented to go ; for, whereas he saw that all Europe besides was either actually in foreign or domestic wars, or just upon the point of being so, this one corner of the world was, in his opinion, likeliest to be free from tumults and combustions. Besides, his companions in that journey were such, that they seemed rather his acquaintances and familiar friends, than strangers or aliens to him ; for many of them had been his intimates for several years, and are well known to the world by their learned works, as Nicholaus Gruchius, Gulielmus Garentæus, Jacobus Tevius, and Elias Venetus. This was the reason that he did not only make one of their society, but also persuaded his brother Patrick to do the same.

And truly the matter succeeded excellently well at first ; till, in the midst of the enterprise, Andrew Govean was taken away by a sudden death, which proved most prejudicial to his companions.

For, after his decease, all their enemies endeavoured first to ensnare them by treachery, and soon after ran violently upon them as it were with open mouth; and their agents and instruments, being great enemies to the accused, laid hold of three of them, and haled them to prison; whence, after a long and loathsome confinement, they were called out to give in their answers; and, after many bitter taunts, were remanded to prison again; and yet no accuser did appear in court against them. As for Buchanan, they exulted most bitterly over him, as being a stranger, and knowing also that he had very few friends in that country, who would either rejoice in his prosperity, sympathise with his grief, or revenge the wrongs offered to him. The crime laid to his charge was the poem he wrote against the Franciscans, which he himself, before he went from France, took care to get excused to the King of Portugal; neither did his accusers perfectly know what it was, for he had given but one copy of it to the King of Scots, by whose command he wrote it. They farther objected to his eating of flesh in Lent; though there was not a man in all Portugal but used the same liberty. Besides, he had given some sly side-blows to the monks; which, however, nobody but a monk himself could well except against. Moreover, they took it heinously ill, that in a certain familiar discourse with some young Portuguese gentlemen, upon mention made of the eucharist, he affirmed that, in his judgment, Augustine was more inclinable to the party condemned by the Church of Rome. Two other persons (as some years after came to his knowledge) viz., John Tulpin, a Norman, and John Ferrerius of Sub Alpine Liguria, had witnessed against him, that they had heard, from divers creditable persons, that Buchanan was not orthodox as to the Roman faith and religion.

After the inquisitors had wearied both themselves and him for almost half a year, that they might not seem to have causelessly vexed a man of name and note in the world, they shut him up in a monastery for some months, there to be more exactly disciplined and instructed by the monks; who, to give them their due, though very ignorant in all matters of religion, were men otherwise neither bad in their morals, nor rude in their behaviour. This was the time he took to form the principal part of David's Psalms into Latin verse.

At last he was set at liberty; and suing for a pass, and accommodations from the crown, to return to France, the King desired him to stay where he was, and allotted him a small sum for daily necessaries and pocket expenses, till some better provision might be made for his subsistence. But he, tired out with delay, and having got the opportunity of a passage in a ship then riding in the bay of Lisbon, was carried over into England. He made no long stay in that country, though fair offers were made him there; for he saw that all things were in a hurry and combustion, under a very young King (Edward VI.), the nobles being at variance one with another, and the minds of the commons yet in a ferment, upon the account of their civil commotions. Whereupon he returned into France, about the time that the siege of Metz was raised. There he was in a manner compelled by his friends to write a poem concerning that siege; which he did, though somewhat unwillingly, because he was loath to interfere with several of his acquaintances, and especially with Mellinus Sangelasius, who had composed a learned and elegant poem on that subject. From thence he was called over into Italy, by Charles de Cossé, Marshal de Brisac, who then presided with very good success over the Gallic and Ligurian countries about the Po. He lived with him and his son Timoleon, sometimes in Italy, and sometimes in France, for the space of five years, till the year 1560; the greatest part of which time he spent in the study of the Holy Scriptures, that so he might be able to make a more exact judgment of the controversies in religion, which employed the thoughts, and took up the time, of most of the men of these days. These disputes were silenced a little in Scotland, when that kingdom was freed from the tyranny of the Guises of France; so he returned thither, and became a member of the Church of Scotland, 1560.

[After his return, George Buchanan occupied many important situations of trust and influence. In 1562, he officiated as classical tutor to Mary Queen of Scots, who was then in the 20th year of her age, and whose fascinating manners produced the deepest impression upon him. In 1564, he received from Queen Mary the temporalities of the abbey of Crossraguel, amounting in annual value to the sum of £500; and in 1566 he was appointed by Regent Moray as principal of St Leonard's College, St Andrews. In the General Assemblies convened at Edinburgh, during the years 1563 to 1567, he was a constant member of their most important committees, and in this last year he was chosen Moderator. In 1568, he attended the Regent to England, when the latter was forced by circumstances to appear as the accuser of his sister Queen Mary, and in this capacity he prepared a Latin treatise entitled, "A Detection of the Doings of Mary Queen of Scots," which was largely circulated by the English Court. After the

RUINS OF CROSSRAGUEL ABBEY.

assassination of Regent Moray, Buchanan, in the year 1570, was appointed one of the tutors of the young King James VI., who was
then only four years of age.   He was also elevated to the office of
Lord Privy Seal, which was honourable and lucrative, and entitled
him to a seat in Parliament, in whose proceedings he took an active
interest.   In 1579, he dedicated to the young King his treatise, "De
Jure Regni apud Scotos," in which, as Sir James Mackintosh says, "the
principles of popular politics, and the maxims of a free government,
are delivered with a preciseness and enforced with an energy which
no former age had equalled, and no succeeding has surpassed."—ED.]

A little before his death he left the Court to visit his friends, during which time King James sent him several messages, and at last a
threatening letter, to return in twenty days.   But he, finding his death
approaching, sent him back a letter of admonition relative to the government of his kingdom and well-being of his council; and in the end told
him that he could run the hazard of his Majesty's displeasure without
danger, for that, "by the time limited, he would be where few kings or
great men should be honoured to enter," at reading which it is said the
King wept.   He died at Edinburgh, September 28th, 1582, and was
buried in the common place, though worthy to have been laid in marble,
for in his lifetime he used to condemn and despise pompous monuments.

Sir James Melville, in his memoirs, gives him the following

character: " He was a stoic philosopher who looked not far before him ; too easy in his old age ; somewhat revengeful against those who had offended him . . . . But, notwithstanding, he was a man of notable endowments, great learning, and an excellent Latin poet ; he was much honoured in foreign countries, pleasant in conversation, into which he happily introduced short moral maxims which his invention readily supplied him with upon any emergency."

Robert Rollock.

ROBERT ROLLOCK was descended from the ancient family of the Livingstons. He was born about the year 1555. His father, David Rollock, sent him to Stirling, to be educated for the university, under Thomas Buchanan ; where his genius, modesty, and sweetness of temper, soon procured to him the particular friendship of his master, which subsisted ever after. From this school he went to the University of St Andrews. where he prosecuted his studies for four years; at the end of which, his progress had been so great, that he was chosen professor of philosophy; the duties of which office he discharged with applause for other four years.

About the year 1583, he was invited by the magistrates of Edinburgh to a professorship in their University, which, shortly before this time, had been founded by King James VI. He complied with their invitation, at the earnest desire of Mr James Lawson, who succeeded John Knox. His reputation as a teacher soon drew a number of students to that college, which was soon afterwards much enlarged by being so conveniently situated in the capital of the kingdom. At first he had the principal weight of academical business laid upon him; but in process of time other professors were chosen from among the scholars whom he had educated; after which his chief employment was to exercise the office of Principal, and, by superintending the several classes, to observe the proficiency of the scholars, to compose such differences as would arise among them, and to keep every one to his duty. Thus was the principality of that college, in his time, a useful institution, and not what it is now, little better than a mere sinecure. Every morning he called the students together, when he prayed among them; and one day in the week, he explained some passage of Scripture to them, in the close of which, he was frequently very warm in his exhortations; which wrought more reformation upon the students than all the laws which were made, or the discipline which was exercised. After the lecture was over, it was his custom to reprove such as had been guilty of any misdemeanour through the week. "How is the gold become dim! how is the most fine gold changed!" He was likewise very attentive to such as were advanced in their studies, and intended the ministry, and his care was productive of much good to the Church, while he was as diligent in his own studies, as he was careful to promote those of others.

Notwithstanding all this business in the university, he preached every Lord's day in the church, with such fervency and demonstration of the Spirit, that he became the instrument of converting many to God. About this time also he wrote several commentaries on different passages of Scripture. His exposition of the epistles to the Romans and Ephesians, coming into the hands of the learned Beza, he wrote to a friend of his, telling him, that he had an incomparable treasure, which, for its judiciousness, brevity, and elegance of style, had few equals.

He was chosen Moderator to the Assembly held at Dundee in 1567, wherein matters were not altogether in favour of Presbytery; but this cannot be imputed to him; although Calderwood, in his History, calls him "a man simple in matters of the Church." He was one of those commissioned by the Assembly to wait upon his Majesty, about seating the churches of Edinburgh; but in the meantime, he sickened, and was confined to his house. Afterwards, at the entreaty of his friends, he went to the country for the benefit of the air: at first he seemed as if growing better, but his distemper returned upon him with greater violence than before, and confined him to bed. He committed his wife (for he had no children) to the care of his friends, and desired two noblemen who came to visit him, to go to the King, and entreat him, in his name, to take care of religion, and preserve it to the end; that he would esteem and comfort the pastors of the church; for the ministry of Christ, though low and base in the eyes of men, should yet shine with great glory. When the ministers of Edinburgh came to him, he spoke of the sincerity of his intentions, in everything done by him in discharge of the duties belonging to the office with which he had been vested.

As night drew on his distemper increased; and together therewith, his religious fervour was likewise augmented. When the physicians were preparing some medicines, he said, "Thou, Lord, wilt heal me," and then began praying for the pardon of his sins through Christ; professing that he counted all things but dung for the cross of Christ. He prayed farther, that he might have the presence of God in his departure, saying, "Hitherto have I seen thee darkly, through the glass of Thy word: O Lord, grant that I may have the eternal enjoyment of Thy countenance, which I have so much desired and longed for." He then spoke of the resurrection and eternal life; after which he blessed and exhorted every one present, according as their respective circumstances required.

The day following, when the magistrates of Edinburgh came to see him, he exhorted them to take care of the University, and nominated a successor to himself. He recommended his wife to them, declaring, that he had not laid up one halfpenny of his stipend, and therefore hoped they would provide for her; to which request they assented, and promised to see her comfortably supplied. After this he said, "I bless God that I have all my senses entire, but my heart is in heaven; and, Lord Jesus, why shouldst not Thou have it? it has been my care all my life to dedicate it to Thee; I pray Thee, take it, that I may live with Thee for ever." Then, after a little sleep, he awakened, crying, "Come, Lord Jesus, put an end to this miserable life; haste, Lord, and tarry not; Christ hath redeemed me, not unto a frail and momentary life, but unto eternal life. Come Lord Jesus, and give that life for which Thou hast redeemed me." Some of the people present bewailing their condition when he should be taken away, he said to them, "I have gone through all the degrees of this life, and am come to my end, why should I go back again? help me, O Lord, that I may go through this last degree, with Thy assistance." And when some told him, that the next day was the Sabbath, he said, "O Lord, shall I begin my eternal Sabbath from Thy Sabbath here?"

Next morning, feeling his death approaching, Rollock sent for Mr Balcanquhal; who, in prayer with him, desired the Lord, if He pleased, to spare his life for the good of the Church. He said, "I am weary of this life, all my desire is, that I may enjoy the celestial life that is hid with Christ in God;" and a little after, "Haste, Lord, and do not tarry, I am weary both of nights and days. Come, Lord Jesus, that I may come to thee : break these eye-strings, and give me others. I desire to be dissolved, and to be with Thee. O Lord Jesus, thrust Thy hand into my body, and take my soul to Thyself? O my sweet Lord, set this soul of mine free, that it may enjoy her husband." And when one of the bystanders said, "Sir, let nothing trouble you, for now your Lord makes haste," he said, " O welcome message ! would to God my funeral might be to-morrow." And thus he continued in heavenly meditation and prayer till he resigned up his spirit to God, on the 8th of February 1598, in the forty-third year of his age.

His works are, a Commentary on some select Psalms, on the Prophecy of Daniel, and the Gospel of John, with its Harmony. He wrote also on the Epistles to the Ephesians, Colossians, Thessalonians, and Galatians ; and an Analysis of the Epistles to the Romans and the Hebrews, with respect to Effectual Calling.

John Craig.

OHN CRAIG was a man of considerable learning and singular abilities. [He was born about the year 1512, and having obtained a good education, removed to England, and became tutor to the children of Lord Dacre. In consequence of war arising between that country and Scotland, he returned home, and entered a Dominican monastery, but being suspected of heresy he was cast into prison, and kept there for a time. On obtaining his liberty he travelled first to England and France, and then removed to Rome, where he was in such favour with Cardinal Pole, that he was appointed to instruct the novices of the Dominican cloister at Bologna. Here, being advanced to the rectorate, he had access to the library, where, happening to read " Calvin's Institutes," he soon imbibed and openly professed the Protestant doctrines. He was sent to Rome, tried, and condemned to be burned ; but the

PORTRAIT OF MARY QUEEN OF SCOTS.

Pope (Paul IV.) having died the day before his intended execution, the people broke open all the prisons, and set the prisoners free. Craig immediately left the city, and it was when on his way to Milan that the incident recorded below occurred. He went afterwards to Vienna, and was permitted to preach before the Emperor, with whom he became a favourite, and who, on being commanded by the Pope to send him back to Rome, generously refused, giving him a safe-conduct out of Germany.—ED.]

During his travels abroad he was frequently delivered out of very great dangers, by the kind interposition of a gracious Providence : an instance of which we have while he was in Italy. Being obliged to flee out of that country, on account of his regard for the Reformation, in order to avoid being apprehended, he was obliged to lurk in obscure places in the day-time, and travel over night. By this means any little money he had was soon exhausted, and being in the extremity of want, a dog brought a purse to him with some gold in it, by which he was supported until he escaped the danger of being taken.

After his return home, he was settled as John Knox's colleague at Edinburgh, where he continued many years, and met with many trials of his fortitude and fidelity. In the year 1567, the Earl of Bothwell, having obtained a divorce from his lawful wife, as preparatory to his marriage with Queen Mary, she sent a letter to John Craig, commanding him to publish the banns of matrimony betwixt her and Bothwell. But the next Sabbath, having declared at length that he had received such a command, he added, that he could not in conscience obey it, the marriage being altogether unlawful : and he would declare that to the parties if present. He was immediately sent for by Bothwell, unto whom he declared his reasons with great boldness ; and the very next Lord's-day, he told the people what he had said before the Council, and took heaven and earth to witness, that he detested that scandalous marriage, and that he had discharged his duty to the Lords. Upon this, he was again called before the Council, and reproved by them, as having exceeded the bounds of his calling. He boldly answered, that the bounds of his commission were the Word of God, right reason, and good laws, against which he had said nothing ; and, by all these, offered to prove the said marriage scandalous ; at which he was silenced, and set out of the Council. Thus John Craig continued not only a firm friend to the Reformation, but a bold opposer of every encroachment made upon the crown and dignity of the Lord Jesus Christ.

In the year 1584, an Act of Parliament was made, that all ministers, masters of colleges, etc., should, within forty-eight hours, compear and subscribe the Act of Parliament, concerning the King's power over all estates, spiritual and temporal, and submit themselves to the Bishops. Upon this, John Craig, John Brand, and some others, were called before the Council, and interrogated, how they could be so bold as to controvert the late Act of Parliament? Craig answered, that they would find fault with anything repugnant to God's Word : at which the Earl of Arran started upon his feet, and said, they were too pert, that he would shave their heads, pare their nails, and cut their toes, and make them an example unto all who should disobey the King's command, and his Council's orders ; and forthwith charged them to appear before King James VI. at Falkland on the 4th of September following.

Upon their appearance at Falkland, they were again accused of transgressing the foresaid Act of Parliament, and disobeying the Bishops' injunctions ; when there arose some hot speeches betwixt Craig and the Archbishop of St Andrews. On this the Earl of Arran spake again most outrageously against the former; who coolly replied, that there had been as great men set up higher, that had been brought low. Arran returned, " I shall make thee, of a false friar, a true prophet;" and sitting down on his knee, he said, " now am I humbled." " Nay," said Craig; " mock the servants of God as thou wilt, God will not be mocked, but shall make thee find it in earnest, when thou shall be cast down from the high horse of thy pride, and humbled." This came to pass a few years after, when he was thrown from off his horse with a spear, by James Douglas of Parkhead, killed, and his corpse exposed to dogs and swine before it was buried.

John Craig was forthwith discharged from preaching any more in Edinburgh, and the Archbishop of St Andrews was appointed to preach in his place; but as soon as the latter entered the great church of Edinburgh, the whole congregation, except a few court parasites, went out, and it was not long before Craig was restored to his place and office.

In the year 1591, when the Earl of Bothwell and his accomplices, on the 27th December, came to the King and Chancellor's chamber-doors, with fire, and to the Queen's with a hammer, in the palace of Holyrood House, with a design to seize the King and the Chancellor, John Craig, upon the 29th, preaching before the King upon the two brazen mountains in Zechariah, said, " As the King had lightly regarded the many bloody shirts presented to him by his subjects craving justice, so, God, in His providence, had made a noise of crying and fore-hammers to come to his own doors." The King would have the people to stay after sermon, that he might purge himself, and said, " If he had thought his hired servant (meaning Craig, who was his own minister) would have dealt in that manner with him, he should not have suffered him so long in his house." Craig, by reason of the throng, not hearing what he said, went away.

In the year 1595, John Craig being quite worn out by his labours, and the infirmities of age, the King's Commissioner presented some articles to the General Assembly; wherein, amongst other things, it was stated, that in respect Mr Craig was awaiting what hour God should please to call him, and was unable to serve any longer, and his Majesty designed to place John Duncanson, Mr Craig's colleague, with the prince, therefore his Highness desired an ordinance to be made, granting any two ministers he should choose. This was accordingly done, and Craig died a short time after this.

John Craig will appear, from this short memoir, to have been a man of uncommon resolution and activity. He was employed in the most part of the affairs of the Church during the reign of Queen Mary, and in the beginning of that of her son. He compiled the National Covenant, and a Catechism commonly called Craig's Catechism, which was first printed by order of the Assembly in the year 1591.

GATEWAY OF THE ABBEY CHURCH OF HOLYROOD.

David Black.

DAVID BLACK was for some time colleague to the worthy Mr Andrew Melville, minister of St Andrews. He was remarkable for zeal and fidelity in the discharge of his duty as a minister, applying his doctrine closely against the corruptions of that age, whether prevailing among the highest or lowest of the people; in consequence of which, he was, in the year 1596, cited before the Council, for some expressions uttered in a sermon, alleged to strike against King James VI. and his Council. but his brethren in the ministry thinking that, by this method of procedure with him, the spiritual government of the house of God was intended to be subverted, resolved that Black should decline answering the citation; and that, in the meantime, the brethren should be preparing themselves to prove from the Holy Scriptures that the judgment of all doctrine, in the first instance, belonged to the pastors of the Church.

Accordingly David Black, on the 18th November 1596, gave in a declinature to the Council to this effect: that he was able to defend all that he had said; yet, seeing his answering before them to that accusation might be prejudicial to the liberties of the Church, and would be taken for an acknowledgment of his Majesty's jurisdiction in matters merely spiritual, he was constrained to decline that judicatory—1. Because the Lord Jesus Christ had given him His word for a rule, and that, therefore, he could not fall under the civil law, only in so far as, after trial, he should be found to have passed from his instructions, which trial only belonged to the prophets, etc. 2. The liberties of the Church, and discipline presently exercised, being confirmed by divers acts of Parliament, approved of by the Confession of Faith, and the office-bearers of the Church being now in the peaceable possession thereof, the question of his preaching ought first, according to the grounds and practice foresaid, to be judged by the ecclesiastical senate, as the competent judges thereof at the first instance.

This declinature, with a letter sent to the different presbyteries, was, in a short time, subscribed by between three and four hundred ministers, all assenting to and approving of it.

The Commissioners of the General Assembly, then sitting at Edinburgh, knowing that the King was displeased at this proceeding, sent some of their number to speak with his Majesty, unto whom he answered, that if Mr Black would pass from his declinature, he would pass from the summons. This they would not consent to do. Upon which, the King summoned Mr Black again, on the 27th of November, to the Council to be held on the 30th. This summons was given with sound of trumpet, and open proclamation at the Cross of Edinburgh; and the same day, the Commissioners of the Assembly were ordered to depart thence in twenty-four hours, under pain of rebellion.

Before the day of David Black's second citation before the Council, he prepared a still more explicit declinature, especially as it respected the King's supremacy, declaring, that there are two jurisdictions in the realm, the oné spiritual, and the other civil: the one respecting the conscience, and the other concerning external things; the one persuading by the spiritual word, the other compelling by the temporal sword; the one spiritually procuring the edification of the Church, the other by justice procuring the peace and quiet of the commonwealth. The latter being grounded in the light of nature, proceeds from God as He is Creator, and is so termed by the Apostle (1 Pet. ii.), but varies according to the constitution of men; the former, being above nature, is grounded upon the grace of redemption, proceeding immediately from the grace of Christ, the only King and only Head of His Church (Eph. i., Col. ii.). Therefore, in so far as he was one of the spiritual office-bearers, and had discharged his spiritual calling in some measure of grace and sincerity, he should not, and could not lawfully be judged for preaching and applying the Word of God by any civil power, he being an ambassador and messenger of the Lord Jesus, having his commission from the King of kings; and all his commission is set down and limited in the Word of God, that cannot be extended or abridged by any mortal king or emperor, they being sheep, not pastors, who are to be judged by the Word of God, and not to be the judges thereof.

A decree of council was passed against him, upon which his brethren of the Commission directed their doctrines against the Council. The King sent a message to the commissioners, signifying that he would rest satisfied with Black's simple declaration of the truth; but Robert Bruce and the rest replied: That if the affair concerned Mr Black alone, they should be content; but the liberty of Christ's kingdom had received such a wound by the proclamation of last Saturday, that if Mr Black's life, and a dozen of others besides, had been taken, it had not grieved the hearts of the godly so much, and that either these things behoved to be retracted, or they would oppose so long as they had breath. But, after a long process, no mitigation of the Council's severity could be obtained; for Black was charged by a macer to enter his person in ward on the north of the Tay, there to remain at his own expense during his Majesty's pleasure; and though he was next year restored to his place at St Andrews, yet he was not suffered to continue, for, about the month of July that same year, the King and Council again proceeded against him; and he was removed to Angus, where he continued until the day of his death. He had always been a severe check on the negligent and unfaithful part of the clergy, but now they had found means to get free of him.

After his removal to Angus, he continued the exercise of his ministry, preaching daily unto such as resorted to him, with much success, and an intimate communion with God, until a few days before his death.

In his last sickness, the Christian temper of his mind was so much improved by large measures of the Spirit, that his conversation had a remarkable effect in humbling the hearts, and comforting the souls of those who attended him, engaging them to take the easy yoke of Christ upon themselves. He found in his own soul also such a sensible taste of eternal joy, that he was seized with a fervent desire to depart and to be with the Lord, longing to have the earthly house of this his tabernacle put off, that he might be admitted into the mansions of everlasting rest. In the midst of these earnest breathings after God, the Lord was wonderfully pleased to condescend to the importunity of His servant, to let him know that the time of his departure was near. Upon this, he took a solemn farewell of his family and flock, with a discourse, as Melville says, that seemed to be spoken out of heaven, concerning the misery and grief of this life, and the inconceivable glory which is above.

The night following, after supper, having read and prayed in his family with unusual continuance, strong crying, and heavy groans, he went a little while to bed: and the next day, having called his people to the celebration of the Lord's Supper, he went to church. Having brought the communion service near a close, he felt the approach of death, and all discovered a sudden change in his countenance, so that some ran to support him. But pressing to be on his knees, with his hands and eyes lifted up to heaven, in the very act of devotion and adoration, as in a transport of joy, he was taken away, with scarcely any pain at all. Thus this holy man, who had so faithfully maintained the interest of Christ upon earth, breathed forth his soul in this extraordinary manner, so that it seemed rather like a translation than a real death. See more of him in Calderwood's History ; De Foe's Memoirs ; and "Hind Let Loose."

John Davidson.

OHN DAVIDSON was minister at Salt Preston (now known by the name of Prestonpans), and began very early to discover uncommon piety and faithfulness in the discharge of his duty. He was involved in the sufferings brought upon several ministers on account of the "Raid of Ruthven," and the enterprise at Stirling, in 1584. Robert Montgomery, minister in Stirling, had made a simoniacal purchase of the archbishopric of Glasgow, from the Earl of Lennox, for which he was to

ST GILES, EDINBURGH, SOUTH VIEW.

give him £500 sterling of yearly rent. Accordingly, on March 8, 1582, Montgomery came to Glasgow with a number of soldiers, and pulled the minister in the pulpit by the sleeve, saying, "Come down, sirrah." The minister replied, "He was placed there by the Kirk, and would give place to none who intruded themselves without order." Much confusion and bloodshed ensued in the town. The presbytery of Stirling suspended Montgomery, in which the General Assembly supported them, but Lennox obtained a commission from King James VI. to try and bring the offenders to justice. Before that commission court met, the Earls of Mar and Gowrie, the Master of Oliphant, young Lochleven, etc., carried the King to Ruthven Castle, and there constrained him to revoke his commission to Lennox, and to banish him from the kingdom. Afterwards, however, the persons concerned in the affair at Ruthven, being charged to leave the realm upon pain of corporal punishment, assembled an army at Stirling, took the castle, and from thence sent a supplication to the King to redress their grievances. In the meantime, the Earl of Gowrie, lingering about Dundee, was apprehended, and committed to prison, which discouraged the party at Stirling so much, that they fled in the night, and got to Berwick. The captain of the castle and three others were hanged. Gowrie was likewise executed on the 2d of May 1584.

[The part which Davidson had to play in this important affair was rather a prominent one. Being then minister at Liberton, near Edinburgh, he was appointed by the metropolitan presbytery to pronounce the sentence of deposition and excommunication upon Montgomery. Afterwards he was one of a Commission sent by the Assembly to Stirling to remonstrate with the King on account of the favour he was showing to Montgomery's friends, and it was in consequence of the fearlessness with which on this occasion he addressed his Majesty, that it was thought expedient for him to seek refuge in England for a time.—ED.]

Having returned to Scotland in the year 1596, when the ministers and other commissioners of the General Assembly were met at Edinburgh for prayer, in order to a general and personal reconciliation (there were about four hundred ministers, besides elders and private Christians), John Davidson was chosen to preside amongst them. He caused the 33d and 34th chapters of Ezekiel to be read, and discoursed upon them in a very affecting manner, showing what was the end of their meeting, in confessing sin, and resolving to forsake it, and that they should turn to the Lord, and enter into a new league and covenant with Him, that so, by repentance, they might be the more meet to stir up others to the same duty. In this he was so assisted by the Spirit working upon their hearts, that within an hour after they had convened, they began to look with another countenance than at first, and while he was exhorting them to these duties, the whole meeting was in tears, every one provoking another by his example, whereby that place might have justly been called Bochim. After prayer, he treated on Luke xii. 22; wherein the same assistance was given him. Before they dismissed, they entered into a new League and Covenant, holding up their hands, with such signs of sincerity as moved all present. That afternoon, the Assembly enacted the renewal of the Covenant by particular synods.

In the General Assembly held at Dundee, 1598, where King James VI. was present, it was proposed whether ministers should vote in Parliament in the name of the Church. John Davidson entreated them not to be rash in concluding so weighty a matter. He said, " Brethren, see you not how readily the bishops begin to creep up." Being desired to give his vote, he refused, and protested in his own name, and in the name of those who should adhere to him, and required that his protest should be inserted in the books of Assembly. Here the King interposed, and said, " That shall not be granted; see if you have voted and reasoned before." "Never, sire," said Mr Davidson, "but without prejudice to any protestation made or to be made." He then presented his protestation in writing, which was handed from one to another, till it was laid down before the clerk. The King taking it up, and reading it, showed it to the Moderator and others about, and at last put it into his pocket.

This protest and letter was the occasion of farther trouble to him; for, in May following, he was charged to compear before the Council on the 26th, and answer for the same, and was by the King committed prisoner to the castle of Edinburgh, but on account of bodily infirmity, this place of confinement was changed to his own dwelling-house, after which he obtained liberty to exercise his ministry in his own parish. When the King was departing for England in 1603, as he was passing through Prestonpans, the laird of Ormiston entreated him to relieve Davidson from his confinement to the bounds of his own parish, but this could not be obtained.

He likewise, in some instances, showed that he was possessed, in a considerable measure, of the spirit of prophecy. While in Preston, he was very anxious about the building of a church in that parish, and had from his own private means contributed liberally to it. Lord Newbattle, having considerable interest in that parish, likewise promised his assistance, but afterwards receded from his engagements; upon which Davidson told him, that these walls there begun should stand as a witness against him, and that ere long God should root him out of that parish, so that he should not have one bit of land in the same; which was afterwards accomplished.

At another time, being moderator of the synod of Lothian, Mr John Spottiswoode, minister at Calder, and Mr James Law, minister at Kirkliston, were brought before them, for playing at football on the Sabbath. Davidson urged that they might be deposed, but the synod, because of the fewness of the ministers present, agreed that they should only be rebuked; which having accordingly done, he turned to his brethren and said, "Now, let me tell you what reward you shall have for your lenity. These two men shall trample on your necks, and on the necks of the ministers of Scotland." How true this proved was afterwards too well known, when Spottiswoode was made archbishop of St Andrews, and Law of Glasgow.

Being at dinner one time with Robert Bruce, who was then in great favour with the King, he told him, he should soon be in as great discredit, which was likewise accomplished. At another time, when dining in the house of one of the magistrates of Edinburgh with the same eminent minister, in giving thanks, he brake forth in these words, "Lord, this good man hath respect, for Thy sake, to Thy servants; but he little knoweth, that in a short time he shall carry us both to prison;" which afterwards came to pass, although at the time it grieved the Bailie exceedingly.

Robert Fleming, in his Fulfilling of the Scriptures, relates another remarkable instance of this kind. A gentleman nearly related to a great family in the parish of Preston, but a most violent hater of true piety, did, on that account, beat a poor man who lived there, although he had no manner of provocation. Among other strokes which he gave him, he gave him one on the back, saying, "Take that for Mr Davidson's sake." This maltreatment obliged the poor man to take to his bed, complaining most of the blow which he had received on his back. In the close of his sermon on the Sabbath following, Davidson, speaking of the oppression of the godly, and the enmity which the wicked had to such, in a particular manner mentioned this last instance, saying, "It was a sad time, when a profane man would thus openly adventure to vent his rage against such as were seekers of God in the place, whilst he could have no cause but the appearance of His image;" and then said, with great boldness, "He who hath done this, were he the laird or the laird's brother, ere a few days pass, God shall give him a stroke, that all the monarchs on earth dare not challenge." Which accordingly came to pass in the close of that very same week; for this gentleman, while standing before his own door, was struck dead with lightning, and had all his bones crushed to pieces.

A little before his death, he happened occasionally to meet with Mr Kerr, a young gentleman lately come from France, and dressed in the court fashion. Davidson charged him to lay aside his scarlet coat and gilt rapier; for, said he, "You are the man who shall succeed me in the ministry of this place;" which surprised the youth exceedingly, but was exactly accomplished; for he became an eminent and faithful minister at that place.

Such as would see more of John Davidson's faithful labours in the work of the ministry, may consult the Apologetical Relation, and Calderwood's History.

PARLIAMENT HOUSE, STIRLING CASTLE.

William Row.

WILLIAM ROW was a son of Mr John Row, minister at Perth, who gave him a very liberal education under his own eye. [As this family occupies a
very prominent place in the ecclesiastical history of
Scotland, a few additional particulars may be furnished
regarding it. The founder of the family was John
Row, who in his earlier years was a staunch and zealous adherent of the Romish Church. At the commencement of the Reformation in Scotland, he was residing in Rome,
where he had been for seven or eight years; and so great was the
confidence reposed in him by the Pope and Cardinals, that, on his
proposing to return to his native country, he was invested with the
character of Legate or Nuncio, and was instructed to inquire minutely
into the nature and causes of the prevailing disaffection, and report.
As his son remarks, however, he proved "a corbie messenger to his
master;" for not only did he not return to Rome, but he speedily
embraced the great principles of the Reformation himself, and became
one of their ablest and most strenuous supporters. He was one of
the six ministers selected to draw up the Confession of Faith, and the
First Book of Discipline; and for a period of twenty years, besides

discharging his ordinary pastoral duties in Perth, he took an active and prominent part in all the proceedings of the Church. On his death, which occurred at Perth on the 16th October 1580, he left several children, five of whom afterwards became ministers. One of these was John, who for fifty years was minister of Carnock in Fife, and is known as the author of the " History of the Kirk of Scotland," and as the father of John Row, principal of King's College, Aberdeen. Another was William, the subject of the present memoir. —ED.]

William Row was settled minister at Forgandenny, in the shire of Perth, about the year 1600, and continued there for several years. He was one of those ministers who refused to give public thanks for King James VI.'s deliverance from his danger in Gowrie's conspiracy, until the truth of that conspiracy was made to appear. This refusal brought upon him the King's displeasure. He was summoned to appear before the King and Council at Stirling, soon after. On the day appointed for his compearance, two noblemen were sent, the one before the other, to meet him on the road, and, under the pretence of friendship, to inform him that the Council had a design upon his life, that he might be prevailed on to decline going up thither. The first met him near his own house, the second a few miles from Stirling; but Row told them that he would not, by disobedience to the summons, make himself justly liable to the pains of law, and proceeded to Stirling, to the amazement of the King and his Court. When challenged for disbelieving the truth of the Gowrie conspiracy, he told them one reason of his hesitation was, that Henderson, who was said to have confessed that Gowrie hired him to kill the King, and to have been found in his Majesty's chamber for that purpose, was not only suffered to live, but rewarded: "Whereas," said he, "if I had seen the King's life in hazard, and not ventured my life to rescue him, I think I deserve not to live."

The two following anecdotes will show what an uncommon degree of courage and resolution he possessed.

Being at Edinburgh, before the Assembly there, at which the King wanted to bring in some innovation, and meeting with James Melville, who was sent for by the King, he accompanied him to Holyrood House. While Melville was with the King, Row stood behind a screen, and not getting an opportunity to go out with his brother undiscovered, he overheard the King say to some of his courtiers, " This is a good simple man; I have stroked cream on his mouth, and he will procure me a good number of voters, I warrant you." This said, Mr Row got off; and overtaking James Melville, asked him what had passed? Melville told him all; and said, "the King is well disposed to the Church, and intends to do her good by all his schemes." Row replied, "the King looks upon you as a fool and a knave, and wants to use you as a coy-duck to draw in others;" and told him what he had overheard. Melville suspecting the truth of this report, Mr Row offered to go with him and avouch it to the King's face. Accordingly, they went back to the palace, when Melville, seeing Row as forward to go in as he was, believed his report, and stopped him; and next day, when the Assembly proceeded to voting, Melville having voted against what the King proposed, his Majesty would not believe that such was his vote, till he, being asked again, did repeat it.

Again, being deputed to open the Synod of Perth, in 1607, to which King James sent Lord Scone, captain of his guards, to force them to accept a Constant Moderator, Scone sent notice to Row, that if, in his preaching, he uttered aught against constant moderators, he should cause ten or twelve of his guards to discharge their culverins at his nose; and when he attended the sermon which preceded that synod, he stood up in a menacing posture to outbrave the preacher. But Row, no way dismayed, knowing what vices Scone was charged with, particularly that he was a great belly-god, drew his picture so like the life, and condemned what was culpable with so much severity, that Scone thought fit to sit down, and even to cover his face. After which Row proceeded to prove, that no constant moderator ought to be suffered in the Church; but knowing that Scone understood neither Latin nor Greek, he wisely avoided naming the constant moderator in English, and always gave the Greek or Latin name for it. Sermon being ended, Scone said to some of the nobles attending him, " You see I have scared the preacher from meddling with the constant moderator; but I wonder who he spoke so much against by the name of *præstes ad vitam.*" They told him that it was Latin for the constant moderator; which so incensed him, that when Row proceeded to constitute the Synod in the name of our Lord Jesus Christ, Scone said, "the devil a Jesus is here:" and when Row called over the roll to choose their moderator after the ancient form, Scone would have pulled it from him, but he, being a strong man, held off Scone with one hand, and holding the synod-roll in the other, called out the names of the members.

After this William Row was put to the horn, and on the 11th of June following, he and Henry Livingstone, the moderator, were summoned before the Council, to answer for their proceedings at the Synod above mentioned. Livingstone compeared, and with great difficulty obtained the favour to be warded in his own parish. But Row was advised not to compear, unless the Council would relax him from the horning, and make him free of the Scone comptrollers, who had letters of caption to apprehend him, and commit him to Blackness. This was refused, and a search made for him; which obliged him to abscond, and lurk among his friends for a considerable time.

Row was subjected to several other hardships during the remainder of his life, but still maintained that steady faithfulness and courage in the discharge of his duty, which is exemplified in the above instances, until the day of his death, of which, however, we have no certain account.

Andrew Melville.

ANDREW MELVILLE, after finishing his classical studies, went abroad, and taught for some time, both at Poitiers in France, and at Geneva. He returned to Scotland in July 1574, after having been absent from his native country nearly ten years. Upon his return, the learned Beza, in a letter to the General Assembly of the Church of Scotland, said, "The greatest token of affection the kirk of Geneva could show to Scotland was, that they had suffered themselves to be spoiled of Mr Andrew Melville."

Soon after his return, the General Assembly appointed him to be the Principal of the College of Glasgow, where he continued for some years. In the year 1576, the Earl of Morton being then Regent, and thinking to bring Andrew Melville into his party, who were endeavouring to introduce Episcopacy, he offered him the parsonage of Govan,

VIEW OF GENEVA.

a benefice of twenty-four chalders of grain yearly, besides what he enjoyed as Principal, providing he would not insist against the establishment of bishops; but Melville rejected his offer with scorn.

He was afterwards translated to St Andrews, where he served in the same station as he had done at Glasgow.; and was likewise a minister of that city. Here he taught the divinity class, and, as a minister, continued to witness against the encroachments then making upon the rights of the Church of Christ.

When the General Assembly sat down at Edinburgh in 1582, Andrew Melville inveighed against the absolute authority which was making its way into the Church: whereby, he said, they intended to pull the crown from Christ's head, and wrest the sceptre out of His hand. When several articles, of the same tenor with his speech, were presented by the commission of the Assembly to King James VI. and Council, craving redress, the Earl of Arran cried out, "Is there any here that dare subscribe these articles." Melville went forward and said, "We dare, and will render our lives in the cause;" and then took up the pen and subscribed. We do not find that any disagreeable consequences ensued at this time.

But in the beginning of February 1584, he was summoned to

appear before the Secret Council, on the 11th of that month, to answer for some things said by him in a sermon on a fast-day, from Dan. iv. At his first compearance, he made a verbal defence; but being again called, he gave in a declaration, with a declinature, importing that he had said nothing, either in that or any other sermon, tending to dishonour King James VI., but had regularly prayed for the preservation and prosperity of his Majesty; that, as by acts of Parliament and laws of the Church, he should be tried for his doctrine by the Church, he therefore protested for, and craved, a trial by them, and particularly in the place where the offence was alleged to have been committed; and that as there were special laws in favour of St Andrews to the above import, he particularly claimed the privilege of them. He further protested, that what he had said was warranted by the word of God; that he appealed to the congregation who heard the sermon; that he craved to know his accusers; that, if the calumny was found to be false, the informers might be punished; that the rank and character of the informer might be considered, etc., after which he gave an account of the sermon in question; alleging that his meaning had been misunderstood, and his words perverted.

When he had closed his defence, the King, and the Earl of Arran, who was then Chancellor, raged exceedingly against him. Melville remained undisquieted, and replied, "You are too bold, in a constituted Christian kirk, to pass by the pastors, and take upon you to judge the doctrine, and control the messengers of a Greater than any present. That you may see your rashness, in taking upon you that which you neither ought nor can do" (taking out a small Hebrew Bible, and laying it down before them), "there are," said he, "my instructions and warrant,—see if any of you can control me, that I have passed my injunctions." The Chancellor opening the book, put it into the King's hand, saying, "Sire, he scorneth your Majesty and the Council." "Nay," said Andrew Melville, "I scorn not, but I am in good earnest." He was, in the time of this debate, frequently removed, and instantly recalled, that he might not have time to consult with his friends. They proceeded against him, and admitted his avowed enemies to prove the accusation; and though the whole train of evidence which was led proved little or nothing against him, yet they resolved to involve him in troubles, because he had declined their authority, as the competent judges of doctrine, and therefore remitted him to ward in the Castle of Edinburgh, during the King's will. Being informed, that if he entered into ward, he would not be released, unless it should be to bring him to the scaffold, and that the decree of the Council being altered, Blackness was appointed for his prison, which was kept by some dependants of the Earl of Arran, he resolved to get out of the country. A macer gave him a charge to enter Blackness in twenty-four hours; and, in the meanwhile, some of Arran's horsemen were attending at the West Port to convoy him thither; but, by the time he should have entered Blackness, he had reached Berwick. Messrs Lawson and Balcanquhal gave him the good character he deserved, and prayed earnestly for him in public, in Edinburgh; which both moved the people and galled the Court exceedingly.

After the storm had abated, he returned to St Andrews in 1586, when the Synod of Fife had excommunicated Patrick Adamson, pretended Archbishop of St Andrews, on account of some immoralities. Adamson having drawn up the form of an excommunication against Andrew Melville, and James, his brother, sent out a boy with some of his own creatures to the kirk to read it, but the people paying no regard to it, the Archbishop, though both suspended and excommunicated, would himself go to the pulpit to preach; whereupon some gentlemen, and others in town, convened in the new college, to hear Andrew Melville. The Archbishop being informed that they were assembled on purpose to put him out of the pulpit and hang him, for fear of this called his friends together, and betook himself to the steeple; but at the entreaty of the magistrates and others, he retired home.

This difference with the Archbishop brought the Melvilles again before the King and Council, who, pretending that there was no other method to end that quarrel, ordained Mr Andrew to be confined to Angus and the Mearns, under pretext that he would be useful in that country in reclaiming Papists. Because of his sickly condition, Mr James was sent back to the new college; and the University sending the Dean of Faculty and the masters with a supplication to the King in Mr Andrew's behalf, he was suffered to return, but was not restored to his place and office until the month of August following.

The next winter, he laboured to give the students in divinity under his care a thorough knowledge of the discipline and government of the Church; which was attended with considerable success. The specious arguments of Episcopacy vanished, and the serious part, both of the town and University, repaired to the college to hear him and Robert Bruce, who began preaching about this time.

After this he was chosen moderator in some subsequent Assemblies of the Church; in which several acts were made in favour of religion, as maintained at that period.

When the King brought home his Queen from Denmark in 1590, Andrew Melville made an excellent oration upon the occasion in Latin, which so pleased the King, that he publicly declared, he had therein both honoured him and his country, and that he should never be forgotten; yet such was the instability of this prince, that, in a little after this, because Melville opposed his arbitrary measures in grasping after an absolute authority over the church, he conceived a daily hatred against him ever after, as will appear from the sequel.

When Andrew Melville went with some other ministers to the Convention of Estates at Falkland in 1596 (wherein they intended to bring home the excommunicated lords who were then in exile), though he had a commission from last Assembly to watch against every imminent danger that might threaten the Church, yet, whenever he appeared at the head of the ministers, the King asked him, who sent for him there? to which he resolutely answered, " Sire, I have a call to come from Christ and His Church, who have a special concern in what you are doing here, and in direct opposition to whom ye are all here assembled; but, be ye assured, that no counsel taken against Him shall prosper; and I charge you, Sire, in His name, that you and your Estates here convened favour not God's enemies, whom He hateth." After he had said this, turning himself to the rest of the members, he told them, that they were assembled with a traitorous design against Christ, His Church, and their native country. In the midst of this speech, he was commanded by the King to withdraw.

The Commission of the General Assembly was now sitting, and understanding how matters were going on at the Convention, they sent some of their members, among whom Andrew Melville was one, to expostulate with the King. When they came, he received them in his closet. James Melville, being first in the commission, told the King his errand; upon which he appeared angry, and charged them with sedition. Mr James, being a man of cool passion and genteel behaviour, began to answer the King with great reverence and respect; but Mr Andrew, interrupting him, said, " This is not a time to flatter, but to speak plainly, for our commission is from the living God, to whom the King is subject; " and then, approaching the king; said,

COURTYARD OF FALKLAND PALACE.

"Sire, we will always humbly reverence your Majesty in public, but having opportunity of being with your Majesty in private, we must discharge our duty, or else be enemies to Christ. And now, Sire, I must tell you, that there are two kings and two kingdoms in Scotland : there is King James, the head of the Commonwealth, and there is Christ Jesus, the Head of the Church, whose subject King James VI. is, and of whose kingdom he is not a head, nor a lord, but a member; and they whom Christ hath called, and commanded to watch over His Church, and govern His spiritual kingdom, have sufficient authority and power from Him so to do, which no Christian king nor prince should control or discharge, but assist and support, otherwise they are not faithful subjects to Christ. And, Sire, when you was in your swaddling clothes Christ reigned freely in this land in spite of all His enemies ; His officers and ministers were convened for ruling His Church, which was ever for your welfare. Will you now challenge Christ's servants, your best and most faithful subjects, for convening together, and for the care they have of their duty to Christ and you? The wisdom of your counsel is, that you may be served with all sorts of men, that you may come to your purpose, and because the ministers and Protestants of Scotland are strong, they must be weakened and brought low, by stirring up a party against them. But, Sire, this is not the wisdom of God, and His curse must light upon it; whereas, in cleaving to God, his servants shall be your true friends, and He shall compel the rest to serve you."

There is little difficulty to conjecture how this discourse was relished by the King. However, he kept his temper, and promised fair things to them for the present; but it was the word of him whose standard maxim was, *Qui nescit dissimulare, nescit regnare*, " He who knows not how to dissemble, knows not how to reign." In this sentiment, unworthy of the meanest among men, he gloried, and made it his constant rule of conduct; for in the Assembly at Dundee in 1598, Andrew Melville being there, he discharged him from the Assembly, and would not suffer business to go on till he was removed.

There are other instances of the magnanimity of this faithful witness of Christ, which are worthy of notice. In the year 1606, he, and seven of his brethren, who stood most in the way of having Prelacy advanced in Scotland, were called up to England, under pretence of having a hearing granted them by the King, who had now succeeded to that throne, with respect to religion, but rather to be kept out of the way, as the event afterwards proved, until Episcopacy should be better established in Scotland. Soon after their arrival they were examined by the King and Council, at Hampton Court, on the 20th of September, concerning the lawfulness of the late Assembly at Aberdeen. The King, in particular, asked Andrew Melville, whether a few clergy, meeting without moderator or clerk, could make an Assembly? He replied, there was no number limited by law; that fewness of number could be no argument against the legality of the court; especially when the promise was in God's word given to two or three convened in the name of Christ; and that the meeting was ordinarily established by his Majesty's laws. The rest of the ministers delivered themselves to the same purpose; after which Andrew Melville, with his usual freedom of speech, supported the conduct of his brethren at Aberdeen, recounting the wrongs done them at Linlithgow, whereof he was a witness himself. He blamed the King's Advocate, Sir Thomas Hamilton, who was then present, for favouring Popery, and maltreating the ministers, so that the Accuser of the brethren could not have done more against the saints of God than had been done; that prelatists were encouraged, though some of them were promoting the interests of Popery with all their might, and the faithful servants of Christ were shut up in prison: and, addressing the Advocate personally, he added, " Still you think all this is not enough, but you continue to persecute the brethren with the same spirit you did in Scotland." After some conversation betwixt the King and the Archbishop of Canterbury, they were dismissed, with the applause of many present for their bold and steady defence of the cause of God and truth; for they had been much misrepresented to the English.

They had scarcely retired from before the King, until they received a charge not to return to Scotland, nor come near the King's, Queen's, or Prince's Court, without special license, and being called for. A few days after, they were again called to Court, and examined before a select number of the Scots nobility; where, after Mr James Melville's examination, Mr Andrew being called, told them plainly, "That they knew not what they were doing; they had degenerated from the ancient nobility of Scotland, who were wont to hazard their lives and lands for the freedom of their country, and the Gospel which they were betraying and overturning." But night drawing on, they were dismissed.

Another instance of his resolution is this: He was called before the Council for having made a Latin epigram upon seeing the King and Queen making an offering at the altar, whereon were two books, two basins, and two candlesticks, with two unlighted candles, it being a day kept in honour of St Michael. The epigram is as follows:

> " Cur stant clausi Anglis, libri duo, regia in ara,
>   Lumina cœca duo, pollubra sicca duo?
>   Num sensum cultumque Dei tenet Anglia clausum
>   Lumine cœca suo, sorde sepulta sua,
>   Romano et ritu, Regalem dum instruit Aram?
>   Purpuream pingit religiosa lupam ! "

The following is an old and literal translation:

> " Why stand there on the Royal Altar hie,
>   Two closed books, blind lights, two basins drie?
>   Doth England hold God's mind and worship closse,
>   Blind of her sight, and buried in her dross?
>   Doth she, with Chapel put in Romish dress,
>   The purple whore religiously express ! "

When he compeared, he avowed the verses, and said, he was much moved with indignation at such vanity and superstition in a Christian church, under a Christian King, born and brought up under the pure light of the Gospel, and especially before idolaters, to confirm them in idolatry, and grieve the hearts of true professors. The Archbishop of Canterbury began to speak, but Andrew Melville charged him with a breach of the Lord's-day, with imprisoning, silencing, and bearing down of faithful ministers, and with upholding Antichristian hierarchy and Popish ceremonies; shaking the white sleeve of his rochet, he called them Romish rags, told him that he was an avowed enemy to all the Reformed Churches in Europe, and therefore he would profess himself an enemy to him in all such proceedings, to the effusion of the last drop of his blood; and said, he was grieved to the heart to see such a man have the King's ear, and sit so high in that honourable Council. He also charged Bishop Barlow with having stated, after the conference at Hampton Court, that the King had said he was in the Church of Scotland, but not of it; and wondered that he was suffered to go unpunished, for making the King of no religion. He refuted the sermons, which Barlow had preached before the King, and was at last removed; and order was given to Dr Overwall, Dean of St Paul's, to receive him into his house, there to remain, with injunctions not to let any have access to him, till his Majesty's pleasure was signified. Next year he was ordered from the Dean's house to the Bishop of Winchester's, where, being not so strictly guarded, he sometimes kept company with his brethren; but was at last committed to the Tower of London, where he remained for the space of four years.

While Andrew Melville was in the Tower, a gentleman of his acquaintance got access to him, and found him very pensive and melancholy concerning the prevailing defections among many of the ministers of Scotland, having lately got account of the proceedings at the General Assembly held at Glasgow in 1610, where the Earl of Dunbar had an active hand in corrupting many with money. The gentleman desired to know what word he had to send to his native country, but got no answer at first; but upon a second inquiry, he said, " I have no word to send, but am heavily grieved that the glorious government of the Church of Scotland should be so defaced, and a Popish tyrannical one set up; and thou, Manderston (for out of that family Lord Dunbar had sprung), hadst thou no other thing to do, but to carry such commissions down to Scotland, whereby the poor Church is wrecked? The Lord shall be avenged on thee; thou shalt never have that grace to set thy foot in that kingdom again !" These last words impressed the gentleman to such a degree, that he desired some who attended the Court to get their business, which was managing through Dunbar's interest, expedited without delay, being persuaded that the word of that servant of Christ should not fall to the ground; which was the case, for the Earl died at Whitehall a short time after, while he was building an elegant house at Berwick, and making grand preparations for his daughter's marriage with Lord Walden.

In 1611, after four years' confinement, Andrew Melville was, by the interest of the Duke de Bouillon, released, on condition that he would go with him to the University of Sedan ; where he continued enjoying that calm repose denied him in his own country, but maintaining the usual constancy and faithfulness in the service of Christ, which he had done through the whole of his life.

The reader will readily observe, that a high degree of fortitude and boldness appeared in all his actions ; where the honour of his Lord and Master was concerned, the fear of man made no part of his character. He is by Spottiswoode styled the principal agent, or Apostle of the Presbyterians in Scotland. He did, indeed, assert the rights of Presbytery to the utmost of his power against diocesan Episcopacy. He possessed great presence of mind, and was superior to all the arts of flattery that were sometimes tried with him. Being once blamed as being too fiery in his temper, he replied, " If you see my fire go downward, set your foot upon it; but if it goes upward, let it go to its own place." He died at Sedan, in France, in the year 1622, at the advanced age of 77 years.

THE PALACE OF HAMPTON COURT.

FALKLAND PALACE.

Patrick Simpson.

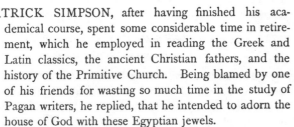

ATRICK SIMPSON, after having finished his academical course, spent some considerable time in retirement, which he employed in reading the Greek and
Latin classics, the ancient Christian fathers, and the
history of the Primitive Church. Being blamed by one
of his friends for wasting so much time in the study of
Pagan writers, he replied, that he intended to adorn the
house of God with these Egyptian jewels.

He was first ordained minister of Cramond, but was afterwards
translated to Stirling, where he continued until his death. He was
a faithful contender against the lordly encroachments of Prelacy. In
the year 1584, when there was an express charge given by King
James VI. to the ministers, either to acknowledge Patrick Adamson as Archbishop of St Andrews, or else lose their benefices, Mr
Simpson opposed that order with all his power, although Adamson
was his uncle by the mother's side ; and when some of his brethren
seemed willing to acquiesce in the King's mandate, and subscribe
their submission to Adamson, so far as it was agreeable to the Word
of God, he rebuked them sharply, saying, that would be no salve to
their consciences, seeing it was altogether absurd to subscribe an

agreement with any human invention, when it was condemned by the Word of God. A bishopric was offered him, and a yearly pension besides, from the King, in order to bring him into his designs, but he positively refused both, saying that he regarded preferment and profit as a bribe to enslave his conscience, which was dearer to him than anything whatever. He did not stop with this; but having occasion, in 1598, to preach before the King, he publicly exhorted him to beware that he drew not the wrath of God upon himself, in patronising a manifest breach of Divine laws. Immediately after sermon, the King stood up, and charged him not to intermeddle in these matters.

When the Assembly, which was held at Aberdeen in 1604, was condemned by the State, he, in a very solemn manner, denounced the judgment of God against all such as had been concerned in distressing and imprisoning the ministers at Linlithgow, who maintained the lawfulness, and justified the conduct of that Assembly. And the protestation given in to the Parliament in 1606 (which Parliament did many things to the further establishment of Prelacy), was written by him, and, having been signed by forty-two ministers, was by him delivered into the hands of the Earl of Dunbar. It was as follows:

" The Protestation offered to the Estates convened in Parliament at Perth, in the beginning of July 1606.

" The earnest desire of our hearts is to be faithful, and in case we would have been silent and unfaithful at this time, when the undermined estate of Christ's kirk craveth a duty at our hands, we should have locked up our hearts with patience and our mouths with taciturnity, rather than to have impeached any with our admonition. But that which Christ commandeth, necessity urgeth, and duty wringeth out of us, to be faithful office-bearers in the kirk of God, no man can justly blame us, providing we hold ourselves within the bounds of that Christian moderation which followeth God without injury done to any man, especially those whom God hath lapped up within the skirts of His own honourable styles and names, calling them gods upon earth.

" Now, therefore, my Lords, convened in the present Parliament, under the most high and excellent Majesty of our dread Sovereign, to your Honours is our exhortation, that ye would endeavour, with all singleness of heart, love, and zeal, to advance the building of the house of God, reserving always unto the Lord's own hand that glory which He will communicate neither with man nor angel, viz., to prescribe from His holy mountain a lively pattern, according to which His own tabernacle should be formed. Remembering always, that there is no absolute and undoubted authority in this world, excepting the sovereign authority of Christ, the King, to whom it belongeth as properly to rule the kirk, according to the good pleasure of His own will, as it belongeth to Him to save His kirk by the merit of His own sufferings. All other authority is so intrenched within the marches of divine commandment, that the least overpassing of the bounds set by God himself, bringeth men under the fearful expectation of temporal and eternal judgments. For this cause, my Lords, let that authority of your meeting in this present Parliament be like the ocean, which, as it is the greatest of all other waters, so it containeth itself better within the coasts and limits appointed by God, than any rivers of fresh running water have done.

" Next, remember that God hath set you to be nursing fathers to the kirk, craving of your hands that ye would maintain and advance, by your authority, that kirk which the Lord hath fashioned by the uncounterfeited work of His own new creation, as the prophet speaketh, *He hath made us, and not we ourselves ;* but not that ye should presume to fashion and shape a new portraiture of a kirk, and a new form of divine service, which God in his word hath not before allowed ; because, that were you to extend your authority farther than the calling ye have of God doth permit, as namely, if ye should (as God forbid) authorise the authority of bishops, and their pre-eminence above their brethren, ye should bring into the kirk of God the ordinance of man, and that thing which the experience of preceding ages hath testified to be the ground of great idleness, palpable ignorance, insufferable pride, pitiless tyranny, and shameless ambition in the kirk of God ; and, finally, to have been the ground of that Antichristian hierarchy which mounteth up on the steps of pre-eminence of bishops ; until that man of sin came forth, as the ripe fruit of man's wisdom, whom God shall consume with the breath of his own mouth. Let the sword of God pierce that belly which brought forth such a monster, and let the staff of God crush that egg which hath hatched such a cockatrice ; and let not only that Roman Antichrist be thrown down from the high bench of his usurped authority, but also let all the steps whereby he mounteth up to that unlawful pre-eminence, be cut down and utterly abolished in this land.

"Above all things, my Lords, beware to strive against God with an open and displayed banner, by building up again the walls of Jericho, which the Lord hath not only cast down, but hath also laid them under a horrible interdiction and execration ; so that the building of them again must needs stand to greater charges to the builders, than the re-edifying of Jericho to Hiel the Bethelite, in the days of Ahab ; for he had nothing but the interdiction of Joshua, and the curse pronounced by him, to stay him from the building again of Jericho ; but the Noblemen and States of this realm have the reverence of the oath of God, made by themselves, and subscribed with their own hands in the Confession of Faith, called the King's Majesty's, published oftener than once or twice, subscribed and sworn by his most excellent Majesty, and by his Highness, the Nobility, Estates, and whole subjects of this realm, to hold them back from setting up the dominion of Bishops ; because it is of verity that they subscribed and swore the said Confession, containing not only the maintenance of the true doctrine, but also of the discipline professed within the realm of Scotland

"Consider also, that this work cannot be set forward without great slander of the Gospel, defamation of many preachers, and evident hurt and loss of the people's souls committed to our charge. For the people are brought almost to the like case as they were in Syria, Arabia, and Egypt about the year of our Lord 600, when the people were so shaken and brangled with contrary doctrines, some affirming and others denying the opinion of Eutyches, that in the end they lost all assured persuasion of true religion, and within a short time thereafter, did cast the gates of their hearts open to the peril, to receive that vile and blasphemous doctrine of Mahomet ; even so the people of this land are cast into such admiration to hear the preachers, who damned so openly this stately pre-eminence of bishops, and then, within a few years after, accept the same dignity, pomp, and superiority, in their own persons, which they before had damned in others, that the people know not what way to incline, and in the end will become so doubtful, in matters of religion and doctrine, that their hearts will be like an open tavern, patent to every guest that chooses to come in.

"We beseech your Honours to ponder this in the balance of a godly and prudent mind, and suffer not the Gospel to be slandered by the behaviour of a few preachers, of whom we are bold to affirm, that if they go forward in this defection, not only abusing and appropriating the name of bishops to themselves, which is common to all the pastors of God's kirk ; but also taking upon themselves such offices that carry with them the ordinary charge of governing the civil affairs of the country, neglecting their flock, and seeking to subordinate their brethren to their jurisdiction ; if any of them, we say, be found to step forward in this cause of defection, they are more worthy, as rotten members, to be cut off from the body of Christ, than to have superiority and dominion over their brethren within the kirk of God.

" This pre-eminence of bishops is that Dagon which once already fell before the ark of God in this land, and no band of iron shall be able to hold him up again. This is that pattern of that altar brought from Damascus, but not shewed to Moses in the mountain ; and, therefore, it shall fare with it as it did with that altar of Damascus, it came last into the temple and went first out. Likewise the institution of Christ was anterior to this pre-eminence of bishops, and shall consist and stand within the house of God when this new fashion of the altar shall go to the door.

" Remember, my Lords, that in times past your authority was for Christ, and not against him. Ye followed the light of God, and strived not against it ; and, like a child in the mother's hand, ye said to Christ, *Draw us after thee.* God forbid that ye should now leave off, and fall away from your former reverence borne to Christ, in presuming to lead Him whom the Father hath appointed to be leader of you, and far less to trail the holy ordinances of Christ, by the cords of your authority, at the heels of the ordinances of men.

"And albeit your Honours have no such intention to do anything which may impair the honour of Christ's kingdom ; yet remember, that spiritual darkness, flowing from a very small beginning, doth so insinuate and thrust itself into the house of God, as men can hardly discern by what secret means the light was dimmed, and darkness, creeping in, got the upper hand ; and in the end, at unawares, all was involved in a misty cloud of horrible apostacy.

"And lest any should think this our admonition out of time, in so far as it is statute and ordained already by his Majesty, with advice of his Estates in Parliament, that all ministers, provided to prelacies, should have vote in parliament ; as likewise, the General Assembly (his Majesty being present thereat) hath found the same lawful and expedient, we would humbly and earnestly beseech all such to consider,

First, That the kingdom of Jesus Christ, the office-bearers and laws thereof, neither should nor can suffer any derogation, addition, diminution, or alteration, besides the prescript of his holy word, by any inventions or doings of men, civil or ecclesiastical.   And we are able, by the grace of God, and will offer ourselves to prove, that this bishopric to be erected, is against the word of God, the ancient fathers, and canons of the kirk, the modern, most learned, and godly divines, the doctrine and constitution of the kirk of Scotland, since the first reformation of religion within the same country, the laws of the realm, ratifying the government of the kirk by the general and provincial assemblies, presbyteries, and sessions; also against the weal and honour of the King's most excellent Majesty, the weal and honour of the realm, and quietness thereof; the established estate and weal of the kirk, in the doctrine, discipline, and patrimony thereof; the weal and honour of your Lordships, the most ancient estate of this realm; and finally, against the weal of all, and every one, the good subjects thereof, in soul, body, and substance.

" *Next*, That the Act of Parliament, granting vote in Parliament to ministers, is with a special provision, that nothing thereby be derogatory or prejudicial to the present established discipline of the kirk, and jurisdiction thereof, in general and synodical assemblies, presbyteries, and sessions.

" *Thirdly* and *lastly*, The General Assembly (his Majesty sitting, voting, and consenting therein), fearing the corruption of that office, hath circumscribed and bounded the same with a number of cautions; all which, together with such others as shall be concluded upon by the Assembly, were thought expedient to be inserted in the body of the Act of Parliament that is to be made for confirmation of their vote in Parliament, as most necessary and substantial parts of the same.   And the said Assembly hath not agreed to give thereunto the name of bishops, for fear of importing the old corruption, pomp and tyranny of Papal bishops, but ordained them to be called commissioners for the kirk to vote in Parliament.   And it is of verity, that according to these cautions, neither have these men, now called bishops, entered to that office of commissionary to vote in Parliament, neither since their ingoing have they behaved themselves therein. And therefore, in the name of the Lord Jesus Christ, who shall hold that great court of parliament to judge both the quick and the dead, at His glorious manifestation, and in the name of His kirk in general, so happily and well established within this realm, and whereof the said realm hath reaped the comfortable peace and unity, free from heresy, schism, and dissention, these forty-six years bypast; also in name of our presbyteries, from which we have our commission; and in our own names, office-bearers and pastors within the same, for discharging of our necessary duty, and disburdening of our consciences in particular; we except and protest against the said bishopric and bishops, and the erection, or confirmation, or ratification thereof, at this present Parliament; most humbly craving that this our protestation may be admitted by your Honours, and registered among the statutes and acts of the same, in case (as God forbid) these bishoprics be erected, ratified, or confirmed therein."

Patrick Simpson was not more distinguished for zeal in the cause of Christ, than for piety and an exemplary life, which had a happy effect upon the people with whom he stood connected. He was in a very eminent degree blessed with the spirit and return of prayer; and the following fact, attested by old Mr Row of Carnock, shows how much of the Divine countenance he had in this duty.

His wife, Martha Barron, a woman of singular piety, fell sick, and under her indisposition was strongly assaulted by the common enemy of salvation, suggesting to her that she should be delivered up to him. This soon brought her into a very distracted condition, which continued for some time increasing; she breaking forth into very dreadful expressions. She was in one of those fits of despair one Sabbath morning, when Mr Simpson was going to preach; he was exceedingly troubled at her condition, and went to prayer; which she took no notice of. After he had done, he turned to the company present, and said, that they, who had been witnesses to that sad hour, should yet see a gracious work of God on her, and that the devil's malice against that poor woman should have a shameful foil. Her distraction continued for some days after. On a Tuesday morning about daybreak, he went into his garden as privately as possible, and Helen Gardiner, wife to one of the bailies of the town, a godly woman, who had sat up that night with Mrs Simpson, being concerned at the melancholy condition he was in, climbed over the garden wall, to observe him in this retirement; but, coming near the place where he was, she was terrified with a noise which she heard, as of the rushing of multitudes of people together, with a most melodious sound intermixed; she fell on her knees, and prayed that the Lord would pardon her rashness, which her regard for His servant had caused. Afterwards, she went forward and found him lying on the ground; she entreated him to tell her what had happened unto him, and after many promises of secrecy, and an obligation that she would not reveal it in his lifetime, but if she survived him, she would be at liberty, he said, " O! what am I! being but dust and ashes! that holy ministering spirits should be sent with a message to me!" He then told her that he had seen a vision of angels, who gave him an audible answer from the Lord, respecting his wife's condition; and then returning to the house, he said to the people who attended his wife, " Be of good comfort, for I am sure that ere ten hours of the day this brand shall be plucked out of the fire;" after which he went to prayer at his wife's bedside. She continued for some time quiet, but upon his mentioning Jacob's wrestling with God, she sat up in the bed, drew the curtain aside, and said, " Thou art this day a Jacob, who hast wrestled and hast prevailed; and now God hath made good His word, which He spoke this morning to you, for I am plucked out of the hands of Satan, and he shall have no power over me." This interruption made him silent for a little, but afterwards, with great melting of heart, he proceeded in prayer, and magnified the riches of grace towards him. From that hour she continued to utter nothing but the language of joy and comfort until her death, which was on the Friday following, August 13th, 1601.

Patrick Simpson lived for several years after this, fervent and faithful in the work of the ministry. In the year 1608, when the bishops, and some Commissioners of the General Assembly convened in the palace of Falkland, the ministers assembled in the kirk of the town, and chose him for their moderator; after which they spent some time in prayer, and tasted some of the comfort of their former meetings. They then agreed upon some articles for concord and peace, to be given in to the bishops. This Mr Simpson and some others did in the name of the rest, but the bishops shifted them off till the next assembly, and, in the meantime, took all possible precautions to strengthen their own party, which they effected.

In 1610 the noblemen and bishops came to Stirling, after dissolving the Assembly. In preaching before them, Mr Simpson openly charged the bishops with perjury and gross defection. They hesitated for some time whether they should delate him, or compound the matter; but, after deliberation, they dropped the affair altogether for the present. There is no reason to doubt but he would have been subjected to the same sufferings with many others of his brethren, had he lived; but before the copestone was laid on Prelacy in Scotland, he had entered into the joy of his Lord. For, in the month of

March 1618, which was about four months before the Perth Assembly when the five articles were agreed upon, viz., (1.) kneeling at the communion; (2.) private communion; (3.) private baptism; (4.) observance of holidays; (5.) confirmation of children,—he said that this month should put an end to all his troubles ; and he accordingly died about the end of it, blessing the Lord that he had not been perverted by the sinful courses of these times, and testifying, that as the Lord had said to Elijah in the wilderness, so, in some respects, He had dealt with him all the days of his life.

He wrote a History of the Church, for the space of about ten centuries. There are some other little tracts, besides a History of the Councils of the Church, which are nearly out of print. Upon some of his books he had written, " Remember, O my soul, and never forget the 9th of August, what consolation the Lord gave thee, and how he performed what he spake, according to Zech. iii. 2: Is not this a brand plucked out of the fire ?"

MARKET-CROSS OF ABERDEEN.

BLACKNESS CASTLE.

Andrew Duncan.

NDREW DUNCAN was settled minister of Crail, in the shire of Fife, and was afterwards summoned before the High Commission Court at St Andrews, in 1619, on account of his faithfulness in opposing the five articles of Perth. [Previous to this, however, he had suffered much for conscience' sake. In 1606 he was one of six ministers who were tried and found guilty of high treason, for having attended the famous Assembly at Aberdeen the preceding year. After suffering imprisonment for fourteen months in Blackness Castle, he was, with his five brethren, banished to France, but was afterwards allowed to return to his native land.—Ed.]

At the first time of his compearance he declined their authority; and at the second, adhered to his former declinature; upon which the High Commission Court passed the sentence of deposition against him, and ordained him to enter himself in ward at Dundee. After this sentence was pronounced, he gave in a protestation, which was as follows: "Now seeing I have done nothing of this business, whereof I have been accused by you, but have been serving Jesus Christ, my Master, in rebuking vice, in simplicity and righteousness of heart, I protest, seeing ye have done me wrong, for a remedy at God's hand, the righteous Judge, and summon you before His dreadful judgment-seat, to be censured and punished for such unrighteous dealings, at such a time as His Majesty shall think expedient; and in the meantime decline this your judgment *simpliciter*, now as before, and appeal to the Ordinary Assembly of the Church, for reasons before produced in writ. Pity yourselves for the Lord's sake; lose not your own dear souls, I beseech you, for Esau's pottage. Remember Balaam, who was cast away by the deceit of the wages of unrighteousness; forget not how miserable Judas was, who lost himself for a trifle of money, that never did him good. Better be pined to death by hunger, than for a little pittance of the earth to perish for ever, and never be recovered so long as the days of heaven shall last, and the years of eternity shall endure. Why should ye distress your own brethren, sons and servants of the Lord Jesus? This is not the doing of the shepherds of the flock of Christ: if ye will not regard your souls nor consciences, look, I beseech you, to your fame. Why will ye be miserable both in this life, and in the life to come?"

When the Archbishop of St Andrews had read some few lines of this admonition, he cast it from him; the Bishop of Dunblane took it up, and reading it, said, "he calls us Esaus, Balaams, and Judases." "Not so," said Mr Duncan; "read again; beware that ye be not like them." In the space of a month after, he was deposed for nonconformity.

In the month of July 1621, he presented a large supplication, in name of himself, and some of his faithful brethren, who had been excluded the General Assembly, to Sir George Hay, clerk-register, on which account he was in a few days after apprehended by the captain of the guard, and brought before the Council, who accused him for breaking ward, after he was suspended and confined to Dundee, because he had preached the week before at Crail. Mr Duncan denied that he had been put to the horn: and as for breaking ward, he said, "that, for the sake of obedience, he stayed at Dundee, separated from a wife and six children for half a year, and the winter approaching forced him to go home. In the end, he requested them not to imprison him on his own charges; but the sentence had been resolved on before he compeared. He was conveyed to Dumbarton Castle next day, some say to Blackness Castle; here he remained until the month of October thereafter, when he was again brought before the Council, and by them was confined to Kilrennie, upon his own charges. This was a parish neighbouring to his own.

Upon another occasion, of the same nature with this just now narrated, this worthy man was banished out of the kingdom, and went to settle at Berwick; but having several children, and his wife being near her confinement, they were reduced to great hardships, being obliged to part with their servant, having scarcely subsistence for themselves. One night in particular, the children asked for bread, and there being none to give them, they cried very sore; the mother was likewise much depressed in spirits; as for Mr Duncan, he had recourse sometimes to prayer, and in the intervals endeavoured to cherish his wife's hope, and please the children, and at last got them to bed; but she continued to mourn heavily. He exhorted her to wait patiently upon God, who was now trying, but would undoubtedly provide for them; and added, that though the Lord should rain down bread from heaven, they should not want. This confidence was the more remarkable, because they had neither friend nor acquaintance in that place to whom they could make their case known. And yet, before morning, a man brought them a sackful of provision, and went off, without telling them from whence it came, though entreated to do so. When Mr Duncan opened the sack, he found in it a bag with twenty pounds Scots, two loaves of bread, a bag of flour, another of barley, and such like provisions; and having brought the whole to his wife, he said, "See what a good Master I serve." After this she hired a servant again, but was soon reduced to a new extremity; the pains of childbearing came upon her, before she could make any provision for her delivery; but Providence interposed on their behalf at this time also. While she travailed in the night season, and the good man knew not where to apply for a midwife, a gentlewoman came early in the morning riding to the door; and having sent her servant back with the horse, with orders when to return, she went in, and asked the maid of the house how her mistress was, and desired access to her, which she obtained. She first ordered a good fire to be made, and directing Mrs Duncan to rise, without any other assistance than the house afforded, she delivered her, and afterwards accommodated Mrs Duncan and the child with abundance of very fine linen, which she had brought along with her. She gave her likewise a box, containing some necessary cordials, and five pieces of gold, bidding them both be of good comfort, for they should not want. After which she went away on the horse, which was by this time returned for her, but would not tell her name, nor from whence she came.

Thus did God take His own servant under His immediate care and providence, when men had wrongfully excluded him from enjoying his worldly comforts. He continued zealous and steadfast in the faith, and to the end of his life his conduct was uniform with the circumstances of this narrative. The following is a copy of the last will and testament of Mr Duncan, a valuable memorial of the piety of this worthy :

" I, Andrew Duncan, a sinful wight, Christ's unworthy minister in His glorious Gospel, being sickly and weak, worn out with years, and heaviness of heart in this pilgrimage ; and being now weary of this loathsome prison, and body of death because of sin ; and having received sundry advertisements and summonses of my Master to flit out of this uncouth country, the region of death, home to my native land ; and now sitting upon the prison-door threshold, ready to obey, waiting till the sad messenger be sent to convey me home to that glorious palace, even the heavenly Jerusalem, that I may enter into possession of my heritage, even that glorious kingdom of eternity, which Christ came down from heaven to conquer for me, and then went up to prepare and possess it in my name, as my attorney, until it please his Majesty to take me thither, that I may in my own person possess it :

" I set down the declaration of my latter will, concerning these things, which God hath lent me in this world ; in manner following, —First, as touching myself, body and soul ; my soul I leave to Christ Jesus, who gave it, and when it was lost, redeemed it, that He may send His holy angels to transport it to the bosom of Abraham, there to enjoy all happiness and contentment ; and as for this frail body, I commend it to the grave, there to sleep and rest, as in a sweet bed, until the day of refreshment, when it shall be reunited to the soul, and shall be set down at the table with the holy patriarchs, prophets, and apostles ; yea, shall be placed on the throne with Christ, and get on the crown of glory on my head. As for the children whom God hath given me, for which I thank His Majesty, I leave them to His providence, to be governed and cared for by Him, beseeching Him to be the tutor, curator, and agent, in all their adoes, yea, and a father ; and that He would lead them by His gracious Spirit, through this evil world ; that they be profitable instruments, both in kirk and commonwealth, to set out His glory ; beseeching them on the other part, as they would have God's blessing and mine in all their affairs, to set Him before their eyes, and to walk in His ways, living peaceably in His fear, in all humility and meekness, with all those they have ado with; holding their course to heaven, and comforting themselves with the glorious and fair-to-look-on heritage, which Christ hath conquered for them, and for all that love Him. Under God, I leave John Duncan, my eldest son, to be tutor to my youngest daughter, Bessie Duncan, his youngest sister, to take a care of her, and to see that all turns go right, touching her person and gear. My executors I leave my three sons, John, William, and David Duncan, to do my turns after me, and to put in practice my directions; requesting them to be good and comfortable to their sisters, but chiefly to the two that are at home, as they would have God's blessing and mine. As concerning my temporal goods, the baggage and blathrie of the earth, as I have gotten them in the world off God's liberal hand, so I leave them behind me in the world; giving most humble and hearty thanks unto my heavenly Father for so long and comfortable loan of the same."— 14th April, 1626.

John Scrimgeour.

OHN SCRIMGEOUR was settled minister at Kinghorn, in the shire of Fife, and went as chaplain with King James VI., in 1590, to Denmark, when he brought home his Queen. He was afterwards concerned in several important affairs of the Church, until that fatal year 1618, when the five articles of Perth were agreed on in an Assembly held at that place. He attended this Assembly, and gave in some proposals (*see* Calderwood's History), upon being, along with others of his faithful brethren, excluded from having a vote by the prevailing party of that Assembly.

In 1620, he was, with some others, summoned before the High Commission Court, for not preaching upon holidays, and not adminis-

PORTRAIT OF JAMES VI.

tering the communion, conform to the agreement at Perth; with certification, if this was proven, that they should be deprived of exercising the functions of a minister in all time coming. But there being none present on the day appointed, except the Archbishops of St Andrews and Glasgow, the Bishop of the Isles, and Mr Walter Whiteford, they were dismissed at that time; but were warned to compear again on the 1st of March. The bishops caused the clerk to exact their consent to deprivation, in case they did not compear against that day. Nevertheless, they all protested with one voice, that they would never willingly renounce their ministry; and such was the resolution and courage of Mr Scrimgeour, that, notwithstanding all the threatenings of the bishops, he celebrated the communion conform to the ancient practice of the Church a few days thereafter.

On the day appointed for their next compearance, the Archbishop of St Andrews, the Bishops of Dunkeld, Galloway, the Isles, Dunblane, Mr Hewison, Commissary of Edinburgh, and Dr Blair, being assembled in the archbishop of St Andrews' lodging in Edinburgh, John Scrimgeour was again called upon to answer, and the Archbishop of St Andrews alleged against him, that he had promised either to conform or quit his ministry, as the act at his last compearance in January 26th reported. He replied, " I am sore straitened; I never saw reason to conform; and as for my ministry, it was not mine, and so I could not quit it." After long reasoning betwixt him and the bishops, concerning Church policy and the keeping of holidays, he was removed for a little. Being called in again, the Archbishop of St Andrews said to him, " You are deprived of all function within the Kirk, and ordained within six days to enter in ward at Dundee." " It is a very summary and peremptory sentence," said Scrimgeour ; "ye might have been advised better, and first have heard what I would have said." "You shall be heard," said the Archbishop. This brought on some further reasoning, in the course of which Scrimgeour gave a faithful testimony against the King's supremacy over the Church, and among other things, said, "I have had opportunity to reason with the King himself on this subject, and have told him that Christ was the Sovereign and only director of His house ; and that his Majesty was subject to Him. I have had occasion to tell other men's matters to the King, and could have truly claimed this great preferment." "I tell you, Mr John," said the Archbishop of St Andrews, "that the King is Pope, and shall be so now." He replied, "That is an evil style you give him." He then gave in his reason in writing, which they read at leisure, and afterwards the Archbishop of St Andrews said to him, "Take up your reasons again : if you will not conform, I cannot help it; the King must be obeyed ; the lords have given sentence, and will stand to it." You cannot deprive me of my ministry," said Scrimgeour ; "I received it not from you ; I received it from the whole Synod of Fife, and, for anything ye do, I will never think myself deposed." The Archbishop of St Andrews replied, " You are deprived only of the present exercise of it." Then Scrimgeour presented the following protestation : " I protest before the Lord Jesus, that I get manifest wrong ; my reasons and allegations are not considered and answered. I attest you to answer at His glorious appearance, for this and such dealings; and protest that my cause should have been heard as I pled, and still plead and challenge. I likewise appeal to he Lord Jesus, His eternal word; to the King my dread Sovereign, His law; to the constitution of this Kirk and kingdom, and to the Councils and Assemblies of both; and protest, that I stand minister of the evangel, and only by violence I am thrust from the same." " You must obey the sentence," said the Archbishop of St Andrews. He answered, that Dundee was far off, and he was not able for far journeys, as physicians could witness ; and added, " Little know ye what is in my purse." " Then where will you choose your place of confinement," said the Archbishop. He answered, " At a little room

of my own, called Bowhill, in the parish of Auchterderran." "Then,"
said the Archbishop, "Write, at Bowhill, during the king's pleasure."

Thus this worthy servant of Christ lived the rest of his days in
Auchterderran. In his old age he was grievously afflicted with the
stone. He said to a godly minister, who went to see him a little
before his death, "I have been a rude stunkard all my life, and now
by this pain the Lord is humbling me, to make me as a lamb before
He take me to Himself." He was a man somewhat negligent in his
clothing, and in some of his expressions and behaviour; and yet was
a very loving, tender-hearted man; of a deep natural judgment, and
very learned, especially in Hebrew. He often wished that most part
of books were burnt, except the Bible, and some short notes thereon.
He had a peculiar talent for comforting the dejected. He used a
very familiar, but pressing manner of preaching. He was also an
eminent wrestler with God, and had more than ordinary power and
familiarity with Him, as appears from the following instances:

When he was minister at Kinghorn, there was a certain godly
woman under his charge, who fell sick of a very lingering disease, and
was all the while assaulted with strong temptations, leading her to
think that she was a castaway, notwithstanding that her whole conversation had put the reality of grace in her beyond a doubt. He
often visited her while in this deep exercise, but her trouble and
terrors still remained. As her dissolution drew on, her spiritual trouble
increased. He went with two of his elders to her, and began first,
in their presence, to comfort and pray with her; but she still grew
worse. He ordered his elders to pray, and afterwards prayed himself, but no relief came. Then sitting pensive for a little space, he
thus broke silence: "What is this! Our laying grounds of comfort
before her will not do; prayer will not do; we must try another
remedy. Sure I am, this is a daughter of Abraham; sure I am, she
hath sent for me; and, therefore, in the name of God, the Father of
our Lord Jesus, who sent Him to redeem sinners; in the name of
Jesus Christ, who obeyed the Father, and came to save us; and in
the name of the Holy and blessed Spirit, our Quickener and Sanctifier,
I, the elder, command thee, a daughter of Abraham, to be loosed from
these bonds." And immediately peace and joy ensued.

Mr Scrimgeour had several friends and children taken away by
death. The only daughter who at that time survived, and whom
he dearly loved, was seized with the king's evil, by which she was
reduced to the very point of death, so that he was called up to see

her die. Finding her in this condition, he went out to the fields, as he himself told, in the night-time, in great grief and anxiety, and began to expostulate with the Lord, with such expressions as for all the world he durst not again utter. In a fit of displeasure, he said, "Thou, O Lord, knowest that I have been serving Thee in the uprightness of my heart, according to my power and measure; nor have I stood in awe to declare Thy mind even unto the greatest in the time, and Thou seest that I take pleasure in this child. O that I could obtain such a thing at Thy hand, as to spare her!" And being in great agony of spirit, at last it was said to him from the Lord, "I have heard thee at this time, but use not the like boldness in time coming, for such particulars." When he came home the child was recovered, and, sitting up in the bed, took some meat; and when he looked at her arm, it was perfectly whole.

[The name of John Scrimgeour occurs among the forty-two appended to the Protest referred to at p. 100. He is also mentioned in Row's History of the Kirk of Scotland as one of those who frequently assisted Mr John Row on communion occasions at Carnock. These communions, it is said, were "very famous and much frequented, many nobles resorting thither, and persons of all ranks that were nonconformists."—ED.]

John Welch.

OHN WELCH was by birth a gentleman, his father being Laird of Collieston, in Nithsdale, an estate rather competent than large. He was born about the year 1570, the dawning of our Reformation being then but dark, and became a rich example of grace and mercy, although with him the night went before the day, being a most hopeless extravagant boy It was not enough for him, frequently, when he was a young stripling, to run away from school, and play the truant, but

PORTRAIT OF JOHN WELCH.

after he had passed his grammar, and was come to be a youth, he left the school, and his father's house, and went and joined himself to the thieves on the English border, who lived by robbing the two nations, and amongst them he stayed until he spent a suit of clothes. Then when he was clothed only with rags, the prodigal's misery brought him to the prodigal's resolution, so he resolved to return to his father's house, but durst not adventure till he should interpose a reconciler.

In his return homewards he took Dumfries in his way, where he had an aunt, Mrs Agnes Forsyth, and with her he spent some days, earnestly entreating her to reconcile him to his father. While he lurked in her house, his father came providentially to the house to visit Mrs Forsyth; and after they had talked a while, she asked him, whether he had ever heard any news of his son John. To her he replied with great grief, "O cruel woman, how can you name him to me! The first news I expect to hear of him is, that he is hanged for a thief." She answered that many a profligate boy had become a virtuous man, and comforted him. He insisted upon his sad complaint, but asked whether she knew if his lost son were yet alive. She answered yes, he was, and she hoped he should prove a better man than he was a boy, and with that she called upon him to come to his father. He came weeping, and kneeled, beseeching his father, for Christ's sake, to pardon his misbehaviour, and deeply engaged to be a new man. His father reproached and threatened him, yet at length by his tears, and Mrs Forsyth's importunities, he was persuaded to a reconciliation. The boy entreated his father to send him to college, and there try his behaviour, and if ever thereafter he should break, he said he should be content that his father should disclaim him for ever. So his father carried him home, and put him to the college, and there he became a diligent student, of great expectation, showing himself also a sincere convert; and so he proceeded to the ministry.

His first settlement was at Selkirk, while he was yet very young, and the country rude. His ministry was rather admired by some, than received by many, for he was always attended by the prophet's shadow, the hatred of the wicked; yea, even the ministers of that country were more ready to pick a quarrel with his person, than to follow his doctrine, as may appear to this day in their synodical records, where we find he had many to censure, and few to defend him. Yet it was thought his ministry in that place was not without fruit, though he stayed but a short time there. Being a young man unmarried, he boarded himself in the house of a man named Mitchelhill, and took a young boy of his to be his bedfellow, who, to his dying day, retained both a respect to John Welch and his ministry, from the impressions Mr Welch's behaviour made upon his apprehension, though but a child. His custom was, when he went to bed at night, to lay a Scots plaid above his bed clothes, and when he went to his night-prayers, to sit up and cover himself negligently therewith, and so to continue; for, from the beginning of his ministry to his death, he reckoned the day ill-spent if he stayed not seven or eight hours in prayer. This the boy did not forget even to old age.

An old man of the name of Ewart, in Selkirk, who remembered Mr Welch's being in that place, said, "He was a type of Christ;" an expression more significant than proper, for his meaning was, that he was a man who imitated Christ, as indeed in many things he did. He also said, that Welch's custom was to preach publicly once every day, and to spend his whole time in spiritual exercises; that some in that place waited well upon his ministry with great tenderness, but that he was constrained to leave, because of the malice of the wicked.

The special cause of his departure was a profane gentleman in the country, Scot of Headschaw, whose family is now extinct. Either because Welch had reproved him, or merely from hatred, he was most unworthily abused by the unhappy man, and among the rest of the injuries he did him, this was one. Mr Welch kept always two good horses for his own use, and the wicked gentleman, when he could do no more, either with his own hand, or by his servants, cut off the rumps of the two innocent beasts, upon which they both died. Such base usage as this persuaded him to listen to a call to the ministry at Kirkcudbright, which was his next post.

When he was preparing to leave Selkirk, he could not find a man in the whole town to transport his furniture, except Ewart, who was at that time a poor young man, but master of two horses, with which he transported Mr Welch's goods, and so left him; but as he took his leave, Welch gave him his blessing, and a piece of gold for a token, exhorting him to fear God, and promised he should never want, which promise Providence made good through the whole course of the man's life, as was observed by all his neighbours.

At Kirkcudbright he stayed not long; but there he reaped a harvest of converts, who continued long after his departure, and became a part of Samuel Rutherford's flock, though not in his parish, while he was minister of Anwoth; yet when his call to Ayr came, the people of the parish of Kirkcudbright never offered to detain him, so his translation to Ayr was the more easy.

While he was at Kirkcudbright, he met with a young gentleman in scarlet and silver lace named Mr Robert Glendinning, newly come home from his travels. He much surprised the young man by telling him that he behoved to change his garb and way of life, and betake himself to the study of the Scriptures, which at that time was not his business, for he should be his successor in the ministry at Kirkcudbright; which accordingly came to pass sometime thereafter.

John Welch was translated to Ayr in the year 1590, and there he continued till he was banished. There he had a very hard beginning, but a very sweet end; for when he came first to the town, the country was so wicked and the hatred of godliness so great, that there could not be found one in all the town who would let him a house to dwell in, so he was constrained to accommodate himself for a time, as best he might, in part of a gentleman's house, whose name was John Stuart, merchant, and some time provost of Ayr, an eminent Christian, and great assistant of Mr Welch.

When he first took up his residence in Ayr, the place was so divided into factions, and filled with bloody conflicts, that a man could hardly walk the streets with safety. Welch made it his first undertaking to remove the bloody quarrellings, but found it a very difficult work; yet such was his earnestness to pursue his design, that many times he would rush betwixt two parties of men fighting, even in the midst of blood and wounds. He used to cover his head with a head-piece before he went to separate these bloody enemies, but would never use a sword, that they might see he came for peace and not for war; and so, by little and little, he made the town a peaceable habitation. His manner was, after he had ended a skirmish amongst his neighbours, and reconciled them, to cause a table to be covered upon the street; he there brought the enemies together, and, beginning with prayer, persuaded them to profess themselves friends, and eat and drink together; then last of all he ended the work with singing a psalm. After the rude people began to observe his example, and listen to his heavenly doctrine, he came quickly to such respect amongst them, that he became not only a necessary counsellor, without whose advice they would do nothing, but also an example to imitate.

He gave himself wholly to ministerial exercises, preaching once every day; he prayed the third part of his time, and was unwearied in his studies. For a proof of this, it was found among his papers, that he had abridged Suarez's metaphysics when they came first to his hand, even when he was well stricken in years. By all this it appears, that he has been not only a man of great diligence, but also of a strong and robust natural constitution, otherwise he had never endured the fatigue.

Sometimes, before he went to sermon, he would send for his elders, and tell them he was afraid to go to the pulpit, because he found himself sore deserted; he would therefore desire one or more of them to pray, and then he would venture to the pulpit. But it was observed that this humble exercise used ordinarily to be followed by a flame of extraordinary assistance; so near neighbours are, many times, contrary dispositions and frames. He would often retire to the church of Ayr, which was at some distance from the town, and there spend the whole night in prayer; for he used to allow his affections full expression, and prayed not only with an audible, but sometimes a loud voice.

There was in Ayr, before he came to it, an aged man, a minister of the town, named Porterfield. He was judged no bad man for his personal inclinations, but was of so easy a disposition, that he frequently used to go too great a length with his neighbours in many dangerous practices; and, amongst the rest, he used to go to the bow butts and archery on the Sabbath afternoon, to Welch's great dissatisfaction. But the way he used to reclaim him was not by bitter severity, but this gentle policy. Welch, together with John Stuart, and Hugh Kennedy, his two intimate friends, used to spend the Sabbath afternoon in religious conference and prayer, and to this exercise they invited Porterfield, which he could not refuse; by which means he was not only diverted from his former sinful practices, but likewise brought to a more watchful and edifying behaviour in his course of life.

While Welch was at Ayr, the Lord's day was greatly profaned at a gentleman's house about eight miles distant, by reason of a great confluence of people playing at the football, and other pastimes. After writing several times to him, to suppress the profanation of the Lord's day at his house, which he slighted, not loving to be called a puritan, Welch came one day to his gate, and, calling him out, told him that he had a message from God to show him; because he had slighted the advice given him from the Lord, and would not restrain the profanation of the Lord's day committed in his bounds, therefore the Lord would cast him out of his house, and none of his posterity should enjoy it. This accordingly came to pass ; for although he was in a good external situation at this time, yet henceforth all things went against him, until he was obliged to sell his estate; and when giving the purchaser possession thereof, he told his wife and children that he had found Welch a true prophet.

He married Elizabeth Knox, daughter of the famous John Knox, minister at Edinburgh, who lived with him from his youth till his death, and by whom he had three sons. The first was called Dr Welch, a doctor of medicine, who was unhappily killed upon an innocent mistake in the Low Countries. Another son was most lamentably lost at sea; for, when the ship in which he was sunk, he swam to a rock in the water, and starved there for want of necessary food and refreshment. When, some time afterwards, his body was found, he was in a praying posture, upon his bended knees, with his hands stretched out ; and this was all the satisfaction his friends and the world had upon his lamentable death. Another he had, who was heir to his father's graces and blessings, and this was Mr Josias Welch, minister at Temple-Patrick, in the north of Ireland, commonly called the Cock of the Conscience by the people of that country, because of his extraordinary, awakening, and rousing gift. He died in his youth, and left for his successor his son, Mr John Welch, minister of Irongray in Galloway, the place of his grandfather's nativity.

As the duty wherein John Welch abounded and excelled most was prayer, so his greatest attainments fell that way. He used to say, he wondered how a Christian could lie in bed all night, and not rise to pray; and many times he rose, and many times he watched. One night he rose and went into the next room, where he stayed so long at secret prayer, that his wife, fearing he might catch cold, was constrained to rise and follow him, and, as she hearkened, she heard him speak as by interrupted sentences, " Lord, wilt Thou not grant me Scotland?" and, after a pause, " Enough, Lord, enough." She asked him afterwards what he meant by saying, " Enough, Lord, enough?" He showed himself dissatisfied with her curiosity; but told her that he had been wrestling with the Lord for Scotland, and found there was a sad time at hand, but that the Lord would be gracious to a remnant. This was about the time when bishops first overspread the land, and corrupted the Church. This is more wonderful still: An honest minister, who was a parishioner of his for many a day, said, that one night as Welch watched in his garden very late, and some friends were waiting upon him in his house, and wearying because of his long stay, one of them chanced to open a window toward the place where he walked, and saw clearly a strange light surround him, and heard him speak strange words about his spiritual joy.

But though John Welch, on account of his holiness, abilities, and success, had acquired among his subdued people a very great respect, yet was he never in such admiration as after the great plague which raged in Scotland in his time. And one cause was this: The magistrates of Ayr, for as much as this town alone was free, and the country around infected, thought fit to guard the ports with sentinels and watchmen. One day two travelling merchants, each with a pack of cloth upon a horse, came to the town desiring entrance, that they might sell their goods, producing a pass from the magistrates of the town from whence they came, which was at that time sound and free. Notwithstanding all this, the sentinels stopped them till the magistrates were called, and when they came they would do nothing without their minister's advice; so John Welch was called, and his opinion asked. He demurred, and putting off his hat, with his eyes towards heaven for a pretty space, though he uttered no audible words, yet he continued in a praying posture, and after a little space told the magistrates that they would do well to discharge these travellers their town, affirming, with great asseveration, that the plague was in these packs. So the magistrates commanded them to be gone, and they went to Cumnock, a town about twenty miles distant, and there sold their goods, which kindled such an infection in that place, that the living were hardly able to bury their dead. This made the people begin to think of Mr Welch as an oracle. Yet, though he walked with God, and kept close with Him, he forgot not man, for he used frequently to dine abroad with such of his friends as he thought were persons with whom he might maintain the communion of the saints; and once in the year he used to invite all his familiar acquaintances in the town to a treat in his house, where there was a banquet of holiness and sobriety.

He continued the course of his ministry in Ayr till King James's purpose of destroying the Church of Scotland, by establishing bishops, was ripe, and then it became his duty to edify the Church by his sufferings, as formerly he had done by his doctrine.

The reason why King James VI. was so violent for bishops, was neither their divine institution, which he denied they had, nor yet the profit the Church should reap by them, for he knew well both the men and their communications, but merely because he believed they were useful instruments to turn a limited monarchy into absolute dominion, and subjects into slaves; the design in the world which he had most at heart. Always in the pursuit of his design, he resolved first to destroy General Assemblies, knowing well that so long as assemblies might convene in freedom, bishops could never get their designed authority in Scotland; and the dissolution of assemblies he brought about in this manner:

The General Assembly at Holyroodhouse, in 1602, with the King's consent, appointed their next meeting to be kept at Aberdeen, on the last Tuesday of July 1604; but before that day came, the King, by his commissioner, the laird of Laurieston, and Mr Patrick Galloway, moderator of the last General Assembly, in a letter directed to the several presbyteries, prorogued the meeting till the first Tuesday of July 1605, at the same place. In June 1605, the expected meeting, to have been kept in the month following, was, by a new letter from the King's commissioner, and the commissioners of the General Assembly, absolutely discharged and prohibited, but without naming any day or place for another assembly; and so the series of our assemblies expired, never to revive again in due form till the Covenant was renewed in 1638. However, many of the godly ministers of Scotland, knowing well, if once the hedge of the government was broken, that corruption of the doctrine would soon follow, resolved not to quit their assemblies so. And therefore a number of them convened at Aberdeen upon the first Tuesday of July 1605, being the last day that was distinctly appointed by authority; and when they had met, did no more but constitute themselves, and dissolve. Amongst these was John Welch, who, though he had not been present upon that precise day, yet, because he came to the place, and approved of what his brethren had done, was accused as guilty of the treasonable act committed by them. So dangerous a point was the name of a General Assembly in King James' jealous judgment.

Within a month after this meeting, many of these godly men were incarcerated, some in one prison, some in another. Mr Welch was sent to Edinburgh Tolbooth, and then to Blackness; and so from prison to prison, till he was banished to France, never to see Scotland again.

And now the scene of Welch's life begins to alter; but before his sufferings he had this strange warning: After the meeting at Aberdeen was over, he retired immediately to Ayr. One night he rose from his wife and went into his garden, as his custom was, but stayed longer than ordinary, which troubled his wife, who, when he returned, expostulated with him very hard for his staying so long to wrong his health. He bade her be quiet, for it should be well with them; but he knew well that he should never preach more in Ayr; and accordingly, before the next Sabbath he was carried prisoner to Blackness Castle. After this he, with many others who had met at Aberdeen, were brought before the Council of Scotland at Edinburgh, to answer for their rebellion and contempt, in holding a General Assembly not authorised by the king. And because they declined the secret council, as judges incompetent in causes purely spiritual, such as the nature and constitution of a General Assembly is, they were first remitted to the prison at Blackness, and other places. Thereafter, six of the most considerable of them, were brought under night from Blackness to Linlithgow before the criminal judges, to answer an accusation of high treason, at the instance of Sir Thomas Hamilton, the King's advocate, for declining, as he alleged, the King's lawful authority, in refusing to admit the council judges competent in the cause of the nature of church judicatories; and after their accusation and answer were read, they were condemned by the verdict of a jury of very considerable gentlemen, as guilty of high treason, the punishment being deferred till the King's pleasure should be known. Their punishment was made banishment, that the cruel sentence might somewhat seem to soften their severe punishment, as the King had contrived it.

While he was in Blackness, he wrote his famous letter to Lilias Graham, Countess of Wigton, in which he utters, in the strongest terms, his consolation in suffering; his desire to be dissolved that he might be with the Lord; and the judgments he foresaw coming upon Scotland. He almost seems most positively to show the true cause of their sufferings, and state of the testimony, in these words:

"Who am I, that He should first have called me, and then constituted me a minister of the glad tidings of the Gospel of salvation these years already, and now, last of all, to be a sufferer for His cause and kingdom. Now, let it be so that I have fought my fight, and run my race, and now from henceforth is laid up for me that crown of righteousness, which the Lord, that righteous God, will give; and not to me only, but to all that love His appearance, and choose to witness this, that Jesus Christ is the King of saints, and that His Church is a most free kingdom, yea, as free as any kingdom under heaven, not only to convocate, hold, and keep her meetings, and conventions, and assemblies; but also to judge all her affairs, in all her meetings and conventions, amongst her members and subjects. These two points: 1. That Christ is the head of His Church; 2. That she is free in her government from all other jurisdiction except Christ's; these two points, I say, are the special cause of our imprisonment being now convicted as traitors for the maintaining thereof. We have been ever waiting with joyfulness to give the last testimony of our blood in confirmation thereof, if it should please our God to be so favourable as to honour us with that dignity; yea, I do affirm, that these two points above written, and all other things which belong to Christ's crown, sceptre, and kingdom, are not subject, nor cannot be, to any other authority, but to His own altogether. So that I would be most glad to be offered up as a sacrifice for so glorious a truth: it would be to me the most glorious day, and the gladdest hour I ever saw in this life; but I am in His hand, to do with me whatsoever shall please His Majesty.

AYR.

"I am also bound and sworn, by a special covenant, to maintain the doctrine and discipline thereof, according to my vocation and power, all the days of my life, under all the pains contained in the book of God, and danger of body and soul, in the day of God's fearful judgment; and therefore, though I should perish in the cause, yet will I speak for it, and to my power defend it, according to my vocation."

He wrote about the same time to Sir William Livingstone of Kilsyth. There are some prophetical expressions in his letter that merit notice.

"As for that instrument, Spottiswoode, we are sure the Lord will never bless that man, but a malediction lies upon him, and shall accompany all his doings; and it may be, sir, your eyes shall see as great confusion covering him, ere he go to his grave, as ever did his predecessors. Now, surely, sir, I am far from bitterness, but here I denounce the wrath of an everlasting God against him, which assuredly shall fall, except it be prevented. Sir, Dagon shall not stand before the ark of the Lord, and these names of blasphemy that he wears, of Arch, and Lord Bishop, will have a fearful end. Not one beck is to be given to Haman, suppose he were as great a courtier as ever *he* was. Suppose the decree was given out, and

VIEW OF EDINBURGH CASTLE.

sealed with the King's ring, deliverance will come to us elsewhere and not by him, who has been so sore an instrument; not against our persons; that were nothing, for I protest to you, sir, in the sight of God, I forgive him all the evil he has done, or can do, to me; but unto Christ's poor Kirk, in stamping under foot so glorious a kingdom and beauty as was once in this land. He has helped to cut Sampson's hair and to expose him to mocking; but the Lord will not be mocked. He shall be cast away as a stone out of a sling, his name shall rot, and a malediction shall fall upon his posterity, after he is gone. Let this, sir, be a monument of it that it was told before, that when it shall come to pass, it may be seen there was warning given him; and therefore, sir, seeing I have not the access myself, if it would please God to move you, I wish you would deliver this hand-message to him, not as from me, but from the Lord."

The man of whom he complains, and threatens so sore, was John Spottiswoode, at that time designed Archbishop of Glasgow; and this prophecy was literally accomplished, though after the space of forty years. For, first the Archbishop himself died in a strange land, and, as many say, in misery; next his son Robert Spottiswoode, sometime President of Session, was beheaded by the Parliament of Scotland, at the market-cross of St Andrews, in the winter after the battle of Philiphaugh. As soon as ever he came upon the scaffold, Mr Blair, the minister of the town, told him, that now Welch's prophecy was fulfilled upon him; to which he replied in anger, that Welch and he were both false prophets.

Before John Welch left Scotland, some remarkable passages in his behaviour are to be remembered. And first, when the dispute about Church-government began to be warm, as he was walking upon the street of Edinburgh, betwixt two honest citizens, he told them that they had in their town two great ministers, who were no great friends to Christ's cause presently in controversy, but, it should be seen, the world should never hear of their repentance. The two men were Mr Patrick Galloway and Mr John Hall, and, accordingly, it came to pass; for Patrick Galloway died suddenly, and John Hall, being at that time in Leith, and his servant woman having left him alone in his house while she went to market, he was found dead at her return.

John Welch was some time prisoner in Edinburgh Castle before he went into exile. One night sitting at supper with Lord Ochiltree, he entertained the company with godly and edifying discourse, as his manner was, which was well received by them all, except a debauched Popish young gentleman, who sometimes laughed, and sometimes mocked and made wry faces. Thereupon Mr Welch brake out into a sad abrupt charge upon all the company to be silent, and observe the work of the Lord upon that mocker, which they should presently behold ; upon which the profane wretch sunk down and died beneath the table, to the great astonishment of all the company.

Another wonderful story they tell of him at the same time : Lord Ochiltree, the Governor of the Castle, being both son to the good Lord Ochiltree, and Mr Welch's uncle-in-law, was indeed very civil to him; but being for a long time, through the multitude of affairs, kept from visiting Welch, as he was one day walking in the court, and espying him at his chamber-window, he asked him kindly how he did, and if in anything he could serve him? Welch answered, that he would earnestly entreat his Lordship, being at that time about to go to Court, to petition King James in his name that he might have liberty to preach the Gospel; which my Lord promised to do. Mr Welch then said, " My Lord, both because you are my kinsman, and for other reasons, I would earnestly entreat and obtest you not to promise, except you faithfully perform." His Lordship answered, he would faithfully perform his promise; and so went for London.

But though, at his first arrival, he really purposed to present the petition to the King, he found the King in such a rage against the godly ministers, that he durst not at that time present it; so he thought fit to delay, and thereafter entirely forgot it.

The first time that Welch saw his face after his return from Court, he asked him what he had done with his petition. His Lordship said that he had presented it to the King, but that the King was in so great a rage against the ministers at that time, he believed it had been forgotten, for he had got no answer. "Nay," said Welch to him, "my Lord, you should not lie to God, and to me; for I know you never delivered it, though I warned you to take heed not to undertake it except you would perform it; but because you have dealt so unfaithfully, remember God shall take from you both estate and honours, and give them to your neighbour in your own time." This accordingly came to pass, for both his estate and honours were in his own time translated to James Stuart, son of Captain James, who was indeed a cadet, but not the lineal heir of the family.

While Welch was detained prisoner in Edinburgh Castle, his wife used for the most part to stay in his company, but upon a time fell into a longing to see her family in Ayr, to which with some difficulty he yielded. When she was to take her journey, he strictly charged her not to take the ordinary way when she came to Ayr, nor to pass by the bridge through the town, but to cross the river above the bridge, and so reach his own house, without going into the town; " for," said he, " before you come thither, you shall find the plague broken out in Ayr," which accordingly came to pass. The plague was at that time very terrible, and being necessarily separate from his people, it was to him the more grievous ; but when the people of Ayr came to him to bemoan themselves, his answer was, that Hugh Kennedy, a godly gentleman in their town, should pray for them, and God would hear him. This counsel they accepted, and the gentleman, convening a number of the honest citizens, prayed earnestly for the town. He was a mighty wrestler with God, and accordingly after that, the plague decreased.

Now the time had come when John Welch must leave Scotland, never to see it again. Upon the 7th of November 1606, he with his neighbours took ship at Leith ; and though it was but two o'clock in the morning, many were waiting with their afflicted families, to bid them farewell. With Mr Welch, other five godly ministers were banished for the same cause, viz., John Forbes, who went to Middle-

burgh, to the English chapel there; Robert Dury, who went to
Holland, and was minister to the Scots congregation in Leyden;
John Sharp, who became minister and Professor of Divinity at Die
in the Dauphinate, where he wrote " Carfus Theologicus," etc; and
Andrew Duncan and Alexander Strachan, who, in about a year,
got liberty to return unto their former places. After prayer they
sung the 23d Psalm, and so, to the great grief of the spectators,
set sail for the south of France, and landed in the river of Bordeaux. Within fourteen weeks after his arrival, such was the Lord's
blessing upon his diligence, Welch was able to preach in French, and
accordingly was speedily called to the ministry, first in a village
called Nerac, thereafter in St Jean d'Angely, a considerable walled
town, where he continued the rest of the time he sojourned in
France, which was about sixteen years. When he began to preach,
it was observed by some of his hearers, that while he continued
in the doctrinal part of his sermon, he spoke very correct French,
but when he came to his application, and when his affections kindled,
his fervour made him sometimes neglect the accuracy of the
French construction. But there were godly young men who admonished him of this, which he took in very good part, so for preventing mistakes of that kind, he desired them when they perceived
him beginning to decline, to give him a sign, by standing up; and
thereafter he was more exact in his expression through the whole
sermon. So desirous was he, not only to deliver good matter, but
to recommend it by neat expression.

There were frequently persons of great quality in his auditory,
before whom he was just as bold as ever he had been in any Scottish
village. This moved Mr Boyd of Trochrig once to ask him, after he
had preached before the University of Saumur with boldness and
authority, as if he had been before the meanest congregation, how he
could be so confident among strangers and persons of such quality.
To which he answered, he was so filled with the dread of God, that
he had no apprehensions for man at all. " This answer," said Mr
Boyd, " did not remove my admiration, but rather increased it."

There was in his house, amongst many others who boarded with
him for good education, a young gentleman of great quality and
suitable expectations, the heir of Lord Ochiltree, Governor of the
Castle of Edinburgh. This young nobleman, after he had gained
very much upon Mr Welch's affections, fell ill of a grievous sickness, and after he had been long wasted by it, closed his eyes

and expired, to the apprehension of all spectators; and was therefore taken out of his bed, and laid on a pallet on the floor, that his body might be more conveniently dressed. This was to Mr Welch a very great grief, and therefore he stayed with the body fully three hours, lamenting over him with great tenderness. After twelve hours, the friends brought in a coffin, whereinto they desired the corpse to be put, as the custom was; but Mr Welch desired that, for the satisfaction of his affections, they would forbear for a time; which they granted, and returned not till twenty-four hours after his death. Then they desired with great importunity, that the corpse might be coffined and speedily buried, the weather being extremely hot; yet he persisted in his request, earnestly begging them to excuse him once more, so they left the corpse upon the pallet for full thirty-six hours; but even after all that, though he was urged not only with great earnestness, but displeasure, they were constrained to forbear for twelve hours more. After forty-eight hours were past, Mr Welch still held out against them; and then his friends, perceiving that he believed the young man was not really dead, but under some apoplectic fit, proposed to him for his satisfaction, that trial should be made upon his body by doctors and chirurgeons, if possibly any spark of life might be found in him; and with this he was content. So the physicians were set to work, who pinched him with pinchers in the fleshy parts of his body, and twisted a bow-string about his head with great force; but no sign of life appearing in him, the physicians pronounced him stark dead, and then there was no more delay to be made. Yet Mr Welch begged of them once more that they would but step into the next room for an hour or two, and leave him with the dead youth; and this they granted.

Then Mr Welch fell down before the pallet, and cried to the Lord with all his might, and sometimes looked upon the dead body, continuing to wrestle with the Lord, till at length the dead youth opened his eyes, and cried out to Mr Welch, whom he distinctly knew, "O sir, I am all whole, but my head and legs;" and these were the places they had sorely hurt with their pinching. When Mr Welch perceived this, he called upon his friends; and showed them the dead young man restored to life again, to their great astonishment. And this young nobleman, though he lost the estate of Ochiltree, lived to acquire a great estate in Ireland, became Lord Castlestuart, and was a man of such excellent parts, that he was courted by the Earl of Stafford to be a counsellor in Ireland. This he refused to be, until the godly silenced Scottish ministers, who suffered under the bishops in the north of Ireland, were restored to the exercise of their ministry ; and then he engaged, and continued so all his life, not only in honour and power, but in the profession and practice of godliness, to the great comfort of the country where he lived. This story the nobleman himself communicated to his friends in Ireland.

While Mr Welch was minister in one of these French villages, upon an evening, a certain Popish friar, travelling through the country, because he could not find a lodging in the whole village, addressed himself to Mr Welch's house for one night. The servants acquainted their master, and he was content to receive the guest. The family had supped before he came, and so the servants conveyed the friar to his chamber ; and after they had made his supper, they left him to his rest. There was but a timber partition betwixt him and Mr Welch, ʻand after the friar had slept his first sleep, he was surprised with the hearing of a silent but constant whispering noise ; at which he wondered very much, and was not a little troubled.

The next morning he walked in the fields, where he chanced to meet with a country man, who, saluting him because of his habit, asked him where he had lodged that night ? The friar answered, he had lodged with the Huguenot minister. Then the countryman asked him, what entertainment he had ? The friar answered, " Very bad ; " for, said he, " I always held that devils haunted these ministers' houses, and I am persuaded there was one with me this night, for I heard a continual whisper all the night over, which I believe was no other thing than the minister and the devil conversing together." The countryman told him he was much mistaken, and that it was nothing else than the minister at his night prayer. " O," said the friar, " does the minister pray?" " Yes, more than any man in France," answered the countryman ; " and if you please to stay another night with him you may be satisfied." The friar got home to Mr Welch's house, and, pretending indisposition, entreated another night's lodging, which was granted him.

Before dinner Mr Welch came from his chamber, and made his family exercise, according to his custom. And first he sung a psalm, then read a portion of Scripture, and discoursed upon it ; thereafter he prayed with great fervour, to all which the friar was an astonished witness. After exercise they went to dinner, where the friar was very civilly entertained, Mr Welch forbearing all question and dispute with him for the time. When the evening came, Mr Welch made exercise as he had done in the morning, which occasioned more wonder to the friar, and after supper they went to bed; but the friar longed much to know what the night-whisper was, and therein he was soon satisfied ; for after Mr Welch's first sleep, the noise began. The friar resolved to be certain what it was, and to that end he crept silently to Mr Welch's chamber door, and there he heard not only the sound, but the words distinctly, and communications betwixt God and man, such as he thought had not been in this world. The next morning, as soon as Mr Welch was ready, the friar came, and confessed that he had lived in ignorance the whole of his life, but now he was resolved to adventure his soul with him ; and thereupon declared himself a Protestant. Mr Welch welcomed and encouraged him, and he continued a Protestant to his death.

When Louis XIII., King of France, made war upon his Protestant subjects, because of their religion, the city of St Jean d'Angely was besieged by him with his whole army, and brought into extreme danger. Mr Welch was minister of the city, and mightily encouraged the citizens to hold out, assuring them that God would deliver them. In the time of the siege, a cannon-ball pierced the bed where he was lying, upon which he got up, but would not leave the room till he had, by solemn prayer, acknowledged his deliverance. During this siege, the citizens made stout defence, till one of the King's gunners planted a great gun so conveniently upon a rising ground, that he could command the whole wall upon which they made their greatest defence. Upon this they were constrained to forsake the wall in great terror, and though they had several guns planted upon the wall, no man durst undertake to manage them. This being told to Mr Welch, he, notwithstanding, encouraged them still to hold out; and running to the wall, found the cannonier, who was a Burgundian, near the wall. Him he entreated to mount the wall, promising to assist in person. The cannonier told Mr Welch, that they behovd to dismount the gun upon the rising ground, else they were surely lost. Welch desired him to aim well, and he would serve him, and God would help them. The gunner fell to work, and Welch ran to fetch powder for a charge, but as he was returning, the king's gunner fired his piece, which carried the ladle with the powder out of his hands. This did not discourage him, for, having left the ladle, he filled his hat with powder, wherewith the gunner dismounted the King's gun at the first shot, and the citizens returned to their posts of defence. This discouraged the King so much, that he sent to the citizens to offer them fair conditions, viz., that they should enjoy the liberty of their religion, their civil privileges, and their walls should not be demolished, the king only desiring that he might enter the city in a friendly manner with his servants. This the citizens thought fit to grant, and the King and a few more entered the city for a short time.

While the King was in the city, Welch preached as usual. This offended the French Court; and, while he was at sermon, the King sent the Duke d'Espernon to fetch him out of the pulpit into his presence. The Duke went with his guard, and when he entered the church where he was preaching, Mr Welch commanded to make way, and to place a seat, that the Duke might hear the word of the Lord. The Duke, instead of interrupting him, sat down, and gravely heard the sermon to an end; and then told Welch that he behoved to go with him to the King, which he willingly did. When the Duke returned, the King asked him, why he brought not the minister with him? and why he did not interrupt him? The Duke answered, " Never man spake like this man:" but that he had brought him along with him. Whereupon Mr Welch was called; and when he had entered the King's presence, he kneeled, and silently prayed for wisdom and assistance. Thereafter the King challenged him, how he durst preach in that place, since it was against the laws of France that any man should preach within the verge of his court? Mr Welch answered, "Sire, if you did right, you would come and hear me preach, and make all France hear me likewise. For," said he, " I preach, that you must be saved by the death and merits of Jesus Christ, and not your own; and I preach, that as you are King of France, you are under the authority of no man on earth. Those men whom you hear, subject you to the Pope of Rome, which I will never do." The King replied, " Well, well, you shall be my minister," and, as some say, called him father, which is an honour bestowed upon few of the greatest prelates in France. However, he was favourably dismissed at that time, and the King also left the city in peace.

But within a short time thereafter the war was renewed, and then Welch told the inhabitants of the city, that now their cup was full, and they should no more escape. This accordingly came to pass, for the King took the town, but commanded Vitry, the captain

THE PALACE OF WHITEHALL, LONDON.

of his guard, to enter and preserve his minister from all danger; horses and waggons were provided for Mr Welch, to transport him and his family to Rochelle, whither he went, and there sojourned for a time.

After his flock in France was scattered, Welch obtained liberty to go to England, and his friends entreated King James VI. that he might have permission to return to Scotland, because the physician declared there was no other method to preserve his life, but by the freedom he might have in his native air. [The following incident is mentioned by Dr M'Crie in his biography of Knox: Mrs Welch, by means of some of her mother's relations at court, obtained access to James VI., and petitioned him to grant this liberty to her husband. The following singular conversation took place on that occasion. His Majesty asked who was her father. She replied, " Mr Knox." " Knox and Welch ! " exclaimed he, " the devil never made such a match as that." " It's right like, sir," said she, " for we never speired his advice." He asked her how many children her father had left, and if they were lads or lasses. She said three, and they were all lasses. "God be thanked," cried the King, lifting up both his hands; "for an' they had been three lads, I had never bruiked my three kingdoms in peace." She again urged her request, that he would give her husband his native air. " Give him his native air ! " replied the King, " give him the devil ! " a morsel which James had often in his mouth. "Give that to your hungry courtiers," said she, offended at his profaneness. He told her at last, that, if she would persuade her husband to submit to the bishops, he would allow him to return to Scotland. Mrs Welch, lifting up her apron, and holding it towards the King, replied, in the true spirit of her father, "Please your Majesty, I'd rather kep his head there."—ED.]

King James would never yield his consent, protesting that he would be unable to establish his beloved bishops in Scotland, if Mr Welch were permitted to return thither; so he languished at London a considerable time. His disease was considered by some to have a tendency to leprosy; physicians said he had been poisoned. He suffered from an excessive languor, together with a great weakness in his knees, caused by his continual kneeling at prayer, by which it came to pass, that though he was able to move his knees, and to walk, yet he was wholly insensible in them, and the flesh became hard like a sort of horn. But when, in the time of his weakness, he was desired to remit somewhat of his excessive labours, his answer was, he had his life of God, and therefore it should be spent for Him.

His friends importuned King James very much, that if he might not return to Scotland, at least he might have liberty to preach in London; which he would not grant till he heard all hopes of life were past, and then he allowed him liberty to preach, not fearing his activity. As soon as ever Welch heard he might preach, he greedily embraced this liberty; and having access to a lecturer's pulpit, he went and preached both long and fervently. This was his last performance; for after he had ended his sermon, he returned to his chamber, and within two hours, quietly, and without pain, resigned his spirit into his Master's hands, and was buried near Mr Deering, the famous English divine, after he had lived little more than fifty-two years.

During his sickness, he was so filled and overcome with the sensible enjoyment of God, that he was overheard to utter these words: "O Lord, hold Thy hand, it is enough; Thy servant is a clay vessel, and can hold no more." As his diligence was great, so it may be doubted, whether his sowing in painfulness, or his harvest in success, was greatest; for if either his spiritual experiences in seeking the Lord, or his fruitfulness in converting souls, be considered, they will be found unparalleled in Scotland. And, many years after his death, Mr David Dickson, at that time a flourishing minister at Irvine, was frequently heard to say, when people talked to him of the success of his ministry, that the grape gleanings in Ayr, in Mr Welch's time, were far above the vintage of Irvine in his own.

John Welch, in his preaching, was spiritual and searching, his utterance tender and moving; he did not much insist upon scholastic purposes, and made no show of his learning. One of his hearers, who was afterwards minister at Muirkirk, in Kyle, used to say, that no man could hear him and forbear weeping, his conveyance was so affecting. There are a large number of his sermons now in Scotland, only a few of which have come to the press. Nor did he ever himself appear in print, except in his dispute with Abbot Brown, wherein he makes it appear that his learning was not behind his other virtues; and in another treatise, called Dr Welch's Armageddon, supposed to have been printed in France, wherein he gives his meditation upon the enemies of the Church, and their destruction, but it is now rarely to be found.

Robert Boyd.

ROBERT BOYD of Trochrig, was born at Glasgow in the year 1578. Having gone to France at an early age, he was first settled at Angouleme, but was afterwards, by the interest of Sieur du Plessis, translated to be professor of divinity at Saumur. Some time after, he was invited home by King James VI., and settled principal of the College of Glasgow, and minister of Govan. At this place he ordinarily wrote his sermons in full; and yet when he came to the pulpit, he appeared with great life and power of affection. While he was in France, the Popish controversy employed his thoughts; but after his return home, the Church of Scotland engrossed almost his whole attention; and he became a zealous friend and supporter of the more faithful part of the ministry against the usurpation of the bishops and their ceremonies. The prelatists, knowing that the eminence of his place, his piety,

PORTRAIT OF ROBERT BOYD.

and learning, would influence many to take part with that way, laboured with great assiduity, by entreaties, threatenings, and the persuasions of some of his friends, to gain him over to their side; insomuch that at length he gave in a paper to Law, Archbishop of Glasgow, in which he seemed in some sort to acknowledge the pre-eminence of bishops. However, getting no rest the next night after this, being so troubled for what he had done, he went back and sought his paper again with tears; but the Archbishop pretended that he had already sent it up to the King, so that he could not obtain it.

Mr Boyd, finding that, from this time forward, he could enjoy no peace in this place, demitted both his charges, and was chosen principal of the college of Edinburgh, and one of the ministers of that city, being succeeded in Glasgow by Dr Cameron, in October 1622. Some of the other ministers of Edinburgh, particularly Andrew Ramsay, envied him on account of his high reputation, both as a preacher and as a teacher (the well affected part of the people both in town and country crowding to his church), and gave the King information against him as a nonconformist. The King sent a letter, December the 13th, to the magistrates of the city, rebuking them for admitting him, and commanding him to be removed. The magistrates were not obedient to the command, and by a courtier, entreated he might be continued; but the King would not grant their request. Accord-

THE ABBEY CHURCH OF PAISLEY.

ingly, on the last day of January 1623, he renewed the order to remove him; and he was in a little time after turned out of his place and office.

Some short time after this Archbishop Law was prevailed on to admit Mr Boyd to be minister of Paisley; for although no man was more opposed to the Perth Articles than he, as he had refused conformity to them both at Glasgow and Edinburgh, yet his learning and prudence recommended him to the Archbishop's esteem. Here he remained in security and peace, until the Earl of Abercorn's brother, a zealous Papist, dispossessed him on a Sabbath afternoon, while he was preaching, and threw all his books out of the house where he had his residence. Upon complaining to the Privy Council, the offender was imprisoned, and the Court and bailies of Paisley having undertaken to repossess him, and the gentleman professing his sorrow for what he had done, Mr Boyd interceded with them for him, and the Council passed the matter over.

But no sooner did he go to take possession, than he found the church doors secured, so that no access could be had; and though the magistrates would have broken them open, yet the mob (urged on, as was supposed, by the Earl's mother) pressed so hard upon the good man, not only by opprobrious speeches, but also by throwing stones at him, as if he had been a malefactor, that he was forced to fly to Glasgow. Afterwards, seeing no prospect of a peaceable settlement at Paisley, he returned to his own house at Trochrig in Carrick, where he probably continued to his death, which was some years later. [He died on the 5th of January 1627, his death having been hastened by the successive disappointments and annoyances to which he had been exposed. " His sickness," says a biographer, "was but short, but his pain very great—his patience and submission much greater. He had been but tender and weakly through life, and much inured to the cross. He had learned to bear it with joy, and great was his enlargement during his three weeks' trouble at Edinburgh. He was under the foretaste of the glory to be revealed, and under much heavenly ravishment and holy rapture."—ED.]

He was a man of great learning for that time, as his Commentary on the Ephesians testifies. He would sometimes say, if he had his choice of languages wherein to deliver his sentiments, it would be in Greek. He was of an austere countenance and carriage, and yet very tender-hearted. He had but a mean opinion of himself, but a high esteem of others in whom he perceived any signs of grace and ingenuity. In the time of that convincing and converting work of the Lord, commonly called the Stewarton sickness, he came from his own house in Carrick, and met with many of the people; and having conversed with them, he heartily blessed the Lord for the grace that was given unto them.

Robert Bruce.

OBERT BRUCE was born about the year 1554. He was second son to Sir Alexander Bruce, the Laird of Airth (of whom he had the estate of Kinnaird), who being at that time a baron of the best quality in the kingdom, educated him with the intention of becoming one of the Lords of Session, and for his better accomplishment sent him to France to study the civil law. After his return home, his father enjoined him to wait upon some affairs of his that were then before the Court of Session, as he had got a patent ensured for his being one of these Lords. But God's thoughts being not as men's thoughts, and having other designs for him, He began then to work mightily upon his conscience, so that he could get no rest till he was suffered to attend Andrew Melville at St Andrews, to study divinity under him. To this his mother was averse, for she would not consent until he first gave up some lands and casualties wherein he was infeft. This he most willingly did, and shaking off all impediments, he fully resolved upon an employment more fitted to the serious turn of his mind.

He went to St Andrews some time before Andrew Melville left the country, and continued there until his return. Here he wanted not some sharp conflicts on this head; insomuch that upon a certain time, walking in the fields with that holy and religious man James Melville, he said to him: "Before I throw myself again into such torment of conscience, as I have had in resisting the call to the ministry, I would rather choose to walk through a fire of brimstone, even though it were half-a-mile in length." After he was accomplished for the ministry, Andrew Melville, perceiving how the Lord wrought with him, brought him over to the General Assembly, in 1587, and moved the Church of Edinburgh to call him to a charge there, in the place of James Lawson, the successor of John Knox.

He could not, however, be prevailed upon to take the charge *simpliciter* (although he was willing to bestow his labour thereon for a time), until, by the joint advice of the ministry of the city, and this stratagem, he was, as it were, trapped into it. Thus, on a time when the sacrament was to be dispensed at Edinburgh, one of the ministers desired Robert Bruce, who was to preach in the afternoon, to sit by him; and after having served two or three tables, he went out of the church, as if he had been to return in a little; but instead of this, he sent notice to Bruce, that unless he served the rest of the tables, the work behoved to stop. Bruce, not knowing but the minister had been seized on a sudden with some kind of sickness, and the eyes of all the people being fixed on him, many entreating him to supply the minister's place, proceeded to the administration of the remainder, and that with such assistance to himself and emotion amongst the people, that the like had never before been seen in that place. When he was afterwards urged by the rest of his brethren to receive, in the ordinary way, the imposition of hands, he refused; because he already had the material part of ordination, viz., the call of the people, and the approbation of the ministry; and besides, he had already celebrated the sacrament of the supper, which was not by a new ordination to be made void. So, having made trial of the work, and finding the blessing of God upon his labours, he accepted the charge, and was from that time forth principal actor in the affairs of the Church, and a constant and strenuous maintainer of the established doctrine and discipline thereof.

While he was a minister at Edinburgh, he shone as a great light through all these parts of the land; the power and efficacious energy of the Spirit accompanied the word preached by him in a most sensible manner, so that he was a terror to evil doers, the authority of God appearing with him; insomuch that he forced fear and respect even from the greatest in the land. Even King James VI. himself, and his Court, had such high thoughts of him, that when he went to Denmark to bring home his Queen in 1590, he expressly desired Robert Bruce to acquaint himself with the affairs of the country and the proceedings of the Council, professing that he reposed more in him than the rest of his brethren, or even all his nobles. And, indeed, in this his hopes were not disappointed; for the country was more quiet during his absence than either before or afterwards; in gratitude for which, Bruce received a congratulatory letter, dated February 19, 1590, wherein the King acknowledged, that he would be obligated to him all his life for the pains he had taken in his absence to keep his subjects in good order. Yea, it is well known that the King had such esteem for Mr Bruce, that upon a certain time, before many witnesses, he gave him this testimony, that he judged him worthy of the half of his kingdom; but in this, as in others of his fair promises, he proved no slave to his word; for not many years after he obliged this good man, for his faithfulness, to leave the kingdom.

Robert Bruce being a man of public spirit and heroic mind, was always on that account pitched upon to deal in matters of high moment. Among other things, upon the 19th of November 1596, he, Andrew Melville, and John Davidson, were directed by the council of the brethren to deal with the Queen concerning her religion, and, for want of religious exercises and virtuous occupations amongst her maids, to move her to hear now and then the instructions of godly and discreet men. They went to her, but were refused admittance until another time.

About the same time he was sent to the King, then sitting with the Lords of Session, to present some articles for redress of the wrongs then done to the Church; but, in the meantime, a bustle falling out

VIEW OF LINLITHGOW.

at Edinburgh by the mob, the King removed to Linlithgow. Upon the Sabbath following, Mr Bruce, preaching upon the 51st Psalm, said, " The removal of your ministers is at hand ; our lives shall be bitterly sought after ; but ye shall see with your eyes, that God shall guard us, and be our buckler and defence." The day following, this was in part accomplished ; for the King sent a charge from Linlithgow to Robert Bruce, and the rest of the ministers of Edinburgh, to enter in ward at the Castle there within six hours after the proclamation, under pain of horning. The rest of the ministers, knowing the King's anger was kindled against them, thought proper to with- draw ; but Bruce, knowing his own innocence, stayed and gave in an Apology for himself and the rest of his faithful brethren. On the 13th April 1599, the King returned to Edinburgh, and was entertained in the house of Mr Bruce, although he himself was not yet released.

But all this was nothing more than the drops before the shower, or as the gathering of waters before an inundation breaks forth ; for the King having for some time laboured to get Prelacy established in Scotland, and because Bruce would not comply with his measures, and refused to give praise to God in public for the King's deliverance from the pretended Gowrie conspiracy in 1600, until he was better assured of the fact, he not only discharged him from preaching in Edinburgh, but also obliged him to leave the kingdom. When he embarked at the Queensferry, on the 3d of November the same year, there appeared such a great light as served him and the company to sail, although it was near midnight. He arrived at Dieppe on the 8th of November.

Although, by the King's permission, he returned home the year following, yet, because he would not (1.) Acknowledge Gowrie's conspiracy; (2.) Purge the King in such places as he should appoint; and (3.) Crave pardon of the King for his long distrust and disobedience; he could not be admitted to his place and office again, but was commanded by the King to keep ward in his own house of Kinnaird. After the King's departure to England, he had some respite for about a year or more; but in the year 1605, he was summoned to compear at Edinburgh, on the 29th of February, before the commission of the General Assembly, to hear and see himself removed from his function at Edinburgh. They had before, in his absence, decerned his place vacant, but now they intimated the sentence, and Livingstone had a commission from the King to see it put in execution. He appealed; they prohibited him to preach; but he obeyed not. In July thereafter, he was advertised by Chancellor Seaton of the King's express order, discharging him from preaching any more, who said, he would not use his authority in this, but only request him to desist for nine or ten days; to which he consented, thinking it but of small moment for so short a time. But he quickly knew how deep the smallest deviation from his Master's cause and interest might go; for that night, as he himself afterwards declared, his body was cast into a fever, with such terror of conscience, that he promised and fully resolved to obey such commands no more.

Upon the 18th of August following, he was charged to enter ward at Inverness, within the space of ten days, under pain of horning; which order he obeyed upon the 27th following; and in this place he remained for the space of four years, teaching every Wednesday and Sabbath forenoon, and was exercised in reading public prayers every other night. These labours were blessed; for this dark country was wonderfully illuminated, and many brought to Christ by means of his ministry, and seed was sown in these remote places, which remained for many years afterwards.

Bruce returned from Inverness to his own house, and though his son had obtained a license for him, yet here he could find nothing but grief and vexation, especially from the ministers of the Presbyteries of Stirling and Linlithgow, and all for curbing the vices some of them were subject to. At last he obtained liberty of the Council to transport his family to another house he had at Monkland, but, because of the Archbishop of Glasgow, he was forced to retire back again to Kinnaird. Thus this good man was tossed about, and obliged to go from place to place.

In this manner he continued, until he was by the King's order summoned before the Council, in September 19th, 1621, to answer for transgressing the law of his confinement. When he compeared, he pleaded the favour granted him by his Majesty when in Denmark, and withal purged himself of the accusation laid against him ; "and yet, notwithstanding of all these," said he, "the King hath exhausted both my estate and person, and has left me nothing but my life, and that apparently he is seeking. I am prepared to suffer any punishment, only, I am careful not to suffer as a malefactor or evil-doer." A warrant was delivered to him to enter ward in the Castle of Edinburgh,—the bishops absenting themselves from the Council that day, although they were his delators. Here he continued till the 1st of January. He was again brought before the Council, where the King's will was intimated to him, that he should return to his own house until the 21st of April, and then transport himself again to Inverness, and remain within four miles thereof during the King's pleasure.

He remained at Inverness, for the most part, until September 1624, when he obtained license to return from his confinement, in order to settle some of his domestic affairs. The condition of his license was so strait, that he purposed to return to Inverness; but in the meantime the King dying, he was not urged to go back ; and although King Charles I. did again renew the charge against him some years after, yet he continued mostly in his own house, preaching and teaching wherever he had occasion.

About this time the parish of Larbert, having neither minister nor stipend, Mr Bruce repaired the church, and discharged all the parts of the ministry there with great success,—many besides the parishioners attending upon his ministrations ; and it would appear that, about this time, Alexander Henderson, then minister at Leuchars, was converted by his ministry.

At Larbert it was his custom, after the first sermon, to retire by himself some time for private prayer ; and on a time, some noblemen who had far to ride, sent the beadle to learn if there was any appearance of his coming in. The man returned, saying, " I think he shall not come out this day, for I overheard him say to some one, 'I protest I will not go unless thou goest with me.' " However, in a little time he came, accompanied by no man, but in the fulness of the blessing of the Gospel of Christ; for his very speech was with much evidence and demonstration of the Spirit. It was easy for his hearers to perceive that he had been in the mount with God, and that, indeed, he had brought that God whom he had met in private, " into his mother's house, and into the chambers of her that conceived him."

Robert Bruce was also a man who had somewhat of the spirit of discerning future events, and did prophetically speak of several things that afterwards came to pass; yea, and divers persons distracted, says Fleming, in his " Fulfilling of the Scripture," and those who were past all recovery with epileptic disease, or falling sickness, were brought to him, and were, after prayer by him in their behalf, fully restored from that malady. This may seem strange, but it is true, for he was such a wrestler with God, and had more than ordinary familiarity with Him.

Some time before his death, being at Edinburgh, where, through weakness, he often kept his chamber, a meeting of godly ministers having been held anent some matter of Church concernment, they, hearing he was in town, came and gave him an account of the prelates' actings. Mr Bruce prayed, and in his prayer he repeated over again to the Lord the substance of their discourse, which was a very sad representation of the case of the Church; when there came an extraordinary motion on all present, and such sensible down-pouring of the Spirit, that they could hardly contain themselves. Mr Wemyss of Lathocker, who was present, said at departing, " O how strange a man is this, for he knocked down the Spirit of God upon us all !" This he said, because Mr Bruce, in the time of that prayer, divers times knocked with his fingers upon the table.

About this time Robert Bruce related a strange dream, how he had seen a long broad book, with black boards, flying in the air, with many black fowls like crows flying about it; and as it touched any of them, they fell down dead. Upon this he heard an audible voice speak to him, saying, *Hæc est ira Dei contra pastores ecclesiæ Scoticanæ,* (this is the anger of God against the pastors of the Scottish Church); upon which he fell a-weeping, and prayed that he might be kept faithful; and not be one of those who were thus struck down by a torch of His wrath, through deserting the truth. He said, when he awakened, he found his pillow all wet and drenched with tears. The accomplishment of this dream I need not describe. All acquainted with our

Church history know, that soon after that, Prelacy was introduced into Scotland, Bishops set up, and Popish and Arminian tenets ushered in, with all manner of corruptions and profanity, which continued in Scotland a number of years.

" One time," says Mr Livingstone, " I went to Edinburgh to see Robert Bruce, in the company of the tutor of Bonnington. When we called on him at eight o'clock in the morning, he told us he was not for any company; and when we urged him to tell us the cause, he answered, that when he went to bed he had a good measure of the Lord's presence, and that he had wrestled with Him about an hour or two before we came in, and had not yet got access ; and so we left him. At another time I went to his house, but saw him not till very late; when he came out of his closet, his face was foul with weeping, and he told me, that he had been thinking on what torture and hardships Dr Leighton, our countryman, had been put to at London ;* and added, 'if I had been faithful, I might have had the pillory, and some of my blood shed for Christ, as well as he; but he hath got the crown from us all.' I heard him once also say, 'I would desire no more at my first appeal from King James, but one hour's converse with him : I know he has a conscience ; I made him once weep bitterly at Holyrood House.' On another occasion, in reference to his death, he said, 'I wonder how I am kept so long here : I have lived two years already in violence ;' meaning, that he was that much beyond seventy years of age."

When the time of his death drew near, which was in the month of August 1631, he was mostly confined to his chamber, through age and infirmity, where he was frequently visited by his friends and acquaintances. Being asked by one of them, how matters

---

* This was the famous Leighton, Doctor of Divinity in the two Universities of St Andrews and Leyden, who, for writing of Zion's Plea against Prelacy, was apprehended at London by two ruffians, and brought before Archbishop Laud, who sentenced him, besides a fine of £10,000, to be tied to a stake, and receive thirty-six stripes with a triple cord, and then to stand two hours in the pillory, (which he did in a cold winter night), and then to have his ear cut, his face fired, and his nose slit, and the same to be repeated that day se'nnight, and his other ear cut off, with the slitting of the other side of his nose, and burning his other cheek. All this was done with the utmost rigour, and then he was sent prisoner to the Fleet, where he continued, till upon a petition to the Parliament in 1640, he was released, and got for his reparation a vote of £6000 (which, it is said, was never paid), and made warden of that prison wherein he had been so long confined ; but through infirmity and bad treatment he did not long survive, being then seventy-two years of age. *See* this more at length in Stevenson's History.

stood betwixt God and his soul? he answered: "When I was young, I was diligent, and lived by faith on the Son of God; but now I am old, and am not able to do so much, yet He condescends to feed me with lumps of sense." On the morning before he was removed, his sickness being mostly a weakness through age, he came to breakfast; and having, as usual, eaten an egg, he said to his daughters, "I think I am yet hungry, ye may bring me another egg." But instantly thereafter falling into deep meditation, and after having mused a little, he said, "Hold, daughter; my Master calls me." With these words, his sight failed him, and calling for his family Bible, but finding he could not see, he said "Cast up to me the eighth chapter of the epistle to the Romans, and set my finger on these words, 'I am persuaded, that neither death, nor life, nor angels, nor principalities, nor powers, nor things present, nor things to come, nor height, nor depth, nor any other creature, shall be able to separate us from the love of God which is in Christ Jesus our Lord.' "Now," said he, "is my finger upon them?" and being told it was, he said, "Now, God be with you, my children; I have breakfasted with you, and shall sup with my Lord Jesus Christ this night." And so, like Abraham of old, he gave up the ghost in a good old age, and was gathered to his people.

In such manner did this occidental star set in our horizon. There were none in his time, who preached with such evidence of the power of the Spirit; and no man had more seals of his ministry; yea, many of his hearers thought that no man, since the days of the Apostles, ever spoke with such power. And although he was no Boanerges, being of a slow but great delivery, yet he spoke with such authority and weight as became the oracles of the living God; so that some of the most stout-hearted of his hearers were ordinarily made to tremble, and by having the door, which had formerly been shut against Jesus Christ, as by an irresistible power broken open, and the secrets of their hearts made manifest, they oftentimes went away under deep conviction. He had a very majestic countenance; in prayer he was short, especially when in public, but every word or sentence he spoke was as a bolt shot from heaven. He spent much of his time in private prayer; he had a very notable faculty in searching the Scriptures, and explaining the most obscure mysteries therein; and was a man who had much inward exercise of conscience anent his own personal case. He was oftentimes assaulted even anent that grand fundamental truth—the being of a God; insomuch that it was almost customary for him to say, when he first spoke in the pulpit, "I think it a great matter to believe there is a God ;" and by this he was the more fitted to deal with others under the like temptations.

Robert Bruce was also an elegant and substantial writer, as the fore-mentioned Apology, and his excellent Letters to M. Espignol, the Duke of Parma, Colonel Semple, and others, copiously evidence. He was also deeply affected with the public cause and interest of Jesus Christ, and much depressed in spirit when he beheld the naughtiness and profanity of many ministers then in the Church, and the carriage and deportment of others unsuitable to so great a calling; which made him express himself with much fear, that the ministry in Scotland would prove the greatest persecutors it had; and which, indeed, came to pass.

GATEWAY OF LINLITHGOW PALACE.

Josias Welch.

OSIAS WELCH was a younger son of the famous Mr John Welch, sometime minister of the Gospel at Ayr, and Elizabeth Knox, daughter of Mr John Knox, our great Reformer. From them he received a most liberal and religious education, but what enhanced his reputation more, was, that he was heir to his father's graces and virtues. Although he had received all the branches of useful learning, in order to the ministry, yet, Prelacy being then prevalent in Scotland, he was detained for some time from that function, seeing he was not clear in his own mind to enter into office by the door of Episcopacy. But some time after, it so fell out, that meeting with Robert Blair, who was then minister at Bangor in Ireland, he discovered how zealous a spirit Josias Welch was of, and exhorted and solicited him much to hasten over there, where he would find work enough, and he hoped, success likewise. This accordingly came to pass; for upon his going to Ireland, he was highly honoured and provided of the Lord, to bring the covenant of grace to the people at the Six-Mile Water, on whom Mr Glendinning, formerly minister there, had wrought some conviction ; and having preached sometime at Oldstone, he was settled at Temple-Patrick, where he with great vigilance and diligence exercised his office, and, by the blessing of God upon his labours, gained many seals of his ministry.

But the devil, envying the success of the Gospel in that quarter, stirred up the prelatical clergy; whereupon the Bishop of Down, in May 1632, cited Josias Welch, Blair, Livingstone, and Dunbar before him, and urged them to conform, and give their subscription to that effect; but they answered with great boldness, that there was no law nor canon in that kingdom requiring this; yet, notwithstanding, they were all four deposed by him from the office of the holy ministry.

After this, Josias Welch continued for some time preaching in his own house, where he had a large auditory; and such was his desire to gain souls to Christ, that he commonly stood in a door looking towards a garden, so that he might be heard without as well as within, by means of which, being of a weakly constitution, he contracted such a cold as ultimately occasioned his death. He continued in this way until May 1634, when, by the intercession of Lord Castlestuart with King Charles I. in their behalf, the foresaid ministers received a grant from the Bishop of six months' liberty; which freedom none more willingly embraced than Josias Welch; but he had preached only a few weeks in his own pulpit before he sickened on the Sabbath afternoon before his death, which was on the Monday following. " I heard of his sickness," says John Livingstone, " and came to him about eleven o'clock at night, and Mr Blair came about two hours thereafter. He had many gracious discourses, as also some wrestling and exercise of mind. One time he cried out, 'Oh! for hypocrisy;' on which Mr Blair said, 'See how Satan is nibbling at his heels before he enters into glory.' A very little before he died, being at prayer by his bedside, and the word victory coming out of my mouth, he took hold of my hand, and desiring me to forbear a little, and clapping his hands, cried out, Victory ! victory ! victory for evermore! Then he desired me to go on, and in a little expired, on June 23d, 1634."

Thus died the pious and faithful Josias Welch, in the flower of his youth, leaving only one son behind him, John Welch, who was afterwards minister of Irongray, in Galloway.

John Gordon, Viscount Kenmuir.

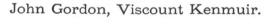

OHN GORDON of Lochinvar (afterwards Viscount Kenmuir) was born about the year 1599. He received a reasonable measure of education; and yet, through the circumstance of his birth, the corruption of the age, but above all, the depravity of nature, and want of restraining grace in his younger years, he became somewhat irreligious and profane, which, when he arrived at manhood, broke out into more gross acts of wicked-ness. Yet all the while the Lord never left him altogether without a

PORTRAIT OF CHARLES I.

check or witness in his conscience ; yea, sometimes when at ordinances, particularly sacramental occasions, he would be filled with a sense of sin, which, being borne powerfully in upon his soul, he was scarcely able to hold out against. But for a long time he was a stranger to true and saving conversion, and the most part of his life, after he advanced in years, he spent like the rich man in the Gospel, casting down barns, and building greater ones; for at his houses of Rusco and Kenmuir, he was much employed in building, parking, planting, and seeking worldly honours.

About the year 1628, he married that virtuous and religious lady Jean Campbell, sister to the worthy Marquis of Argyle, by whom he had some children (two at least), one of whom it appears died about the beginning of the year 1635 ; for we find Samuel Rutherford, in one of his letters, about that time, comforting this noble lady upon such a mournful occasion.

In 1633, Charles I., to honour his coronation in the place of his birth and first Parliament, dignified many of the Scots nobility and gentry with higher titles, and places of office and honour, among whom was Sir John Gordon, who, upon the 8th of May, was created Viscount Kenmuir, and Lord Gordon of Lochinvar. Accordingly, the Viscount came to the Parliament which sat down at Edinburgh, June 16th, 1633, and was present the first day, but stayed only a few days thereafter ; for being afraid to displease the King, from whom he had both received some, and expected more honours, and not having the courage to glorify God by his presence, when His cause was at stake, he deserted the Parliament under pretence of indisposition of body, and returned home to his house at Kenmuir in Galloway, and there slept securely for about a year, without check of conscience, till August 1634, when his affairs occasioned his return to Edinburgh. Here he remained some days, not knowing that with the ending of his affairs he was to end his life, returning home with some alteration of bodily health ; and from that day his sickness increased until September 12th ensuing, which was the day of his death.

But the Lord had other thoughts than that this nobleman should die without some sense of his sin, or yet go out of this world unobserved. And therefore it pleased Him, with his bodily affliction, to shake his soul with fears, making him sensible of the power of eternal wrath, for his own good, and for an example to others in after ages, never to wrong their consciences, or to be wanting to the cause or interest of God, when He gives them an opportunity to that purpose.

Upon the Sabbath, August 31st, being much weakened, he was visited by a religious and learned minister, who then lived in Galloway, not far from the house of Kenmuir. His Lordship much rejoiced at his coming, observing God's over-ruling providence in sending such a man (who had been abroad from Galloway some time) sooner home than he expected. After supper, his Lordship drew on a conference with the minister, showing he was much taken up with the fear of death, and extremity of pain. "I never dreamed," said he, "that death had such a terrible, austere, and gloomy countenance. I dare not die ; howbeit, I know I must die. What shall I do, for I dare not venture in grips with death, because I find my sins grievous, and so many, that I fear my account is out of order, and not so as becomes a dying man."

The minister for some time discoursed to him anent this weakness of nature, which was in all men, believers not excepted, and made them afraid of death ; but he hoped Christ would be his second in the combat, willing him to rely upon His strength ; and withal said, "My lord, I fear more the ground of your fear of death, which is, as you say, the consciousness of your sins, for there can be no plea betwixt you and your Lord, if your sins be not taken away in Christ; therefore make that sure, and fear not." My lord answered : "I have been too late in coming to God ; and have deferred the time of making my account so long, that I fear I have but the foolish virgins' part of it, who came and knocked at the door of the bridegroom so late, and never got in."

The minister having recounted somewhat both of his own and his father's sins, particularly their cares for this world and worldly honours, and thinking his lordship designed to extenuate his fault in this, he drew several weighty propositions, in way of conference, about the fears of death and his eternal all, which depended upon his being in or out of Christ. He then addressed him in these words, "Therefore, I entreat you, my lord, by the mercies of God, by your appearing before Christ your Judge, and by the salvation of your soul, that you would look ere you leap, and venture not into eternity, without a certificate under Jesus Christ's hand ; because it is said of the hypocrite : ' He lieth down in the grave, and his bones are full of the sins of his youth.' "

My lord replied, " When I begin to look upon my life, I think all is wrong in it, and the lateness of my reckoning affrighteth me ; therefore stay with me, and show me the marks of a child of God, for you must be my second in this combat, and wait upon me." His lady answered, " You must have Jesus Christ to be your second ; " to which he heartily said, " Amen ; but," continued he, " how shall I know that I am in the state of grace ? for while I be resolved, my fears will still overburden me." The minister said, " My lord, scarcely or never doth a castaway anxiously and carefully ask the question, whether he be a child of God or not." But my lord excepted against that, saying, " I do not think there is any reprobate in hell, but would, with all his heart, have the kingdom of heaven." The minister having explained the different desires in reprobates, his lordship said, " You never saw any tokens of true grace in me ; and that is my great and only fear."

The minister said, " I was indeed sorry to see you so fearfully carried away with temptation, and you know I gave 'you faithful warning that it would come to this. I wish your soul was deeply humbled for sin ; but to your demand, I thought you ever had a love for the saints, even to the poorest, who carried Christ's image, although they could never serve nor profit you in any way. ' We know we have passed from death unto life, because we love the brethren'" (1 John iii 14). And at last, with this mark, after some objections, he seemed convinced. The minister asked him, "My lord, dare you now quit your part in Christ, and subscribe an absolute re-signation of Him?" My lord said, " O Sir, that is too hard; I hope He and I have more to do together, and I will be advised ere I do that ;" and then asked, " What mark is it to have judgment to discern a minister called and sent of God from an hireling?" The minister allowed it to be a good mark, and cited John x. 4, " My sheep know my voice."

At the second conference, the minister urged deep humiliation. He acknowledged the necessity thereof; but said, " Oh! if I could get Him! But sin causeth me to be jealous of His love to such a man as I have been." The minister advised him " to be jealous of him-self, but not of Jesus Christ, there being no meeting between them without a sense of sin" (Isa. lxi. 2, 3). Whereupon my lord said, with a deep sigh accompanied with tears, " God send me that!" and thereafter reckoned out a certain number of his sins, which were as serpents or crocodiles before his eyes. The minister told him that death and he were yet strangers, and hoped that he would tell another tale ere all the play was ended, and he should think death a sweet messenger to carry him to his Father's house. He said with tears, " God make it so!" and desired him to pray.

At the third conference, he said, " Death bindeth me straight. O how sweet a thing it is to seek God in health, and in time of pro-sperity to make our accounts, for now I am so distempered, that I cannot get my heart framed to think on my account, and the life to come." The minister told him that he behoved to fight against sick-ness and pain, as well as sin and death, seeing it is a temptation. He answered, " I have taken the play long; God hath given me thirty-five years to repent ; but, alas! I have misspent it ;" and with that he covered his face and wept. The minister assured him, that although his day was far spent, yet he behoved in the afternoon, yea, when near evening, to run fast and not to lie in the field and miss his lodging, upon which he, with uplifted eyes, said, " Lord, how can I run ? Lord, draw me, and I shall run" (Cant i. 4). The minister, hearing this, desired him to pray, but he answered nothing ; yet, within an hour, he prayed before him and his own lady very devoutly, and bemoaned his own weakness, both inward and outward, saying, " I dare not knock at thy door ; I lie at it scrambling as I may, till thou come out and take me in ; I dare not speak ; I look up to thee and look for one kiss of Christ's fair face. Oh, when wilt thou come !"

At the fourth conference, he charged the minister to go to a
secret place and pray for him, and do it not for the fashion. " I
know," said he, " prayer will pull Christ out of heaven." The
minister said, " What shall we seek ? Give us a commission." He
answered, " I charge you to tell my Beloved that I am sick of love."
The minister desired if they should seek life or recovery. He said,
" Yea, if it be God's good pleasure ; for I find my fear of death now
less, and I think God is now loosing the root of the deep-grown tree
of my soul, so firmly fastened to this life." The minister told him, if
it were so, he behoved to covenant with God, in dedicating himself
and all he had to God and His service, to which he heartily consented;
and after the minister had recited several Scriptures for that purpose,
such as Ps. lxxviii. 36, etc., he took the Bible, and said, " Mark
other Scriptures for me." Having marked 2 Cor. v., Rev. xxi. and
xxii., Psalm xxxviii., John xv., he turned over these places, and
cried often for one love-blink—" O Son of God, for one sight of Thy
face."

When the minister told him his prayers were heard, he took
hold of his hand, and drew him to him, and said with a sigh, " Good
news indeed;" and desired him and others to tell him what access
they had got to God in Christ for his soul. They told him they had
got access, at which he rejoiced and said, " Then will I believe and
wait on. I cannot think but my Beloved is coming, leaping over the
hills."

When friends or others came to visit him, whom he knew feared
God, he would cause them to go and pray for him, and sent some of
them expressly to the wood of Kenmuir on that errand. After some
cool of a fever (as was thought), he caused one of his attendants to
call for the minister, to whom he said, smiling, " Rejoice now, for
He is come. Oh! if I had a tongue to tell the world what Jesus
Christ hath done for my soul ! "

And yet, after all this, conceiving hopes of recovery, he became
more careless, remiss, and dead, for some days, and seldom called
for the minister, though he would not suffer him to go home to his
flock. His lady and others perceiving this, went to the physician,
and asked his judgment anent him. He plainly told them, there was
nothing but death for him, if the flux returned, as it did. This made
the minister go to him, and give him faithful warning of his approaching danger, telling him his glass was shorter than he was aware of,
and that Satan would be glad to steal his soul out of the world sleep-

ing. This being seconded by the physician, he took the minister by the hand, thanked him for his faithful and plain dealing, and acknowledged the folly of his deceiving heart, in looking over his affection to this life, when he was so fairly once on his journey toward heaven; then, ordering them all to leave the chamber except the minister, and causing him to shut the door, he conferred with him anent the state of his soul.

After prayer, the minister told him, he feared that his former joy had not been well grounded, nor his humiliation deep enough; and therefore desired him to dig deeper, representing his offence both against the first and second table of the law, etc. Thereupon his Lordship reckoned out a number of great sins, and, amongst the rest, freely confessed his sin in deserting the last Parliament, saying, "God knoweth, I did it with fearful wrestling of conscience, my light paying me home within when I seemed to be glad and joyful before men." The minister being struck with astonishment at this reckoning, after such fair appearance of sound marks of grace in his soul, stood up and read the first eight verses in the sixth chapter of the epistle to the Hebrews, and discoursed thereon; then cited the eighth verse of the twenty-first chapter of Revelation, and told him he had not one word of mercy from the Lord to him, and so turned his back. At this he cried out with tears, that they heard him at some distance, saying, "God armed is coming against me to beat out my brains! I would die—I dare not die! I would live—I dare not live! O what a burden is the hand of an angry God! Oh! what shall I do? Is there no hope of mercy?" In this agony he lay for some time. Some said that the minister would kill him; others, that he would make him despair; but he bore with them, and went to a secret place, where he sought words from God to speak to this patient.

After this another minister came to visit him, to whom he said, "He hath slain me;" and, before the minister could answer for himself, added, "Not he, but the Spirit of God in him." The minister said, "Not I, but the law hath slain you;" and withal told him of the process the Lord had against the house of Kenmuir. The other minister read the history of Manasseh, and of his wicked life, and how the Lord was entreated of by him. But the former minister—supposed to have been Samuel Rutherford—went still upon wrath, telling him he knew he was extremely pained both in body and mind, but what would he think of the lake of fire and brimstone, of everlasting burning, and of utter darkness, with the devil and his angels. My lord answered, "Woe is me if I should suffer my thoughts to dwell upon it at any time ; it were enough to cause me to go out of my senses. But I pray you, what shall I do?" The minister told him he was still in the same situation, only the sentence was not given out, and, therefore, desired him to mourn for offending God ; and further said, "What, my lord, if Christ had given out the sentence of condemnation against you, and come to your bedside, and told you of it ; would you not still love Him, trust in Him, and hang upon Him?" He answered, "God knoweth, I durst not challenge Him ; howbeit He should slay me, I will still love Him—yea, though the Lord should slay me, yet will I trust in Him. I will lie down at God's feet, let Him trample upon me ; if I die, I will die at Christ's feet." The minister—finding him claiming kindness to Christ, and hearing him often cry, " O Son of God, where art Thou? when wilt Thou come to me? Oh! for a love-look !"—said, "Is it possible, my lord, that you can love and long for Christ, and He not love and long for you? Can love and kindness stand only on your side? Is your poor love more than infinite love, seeing He hath said (Isa. xlix. 15) 'Can a woman forget her sucking child, that she should not have compassion on the son of her womb? yea, they may forget, yet will I not forget thee. Behold, I have graven thee upon the palms of my hands; thy walls are continually before me.' My lord, be persuaded; you are graven upon the palms of God's hands." Upon this, he, with a hearty smile, looked about to a gentleman, one of his attendants, and said, " I am written, man, upon the palms of Christ's hands—He will not forget me. Is not this brave talking?"

Afterwards, the minister, finding him weaker, said, "My lord, the marriage-day is drawing near; make ready; set aside all care of your estate and the world, and give yourself to meditation and prayer and spiritual conference." After that he was observed to be still on that exercise, and when none were near him he was found praying; yea, when to appearance sleeping, he was overheard to be engaged in that duty. After some sleep he called for one of his kinsmen, with whom he was not reconciled, and also for a minister, who had before offended him, that they might be friends again, which was done quickly. To the preacher he said, "I have ground of offence against you as a natural man, and I do to you that which all men breathing could not have moved me to do; but now, because the Holy Spirit commands me, I must obey, and therefore freely forgive you, as I would

THE PALACE OF HOLYROOD.

wish you to forgive me. You are in an eminent station, walk before God and be faithful to your calling; take heed to your steps; walk in the right road; hold your eye right; for all the world, decline not from holiness, and take example by me." To his cousin he said, "Serve the Lord, and follow not the footsteps of your father-in-law" (for he had married the Bishop of Galloway's daughter); "learn to know that you have a soul, for I say unto you, the thousandth part of the world know not that they have a soul. The world liveth without any sense of God."

He desired the minister to sleep in a bed made upon the floor in the chamber by him, and urged him to take a sleep, saying, "You and I have a far journey to go, make ready for it." Four nights before his death he would drink a cup of wine to the minister, who said, "Receive it, my lord, in hope you shall drink of the pure river of the water of life, proceeding from the throne of God and from the Lamb;" and when the cup was in his hand, with a smiling countenance, he said "I think I have good cause to drink with a good will to you." After some heaviness the minister said, "My lord, I have good news to tell you. Be not afraid of death and judgment, because the process that your Judge had against you is cancelled and rent in pieces, and Christ hath trampled it under his feet." My lord answered, with a smile, "Oh! that is a lucky tale. I will then believe and rejoice, for sure I am, that Christ and I once met, and will He not come again?" The minister said, "You have gotten the first fruit of the Spirit, the earnest thereof, and Christ will not lose his earnest, therefore the bargain betwixt him and you holdeth." Then he asked, "What is Christ like, that I may know him?" The minister answered, "He is like love, and altogether lovely" (Cant. v.).

The minister said, "My lord, if you had the man Christ in your arms, would your heart, your breast, and sides be pained with a stitch?" He answered, "God knoweth I would forget my pain, and thrust Him to my heart; yea, if I had my heart in the palm of my hand I would give it to Him, and think it a gift too unworthy of Him." He complained of Jesus Christ in coming and going. "I find," said he, "my soul drowned in heaviness; when the Lord cometh He stayeth not long." The minister said, "Wooers dwell not together, but married folk take up house and sunder not; Jesus Christ is now wooing, and therefore He feedeth His own with hunger, which is as growing meat as the sense of His presence." He said often, "Son of God, when wilt thou come? God is not a man that he should change, or as the son of man that He should repent. Them that come to Christ He casteth not away, but raiseth them up at the last day." He was heard to say in his sleep, "My Beloved is mine, and I am His." Being asked if he had been sleeping, he said he had; but he remembered he had been giving a claim to Christ. He asked, "When will my heart be loosed and my tongue untied, that I may express the sweetness of the love of God to my own soul?" and before the minister answered any thing, he himself answered, "Even when the wind bloweth."

At another time, being asked his judgment anent the ceremonies then used in the Church, he answered, "I think, and am persuaded in my conscience, they are superstitious, idolatrous, and antichristian, and come from hell. I repute it a mercy that my eyes shall not see the desolation that shall come upon this poor Church. It is plain Popery that is coming among you. God help you. God forgive the nobility, for they are either very cold in defending the true religion, or ready to welcome Popery, whereas they should resist; and woe be to a dead, time-serving, and profane ministry."

He called his lady, and a gentleman who had come from the east country to visit him, and caused shut the door; then from his bed directed his speech to the gentleman thus: "I ever found you faithful and kind to me in my life; therefore I must now give you a charge, which you shall deliver to all noblemen you are acquainted with; go through them, and show them from me that I have found the weight of the wrath of God for not giving testimony for the Lord my God when I had occasion, once in my life, at the last Parliament, for which fault how fierce have I found the wrath of the Lord. My soul hath raged and roared; I have been grieved at the remembrance of it. Tell them that they will be as I am now; encourage my friends that stood for the Lord; tell them that failed, if they would wish to have mercy when they are as I am now, they must repent, and crave mercy of the Lord. For all the earth I would not do as I have done."

To a gentleman, one of his kinsmen, he said: "I love you, soul and body; you are a blessed man if you improve the blessed means of the Word preached beside you. I would not have you drown yourself so much with the concerns of this world, as I did. My grief is, that I had not the occasion of good means as you have, and if you yourself make not a right use of them, one day they shall be a witness against you."

To Lord Herries, his brother-in-law, he said: "Mock not at my counsel, my lord. In case you follow the course you are in, you shall never see the face of Jesus Christ; you are deceived with the merchandise of the whore, that makes the world drunk out of the cup of her fornication; your soul is built upon a sandy foundation. When you come to my state you will find no comfort in your religion. You know not what wrestling I have had, before I came to this state of comfort. The kingdom of heaven is not gotten with a skip or leap, but with much seeking and thrusting."

To his own sister he said: "Who knows, sister, but the words of a dying brother may prevail with a loving sister. Alas! you incline to a rotten religion; cast away these rotten rags, they will not avail you when you are brought to this case as I am. The half of the world are ignorant and go to hell, and know not that they have a soul. Read the Scriptures, they are plain easy language to all who desire wisdom from God, and to be led to heaven."

To a gentleman, his neighbour, he said: "Your soul is in a dangerous case, but you see it not. Leave these sinful courses. There are small means of instruction to be had, seeing the most part of the ministry are profane and ignorant. Search God's word for the good old way, and search and find out all your own ways."

To a gentleman, his cousin, he said: "You are a young man, and know not well what you are doing. Seek God's direction for wisdom in your affairs, and you shall prosper; and learn to know that you have need of God to be your friend."

To another cousin he said: "David, you are an aged man, and you know not well what an account you have to make. I know you better than you believe, for you worship God according to men's devices; you believe lies of God; your soul is in a dreadful case, and till you know the truth, you shall never see your own way aright."

To a young man, his neighbour: "Because you are but young, beware of temptation and snares; above all, be careful to keep yourself in the use of means; resort to good company, and howbeit you be named a Puritan, and mocked, care not for that, but rejoice and be glad that they would admit you to their society; for I must tell you, when I am at this point in which you see me, I get no comfort to my soul from any other second means under heaven, but from those who are nick-named Puritans; they are the men that can give a word of comfort to a wearied soul in due season, and that I have found by experience."

To one of his natural sisters: "My dove, thou art young, and, alas, ignorant of God. I know thy breeding and upbringing well enough. Seek the spirit of regeneration. Oh! if thou knew it, and felt the power of the Spirit as I do now! Think not all is gone because your brother is dead. Trust in God, and beware of the follies of youth. Give yourself to reading and praying, and be careful in hearing God's word, and take heed whom you hear, and how you hear; and God be with you."

To a minister he said: "Mr James, it is not holiness enough to be a minister, for you ministers have your own faults, and those more heinous than others. I pray you, be more painful in your calling, and take good heed to the flock of God; know that every soul that perisheth by your negligence, shall be counted to your soul, murdered before God. Take heed in these dangerous days how you lead the people of God, and take heed to your ministry."

To Mr George Gillespie, then his chaplain: "You have carried yourself discreetly to me, so that I cannot blame you. I hope you shall prove an honest man. If I have been at any time harsh to you, forgive me. I would I had taken better heed to many of your words; I might have gotten good by the means God gave me, but I made no use of them. I am grieved for my ingratitude against my loving

Lord, and that I should have sinned against Him who came down from heaven to the earth for my cause, to die for my sins; the sense of this love borne in upon my heart hath a reflex, making me love my Saviour, and grip to Him again."

To another kinsman he said: " Learn to use your time well. Oh, alas! the ministry in this country is dead ; God help you, ye are not led right; ye had need to be busy among yourselves. Men are as careless in the practice of godliness as it were but words, fashions, signs, and shows ; but all these will not do the turn. Oh! but I find it hard now to thrust in and take the kingdom of heaven by force."

To two neighbouring gentlemen he said : " It is not rising soon in the morning, and running to the park or stone-dyke that will bring peace to the conscience, when it comes to this part of the play. You know how I have been beguiled with this world. I would counsel you to seek that one thing necessary, even the salvation of your souls."

To a cousin, bailie of Ayr, he said : " Robert, I know you have light and understanding ; and though you need not be instructed by me, yet you need to be incited. Care not overmuch for the world, but make use of good means which you have in your country ; for here is a pack of dumb dogs that cannot bark ; they tell over a clash of terror, and clatter of comfort, without any sense or life."

To a cousin, and another gentleman who was along with him, he said : " Ye are young men, and have far to go, but it may be, some of you have not far to go ; and though your journey be short, howsoever it is dangerous. Now are you happy, because you have time to lay your accounts with Jesus Christ. I entreat you to give your youth to Christ, for it is the best and most acceptable gift you can give him. Give not your youth to the devil and your lusts, and then reserve nothing to Jesus Christ but your rotten bones ; it is to be feared that then He will not accept you. Learn, therefore, to watch and take example by me."

He called Mr Lamb, who was then Bishop of Galloway, and commanding all others to leave the room, he had a long conference with him, exhorting him earnestly not to molest or remove the Lord's servants, or enthral their consciences to receive the five articles of Perth, or do anything against their consciences, as he would wish to have mercy from God. The Bishop answered, " My lord, our ceremonies are, of their own nature, but things indifferent, and we impose them for decency and order in God's kirk. They need not stand so scrupulously on them as matter of conscience in God's worship." My lord replied, " I will not dispute with you, but one thing I know, and can tell you from dear experience, that these things indeed are matters of conscience, and not indifferent; and so I have found them. For since I lay on this bed, the sin that lay heaviest on my soul was withdrawing myself from the Parliament, and not giving my voice for the truth, against these things which they call indifferent ; and in so doing I have denied the Lord my God." When the Bishop began to commend him for his well-led life, putting him in hopes of health, and praising him for his civil carriage and behaviour, saying, he was no oppressor, and without any known vice, he answered : " No matter, a man may be a good civil neighbour, and yet go to hell." The Bishop answered : " My lord, I confess we have all our faults ;" and thereafter he insisted so long that my lord thought him impertinent. This made him interrupt the Bishop, saying : " What should I more ? I have got a grip of Jesus Christ, and Christ of me." On the morrow the Bishop came to visit him, and upon asking how he did, he answered, " I thank God, as well as a saved man hastening to heaven can be."

After he had given the clerk of Kirkcudbright some suitable advice, anent his Christian walk and particular calling, he caused him swear, in the most solemn terms, that he should never consent to, but oppose, the election of a corrupt minister or magistrate. To his coachman, he said, " You will go to any one who will give you the most hire ; but do not so : go where you can get the best company ; though you get less wages, yet you will get the more grace." Then he made him hold up his hand, and promise before God so to do. To two young serving-men, who came to him weeping, to get his last blessing, he said, " Content not yourselves with a superficial view of religion, blessing yourselves in the morning only for a fashion ; yea, though you would pray both morning and evening, yet that will not avail you, except likewise ye make your account every day. Oh ! ye will find few to direct or counsel you ; but I will tell you what to do ; first pray to the Lord fervently, to enlighten the eyes of your mind, then seek grace to rule your affections ; you will find the good of this when you come to my situation." Then he took both their oaths to do so.

He gave many powerful exhortations to several persons, and caused each man to hold up his hand, and swear in his presence, that by God's grace he should forbear his former sins, and follow his counsel.

When giving a divine counsel to a friend, he rested in the midst of it, and looking up to heaven, prayed for a loosened heart and tongue to express the goodness of God to men ; and thereafter went on in his counsel, not unlike Jacob, Gen. xlix. 18, who, in the midst of a prophetical testament, rested a little and said, " I have waited for thy salvation."

He gave his lady divers times openly an honourable and ample testimony of her holiness, goodness, and respectful kindness to him, earnestly craved her forgiveness wherein he had offended her, and desired her to make the Lord her comforter ; and said, he was but gone before, and it was but fifteen or sixteen years up or down.

He spoke to all the boys of the house, the butler, cook, etc., omitting none, saying, " Learn to serve and fear the Lord, and use carefully the means of your salvation. I know what is ordinarily your religion ; ye go to kirk, and when ye hear the devil or hell named in the preaching, ye sigh and make a noise, and it is forgot by you before you come home, and then ye are holy enough. But I can tell you, the kingdom of heaven is not got so easily. Use the means yourselves, and win to some sense of God, and pray as you can, morning and evening. If you be ignorant of the way to salvation, God forgive you, for I have discharged myself in that point towards you, and appointed a man to teach you ; your blood be upon yourselves." He took an oath of his servants, that they should follow his advice, and said to them severally, " If I have been rough to or offended you, I pray you, for God's sake, to forgive me." Amongst others, one to whom he had been rough said, " Your lordship never did me wrong ; I will never get such a master again." Yet he urged him to say, " My lord, I forgive you ;" although the boy was hardly brought to utter these words, and said to all the beholders about him, "Sirs, behold how low the Lord hath brought me."

To a gentleman burdened in his estate, he said ; " Sir, I counsel you to cast your burden upon the Lord your God." To a religious gentleman of his own name coming to visit him four days before his death, he said, " Robert, come to me, and leave me not till I die." Being much comforted with his speeches, he said, " Robert, you are a friend to me both in soul and body." The gentleman asked him what comfort he had in his love towards the saints. He answered, " I rejoice at it." Then he asked him what comfort he had in bringing the minister who attended him from Galloway. He answered, "God knoweth that I rejoice that ever He put it in my heart so to do, and now because I aimed at God's glory in it, the Lord hath made me find comfort to my soul in the end; the ministers of Galloway murdered my father's soul, and if this man had not come they had murdered mine also."

Before his sister Lady Herries, who was a Papist, he testified his willingness to leave the world, "that Papists may see," said he, "that we who die in this religion both see and know whither we go for the hope of our Father's house." When letters were brought him from friends, he caused deliver them to his lady, saying, "I have nothing to do with them. I had rather hear of news from heaven concerning my eternal salvation." It was observed, that when any came to him anent worldly business, before they were out of doors, he was returned to his spiritual exercises, and was exceedingly short in despatching all needful writs. He recommended the case of the poor to his friends. Upon coming out of a fainting-fit, into which his weakness had thrown him, he said, with a smiling countenance to all about him, "I would not exchange my life with you all; I feel the smell of the place whither I am going."

Upon Friday morning, the day of his departure from this life, he said, "This night I must sup with Jesus Christ in paradise." The minister read to him 2 Cor. v., and Rev. xxii., and made some observations on such places as concerned his state. After prayer, he said, "I conceive good hopes that God looketh upon me, when He granteth such liberty to pray for me. Is it possible that Jesus Christ can lose His grip of me? neither can my soul get itself plucked from Jesus Christ." He earnestly desired a sense of God's presence; and the minister said, "What, my lord, if that be suspended till you come to your own home, and be before the throne, clothed in white, and get your harp in your hand, to sing salvation to the Lamb, and to Him that sitteth on the throne, for that is heaven; and who dare promise it to you upon earth? There is a piece of nature in desiring a sense of God's love, it being an apple that the Lord's children delight to play with. But, my lord, if you would have it only as a pledge of your salvation, we shall seek it from the Lord for you, and you may lawfully pray for it." Earnest prayers were made for him, and he testified that he was filled with the sense of the Lord's love. Being asked what he thought of the world? he answered, "It is more bitter than gall or wormwood." And being demanded, if he now feared death, he answered, "I have tasted death; it is not a whit bitter; welcome! the messenger of Jesus Christ."

The minister said: " There is a process betwixt the Lord and your father's house, but your name is taken out of it. How dear was heaven bought for you by Jesus Christ." He frequently said, " I know there is wrath against it, but I shall get my soul for a prey." Ofttimes he said, " It is a sweet word God saith, ' As I live, I delight not in the death of a sinner.' I will not let go the hold I have got of Jesus Christ ; though He should slay me, yet will I trust in Him."

In deep meditation on his change, he put this question, " What will Christ be like when He cometh ?" It was answered, " Altogether lovely." Before he died, he was heard praying very fervently, and said to the doctor, " I thought to have been dissolved ere now." The minister said, " Weary not of the Lord's yoke; Jesus Christ is posting fast to be at you ; He is within a few miles." He answered, " This is my infirmity. I will wait on ; He is worth the on-waiting ; though He be long in coming, yet I dare say He is coming, leaping over the mountains, and skipping over the hills." The minister said, " Some have gotten their fill of Christ in this life ; howbeit He is often under a mask to His own ; even His best saints, Job, David, Jeremiah, were under desertions." My lord said, " But what are these examples to me? I am not in holiness near to them." The minister said, " It is true, you cannot take so wide steps as they did, but you are in the same way with them ; a young child followeth his father at the back, though he cannot take such wide steps as he. My lord, your hunger overcometh your faith : only but believe His word ; you are longing for Christ; only believe that He is faithful, and will come quickly." To this he answered, " I think it is time ; Lord Jesus, come !"

Then the minister said, " My Lord, our nature is anxious for our own deliverance ; whereas God seeketh first to be glorified in our faith, patience, and hope." He answered, " Good reason to be first served. Lord, give me to wait on ; only, Lord, turn me not to dross."

Another said, " Cast back your eyes, my lord, on what you have received, and be thankful ;" at the hearing of which he brake forth in praising of God ; and finding himself now weak—his speech failing more than an hour before his death—he desired the minister to pray. After prayer, the minister cried in his ear, " My lord, may you now sunder with Christ?" To this he answered nothing, nor was it expected he would speak any more. Yet, in a little the minister asked him, " Have you any sense of the Lord's love?" He answered,

"I have." The minister said, "Do you now enjoy?" He answered, "I do enjoy." Therefore he asked him, "Will ye not sunder with Christ?" He answered, "By no means." This was his last word, not being able to speak any more. The minister asked if he should pray, and he turned his eyes towards him. In the time of the last prayer he was observed joyfully smiling and looking upward. He departed this life about sun-setting, September 12, 1634, aged thirty-five years. It was observed that he died at the same instant that the minister concluded his prayer.

Samuel Rutherford, in one of his letters to the Viscountess of Kenmuir, a little after the death of her husband, to comfort her, among other things lets fall this expression: "In this late visitation that hath befallen your ladyship, ye have seen God's love and care in such a measure, that I thought our Lord brake the sharp point of the cross, and made us and your ladyship see Christ take possession and infeftment upon earth, of him who is reigning and triumphing with the hundred and forty and four thousand who stand with the Lamb on Mount Zion."

Some may object—What did this nobleman for the cause of Christ, or Scotland's covenanted work of Reformation, that he should be inserted among the Scots Worthies? To this it may be answered, —What did the most eminent saint that ever was in Scotland, or anywhere else, until enabled by the grace of God? So it was with reference to him; for no sooner was he made partaker of this, than he gave a most ample and faithful testimony for his truths and interest; and although the Lord did not see it proper that he should serve Him after this manner in his day and generation, yet He, no doubt, accepted of the will for the deed; and why should we not enrol his name among these Worthies on earth, seeing He hath written his name among the living in Jerusalem.

BELFAST LOUGH.

Robert Cunningham.

OBERT CUNNINGHAM, having received a good education, first became chaplain to the Duke of Buccleuch's regiment in Holland.   He was soon afterwards settled minister at Holywood in Ireland, sometime before Mr Blair was settled at Bangor, and with him Mr Blair, after his settlement at that place, contracted such an acquaintance as was comfortable to them both.

He applied himself closely unto the work of the ministry, which no doubt to him was the most desirable of all employments, being in his own element in the pulpit, like a fish in the water, or a bird in the air; always judging that therein a Christian might enjoy much fellowship with Christ, and have an opportunity of doing Him the best of services, considering what Christ said to Peter : " Lovest thou Me more than these?—feed my lambs—feed my sheep" (John xxi. 15, etc.).

He continued to exercise his office as a faithful pastor over the flock to whom he was appointed overseer, until the time that several of his faithful brethren were deposed and ejected by the Bishops. The Bishop of Down threatened Mr Blair with a prosecution against himself, Mr Cunningham, and some others, to whom Mr Blair said " Ye may do with me and some others as ye please, but if ever ye meddle with Mr Cunningham, your cup will be full." And, indeed, he was longer spared than any of the rest, which was a great benefit to their flocks, for, after they were deposed, he preached every week in one or other of their kirks. So, with great pains both at home and abroad, he wore out his body, which before was not very strong.

When Blair and Livingstone were summoned before Bishop Ecklim to be deposed, they went the night before their appearance to take their leave of Mr Cunningham. Next day, as they were going to the church of Parphilips, he came up to them ; whereat, being surprised, they asked him why he came thither. To this he answered : " All night long I have been troubled with that passage, ' At my first answer no man stood with me,' therefore I am come to stand by you." But being the eye-sore of the devil and the prelatical clergy in that part of the country, he could not be suffered long to exercise his ministry ; and in August 1636, he, with others of his faithful brethren, were thrust out and deposed. He continued mostly after this with the rest of the suffering brethren, until, after the defeat of their enterprise to New England, they were obliged to leave Ireland, and come over to Scotland, and not long after, he took his last sickness in Irvine, whereof he soon died.

During his sickness, besides many other gracious expressions, he said : " I see Christ standing over Death's head, saying, ' Deal warily with my servant ; loose thou this pin, then that pin, for his tabernacle must be set up again.' "

The day before his death, the members of the Presbytery of Irvine paid him a visit, whom he exhorted to be faithful to Christ and His cause, and to oppose the Service Book, then pressed upon the Church. "The Bishop," said he, " hath taken my ministry from me, and I may say, my life also ; for my ministry is dearer to me than my life." A little before his departure, his wife sitting by his bed-side, with his hand in hers, he did by prayer recommend the whole Church of Ireland, the parish of Holywood, his suffering brethren in the ministry, and his children, to God; and withal added, " Lord, I recommend this gentlewoman to thee, who is no more my wife," and with that he softly loosed his hand from hers, and thrust it a little from him, at which she and several of the company fell a-weeping. He endeavoured to comfort them with several gracious expressions ; and, with the Lord's servant of old, mentioned in Acts

xiii. 36, " Having served his own generation, by the will of God he fell on sleep," March 27, 1637.

Mr Cunningham was a man much under deep exercise of mind, and although in public preaching he was, to his own sense, sometimes not so assisted as at other times, yet even then the matter he treated of was edifying and refreshful, being carried through with a full gale, and using more piercing expressions than many others. For meekness he was like Moses, and for patience another Job. " To my discerning," says John Livingstone, " he was the man who most resembled the meekness of Jesus Christ in all his carriage, that I ever saw ; and was so far reverenced of all, even by the wicked, that he was often troubled with that Scripture, ' Woe to you when all men speak well of you.' "

James Mitchell.

AMES MITCHELL was the son of Mr James Mitchell of Dykes, in the parish of Ardrossan, and was born about the year 1621. His father, being factor to the Earl of Eglinton, and a very religious man, gave his son a most liberal and religious education ; for being sent to the University of St Andrews when very young, he profited to such a degree, that by the time that he was eighteen years of age, he was made Master of Arts.

After this he returned home to his father's house, where he studied nearly two years and a half; the Lord in a good measure blessing his pains and endeavours therein. Robert Baillie, then minister of Kilwinning, showed him no small kindness, by the loan of his books, by his counsel, and by superintending his studies.

Thereafter, he was called by the Lady Houston to attend her eldest son at the college, in which employment he continued over two years and a half; in the which time the Lord blessed his studies exceedingly; and the great pains taken with him by Mr David Dickson (then Professor of the University of Glasgow), Mr Baillie, and others, had such a blessing from heaven, that he passed both his private and public trials in order for the ministry, to their great contentment. After he was licensed, he came west and preached in Kilwinning and Stevenston, to the satisfaction of all who heard him; so that they blessed God on his behalf, and were very hopeful of his great abilities.

Before Martinmas 1643, he went back to Glasgow, where he both attended his studies, and his pupil. He preached some few times in Glasgow, and all those who loved Christ and His cause and Gospel were exceedingly well pleased. At this time, Mr Dickson, Mr Baillie, and Mr Robert Ramsay, having great hopes of his gifts in preaching, told his father that he had good reason to bless God for the gifts and graces bestowed upon his son, above all their expectation; for besides these, the Lord had taken him truly by the heart, and wrought graciously with his soul. He had given himself much up to fasting and prayer; and the study of the Word of God, and reading thereof, was now become his delight.

But the Lord having other thoughts concerning him, in a short time all their great expectations of him in the ministry were frustrated; for, by his extreme abstinence, drinking of water, and indefatigable application, he contracted that sickness of which he died soon after. His body began to languish, his stomach to refuse all meat, and his constitution to alter. Mr Dickson laid his condition much to heart (Mr Baillie being at London), and kept him fifteen days with him; thereafter he went to Houston, and stayed as long there, where the Lady and her daughter showed more love and kindness than can be expressed, and that not only for the care he had of her son, but also for the rare gifts and graces God had bestowed on him. His father having sent for him, he returned home. The first night on his journey he was with Ralston; and the Laird of Ducathall, being there occasionally, attended him all the rest of the way homeward; for not being able to ride two miles together, he behoved to go into a house to rest himself for an hour; such was his weakly condition.

After his arrival at home, he put on his clothes every day, for fifteen days, but after that lay bedfast for ten weeks, until the day of his death; during which time the Lord was very merciful and gracious to him, both in an external and internal way. His body, by degrees, daily languished, till he became like a skeleton; and yet his face remained ever pleasant, beautiful, and well coloured, even to the last.

The last five or six weeks he lived, there were always three or four waiting on him, and sometimes more ; yet they never had occasion to weary of him, but were rather refreshed with every day's continuance, by the many wise, sweet, and gracious discourses which proceeded out of his mouth.

In the time of his sickness, the Lord was graciously pleased to guard his mind and heart from the malice of Satan, so that his peace and confidence in God were not much disturbed ; or if the Lord was pleased to suffer any little assault, it soon vanished. His feeling and sense were not frequent nor great, but his faith or confidence in God, through Jesus Christ, was ever strong, which he told his father divers times was more sure and solid than the other. He said, that the Lord, before his sickness, had made fast work with him about the matters of his soul ; that he had been under sore exercise of mind, by the sense of his own guiltiness, for a long time before ever he had solid peace and clear confidence, and often said, " Unworthy I, and naughty I, am freely beloved of the Lord ; and the Lord knows, my soul dearly loves Him back again."

He was also possessed of great patience and submission under all this sore trouble, and never was heard to murmur in the least, but often thought his Master's time well worth the waiting on, and was frequently much refreshed with the seeing and hearing of honest and gracious neighbours who came to visit him ; so that he had little reason with Heman to complain, " Lover and friend hast thou put far from me, and mine acquaintance into darkness " (Psa. lxxxviii. 18).

Among other of his gracious discourses he declaimed much against imprudent speaking, wishing it might be amended, especially in young scholars and young ministers, and as being but the froth and vanity of the foolish mind. Among other things he lamented the pride of many young preachers and students, in usurping priority of place, which became them not ; and exclaimed frequently against himself for his own practice ; yet said that he was, in the strength of God, brought to mortify the same. He frequently exhorted his parents to carry themselves to one another as the word of God required, and above all things to fear God and delight in His word ; and often said that he dearly loved the Book of God, and sought them to be earnest in prayer, showing that it was an unknown thing, and a thing of another world, and that the influence of prayer behoved to come out of heaven ; therefore the spirit of supplication must be wrestled for, or else all prayer would be but lifeless and natural. He said, that being once with the Lady Houston and some country gentlemen at Baglas, the spirit of prayer and supplication was poured upon him in such a powerful and lively manner, two several days before they went to dinner, that all present were much affected, and shed tears in abundance, and yet at night he found himself so emptied and dead, that he durst not venture to pray at all these two nights, but went to bed, and was much vexed and cast down, not knowing the reason. By this he was from that time convinced, that the dispensation and influence of spiritual and lively prayer came only from heaven, and from no natural abilities that were in man.

The Laird of Cunningham coming to visit him, as he did frequently, he enumerated all the remarkable passages of God's goodness to him, especially since he contracted sickness, as in showing infinite mercies to his soul, tender compassion towards his body and natural spirits, patience and submission to His will without grudging, calmness of spirit without passion, solid and constant peace within and without. He said, "This is far beyond the Lord's manner of dealing with many of His dear saints. Now, Sir, think ye not but I stand greatly indebted to the goodness and kindness of God, who deals thus graciously and warmly with me every way?" Then he burst out in praise to God in a sweet and lively manner.

At another time, the laird being present, looking out of his bed to the sun shining brightly on the opposite side of the house, he said, "Oh! what a splendour and glory will all the elect and redeemed saints have one day; and oh! how much more will the glory of the Creator be, who shall communicate that glory to all His own; but the shallow thoughts of silly men are not able to conceive the excellency thereof."

Again, Mr Macqueen being present, his father asked wherein our communion with God stood? He said, in reconciliation and peace with him, which is the first effect of our justification; then there were access and love to God, patience and submission to his will; then the Lord's manifestation of Himself to us, as Christ says, John xiv. 21. See the 20th verse, which he instanced.

He said one morning to Mr Hugh Macgavin and his father, "I am not afraid of death; for I rest on infinite mercy, procured by the blood of the Lamb." Then he spake as to himself, "Fear not, little flock, it is the Father's good pleasure to give you the kingdom." Then he said, "What are these who are of this little flock? Even sinners. 'I came not to call the righteous, but sinners to repentance.'

But what kind of sinners? Only those who are sensible of sin and wrath, and see themselves to be lost; therefore, says Christ, ' I came to seek and to save them that are lost!' And who are these? Even those who are lost bankrupts, who have nothing to pay. These are they whom Christ seeks, and who are of His flock."

To John Kyle, another morning, he said twice over, " My soul longeth for the Lord more than they that watch for the morning." And at another time, perceiving his father weeping, he said, "I cannot blame you for mourning, for I know that you have thought that I might, with God's blessing, have proved a comfortable child to you ; but comfort yourself in this, that ere it be long I will be at a blessed rest, and in a far better state than I can be in this life, free from sin and every kind of misery, and within a short time ye will follow after me. In the meantime, encourage yourself in the Lord, and let not your mourning be like those who have no hope ; the Lord by degrees will assuage your grief, for so He has appointed, else we would be swallowed up and come to nought. I could never have been removed out of this life in a more seasonable time than now, having both the favour of God and man ; being hopeful that my name shall not be unsavoury when I am gone, for none know what affronts, grief, and calamities I might fall into, did I live much longer in this life. And for crosses and trouble ; how might my life have been made bitter to me ! For when I think what opposition I might have ere I was an actual minister, by divisions of the people, the patron, and the presbytery, it could not but overwhelm me ; and then being entered, what a fighting life with a stubborn people might be my lot, I know not ; and then what discontentment I might have in a wife, which is the lot of many an honest man, is uncertain ; then cares, fears, straits of the world, reproaches of men, personal desires, and the devil and an evil world to fight with—these, and many more, cannot but keep a man in a struggling state in this life. And now, lest this should seem a mere speculation, I could instance these things in the persons of many worthy men ; I pass all, and only point out one, whose gifts and graces are well known to you, namely, Mr David Dickson, whom I am sure God has made the instrument of the conversion of many souls, and of much good to the country, and yet this gracious person has been tossed to and fro. You know that the Lord made him a gracious instrument in this late Reformation, and yet he has, in a great measure, been slighted by the state and the kirk also. What reason have I then to bless God, who in mercy is timeously removing me from all trouble, and will make me as welcome to heaven as if I had preached forty years, for He knows it was my intention, by His grace, to have honoured Him in my ministry. And seeing He has accepted the will for the deed, what reason have I to complain? for now I am willing and ready to be dissolved and to be with Christ, which is best of all; wherefore, dear father, comfort yourself with this."

One time, in conference concerning sin in the godly, his father said to him, "I am sure you are not now troubled with corruption, being so near death." He answered, "Ye are altogether deceived, for so long as my foot remaineth on this earth, though the other were translated above the clouds, my mind would not be free of sinful motions." Whereupon he regretted that he could not get his mind and his affections so lifted up, to dwell or meditate on God, His word, or that endless life, as he could have wished, and that he could not find that spirituality by entertaining such thoughts of God's greatness and goodness as became him, and was often much perplexed with vain thoughts; but he was confident that the Lord, in His rich mercy, would pity and pass by this his weakness and infirmity.

Some time before his death, he fell into several fainting fits. About ten or twelve days before it, having fallen into one, he was speechless near an hour, so that none present had any hope that he would again recover; but, in the meantime, he was wrapt up in divine contemplation. At last he began to recover, and his heart being enlarged, he opened his mouth with such lively exhortations as affected all present, and directing his speech to his father, he said, "Be glad, sir, to see your son, yea, I say, your second son, made a crowned king." And to his mother he said, "Be of good courage, and mourn not for want of me, for you will find me in the all-sufficiency of God." Then he said, "O death, I give thee a defiance, through Jesus Christ;" and then again he said to onlookers, "Sirs, this will be a blythe and joyful good-night."

In the meantime Mr Bell came in, to whom he said, "Sir, you are welcome to be witness to see me fight out my last fight;" after which he fell quiet, and got some rest. Within two days Mr Bell having again come to visit him, he said, "O Sir, but I was glad the last night when you were here, when I thought to be dissolved, that I might have met with my Master, and have enjoyed His presence for ever; but I was much grieved, when I perceived a little reverting, and that I was likely to live longer."

To Mr Gabriel Cunningham, when conferring about death and

the manner of the dissolution, he said, " Oh! how sweet a thing it were for a man to sleep till death in the arms of Christ." He had many other lively and comfortable speeches, which were not remembered, the day never passing, during the time of his sickness, but the on-waiters were refreshed by him.

The night before his departure, he was sensible of great pain; whereupon he said, " I see it is true, that we must enter into heaven through trouble, but the Lord will help us through it." Then he said, " I have great pain, but mixed with great mercy, and strong confidence." He called to mind that saying of John Knox, on his death-bed, " I do not esteem that pain, which will be to me an end of all trouble, and the beginning of eternal felicity."

His last words were these, " Lord, open the gates that I may enter in." And a little after, his father asked what he was doing? Whereupon he lifted up his hands, and caused all his fingers shiver and twinkle, and in presence of many honest neighbours, he yielded up his spirit, and went to his rest, a little after sun-rising, upon the 11th of June 1643, being twenty-three years of age.

Thus, in the bloom of youth, he ended his Christian warfare, and entered into the heavenly inheritance, a young man, but a ripe Christian. There were three special gifts vouchsafed to him by the Lord; a notable invention, a great memory, and a ready expression.

Among other fruits of his meditation and pains, he drew up a model and frame of preaching, which he entitled, " The Method of Preaching." Many other manuscripts he left behind him as evidences of his indefatigable labour, which, if yet preserved in safe custody, might be of no small benefit to the public, as it appears that they have not hitherto been published.

CHURCH AT LEUCHARS.　　　　　　　*From a Photograh by Valentine.*

Alexander Henderson.

WHEN Alexander Henderson had passed his degrees at the university with great applause, he was, by the Archbishop of St Andrews, about the year 1620,* preferred to be minister of Leuchars, in the shire of Fife.　But he was brought in against the consent of the parish, to such a degree, that on the day of his ordination, the church doors were shut so fast by the people, that they were obliged to break in by a window.

He was very prelatical in his judgment at this time ; but a little after, upon the report of a communion service in the neighbourhood, where Robert Bruce was to be a helper, he went thither secretly, and placed himself in a dark corner of the church, where he might not be readily seen or known.　When Bruce was come to the pulpit, he kept silence for some time as his usual manner was, which did astonish Mr Henderson ; but it astonished him much more, when he heard him begin with these words, "He that entereth not in by the door, but climbeth up some other way, the same is a thief and a robber."

* [There is good reason for believing that he entered upon his charge during the year 1615, or perhaps sooner.　He was present at the famous Perth Assembly in 1618, and both spoke and voted against the Articles.—ED.]

This by the blessing of God, and the effectual working of the Holy Spirit, took such hold on him at that very instant, and made such impression on his heart afterwards, as proved the first means of his conversion unto Christ.

After this, he became not only a most faithful and diligent minister of the Gospel, but also a stanch Presbyterian, and had a very active hand in carrying on the covenanted work of Reformation, from the year 1638 to the day of his death. He was among the very first who got a charge of horning preferred against him by the Archbishop of St Andrews, for refusing to buy and use the Service-Book, and the Book of Canons, then imposed by King Charles I. upon the Church. This prompted him, and some others, to give in several petitions and complaints to the Council, both craving some mitigation therein, and showing the sinfulness thereof; for which, and some other considerations and overtures for relief (mostly compiled by Henderson), they were, by order of proclamation, charged, within twenty-four hours, to leave the city of Edinburgh, under pain of rebellion.

[The events which occurred at this time in Scotland were so important in themselves and their consequences, that no apology need be offered for referring to them more fully. In the years 1636 and 1637, a deliberate attempt was made by the King and his advisers to impose the worst and most hated form of Prelacy upon the Scottish Church and nation. First, a book of ecclesiastical canons was sent down from England, and after a little delay this was followed by an Anglo-Popish Liturgy or Service Book, specially prepared under the auspices of Archbishop Laud, and largely impregnated with Romish doctrines and ceremonies. The day fixed for the introduction of the Service Book was the 23d of July 1637, and the events of that day made an impression on the mind of the nation which time has not been able to obliterate. In the Greyfriars Church of Edinburgh, where the Bishop of Argyle officiated, the people gave utterance to their feelings only in tears and groans; but in St Giles, where a similar service was being conducted, an incident occurred, small in itself, but mighty in its results. The Dean of Edinburgh, arrayed in his surplice, had just begun to read the prayers, when an old woman, by name Janet Geddes, snatching up the stool on which she sat, hurled it at his head with the exclamation, "Villain, dost thou say mass at my lug?" This was the spark which alone was needed to produce an explosion which now shook the kingdom to its very centre, and made the Archbishop of St Andrews exclaim, in accents of despair, " All that we have been doing these thirty years past is at once thrown down." No sooner had the tumult in Edinburgh, occasioned by this incident, subsided, than indications were received from other quarters of the impression it had produced. From every part of the kingdom petitions against the innovations were showered upon the Privy Council, and multitudes of every class flocked to the capital, ready to support their petitions, if necessary, with their lives. Even one of the bishops acknowledged that " besides the increase of noblemen who had not been formerly there, there were few or no shires on the south of the Grampian hills from which came not gentlemen, burghers, ministers, and commons." Indeed, so large was the concourse of petitioners that it was found necessary to divide them into four classes (the nobles, gentry, ministers, and burgesses), and to commit the prosecution of their petitions to a certain number of deputies or commissioners, appointed by each of them. This was done with the approbation of the Privy Council, and as these deputies met separately in the Parliament House, and sat around four tables (meeting only from time to time for joint conference) they received the name of " The Tables," a name which occurs again in this book, and which without this explanation it might be difficult to understand. On learning that these petitions, though supported by the Privy Council, had been rejected by the King, and that a proclamation had been issued prohibiting their meetings under pain of rebellion, the noblemen, gentlemen, burgesses, and ministers agreed upon taking another and very decisive step. Remembering that on a former occasion of public danger (A.D. 1580-1) the nation had entered into a solemn Covenant, in which they had bound themselves to defend and support the Protestant religion against any and every enemy, it was resolved to renew this Covenant, adapting it to recent innovations, and the somewhat altered circumstances of the time. This memorable document, which may justly be called the Magna Charta of Scottish liberty, was prepared by Alexander Henderson and Archibald Johnstone, afterwards Lord Warriston. Having been approved by " The Tables," it was publicly subscribed in the Greyfriars Churchyard of Edinburgh, on the last day of February 1638. The occasion was one of intense and absorbing interest. After devotional exercises, conducted by Alexander Henderson (who has been called the Knox of the second Reformation), the Covenant was produced and read, and so great was the enthusiasm of the assembled multitude that they were unable to restrain their feelings. Some wept aloud :

others raised a shout of congratulation ; many added to their signature the words "till death ;" and some more enthusiastic than the rest, opened their veins and subscribed their names with their own blood. This Covenant, the main design of which was to promote the restoration, "by all means lawful, of the purity and liberty of the Gospel, as it was established and professed," before the recent innovations, was afterwards ratified by Act of Parliament in 1641, and made the law of the land. It was also subscribed by Charles II. at his coronation in 1651, although, as the sequel showed, this was only one of the many acts of falsehood and perjury which characterised the life of that wicked king.—Ed.]

When the national confession or Covenant was agreed upon, and sworn unto by almost all ranks in the land, the Marquis of Hamilton was sent by the King to suppress the Covenanters, who, having held several conferences to little or no purpose, at last told them that the Book of Canons and Liturgy would be discharged, on condition they should yield up their Covenant. This proposition did not only displease them, but also made them more vigilant to support and vindicate that solemn deed ; whereupon Mr Henderson was again set to work, and in a short time favoured the public with sufficient grounds and reasons why they could not recede from any part of it.

Some time after this, the Tables erected at Edinburgh for carrying on the work of the Reformation, being sorry that the town and shire of Aberdeen (excited by the persuasion of their doctors) stood out and opposed the Covenant and work of Reformation, sent some Earls, with Messrs Henderson, Dickson, and Cant, to deal with them once more, and try to reclaim that town and county. Upon their arrival there, they could have no access to preach in any church, whereupon the three ministers resolved to preach in the Earl Marischal's close and hall, as the weather favoured them. Accordingly, they preached by turns ; Mr Dickson preached in the morning to a very numerous multitude ; at noon Mr Cant preached ; and Mr Henderson preached at night to no less an auditory than was in the morning ; and all of them pressed and produced arguments for subscribing the Covenant, which had such an effect upon the people, that, after public worship was over, about 500 persons subscribed the Covenant at one table, of whom several were people of the best quality.

And here one thing was very observable, that while Mr Henderson preached, the crowd being very great, there were several mockers.

PORTRAIT OF ALEXANDER HENDERSON.

Among the rest was John Logie, a student, who threw clods at the commissioners; but it was remarked, that within a few days after, he killed one Nichol Torrie, a young boy, because the boy's father had beat him for stealing his peas, and though at that time he escaped justice, yet he was taken and executed in 1644. Such was the consequence of disturbing the worship of God, and mocking at the ambassadors of Jesus Christ.

In the same year, at that famous General Assembly convened at Glasgow, where many of the nobility were present, Mr Henderson, without one contrary vote, was chosen moderator, when he did, by solemn prayer, constitute the Assembly in the name of the Lord Jesus Christ, for, "among that man's other qualifications," said Mr Baillie, "he had a faculty of grave, good, and fervent prayer, which he exercised without fainting unto the end of the Assembly."

[" On the 21st of November," says Mr Baillie in his letters, who was an eye-witness of what he thus describes, "the Assembly convened in the High Church, which day, and for two weeks thereafter, the multitudes assembled were so exceeding great, that the members could not get access without the assistance of the magistrates and town guard, of the nobles and gentry, and sometimes, at first, the Lord Commissioner in person was pleased to make way for the members, but they were well accommodated after they got in. The Lord

GREYFRIARS' CHURCH, EDINBURGH.

Commissioner sat in a chair of state, and at his feet, before and on each side, the Lords of the Privy Council. The Covenanting Lords and Barons sat at a long table in the floor, with their assessors, which consisted of almost the whole Barons of note through Scotland ; and, in general, from all the fifty-three presbyteries, there were three commissioners, except from a very few, who sat all commodiously in seats, rising up by degrees round the long table. A little table was set in the midst for the Moderator and Clerk. At the end was a high room, prepared chiefly for the young nobility, but the same was crowded with great numbers of other gentleman, and the vaults above were filled with ladies and gentlemen. Mr Bell of Glasgow, as the oldest minister, was appointed to preach, a wise choice, which prevented any inflammatory harangue from younger men of fiery zeal and stouter lungs. His sermon was lost to the greater part of the auditory, not above a sixth part of whom could hear him distinctly." According to Crookshanks, the Assembly consisted of 143 ministers, together with professors from the universities, and 95 ruling elders from the presbyteries and burghs. This Assembly was distinguished, not only for the important acts which were passed for completing the work of Reformation, according to the National Covenant sworn in the same year, but also for asserting the inherent right of the church to hold her assemblies independently of civil authority, by continu-ing its sittings after the Marquis of Hamilton, the Lord Commissioner, had thought fit to dissolve it in the King's name. The words of Mr Henderson, the Moderator, on that occasion, were worthy so great a man, and the important and honourable stituation which he filled. " Seeing," said he, " we perceive his Grace, my Lord Commissioner, to be zealous of his royal master's commands, have not we as good reason to be zealous toward our Lord, and to maintain the liberties and privileges of His kingdom ?"—ED.]

It was in the 20th session of this Assembly, that Mr Henderson, the Moderator, after a most pious and learned sermon, to a very great auditory, from Psalm cx. 1, " The Lord said to my lord, sit thou at my right hand," did, in a most grave and solemn manner, excom-municate and depose the bishops, according to the form published among the printed acts of that Assembly. In the 21st session, a supplication was given in for liberty to transport him from Leuchars to Edinburgh, but this he was unwilling to accede to, having been nearly eighteen years minister there. He pled that he was now too old a plant to take root in another soil ; but after much contest betwixt the two parties for some days, Edinburgh carried it by seventy-five votes, very much against his own inclination. However, he submitted, on condition, that when old age should overtake him, he should again be removed to a country charge. At the conclusion of this Assembly, he said, "We have now cast down the walls of Jericho" (meaning Prelacy), "let him that rebuildeth them beware of the curse of Hiel the Bethelite."

In 1639 he was one of those commissioned by the Church, to treat upon the articles of pacification with the King and his commis-sioners, at Birks, near Berwick, where he behaved with great pru-dence and candour.

When the General Assembly, the same year, sat down at Edin-burgh, August 12, Mr Henderson having been the former Moderator, preached to them from Acts v. 33, " When they heard that, they were cut to the heart." Towards the close of his discourse, he addressed John Earl of Traquair, his Majesty's Commissioner, in these words : "We beseech your Grace to see that Cæsar have his own, but let him not have what is due to God, by whom kings reign. God hath exalted your Grace unto many high places within these few years, and is still doing so. Be thankful, and labour to exalt Christ's throne. Some are exalted like Haman, some like Mordecai. . . . . . When the Israelites came up out of Egypt, they gave all the silver and gold they had carried thence for the building of the tabernacle ; in like manner your grace must employ all your parts and endowments for building up the Church of God in this land."

And to the members chosen, he said : " Right honourable, worshipful, and reverend, go on in your zeal and constancy. True zeal doth not cool, but the longer it burns the more fervent it will grow. If it shall please God that by your means the light of the Gospel shall be continued, and that you have the honour of being instrumental of a blessed Reformation, it shall be useful and comfortable to yourselves and your posterity. But let your zeal be always tempered with moderation ; for zeal is a good servant, but a bad master ; like a ship that hath a full sail, but no rudder. We have much need of Christian prudence, for we know what advantage some have attempted to take of us this way. For this reason, let it be seen to the world, that Presbytery, the government we contend for in the Church, can consist very well with Monarchy in the State ; and thereby we shall gain the favour of our King, and God shall get the glory." After this discourse, and the calling of the commissions, Traquair desired that Mr Henderson might be continued Moderator. Whether this was to corroborate his master's design, or from a regard to Henderson's abilities, as he himself professed, is not certain ; but the Assembly opposed this, as savouring too much of the Constant Moderator, the first step taken of late to introduce Prelacy ; and no man opposed Traquair's motion more than Henderson himself, by which means it was overruled.

Alexander Henderson was one of those ministers who went with the Scots army to England, in the year 1640, every regiment having one of the most able ministers, in the bounds where they were raised, as chaplain. When the treaty was set on foot which began at Ripon, and ended at London, he was also nominated as one of the commissioners for the Church ; the duties of which he discharged with great prudence and advantage. The very next year, he was, by the commission of the General Assembly, authorised to go with Lord Loudon, Warriston, and Barclay, to the King, to importune him to call his English Parliament as the only and best expedient to obtain an honourable and lasting peace ; but his embassy had not the desired effect.

After his return, he was chosen moderator to the General Assembly in 1643 ; and when the English commissioners, viz., Sir William Armyn, Sir Harry Vane the younger, Mr Hatcher, and Mr

Darley, from the Parliament; and two ministers, Mr Stephen Marshall, a Presbyterian, and Philip Nye, an Independent, from the Westminster Assembly of Divines, arrived at Edinburgh, where the General Assembly of the Church of Scotland was then sitting, craving their aid and counsel upon such an emergent occasion, he was among the first of those nominated as commissioners, to go up to the Parliament and Assembly of England. And so in a little after, Mr Henderson, and Mr Gillespie, with Mr Hatcher, and Mr Nye, set out for London, to get the Solemn League ratified there, the rest of the commissioners staying behind, until it should be returned.'

[This important document, which Hetherington characterises as "the wisest, the sublimest, and the most sacred ever framed by uninspired men," was the bond of union or alliance between the Covenanters and the English Puritans. It had for its twofold object the defence of the people's civil and religious liberties, and the promotion of uniformity among the churches of England, Scotland, and Ireland. It was drawn up with great care by Henderson, and having been finally adjusted between the Scottish Parliament and the English Commissioners, it was solemnly sworn to and subscribed in St Margaret's Church, Westminster, by the assembled statesmen and divines of England on the 25th September 1643. The following is the analysis which Hallam has given of it in his "Constitutional History of England:" "The Covenant consisted in an oath, to be subscribed by all parties in both kingdoms, whereby they bound themselves to preserve the Reformed religion in the Church of Scotland, in doctrine, worship, discipline, and government, according to the word of God, and practice of the best Reformed Churches; and to endeavour to bring the Churches of God, in the three kingdoms, to the nearest conjunction and uniformity in religion, confession of faith, form of Church government, directory for worship, and catechising; to endeavour, without respect of persons, the extirpation of Popery, Prelacy, and whatsoever should be found contrary to sound doctrine and the power of godliness; to preserve the rights and privileges of the Parliaments, and the liberties of the kingdoms, and the King's person and authority in the preservation and defence of the true religion and liberties of the kingdoms; to endeavour the discovery of incendiaries and malignants, who hinder the reformation of religion, and divide the King from his people, that they may be brought to punishment; finally, to assist and defend all such as should enter into this Covenant, and not suffer themselves to be withdrawn from it, whether to revolt to the opposite party, or to give in to a detestable indifference and neutrality." Such is Hallam's admirable analysis of this important document, usually known as "The Solemn League and Covenant." To be able to form a just estimate of its nature and importance, we must bear in mind the peculiar circumstances of the times, and the cruel and oppressive character of those evils with which our fathers had to contend.—ED.]

Upon their arrival at London, and having received a warrant from the Parliament to sit in the Westminster Assembly (which warrant was presented by Mr Henderson), the Assembly sent out three of their number to introduce them. At their entry, Dr Twisse, the prolocutor, welcomed them into the Assembly, and complimented them for the hazard they had undergone on their account, both by sea and land, in such a rigorous season, it being then November ; after which they were led to a place the most convenient in the house, upon the prolocutor's right hand.

Again, in the year 1646, Henderson was sent down from London to attend the King, who was then with the Scots army at Newcastle, at which time the General Assembly of Scotland appointed also Messrs Robert Blair, James Guthrie, Robert Douglas, and Andrew Cant, to wait on his Majesty. Here Henderson officiated for some time as his chaplain ; and although he and Mr Blair, of all the Presbyterians, were the best beloved of the King, yet they could by no means prevail upon him to grant the first demand of his subjects : yea, he obstinately refused, though they besought him on their knees.

In the interval of these affairs, a series of letters was continued betwixt the King (who was assisted by Sir Robert Murray) on the one hand, and Henderson on the other—the one in defence of Episcopacy, and the other of Presbytery. These were exchanged from the 19th of May to the midst of July, as each person was in readiness. During this controversy, Mr Henderson's constitution being much worn out with fatigue and travel, he was obliged to break off an answer to the King's last paper, and return to Edinburgh, where, in a little time after his arrival, he laid down his earthly tabernacle in exchange for a heavenly crown, about the middle of August 1646.

Some of the abettors of Prelacy, sensible of his great abilities, were earnestly desirous to bring him over to their side at his death ; and for that purpose palmed upon the world most groundless stories of his changing his principles at his last hours. Yea, the anonymous author of the " Civil Wars of Great Britain " goes further, when

HENDERSON'S MONUMENT IN GREYFRIARS' CHURCHYARD.

he says: "Mr Henderson had the honour to be converted by his Majesty's discourse at Newcastle, and died reconciled to the Church of England." But from these false calumnies he hath been sufficiently vindicated a long time ago, by a declaration in the 9th Act of the General Assembly in 1648.

Some time after his death, a monument was erected on his grave, in the Greyfriars' Churchyard of Edinburgh, in form of a quadrangular urn, inscribed on three sides; and because there was some mention thereon of the Solemn League and Covenant, or rather because Mr Henderson had done much for and in behalf of the Covenant, Commissioner Middleton, some time in June or July 1662, stooped so low as to procure an order of Parliament to raze and demolish it. This was all the length their malice could go against a man who had been nearly sixteen years in his grave. Hard enough (if he had died in the Prelatical persuasion), from those who pretended to be the chief promoters of the same! This monument was afterwards repaired, and now stands entire, a little to the westward of the Church.

Mr Henderson was a man who spared no pains in carrying on the work of Reformation in the land; for whether he was called forth to church-judicatories, to the pulpit, or any other business, no trouble or danger could make him decline the work. One of his colleagues and intimate acquaintances, Mr Baillie, in his speech to the General Assembly, 1647, gives him no mean testimony when he says : " May I be permitted to conclude with my earnest wish, that that glorious soul of worthy memory, who is now crowned with the reward of all his labours for God and us, may be fragrant among us, as long as free and pure Assemblies remain in this land, which I hope shall be till the coming of our Lord. You know he spent his strength, wore out his days, and did breathe out his life in the service of God, and of this Church. This binds it on us and posterity to account him the fairest ornament, after John Knox of incomparable memory, that ever the Church of Scotland did enjoy."

Besides being author of the forenamed papers, with another entitled The Remonstrance of the Nobility, a Tract on Church Government, and an Instruction for Defensive Arms, the General Assembly appointed him, along with Mr Calderwood and Mr Dickson, to prepare a Directory for the worship of God ; which not only had the desired effect, but at length brought about uniformity in all our Churches. There are also some few of his sermons in print, some of which were preached before the Parliament.

George Gillespie.

EORGE GILLESPIE was the son of Mr John Gillespie, some time minister of the Gospel at Kirkcaldy. After he had been for some time at the University, where he surpassed the most part of his fellow-students, he was licensed to preach some time before the year 1638, but could have no entry into any parish, because the Bishops had then the ascendant in the affairs of the Church. This obliged him to remain for some time chaplain in the family of the Earl of Cassilis. Here it was that he wrote that elaborate piece, though he was scarcely twenty-five years

ST GILES, NORTH VIEW.

of age, entitled " A Dispute against the English Popish Ceremonies,"
which book was, in the year 1637, discharged, by order of proclamation, from being used, as being of too corrosive a quality to be
digested by the Bishops' weak stomachs.

After this, he was ordained minister of Wemyss, by Mr Robert
Douglas, April 26, 1638, being the first who was admitted by a presbytery at that period without an acknowledgment of the Bishops. And
now Gillespie began in a more public way to exert himself in defence
of the Presbyterian interest, when, at the 11th session of that venerable Assembly, held at Glasgow, 1638, he preached a very learned
and judicious sermon from these words : " The King's heart is in the
hand of the Lord." In this sermon, the Earl of Argyle thought that
he touched the royal prerogative too near, and did very gravely
admonish the Assembly concerning the same ; which they all took
in good part, as appeared from a discourse then made by the Moderator, for the support of that admonition.

At the General Assembly held at Edinburgh, 1641, Gillespie had
a call tabled from the town of Aberdeen, but the Lord Commissioner
and himself pled his cause so well, that he was for some time continued at Wemyss. Yet he got not staying there long ; for the
General Assembly, in the following year, ordered him to be trans-

WESTMINSTER ABBEY.

lated to the city of Edinburgh, where it appears he continued until the day of his death, about six years after.

George Gillespie was one of those four ministers who were sent as commissioners from the Church of Scotland to the Westminster Assembly, in the year 1643, where he showed himself to be one of great parts and learning, debating with such perspicuity, strength of argument, and calmness of spirit, that few could equal, yea, none excel him, in that Assembly. As for instance, one time, when both the Parliament and the Assembly were met together, and a long studied discourse being made in favour of Erastianism, to which none seemed ready to make an answer, Gillespie, being urged thereunto by his brethren the Scots commissioners, repeated the subjectmatter of the whole discourse, and refuted it, to the admiration of all present. And that which surprised them most was, that though it was usual for the members to take down notes of what was spoken in the Assembly for the help of their memory, and though Gillespie seemed to be so employed during the time of the speech; yet those who sat next him declared, that having looked into his note-book, they found nothing of that speech written, but here and there, " Lord, send light—Lord, give assistance—Lord, defend Thine own cause."

And although the practice of our Church gave all the Scots commissioners great advantages (the English divines having so great a difference) in that they had the first forming of all these documents which were afterwards compiled and approved of by that Assembly, yet no one was more useful in supporting them therein than George Gillespie, the youngest of them. "None," says one of his colleagues, Robert Baillie, "in all the Assembly did reason more, nor more pertinently, than Mr Gillespie: he is an excellent youth; my heart blesses God in his behalf." Again, he states that when Acts xiv. 23 was brought for the proof of the power of ordination, and keen disputing arose upon it, "the very learned and accurate Gillespie, a singular ornament to our Church, than whom not one in the Assembly spoke to better purpose, nor with better acceptance of all the hearers, showed that the Greek word by the Episcopals purposely translated *ordination*, was truly *choosing*, importing the people's suffrage in selecting their own office-bearers." And elsewhere he says, "We get good help in our Assembly debates of Lord Warriston, an occasional commissioner, but of none more than that noble youth Mr Gillespie. I admire his gifts, and bless God, as for all my colleagues, so for him in particular, as equal in these to the first in the Assembly."

After his return from the Westminster Assembly, he was employed mostly in the public affairs of the church, until the year 1648, when he was chosen Moderator of the General Assembly of Scotland; in which Assembly several famous acts were made in favour of the covenanted work of Reformation, particularly that against the unlawful engagement then made against England by the Duke of Hamilton and those of the malignant faction. In this Assembly he was one of those nominated to prosecute the treaty of uniformity in religion with England; but in a short time after this, the sickness seized him whereof he died about the 17th of December following.

Samuel Rutherford writes to him, when on his death-bed, "Be not heavy; the life of faith is now called for; doing was never reckoned on your accounts, though Christ in and by you hath done more than by twenty, yea, an hundred grey-haired and godly pastors. Look to that word, Gal. ii. 20: 'Nevertheless, I live; yet not I, but Christ liveth in me.'"

In his lifetime, Gillespie was always firmly attached to the work of Reformation, and continued so to the end of his life. About two months before his decease, he sent a paper to the Commission of the General Assembly, wherein he gave faithful warning against every sin and backsliding that he then perceived to be growing both in Church and State. And last of all, he emitted the following faithful testimony against association and compliance with the enemies of truth and true godliness, in these words :

"Seeing now, in all appearance, the time of my dissolution draweth near, although I have in my latter will declared my mind of public affairs, yet I have thought good to add this further testimony, that I esteem the malignant party in these kingdoms to be the seed of the serpent, enemies to piety and Presbyterian government (pretend what they will to the contrary), a generation who have not set God before them. With the malignant are to be joined the profane and scandalous ; from all which, as from heresy and error, the Lord, I trust, is about to purge His church. I have often comforted myself, and still do, with the hopes of the Lord's purging this polluted land. Surely the Lord hath begun, and will carry on that great work of mercy, and will purge out the rebels. I know there will be always a mixture of hypocrites, but that cannot excuse the conniving at gross and scandalous sinners. . . . I recommend to them that fear God, seriously to consider, that the Holy Scriptures do plainly hold forth : 1. That the helping of the enemies of God, joining or mingling with wicked men, is a sin highly displeasing ; 2. That this sin hath ordinarily ensnared God's people into divers other sins ; 3. That it hath been punished of God with grievous judgments ; and, 4. That utter destruction is to be feared, when a people, after great mercies and judgments, relapse into this sin (Ezra ix. 13, 14) :

"Upon these and the like grounds, for my own exoneration, that so necessary a truth want not the testimony of a dying witness of Christ, although the unworthiest of many thousands, and that light may be held forth, and warning given, I cannot be silent at this time, but speak by my pen when I cannot by my tongue ; yea, now also by the pen of another, when I cannot by my own ; seriously, and in the name of Jesus Christ, exhorting and obtesting all that fear God, and make conscience of their ways, to be very tender and circumspect, to watch and pray, that they be not ensnared in that great and dangerous sin of compliance with malignant or profane enemies of the truth. . . . . . which if men will do, and trust God in His own way, they shall not only not repent it, but, to the greater joy and peace of God's people, they shall see His work go on and prosper gloriously. In witness of the premises, I have subscribed the same. At Kirkcaldy, December 15, 1648, before these witnesses." In about two days after he gave up the ghost, death shutting his eyes, that he might then see God, and be for ever with Him.

Thus died George Gillespie, very little past the prime of life; a pregnant divine, a man of much boldness, and great freedom of expression. He signalised himself on every occasion where he was called forth to exercise any part of his ministerial function. No man's death, at that time, was more lamented than his; and such was the sense the public had of his merit, that the Committee of Estates, by an act dated December 20, 1648, did, "as an acknowledgment for his faithfulness in all the public employments entrusted to him by this church, both at home and abroad, his faithful labours, and indefatigable diligence in all the exercises of his ministerial calling for his Master's service, and his learned writings published to the world, in which rare and profitable employments, both for Church and State, he truly spent himself, and closed his days, ordain, That the sum of one thousand pounds sterling be given to his widow and children." But though the Parliament did, by their act, dated June 8, 1650, unanimously ratify the above act, and recommended to their committee to make the same effectual; yet, the usurper Cromwell, presently overrunning the country, this good design was frustrated, as his grandson, the Rev. George Gillespie, minister at Strathmiglo, did afterwards declare.

Besides the " English Popish Ceremonies," already mentioned, he wrote also " Aaron's Rod Blossoming," and his " Miscellaneous Questions," first printed in 1649; all which, with the fore-cited testimony and some other papers, show that he was a man of most profound parts, learning, and abilities.

KIRKCUDBRIGHT.

John M'Clelland.

OHN M'CLELLAND having gone through several branches of useful learning, kept a school for some time at Newton, in Ireland, where he became instrumental in training up several hopeful young men for the university. Afterwards he was tried and approved of by the honest ministers in the county of Down, and being licensed, he preached in their churches, until, among others, for faithfulness, he was deposed and excommunicated by the Bishops.

He was also engaged with the rest of his faithful brethren in their intended voyage to New England, in the year 1636; but that enterprise proving abortive, by reason of a storm, which forced them to return back to Ireland, he preached for some time through the counties of Down, Tyrone, and Donegal, in private meetings, till being pursued by the Bishops' official, he was obliged to come over in disguise to Scotland, where, about the year 1638, he was admitted minister at Kirkcudbright, in which place he continued till the day of his death.

It would appear that he was married to one of Mr Livingstone's wife's sisters, and the strictest friendship subsisted betwixt these two worthy men, both while in Ireland, and after their return to Scotland. While he was at Kirkcudbright, he discovered more than ordinary diligence, not only in testifying against the corruptions of the time, but also in his own singular walk and conversation, being one who was set for the advancement of all the practical parts of religion, as well in public as in private duties. For instance, when Mr Henry Guthrie, then minister at Stirling (but afterwards Bishop of Dunkeld), thought to have brought in a complaint to the General Assembly, 1639, against private society meetings, which were then become numerous through the land, some of the leading members, knowing that Guthrie did it partly out of resentment against the laird of Leckie, who was a great practiser and defender of these meetings, thought proper, rather than that it should come to the Assembly, to agree that Guthrie should preach up the duty of religious exercise in families, and that Messrs M'Clelland, Blair, and Livingstone, should preach against night meetings and other abuses. These brethren endeavoured, by conference, to gain such as had offended by excess in this matter, but by no means could be prevailed on to preach against them; which so offended Guthrie, that he gave in a charge or complaint to the General Assembly, 1640, wherein he alleged that these three ministers were the only encouragers of the meetings. M'Clelland roundly took him up, and craved that a committee might be appointed to try these disorders, and to censure the offenders, whether those complained of, or the complainers; which so nettled Guthrie, the Earl of Seaforth, and others of their fraternity, that nothing was heard in the Assembly for some time for confusion and noise stirred up by them.

John M'Clelland was also one who was endued with the spirit of discerning what should afterwards come to pass, as is evident from some of his prophetical expressions, particularly that letter which he wrote to John, Lord of Kirkcudbright, dated February 20, 1649, a little before his death, an abstract of which may not be improper, and is as follows:

"MY NOBLE LORD, I received yours, and do acknowledge my obligation to your Lordship is redoubled. I long much to hear what decision followed on that debate concerning patronages. Upon the most exact trial, they will be found a great plague to the kirk, an obstruction to the propagation of religion. I have reason to hope that such a wise and well-constituted Parliament will be loath to lay such a yoke upon the churches, of so little advantage to any man, and so prejudicial to the work of God, as hath been many times represented.   Certainly the removing of it were the stopping the way of simony, except we will apprehend that whole presbyteries will be bribed for patronage.   I can say no more but what Christ said to the Pharisees, ' It was not so from the beginning;' the primitive Church knew nothing of it.

"But as for their pernicious disposition to a rupture among sectaries, I can say nothing to them; only this, I conclude their judgment sleeps not.   'Shall they escape, shall they break the covenant, and be delivered?' (Ezek. xvii. 15); which I dare apply to England, I hope, without wresting of Scripture.   'Therefore thus saith the Lord God : As I live, surely mine oath that he hath despised, and covenant that he hath broken, even it will I recompense upon his own head (Ezek. xvii. 19).'   This covenant was made with Nebuchadnezzar; the matter was civil, but the tie was religious; wherefore the Lord owns it as His covenant, because God's name was invoked and interponed in it; and he calls England to witness.   England's covenant was not made with Scotland only, but with the high and mighty God, principally for the reformation of His house, and it was received in the most solemn manner that I have heard; so that they may call it God's covenant both formally and materially : and the Lord did second the making of it with more than ordinary success to that nation.   Now, it is manifestly despised and broken in the sight of all nations; therefore, it remains that the Lord avenge the quarrel of his covenants.   England hath had to do with the Scots, French, Danes, Picts, Normans, and Romans, but they never had such a party to deal with as the Lord of armies, pleading for the violation of His Covenant. . . . Englishmen shall be made spectacles to all nations for a broken Covenant, when the living God swears; 'As I live, even the Covenant that he hath despised, and the oath that he hath broken, will I recompense upon his own head.'   There is no place left for doubting.   'Hath the Lord said it, hath the Lord sworn it? and will he not do it?'   His assertion is a ground for faith, His oath a ground of full assurance of faith : if all England were as one man united in judgment and affection, and if it had a wall round about it reaching to the sun, and if it had as many armies as it has men, and every soldier had the strength of Goliath, and if their navies could cover the ocean, and if there were none to peep out or move the tongue against them, yet I dare not doubt of their destruction; when the Lord hath sworn by His life, that He will avenge the breach of Covenant. When, and by whom, and in what manner He will do it, I do profess ignorance, and leave it to his glorious Majesty, his own latitude, and will commit it to Him.

"My Lord, I live and will die, and if I be called home before that time, I am in the assured hopes of the ruin of all God's enemies in the land; so I commit your Lordship and your Lady to the grace of God.   JOHN M'CLELLAND."

A very little after he had written this letter, in one of his sermons he expressed himself much to the same purpose, thus: "The judgments of England shall be so great, that a man shall ride fifty miles through the best plenished parts of England before he hear a cock crow, a dog bark, or see a man's face." Also, he farther asserted, that if he had the best land of all England, he would make sale of it for two shillings the acre, and think he had come to a good market. And although this may not have had its full accomplishment as yet, yet there is ground to believe that it will be fulfilled; for the Lord will not alter the word that is gone out of His mouth.

John M'Clelland continued nearly twelve years at Kirkcudbright. About the year 1650 he was called home to his Father's house, to the full fruition of that which he had before seen in vision.

He was a man most strict and zealous in his life, and knew not what it was to be afraid of any man in the cause of God, being one who was most nearly acquainted with Him, and knew much of his Master's will. Surely the Lord doeth nothing but what He revealeth to His servants the prophets.

A little before his death he made the following epitaph on himself :—

> Come, stingless death, have o'er, lo! here's my pass,
> In blood character'd, by His hand who was,
> And is, and shall be. Jordan, cut thy stream;
> Make channels dry. I bear my Father's name
> Stamp'd on my brow. I'm ravished with my crown,
> I shine so bright. Down with all glory, down,
> That world can give. I see the peerless port,
> The golden street, the blessed soul's resort,
> The tree of life. Floods, gushing from the throne,
> Call me to joys. Begone, short woes, begone;
> I live to die, but now I die to live;
> I do enjoy more than I did believe.
> The promise me into possession sends;
> Faith in fruition, hope in having, ends.

JEDBURGH ABBEY.

David Calderwood.

AVID CALDERWOOD, having spent some time at the grammar-school, went to the university to study theology, in order for the ministry. After a short space, being found fit for that office, he was made minister of Crailing, near Jedburgh, where for some considerable time he preached the word of God with great wisdom, zeal, and diligence, and as a faithful wise husbandman brought in many sheaves into God's granary. But it being then a time when prelacy was upon the advance in the Church, and faithful ministers were everywhere thrust out and suppressed, he, among the rest, gave in his declinature in the year 1608, and thereupon took instruments in the hands of James Johnston, notary-public, in presence of some of the magistrates and council of the town. Whereupon, information being sent to King James VI. by the bishops, a direction was sent down to the council to punish him, and another minister who declined, exemplarily; but by the earnest dealing of the Earl of Lothian with the Chancellor in favour of Mr Calderwood, their punishment resolved itself only into confinement within their own parishes.

Here he continued until June 1617, when he was summoned to

appear before the High Commission Court at St Andrews, upon the 8th of July following. Being called upon (the King being present), and his libel read and answered, the King, among other things, said, "What moved you to protest?" "An article concluded among the Lords of the Articles," Mr Calderwood answered. "But what fault was there in it?" said the King. "It cutteth off our General Assemblies," he answered. The King, having the protestation in his hand, challenged him for some words of the last clause thereof. He answered, that whatsoever was the phrase of speech, it meant no other thing but to protest that they would give passive obedience to his Majesty, but could not give active obedience unto any unlawful thing which should flow from that article. "Active and passive obedience?" said the King. "That is, we will rather suffer than practise," said Calderwood. "I will tell thee," said the King, "what is obedience, man; what the centurion said to his servant, To this man, Go, and he goeth, and to that man, Come, and he cometh; that is obedience." He answered, "To suffer, Sire, is also obedience, howbeit not of the same kind; and that obedience was not absolute, but limited, with the exception of a countermand from a superior power." "I am informed," said the King, "ye are a refractor; the Archbishop of Glasgow your ordinary, the Bishop of Caithness, the Moderator, and your presbytery, testify ye have kept no order; ye have repaired to neither presbytery nor synod, and are no way conform." He answered, "I have been confined these eight or nine years, so my conformity or nonconformity in that point could not well be known." "Gude faith! thou art a very knave," said the King. "See these same false puritans, they are ever playing with equivocations." The King asked, whether, if he was released, he would obey or not? He answered, "I am wronged in that I am forced to answer such questions, which are beside the libel;" after which he was removed.

When called in again, it was intimated to him, that if he did not repair to synods and presbyteries between this and October, conform during that time, and promise obedience in all time coming, the Archbishop of Glasgow was to deprive him. Then Calderwood begged leave to speak to the bishops; which being granted, he reasoned thus; "Neither can ye suspend or deprive me in this Court of High Commission, for ye have no power in this court but by commission from his Majesty; and his Majesty cannot communicate that power to you which he claims not to himself." At this the King wagged his head, and said to him, "Are there not bishops and fathers in the church, persons clothed with power and authority to suspend and depose?" "Not in this court," answered Calderwood; at which words there arose a confused noise, so that he was obliged to extend his voice, that he might be heard. In the end the King asked him, if he would obey the sentence? To which he answered, "Your sentence is not the sentence of the Kirk, but a sentence null in itself, and therefore I cannot obey it." At this some, reviling, called him a proud knave; others were not ashamed to shake his shoulders, in a most insolent manner, till at last he was removed a second time.

Being again called in, the sentence of deprivation was pronounced, and he was ordained to be committed to close ward in the tolbooth of St Andrews, till farther orders were taken for his banishment; after which he was upbraided by the Archbishop, who said, that he deserved to be used as Ogilvy the Jesuit, who was hanged. When he would have answered, the bishops would not allow him, and the King, in a rage, cried, "Away with him;" and Lord Scone, taking him by the arm, led him out, where they stayed some time waiting for the bailiffs of the town. In the meantime Calderwood said to Scone, "My lord, this is not the first like turn that hath fallen into your hands." "I must serve the King," said Scone. To some ministers then standing by, Calderwood said, "Brethren, ye have Christ's cause in hand at this meeting; be not terrified with this spectacle, prove faithful servants to your Master." Scone took him to his house till the keys of the tolbooth were had. By the way one demanded, "Whither with the man, my lord?" "First to the tolbooth, and then to the gallows," said Scone.

He was committed close prisoner, and the same afternoon a charge was given to transport him to the jail of Edinburgh. After the charge, he was delivered to two of the guard to be transported thither, although several offered to bail him, that he might not go out of the country. But no order of Council could be had for that end, for the King had a design to keep him in close ward till a ship was ready to convey him first to London, and then to Virginia; but Providence had ordered otherwise; for, upon several petitions in his behalf, he was liberated from prison, Lord Cranston being bail that he should depart out of the country.

After this, Calderwood went with Lord Cranston to the King at Carlisle, where the said Lord presented a petition to him, that Mr David might only be confined to his parish; but the King inveighed against him so much, that at last he repulsed Cranston with his elbow. He insisted again for a prorogation of time for his departure till the last of April, because of the winter-session, that he might have leisure to get up his year's stipend. The King answered, that however he begged, it were no matter; he would know himself better the next time; and, for the season of the year, if he drowned in the seas, he might thank God that he had escaped a worse death. Yet Cranston being so importunate for the prorogation, the King answered, "I will advise with my bishops." Thus the time was delayed until the year 1619, that he wrote a book, called "Perth Assembly," which was condemned by the Council in December that same year; but, as he himself says, neither the book nor the author could be found, for in August preceding he had embarked for Holland.

During his abode there, Patrick Scot, a landed gentleman near Falkland, having wasted his patrimony, had no other means to recover his estate, but by some unlawful shift at Court; and for that end in the year 1624, he set forth a recantation, under the name of David Calderwood, who, because of his long sickness before, was supposed by many to have been dead. The King (as Scot alleged to some of his friends), furnished him with the matter, and he set it down in form. This project failing, Scot went over to Holland, in November, and sought Calderwood in several towns, particularly in Amsterdam, in order to despatch him, as afterwards appeared. After he had stayed twenty days in Amsterdam, making all the search he could, he was informed that Calderwood had returned home privately to his native country, which frustrated his intention. After the death of King James, Scot published a pamphlet full of this, entitled *Vox vera;* and yet, notwithstanding of all his wicked and unlawful pursuits, he died soon after, so poor that he left not wherewith to defray the charges of his funeral.

David Calderwood being now returned home, after the death of King James VI., remained as private as possible, and was mostly at Edinburgh, where he strengthened the hands of nonconformists, being also a great opposer of sectarianism, until after the year 1638, when he was admitted minister of Pencaitland, in East Lothian.

He contributed very much to the covenanted work carried on in that period. For first he had an active hand in drawing up several excellent papers, wherein were contained the records of church-policy betwixt the year 1576 and 1596, which were presented and read by Mr Johnston, the clerk, at the General Assembly at Glasgow, in

1638. He was also, by recommendation of the General Assembly 1646, required to consider the order of the visitation of kirks, and trials of Presbyteries, and to make report thereof unto the next General Assembly; and likewise, at the General Assembly 1648, a further recommendation was given to him, to make a draft of the form of visitation of particular congregations, against the next Assembly. He was also one of those appointed, with Mr David Dickson, to draw up the form of the Directory for the public worship of God, by the General Assembly 1643.

After he had both spent and been spent, with the apostle, for the cause and interest of Jesus Christ, when the English army lay at Lothian in 1651, he went to Jedburgh, where he sickened, and died in a good old age. He was another valiant champion for the truth, who, in pleading for the crown and interest of Jesus Christ, knew not what it was to be daunted by the face and frowns of the highest and most incensed adversaries.

Before he went to Holland, he wrote the book entitled, "Perth Assembly." While in Holland, he wrote that learned book called *Altare Damascenum*, with some other pieces in English, which contributed somewhat to keep many straight in that declining period. After his return, he wrote the history of our Church as far down as the year 1625, of which the printed copy that we have is only a short abstract of that large *written* history, which both as to the style and the manner wherein it is executed, is far preferable to the printed copy. Whoever compares the two, or the last, with his *Altare Damascenum*, both of which are yet in the hands of some, will readily grant the truth of this assertion; and yet all this derogates nothing from the truth of the facts reported in the printed copy; and therefore no offence need be taken at the information, that there is a more full and better copy than has yet been printed.

[This better copy, which is here referred to, has since been published by the Wodrow Society in seven volumes. These form an interesting memorial of him whom Baillie describes as "that living magazine of our ecclesiastical history, most Reverend Master Calderwood." From the valuable appendix contained in the eighth volume, we borrow the following elegy on his death.—ED.]

> " The Wood is fallin, the Church not built,
>   Nor Reformation endit ;
>   The Cedar great is now cutt doun,
>   Who first that Work intendit.

" By toung and pen he did not fear
    T' oppose proud Prelacie ;
His Scriptural arguments did prevail
    Against their Hierarchie.

" Both Sectaries and Schismaticks
    He did convince with reasoun ;
His Lyff and Papers weil record
    He did abhor their treasoun,

" Sing hymnes of joy, sweit soul, in peace,
    Unto thy great Redeemer ;
Untill this persecuted clay
    Be joyn'd with Thee for ever."

WEST PORT, ST ANDREWS.

GLASGOW COLLEGE.

Hugh Binning.

HUGH BINNING was son of John Binning of Dalvennan, and Margaret M'Kell, daughter of Matthew M'Kell, minister of Bothwell, and sister of Hugh M'Kell, one of the ministers of Edinburgh. His father's worldly circumstances were so good (being possessed of no inconsiderable estate in the shire of Ayr) that he was enabled to give his son Hugh a very liberal education, the good effects of which appeared very early upon him ; for the greatness of his spirit and capacity of judgment gave his parents good grounds to conceive the pleasing hope of his being a promising child.

While he was at the grammar school, he made so great proficiency in the knowledge of the Latin tongue, and the Roman authors, that he outstripped his fellow-scholars, even such as were by some years older than himself. When they went to their diversions, he declined their society, and chose to employ himself either in secret duty with God, or conference with religious people, thinking time was too precious to be lavished away in these things. He began to have sweet familiarity with God, and to live in near communion with Him, before others of his years began seriously to lay to heart their lost and undone state and condition by nature; so that before he arrived at the thirteenth or fourteenth year of his age, he had even attained to such experience in the ways of God, that the most judicious and exercised Christians in the place confessed they were much edified, strengthened, and comforted by him; nay, he provoked them to diligence in the duties of religion, being abundantly sensible that they were much outrun by such a youth.

Before he was fourteen years of age, he entered upon the study of philosophy in the University of Glasgow, wherein he made very considerable progress, by which means he came to be taken notice of in the college by the professors and students, and at the same time advanced remarkably in religion also. The abstruse depths of philosophy, which are the torture of a slow genius and a weak capacity, he dived into without any pain or trouble; so that, by his ready apprehension of things, he was able to do more in one hour than some others could do in many days by hard study and close application; and yet he was ever humble, and never exalted with self-conceit, the common foible of young men.

As soon as his course of philosophy was finished, he obtained the degree of Master of Arts with great applause; and began the study of divinity with a view to serve God in the holy ministry. At this time there happened to be a vacancy in the chair of Philosophy at the college of Glasgow, by the resignation of Mr James Dalrymple of Stair, who had for some time been his master; and though Binning was but lately his scholar, yet he determined, after much entreaty, to stand as a candidate for that post. According to the usual laudable custom, the masters of the college emitted a programme, and sent it to all the universities of the kingdom, inviting such as had a mind for a professorship of philosophy, to sist themselves before them, and offer to compete for the preferment; giving assurance, that without partiality the place would be conferred upon him who should be found most worthy and most learned.

The ministers of the city of Glasgow, considering how much it was the interest of the Church that well qualified persons should be put into the profession of philosophy, and knowing that Mr Binning was eminently pious, and of a bright genius, as well as of solid judgment, requested him to sist himself among the other competitors. They had difficulty to overcome his modesty, but at last prevailed upon him to declare his willingness to undertake the dispute before the masters. Among others, there were two candidates, one of

GLASGOW COLLEGE, OUTER QUADRANGLE.

whom had the advantage of having great interest with Dr Strang, principal of the college at that time; and the other, a scholar of great ability; yet Mr Binning so managed the dispute, and so acquitted himself in all parts of his trial, that, to the conviction of the judges, he distanced his rivals, and threw them completely into the shade. But the doctor, and some of the faculty who joined him, though they could not pretend that the person they inclined to prefer had an equality, much less a superiority, in the dispute, yet argued, that this person they intended was a citizen's son, of a competency of learning, and a person of more years, and by that means had greater experience than what Mr Binning, who was in a manner but of yesterday, could be supposed to have. To this it was replied, that Mr Binning was such a pregnant scholar, so wise and sedate, as to be above all the follies and vanities of youth, and what was wanting in years was made up sufficiently by his more than ordinary and singular endowments. Whereupon, a member of the faculty, perceiving the struggle to be great (as, indeed, there were plausible reasons on both sides), proposed a dispute betwixt the two candidates *extempore*, upon any subject they should be pleased to prescribe. This being considered, soon put a period to the division amongst them, and those who had opposed him, not being willing to engage their friend with such an able antagonist a second time, Mr Binning was elected.

Binning was not quite nineteen years of age when he became regent and professor of philosophy; and though he had not time to prepare a system of any part of his profession, as he had instantly to begin his class, yet such was the quickness and fertility of his invention, the tenacity of his memory, and the solidity of his judgment, that his dictates to his scholars had depth of learning, and perspicuity of expression. He was among the first in Scotland who began to reform philosophy from the barbarous terms and unintelligible jargon of the schoolmen.

Binning continued in this profession three years, and discharged his trust so as to gain the general applause of the university for academical exercises; and this was the more remarkable, for, having turned his thoughts towards the ministry, he carried on his theological studies at the same time, and made great improvements therein ; his memory being so retentive that he scarcely forgot anything he had read or heard. It was easy and ordinary for him to transcribe any sermon, after he returned to his chamber, at such a length that the intelligent and judicious reader, who had heard it preached, would not find one sentence wanting.

During this period, he gave full proof of his progress and knowledge in divinity, by a composition from 2 Cor. v. 14, " For the love of Christ constraineth us," which performance he sent to a gentlewoman, who had been some time at Edinburgh, for her private edification. Having perused the same, she judged it to have been a sermon of some eminent minister in the west of Scotland, and put it into the hands of the then provost of Edinburgh, who judged of it in the same manner; but when she returned to Glasgow she found her mistake, by Mr Binning asking it from her. This was the first discovery he had given of his dexterity and ability in explaining the Scriptures.

At the expiration of three years as a professor of philosophy, the parish of Govan, which lies adjacent to the city of Glasgow, happened to be vacant. Before this time, whoever was Principal of the College of Glasgow, was also minister there ; but this being attended with inconveniences, an alteration was made ; and the presbytery having a view to supply that vacancy with Mr Binning, took him upon trials, in order to be licensed a preacher. Having preached there to the great satisfaction of the people, he was some time after called to be minister of Govan ; which call the presbytery approved of, and entered him upon trials for ordination about the twenty-second year of his age. These he went through to the unanimous approbation of the presbytery, who gave their testimony to his fitness to be one of the ministers of the city upon the first vacancy, having a view at the same time to bring him back to the university, whenever the professorship of divinity should be vacant.

He was, considering his age, a prodigy of learning, for before he had arrived at the twenty-sixth year of his life, he had such a large stock of useful knowledge, as to be *philologus, philosophus, et theologus eximius* (philologist, philosopher, and excellent theologian), and might well have been an ornament to the most famous and flourishing university in Europe. This was the more surprising, considering his weakness and infirmity of body, as not being able to read much at a time, nor to undergo the fatigue of continual study; insomuch that his knowledge seemed rather to have been born with him, than to have been acquired by hard and laborious study.

Though he was bookish and much intent upon the fulfilling of his ministry, yet he turned his thoughts to marriage, and did espouse a virtuous and excellent person, Barbara Simpson, daughter of Mr James Simpson, a minister in Ireland. Upon the day he was to be married, he went, accompanied with his friend and some others (among whom were several worthy ministers), unto an adjacent country congregation, upon the day of the weekly sermon. The minister of the parish delayed sermon till they would come, hoping to put the work upon one of them; but all declining it, he tried next to prevail on the bridegroom, with whom he succeeded, though the invitation was not expected. It was no difficult task to him to preach upon a short warning. Stepping aside a little to premeditate, and implore his Master's presence and assistance (for he was ever afraid to be alone in this work), he entered the pulpit immediately, and preached upon 1 Pet. i. 15 : " But as He that called you is holy," etc. At which time he was so remarkably helped, that all acknowledged that God was with him of a truth.

When the unhappy differences occurred betwixt the Resolutioners and Protesters, Binning espoused the cause of the latter party.

[This serious division is so often referred to in the present volume, that a few explanatory remarks regarding it may here be introduced with advantage. The origin of the controversy may be traced as far back as the year 1647. In that year, when it became known that King Charles I. was a prisoner in the hands of the English, the tide of feeling, which had run strong against him for a considerable time, began to turn in his favour. A party was formed, headed by the Marquis of Hamilton, and supported by almost all the nobles, except Argyle, for the purpose of delivering the king from his unworthy bondage, and restoring him to his constitutional rights and privileges. The best of the Covenanters foresaw the danger, and sounded the alarm; but nothing could resist the tide of loyalty which had now set in, and already swept with mighty force over the land. The Marquis of Hamilton was soon at the head of an army, consisting not only of the old Royalists, but of many who had signed the Covenant. With this army he entered England, but was soon totally routed by Cromwell at the battle of Preston. This defeat, while it extinguished the hopes of his party, also widened the breach which had already been made between them and those who had stood aloof from their movement, and whom they not unnaturally blamed for their want of success. The once united body of Covenanters was thus split into two great parties: the Engagers, so called from the engagement which the Marquis of Hamilton had entered into with the king, and the strict Covenanters, who were under the leadership of Warriston and Argyle. This breach was still further widened by an Act passed in the Parliament of 1649, called the "Act of Classes," according to which the various classes of Malignants (as they were called) or Engagers, were declared incapable of holding any office of public trust or employment for a longer or shorter period. The immediate result of this Act was to throw the entire management of public affairs into the hands of the strict Covenanters; but these having taken up the cause of King Charles II., and having been defeated by Cromwell at the fatal battle of Dunbar (Sept. 1, 1650), the Engagers returned to power, the "Act of Classes" was repealed, and a new army was levied, which to a great extent was commanded, officered, and filled by Malignants or Anti-Covenanters. Strange to say, this met with the approval of the Church. Forsaking her proper sphere, and forgetful of the spirit by which hitherto she had been animated, the Church now issued *Resolutions* in favour of these proceedings, against which, however, a large and influential minority boldly and strenuously *protested*. Such was the origin of the controversy between the Resolutioners and Protesters, a controversy which raged with unabated animosity for many years, and which bred most disastrous results to the Scottish Church and nation.—ED.]

Binning saw some of the fatal consequences of these divisions in his own time, and being of a catholic and healing spirit, he wrote, with a view to the cementing of differences, an excellent treatise on Christian love, which contains very strong and pathetic passages, most apposite to the subject. He was no fomenter of factions, but was studious of the public tranquillity. He was a man of moderate principles and temperate passions, never imposing upon or overbearing others, but willingly hearkened to advice, and always yielded to reason.

The prevailing of the English sectaries under Oliver Cromwell, to the overthrow of the Presbyterian interest in England, and the various attempts which they made in Scotland on the constitution and discipline of the Church, were the greatest difficulties which the ministers had then to struggle with. Upon this he hath many excellent reflections in his sermons, particularly in that from Deut. xxxii. 4, 5.

It is said that the Presbyterians and Independents, disputing before Cromwell while he was in Scotland, in or about Glasgow, Mr Binning, being present, so managed the points controverted, that he not only nonplussed Cromwell's ministers, but even put them to shame ; which, after the dispute, made Cromwell ask the name of that learned and bold young man ; and being told his name was Hugh Binning, he said, " He hath bound well indeed," but, clapping his hand on his sword, said, " This will loose all again."

After he had laboured four years in the ministry, serving God with his spirit in the gospel of His Son, he died in 1653, of a consumption, when he was scarcely come to the prime and vigour of his life, being only in the 26th year of his age ; leaving behind him a sweet savour, and an epistle of commendation, upon the hearts of those who were his hearers.

He was a person of singular piety, of a humble, meek, and peaceable temper ; a judicious and lively preacher ; nay, so extraordinary a person, that he was justly accounted a prodigy of human learning and knowledge of divinity. From his childhood he knew the Scriptures, and from a boy had been much under deep and spiritual exercise, until the time, or a little before, that he entered upon the office of the ministry ; when he came to a great calm and tranquillity of mind, being mercifully relieved from all these doubtings which for a long time he had been exercised with. Though he studied in his discourses to condescend to the capacity of the meaner sort of hearers, yet it must be owned, that his gift of preaching was not so much accommodated to a country congregation, as it was to the judicious and learned. Binning's method was peculiar to himself, much after the haranguing way. He was no stranger to the rules of art, and knew well how to make his matter subservient to the subject he handled. His diction and language were easy and fluent, void of all affectation and bombast, and had a kind of undesigned negligent elegance, which arrested the hearers' attention. Considering the time he lived in, it might be said, that he carried the orator's prize from his contemporaries in Scotland, and was not inferior to the best pulpit orator in England at that time. While he lived he was highly esteemed, having been a successful instrument of saving himself, and them that heard him; of turning sinners unto righteousness, and of perfecting the saints. He died much lamented by all good people who had the opportunity of knowing him. That great divine, Mr James Durham, gave him this verdict : " That there was no speaking after Mr Binning ;" and truly he had the tongue of the learned, and knew how to speak a word in season.

Besides his " Works," and a paper written upon occasion of the already mentioned dispute between the Resolutioners and the Protesters, some other little pieces of his have been published since. There is also a book in quarto, said to be his, entitled, " A Useful Case of Conscience, learnedly and acutely discussed and resolved, concerning association and confederacies with idolaters, heretics, malignants, etc.," first printed in 1693, which was like to have had some influence at that time upon King William's soldiers while in Flanders, which made him suppress it, and raise a prosecution against Mr James Kid, for publishing the same at Utrecht, in the Netherlands.

GLASGOW CATHEDRAL.

Andrew Gray.

ANDREW GRAY (by the calculation of his age and the date of his entry into the ministry) seems to have been born about the year 1634; and being very early sent to school, he learned so fast, that in a short time he was ripe for the university; where, by the vivacity of his parts and ready genius, he made such proficiency, both in scholastic learning and divinity, that before he was twenty years of age, he was found accomplished for entering into the holy office of the ministry.

From his very infancy he had studied to be acquainted with the Scriptures, and, like another young Samson, the Spirit of God began very early to move him; there being such a delightful gravity in his conversation, that what Gregory Nazianzen once said of the great Basil might be applied to him: "He held forth learning beyond his age, and fixedness of manners beyond his learning." The earthly vessel being thus filled with heavenly treasure, he was quickly licensed to preach, and got a call to be minister of the outer kirk of the High Church of Glasgow, though he was scarcely twenty years of age, and therefore below the age appointed by the constitution of the Church, unless in extraordinary cases.

No sooner was this young servant of Christ entered into his Master's vineyard, than the people from all quarters flocked to attend his sermons, it being their constant emulation who should be most under the refreshing drops of his ministry. As he and his learned colleague Mr Durham were one time walking together, Durham, observing the multitude thronging into that church where Andrew Gray was to preach, and only a very few going into the church in which he was to preach, said to him, "Brother, I perceive you are to have a throng church to-day." To which he answered, "Truly, brother, they are fools to leave you and come to me." Durham replied, "Not so, dear brother, for none can receive such honour and success in his ministry, except it be given him from heaven. I rejoice that Christ is preached and that His kingdom and interest is getting ground, for I am content to be anything, or nothing, that Christ may be all in all."

And indeed, Andrew Gray had a notable and singular gift in preaching, being one experienced in the most mysterious points of Christian practice and profession; in handling of all his subjects being free of youthful vanity, or affectation of human literature, though he had a most scholastic genius and more than ordinary abilities. He did outstrip many that entered into the Lord's vineyard before him. His expression was every way warm and rapturous, and well adapted to affect the hearts of his hearers; yea, he had such a faculty, and was so helped to press home God's threatenings upon the consciences of his hearers, that his contemporary, the foresaid Mr Durham, observed, "That many times he caused the very hairs of their heads to stand up."

Among his other excellences in preaching, which were many, this was none of the least, that he could so order his subject as to make it be relished by every palate. He could so dress a plain discourse as to delight a learned audience, and at the same time preach with a learned plainness. He had such a clear notion of high mysteries, as to make them stoop to the meanest capacity. He had so learned Christ; and being a man of a most zealous temper, the great bent of his spirit and that which he did spend himself anent, was to make people know their dangerous state by nature, and to persuade them to believe and lay hold of the great salvation.

All these singularities seem to have been his peculiar mercy from the Lord, to make him a burning and shining light, though for about the space of two years only; the Spirit of the Lord as it were stirring up a lamp unto a sudden blaze, that was not to continue long in His Church. On which a late prefacer of some of his sermons has very pertinently observed, "Yea, how awakening, convincing, and reproving may the example of this very young minister be to many ministers of the Gospel, who have been many years in the vineyard, but fall far short of his labours and progress. God thinks fit now and then to raise up a child to reprove the sloth and negligence of many thousands of advanced years, and shows that He can perfect His own praise out of the mouths of babes."

His sermons are now in print, and well known in the world. His works do praise him in the gates, and though they are free from the metaphysical speculations of the schools, yet it must be granted that the excellences of the ancient fathers and schoolmen do all con-centre in them. For his doctrine carries light, his reproofs are weighty, and his exhortations powerful; and though they are not in such an accurate or grammatical style as some may expect, yet this may be easily accounted for, if we consider the great alteration and embellishment in the style of the English language since his time. There can be no ground, also, to doubt but they must be far inferior to what they were when delivered by the author, who neither corrected them, nor, as appears, intended that they should ever be published. Yet all this is sufficiently made up otherwise, for what is wanting in symmetry of parts or equality of style is made up in the pleasure of variety, like the grateful odours of various flowers, or the pleasant harmony of different sounds, for so is truth in its own native dress.

It hath been often said that Mr Gray many times longed for the twenty-second year of his age, wherein he expected to rest from his labours, and, by a perpetual jubilee, to enjoy his blessed Lord and Master. It is certain that in his sermons we often find him longing for his majority, that he might enter into the possession of his heavenly Father's inheritance, prepared for him before the founda-tions of the world were laid.

He escaped death very narrowly when going to Dundee, in com-pany with Mr Robert Fleming (some time minister at Cambuslang), which remarkable sea-deliverance was matter of thankfulness to God all his life after.

There is one thing that may be desiderated by the inquisitive, namely, what Andrew Gray's sentiments were concerning the public resolutions, seeing he entered the ministry about the third year after they were passed. Whatever his contentions in public were, it is credibly reported that he debated in private against these defections, with his learned colleague Mr Durham, who afterwards, when on his death-bed, asked him, What he thought of these things? He answered, that he was of the same mind as formerly, and did much regret that he had been so sparing in public against these woeful resolutions, speaking so pathetically of their sinfulness and the calamities they would procure, that Mr Durham, contrary to his former practice, durst never after speak in defence of them.

But the time now approached that the Lord was about to accomplish the desire of His servant. He fell sick, and was in a high fever for several days, being much tossed with sore trouble, without any intermission ; but all the time continuing in a most sedate frame of mind.

It is a loss that his last dying words were neither written nor remembered ; only we may guess what his spiritual exercises were, from the short but excellent letter sent by him, a little before his death, to Lord Warriston, bearing date February 7, 1656. In this he shows that he not only had a most clear discovery of the toleration then granted by Cromwell, and the evils that would come upon the land for all these things, but also was most sensible of his own case and condition, as appears from the conclusion of it, where he accosts his Lordship thus : " Now, not to trouble your lordship, whom I highly reverence, and my soul is knit to you in the Lord, but that you will bespeak my case to the great Master of requests, and lay my broken state before Him who hath pled the desperate case of many, according to the sweet words in Lamentations iii. 56 : 'Thou hast heard my voice : hide not thine ear at my breathing, at my cry.' This is all at this time from one in a very weak condition, in a great fever, who, for much of seven nights, hath slept little at all, with many other sad particulars and circumstances."

Thus in a short time, according to his desire, it was granted to him, by death, to pass unto the Author of life, his soul taking its flight into the arms of his blessed Saviour, whom he had served faithfully in his day and generation, though only about twenty-two years old. He shone too conspicuous to continue long, and burned so intensely, that he behoved soon to be extinguished ; but he now shines in the kingdom of his Father, in a more conspicuous refulgent manner, even as the brightness of the firmament and the stars for ever and ever.

He was, in his day, a most singular and pious youth ; and though he died young, yet was old in grace, having lived and done much for

God in a little time. He was one, both in public and private life, who possessed, in a high degree, every domestic and social virtue that could adorn the character of a most powerful and pathetic preacher, a loving husband, an affable friend ; ever cheerful and agreeable in conversation, always ready to exert himself for the relief of all who asked or stood in need of his assistance. These uncommon talents not only endeared him to his brethren the clergy, but also to many others from the one extremity of the land to the other that heard or knew anything of him, who considered and highly esteemed him as one of the most able advocates for the propagation and advancement of Christ's kingdom.

His well-known sermons are printed in several small portions. Those called his Works are bound in one volume 8vo. In addition to the Eleven Sermons printed some time ago, a large collection, to the number of fifty-one, are lately published, entitled his Select Sermons, whereof only three, for connection's sake, and his letter to Lord Warriston, are inserted, which were before published in his works. So that by this time most if not all of the sermons are now in print that ever were preached by him.

James Durham.

AMES DURHAM was born about the year 1622, and was lineally descended from the ancient and honourable family of Grange Durham, in the parish of Monifeith in the shire of Angus. He was the eldest son of John Durham of Easter Powrie, now called Wedderburn, after the gentleman's name who is the present possessor thereof.

Having gone through all the parts of useful learning with success and applause, he left the university before he was graduate, and for some time lived as a private gentleman at his own dwelling-house in the country, without any thought then of farther prosecuting his studies, especially for the ministry. And though he

THE OLD STEEPLE, DUNDEE.

was always blameless and moral in his life, both in the university and
when he left it, yet he was much a stranger to religion in the serious
exercise and power of it, and, through prejudice of education, did not
stand well affected to the Presbyterian Government. He was first
married to a daughter of the laird of Duntervie : his wife and her
mother were both very pious women.

His conversion to the Lord was very remarkable : for, going
with his lady to visit her mother in the parish of Abercorn, some
miles west from Edinburgh, it happened that at this time the sacrament was to be administered in the parish. Upon Saturday his
mother-in-law earnestly pressed him to go with them to church and
hear sermon. At first he showed much unwillingness ; but, partly by
their persuasion, and partly from his complaisant disposition, he went
along with them. The minister who preached that day was extremely
affectionate and serious in his delivery ; and though the sermon was
a plain familiar discourse, yet his seriousness fixed Mr Durham's
attention very closely, and he was much affected therewith. But the
change was reserved till the morrow. When he came home, he said
to his mother-in-law, " The minister hath preached very seriously this
day, I shall not need to be pressed to go to church to-morrow."
Accordingly, on Sabbath morning, rising early, he went to church,

where Mr Melville preached from 1 Pet. ii. 7, "Unto you therefore which believe He is precious," when he so sweetly and seriously opened up the preciousness of Christ, and the Spirit of God wrought so effectually upon Mr Durham's spirit, that in hearing of this sermon, he first closed with Christ, and then went to the Lord's table and took the seal of God's covenant. After this he ordinarily called Mr Melville "father," when he spoke of him.

Afterwards he made serious religion his business in secret, in his family, and in all places and companies where he came, and did cordially embrace the interest of Christ and His Church, as then established, and gave himself much up to reading ; for which reason, that he might be free of all disturbance, he caused build a study for himself. In this little chamber he gave himself to prayer, reading, and meditation, and was so close a student that he often forgot to eat his bread, being sometimes so intent upon his studies, that servants who were sent to call him down often returned without an answer ; yea, his lady frequently called on him with tears before he would come. Such sweet communion he had sometimes with the Lord in that place.

James Durham made great proficiency in his studies, and not only became an experimental Christian, but also a very learned man ; one evidence of which he gave in a short dispute with one of the ministers of Dundee, while he was in that town. He met there with the parson of the parish (for so the ministers were then called) who knew him not. After some discourse, he fell upon the Popish controversy with him, and so put him to silence, that he could not answer a word, but went sneakingly out of the room to the provost, craving his assistance to apprehend Durham as a Jesuit, assuring the provost, that if ever there was a Jesuit in Rome, he was one ; and that if he were suffered to remain in the town or country, he might pervert many from the faith. Upon this, the provost going along with him to the house where the pretended Jesuit was, and entering the room, he immediately knew Mr Durham, and saluted him as laird of Easter Powrie, craving his pardon for their mistake ; and turning to the parson, asked where the person was whom he called the Jesuit? Mr Durham smiled, and the parson, ashamed, asked pardon of them both ; and was rebuked by the provost, who said, " Fy, fy! that any country gentleman should be able to put our parson thus to silence."

His call and coming forth to the ministry were somewhat remarkable, for at the time when the civil wars broke out, several gentlemen being in arms for the cause of religion, he was chosen and called to be a captain, in which station he behaved himself like another Cornelius, being a devout man and one that feared God with all his house, and prayed to God always with his company. When the Scots army were about to engage with the English, he judged meet to call his company to prayer before the engagement, and as he began to pray, Mr David Dickson, then professor of divinity at Glasgow, on his way past, seeing the soldiers addressing themselves to prayer, and hearing the voice of one praying, drew near, alighted from his horse, and joined with them. He was so much taken with the prayer, that he called for Mr Durham, and having conversed with him a little, he solemnly charged him, that as soon as this piece of service was over, he should devote himself to serve God in the holy ministry, for to that he judged the Lord called him.

But though, as yet, Durham had no clearness to hearken to Mr Dickson's advice, yet two remarkable providences fell out just upon the back of this solemn charge, which served very much to clear the way to comply with his desire. The first was, that in the engagement his horse was shot under him and he was mercifully preserved; the second, that in the heat of the battle an English soldier was on the point of striking him down with his sword, but apprehending him to be a minister by his grave carriage, black cloth and band (as was then in fashion with gentlemen), he asked him if he was a priest? Durham replied, "I am one of God's priests," and he spared his life. Durham, upon reflecting how wonderfully the Lord had thus preserved his life, and that his saying he was a priest had been the means thereof, resolved, as a testimony of his grateful sense of the Lord's goodness to him, henceforth to devote himself to the service of God in the holy ministry, if the Lord should see meet to qualify him for the same.

Accordingly, in pursuance of this resolution, he quickly went to Glasgow, and studied divinity under Mr David Dickson, then professor there, and made such proficiency, that in a short time, he humbly offered himself to trials in 1646, and was licensed by the presbytery of Irvine to preach the Gospel. Next year, upon Mr Dickson's recommendation, the session of Glasgow appointed Mr Ramsay, one of their ministers, to entreat Mr Durham to come and preach in Glasgow. Accordingly he came, and preached two Sabbath-days and one week day. The session being fully satisfied with his doctrine, and the gifts bestowed on him by the Lord for serving him in the holy ministry, did unanimously call him to the ministry of the Blackfriars church, then vacant; and he was ordained minister there in November 1647.

James Durham applied himself to the work of the ministry with great diligence; so that his profiting did quickly appear to all; but considering that no man that warreth should entangle himself with the affairs of this life, he obtained leave of his people to return to his own country for a little time, to settle his worldly affairs. Yet even there he was not idle, but preached every Sabbath. First, he preached at Dundee, before a great multitude, from Rom. i. 16, "I am not ashamed of the Gospel of Christ;" from which he showed that it was no disparagement for the greatest to be a Gospel minis ter. The second time he preached at Tealing, in his own country, upon 2 Cor. v. 18, "And hath given to us the ministry of reconciliation;" and the third time at Monifeith, at the desire of the minister there, from 2 Cor. v. 20, "Now then we are ambassadors for Christ." In all these places, he indeed acted like an ambassador for Christ, and managed the Gospel treaty of peace to good purpose. The next Sabbath he designed to have preached at Montrose; but receiving an express to return to Glasgow in haste, his wife being dangerously sick, he came away, leaving his affairs to the care of his friends, and returned to Glasgow, where in a few days, his wife, who had been the desire of his eyes, died. His Christian submission under this afflicting dispensation was most remarkable; for after a short silence, he said to some about him, "Now, who could persuade me that this dispensation of God's providence was good for me, if the Lord had not said it was so?" He was afterwards married to Margaret Muir, relict of Mr Zachariah Boyd, minister of the Barony Church of Glasgow.

In 1650, Mr David Dickson, Professor of Divinity in the college of Glasgow, being called to be Professor of Divinity in the University of Edinburgh, the commissioners of the General Assembly, authorised for visiting the University of Glasgow, unanimously designed and called Mr Durham to succeed Mr Dickson as Professor there. But before he was admitted to that charge, the General Assembly being persuaded of his eminent piety and steadfastness, prudence and moderation, did, after mature deliberation, that same year, pitch upon him, though then but about twenty-eight years of age, as among the ablest and best accomplished ministers then in the Church, to attend the King's family as chaplain; in which station, though the

GLASGOW COLLEGE, INNER QUADRANGLE.

times were most difficult, as abounding with snares and temptations, he did so wisely and faithfully acquit himself, that there was a conviction left upon the consciences of all who observed him. Yea, during his stay at Court, and whenever he went about the duty of his place, they did all carry gravely, and did forbear all lightness and profanity, none allowing themselves to do anything offensive before him; so that while he served the Lord in the holy ministry, and particularly in that post and character of the King's chaplain, his ambition was to have God's favour rather than the favour of great men, and studied more to profit and edify their souls, than to tickle their fancies, as some court parasites in their sermons do. One instance whereof was, that being called to preach before the Parliament, where many rulers were present, he preached from John iii. 10 : " Art thou a master of Israel, and knowest not these things?" On this occasion he mostly insisted, that it was a most unaccountable thing for rulers and nobles in Israel, to be ignorant of the great and necessary things of regeneration, and being born again of the Spirit; and did most seriously press all, from the king to the beggar, to seek and know experimentally these things—a good pattern for all ministers who are called to preach on the like occasion. He continued with King Charles II. till he went to England, and then returned.

PORTRAIT OF OLIVER CROMWELL.

Towards the end of January 1651, the common session of Glasgow appointed Patrick Gillespie to write him, concerning Robert Ramsay's being Professor of Divinity in his place in the University of Glasgow. In consequence of this, Durham came to Glasgow; for he is mentioned as present in the session in the beginning of April after. At the same time, Cromwell and his army were in Glasgow, and on the Lord's day, Cromwell heard Durham preach, when he testified against his invasion to his face. Next day he sent for Durham, and told him, he always thought he had been a wiser man than to meddle with matters of public concern in his sermons. To this he answered, it was not his practice, but that he judged it both wisdom and prudence to speak his mind on that head, seeing he had the opportunity to do it in his presence. Cromwell dismissed him very civilly, but desired him to forbear insisting on that subject in public. At the same time sundry ministers, both in town and country, met with Cromwell and his officers, and represented, in strong terms, the injustice of his invasion.

It would appear that James Durham, some time after this, had withdrawn from Glasgow. A letter was therefore in August next ordered to be sent to him, to come and preach; and in September after, there being a vacancy in the Inner Kirk by the death of Mr Ramsay, the common session gave him an unanimous call, with which the town council agreed. Some time after this, he was received as minister, Mr John Carstairs, his brother-in-law, being his colleague in that church.

In the whole of his ministry he was a burning and shining light, and particularly he shone in humility and self-denial. He was also a person of the utmost gravity, and scarcely smiled at anything. Once when Mr William Guthrie, being exceedingly merry, made Mr Durham smile with his pleasant, facetious, and harmless conversation, the latter was at first a little disgusted, but it being the laudable custom of that family to pray after dinner, which Mr Guthrie did, upon being desired, with the greatest measure of seriousness and fervency, to the astonishment of all present, Mr Durham embraced him, when they arose from prayer, and said: "O William, you are a happy man; if I had been so merry as you have been, I could not have been in such a serious frame for prayer for the space of forty-eight hours."

James Durham was devout in all parts of his ministerial work, but more eminently so at communion occasions. Then he endeavoured, through grace, to rouse and work himself up to such a divineness of frame, as very much suited the spiritual nature and majesty of that ordinance. Yea, at some of these solemn and sweet occasions, he spoke some way as a man that had been in heaven, commending Jesus Christ, making a glorious display of grace, and bringing the offers thereof so low, that his hearers were made to think that the rope or cord of the salvation offered was let down to sinners, so that those of the lowest stature might catch hold of it. He gave himself much up to meditation, and usually said little to persons that came to propose their cases to him, but heard them patiently, and was sure to handle their cases in his sermons.

His healing disposition, and great moderation of spirit, remarkably appeared when this Church was grievously divided betwixt the Resolutioners and Protesters; he would never give his judgment on either side, and used to say, that "division was worse by far than either." He was equally respected by both parties; for at a meeting of the synod in Glasgow, when those of the different sides met separately, each of them made choice of Mr Durham for their moderator; but he refused to join either of them, till they would unite; which they accordingly did. At this meeting he gave in some overtures for peace, the substance of which was, that they should eschew all public awakening, or lengthening out the debate, by preaching or spreading of papers on either side, and that they should forbear practising, executing, or pressing of acts made in the last Assembly at St Andrews and Dundee, and also pressing or spreading appeals, declinatures, etc., against the same, and that no church-officer should be excepted against on account of these things, they being found otherwise qualified.

[The unhappy character and results of the dispute between the Resolutioners and Protesters, and the spirit with which Durham regarded it, may be illustrated by a reference to the last book he penned, entitled, "The Dying Man's Testament to the Church of Scotland; or, a Treatise concerning Scandal." In the concluding part, which speaks of " scandalous divisions," the following passages occur; and it is hoped that the relation of the subject to the present state of ecclesiastical affairs in Scotland, as well as the scarcity of the work, will be regarded as a sufficient reason for introducing them at length. Speaking of the sad effects of division, he says: " Having now someway discovered the nature and causes of the evil of division, it may be easily conjectured what will be the effects thereof, which have ever been most deplorable, as to the torturing of them that are engaged, to the scandalising of the weak, to the hardening and breaking of the neck of many profane, light persons, to the spoiling of the Church in its purity, government, order and beauty of its ordinances, and, which is more, to the wearing out of the life and power of religion. Yea, which is above all, there is nothing that doth more tend to the reproach of the blessed name of our Lord Jesus, that maketh Christianity more hateful, that rendereth the Gospel more unfruitful, and more marreth the progress and interest of the kingdom of our Lord Jesus, and, in one word, doth more shut out all good, and let in by an open door everything that is evil into the Church, than this woful evil of division, according to the Word (James iii. 16), 'Where envying and strife is, there is confusion and every evil work.' And we are persuaded, that all who have read the Scriptures, and the many and great motives whereby union is pressed, and have considered the Fathers, what great weight they lay upon unity, and with what horror they mention division, even as *maximum malum*, or the greatest evil that can befall the Church; or have observed in Church history the many sad consequents and efforts that have followed upon this, and the lamentable fall of the Church under the same, when friends thought shame and were made faint, enemies were encouraged and delighted, and onlookers were either provoked to mock at or pity the same; or who have had some taste in experience of the bitter fruits thereof, will, and, if they be not altogether stupid, cannot but be convinced of the many horrible evils that are in this one evil of division. Sure there is no evil doth more suddenly and inevitably overturn the Church than this; which maketh her fight against herself, and eat her own flesh, and tear her own bowels; for, that a kingdom divided against itself cannot stand, is the infallible maxim of Him that was greater and wiser than Solomon. And, when things are compared, it will be found there is no more compendious way to blast the fruit of ordinances, when they cannot be removed or corrupted, and by so doing to destroy and carry souls headlong than this; that a Church, in her ministers and members, should be engaged thus to bite and devour one another, and to counteract the actings one of another. This, we suppose, will not be denied. . . . . Oh! how many temptations have such divisions accompanying them, especially to ministers! and also how many afflictions, crosses, and reproaches upon the back of these! Might it not make a minister tremble to think upon the matter of division; that now, besides all his former difficulties, and straits, there is a snare and trial in everything. In every sermon that he preacheth it is thus, lest his own affection steal in for the zeal of God, to make him hotter and more vehement against those that oppose him in such things as are controverted, than he useth to be in things more nearly concerning the glory of God; and lest, by discovering his carnality, he make his ministry despicable before others. When he heareth he is in hazard to be irritated by a contradiction, and though there be no contradiction, he is in hazard to lay the less weight upon what might be for his edification, because it is spoken by one who in such and such things differeth from him. When he is in any judicatory (or Church court) there is a temptation waiting on, by the least motion of such things, to discompose all, and make such meetings scandalous and burdensome; by this all conversations almost becometh heartless and comfortless; the most intimate brother is either suspicious or suspected; all construction of men's ingenuity and sincerity in anything, is for the most part grounded on men's interests; as if men after that had no conscience of sinning; there is a failing of sympathy amongst brethren," etc. After speaking of union as "a commanded duty," and "a thing attainable," he makes the following important observations: "We premise that, in endeavouring union and healing, men would not straiten it to a universal union in everything, in judgment and practice, but would resolve to have it with many things defective that need forbearance in persons that are united, which we may take up in these particulars: 1. There may be difference of judgment in many things—I mean in such things as are consistent with the foundation and edification. In such, a forbearance would be resolved upon, and to do otherwise were to think that either men had no reason at all, or that their understandings were perfect, or, at least, of equal reach. 2. There may be dissatisfaction with many persons, whether officers or members; and to expect a Church free of unworthy officers or members, and to defer Church-union thereupon, is to expect the barn-floor shall be without chaff, and to frustrate the many commands whereby this duty is pressed, for so this command should be obligatory on no Church but that which is triumphant. 3. It may also be consistent with many particular failings and defects in the exercise of government, as possibly the sparing of some corrupt officers and members, yea, the censuring of some unjustly, or the admission of some that are unfit for the ministry, and such like. These, indeed, are faults, but they are not such as to make a Church to be no Church; and though these have sometimes been pretended to be the causes of schisms and divisions in the Church in practice, yet were they never defended on just ground of schisms and divisions, but were ever condemned by all Councils and Fathers, and cannot be in reason sustained. 4. It may stand with some defects of worship, manner of government, and rules, that are necessary for good government in a Church. It is likely that many things of that kind were defective in the Church of Corinth, where the Sacrament was so dividedly administered, confusion in many things of worship, and some things still to be set in order; yet doth the Apostle nowhere press union more than in his Epistles to that Church. Neither can it be thought that perfection in all these is ever to be expected, or that union until such time is to be delayed. And, if there be defects of that kind, it is union, and not division that is to be looked upon as the commended mean of redressing of the same." He concludes this interesting and very valuable treatise with sundry considerations, which he commends to the prayerful attention of the reader who is still in doubt regarding the lawfulness of the union proposed. Among other questions he asks, "If all the present Reformed Churches, being appealed to in such a case, were singly and impartially to give judgment thereanent, whether it could upon any ground be thought that they would judge such condescending for mutual forbearance unlawful upon either side, if by it and no other way union were to be attained?"—ED.]

So weighty was the ministerial charge upon his spirit, that he said if he were to live ten years longer, he would choose to live nine years in study for preaching the tenth; and it was thought his close study and thoughtfulness cast him into that decline whereof he died. In the time of his sickness, the better part being afraid that the magistrates, and some of the ministry who were for the public resolutions, would put in one of that stamp after his death, moved Mr Carstairs, his colleague, to desire him to name his successor. After some demur, enjoining secrecy till it was nearer his death, he at last named Mr David Veitch, then minister of Govan; but afterwards, when dying, to the magistrates, ministers, and some of the people, he named other three, to take any of them they pleased. This alteration made Mr Carstairs inquire the reason, after the rest were gone; to whom Durham replied, " O brother, Mr Veitch is too ripe for heaven to be transported to any church on earth; he will be there almost as soon as I." And so it proved, for Durham died the Friday after; and next Sabbath Veitch preached; though knowing nothing of this, he told the people in the afternoon that it would be his last sermon to them; and the same night taking bed, he died next Friday morning about three o'clock, the time that Durham died, as Dr Rattray, who was witness to both, did declare.

When on his death-bed, Mr Durham was under considerable darkness about his state, and said to Mr John Carstairs' brother, "For all that I have preached or written, there is but one Scripture I can remember or dare grip unto; tell me if I dare lay the weight of my salvation upon it: 'Whosoever cometh unto Me, I will in no wise cast out?' Mr Carstairs answered, "You may depend upon it, though you had a thousand salvations at hazard." When he was drawing towards his departure, though in great conflict and agony, yet he sensibly, through the strength of God's grace, triumphantly overcame, and cried, in a rapture of holy joy, some little time before he committed his soul to God, " Is not the Lord good? Is he not infinitely good? See how he smiles! I do say it, and I do proclaim it." He died on Friday the 25th of June 1658, in the thirty-sixth year of his age.

Thus died the eminently pious, learned, and judicious James Durham, whose labours did always aim at the advancement of practical religion, and whose praise in the Gospel is throughout all the churches, both at home and abroad. He was a burning and a shining light, a star of the first magnitude, and of him it may be said (without derogating from the merit of any) that he attained unto the first three, and had a name among the mighty. He was also one of great integrity and authority in the country where he lived ; insomuch, that when any difference fell out, he was always chosen by both parties as their great referee or judge, unto whose sentence all parties submitted. Such was the quality of his calm and healing spirit.

His colleague, Mr John Carstairs, in his funeral sermon, from Isa. lvii. 1, 2 : "The righteous perisheth, and no man layeth it to heart," gives him this character : "Know ye not that there is a prince among pastors fallen to-day! a faithful and wise steward, who knew well how to give God's children their food in due season, a gentle and kind nurse, a faithful admonisher and reprover, a skilful counsellor in all straits and difficulties ; in dark matters he was eyes to the blind, feet to the lame, a burning and shining light in the dark world, an interpreter of the word among a thousand ; to him men gave ear, and after his words no man spake again."

His learned and pious works, wherein all the excellences of the primitive and ancient fathers seem to concentrate, are a Commentary on the Revelation ; Seventy-two Sermons on the fifty-third chapter of the Prophecy of Isaiah ; an Exposition of the Ten Commandments ; an Exposition of the Song of Solomon ; his Sermons on Death and on the Unsearchable Riches of Christ ; his Communion Sermons ; Sermons on Godliness and Self-Denial ; a Sermon on a Good Conscience. There are also a great many of his Sermons in manuscript, never yet published, viz., three Sermons upon Resisting the Holy Ghost, from Acts vii. 51 ; eight on Quenching the Spirit ; five upon Giving the Spirit ; thirteen upon Trusting and Delighting in God ; two against Immoderate Anxiety ; eight upon the One Thing Needful ; with a Discourse upon Prayer ; and several other sermons and discourses from Eph. v. 15 ; 1 Cor. xi. 24 ; Luke i. 6 ; Gal. v. 16 ; Psalm cxix. 67 ; 1 Thess. v. 19 ; 1 Pet. iii. 14 ; Matt. viii. 7. There is also a Treatise on Scandal, and an Exposition, by way of Lecture, upon Job, said to be his ; but whether these, either as to style or strain, cohere with the other works of the laborious author, must be left to the impartial and unbiassed reader.

KING'S COLLEGE, ABERDEEN.

Samuel Rutherford.

AMUEL RUTHERFORD, a gentleman by extraction, having spent some time at the grammar school, went to the University of Edinburgh, where he was so much admired for his pregnancy of parts, and deservedly looked upon as one from whom some great things might be expected, that in a short time, though then but very young, he was made Professor of Philosophy in that University.

Some time after this he was called to be minister at Anwoth, in the shire of Galloway, unto which charge he entered by means of the then Viscount Kenmuir, without any acknowledgment or engagement to the bishops. There he laboured with great diligence and success, both night and day, rising usually by three o'clock in the morning, spending the whole time in reading, praying, writing, catechising, visiting, and other duties belonging to the ministerial profession and employment.

Here he wrote his *Exercitationes de Gratia*, for which he was summoned, as early as June 1630, before the High Commission Court at Edinburgh; but the weather was so tempestuous as to obstruct the passage of the Archbishop of St Andrews hither, and Mr Colvil, one of the judges, having befriended him, the diet was deserted. About the same time, his first wife died, after a sore sickness of thirteen months ; and he himself was so ill of a tertian fever for thirteen weeks, that he could not preach on the Sabbath-day without great difficulty.

Again, in April 1634, he was threatened with another prosecution at the instance of the bishop of Galloway, before the High Commission Court ; and neither were these threatenings all the reasons Mr Rutherford had to lay his account with suffering ; for as the Lord would not hide from his faithful servant Abraham the things he was about to do, neither would he conceal from this son of Abraham what his purposes were concerning him. In a letter to the provost's wife of Kirkcudbright, dated April 20, 1633, he says, that upon the 17th and 18th of August, he got a full answer of his Lord to be a graced minister, and a chosen arrow hid in his quiver. Accordingly, the thing he looked for came upon him ; for he was again summoned before the High Commission Court for his non-conformity, his preaching against the five articles of Perth, and the forementioned book of *Exercitationes Apologeticæ pro Divina Gratia*, which book they alleged did reflect upon the Church of Scotland. But " the truth was," says a late historian, " the argument of that book did cut the sinews of Arminianism, and galled the Episcopal clergy to the very quick ; and so Bishop Sydserff could endure him no longer." When he came before the Commission Court, he altogether declined it as a lawful judicatory, and would not give the chancellor (being a clergyman) and the bishops their titles, by lording of them. Some had the courage to befriend him, particularly the Lord Lorne, afterwards the famous Marquis of Argyle, who did as much for him as was within his power to do ; but the Bishop of Galloway, threatening that if he got not his will of him, he would write to the King, it was carried against him ; and upon the 27th of July 1636, he was discharged from exercising any part of his ministry within the kingdom of Scotland, under pain of rebellion ; and ordered within six months to confine himself within the city of Aberdeen, during the King's pleasure ; which sentence he obeyed, and forthwith went toward the place of his confinement.

From Aberdeen he wrote many of his famous letters, from which it is evident that the consolation of the Holy Spirit did greatly abound with him in his sufferings. Yea, in one of these letters, he expresses it in the strongest terms, when he says, " I never knew before, that His love was in such a measure. If He leave me, He leaves me in pain, and sick of love; and yet my sickness is my life and health. I have a fire within me; I defy all the devils in hell, and all the prelates in Scotland, to cast water on it." Here he remained upwards of a year and a-half, by which time he made the doctors of Aberdeen know, that the Puritans, as they called them, were clergymen as well as they. But upon notice that the Privy Council had received a declinature against the High Commission Court in the year 1638, he adventured to return to his flock at An-woth, where he again took great pains, both in public and private, amongst the people who from all quarters resorted to his ministry, so that the whole country side might be accounted as his particular flock; and (it being then in the dawning of the Reformation) men found no small benefit by the Gospel; that part of the ancient pro-phecy being farther accomplished, " For in the wilderness shall the waters break out, and streams in the desert" (Isa. xxxv. 6).

He was before that Venerable Assembly held at Glasgow in 1638, and gave an account of all these his former proceedings, with respect to his confinement, and the causes thereof. By them he was ap-pointed to be professor of divinity at St Andrews, and colleague in the ministry with the worthy Mr Blair, who was translated thither about the same time. And here God did again so second this his eminent and faithful servant, that by his indefatigable pains both in teaching in the schools and preaching in the congregation, St Andrews, the seat of the archbishop, and the nursery of all supersti-tion, error, and profaneness, soon became forthwith a Lebanon, out of which were taken cedars for building the house of the Lord, almost throughout the whole land. Many of those who received the spiritual life by his ministry he guided to heaven before himself, and many others did walk in that light after him.

As Samuel Rutherford was mighty in the public parts of religion, so he was a great practiser and encourager of the private duties thereof. Thus, in the year 1640, when a charge was foisted in before the General Assembly, at the instance of Mr Henry Guthrie, minister at Stirling, afterwards Bishop of Dunkeld, against private society meetings, which were then abounding in the land, on which ensued much reasoning; the one side yielded that a paper before drawn up by Mr Henderson should be agreed unto, concerning the order to be kept in these meetings; but Guthrie and his adherents opposing this, Mr Rutherford, who was never much disposed to speak in judicatories, threw in this syllogism, " What the Scriptures do warrant, no Assembly may discharge; but private meetings for religious exercises, the Scriptures do warrant," " Then they that feared the Lord spake often one to another " (Mal. iii. 16). " Confess your faults one to another, and pray one for another " (James v. 16). And although the Earl of Seaforth there present, and those of Guthrie's faction, upbraided the good man for this, yet it had influence upon the majority of the members ; so all that the opposite party got done, was an act anent the ordering of family worship.

Samuel Rutherford was also one of the Scots commissioners, appointed in 1643 to the Westminster Assembly, and was very much beloved there for unparalleled faithfulness and zeal in going about his Master's business. It was during this time that he published *Lex Rex*, and several other learned pieces, against the Erastians, Anabaptists, Independents, and other sectaries, that began to prevail and increase at the time ; and none ever had the courage to take up the gauntlet of defiance thrown down by this champion.

It is reported, that when King Charles saw *Lex Rex*, he said, it would scarcely ever get an answer ; nor did it ever get any, except what the parliament in 1661 gave it, when they caused it to be burned at the cross of Edinburgh, by the hands of the hangman.

When the principal business of the Westminster Assembly was pretty well settled, Samuel Rutherford, in October 24, 1647, moved, that it might be recorded in the scribe's book, that the Assembly had enjoyed the assistance of the commissioners of the Church of Scotland, all the time they had been debating and perfecting these four things mentioned in the solemn league, viz., their composing a Directory for Worship, a uniform Confession of Faith, a Form of Church Government and Discipline, and the Public Catechism ; which was done in about a week after he and the rest returned home.

Upon the death of the learned Dematius, in 1651, the magistrates of Utrecht in Holland, being abundantly satisfied as to the learning, piety, and true zeal of the great Mr Rutherford, invited him to the divinity-chair there ; but he could not be persuaded. His reasons (elsewhere, when dissuading another gentleman from going abroad) seem to be expressed in these words : " Let me entreat you to be far from the thoughts of leaving this land. I see it, and find it, that the Lord hath covered the whole land with a cloud in his anger ; but though I have been tempted to the like, I had rather be in Scotland beside angry Jesus Christ, knowing He mindeth no evil to us, than in any Eden or garden on the earth." From this it is evident, that he chose rather to suffer affliction in his own native country, than to leave his charge and flock in time of danger. He continued with them till the day of his death, in the free and faithful discharge of his duty.

When the unhappy difference fell out between those called the Resolutioners and the Protesters, in 1650 and 1651, he espoused the protesters' quarrel, and gave faithful warning against the public resolutions; and likewise during the time of Cromwell's usurpation, he contended against all the prevailing sectaries that were then ushered in by virtue of his toleration. And such was his unwearied assiduity and diligence, that he seemed to pray constantly, to preach constantly, to catechise constantly, and to visit the sick, exhorting them from house to house; to teach as much in the schools, and spend as much time with the students and young men in fitting them for the ministry, as if he had been sequestered from all the world besides; and yet withal to write as much as if he had been constantly shut up in his study.

But no sooner did the restoration of Charles II. take place than the face of affairs began to change; and after his fore-mentioned book *Lex Rex* was burnt at the cross of Edinburgh, and at the gates of the new college of St Andrews, where he was professor of divinity, the parliament, in 1651, were to have an indictment laid before them against him; and such was their humanity, when everybody knew he was a-dying, that they summoned him to appear before them at Edinburgh, to answer to a charge of high treason! But he had a higher tribunal to appear before, where his Judge was his friend. He was dead before the time came, being taken away from the evil to come.

It is commonly said that, when the summons came, he spoke out of his bed and said, "Tell them I have got a summons already before a superior Judge and judicatory, and I behove to answer my first summons, and ere your day come I will be where few kings and great folks come." When they returned and told he was a-dying, the parliament was put to a vote, whether or not to let him die in the college. It was carried, "put him out," only a few dissenting. My Lord Burleigh said, "Ye have voted that honest man out of the college, but ye cannot vote him out of heaven." Some said, He would never win there, hell was too good for him. Burleigh said, "I wish I were as sure of heaven as he is, I would think myself happy to get a grip of his sleeve to haul me in."

When on his deathbed, he lamented much that he was withheld

from bearing witness to the work of Reformation since the year 1638; and upon the 28th of February, he gave a large and faithful testimony against the sinful courses of that time; which testimony he subscribed twelve days before his death; being full of joy and peace in believing.

During the time of his last sickness, he uttered many savoury speeches, and often broke out in a kind of sacred rapture, exalting and commending the Lord Jesus, especially when his end drew near. He often called his blessed Master his kingly King. Some days before his death, he said, "I shall shine—I shall see Him as He is—I shall see Him reign, and all his fair company with Him; and I shall have my large share. Mine eyes shall see my Redeemer : these very eyes of mine, and none other for me. This may seem a wide word; but it is no fancy or delusion; it is true. Let my Lord's name be exalted; and, if He will, let my name be grinded to pieces, that He may be all in all. If He should slay me ten thousand times, I will trust." He often repeated Jer. xv. 16 : "Thy words were found, and I did eat them."

When exhorting one to diligence, he said, "It is no easy thing to be a Christian. For me, I have got the victory, and Christ is holding out both His arms to embrace me." At another time, to some friends present, he said, "At the beginning of my sufferings I had mine own fears, like other sinful men, lest I should faint, and not be carried creditably through, and I laid this before the Lord; and as sure as ever He spoke to me in His word, as sure as His Spirit witnesseth to my heart, He hath accepted my sufferings. He said to me, Fear not, the outgate shall not be simply matter of prayer, but matter of praise. I said to the Lord, if He should slay me five thousand times five thousand, I would trust in Him; and I speak it with much trembling, fearing I should not make my part good; but as really as ever He spoke to me by His Spirit, He witnessed to my heart, that His grace should be sufficient." The Thursday night before his death, being much grieved with the state of the land, he had this expression, "Horror had taken hold on me." And afterwards, falling on his own condition, he said, "I renounce all that ever He made me will and do, as defiled and imperfect, as coming from me; I betake myself to Christ for sanctification, as well as justification; repeating these words (1 Cor. i. 30)—"He is made of God to me wisdom, righteousness, sanctification, and redemption;" adding, "I close with it, let Him be so : He is my all in all."

March 17. Three gentlewomen came to see him; and after exhorting them to read the Word, and be much in prayer, and much in communion with God, he said, "My honourable Master and lovely Lord, my great royal King, hath not a match in heaven or in earth. I have my own guilt, even like other sinful men; but He hath pardoned, loved, washed, and given me joy unspeakable and full of glory. I repent not that ever I owned His cause. These whom ye call protesters are the witnesses of Jesus Christ. I hope never to depart from that cause, nor side with those who have burnt the "Causes of God's Wrath." They have broken their covenant oftener than once or twice, but I believe the Lord will build Zion, and repair the waste places of Jacob. Oh! to obtain mercy to wrestle with God for their salvation. As for this presbytery, it hath stood in opposition to me these years past. I have my record in heaven. I had no particular end in view, but was seeking the honour of God, the thriving of the Gospel in this place, and the good of the new college; that society which I have left upon the Lord. What personal wrongs they have done me, and what grief they have occasioned to me, I heartily forgive them, and desire mercy to wrestle with God for mercy to them, and for the salvation of them all."

The same day James M'Gill, John Wardlaw, William Vilant, and Alexander Wedderburne, all members of the same presbytery with him, coming to visit him, he made them welcome, and said, "My Lord and Master is the chief of ten thousand, none is comparable to Him in heaven or earth. Dear brethren, do all for Him; pray for Christ, preach for Christ, feed the flock committed to your charge for Christ, do all for Christ; beware of men-pleasing—there is too much of it amongst us. The new college hath broken my heart; I can say nothing of it; I have left it upon the Lord of the house; and it hath been, and still is, my desire that He may dwell in this society, and that the youth may be fed with sound knowledge." After this he said, "Dear brethren, it may seem presumptuous in me, a particular man, to send a commission to a presbytery;"—and Mr M'Gill, replying, that it was no presumption, he continued,—"Dear brethren, take a commission from me, a dying man, to them to appear, for God and His cause, and adhere to the doctrine of the covenant, and have a care of the flock committed to their charge. Let them feed the flock out of love, preach for God, visit and catechise for God, and do all for God; beware of men-pleasing—the chief Shepherd will appear shortly. . . . I have been a sinful man, and have had mine own failings; but my Lord hath pardoned me and accepted my labours. I adhere to the Cause and Covenant, and resolve never to depart from the protestation against the controverted Assemblies. I am the man I was. I am still for keeping the government of the Kirk of Scotland entire, and would not for a thousand worlds have had the least hand in the burning of the 'Causes of God's Wrath.' Oh! for grace to wrestle with God for their salvation."

Mr Vilant having prayed at his desire, as they took their leave he renewed his charge to them to feed the flock out of love. The next morning, as he recovered out of a fainting, in which they who looked on expected his dissolution, he said, " I feel, I feel, I believe, I joy and rejoice, I feed on manna." Mr Blair, whose praise is in the Churches, being present, when he took a little wine in a spoon to refresh himself, being then very weak, said to him, " Ye feed on dainties in heaven, and think nothing of our cordials on earth." He answered, " They are all but dung; but they are Christ's creatures, and, out of obedience to His command, I take them. Mine eyes shall see my Redeemer; I know He shall stand the last day upon the earth, and I shall be caught up in the clouds to meet Him in the air, and I shall ever be with Him; and what would you have more? there is an end." And stretching out his hands, he said again, " there is an end." And a little after, he said, " I have been a single man, but I stand at the best pass that ever a man did; Christ is mine, and I am His;" and spoke much of the white stone and new name. Mr Blair, who loved with all his heart to hear Christ commended, said to him again—" What think ye now of Christ?" To which he answered, " I shall live and adore Him. Glory! glory to my Creator and my Redeemer for ever! Glory shines in Immanuel's land." In the afternoon of that day, he said, " Oh! that all my brethren in the land may know what a Master I have served, and what peace I have this day. I shall sleep in Christ, and when I awake I shall be satisfied with His likeness. This night shall close the door, and put my anchor within the vail; and I shall go away in a sleep by five of the clock in the morning;" which exactly fell out. Though he was very weak, he had often this expression, " Oh! for arms to embrace Him! Oh! for a well-tuned harp!"

He exhorted Dr Colvil, a man who complied with prelacy afterwards, to adhere to the government of the Church of Scotland, and to the doctrine of the Covenant; and to have a care to feed the youth with sound knowledge. And the Doctor being the professor of the new college, he told him that he heartily forgave all the wrongs he had done him. He spake likewise to Mr Honeyman, afterwards Bishop Honeyman, who came to see him, saying, "Tell the presbytery to answer for God, and His cause and covenant; the case is desperate; let them be in their duty." Then directing his speech to Dr Colvil and Mr Honeyman, he said, "Stick to it. You may think it an easy thing in me, a dying man, that I am now going out of the reach of all that men can do; but He, before whom I stand, knows I dare advise no colleague or brother to do what I would not cordially do myself upon all hazard; and as for the 'Causes of God's Wrath,' that men have now condemned, tell Mr James Wood, from me, that I had rather lay down my head on a scaffold, and have it chopped off many times, were it possible, before I had passed from them." And then to Mr Honeyman he said, "Tell Mr Wood, I heartily forgive him all the wrongs he hath done me; and desire him, from me, to declare himself the man that he is still for the government of the Church of Scotland."

Afterwards, when some spoke to him of his former painfulness and faithfulness in the ministry, he said, "I disclaim all that; the port that I would be at is redemption and forgiveness through His blood; 'Thou shalt show me the path of life, in Thy sight is fulness of joy:' there is nothing now betwixt me and the resurrection, but 'to-day thou shalt be with Me in paradise.'" Mr Blair saying, "Shall I praise the Lord for all the mercies He has done and is to do for you?" He answered, "Oh! for a well-tuned harp." To his child he said, "I have again left you upon the Lord; it may be you will tell this to others, that 'the lines are fallen to me in pleasant places; I have got a goodly heritage.' I bless the Lord that He gave me counsel."

Thus, by five o'clock in the morning, as he himself foretold, it was said unto him, "Come up hither;" and he gave up the ghost, and the renowned eagle took its flight unto the mountains of spices.

Thus died the famous Samuel Rutherford, who may justly be accounted among the sufferers of that time; for surely he was a martyr, both in his own design and resolution, and by the design and determination of men. Few men ever ran so long a race without cessation; so constantly, so unweariedly, and so unblameably. Two things rarely to be found in one man, were eminent in him, viz., a quick invention and sound judgment; and these accompanied with a homely but clear expression, and graceful elocution; so that such

RUTHERFORD'S MONUMENT AT ANWOTH.

as knew him best, were in a strait whether to admire him most for his penetrating wit, and sublime genius in the schools, and peculiar exactness in disputes and matters of controversy, or for his familiar condescension in the pulpit, where he was one of the most moving and affectionate preachers in his time, or perhaps in any age of the Church. To sum up all in a word, he seems to have been one of the most resplendent lights that ever arose in this horizon.

In all his writings he breathes the true spirit of religion; but in his every way admirable Letters, he seems to have outdone himself, as well as everybody else. These, although jested on by the profane wits of this age, because of some homely and familiar expressions in them, it must be owned by all who have any relish for true piety, contain sublime flights of devotion, and must ravish and edify every sober, serious, and understanding reader.

Among the posthumous Works of the laborious Mr Rutherford, are, his Letters; the Trial and Triumph of Faith; Christ's Dying and Drawing of Sinners; a discourse on Prayer; a discourse on the Covenant; on Liberty of Conscience; a Survey of Spiritual Antichrist; a Survey of Antinomianism; Antichrist Stormed; and several other controversial pieces, such as *Lex Rex;* the Due Right of Church Government; the Divine Right of Church Government;

a Peaceable Plea for Presbytery; as also his Summary of Church Discipline, and a treatise on the Divine Influence of the Spirit. There are also many of his sermons in print, some of which were preached before both Houses of Parliament, 1644 and 1645. He wrote also upon Providence; but this being in Latin, is only in the hands of a few, as are also the greater part of his other works, being so seldom republished. There is also a volume of Sermons, Sacramental Discourses, etc.

AN EPITAPH ON HIS GRAVE-STONE.

What tongue, what pen, or skill of men
Can famous Rutherford commend!
His learning justly rais'd his fame—
True goodness did adorn his name.
He did converse with things above,
Acquainted with Immanuel's love.
Most orthodox he was and sound,
And many errors did confound.
For Zion's King, and Zion's cause,
And Scotland's covenanted laws,
Most constantly he did contend,
Until his time was at an end.
At last he wan to full fruition
Of that which he had seen in vision.

The Most Noble Archibald Campbell, Marquis of Argyle.

ARCHIBALD CAMPBELL having, after a good classical education, applied himself to the study of the Holy Scriptures, became well acquainted with the most interesting points of religion, which he retained and cultivated amidst his most laborious and exalted employments, both in Church and State, ever after.

From his early years he stood well affected to the Presbyterian interest, and being still a favourer of the Puritans (as the Presbyterians were then called) when Samuel Rutherford was, for his nonconformity, brought before the High Commission Court in the year 1638, he interposed to the utmost in his behalf, concerning which Rutherford in his Letters says, "My Lord has brought me a friend from the Highlands of Argyle, my Lord of Lorne, who hath done as much as was within the compass of his power. God gave me favour in his eyes." And elsewhere to the Lady Kenmuir, "Write thanks to your brother, my Lord of Lorne, for what he has done for me, a poor unknown stranger to him. I shall pray for him and his house while I live. It is his honour to open his mouth in the streets for his wronged and oppressed Master, Christ Jesus." Nor was this all; for about the same time, he so laboured and prevailed with the Bishop of Galloway, that Gordon of Earlston was released from the sentence of banishment, unto which he was assigned for the same noble cause."

And no sooner did our Reformation, commonly called the second Reformation, begin to dawn in 1637, than he espoused the same cause himself; for we find next year the Earl of Argyle, (his father having died about that time), though a privy councillor, diligently attending all the sessions of that famous General Assembly held at Glasgow, to hear their debates and determinations concerning diocesan episcopacy, and the five articles of Perth, and declaring his full satisfaction with their decisions. And here it was that this noble peer began to distinguish himself by a concern for the Redeemer's glory; in which he continued, and was kept faithful, until he got the crown of martyrdom at last.

At this Assembly, among many other things, his Lordship proposed an explanation of the Confession and Covenant; in which he wished them to proceed with great deliberation, lest (said he) they should bring any under suspicion of perjury, who had sworn it in the sense he had done; which motion was taken in good part by the members, and entered upon in its eighth session. Alexander Henderson, the Moderator, at the conclusion of this Assembly, judging that, after all, the countenance given to their meetings by Argyle deserved a particular acknowledgment, expressed the wish that his Lordship had joined with them sooner; but he hoped God had reserved him for the best times, and would honour him here and hereafter. Whereupon his Lordship rose, and delivered an excellent speech *extempore* before the Assembly; in which, amongst other things, he said, " And whereas you wished I had joined you sooner, truly it was not for want of affection for the good of religion, and my own country, which detained me, but a desire and hope, that, by staying with the Court, I might have been able to bring about a redress of grievances ; and when I saw that I could no longer stay without proving unfaithful to my God and my country, I thought good to do as I have done. I remember I told some of you, that pride and avarice are two evils that have wrought much woe to the Church of Christ; and as they are grievous faults in any man, they are especially so in churchmen. I hope every man here shall walk by the square and rule which is now set before him, observing duty— 1. To superiors ; 2. To equals ; and, 3. To inferiors. Touching our duty to superiors, there needs nothing to be added to what has been wisely said by the Moderator. Next, concerning equals, there is a case much spoken of in the Church, viz., the power of ruling elders; some ministers apprehending it to be a curbing of their power. Truly it may be some elders are not so wise as there is need for. But as unity ought to be the endeavour of us all, let neighbouring parishes and presbyteries meet together for settling the same. And thirdly, for inferiors, I hope ministers will discharge their duty to their flocks, and that people will have a due regard to those that are set over them to watch for their souls, and not to think, that because they want Bishops, they may live as they will."

After this, when the Covenanters were obliged to take arms in their own defence, in 1639, and marched towards the borders of England, under the command of General Alexander Leslie, this noble lord being set to guard the western coast, contributed very much, by his diligence and prudence, to preserve peace ; not only in convening the gentlemen in these quarters, and taking security of them for that purpose, but also by raising four hundred men in the shire of Argyle, whom he took in hand to maintain at his own charges. This number he afterwards increased to nine hundred able men, one-half whereof he set on Kintyre in Argyleshire, to wait on the Marquis of Antrim's design, and the rest on the head of Lorne, to observe the motions of those of Lochaber, and the Western Isles. From thence he himself went over to Arran with some cannon and took the castle of Brodick, belonging to the Marquis of Hamilton ; which surrendered without resistance.

He was again, in the absence of the Covenanters' army, during the year 1640, appointed to the same business, which he managed with no less success ; for he apprehended no less than eight or nine of the ringleaders of the malignant faction, and made them give

bonds for their better behaviour in time coming; which industrious and faithful conduct so stirred up the malice of his adversaries and those of the truth, that they afterwards sought on all
occasions to vent their mischief against him; for, at the very
sitting down of the Scots Parliament, the Earl of Montrose made
a most mischievous attempt to wound his reputation, and to set the
King at perpetual variance with his Lordship.

Among other offensive speeches uttered by Montrose, one was,
that when the Earl of Athole, and the other eight gentlemen arrested
by him last year, for carrying arms against their country, were in
his Lordship's tent at the ford of Lyon, he (Argyle) had said publicly,
"That they (meaning the Parliament) had consulted both lawyers
and divers others, anent the deposing of the King, and had got
resolution that it might be done in three cases, viz. 1. Desertion; 2.
Invasion; and 3. Vendition; and that they once thought to have
done it at the last sitting of Parliament, but would do it at the next
sitting thereof." Montrose condescended on Mr James Stuart, commissary of Dunkeld, one of the foresaid eight taken by Argyle, as
his informer; and some of his Lordship's friends having brought the
said commissary to Edinburgh, he was so foolhardy as to subscribe
the acknowledgment of the above report to Montrose. The Earl
of Argyle denied the truth of this in the strongest terms, and resolved to prosecute Stuart before the Court of Justiciary, where his
Lordship insisted for an impartial trial; which was granted; and,
according to his desire, four Lords of the Session were added *hac
vice* to the Court of Justiciary. Stuart was accused upon the laws of
leasing, particularly of a principal statesman; to escape the imminent
danger of which he wrote to Argyle, wherein he cleared him of the
charge as laid against him, and acknowledged that he himself forged
them, out of malice against his Lordship. But though Argyle's
innocence was thus cleared, it was thought necessary to let the trial
go on; and the fact being proven, he was condemned to die. Argyle
would willingly have seen the royal clemency extended to the
unfortunate wretch: but others thought the crime tended to mar the
design of the late treaty, and judged it needful, as a terror to others,
to make an example. At his execution, he discovered a great deal
of remorse for what he had done; and although Argyle was vindicated
in this, yet we find that after the Restoration it was made one of the
principal handles against this noble martyr.

During these transactions, King Charles I., disagreeing with his

English Parliament, made another tour to Scotland, and attended the Scots Parliament there; in which Parliament, that he might more effectually gain the Scots over to his interest, he not only granted a ratification of all their former proceedings, both in their own defence, and with respect to religion, but also dignified several of the Scots nobility. Being sensible of the many great and good services done by this noble Earl, he was placed at the head of the Treasury; and the day before the rising of the Parliament, all the commissions granted to, and services and employments performed by Archibald Earl of Argyle, in the service of his country, were approved of; and an Act of Parliament made thereon was read and voted, the King giving him this testimony in public, that he dealt over honestly with him, though he was still stiff as to the point in controversy. On the same day, November 15, 1641, the King delivered a patent to Lyon King at Arms, and he to the Clerk-Register, who read it publicly, whereby His Majesty created Archibald Earl of Argyle, Marquis of Argyle, Earl of Kintyre, Lord Lorne, etc.; which being read and given back to the King, His Majesty delivered the same with his own hand to the Marquis; who rose and made a very handsome speech in gratitude to His Majesty, showing that he neither expected nor deserved such honour or preferment.

During the sitting of the foresaid Parliament, another incident occurred, wherein a plot was laid to destroy this nobleman, in the following manner. Some of the nobility, envying the power, preferment, and influence that he and the Marquis of Hamilton had with the King, laid a close design for their lives. The Earl of Crawfurd, Colonel Cochran, and Lieutenant Alexander Stuart, were to have been the actors, and it was insinuated that his Majesty, Lord Almond, and others, were privy to the design, which was, that Hamilton and Argyle should be called for in the dead of the night to speak with the King, and in the way were to be arrested as traitors and delivered to Earl Crawfurd, who was to wait for them with a considerable body of armed men. If any resistance was made he was to stab them immediately; if not, carry them prisoners to a ship of war, in the roads of Leith, where they were to be confined until they should be tried for treason. But this breaking out before it was fully ripe, the two noblemen, the night before, went off to a place of more strength, twelve miles distant, and so escaped the danger, as a bird out of the hands of the fowler. Yet such were their lenity and clemency, that, upon a petition from them, the foresaid persons were set at liberty.

After this, the Marquis of Argyle had a most active hand in carrying on the work of Reformation and uniformity in religion in 1643. While he was busied among the Covenanters in 1644, Montrose and some others associated themselves to raise forces for the King, intending to draw the Scots army from England. To effect this, the Earl of Antrim undertook to send over ten thousand Irish to the north of Scotland, under the command of one Alaster M'Donald, a Scotsman, and a considerable body was accordingly sent, who committed many outrages in Argyle's country. To suppress this insurrection, the Committee of Estates, April 10, gave orders to the Marquis to raise three regiments, which he accordingly did, and with them marched northward, took several of their principal chieftains, and dispersed the rest for some time. But Montrose being still in the field, gained several victories during this and the following year, and in the meantime plundered and laid waste the greater part of Argyleshire and other places belonging to the Covenanters, without mercy. Although he was at last defeated and totally routed by General David Leslie at Philliphaugh, yet such was the cruelty of those cutthroats, that the foresaid M'Donald and his Irish band returned to Argyleshire, in the beginning of the year 1646, and burned and plundered the dwellings of the well-affected, in such a terrible manner, that about twelve hundred of them assembled in a body under Acknalase, who brought them down to Monteith, to live upon the disaffected in that country. But the Athol men falling upon them at Callander, and they being but poorly armed, several of them were killed, and the rest fled towards Stirling, where their master, the noble Marquis, met them, and, commiserating their deplorable condition, carried them through to Lennox, to live upon the lands of the Lord Napier and others of the disaffected, until they were better provided for. In the meantime he himself went over to Ireland and brought over the remains of the Scots forces, and with them landed in Argyleshire, upon which M'Donald soon betook himself to the Isles, and from thence returned to Ireland, whereby peace was restored in those parts.

Again, in the year 1648, when the State fell into two factions, that of the malignants was headed by the Duke of Hamilton, and the Covenanters by the Marquis of Argyle, from which it is easy to conclude that from the year 1643 (when he had such an active hand in calling the Convention of Estates, and entering into the Solemn League and Covenant) to 1648, he was the principal agent amongst the Cove-

PORTRAIT OF ARCHIBALD, MARQUIS OF ARGYLE.

nanters, and never failed on all occasions to appear in defence of the civil and religious liberties of his native country.

It is well known what appearances he made in the year 1649, and what interest he had in the Parliament, and that to the utmost of his power he did employ the same for bringing home Charles II., and possessing him of his crown and the exercise of his royal authority. In this he succeeded to good purpose, as long as the King followed his counsel and advice; but by the King afterwards taking the malignant faction into places of power and trust, all went to shipwreck together, which was no small matter of grief to this worthy and religious nobleman.

As the King was well received by the Marquis of Argyle, so he pretended a great deal of regard and kindness for him, as appears from a letter or declaration given under his own hand at Perth, September 24, 1650, in which he says : " Having taken into my consideration the faithful endeavours of the Marquis of Argyle for restoring me to my just rights, . . . I am desirous to let the world see how sensible I am of his real respect to me, by some particular favour to him. And particularly I do promise that I shall make him Duke of Argyle, a Knight of the Garter, and one of the gentlemen of my bedchamber, and this to be performed when he shall think fit. I do further promise to hearken to his counsel. . . . Whenever it shall

PORTRAIT OF GENERAL ALEXANDER LESLIE, EARL OF LEVEN.

please God to restore me to my just rights in England, I shall see him paid the forty thousand pounds sterling which are due to him. All which I do promise to make good upon the word of a King. C. R."

How all these fair promises were performed will come afterwards to be observed. For this godly nobleman taking upon him to reprove the King for some of his immoralities, his faithful admonition, however well it appeared to be taken at the time, was never forgotten, until it was repaid with the highest resentment. Such was the way to hearken to his counsel ! for if debauchery and dissimulation had ever been accounted among the liberal sciences, then this prince was altogether a master in that faculty.

In the meantime, January 1, 1651, the King was crowned at Scone, where, after an excellent sermon by Mr Robert Douglas, from 2 Kings xi. 12, 17, the King took the coronation oath, then sitting down in the chair of state. After some other ceremonies were performed, the Marquis of Argyle, taking the crown in his hands (Mr Douglas having prayed) set it on the King's head ; and so ascending the stage, attended by the officers of the crown, he was installed into the royal throne by the Marquis, saying, " Stand fast from henceforth, in the place whereof you are the lawful and righteous heir, by a long and lineal succession of your fathers, which is now delivered to you by the authority of God Almighty." Then the solemnity was concluded by a pertinent exhortation, both to King and people, wherein they were certified, that if they should conspire against the kingdom of Jesus Christ, both supporters and supported should fall together.

But the King's forces having been before that defeated by Cromwell at Dunbar, and being no longer able to make head against the English, Charles went to England, and, by his particular allowance, the Marquis of Argyle, after kissing his hand, was left at Stirling. But the King's army being totally routed on the 3d of September at Worcester, and he himself being driven from his dominions, the Parliamentary army overran the whole country, so that the representatives of the nation were either obliged to take the tender, or else suffer great hardships ; which tender the Marquis having refused at Dumbarton, they resolved to invade the Highlands and the shire of Argyle, which were now inclosed on all hands with regiments of foot and horse. Major Dean, coming to the Marquis's house at Inverary where he was lying sick, presented a paper, which he behoved to subscribe against to-morrow, or else be carried off prisoner. This (though sore against his will), for his own and his vassals' and tenants' safety, he was obliged to subscribe with some alterations, which capitulation was made a mighty handle against him afterwards. And although he had some influence with Cromwell, and was present at several meetings wherein he procured an equal hearing to the protesters at London, while he was there in the year 1657, yet he was rather a prisoner on demand than a free agent, and so continued until the Restoration.

Soon after the King's return, the Marquis was very much solicited to repair to court, and no doubt he himself inclined to wait on a prince on whose head he had set the crown. Though some of his best friends used powerful arguments to divert him from his purpose till matters were better settled, yet, from the testimony of a good conscience, knowing that he was able to vindicate himself from all aspersions, if he were but once admitted to the King's presence, he set out for London, where he arrived on the 8th of July, and went directly to Whitehall to salute his Majesty. Whenever the King heard he was come thither (notwithstanding his former fair promises) he ordered Sir William Fleming to apprehend him, and carry him to the Tower, where he continued till toward the beginning of December, when he was sent down in a man-of-war, to abide his trial before the Parliament in Scotland. On the 20th they landed at Leith, and

next day he was marched along the streets of Edinburgh, betwixt two
of the town bailies, to the Castle, where he continued until his trial
came on.

On February 1661, his lordship was brought down from the Castle
in a coach, with three of the magistrates of Edinburgh, attended by
the town-guard, and presented before the bar of the House of Parliament, where the King's advocate, Sir John Fletcher, accused him
in common form of high treason, and producing an indictment,
craved that it might be read. The Marquis begged liberty to
speak before that was done, but the House refused his reasonable
desire, and ordered it to be read; and though he entreated them to
hear a petition he had to present, yet this was too great a favour to
be granted. The indictment, which was more months in forming
than he had days allowed at first to bring his defence, consisted of
fourteen articles, the principal of which were, his entering into the
Solemn League and Covenant with England, and his complying with
Oliver Cromwell; all the rest being a heap of slanders, and perver-
sion of matters of fact, gathered up against this good and great man,
all which he abundantly clears off in his information and answers.

After his indictment was read, he had leave to speak, and discoursed for some time to good purpose. Among other things, he
said that the things laid against him could not be proven; but he
confessed, that in the way allowed by solemn oath and covenant, he
served his God, his king, and his country; and though he owned he
wanted not failings common to all persons in public business in such
a time, yet he blessed God that he was able to make the falsehood
of every article of his charge appear, that he had done nothing with
a wicked mind, but with many others had the misfortune to do many
things, the unforeseen events of which had proved bad.

The Parliament fixed the 26th day of February for bringing in his
defence, which was too short a time for replying to so many articles.
However, at his request, it was put off till the 5th of March, when
he appeared before the Lords of the Articles, who ordered him immediately to produce his defence; whereupon he delivered a very
moving speech, and gave in a most affecting petition, remitting himself to the King's mercy, and beseeching the Parliament to intercede
for him; which are too long here to be inserted. On March the 6th,
being brought before the Parliament, it was reported from the Lords,
that he had offered a submission to His Majesty; but his submission
was voted not satisfactory, and he was commanded on the morrow

to give in his defence to the Lords of the Articles. When he came before them, and told his defence was not ready, he was appointed to give them in on Monday, April 9th, otherwise they would take the whole business before them, without any regard to what he should afterwards say; but it seems, on the day appointed, his defence was given in, which contained fifteen sheets of small print, wherein the Marquis's management was fully vindicated from all the falsehoods and calumnies in the indictment.

Upon the 16th of April he was again before the Parliament, where, after the process was read, he made a very handsome and moving speech, wherein, at a considerable length, he removed several reproaches cast upon him, and touched on some things not in his papers; but whatever he or his lawyers could say had little weight with the members of Parliament. Some of them were already resolved what to do. The House had many messages to hasten his process to an end, but the failure of many of their designed proba tions against this good man embarrassed them mightily for some time. For it appears that there were upwards of thirty different libels all formed against him, and all came to nothing when they began to prove them; so that they were forced to betake themselves to the charge of his innocent but necessary compliance with the English Parliament, after every shire and burgh in Scotland had made the same submission to their conquerors.

In the beginning of May, witnesses were examined and depositions taken against him, after which he was, upon the 25th, brought before the bar of the house to receive sentence from his judges, who were *socii criminis* (or accomplices), as he told the King's advocate. The house was very thin, all withdrawing except those who were resolved to follow the courses of the time. He put them in mind of the prac tice of Theodosius the emperor, who enacted that the sentence of death should not be executed till after thirty days were passed, and added, " I crave but ten, that the King may be acquainted with it ;" but this was refused. Then the sentence was pronounced : " That he was found guilty of high treason, and adjudged to be executed to the death as a traitor, his head to be severed from his body at the Cross of Edinburgh, upon Monday the 27th instant, and affixed on the same place where the Marquis of Montrose's head formerly was, and his arms torn before the Parliament at the Cross." Upon this he offered to speak, but the trumpets sounding, he stopped till they ended, and then said, " I had the honour to set the crown on the

King's head, and now he hastens me to a better crown than his own."
And directing himself to the commissioner and Parliament, he said,
"You have the indemnity of an earthly king among your hands, and
have denied me a share in that; but you cannot hinder me from the
indemnity of the King of kings, and shortly you must be before His
tribunal. I pray He mete not out such measure to you as you have
done to me, when you are called to an account for all your actings,
and this amongst the rest."

After his sentence he was ordered to the common prison, where
his excellent lady was waiting for him. Upon seeing her he said,
"They have given me till Monday to be with you, my dear, therefore
let us make for it." She, embracing him, wept bitterly, and said,
"The Lord will require it : the Lord will require it," which drew
tears from all in the room. But being himself composed, he said,
"Forbear, forbear; I pity them, they know not what they are doing;
they may shut me in where they please, but they cannot shut God
out from me. For my part, I am as content to be here as in the
Castle, and as content in the Castle as in the Tower of London, and
as content there as when at liberty; and I hope to be as content on
the scaffold as any of them all." He added that he remembered a
Scripture cited by an honest minister to him while in the castle,
which he intended to put in practice : "When Ziklag was taken and
burnt, the people spake of stoning David, but he encouraged himself
in the Lord his God."

He spent all his short time till Monday with the greatest serenity
and cheerfulness, and in the proper exercise of a dying Christian.
To some ministers who were permitted to attend him he said, that
shortly they would envy him who was got before them; and added,
"Remember that I tell you; my skill fails me, if you who are ministers will not either suffer much or sin much; for, though you go along
with these men in part, if you do not in all things, you are but where
you were, and so must suffer, and if you go not at all with them, you
must but suffer."

During his life he was reckoned rather timorous than bold to any
excess. In prison he said that in his temper he was naturally inclined
to fear, but desired those about him, as they could not but do, to
observe that the Lord had heard his prayer, and removed all fear from
him. At his own desire, his lady took her leave of him on the Sabbath night. Mr Robert Douglas and Mr George Hutcheson preached
to him in the Tolbooth on the Lord's day, and his dear and much

valued friend, Mr David Dickson (says Wodrow), was his bedfellow the last night he was on earth.

The Marquis had a sweet time in the Tolbooth as to his soul's case, and it still increased nearer his end. As he had slept calmly and pleasantly his last night, so in the intervals of his necessary business he had much spiritual conversation. On Monday morning, though he was much engaged in settling his affairs in the midst of company, yet he was so overpowered with a sensible effusion of the Holy Spirit, that he broke out in rapture, and said, "I thought to have concealed the Lord's goodness, but it will not do. I am now ordering my affairs, and God is sealing my charter to a better inheritance, and is just now saying to me, "Son, be of good cheer, thy sins are forgiven thee."

Some time before he went to the place of execution, he received an excellent letter from a certain minister, and wrote a most moving one to the King, and after dining precisely at twelve o'clock along with his friends with great cheerfulness, he retired for a little. Upon his opening the door, Mr Hutcheson said, "What cheer, my Lord?" He answered, "Good cheer, sir; the Lord hath again confirmed and said to me from heaven, Thy sins be forgiven thee." Upon this, tears of joy flowed in abundance; he retired to the window and wept there; from that he came to the fire, and made as if he would stir it a little to conceal his concern, but all would not do; his tears ran down his face, and coming to Mr Hutcheson, he said, "I think His kindness overcomes me. But God is good to me, that He let not out too much of it here, for He knows I could not bear it. Get me my cloak and let us go." But being told that the clock was kept back till one, till the bailies should come, he answered "They are far in the wrong;" and presently kneeled and prayed before all present, in a most sweet and heavenly manner. As he ended, the bailies sent up word to come down; upon which he called for a glass of wine, and asked a blessing to it, standing, and continuing in the same frame, he said, "Now let us go, and God be with us."

After having taken his leave of such in the room as were not to go with him to the scaffold, when going towards the door he said, "I could die like a Roman, but choose rather to die like a Christian. Come away, gentlemen, he that goes first goes cleanliest." When going down stairs, he called Mr James Guthrie to him, and embracing him in a most endearing way, took his farewell of him. Guthrie, at parting, addressed the Marquis thus, "My lord, God hath

been with you,—He is with you,—and will be with you. And such
is my respect for your lordship, that if I were not under sentence of
death myself, I would cheerfully die for your lordship." So they
parted, to meet again in a better place on the Friday following.

Then the Marquis, accompanied by several noblemen and
gentlemen, dressed in black, with his cloak and hat on, went down
the street, mounted the scaffold with great serenity and gravity, like
one going to his father's house, and saluted all on it. Then Mr
Hutcheson prayed, after which his lordship delivered his speech, in
which among other things he said, "I come not here to justify myself, but the Lord; who is holy in all His ways, righteous in all His
works, holy and blessed be His name. Neither come I to condemn
others. I bless the Lord, I pardon all men, and desire to be pardoned of the Lord myself. Let the will of the Lord be done ; that is
all I desire. I was real and cordial in my desires to bring the King
home, and in my endeavours for him when he was home, and had no
correspondence with the adversaries' army, nor any of them, when his
Majesty was in Scotland ; nor had I any hand in his late Majesty's
murder. I shall not speak much to these things for which I am condemned, lest I seem to condemn others. It is well known it is only
for compliance, which was the epidemical fault of the nation ; I wish
the Lord to pardon them : I say no more. But God hath laid
engagements on Scotland ; we are tied by covenants to religion and
reformation ; those who were then unborn are yet engaged ; and it
passeth the power of all the magistrates under heaven to absolve from
the oath of God. These times are like to be either very sinning or
suffering times ; let Christians make their choice ; there is a sad dilemma in the business—sin or suffer ; and surely he that will choose
the better part will choose to suffer ; others that will choose to sin
will not escape suffering. They shall suffer, but perhaps not as I do
(pointing to the Maiden), but worse. Mine is but temporal, theirs
shall be eternal. When I shall be singing, they shall be howling.
Beware therefore of sin, whatever you beware of, especially in such
times. And hence my condition is such now, as, when I am gone,
will be seen not to be as many imagined. I wish, as the Lord hath
pardoned me, so may He pardon them, for this and other things, that
what they have done to me may never meet them in their accounts.
I have no more to say, but to beg the Lord, that when I go away,
He would bless every one that stayeth behind."

When he had delivered this his seasonable and pathetic speech

THE MAIDEN.

(which, with his last words, is recorded at length in "Naphtali, or the wrestling of the Church of Scotland"), Mr Hamilton prayed, after which he prayed most sweetly himself, and then took his leave of all his friends on the scaffold.　He first gave to the executioner a napkin with some money in it; to his sons-in-law, Caithness and Ker, his watch and some other things out of his pocket; he gave to Loudon his silver pencase, to Lothian a double ducat, and then threw off his coat.　When going to the Maiden, Mr Hutcheson said, " My Lord, now hold your grip sicker."　He answered, " You know, Mr Hutcheson, what I said to you in the chamber.　I am not afraid to be surprised with fear."　The laird of Skelmorlie took him by the hand, when near the Maiden, and found him most composed.　He kneeled down most cheerfully, and after he had prayed a little, gave the signal (which was the lifting up of his hand), and the instrument called the Maiden struck off his head from his body, which was fixed on the west end of the Tolbooth, as a monument of the Parliament's injustice and the land's misery.　His body was by his friends put in a coffin and conveyed, with a good many attendants, through Linlithgow and Falkirk to Glasgow, and from thence to Kilpatrick, where it was put in a boat, carried to Dunoon, and buried in Kilmun church.

Thus died the noble Marquis of Argyle, the proto-martyr to

religion since the Reformation from Popery, the true portrait of whose character cannot be drawn. His enemies themselves will allow him to have been a person of extraordinary piety, remarkable wisdom and prudence, great gravity and authority, and singular usefulness. He was the head of the Covenanters in Scotland, and had been singularly active in the work of Reformation there, and of almost any that had engaged in the work he stuck closest by it, when most of the nation quitted it very much, so that this attack upon him was a stroke at the root of all that had been done in Scotland from 1638 to the usurpation. But the tree of prelacy and arbitrary measures, when planting, behoved to be soaked with the blood of this excellent patriot, stanch Presbyterian, and vigorous asserter of Scotland's liberty; and as he was the greater promoter thereof during his life, and steadfast in witnessing to it at his death, so it was to a great degree buried with him in Scotland for many years. In a word, he had piety for a Christian, sense for a counsellor, courage for a martyr, and soul for a king. If ever any was, he might be said to be a true Scotsman.

James Guthrie.

AMES GUTHRIE, son of the Laird of Guthrie (a very ancient and honourable family) having gone through his course of classical learning at the Grammar School and college, taught philosophy in the University of St Andrews, where for several years he gave abundant proof that he was an able scholar. His temper was very steady and composed; he could reason upon the most subtle points with great solidity, and, when every one else was warm, his temper was never ruffled. At any time when indecent heats or wranglings happened to occur when reasoning, it was his ordinary custom to say, "Enough of this; let us go to some other subject; we are warm, and can dispute no longer with advan-

PORTRAIT OF JAMES GUTHRIE.

tage." Perhaps he had the greatest mixture of fervent zeal and sweet calmness in his temper, of any man in his time.

Being educated in opposition to Presbyterian principles, he was highly prelatical in his judgment when he came first to St Andrews ; but by conversing with Samuel Rutherford and others, and especially through his joining the weekly society's meetings there, for prayer and conference, he was effectually brought off from that way. And perhaps it was this that made the writer of the Diurnal (who was no friend of his) say, " That if James Guthrie had continued fixed to his first principles, he had been a star of the first magnitude in Scotland." When he came to judge for himself, he happily departed from his first principles, and upon examination of that way wherein he was educated, he left it, and thereby became a star of the first magnitude indeed. It is said that while he was regent in the college of St Andrews, James Sharp (afterwards Archbishop Sharp) being then a promising young man there, he several times wrote this verse upon him,

> If thou, Sharp, die the common death of men,
> I'll burn my bill, and throw away my pen.

Having passed his trials, in the year 1638, he was settled minister at Lauder, where he remained for several years. In the year 1646 he was appointed one of those ministers who were to attend the King, while at Newcastle, and likewise he was one of those nominated in the commission for the public affairs of the Church, during the intervals betwixt the General Assemblies. In about three years after this he was translated to Stirling, where he continued until the Restoration, a most faithful watchman upon Zion's walls, who ceased not day and night to declare the whole counsel of God to His people, "showing Israel their iniquities, and the house of Jacob their sins."

After he came to Stirling, he not only evidenced a singular care over his people, but also was a great assistant in the affairs of the Church, being a most zealous enemy to all error and profanity. And when that unhappy difference fell out with the public Resolutioners, he was a stanch Protester, opposing these resolutions to the utmost of his power; insomuch that after the Presbytery of Stirling had written a letter to the Commission of the General Assembly, showing their dislike and dissatisfaction with the resolutions, after they had been concluded upon at Perth, December 14, 1650, James Guthrie and his colleague, Mr Bennett, went somewhat further, and openly preached against them, as a thing involving the land in conjunction with the malignant party. For this they were ordered to repair to Perth, on February 19, 1651, to answer before King Charles II. and the Committee of Estates; but upon the indisposition of one of them, they excused themselves by a letter for their non-appearance that day, and promised to attend about the end of the week. Accordingly, on the 22d they appeared at Perth, where they gave in a protestation; signifying that although they owned His Majesty's civil authority, yet was Mr Guthrie challenged by the King and his Council for a doctrinal thesis which he had maintained and spoken to in a sermon; and they being incompetent judges in matters purely ecclesiastical—such as is the examination and censuring of doctrines—they did decline them on that account.

The matter being deferred for some days till the King returned from Aberdeen, the two ministers were, in the meantime, confined to Perth and Dundee, whereupon they (February 28) presented another paper or protestation, which was much the same, though in stronger terms, and supported by many excellent arguments. After this the King and Committee thought proper to dismiss them, and to proceed no farther in the affair at present; and yet James Guthrie's declining the King's authority in matters ecclesiastical here was made the prin-

cipal article in his indictment some ten years after, to gratify a
personal pique which the Earl of Middleton had against this good
man, the occasion of which was as follows :

By improving an affront the King met with in 1659, some
malignants so prevailed to heighten his fears of the evil designs
of those about him, that, by a correspondence with the Papists,
malignants, and such as were disaffected to the Covenants in the
north, matters came in a little to such a pass, that a considerable
number of noblemen, gentlemen, and others, were to rise and form
themselves into an army, under Middleton's command, and the King
was to cast himself into their arms.   Accordingly, the King, with a
few in his retinue, as if he were going a-hunting, left his best friends,
crossed the Tay, and came to Angus, where he was to have met with
those people : but soon finding himself disappointed, he came back
to the Committee of Estates, where indeed his greatest strength lay.
In the meanwhile several who had been in the plot, fearing punishment, got together under Middleton's command.   General Leslie
marched towards them, and the King wrote them to lay down their
arms.   The Committee sent an indemnity to such as should submit ;
but while the States were thus dealing with them, the Commission of
the Assembly were not wanting to show their zeal against such as
ventured to disturb the public peace.   It is said, that James Guthrie
here proposed summary excommunication, as a censure Middleton
deserved, and as what he thought to be a suitable testimony from the
Church at this juncture.   This highest sentence was carried in the
Commission by a plurality of votes, and Guthrie was appointed
to pronounce the sentence next Sabbath.   In the meantime the
Committee of Estates, not without some debate, had agreed upon
an indemnity to Middleton.   There was an express sent to Stirling,
with an account how things stood, and a letter, desiring Mr Guthrie
to forbear the intimation of the Commission of Assembly's sentence.
But this letter coming to him just as he was going to the pulpit, he did
not open it till the work was over ; and though he had, it is a question
if he would have delayed the Commission's sentence upon a private
missive to himself.   However, the sentence was inflicted, and although
the Commission, January 3, 1651 (being their next meeting), did relax
Middleton from that censure, and laid it on a better man, Colonel
Strachan, yet it is believed that Middleton never forgave or forgot
what Mr Guthrie did upon that day, as will afterwards be made more
fully to appear.

James Guthrie, about this time, wrote several of the papers upon the Protesters' side; for which, and his faithfulness, he was one of three who were deposed by the pretended Assembly of St Andrews, 1657. Yea, such was the malice of these woful Resolutioners, that upon his refusal of one of that party, and accession to the call of Mr Rule to be his colleague at Stirling, upon the death of Mr Bennett in the year 1656, they proceeded to stone this seer in Israel with stones, his testimony while alive so tormenting the men who dwelt npon the earth.

As James Guthrie did faithfully testify against the Resolutioners and the malignant party, so he did equally oppose himself to the sectaries and to Cromwell's usurpation; and although he went up to London in 1657, when the Marquis of Argyle procured an equal hearing betwixt the Protesters and the Resolutioners, yet he so boldly defended the King's right in public debate with Hugh Peters, Oliver's chaplain, and from the pulpit asserted the King's title in the face of the English officers, as was surprising to all gainsayers. Yet for this, and other hardships that he endured at this time, he was poorly rewarded, as by and by will come to be observed.

Very soon after the Restoration, while James Guthrie, and some others of his faithful brethren who assembled at Edinburgh, were drawing up a paper by way of supplication to His Majesty, they were all apprehended (except one who happily escaped), and imprisoned in the Castle of Edinburgh. From thence Guthrie was taken to Stirling Castle, where he continued till a little before his trial, which was upon the 20th of February 1661. When he came to his trial, the Chancellor told him, he was called before them to answer to the charge of high treason (a copy of which charge he had received some weeks before); and the Lord Advocate proposed that his indictment should be read; which the House went into. The heads of it were—

1. His contriving, consenting to, and exhibiting before the Committee of Estates, the paper called the Western Remonstrance.

2. His contriving, writing, and publishing that abominable pamphlet, called the " Causes of the Lord's Wrath."

3. His contriving, writing, and subscribing the paper called the "Humble Petition of the twenty-third of August last."

4. His convocating of the King's lieges, etc.

5. His declaring His Majesty, by his appeals and protestations, presented by him at Perth, incapable to be judge over him. And,

6. Some treasonable expressions he was alleged to have uttered in a meeting in 1650, or 1651.

His indictment being read, he made an excellent speech before the Parliament, wherein he both defended himself, and that noble cause for which he suffered, but it being too nervous to abridge, and too long to insert in this place, the reader will find it in Wodrow's History.

After he had delivered this speech, and being ordered to remove, he humbly craved that some time might be given him to consult with his lawyers. This was granted, and he was allowed till the 29th to give in his defence. It is affirmed, upon very good authority, that when he met with his lawyers to form his defence, he very much surprised them by his exactness in our Scots law, and suggested several things to be added that had escaped his advocate, which made Sir John Nisbet express himself to this purpose : " If it had been in the reasoning part, or in consequences from Scripture and Divinity, I would have wondered the less if he had given us some help; but even in the matter of our own profession, our Statutes and Acts of Parliament, he pointed out several things that had escaped us." And likewise, the day before his first appearance in Parliament, it is said that he sent a copy of the fore-mentioned speech to Sir John, and the rest of his lawyers, of the reasoning and law part, and they could mend nothing therein.

The advocate's considering his defence, and the giving of it in, took up some weeks, until April the 11th, when the process against him was read in the house, upon which he made a speech which was both affecting and close to the purpose, in which he concludes thus :

" My Lords, in the last place, I humbly beg, that having brought so pregnant and clear evidence from the Word of God, so much Divine reason and human laws, and so much of the common practice of kirk and kingdom, in my defence, and being already cast out of my ministry, out of my dwelling and maintenance, myself and my family put to live on the charity of others, and having now suffered eight months' imprisonment, your lordships would put no other burden upon me. I shall conclude with the words of the prophet Jeremiah, ' Behold, I am in your hands, do to me what seemeth good to you.' I know, for certain, that the Lord hath commanded me to speak all these things : and that if you put me to death, you shall bring innocent blood upon yourselves, and upon the inhabitants of this city.

" My Lords, my conscience I cannot submit ; but this old crazy body and mortal flesh I do submit, to do with it whatever ye will, whether by death or banishment, or imprisonment, or anything else ; only I beseech you to ponder well what profit there is in my blood. It is not the extinguishing of me, or many others, that will extinguish the Covenant and work of Reformation since the year 1638. My blood, bondage, or banishment, will contribute more for the propagation of these things, than my life or liberty could do, though I should live many years."

Though this speech had not that influence that might have been expected, yet it made such impression upon some of the members that they withdrew, declaring to one another, that they would have nothing to do with the blood of this righteous man. But his judges were determined to proceed, and accordingly his indictment was found relevant. Bishop Burnet (in the History of his Own Times) says, " The Earl of Tweeddale was the only man that moved against puting him to death. He said that banishment had hitherto been the severest censure laid upon preachers for their opinions,—yet he was condemned to die." The day of his execution was not named till the 28th of May, when the Parliament ordered him and William Govan to be hanged at the cross of Edinburgh, on the 1st of June 1661 ; James Guthrie's head to be fixed on the Netherbow, his estate to be confiscated, and his arms torn ; and the head of the other to be fixed upon the West Port of Edinburgh.

Thus a sentence of death was passed upon James Guthrie, for his accession to the " Causes of God's Wrath," his writing the petition last year, and the protestation above mentioned ; matters in every way agreeable and conform to the Word of God, the principles and practice of this and other Churches, and the laws of the kingdom. After he received his sentence, he accosted the Parliament thus, "My lords, let never this sentence affect you more than it does me, and let never my blood be required of the King's family."

Thus it was resolved that this excellent man should fall a sacrifice to private and personal pique, as the Marquis of Argyle was said to have fallen to a more exalted revenge. It is said, that the Council had no small debate what his sentence should be ; for he was dealt with by some of them to retract what he had done and written, and join with the present measures ; and he was even offered a bishopric. The other side were in no hazard in making the experiment, for they might be assured of his firmness in his principles. A bishopric was a

THE CHURCHES OF STIRLING.

very small temptation to him, and the commissioner improved his inflexibility to have his life taken away, that it might be a terror to others, and that they might have the less opposition in establishing prelacy.

Betwixt James Guthrie's sentence and his execution, he was in perfect composure and serenity of spirit, and wrote a great many excellent letters to his friends and acquaintances. In this interval he uttered several prophetical expressions, which, together with the foresaid religious letters, could they now be recovered, might be of no small use in this apostate and backsliding age. On June 1, the day on which he was executed, upon some reports that he was to buy his life at the expense of retracting some of the things he had formerly said and done, he wrote and subscribed the following declaration:

"These are to declare, that I do own the Causes of God's Wrath, the Supplication at Edinburgh August last, and the accession I had to the Remonstrances. And if any do think, or have reported, that I was willing to recede from these, they have wronged me, as never having any ground from me to think, or to report so. This I attest, under my hand, at Edinburgh, about 11 o'clock forenoon, before these witnesses.   "Mr Arthur Forbes, Mr John Guthrie,
                              "Mr Hugh Walker, Mr James Cowie."

NETHERBOW PORT—WEST FRONT.

That same day he dined with his friends with great cheerfulness. After dinner he called for a little cheese, which he had been dissuaded from taking for some time, as not good for the gravel, which he was troubled with, and said, " I am now beyond the hazard of the gravel." After he had been in secret for some time, he came forth with the utmost fortitude and composure, and was carried down under a guard from the Tolbooth to the scaffold, which was erected at the Cross. Here he was so far from showing any fear, that he rather expressed a contempt of death, and spake an hour upon the ladder with the composure of one delivering a sermon. His last speech is in "Naphtali," where among other things becoming a martyr, he saith, " One thing I warn you all of, that God is very wroth with Scotland, and threatens to depart, and remove His candlestick. The causes of his wrath are many, and would to God it were not one great cause, that causes of wrath are despised. Consider the case that is recorded in Jer. xxxvi. and the consequences of it, and tremble and fear. I cannot but also say that there is a great addition of wrath. (1.) By that deluge of profanity that overfloweth all the land, in so far that many have not only lost all use and exercise of religion, but even of morality. (2.) By that horrible treachery and perjury that are in the matters of the covenant and cause of God. Be ye astonished, O ye heavens, at this! (3.) By our horrible ingratitude. The Lord, after ten years' oppression, hath broken the yoke of strangers from off our necks ; but the fruit of our delivery is to work wickedness, and to strengthen our hands to do evil, by a most dreadful sacrificing to the creature. We have changed the glory of the incorruptible God into the image of a corruptible man, in whom many have placed almost all their salvation. God is also wroth with a generation of carnal, corrupt, time-serving ministers. I know and do bear testimony, that in the church of Scotland there is a true and faithful ministry, and I pray you to honour these for their works' sake. I do bear my witness to the National Covenant of Scotland, and Solemn League and Covenant betwixt the three kingdoms. These sacred, solemn, public oaths of God, I believe can be loosed or dispensed with by no person, or party, or power, upon earth, but are still binding upon these kingdoms, and will be so for ever hereafter, and are ratified and sealed by the conversion of many thousand souls, since our entering thereinto. I bear my testimony to the protestation against the controverted assemblies and the public resolutions. I take God to record upon my soul, I would not exchange this scaffold with the palace or mitre of the greatest prelate in Britain. Blessed be God, who hath shown mercy to me such a wretch, and has revealed his Son in me, and made me a minister of the everlasting Gospel, and that He hath deigned, in the midst of much contradiction from Satan and the world, to seal my ministry upon the hearts of not a few of His people, and especially in the station wherein I was last ; I mean the congregation and presbytery of Stirling. Jesus Christ is my light and my life, my righteousness, my strength, and my salvation, and all my desire. Him! O Him! I do, with all the strength of my soul, commend to you. Bless Him, O my soul, from henceforth, even for ever!" He concluded with the words of old Simeon, "Now lettest thou thy servant depart in peace, for mine eyes have seen thy salvation." He gave a copy of this his last speech and testimony, subscribed and sealed, to a friend to keep, which he was to deliver to his son, then a child, when he came of age. When on the scaffold, he lifted the napkin off his face, just before he was turned over, and cried, "The Covenants, the Covenants, shall yet be Scotland's reviving."

A few weeks after he was executed, and his head placed on the Netherbow-port, Middleton's coach coming down that way, several drops of blood fell from the head upon the coach, which all their art

and diligence could not wipe off; and when physicians were called
and desired to inquire, if any natural cause could be given for this,
they could give none. This odd incident being noised abroad, and
and all means tried, at length the leather was removed, and a new
cover put on. But this was much sooner done than the wiping off
the guilt of this great and good man's blood from the shedders of it,
and this poor nation. Mr Alexander Hamilton, when a student at
the college of Edinburgh, at the hazard of his life, took down Mr
Guthrie's head and buried it, after it had stood a spectacle for twenty-
seven years. And it is observable, that the very same person afterwards succeeded him at Stirling, where he was minister for twelve
years.

Thus fell the faithful Mr James Guthrie, who was properly the
first who suffered unto death in that period, for asserting the kingly
prerogative of Jesus Christ, in opposition to Erastian supremacy.
He was a man honoured of God to be zealous and singularly faithful
in carrying on the work of Reformation, and had carried himself
straight under all changes and revolutions ; and because he had been
such, he must live no longer. He did much for the interest of the
King in Scotland, of which the King no doubt was sensible. When
he got notice of his death, he said with some warmth, "And what
have you done with Mr Patrick Gillespie?" He was answered,
that having so many friends in the House, his life could not be taken.
"Well," said the King, "if I had known you would have spared Mr
Gillespie, I would have spared Mr Guthrie." And indeed he was not
far out with it ; for Mr Guthrie was capable to have done him as
much service, being one accomplished with almost every qualification,
natural or acquired, necessary to complete both a man and a
Christian.

It is a loss that we are favoured with so few of the writings of this
worthy. For besides those papers already mentioned, he wrote several others upon the Protesters' side, among which was also a paper
written against the usurper Oliver Cromwell, for which he suffered
some hardships during the time of that usurpation. His last sermon
at Stirling, preached from Matt. xiv. 22, was published in 1738,
entitled, a Cry from the Dead ; with his Ten Considerations anent the
Decay of Religion, first published by himself in 1660 ; and an authen-
tic paper, written and subscribed by himself, upon the occasion of his
being stoned by the resolution party about 1656, for his accession to
the call of Mr Robert Rule to be his colleague, after the death of Mr

Bennett. He also wrote a Treatise on Ruling Elders and Deacons, about the time he entered into the ministry, which is now affixed to the last edition of his cousin Mr William Guthrie's treatise of a Trial of a Saving Interest in Christ.

John Campbell, Earl of Loudon.

OHN CAMPBELL, Earl of Loudon, was heir to Sir James Campbell of Lawers, and husband of Margaret, Baroness of Loudon.

The first of his state-preferments was in 1633, when King Charles I. came to Scotland, in order to have his coronation performed ; at which time he dignified several of the Scots nobility with higher titles of honour; and among others this nobleman, who was created Earl of Loudon, 12th May 1633.

It appears that from his youth he had been well affected to the Presbyterian interest ; for no sooner did the second Reformation begin to take air, which was about the year 1637, than he appeared, a principal promoter thereof, not only in joining these petitioners, afterwards called the Covenanters, but also, when the General Assembly sat down at Glasgow in November 1638, he thought it his honour to attend at almost every session, and was of great service, both by his advice in difficult cases, and by several excellent speeches which he delivered therein. For instance, upon the very entry, when the difference arose between the Marquis of Hamilton, the King's Commissioner, and some of the rest, anent choosing a clerk to the Assembly, the Marquis, refusing to be assisted by Traquair and Sir Lewis Stewart, urged several reasons for compliance with his Majesty's pleasure, and at last renewed his protest ; whereupon Lord Loudon, in name of the Commissioners to the Assembly, gave in reasons of a pretty high strain, why the Lord Commissioner and his assessors ought to have but one vote in the Assembly. Of these reasons Traquair craved a duplicate, and promised to answer them ; but it appears never found leisure for the employment.

About this time he told the King's Commissioner roundly, " They knew no other bounds betwixt a King and his subjects, but religion and laws ; and if these were broken, men's lives were not dear to them. They would not be so ; such fears were past with them."

The King and the Bishops being galled to the heart to see that by this Assembly Presbytery was almost restored, and Prelacy well-nigh abolished, immediately raised an army, in order to reduce the Covenanters. They, hearing of the preparation, provided as well as they could. Both armies marched towards the Border ; but upon the approach of the Scots, the English were moved with great timidity ; whereupon ensued a pacification ; and commissioners being appointed to treat on both sides, the Scots were permitted to make known their desires. Lord Loudon being one of the Scots commissioners, upon his knees, said, that their demand was only to enjoy their religion and liberties, according to the ecclesiastical and civil laws of the kingdom. The King replied, that if that was all that was desired, peace would soon be made. After several particulars were agreed upon, the King promised, " That all ecclesiastical matters should be decided by an Assembly, and civil matters by the parliament ; which Assembly should be kept once a-year. That on the 6th of August should be held a free General Assembly, when the King would be present, and pass an act of oblivion," etc. The articles of the pacification were subscribed June 18, by the Commissioners of both sides, in view of both armies, at Birks, near Berwick, in the year 1630.

But this treaty was short-lived and ill observed ; for the King, urged on by the Bishops, soon after burned the pacification by the hands of the hangman, charging the Scots with a breach of the articles of the treaty, although the Earl of Loudon gave him sufficient proofs to the contrary. This freedom used by his Lordship no way pleased the King ; but he was suffered to return home, and the King kept his resentment until another opportunity.

In the meantime, the General Assembly sat down at Edinburgh, August 12. Mr Dickson was chosen moderator, and at this Assembly, after several matters were discussed, Messrs Henderson and Ramsay entered upon a demonstration, that Episcopacy hath its beginning from men, and is of human institution. But they had not proceeded far, till they were interrupted by Traquair, the King's commissioner, who declared he did not desire them to fall upon any scholastic dispute, but how far those in the Reformation had found Episcopacy contrary to the constitution of this Church.   Thereupon the truly noble Lord Loudon being present, did most solidly explain the act of the General Assembly 1580, which condemned the office of Bishops in the most express terms, prior to the subscription of the National Covenant, and because of a difficulty raised from words in that act, as it was then used, his Lordship observed, that in the Assemblies 1560, 1575, 1576, 1577, and 1578, Episcopacy came still under consideration, though not directly as to the office, yet as to the corruption of it; and having enlarged upon the office of Bishops as without a warrant from the Word of God, he concluded thus : " The connection between the Assemblies of 1574 and of 1581 is quite clear—Episcopacy is put out as wanting warrant from the Word of God, and Presbytery put in as having that Divine warrant."

The same day on which the Assembly arose, the Parliament sat down ; but falling upon matters that did not correspond with the King's design, Traquair did all he could to stop them, that they might have nothing done ; whereupon they agreed to send up the Earls of Dunfermline and Loudon to implore his Majesty to allow the Parliament to proceed, and to determine what was before them. But ere these two Lords had reached the Court, orders were sent them, discharging them, in the King's name, from coming within a mile of him, on supposition that they had no express warrant from the Lord Commissioner ; and they returned home.

In the meantime, the Parliament, by the King's orders, was prorogued to the 2d of June 1640, and matters continued so till January 1641, when the Committee of Parliament, having obtained leave to send up commissioners to represent their grievances, did again commission the two foresaid Earls, to whom they added Sir William Douglas of Cavers, and Mr Barclay, provost of Irvine. On their arrival they were allowed to kiss the King's hand, and some time after were appointed to attend at the Council Chamber, but understanding they were not to have a hearing of the King himself, they craved a copy of Traquair's information to the Council of England, which was denied.

At last the King gave them audience himself upon the 3d of March, when Lord Loudon, after having addressed his Majesty, showed that his ancient and native kingdom was independent of any other judicatory whatever. He craved his Majesty's protection in

defence of religion, liberty, and the cause of the Church and kingdom ; and then speaking concerning those who had misrepresented or
traduced these his most loyal Scots subjects, he said, " If it please
God for our sins to make our condition so deplorable as they may
get the shadow of your Majesty's authority—as we hope in God they
will not—to palliate their ends, then, as those who are sworn to
defend our religion, our recourse must be only to the God of Jacob,
for our refuge, who is King of kings and Lord of lords, and by whom
kings do reign and princes decree justice. And if, in speaking thus
out of zeal to religion, and the duty we owe to our country, and that
charge which is laid upon us, anything hath escaped us, sith it is
spoken from the sincerity of our hearts, we fall down at your Majesty's
feet, craving pardon for our freedom." Again, having eloquently ex-
patiated upon the desires of his subjects, and the laws of the kingdom, he spake of the laws of God, and the power of the Church,
saying, "Next, we must distinguish betwixt the Church and State,
betwixt the ecclesiastical and civil power, both which are materially
one, yet formally they are contradistinct in power, in jurisdiction,
in laws, in bodies, in ends, in offices, and officers. And although
the Church and ecclesiastic assemblies thereof be formally different
and distinct from the Parliament and civil judicatories, yet there
is so strict and necessary a conjunction betwixt ecclesiastic and
civil jurisdiction, betwixt religion and justice, as the one cannot
firmly subsist and be preserved without the other, therefore they
must stand and fall, live and die together." He enlarged further
upon the privileges of both Church and State, and then concluded with mentioning the sum of their desires, which was :
" That your Majesty may be graciously pleased to command, that
the Parliament may proceed freely to determine all these articles
given in to them, and whatsoever exceptions, objections, or informa-
tions, are made against any of the particular overtures, we are most
willing to receive the same in writing, and are content, in the same
way, to return our answers and humble desires."

On March 11, the Commissioners appeared, and brought their
instructions, whereupon ensued some reasonings betwixt them and
the King, at which time Archbishop Laud, who sat on the King's
right hand, was observed to mock the Scots commissioners, causing
the King to put such questions as he pleased. At last Traquair gave
in several queries and objections to them, unto which they gave most
solid and sufficient answers in every particular.

LOUDON CASTLE.

But this farce being over (for it seems nothing else was here intended by the Court than to entrap the commissioners, and particularly this noble Earl who had so strenuously asserted the laws and liberties of his native country), all the deputies, by the King's order, were taken into custody, and the Earl of Loudon sent to the Tower for a letter alleged to be written by him, and sent by the Scots to the French King, as to their sovereign, imploring his aid against their natural king, of the following tenor:

"SIRE,—Your Majesty being the refuge and sanctuary of afflicted princes and states, we have found it necessary to send this gentleman, Mr Colville, to represent unto your Majesty the candour and ingenuity as well of our actions and proceedings as of our intentions, which we desire to be engraven and written in the whole world, with a beam of the sun, as well as to your Majesty. We therefore beseech you, Sire, to give faith and credit to him, and to all that he shall say on our part, touching us and our affairs. Being much assured, Sire, of an assistance equal to your wonted clemency heretofore, and so often showed to the nation, which will not yield the glory to any other whatsoever, to be eternally, Sire, your Majesty's most humble, most obedient, and most affectionate servants."

This letter, says a historian, was advised to and composed by

YORK MINSTER.

Montrose, when the King was coming against Scotland with a potent army, transcribed by Lord Loudon, and subscribed by them and by the Lords Rothes, Mar, Montgomery, and Forrester, and General Leslie. The translation being found faulty by Lord Maitland, it was dropped altogether, and this copy wanted both the date, which the worst of its enemies' never pretended it had, and a direction, which the Scots confidently affirmed it never had ; but falling into the King's hand (by means of Traquair) he intended to make a handle of it, to make Lord Loudon the first sacrifice. This noble lord being examined before the council, did very honestly acknowledge the handwriting and subscription to be his, but said it was before the late pacification, when his Majesty was marching in hostility against his native country, that in these circumstances it seemed necessary to have an intercessor to mitigate his wrath, and they could think of none so well qualified as the French king, being the nearest relation by affinity to their sovereign of any other crowned head in the world; but being thought on shortly before the arrival of the English on the border it was judged too late, and therefore was never either addressed by them or sent to the French king.

Notwithstanding this, evil was intended against this noble peer, and being remanded back to prison, he was very near being dispatched, and that not only without the benefit of his peers, but without any legal trial or conviction. Burnet fairly acknowledges that the King was advised to proceed capitally against him. But the English historians go still farther, and plainly say that the King, about three o'clock in the afternoon, sent his own letter to William Balfour, lieutenant of the Tower, commanding him to see the Lord Loudon's head struck off within the Tower, before nine the next morning ; a striking demonstration of the just and forgiving spirit for which, by some, King Charles is so much extolled ! Upon this command, the lieutenant of the Tower, that his lordship might prepare for death, gave him notice of it, which awful intimation he, knowing the justice of his cause, received with astonishing composure and serenity of mind. The lieutenant went himself to the Marquis of Hamilton, who he thought was bound in honour to interpose in this matter. The Marquis and the lieutenant made their way to the King, who was then in bed. The warrant was scarcely named, when the King, understanding their errand, stopped them, saying, " By God it shall be executed." But the Marquis laying before him the odiousness of the fact, by the violation of the safe conduct he had granted to that nobleman, and the putting him to death without conviction, or so much as a legal trial, with the dismal consequences that were like to attend an action of that nature, not only in respect of Scotland, which would certainly be lost, but likewise of his own personal safety from the nobility,—the King called for the warrant, tore it, and dismissed the Marquis and the lieutenant somewhat abruptly. After this, about the 28th of June, this noble lord, upon promise of concealing from his brethren in Scotland the hard treatment he had met with from the King, and of contributing his endeavours to dispose them to peace, was liberated from his confinement, and allowed to return home.

But things being now ripened for a new war, the King put himself at the head of another army, in order to suppress the Scots. On the other hand, the Scots resolved not to be behind in their preparations, and entered England with a numerous army, mostly of veteran troops, many of whom had served in Germany under Gustavus Adolphus. A party of the King's forces disputed the passage of the Tyne, but were defeated by the Scots at Newburn ; whereupon the Scots took Newcastle and Berwick, pushing their way as far as Durham. Here the noble Earl of Loudon acted no mean part, for he not only persuaded the citizens of Edinburgh and other places to contribute money and other necessaries for the use and supply of the Scots, but also commanded a brigade of horse, with whom, in the foresaid skirmish at Newburn, he had no small share of the victory. The King retired to York, and finding himself environed on all hands, appointed commissioners to treat with the Scots a second time. On the other side, the Scots nominated the Earls of Dunfermline, Rothes, and Loudon, with some gentlemen, and Messrs Henderson and Johnston, advocates for the Church, as their commissioners for the treaty. Both commissioners, upon October 1, 1640, met at Ripon, where, after agreeing upon some articles for a cessation of arms for three months, the treaty was transferred to London. To this the Scots commissioners, upon a patent granted from the King for their safe conduct, consented and went thither. And because great hopes were entertained by friends in England, from their presence and influence at London, the committee at Newcastle appointed Mr Robert Blair, for his dexterity in dealing with the Independents; Mr Robert Baillie, for his eminence in managing the Arminian controversy; and Mr George Gillespie, for his nervous and pithy confutation of the English ceremonies, to accompany the three noblemen, as their chaplains; and Messrs Smith and Borthwick followed soon after.

After this treaty things went smoothly for some time in Scotland; but the King, not relishing the proceedings of the English Parliament, made a tour next year to Scotland, where he attended the Scots Parliament. When this Parliament sat down (before the King's arrival), Traquair, Montrose, and several other incendiaries, were cited before them for stirring up strife between the King and his subjects, and for undoing the Covenanters; of whom some appeared and some appeared not. In the meanwhile, the noble Earl of Loudon said so much in favour of some of them, discharging himself so effectually of all the orders laid on him last year by the King, that some, forgetting the obligation he came under to steer with an even hand, began to suspect him of changing sides, so that he was well-nigh left out of the commission to England with the Parliament's agreement to the treaty. This so much offended his lordship, that he supplicated the Parliament to be examined by them of his past conduct and negotiations, if they found him faithful (so far was he emboldened, having the testimony of a good conscience), which grieved the members of the house very much. The house declared, indeed, that he had behaved himself faithfully and wisely in all his public employments, and that he not only deserved to have an act of approbation, but likewise to be rewarded by the Estates, that their favour and his merit might be known to posterity. They further considered that the loss of such an eminent instrument could not be easily supplied. The English dealt not so freely with any of our commissioners as with Lord Loudon, nor did ever any of our commissioners use so much ingenuous freedom with his Majesty as he did; and he behoved once more to return to London with the treaty new revised by the Parliament, subscribed by the Lord President and others.

After the return of the commissioners, the King having arrived in Parliament, they began to dignify several of the Scots nobility with offices of State, and because a Lord Treasurer was a-wanting, it was moved that none did deserve that office so well as the Earl of Loudon, who had done so much for his country. But the King, judging more wisely in this, and thinking it more difficult to find a fit person for the Chancery than for the Treasury, was obliged to make the Earl of Loudon Chancellor, contrary both to his own inclination (for he never was ambitious of preferment), and to the solicitation of his friends. But to make amends for the smallness of his fees, an annual pension of £1000 was added to the office.

Accordingly, upon the 2d of October, 1642, this noble lord did solemnly, in the face of the Parliament, on his bended knees before the throne, first swear the oath of allegiance, then that of privy councillor, and lastly, when the great seal (which for two years had been kept by the Marquis of Hamilton) was, with the mace, delivered to him out of his Majesty's hand, he did swear the oath *de fideli administratione officii*, and was, by the Lyon King at Arms, placed in the seat under his Majesty's feet, on the right hand of the lord president of Parliament. On this he immediately arose, and prostrating himself before the King, said, " Preferment comes neither from the east nor from the west, but from God alone. I acknowledge I have this from your Majesty as from God's vicegerent upon earth, and the fountain of all earthly honour here, and I will endeavour to answer that expectation your Majesty has of me, and to deserve the goodwill of this honourable house, in faithfully discharging what you both (without desert of mine) have put on me." Then kissing his Majesty's hand, he retired to his seat.

This was a notable turn of affairs, for he who last year, for the cause of Christ and love of his country, in all submission received the message or sentence of death, was now, for his great wisdom and prudence, advanced by the same person and authority unto the helm of the highest affairs of the kingdom ; which verifies what the wise man saith, " The fear of the Lord is the beginning of wisdom, and before honour is humility" (Prov. xv. 33).

As soon as this excellent nobleman was advanced unto this dignity and office, he not only began to exert his power for the utility and welfare of his own native country, but also, the next year, went up to London to importune his Majesty to call his English Parliament, as the most expedient way to bring about a firm, permanent, and lasting peace betwixt the two kingdoms. And although he was not one of those commissioners nominated and sent up from the Parliament and assembly of the Church of Scotland in the year 1643, yet it is evident from a letter sent from them while at London, bearing the date of January 6, 1645, that he was amongst them there, using his utmost endeavours for bringing about that happy uniformity of religion, in doctrine, discipline, and church-government, which took place, and was established in these nations at that time.

And next year, before the King surrendered himself to the Scots army at Newcastle, Lord Loudon, being sent up as commissioner to the King, after the Lord Leven at the head of 100 officers in the army had presented a petition upon their knees, beseeching his Majesty to give them satisfaction in point of religion, and to take the Covenant, did, in plain terms, accost the King in this manner: "The difference between your Majesty and your Parliament is grown to such a height, that after many bloody battles, they have your Majesty, with all your garrisons and strongholds in their hands. They are in a capacity now to do what they will in Church and State ; and some are afraid, and others unwilling to proceed to extremities, till they know your Majesty's last resolution. Now, sire, if your Majesty shall refuse your assent to the propositions, you will lose all your friends in the house and in the city, and all England will join against you as one man ; they will depose you, and set up another government. They will charge us to deliver up your Majesty to them, and remove our arms out of England ; and upon your refusal, we shall be obliged to settle religion and peace without you, which will ruin your Majesty and your posterity. We own, the propositions are higher in some things than we approve of, but the only way to establish your Majesty is to consent to them at present. Your Majesty may recover, in a time of peace, all that you have lost in a time of tempest and trouble." Whether or not the King found him a true prophet in all this, must be left to the history of these times.

He was again employed on the like errand to the King, in the year 1648, but with no better success, as appears from two excellent speeches to the Scots Parliament at his return, concerning these proceedings. In the same year, in the month of June, he was with a handful of Covenanters at a communion at Mauchline muir, where they were set upon by Callender's and Middleton's forces, after they had given their promise to his Lordship of the contrary.

Although this noble Earl, through the influence of the Earl of Lanark, had given his consent at first to the King, who was setting on foot an army for his own rescue, yet he came to be among those who protested against the Duke of Hamilton's unlawful engagement. To account in some measure for this, he had before received a promise of a gift of the teinds, and a gift sometimes blindeth the eyes, especially of a nobleman whose estate was at that time somewhat burdened; but by conversing with some of the protesting side, and some ministers, who discovered to him his mistake when his foot had well-nigh slipped, he was so convinced that this was contrary to his trust, that he subscribed an admonition to more steadfastness, from the Commission of the Church, in the High Church of Edinburgh.

But at last Charles I. being executed, and his son Charles II. called home by the Scots, a new scene began to appear in 1650; for malignants being then again brought into places of power and trust, it behoved the Lord Chancellor, who never was a friend to malignants, to demit. He had now for nearly the space of ten years presided in Parliament, and had been highly instrumental in the hand of the Lord, to establish in this nation, both in Church and State, the purest reformation that ever was established in any particular nation, under the New Testament dispensation; but now he was turned out, and Lord Burleigh substituted in his place.

In what manner he was mostly employed during the time of Cromwell's usurpation, there is no certain account; only it is probable, that notwithstanding the many struggles he had in asserting the King's interest, he mostly lived a private life, as most of the noblemen and gentlemen of the nation did at that time.

But no sooner was the King restored unto his dominions, than these lands did again return unto the old vomit of Popery, Prelacy, and slavery; and it is impossible to express the grief of heart this godly nobleman sustained when he beheld, not only the carved work of the sanctuary cut down, by defacing that glorious structure of Reformation, which he had such an eminent hand in erecting and building up, but also to find himself at the King's mercy for his accession to the same. He knew that, next to the Marquis of Argyle, he was the butt of the enemies' malice, and he had frequently applied for his Majesty's grace, but was as often refused; so that the violent courses now carried on, and the plain invasions upon the liberties and religion of the nation, made him weary of his life. Being then at Edinburgh, he often exhorted his excellent lady to pray that he might never see the next session of Parliament, else he might follow his dear friend the Marquis of Argyle; and the Lord was pleased to grant his request; for he died, in a most Christian manner, at Edinburgh, March 15, 1652, and his corpse was carried home, and interred beside his ancestors.

The most exaggerated praise that can be at present bestowed on this renowned patriot, the worthy Earl of Loudon, must be far below his merit, as he was possessed of singular prudence, eloquence, and learning, joined with remarkable courage. These excellent endowments he invariably applied for the support of our ancient and admir-

TOWER OF LONDON.

able constitution, which he maintained upon all hazards and occasions; and he might be truly accounted the chief advocate, both for the civil and religious liberties of the people. To sum up all in a few words; he was a most exquisite orator in the senate, a refined politician, an honour to his name, an ornament to this nation, and in every virtue, in political, social, and domestic life, a pattern worthy of imitation. And although his offspring have hitherto all along retained a sense of their civil liberties, yet it is to be lamented, that few or none of our noblemen at this day follow his example. His son James, Earl of Loudon, suffered much after his father's death, during the persecuting period; and at last was obliged to leave his native country, and died an exile at Leyden, after having endured a series of hardships. And there are recent instances of the truly noble and independent spirit for liberty which this worthy family have all along retained, and which, we doubt not, will be transmitted to their posterity.

Robert Baillie.

OBERT BAILLIE was born at Glasgow on Friday the 30th April 1602. His father was a citizen there, being lineally descended from Baillie of Jerviston, a brother of the house of Carphin, and a branch of the ancient house of Lamington, all in the county of Lanark. By his mother's side, he was of the same stock with the Gibsons of Durie, who have made such a figure in the law. He received his education at Glasgow, and at that university plied his studies so hard, that by his industry and uncommon genius he attained to the knowledge of twelve or thirteen languages, and could write a Latin style, that, in the opinion of the learned, might well become the Augustan age.

After his study of divinity, he took orders from Archbishop Law, about the year 1622, and was soon after presented by the Earl of

KILWINNING CHURCH.

Eglinton to the living of Kilwinning. When the Reformation began
in the year 1637, he wanted not his own difficulties, from his education, and tenderness of the King's authority, to see through some of
the measures then taken. Yet, after reasoning, reading, and prayer
(as he himself expressed it), he came heartily into the Covenanting
interest about that time.

Being a man of distinct and solid judgment, he was often employed in the public business of the Church. In the year 1638, he
was chosen by his presbytery to be a member of that memorable
Assembly held at Glasgow, where he behaved himself with great wisdom and moderation.

He was also one of those who attended as chaplains to the army
in 1639 and 1640, and he was present during the whole treaty begun
at Ripon and concluded at London. What comfort he had in these
things he describes in these words, " As for myself, I never found my
mind in a better temper than it was all that time, from my outset
until my head was again homeward. I was as one who had taken
leave of the world, and resolved to die in that service. I found the
favour of God shining on me, and a sweet, meek, and humble, yet
strong and vehement spirit leading me along." The same year, 1640,
he was, by the covenanting Lords, sent to London, to draw up an

accusation against Archbishop Laud, for the innovations he had obtruded upon the Church of Scotland.

[In the year 1642 he accepted an invitation to become Dickson's colleague as Professor of Divinity in the University of Glasgow. The following year he was sent as a Commissioner from the Church of Scotland to the Westminster Assembly at London, where he remained the most of the time. As he himself modestly tells us, he did not take that action and prominent part in the deliberations which was done by his colleagues Rutherford and Gillespie. Still, we are largely indebted to his Letters for much of the information we possess regarding that famous Assembly. The following is the interesting and graphic sketch he gives of its appearance and order of procedure: "The like of that Assembly I did never see, and as we hear say, the like was never in England, nor anywhere is shortly like to be. They did sit in Henry VII.'s chapel, in the place of the convocation ; but since the weather grew cold, they did go to Jerusalem chamber, a fair room, in the abbey of Westminster, about the bounds of the college forehall, but wider. At the one end, nearest the door, and on both sides, are stages of seats, as in the new Assembly house at Edinburgh, but not so high, for there will be room but for five or six score. At the upmost end, there is a chair, set on a frame, a foot from the earth, for the master prolocutor Dr Twisse. Before it, on the ground, stand two chairs, for the two master assessors Dr Burgess and Mr White ; before these two chairs, through the length of the room, stands a table, at which sit the two scribes, Mr Byfield and Mr Roborough. The house is all well hung, and has a good fire, which is some dainties at London. Foranent the table, upon the prolocutor's right hand, there are three or four ranks of forms. On the lowest, we five do sit; upon the other at our backs, the members of Parliament deputed to the Assembly. On the forms foranent us, on the prolocutor's left hand, going from the upper end of the house to the chimney, and at the other end of the house, and backside of the table till it come about to our seats, are four or five stages of forms, whereupon the divines sit as they please, albeit commonly they keep the same place. From the chimney to the door, there are no seats, but a void space for passage. The lords of Parliament used to sit on chairs in that end about the fire. We meet every day of the week, except Saturday. We sit commonly from nine to two or three afternoon. The prolocutor, at beginning and end, has a short prayer. . . . . Ordinarily, there will be present about threescore of their divines. These are divided in three com-

mittees ; in one whereof, every man is a member. No man is
excluded who pleases to come to any of the three. Every committee,
as the Parliament gives orders in writing to take any purpose to consideration, takes a portion, and on the afternoon meeting, prepares
matters for the Assembly, sets down its mind in distinct propositions,
backing these propositions with texts of Scripture. After the prayer,
Mr Byfield, the scribe, reads the propositions, and Scriptures, whereupon the Assembly debates, in a most grave and orderly way. No
man is called upon to speak ; but whosoever stands up of his own
accord speaks so long as he will without interruption. If two or three
stand up at once, then the divines confusedly call on his name whom
they desire to hear first. On whom the loudest and maniest voices
call, he speaks. No man speaks to any, but to the prolocutor. They
harangue long, and very learnedly. They study the question well
beforehand, and prepare their speeches, but withal, the men are
exceedingly prompt and well spoken. I do marvel at the very accurate and extemporal replies that many of them usually make.

"When, upon every proposition by itself, and on every text of
Scripture that is brought to confirm it, every man who will has said
his whole mind, and the replies, and duplies, and triplies are heard,
then the most part call ' To the question.' Byfield, the scribe, rises
from the table, and comes to the prolocutor's chair, who, from the
scribe's book, reads the proposition, and says, ' As many as are in
opinion that the question is well stated in the proposition, let them say
Ay ;' when *Ay* is heard, he says, 'As many as think otherwise say *No.*'
If the difference of ' *Ayes*' and ' *Noes*' be clear, as usually it is, then
the question is ordered by the scribes, and they go on to debate the
first Scripture alleged for proof of the proposition. If the sound of '*Ay*'
and '*No*' be near equal, then says the prolocutor, 'As many as say *Ay*
stand up ;' while they stand, the scribe and others number them in
their minds ; when they are set down, the *Noes* are bidden stand, and
they likewise are numbered. This way is clear enough, and saves a
great deal of time, which we spend in reading our catalogue. When a
question is once ordered, there is no more of that matter ; but if a
man will deviate, he is quickly taken up by Mr Assessor, or many
others, confusedly crying, ' Speak to order.' No man contradicts
another expressly by name, but most discreetly speaks to the prolocutor, and, at most, holds to general terms ; ' As the reverend
brother who lately or last spoke on this hand, on that side, above or
below.' They follow the way of their Parliament."

HENRY VII. CHAPEL—WESTMINSTER ABBEY.

After more than a year's absence from home, it was thought proper that some of the Scottish Commissioners should attend the General Assembly at Edinburgh, to report what progress had been made. Baillie and Gillespie, having been deputed for this purpose, set out from London on horseback on the 6th January 1645, and reached Newcastle on the 18th, "verie wearie, and fashed with a long evil way." On the evening of the 22d they arrived in Edinburgh, and in the course of a speech which he delivered next day before the General Assembly, after referring to the progress which had been made, Baillie proceeded to say: "Such stories lately told would have been counted fancies, dreams, mere impossibilities; yet this day we tell them as deeds done for the great honour of God, and, we are persuaded, the joy of many a godly soul. If any will not believe our report, let them trust their own eyes; for, behold, here is the warrant of our words, written and subscribed by the hands of the clerks of the Parliament of England, and the scribes of the Assembly there." After visiting his family at Glasgow, he was obliged to return to London before the end of March; but two years afterwards we find him again in Scotland addressing the General Assembly. At the meeting of the Commission in January 1647, he presented the Confession of Faith and the new metrical version of the Psalms; and at the meeting of the Assembly in August, he gave an interesting account of their labours, in the course of which he said: " It is one of the Lord's promises to us, that they who sow in tears shall reap in joy: that they who go out weeping, and carry precious seed, shall return with rejoicing, and bring their sheaves. It was the General Assembly's pleasure, some four years ago, to send some of us, their weak brethren and servants, to that venerable and worthy Synod at Westminster, to sow, in that famous place, some of the precious seed, not of our Church, as enemies do slander, but of God, the Father of all light and truth. Our poor labours in that service were so blessed by the good hand of our God, that although the sowing of the seed was often accompanied with much solicitude and perplexity of mind, yea, sometimes with great grief of heart, and tears in a good measure, yet the visible appearance of a fair harvest did .bring a sensible joy, not only to ourselves, but to many thousands more on both sides the sea. The last Assembly wherein my present colleague (Gillespie) and I did appear in this place, we brought with us a bundle of so goodly sheaves as did revive the hearts of many in that very sad time. This day the Lord has sent us again to the same place, burdened with more of these precious fruits, which we trust shall help to refresh all honest spirits, though otherwise exceedingly saddened with the late unhappy and much unexpected occurrences."—ED.]

When the Westminster Assembly terminated, the Parliament of England, as an acknowledgment of his good services, made him a handsome present of silver plate,. with an inscription signifying it to be a token of their great respect to him. This, not long since, was to be seen in the house of Carnbroe, very carefully preserved; and perhaps it remains there to this day.

By his first wife, Lilias Fleming, he had one son and four daughters; by his second wife, Principal Strang's daughter, he had one daughter, who was married to Walkinshaw of Barrowfield.

About this time he was a great confidant of the Marquis of Argyle, the Earls of Cassilis, Eglinton, Lauderdale, and Loudon, Lord Balmerino, and Sir Archibald Johnston (Lord Warriston), with others of the leaders amongst the Covenanters, whereby he obtained the most exact knowledge of the transactions of that time, which he has carefully collected in his Letters. As he expresses himself, there was no one from whom his correspondent could get a more full narrative under Cromwell's usurpation. He joined with the Resolutioners, and composed several of the papers belonging to that party,

1661. He was by Lauderdale's interest made Principal of the College of Glasgow, upon the removal of Mr Patrick Gillespie; about which time, it is commonly said that he had a bishopric offered him, but that he refused it, because, says the writer of the Memorial, he did not choose to enter into a dispute with those whom he had formerly lived with in friendship. But this was only a sly way of wounding an amiable character; for Baillie continued firmly attached to Presbyterian government, and in opposition to Prelacy, to the very last. Several instances could be brought, but a few extracts from some of his own letters, particularly one to Lauderdale, a little before his death, may effectually wipe away that reproach. "Having the occasion of this bearer, I tell you my heart is broken with grief, and I find the burthen of the public weighty, and hastening me to my grave. What need you do that disservice to the King, which all of you cannot recompense, to grieve the hearts of all your godly friends in Scotland, with pulling down all our laws at once, which concerned our Church since 1633. Was this good advice, or will it thrive? Is it wisdom to bring back upon us the Canterburian times, the same designs, the same practices? Will they not bring on the same effects, whatever fools dream?" And again, in the same letter, further on, he says, "My lord, you are the nobleman in all the world I love best, and esteem most. I think I may say I write to you what I please. If you have gone with your heart to forsake your covenant, to countenance the re-introduction of bishops and books, and strengthen the King by your advice in those things, I think you a prime transgressor, and liable among the first to answer for that great sin." When the Archbishop came to visit him on his deathbed, he would not so much as give him the appellation of lord; yea, it appears that the introduction of Prelacy hastened his death, as appears evident from his last public letter to his cousin, Mr Spang, dated May 12, 1662. After some account of the west-country ministers being called into Edinburgh, he says, "The guise is now, the bishops will trouble no man, but the states will punish seditious ministers. This poor Church is in the most hard taking that ever we have seen. This is my daily grief; this hath brought all my bodily trouble on me, and is like to do me more harm." Very shortly after that, in the month of July, he got to his rest and glorious reward, being aged sixty-three years.

Robert Baillie may very justly, for his profound and universal learning, exact and solid judgment, be accounted amongst the great men of his time. He was an honour to his country, and his works do praise him in the gates; among which are his Scripture Chronology, written in Latin; his Canterburian Self-conviction; his Parallels or Comparison of the Liturgy with the Mass Book; his Dissuasive against the Errors of the Times, and a large manuscript collection of Historical Papers and Letters, consisting of four volumes folio, beginning in the year 1637, and ending at the Restoration. To him is, by some, ascribed that book entitled "Historia Motuum in Regno Scotiæ, annis 1634-1640;" and if he was the author of that, then he also wrote another anonymous paper, called "A Short Relation of the State of the Kirk of Scotland, from the Reformation of Religion to the month of October, 1638;" for, from the preface to the last-mentioned book, it appears that both were written by the same hand. He also wrote Laudensium, an Antidote against Arminianism, a Reply to the Modest Inquirer, with other tracts, and some sermons on public occasions.

In the Life and now published Letters of Principal Baillie we have a striking proof of human frailty—nay, more, that even great and good men will be biassed in judgment, and prejudiced in mind at others more faithful than themselves. For instance, those very noblemen and ministers, to whom he gives the highest eulogiums of praise for being the prime instruments in God's hand for carrying on the work of Reformation betwixt 1638 and 1639, no sooner took the Protesters' side, than he not only represents some of them to be of such a character as I shall forbear to mention, but even gives us a very diminutive view of their most faithful contendings about that time; wherein the gallant Argyle, the courageous Loudon, the able statesman Warriston, faithful Guthrie, godly Rutherford, peaceable Livingstone, honest M'Ward, etc., cannot escape their share of reflections. This, no doubt, adds nothing to the credit of the last ten years of his history, and all from a mistaken view of the controversy betwixt these Protesters and his own party, the Resolutioners; taking, as he did, all divisions and calamities that befell the Church, State, and army, at that time, to proceed from the Protesters not concurring with them; whereas, it was just the reverse. The admission of Charles II., that atheistical wretch, and his malignant faction, into the bosom of the Church, proved the Achan in the camp that brought these evils upon the Church, State, and army, at and since that time. The Protesters could not submit their consciences to the arbitrary dictates of the public Resolutioners. They could not agree to violate their almost newly-sworn Covenant, by approving of the admission of these wicked malignants into public places of power and trust; in defence of which many of them faced the awful gibbet, banishment, imprisonment, and other excruciating hardships; whereas, several hundreds of the Resolutioners, on the very first blast of temptation, involved themselves in fearful apostacy and perjury; some of them becoming violent persecutors of their faithful brethren, and not a few of them absolute monsters of iniquity.

David Dickson.

DAVID DICKSON was born about the year 1583. He was the only son of Mr John Dick or Dickson, merchant in Glasgow, whose father was an old feuar and possessor of some lands in the barony of Fintry, and parish of St Ninian's, called the Kirk of the Muir. His parents were religious, of considerable substance, and were many years married before they had David, who was their only child. As he was a Samuel asked of the Lord, so he was early devoted to Him and the ministry; yet afterwards the vow was forgot, till Providence, by a rod and sore sickness on their son, brought their sins to their remembrance, and then he was sent to assume his studies at the University of Glasgow.

Soon after he had received the degree of Master of Arts, he was admitted professor of philosophy in that college, where he was very useful in training up the youth in solid learning; and, with the learned Principal Boyd of Trochrig, the worthy Mr Blair, and other pious members of that society, his labours were singularly blessed in reviving serious piety among the youth in that declining and corrupted time, a little after the imposition of Prelacy upon the Church. Here, by a recommendation of the General Assembly not long after our Reformation from Popery, the regents were only to continue eight

IRVINE.

years in their profession; after which, such as were found qualified were licensed, and upon a call after trial were admitted to the holy ministry; by which constitution the Church came to be filled with ministers well-qualified in all the branches of useful learning. Accordingly, David Dickson was, in 1618, ordained minister to the town of Irvine, where he laboured for about twenty-three years.

That same year, the corrupt Assembly at Perth agreed to the five articles imposed upon the Church by King James IV. and the prelates. David Dickson at first had no great scruple against Episcopacy, as he had not studied those questions much, till the articles were imposed by this Assembly. These he closely examined; the more he looked into them, the more aversion he found to them; and when some time after, by a sore sickness, he was brought within view of death and eternity, he gave open testimony of the sinfulness of them.

But when this came to take air, James Law, Archbishop of Glasgow, summoned him to appear before the High Commission Court, January 29, 1622. Dickson, at his entrance to the ministry at Irvine, had preached upon 2 Cor. v. 11—"Knowing the terrors of the Lord, we persuade men;" and when he perceived at this juncture a separation (at least for a time), the Sabbath before his compearance he chose the next words of that verse—"But we are made manifest unto God." Extraordinary power and singular movings of the affections accompanied that parting sermon.

David Dickson appeared before the Commission, where, after the summons being read, and after some reasoning among the bishops, he gave in his declinature; upon which, some of the bishops whispering in his ear, as if they had favoured him upon the good report they had heard of him and his ministry, said to him, " Take it up, take it up." He answered calmly, " I laid it not down for that end to take it up again." Spottiswoode, Archbishop of St Andrews, asked if he would subscribe it. He professed himself ready. The clerk, at the Archbishop's desire, began to read it; but had scarcely read three lines, till the Archbishop burst forth in railing speeches, full of gall and bitterness; and turning to Mr David, he said, " These men will speak of humility and meekness, and talk of the Spirit of God, but ye are led by the spirit of the devil; there is more pride in you, I dare say, than in all the bishops of Scotland. I hanged a Jesuit in Glasgow for the like fault." Mr David answered, " I am not a rebel; I stand here as the King's subject; grant me the benefit of the law, and of a subject, and I crave no more." But the Archbishop seemed to take no notice of these words. Aberdeen asked him, whether he would obey the King or not? He answered, " I will obey the King in all things in the Lord." "I told you that," said Glasgow, "I knew he would seek to his limitation." Aberdeen asked again, "May not the King give the same authority that we have to as many sutors and tailors in Edinburgh, to sit, and see whether ye be doing your duty or not?" Mr David said, " My declinature will answer to that." Then St Andrews fell again to railing, " The devil," said he, " will devise; he has Scripture enough ;" and then called him knave, swinger, young lad; and said he might have been teaching bairns in the school." " Thou knowest what Aristotle saith," said he, " but thou hast no theology." Because he perceived that Dickson gave him no titles, but once called him Sir, he gnashed his teeth, and said, " Sir! you might have called me Lord; when I was in Glasgow long since, ye called me so, but I cannot tell how, ye are become a puritan now." All this time he stood silent, and once lifted up his eyes to heaven, which St Andrews called a proud look. So after some more reasoning betwixt him and the bishops, St Andrews pronounced his sentence, in these words : " We deprive you of your ministry at Irvine, and ordain you to enter in Turriff, in the north, in twenty days." " The will of the Lord be done," said Mr David; "though ye cast me off, the Lord will take me up. Send me whither ye will, I hope my Master will go with me; and as He has been to me heretofore, He will be with me still, as with His own weak servant."

Mr Dickson continued preaching till the twenty days were expired, and then began his journey. The Earl of Eglinton prevailed with the Archbishop of Glasgow, that he might come to Eglinton, and preach there, but the people from all quarters resorting to his sermons in Eglinton's hall and court-yard, he enjoyed that liberty only two months ; for the Archbishop sent him another charge, and he went to the place of his confinement.

While in Turriff, he was daily employed to preach by Mr Thomas Mitchell, minister there. But he found far greater difficulty, both in studying and preaching, than formerly. Some time after, his friends prevailed with the Archbishop of Glasgow to repone him, upon condition he would take back his declinature, and for that purpose wrote to Mr Dickson to come to Glasgow. He came as desired; but though many wise and gracious persons urged him to yield, yet he could not be persuaded. Yea, at last it was granted to him, that if he, or any friend he pleased, would go to the Archbishop's castle, and either lift the paper, or suffer his friend to take it off the hall-table, without seeing the Archbishop at all, he might return to Irvine. But he found that to be but a juggling in such a weighty matter, in point of public testimony, and resolved to meddle no farther in this matter, but to return to his confinement. Accordingly he began his journey, and was scarcely a mile out of town, till his soul was filled with such joy and approbation from God that he seldom had the like.

Some time after, by the continued intercession of the Earl of Eglinton, and the town of Irvine, with the Archbishop, the Earl got a license to send for him, and a promise that he should stay till the King challenged him. Thus he returned, without any condition on his part, to his flock, about the end of July 1623.

While at Irvine, David Dickson's ministry was singularly countenanced of God, and multitudes were convinced and converted. Few who lived in his day were more instrumental in this work than he ; so that people, under exercise and soul-concern, came from every quarter about Irvine, and attended his sermons. The most eminent Christians, from all corners of the Church, came and joined with him at the communions, which were indeed times of refreshing from the presence of the Lord. Yea, not a few came from distant places, and settled at Irvine, that they might be under his ministry; yet he himself observed, that the vintage of Irvine was not equal to the gleanings of Ayr in Mr Welch's time ; where indeed the Gospel had wonderful success in conviction, conversion, and confirmation.

He commonly had his week-day sermon upon Monday, which

was the market-day then at Irvine. Upon the Sabbath evenings many persons under soul-distress used to resort to his house after sermon, when usually he spent an hour or two in answering their cases, and directing and comforting those who were cast down. In all this he had an extraordinary talent; indeed he had the tongue of the learned, and knew how to speak a word in season to the weary soul. In a large hall, which was in his own house, there would sometimes have been scores of serious Christians waiting for him after he came from church. These, with the people round the town, who came into the market, made the church as throng, if not thronger, on the Mondays than on the Lord's day. By these week-day sermons the famous Stewarton sickness (as it was called) was begun, about the year 1630, and spread from house to house for many miles in the valley where Stewarton water runs. Satan indeed endeavoured to bring a reproach upon such serious persons, as were at this time under the convincing work of the Spirit, by running some, seemingly under serious concern, to excess, both in time of sermon and in families. But the Lord enabled Mr Dickson, and other ministers who dealt with them, to act so prudent a part, that Satan's design was much disappointed, and solid, serious, practical religion flourished mightily in the west of Scotland about this time, under the hardships of Prelacy.

About the years 1630 and 1631, some of our Scottish ministers, Messrs Livingstone, Blair, and others, were settled among the Scots in the North of Ireland, where they were remarkably owned of the Lord in their ministry and communions about the Six-Mile Water, for reviving religion, and the power and practice of it. The Irish bishops, at the instigation of the Scots bishops, got them removed for a season. After they were silenced, and had come over to Scotland, about the year 1637, Mr Dickson employed Messrs Blair, Livingstone, and Cunningham at his communion, for which he was called before the High Commission; but the prelates' power being on the decline he soon got rid of that trouble.

Several other instances might be given concerning Mr Dickson's usefulness in answering perplexing cases of conscience, and in counselling students who had their eyes to the ministry. While he was at Irvine, the prudent directions, cautions, and encouragements given to such, were extremely useful and beneficial. Some examples might also be given of his usefulness to his very enemies; but there is little room here to insist on these things.

It was David Dickson who brought over the Presbytery of Irvine to supplicate the Council in 1637 for a suspension of the service-book. At this time four deputations from different quarters met at the council-house door, to their mutual surprise and encouragement; which were the small beginnings of the happy turn of affairs that next year ensued. In that great revolution Mr Dickson had no small share. He was sent to Aberdeen, with Messrs Henderson and Cant, by the Covenanters, to persuade that town and country to join in renewing the Covenants. This brought him to bear a great part in the debates with the learned Drs Forbes, Barrow, Sibbald, etc., at Aberdeen, which, being in print, need no further notice at present.

When King Charles I. was prevailed upon to allow a free General Assembly at Glasgow, November 1638, Mr Dickson and Mr Baillie, from the Presbytery of Irvine, made no small figure in all the important matters before that grave Assembly. Mr Dickson signalised himself, in a most seasonable and prudent speech, when his Majesty's Commissioner threatened to leave the Assembly; as also, in the 11th session, December 5, he had another most learned discourse against Arminianism.

By this time, not only the Lord's eminent countenancing of Mr Dickson's ministry at Irvine spread abroad, but his eminent prudence, learning, and holy zeal, came to be universally known, especially to ministers, from the part he bore in the Assembly at Glasgow, so that he was almost unanimously chosen moderator to the next General Assembly at Edinburgh, in August 1639. In its 10th session, the city of Glasgow presented a call to him: but, partly because of his own aversion, and the vigorous appearance of the Earl of Eglinton, and his loving people, and mostly for the remarkable usefulness of his ministry in that corner, the General Assembly continued him still at Irvine.

Not long after this, about 1641, he was appointed professor of divinity in the University of Glasgow, where he did great service to the Church by training up young men for the holy ministry; and yet, notwithstanding of his laborious work, he preached on the forenoon of every Sabbath, in the High Church there; where for some time he had the learned Mr Patrick Gillespie for his colleague.

In the year 1643, the Church laid a very great work upon him, together with Messrs Calderwood and Henderson, to form a draft of a directory for public worship, as appears by an Act of the General

Assembly. When the pestilence was raging at Glasgow in 1647, the masters and students, upon Mr Dickson's motion, removed to Irvine. There it was that the learned Mr Durham passed his trials, and was earnestly recommended by David Dickson to the Presbytery and Magistrates of Glasgow. A very strict friendship subsisted between these two great lights of the Church, and among other effects of their religious conversation we have "The Sum of Saving Knowledge," which has been printed with our Confession of Faith and Catechisms. This, after several conversations upon the subject, and manner of handling it, so that it might be useful to vulgar capacities, was dictated by Messrs Dickson and Durham to a reverend minister about the year 1650; and though never judicially approven by the Church, yet it deserves to be much more read and practised than what it at present is. [It was the reading of this treatise that brought M'Cheyne to a clear understanding of the way of acceptance with God, as appears from the following extract from his diary: "March 11th, 1834.—Read in the 'Sum of Saving Knowledge,' the work which I think first of all wrought a saving change in me. How gladly would I renew the reading of it, if that change might be carried on to perfection!"—ED.]

About this time he was translated from the profession of divinity at Glasgow to the same work at Edinburgh; at which time he published his *Prelectiones in Confessionem Fidei* ("Lectures on the Confession of Faith"), which he dictated in Latin to his scholars. There he continued his laborious care of students in divinity, the growing hopes of the Church; and either at Glasgow or at Edinburgh, the most part of the Presbyterian ministers, at least in the west, south, and east parts of Scotland, from 1640, were under his inspection. From the fore-mentioned book, we may perceive his care to educate them in the form of sound words, and to ground them in the excellent standards of doctrine agreed to by the once famous Church of Scotland; and happy had their successors been, had they preserved, and handed down to posterity, the scriptural doctrines, pure and entire, as they were delivered by our first reformers to Mr Dickson and his contemporaries, and from him and them handed down without corruption to their successors.

All this time, viz., in 1650 and 1651, Mr Dickson had a great share in the printed pamphlets upon the unhappy debates betwixt the Resolutioners and the Protesters. He was in favour of the public Resolutioners; and most of the papers on that side were written by him, Baillie, and Douglas; as those on the other side were written by James Guthrie, Patrick Gillespie, and a few others.

David Dickson continued at Edinburgh, discharging his trust with great diligence and faithfulness, until the restoration of Prelacy, upon the return of Charles II.; when, for refusing the oath of supremacy, he was, with many other Worthies, turned out; so that his heart was broken with this heavy change on the beautiful face of that once famed Reformed Church.

He married Margaret Robertson, daughter of Archibald Robertson of Stone-hall, a younger brother of the house of Ernock, in the shire of Lanark. By her he had three sons: John, clerk to the Exchequer in Scotland; Alexander, professor of Hebrew in the College of Edinburgh; and Archibald, who lived with his family afterwards in the parish of Irvine.

On December 1662, he fell extremely sick, at which time worthy Mr Livingstone, now suffering for the same cause, though he had then but forty-eight hours' liberty to stay in Edinburgh, came to see him on his death-bed. They had been intimately acquainted nearly forty years, and now rejoiced as fellow-confessors together. When Livingstone asked the professor, what were his thoughts of the present affairs, and how it was with himself? his answer was—" That he was sure Jesus Christ would not put up with the indignities done against His work and people;" and as for himself, said he, " I have taken all my good deeds, and all my bad deeds, and have cast them together in a heap before the Lord, and have fled from both to Jesus Christ, and in Him I have sweet peace."

Having been very low and weak for some days, he called all his family together, and spoke in particular to each of them; and having gone through them all, he pronounced the words of the apostolical blessing (2 Cor. xiii. 13, 14), with much gravity and solemnity. Then putting up his hand, he closed his eyes; and without any struggle or apparent pain, immediately expired in his son's arms, and, like Jacob of old, was gathered to his people in a good old age, being upwards of seventy-two years.

He was a man singularly endowed with an edifying gift of preaching; and his painful labours had been, in an eminent manner, blessed with success. His sermons were always full of solid and substantial matter, very scriptural, and in a very familiar style; not low, but extremely strong and affecting, being somewhat akin to the style of godly Samuel Rutherford. It is said, that scarce any minister of

KING'S COLLEGE, ABERDEEN—FRONT VIEW.

that time came so near Mr Dickson's style or method of preaching as William Guthrie, minister of Fenwick, who equalled, if not exceeded him. [A story is told of an English merchant who had occasion to visit Scotland about the year 1650. On his return, he was asked what news he had brought with him, when he replied: "Great and good news! I went to St Andrews, where I heard a sweet, majestic-looking man (Blair), and he showed me *the majesty of God*. After him, I heard a little fair man (Rutherford), and he showed me *the loveliness of Christ*. I then went to Irvine, where I heard a well-favoured, proper old man, with a long beard (Dickson), and that man showed me *all my heart*." "The whole General Assembly," says Wodrow, "could not have given a better character of the three men."—ED.]

His works are, a Commentary on the Epistle to the Hebrews, on Matthew's Gospel, on the Psalms of David and on the Epistles; his *Prælectiones in confessionem fidei*, or, Truth's Victory over error; his *Therapeutica sacra*, or, Cases of Conscience Resolved, in Latin and English; and a Treatise on the Promises. Besides these, he wrote a great part of the Answers to the Demands, and Duplies to the Replies of the Doctors of Aberdeen, and some of the pamphlets in defence of the public Resolutioners, as has been

RUINS OF ARCHBISHOP OF GLASGOW'S PALACE.

already observed; also some short poems on pious and serious subjects, such as, the Christian Sacrifice, True Christian Love, to be sung with the common tunes of the Psalms. There are also several other pieces of his, mostly in manuscript, such as, his *Tyrones conscionaturi*, supposed to be dictated to his scholars at Glasgow; *Summarium libri Isaiæ*; his Letters on the Resolutioners; his First Paper on the public Resolutions; his Replies to Mr Gillespie and Mr James Guthrie; his Non-separation from the Well-affected in the army; as also, some sermons at Irvine, upon 1 Tim. i. 5; and his Precepts for the Daily Direction of a Christian, etc., by way of a Catechism for his congregation at Irvine; with a Compend of Sermons upon Jeremiah and the Lamentations, and the first nine chapters of the Romans.

Archibald Johnston, Lord Warriston.

HE first of Archibald Johnston's public appearances in favour of that glorious work of Reformation, commonly called the second reformation period, seems to have been about the beginning of 1638. When it came first to be known that Traquair was going up to King Charles I., the deputies (afterwards called the Covenanters) were desirous that he would carry up an information, which the Lord Balmerino and Mr Johnston (the only advocates as yet trusted by the petitioners) had drawn up, and that he would present the same, with their supplication, to his Majesty. But both of these being rejected by the King, and orders given by him to Traquair to publish a proclamation at Edinburgh and Stirling against the requisitions of the Covenanters, sixteen of the nobles, with many barons, gentlemen, burgesses, and ministers, after hearing the proclamation, caused Mr Johnston to read a protest against the same. And the same year, when the Marquis of Hamilton published another declaration in name of the King, the Covenanters, upon hearing it, gave another protestation in the same place by Mr Johnston; whereupon the Earl of Cassilis, in name of the nobility, Gibson of Durie, in name of the barons, Fletcher, provost of Dundee, in name of the burgesses, Mr Kerr, minister at Preston, in name of the Church, and Mr Archibald Johnston, in name of all others who adhered to the Covenant, took instruments in the hands of three notaries, and, in all humility, offered a copy of the same to the herald at the Cross of Edinburgh.

Upon the 9th of September, a declaration of the same nature being published, the noblemen, gentlemen, and burgesses, gave in another protest, and Mr Johnston, leader and advocate for the Church, in name of all who adhered to the Confession of Faith, and Covenant lately renewed within the kingdom, took instruments in the hands of three notaries there present, and offered a copy thereof to the herald at the Cross of Edinburgh.

In the same year, when the famous General Assembly sat down at Glasgow, in the month of November, Alexander Henderson being chosen moderator, it was moved, that Mr Johnston, who had hitherto served the Tables at Edinburgh without reward, and yet with great diligence, skill, and integrity, deserved the office of clerk above all others. After much reasoning concerning him and some others put on a leet for election, the roll being called, on a vote for clerk, it was carried unanimously for Mr Johnston, who then gave his oath for fidelity, diligence, and a conscientious use of the registers; and was admitted to all the rights, profits, and privileges, which any in that office had formerly enjoyed; and instruments were taken both of his admittance and acceptance.

Mr Johnston being thus installed, the moderator desired, that all who had any acts or books of former Assemblies, would put them into his hands; whereupon Mr Sandihills (formerly clerk) exhibited two books, containing some acts from 1592 to that of Aberdeen in 1618, and being interrogated concerning the rest, he solemnly averred, that he had received no more from the Archbishop, and, to his knowledge, he had no other belonging to the Church. Then a farther motion was made by the Assembly for recovering the rest, and that if any had them, they should give them up; whereupon Mr Johnston gave an evidence how deserving he was of the trust reposed in him, by producing on the table five books, being now seven in all, which were sufficient to make up a register of the Church from the beginning of the Reformation, which was very acceptable to the whole Assembly.

In the twenty-fourth session of this Assembly, a commission was given to Mr Johnston to be their procurator, and Mr Dalglish to be their agent; and in their last session of December 20, an act was passed, allowing him the instruction of all treaties and papers that concerned the Church, and prohibiting all printers from publishing anything of that kind, not licensed by him.

But the King and the Canterburian faction, being highly displeased with the proceedings of this Assembly, advanced with an army towards the Borders, which made the Covenanters, seeing the danger to which they were exposed, raise another army, with which, under the command of General Alexander Leslie, they marched towards the King's, now encamped on the south side of the Tweed, about three miles above Berwick. Upon their approach, the English began to faint; whereupon the King and the English nobility desired a treaty, which was easily granted by the Scots, who appointed the Earls of

PORTRAIT OF EARL OF TRAQUAIR.

Rothes, Dunfermline, and Loudon, the Sheriff of Teviotdale, Mr Henderson, and Mr Archibald Johnston, advocate for the Church, as their commissioners, to treat with the English commissioners, to whom his Majesty granted a safe-conduct upon the 9th of June 1639. The Scots, having made known their demands, condescended upon several particulars, which were answered by the other side. On the 17th, and the day following, the articles of specification were subscribed by both parties, in sight of both armies, at Birks near Berwick.

But this treaty was but short-lived, and as ill kept; for the very next year the King took arms against the Scots, who immediately armed themselves a second time and went for England, where they defeated a party of the English at Newburn, and pushed their way as far as Durham. The King, finding himself in a strait, the English supplicating him behind, and the Scots with a potent army before him, resolved on a second treaty, which was set on foot at Ripon, and concluded at London; and thither Mr Henderson and Mr Johnston were sent again as commissioners for the Church; in which affairs they behaved with great prudence and candour. When the Scots Parliament sat down this year, they by an act appointed a fee of one hundred merks to Mr Johnston as advocate for the Church, and five hundred merks as clerk to the General Assembly; so sensible were they of his many services done to the Church and nation.

WINDSOR CASTLE.

Next year (1641) the King, having fallen out with his English Parliament, came to Scotland, where he attended the Scots Parliament. In this Parliament several offices of state were filled up with persons fit for such employments; the Earl of Argyle being put at the head of the Treasury, and the Earl of Loudon made Chancellor. Among others, Mr Archibald Johnston stood fair for the Register's office, and the generality of the well-affected thought it the just reward of his labours, but the King, Lennox, Argyle, etc., being for Gibson of Durie, he carried the prize. Yet Mr Johnston's disappointment was removed by the King's conferring the order of knighthood upon him, and granting him a commission to be one of the Lords of Session, with an annual pension of £200; and Ormiston was made Justice-Clerk.

During this and the next year, Sir Archibald Johnston had several great employments committed to his trust. He was one of those nominated to conserve the articles of peace betwixt the two kingdoms until the meeting of Parliament; and then he was appointed one of those commissioners who were sent up to London to negotiate with the English Parliament for sending over some relief from Scotland to Ireland, it being then on the back of the Irish rebellion. While at London they waited on his Majesty at Windsor, and offered their mediation betwixt him and his two Houses of Parliament; but for this he gave them little thanks, although he found his mistake afterwards.

When the General Assembly sat down at Edinburgh, in 1643, they, upon a motion from Sir Archibald Johnston, their clerk, emitted a declaration for joining with the English Parliament, for a variety of reasons, of which these were the sum and substance : " (1.) They apprehended the war was for religion. (2.) The Protestant faith was in danger. (3.) Gratitude for the assistance in the time of the former Reformation required a suitable return. (4.) Because the Churches of Scotland and England, being embarked in one cause, if the one were ruined, the other could not subsist. (5.) The prospect of an uniformity between the two kingdoms in discipline and worship would strengthen the Protestant interest at home and abroad. (6.) The present Parliament had been friendly to the Scots, and might be so again. (7.) Though the King had so lately established religion amongst them, according to their desire, yet they could not confide in his royal declaration, having so often found his actions and promises contradictory the one to the other." These reasons the Estates took in good part, and suggested others of their own, as they saw proper.

Toward the latter end of this Assembly, upon the arrival of the commissioners from the Parliament and Assembly at Westminster, the Scots Assembly, by an act of Session 14, commissioned Messrs Henderson, Douglas, Rutherford, Baillie, and Gillespie, ministers ; John, Earl of Cassilis, John Lord Maitland, Sir Archibald Johnston of Warriston, ruling elders ; or any three of them, whereof two should be ministers, " to repair to the kingdom of England, and there to deliver the declaration sent to the Parliament of England, and the letter sent to the Assembly of Divines, now sitting in that kingdom, and to propound, consult, treat, and conclude with that Assembly, or any commissioner deputed, or any committee or commissioner deputed by the House of Parliament, in all matters which may further the union of this island, in one form of church government, one Confession of Faith, one Catechism, one Directory for the Worship of God, according to the instructions they have received from the Assembly, or shall receive from time to time hereafter from the commissioners of the Assembly deputed for that effect." This commission was again renewed by several acts of the subsequent Assemblies, till the year 1648. And it appears that Lord Warriston did not only use all diligence, as a member of the Westminster

Assembly, for bringing about uniformity of religion in worship, discipline, and government, but also, for some time, sat as a member of the English Parliament, for concerting such methods as might bring about a firm and lasting peace between the two kingdoms afterwards ; which was reckoned a most noble piece of service both to Church and State in those days ; yet, we shall find it accounted high treason in this worthy man afterwards. The following is an abstract of a speech, which he made in the Westminster Assembly, after the delivery of some queries from the Parliament :

" MR PROLOCUTOR,—I am a stranger. I will not meddle with the Parliament privileges of another nation, nor the breaches thereof, but as a Christian, under one common Lord, a ruling elder in another church, and a Parliament-man in another kingdom, having commission from both that Church and State, and at the desire of this kingdom assisting in their debates, I entreat for your favour and patience to express my thoughts of what is before you.

" In my judgment, that is before you which concerns Christ and these kingdoms most and above all, and which will be the chiefest mean to end or continue these troubles. And that, not only speaking *humaniter*, and looking to the disposition of these kingdoms, but especially in regard to the divine dispensation, which hath been so special and sensible in the rise and continuance of these commotions, as I can neither be persuaded that they were raised for, or will be calmed upon the settlement of civil rights and privileges, either of kings or princes, whatsoever may seem to be our present success. But I am convinced they have a higher rise, from and for the highest end, the settling of the Crown of Christ in these islands, to be propagated from island to continent ; and until King Jesus be set down on His throne, with His sceptre in His hand, I do not expect God's peace, and so not solid peace from men, in these kingdoms. But establish that, and a durable peace will be found to follow that sovereign truth. Sir, let us lay to heart what is before us, a work which concerns God and man most of anything in agitation now under the sun, and for which we will one day be called to a more strict account than for any other passage of our life. Let us both tremble and rejoice when we reflect upon what is under debate, and now in our hands.

" I was glad to hear the Parliament confess their willingness to receive and observe whatsoever shall be shown from the word of God to be Christ's or His Church's rights or dues ; albeit I was sorry to see any, in the delivery thereof, intermix any of their own personal asperity, any aspersions upon this Assembly, or reflections on another nation; so in this day of law for Christ, wherein justice is offered, if He get not right in not showing His patent from His Father, and His Church's from Himself, it will be counted your fault.

" Sir, all Christians are bound to give a testimony to every truth when called to it, but ye are the immediate servants of the Most High, Christ's proctors and heralds, whose proper function it is to proclaim His name, and preserve His offices, and assert His rights. Christ has had many testimonies given to His prophetical and priestly offices by the pleadings and sufferings of His saints, and in these latter days, seems to require the same unto His kingly office. A king loves a testimony to his crown best of any, as that which is tenderest to him ; and confessors and martyrs for Christ's crown are the most royal and most stately of any state-martyrs ; so, although Christ's kingdom be not of this world, and His servants did not fight therefor when He was to suffer, yet it is in this world, and for this end was He born. To give a testimony to this truth, among others, were we born, and must not be ashamed of it, or deny it, but confess and avouch it, by pleading, doing, and suffering for it, even when what is in agitation seems most to oppose it, and therefore requires a seasonable testimony. But it lies upon you, sir, who have both your calling from Christ for it, and at this time a particular calling from many ; that which the honourable houses require from you at such a time, when the settlement of religion is thereon, and when it is the very controversy of the times ; and the civil magistrates not only call you before them to aver the truth therein, but also, giving you a good example, come before you out of tenderness to their civil trust and duty to maintain the privileges of Parliament ; to give a testimony as sentatory to their civil rights and privileges ; and to forewarn you lest you break the same, and incur civil premunires. Sir, this should teach us to be as tender, zealous, and careful to assert Christ and His Church, their privileges and rights ; and to forewarn all lest they endanger their souls by encroaching thereon, and lest their omissions and remissness bring eternal premunires upon them. Let all know that the Spirit of your Master is upon you, and that Christ hath servants who will not only make pulpits to ring with the sound of His prerogative, but also, if they shall be called to it, make a flame of their bodies burning at the stake for a testimony to it, carry it aloft through the earth, like the voice in Sicily, that *Christ lives and reigns alone in*

His Church, and will have all done therein according to His word and will, and that He has given no supreme headship over His Church to any Pope, King, or Parliament whatsoever.

" Sir, you are often desired to remember the bounds of your commission from man, and not to exceed the same. I am confident you will make as much conscience not to be deficient in the discharge of your commission from Christ. But now, sir, you have a commission from God and man together, to discuss that truth, That Christ is a King, and has a kingdom in the external government of His Church, and that He has set down laws and offices, and other substantials thereof, and a part of the kingdom for the coming of which we daily pray. We must not now before men mince, hold up, or conceal anything necessary for this testimony. All these would seem to me to be retiring and flying, and not to flow from the High Spirit of the Most High, who will not refuse to flinch for one hour, nor quit one hoof, nor edge away a hem of Christ's robe royal. These would seem effects of desertion, tokens of being ashamed, afraid, or politically diverted ; and all these, and every degree of them, sir, I am confident will be very far from the thoughts of every one here who by their votes and petitions, according to their protestations at their entry, have showed themselves so zealous and forward to give their testimony, albeit they easily saw it would not be very acceptable to the powers on earth, who would hamper, stamp, and halve it. But would ye answer to that question, If this were a Parliament, and if it was a full and free one, would he not, and should he not be esteemed a great breaker of privileges, and *contemptor curiæ* ? Albeit we are not so wise, yet let us be as tender and jealous in our day and generation. Truly, sir, I am confident you will not be so in love with a peaceable and external profession of anything that may be granted to the Church, as to conceal, disclaim, or invert your Master's right. That were to lose the substance for a circumstance, to desert and dethrone Christ to serve yourselves, and enthrone others in His place. A tenant doing so to his lord or landlord forfeits all. Ye are commanded to be faithful in little, but now ye are commanded to be faithful in much ; for albeit the salvation of souls be called *cura curarii,* the welfare and happiness of churches (made up of these) is far more. But the kingdom of Christ is *optimum maximum;* and to have it now under your debate, as it is the greatest honour God doth bestow upon an Assembly, so it is in the greatest danger, for according now as God shall assist or direct you, you may and will be the instruments of the greatest good or evil on earth. Let us do all in, with, for, and by Christ. Remember the account we have to make to Him, who subjects the standing or falling of His crown in this island to our debate. I speak *humaniter* for *diviniter.* I know it is impossible, and albeit we should all prove false and faint-hearted, He can, and will, soon raise up other instruments to assert, publish, and propagate His right to a *forum consistorii.* He will have it thoroughly pled and judged betwixt His kingdom and the kingdoms of the earth. And seeing He has begun to conquer, He will prevail over all that stand in His way, whether Pope, King, or Parliament, that will claim any part of Headship, supreme prerogative, and monarchy over His own Church.

"Sir, some may think you have had a design in abstaining so long from asserting the divine right of church government now to come in with it truly. Sir, I look upon this check as a good providence for your great sparing and abstaining in that point, and must bear witness to many passages of God's good hand in it, in not suffering us to make a stand of our desires concerning religion, either in Scotland or here, albeit we have often set down *mensura voti* to ourselves. But He has as often moved us step after step to trace back our defections, and make the last innovations a besom to sweep out the former, and the king refused to be a mean to engage in a covenant with himself and others, and so has drawn us against our wills, and beyond our desires, to perform our duty, and to give a testimony to His truth, that much of God and divine wisdom and design, and little of man and his politic projects, might be seen in the beginning, progress, and continuance of the whole work, by this good hand of God ; and for this end, I hope these queries are brought to your hand at this time.

"Sir, your serving the Parliament a while, I am confident, has been and will be still, not that they may serve you, but for to serve the Lord Jesus Christ, and that Parliament will glory more in their subordination and subservience to Him, than in the empire and command over the world.

"Sir, we may hear much of the breach of privilege and of the Covenant in relation to civil right. Let us remember in the Covenant the three orders in the title and preface, three main duties in the body, and the three effects in the close.—The covenant begins with the advancement, and ends with the enlargement of the kingdom of Christ, as the substantials and overword of the whole.

" The first article of the seven is Christ, an article like *dies Dominica* in the week, all the rest are *in Domino*, and subordinate thereunto. And all laws contrary to the will of Christ are acknowledged to be void in His kingdom, and so they should, with far greater reason than the constable's orders, against the ordinance of Parliament are void in law. But, sir, Christ's throne is highest, and His privileges supreme as the only King and Head of His church, albeit kings and magistrates may be members in it. There is no authority to be balanced with His, nor posts to be set up against His, nor Korahs to be allowed against His Aarons, nor Uzziahs against His Azariahs. Is it so small a thing to have the sword, but they must have the keys also? Truly, sir, I am confident that the Parliament and both nations will acknowledge themselves engaged under this authority; and, as they would not be drawn from it (for we must deny our places, take up our cross, lay aside our love to father and mother, paternal and civil, yea, lay down our lives to aver and confess this truth against all allurements and terrors), so ye would never endeavour to draw us to any other. And whatsoever reflection to the contrary was insinuated by the deliverer of this message, I cannot but impute it to personal passion, which long ago was known to the world, but I will never believe the Honourable House will allow thereof, as being far beneath their wisdom, and contrary to your merit.

"And, sir, seeing these queries are before you, I am confident that whatever diversity of opinion may be among you in any particular, you will all hold out Christ's kingdom distinct from the kingdoms of the earth, and that He has appointed the government of His own house, and should rule the same ; and that none of this Assembly, even for the gaining of their desires in all the points of difference, would, by their silence, concealment and connivance, weaken, commutate or sell a part of this fundamental truth, this sovereign interest of Christ ; and that ye will all concur to demonstrate the same by clear passages of Scripture, or necessary consequences therefrom, and by the constant practice of the apostles, which are rules unto us.

"Sir, I will close with remembering you of two passages of your letter, sent by order of the House of Commons to the General Assembly of the Church of Scotland, that you will set out with such discipline as, to the utmost of your power, you may exalt Christ the only Lord over the Church, His own house, in all His offices, and present the Church as a chaste virgin to Christ ; and for this end that you were not restrained by the Houses in your votes and resolutions, nor bound up to the sense of others, not to carry on a private design in a civil way, but by your oath were secured against all flattering of your judgment, and engaged thereby, according to the House's desire, to use all freedom becoming the integrity of your consciences, the weight of the cause, and the integrity and honour of such an Assembly. I will no more, sir, trouble you; but with one word upon the whole matter, to desire you seriously to consider if this business, whereon the eyes of God are fixed, deserves not a special day of humiliation and prayer for the Lord's extraordinary assistance and direction of this Assembly."

Lord Warriston, for his upright and faithful dealing in the many important matters committed to his charge, received many marks of favour and dignity both from Church and State; and to crown all the rest, the Scots Parliament, in 1646, made an act, appointing his commission to be Lord Advocate, with the conducting of the committee of London and Newcastle, and the general officers of the army; all which evidence what a noble hand he had in carrying on that blessed work of reformation.

He had now been clerk to the General Assembly since the year 1638; and when that unhappy difference fell out in 1650, when the Act of Classes was repealed, and malignants were taken into places of power and trust, which occasioned the rise of the Protesters and Resolutioners, Lord Warriston was one of those who had a principal hand in managing affairs. He wrote a most solid letter to the meeting at St Andrews, July 18, 1651, concerning which, the protesters, in their reasons proving the said meeting to be no lawful, full, or free General Assembly, say, " Sir Archibald Johnston, clerk to the Assembly, a man undeniably faithful, singularly acquainted with the acts and proceedings of this kirk, and with the matters presently in controversy, and who hath been useful above many in all the tracts of the work of reformation, from the beginning, in all the steps thereof, both at home and abroad, having written his mind to the meeting, not being able to come himself, about the things that are to be agitated in the Assembly, and held out much clear light from the Scriptures, and from the acts of former Assemblies, in these particulars; albeit the letter was delivered publicly to the moderator, in the face of the Assembly, and urged to be read by him who presented it, that then the moderator did break it open, and caused it to be read; and that many members did thereafter, upon several occasions, and at several diets, press the reading of it, but it could never be ob-

PORTRAIT OF ANDREW CANT.

tained. . . . And further, those papers bearing the name of representations, propositions, protestations, etc., were by the said Lord Warriston, Messrs Cant, Rutherford, Livingstone, and others, presented to the reverend ministers and elders met at Edinburgh, July 24, 1652, when the Marquis of Argyle, at London, procured an equal hearing to the Protesters; and Mr Simpson, one of the three ministers deposed by the Assembly, 1651, being sent up by the Protesters for that purpose, in the beginning of 1657, Messrs James Guthrie and Patrick Gillespie, the two others who had been deposed by that Assembly, together with Lord Warriston, were sent up to assist Mr Simpson."

Lord Warriston had now, for the space of five years or more, wrestled and acted, with all his power, for the King's interest; and being a man of great resolution, he both spoke and wrote openly against Scotsmen submitting to take offices under Cromwell. But being sent up to London in the foresaid year 1657, with some of the Scots nobility, upon some important affairs, and Cromwell being fully sensible how much it would be for his interest to gain such a man as Warriston over to his side, he prevailed upon him to re-enter the office of Clerk-Register; which was much lamented by this worthy man afterwards, as well as his sitting and presiding in some meeting at London after Oliver's death. Wodrow* has observed, that at the

* Blair's Memoirs.

meeting at Edinburgh, which sent Lord Warriston to London upon business, he reasoned against it, and to the utmost of his power opposed his being sent up, acquainting them with what was his weak side ; that, through the easiness of his temper, he might not be able to resist importunity, craving that he might not be sent among snares; and yet, after all, he was peremptorily named.

To account some way for his conduct in this: his family was numerous ; and very considerable sums were owing him, which he had advanced for the public service, and a good many bygone years' salaries. He was, through importunity, thus prevailed upon to side with the usurper, there being no other door open then for his relief. And yet, after this his compliance, it was observed, he was generally more sad and melancholy than what he had formerly been ; and it is said that his outward affairs did not prosper so well afterwards.

King Charles II. being restored to his dominions in 1660, and the noble Marquis of Argyle imprisoned July 14, orders came down to seize Sir James Stuart, provost of Edinburgh, Sir Archibald Johnston of Warriston, and Sir John Chiesly of Carswell. The first and last were tried, but Lord Warriston escaped for a time, and therefore was summoned, by sound of trumpet, to surrender himself, and a proclamation issued for seizing him, promising a hundred pounds Scots to any one who should do it, and discharging all from concealing or harbouring him, under pain of treason. A most arbitrary step indeed ! for here is not only a reward offered for apprehending this worthy gentleman, but it is declared treason for any to harbour him, and that without any cause assigned.

Upon the 10th of October following, he was, by order of the Council, declared fugitive ; and next year (February 1) the indictment against Lord Warriston, William Dundas, and John Hume, was read in the House, none of them being present. Warriston was forfeited, and his forfeiture publicly proclaimed at the Cross of Edinburgh. The principal articles of his indictment were, his pleading against Newton Gordon, when he had the King's express orders to plead for him ; his assisting to the act of the West Kirk, etc. ; his drawing out, contriving, or assenting to, the paper called the Western Remonstrance, and the book called the "Causes of the Lord's Wrath ;" his sitting in Parliament as a peer in England, contrary to his oath ; his accepting the office of Clerk-Register from Cromwell ; and being president of the Committee of Safety, when Richard Cromwell was laid aside. But none of all these was the proper cause of this good man's sufferings. Personal prejudice and pique was at the bottom of all these bitter proceedings: for the godly freedom he took in reproving vice was what could never be forgotten or forgiven. Wodrow hints, that the Earl of Bristol interceded for him, and says: "I have an account of this holy freedom Lord Warriston used, from a reverend minister who was his chaplain at that time, and took freedom to advise my Lord not to adventure on it. Yet this excellent person, having the glory of God and the honour of religion more in his eyes than his own safety, went on in his designed reproof, and would not, for a compliment, quit the peace he expected in his own conscience, be the event what it would, by disburdening himself. He got a great many fair words, and it was pretended to be taken well from my Lord Register; but, as he was told by his well-wishers, it was never forgot." In his compliance with Cromwell, he was not alone; the greater part of the nation being involved therein as well as he; and several of those who had been named trustees to the Usurper, were all discharged from Court, except Warriston, who was before come to Scotland, and ordered to appear before the Parliament at the sitting down hereof.

This good man, after the sentence of forfeiture and death passed against him by the first Parliament, being obliged to go abroad to escape the fury of his enemies, even there did their crafty malice reach him. For while at Hamburg, being visited with sore sickness, it is certain that Dr Bates, one of King Charles's physicians, intending to kill him, contrary to his faith and office, prescribed poison to him instead of physic, and then caused draw from him sixty ounces of blood, whereby, though the Lord wonderfully preserved his life, he was brought near the gates of death, and so far lost his memory, that he could not remember what he had said or done a quarter of an hour before, and continued so until the day of his martyrdom.

And yet all this did not satisfy his cruel and blood-thirsty enemies. While he was yet in life they sought him carefully; and at last, he having gone unadvisedly to France, one Alexander Murray, being dispatched in quest of him, apprehended him at Roanne, while he was engaged in secret prayer, a duty wherein he much delighted. In January 1663, he was brought over prisoner, and committed to the Tower of London, where he continued till the beginning of June, when he was sent down to Edinburgh to be executed.

His conduct during his passage was truly Christian. He landed at Leith on the 8th, and was committed to the Tolbooth of Edin-

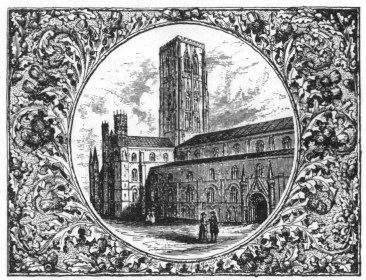

DURHAM CATHEDRAL.

burgh; from which he was brought before the Parliament on the 8th
of July. His nephew, Bishop Burnet, in his History, says, he was so
disordered both in body and mind, that it was a reproach to any
Government to proceed against him.

When at the bar of the House, he discovered such weakness of
memory and judgment, that almost every person lamented him, except
Sharp and the other bishops, who scandalously and basely triumphed
over, and publicly derided him: "although it is well known," says
the author of the Apologetical Relation, "that Lord Warriston was
once in case not only to have been a member, but a president of any
judicatory in Europe, and to have spoken for the cause and interest
of Christ before kings, to the stopping of the mouths of gainsayers."

It seemed that many of the members of Parliament inclined to
spare his life; but when the question was put, whether the time of his
execution should be just now fixed or delayed, Lauderdale interposed, upon calling the rolls, and delivered a most dreadful speech
for his present execution. Sentence was accordingly pronounced,
that he be hanged at the cross of Edinburgh, on the 22d of July, and
his head placed on the Netherbow, beside that of James Guthrie. He
received his sentence with such meekness as filled all with admiration; for then he desired, that the best blessings might be on Church

NETHERBOW PORT—EAST FRONT.

and State, and on his Majesty (whatever might befall himself), and that God would give him true and faithful counsellors.

During the whole time of his imprisonment, he was in a most spiritual and tender frame, to the conviction of his very enemies; and the nearer that his death approached, the composure of his mind became the more conspicuous. He rested agreeably the night before his execution, and in the morning was full of consolation, sweetly expressing his assurance of being clothed with a long white robe, and of getting a new song of the Lamb's praise in his mouth. Before noon he dined with cheerfulness, hoping to sup in heaven, and to drink the next cup fresh and new in his Father's kingdom.

After he had spent some time in secret prayer, about two o'clock he was taken from prison, attended by several of his friends in mourning, though he himself was full of holy cheerfulness and carriage, and in perfect serenity of mind. When going to the scaffold, he said frequently to the people, "Your prayers! your prayers!" When he was on the scaffold, he said, "I entreat you, quiet yourselves a little, till this dying man deliver his last speech among you;" and desired they would not be offended at his making use of the paper to help his memory, it being so much impaired by long sickness and the malice of physicians. Then he read his speech, first on the one side of the scaffold, and then on the other: in which speech, after a short preamble, showing that what he intended to have spoken at his death was not now in his power, being taken from him, and expressing the hope that the Lord would preserve it to be his testimony, he in the first place confessed his sins, pleaded for forgiveness, bewailed his compliance with the usurper, although, as he said, he was not alone in that offence, but had the body of the nation going before him, and the example of all ranks to ensnare him. Then he declared his adherence to the covenanted work of Reformation, earnestly desiring the prayers of all the Lord's praying people ; and vindicated himself from having any accession to the late King's death, and to the making of the change of Government; taking the great God of heaven to witness between him and his accusers. At last he concluded with these words; "I do here now submit, and commit my soul and body, wife and children, and children's children, from generation to generation for ever, with all others, my friends and followers, all His doing and suffering witnesses, sympathising ones in present and subsequent generations, unto the Lord's choice mercies, graces, favours, services, employments, enjoyments, and inheritments on earth, and in heaven, for time and all eternity ; all which suits, with all others which He hath at any time by his Spirit moved and assisted me to put up according to His will, I leave before and upon the Father's merciful bowels, the Son's mediating merits, and the Holy Spirit's compassionate groans, both now and for ever more ! Amen !"

After the reading of his speech, he prayed with great fervency and liberty, and, being in a rapture, he began thus : "Abba, Father! Accept this thy poor sinful servant, coming unto thee, through the merits of Jesus Christ." Then taking leave of his friends, he prayed again with great fervency, being now near the end of that sweet work he had so much through the course of his time been employed in. No ministers were allowed to be with him ; but it was by those present observed that God sufficiently made up that want. He was helped up the ladder by some of his friends in deep mourning ; and, as he ascended, he said, "Your prayers ! your prayers ! Your prayers I desire in the name of the Lord." Such was the esteem he had for that duty.

When got to the top of the ladder, he cried out with a loud voice, "I beseech you all who are the people of God, not to scare at suffering for the interest of Christ, or stumble at any thing of this kind falling out in these days ; but be encouraged to suffer for Him, for I assure you, in the name of the Lord, He will bear your charges."

While the rope was putting about his neck, he repeated these words again; adding, " The Lord hath graciously comforted me." When the executioner desired his forgiveness, he said, " The Lord forgive thee, poor man ;" and withal gave him some money, bidding him do his office if he was ready ; and crying out, " O pray, pray ! Praise, praise, praise," he was turned over ; and died almost without any struggle, with his hands lifted up unto heaven, whither his soul ascended, to enjoy the beatific presence of his Lord and Saviour Jesus Christ.

He was soon cut down, and his head struck off, and set up beside that of his dear friend James Guthrie ; his body being carried to the Greyfriars' Churchyard. But his head soon after, by the interest and intercession of Lieutenant-general Drummond, who married one of his daughters, was taken down and interred with his body.

Thus stood and thus fell, the eminently pious and truly learned Lord Warriston, whose talents as a speaker in the senate, as well as on the bench, are too well known to be here insisted upon. For prayer, he was one among a thousand, and ofttimes met with very remarkable returns ; and though he was for some time borne down with weakness and distress, yet he never came in the least to doubt of his eternal happiness. He used to say, " I dare never question my salvation, I have so often seen God's face in the house of prayer." And, as the last-cited historian observes, " Although his memory and talents were for some time impaired, yet like the sun at his setting, after he had been a while under a cloud, he shone most brightly and surprisingly, and so in some measure the more sweetly ; for that morning he was under a wonderful effusion of the Spirit ; as great, perhaps, as any have had since the primitive times."

He wrote a large diary, which yet remains in the hands of his relations, a valuable treasure both of Christian experience and matters of fact, little known at present, but which might be of great use and light to the history of that period. Therein he records his sure hope (after much wrestling in which he was mightily helped), that the Church of Scotland would be manifestly visited and freed from the evils she fell under after the Restoration. His numerous family, whom he so often left upon the Lord's providence, were, for the most part, as well provided for as could have been expected, though he had continued with them in his own outward prosperity. " He that overcometh shall be clothed in white raiment, and I will not blot out his name out of the book of life ; but I will confess his name before my Father and His angels."

James Wood.

AMES WOOD was, some time after the year 1651, made provost or principal of the Old College of St Andrews, and one of the ministers there. Being one who in judgment fell in with the resolution party, this occasioned some difference betwixt him and Samuel Rutherford, at that time Professor of Divinity in the New College there. And yet the latter had ever a great and high esteem for Mr Wood, as appears from a message he sent him when on his death-bed, wherein he said, "Tell Mr James Wood from me, I heartily forgive him all the wrongs he hath done, and desire him from me to declare himself the man he is, still for the Government of the Church of Scotland." And truly he was not deceived in him, for Mr Wood was true and faithful to the Presbyterian Government. Nothing could prevail upon him to comply in the least degree with abjured Prelacy. So far was he from this, that the apostacy and treachery of others, whom he had too much trusted, broke his upright spirit, particularly the aggravated defection and perfidy of James Sharp, whom he termed Judas, Demas, and Gehazi, all in one, after he had found what part he had acted to the Church of Scotland under trust.

On one occasion, in company with Mr Veitch, he went into one James Glen's shop, in Edinburgh, to see Sharp, whom he had not seen since he became archbishop, and who was expected to pass in the Commissioner's coach. Sharp coming first out of the coach, and uncovering his head to receive the Commissioner, they had a full view of his face, at which Mr Wood looked very seriously, and then, being much affected, uttered these words: " O, thou Judas and apostatised traitor, thou hast betrayed the famous Presbyterian Church of Scotland to its total ruin, as far as thou canst; if I know anything of the mind of God, thou shalt not die the ordinary and common death of men." This, though spoken eighteen years before, was exactly accomplished in 1679.

James Wood continued in the exercise of the foresaid offices until 1663, when, at the instigation of Archbishop Sharp, he got a charge to appear before the Council on the 23d of July, to answer to several things laid to his account. For though Sharp was indebted to him for any reputation he had, and was under as great obligation to him as one man could be to another (for they had been more than ordinarily familiar), yet now he could not bear his continuing any longer there, and he cited him before the Council.

When he compeared, he was interrogated, How he came to be provost of the College of St Andrews? When he began to answer, he was rudely interrupted, and commanded to give in his answer in a word, for the Archbishop and others present could not endure his telling some truths he was entering upon. He told them, he was called by the faculty of that college, at the recommendation of the usurper, as some present (meaning Sharp) very well know. Thereupon he was removed, and a little after, being called in again, his sentence was intimated unto him: " That the Lords of Council, for the present, do declare the said place to be vacant, and ordain and command him to confine himself within the city of Edinburgh, and not to depart from thence until farther orders." He replied, " He was sorry they had condemned a person without hearing him, whom they could not charge with the breach of any law." In September following, Sharp got the charge and privileges of his office; which shows that he had some reason for pushing Mr Wood from it.

Upon the 30th of the same month, Mr Wood presented a petition to the Council, showing that his father was extremely sick, that he had several necessary affairs at St Andrews, and that he desired liberty to go there for that purpose.. This petition being read, with a certificate of his father's infirmity, the Council granted license to the petitioner to go to St Andrews to visit his father, and perform his other necessary affairs ; always returning when he should be called by the Council.

Thus he continued till toward the beginning of the year 1664, when he took sickness, whereof he died. And though he suffered not in his body, as several of his brethren did, yet the Archbishop, it appears, was resolved to ruin his name and reputation after his death, if not sooner ; in order to which he saw good, once or twice, to pay him a visit, when on his death-bed in St Andrews. Being now extremely weak, he spoke very little to Sharp, and nothing at all about the changes made in the state of public affairs. However, the consequence of these visits was, that the Primate spread a rumour that Mr Wood, being now under the views of death and eternity, professed himself very indifferent as to church-government, and declared himself as much for Episcopacy as for Presbytery. And in all companies he asserted, that Mr Wood had declared to himself, that Presbyterian government was indifferent, and alterable at the pleasure of the magistrate, and other falsehoods ; yea, he had the impudence, says Wodrow, to write an account of this to Court, even before Mr Wood's death. These reports, coming to the ears of this good man, added grief unto his former sorrow ; and he could have no rest till he vindicated himself from such a false calumny, by a solemn testimony, which he himself dictated, and subscribed upon the 2d of March, before two witnesses and a public notary ; which testimony, being burned by order of the High Commission, in April following, deserves a place here.

" I, James Wood, being very shortly, by appearance, to render up my spirit to the Lord, find myself obliged to leave a word behind me, for my vindication before the world. It hath been said of me, that I have, in word at least, departed from my wonted zeal for the Presbyterian government, expressing myself concerning it, as if it were a matter not to be accounted of, and that no man should trouble himself therefor in matter of practice. Surely any Christian that knows me in this kirk, will judge that this is a wrong done to me. It is true that I, being under sickness, have said sometimes, in conference about my soul's state, that I was taken up about greater business than anything of that kind ; and what wonder I said so, being under such wrestling anent my interest in Jesus Christ, which is a matter of far greater concernment than any external ordinance ? But for my estimation of Presbyterian government, the Lord knoweth, that since the day He convinced my heart (which was by a strong hand), that it is the ordinance of God, appointed by Jesus Christ, for governing and ordering His visible church, I never had the least change of thought concerning the necessity of it, nor of the necessity of the use of it. And I declare, before God and the world, that I still account so of it; and that, however there may be some more precious ordinances, this is so precious, that a true Christian is obliged to lay down his life for the profession thereof, if the Lord shall see meet to put him to the trial; and for myself, if I were to live, I would account it my glory to seal this word of my testimony with my blood. Of this declaration I take God, angels and men, to be my witnesses; and have subscribed these presents at St Andrews, on the 2d of March, 1664, about seven hours in the afternoon, before these witnesses," etc.

William Tullidaff,

John Carstairs,   JAMES WOOD.

John Pitcairn, *writer.*

After this he uttered many heavenly expressions to several persons who came to see him, all setting forth the sweet experience of his soul, until, upon the 5th of March, he made a happy and glorious exit, exchanging this present life for a crown of righteousness.

James Wood was among the brightest lights of that period. He had been colleague to Sharp, and after the Restoration he lamented much that he had been deceived by that unhappy man. He refuted the Independents, and asserted the Presbyterian government, as is evident from that work of his, written in opposition to Nicholas Lockier's "Little Stone hewed out of the Mountain," and his other books that are in print. It is also said, that before his death he lamented his taking part with the public Resolutioners very much.

"I have been informed," says Wodrow, "that he left some very valuable manuscripts behind him, particularly a complete refutation of the Arminian scheme of doctrine, ready for the press, which doubtless, if published, would be of no small use to this age, when Arminianism has so far got the ascendant."

PORTRAIT OF GENERAL DAVID LESLIE, LORD NEWARK.

William Guthrie.

WILLIAM GUTHRIE was born in the year 1620. He was the eldest son of the laird of Pitfrothy, in the shire of Angus; and by the mother's side was descended from the ancient house of Easter Ogle, of which she was a daughter. God blessed his parents with a numerous offspring, for he had three sisters german, and four brothers, who all, except one, dedicated themselves to the service of the gospel of Christ. Robert was licensed to preach, but never was ordained to the charge of any parish, his tender constitution and numerous infirmities rendering him unfit, and soon bringing him to the end of his days. Alexander was a minister in the presbytery of Brechin, about the year 1645, where he continued a pious and useful labourer in the work of the Gospel, till the introduction of Prelacy; which unhappy change affected him in the tenderest manner, and was thought to have shortened his days, for he died in 1661. John, the youngest, was minister at Tarbolton, in Ayrshire, in which place he continued till the Restoration, 1662. When, by the infamous Act of Glasgow, above a third part of the ministers in Scotland (amounting to nearly 400), were thrust from their charges, he had his share of the hardships that many faithful

BRECHIN CATHEDRAL.

ministers of Jesus Christ at that time were brought under. The next year, being 1663, the Council, at the instigation of the Archbishop of Glasgow, summoned him and other nine to appear before them on the 23d of July, under pain of rebellion; but he and other six did not appear. In the year 1666, he joined with that party, who, on the 26th of November, renewed the Covenants at Lanark. After a sermon preached by him, he tendered the Covenants, which were read, to every article of which, with their hands lifted up to Heaven, they engaged, with great solemnity and devotion. After their defeat at Pentland, he, no doubt, had his share of the violence and cruelty that then reigned, till, in the year 1668, he was removed to a better world.

William, who was the eldest of the sons, soon gave proofs of his capacity and genius, by very considerable progress made in the Latin and Greek languages. He was sent to the University of St Andrews, where he studied philosophy under the memorable James Guthrie, his cousin, afterward minister at Stirling, "and whom," says Mr Trail, "I saw die in and for the Lord, at Edinburgh, June 1, 1661." As the master and scholar were near relations, William was his peculiar care, and lodged, when at the college, in the same chamber with him, and therefore had the principles of learning infused into him with more accuracy than his class-fellows.

Having taken the degree of Master of Arts, he applied himself for some years to the study of divinity, under the direction of Samuel Rutherford. Mr Trail says, " Then and there it pleased the Lord, who separated him from his mother's womb, to call him by his grace, by the ministry of excellent Samuel Rutherford, and this young gentleman became one of the first fruits of his ministry at St Andrews. His conversion was begun with great terror of God in his soul, and completed with that joy and peace in believing that accompanied him through his life. After this blessed change wrought upon him, he resolved to obey the call of God to serve Him in the ministry of His Gospel, which was given him by the Lord's calling him effectually to grace and glory. He did for this end so dispose of his outward estate, to which he was born heir, as not to be entangled with the affairs of this life." He gave his estate to the only brother of the five who was not engaged in the sacred office, that thereby he might be perfectly disentangled from the affairs of this life, and entirely employed in those of the eternal world.

Soon after he was licensed to preach he left St Andrews, with high esteem and approbation from the professors of that university, which they gave proof of by their ample recommendations. After this he became tutor to Lord Mauchline, eldest son to the Earl of Loudon, in which situation he continued for some time, till he entered upon a parochial charge.

The parish of Kilmarnock, in the shire of Ayr, being large, and many of the people belonging to the said parish being no less than six or seven miles distant from their own kirk, the heritors and others procured a disjunction, and called the new parish Fenwick or New Kilmarnock.

William Guthrie was employed to preach at Galston on a preparation day, before the celebration of the Lord's Supper; and several members of the new erected parish being present on that occasion, and being greatly edified by his sermons, conceived such a value for him, that they immediately resolved to make choice of him for their minister, and in consequence thereof, gave him a very harmonious call, which he complied with. It is said that he, along with the people, made choice of the piece of ground for building the church upon, and preached within the walls of the house before it was completed.

He was ordained unto the sacred office, November 7, 1644, and had many difficulties to contend with, many circumstances of his ministry being extremely discouraging; but yet, through the divine blessing, the Gospel preached by him had surprising success, and became in an eminent manner the wisdom and power of God to the salvation of many perishing souls.

After William Guthrie came to Fenwick, many of the people were so rude and barbarous, that they never attended upon divine worship, and knew not so much as the face of their pastor. To such, everything that respected religion was disagreeable; many refused to be visited or catechised by him; they would not even admit him into their houses. To such he sometimes went in the evening disguised in the character of a traveller, and sought lodging, which he could not even obtain without much entreaty, but, having obtained it, he would engage in some general amusing conversation at first, and then ask them how they liked their minister. When they told him that they did not go to church, he engaged them to go and take a trial; others he hired with money to go. When the time of family worship came, he desired to know if they made any, and if not, what reasons they had for it.

There was one person, in particular, whom he would have to perform family worship, but he told him that he could not pray. Mr Guthrie asked what was the reason? He told him that he never was used to pray. Mr Guthrie would not take this for answer, but would have the man to make a trial in that duty before him, to which the man replied, " O Lord, Thou knowest that this man would have me to pray, but Thou knowest that I cannot pray." After this Mr Guthrie bade him stop, and said he had done enough, and prayed himself to their great surprise. When prayer was ended the wife said to her husband that surely this was a minister; for they did not know him. After this he engaged them to come to the kirk on Sabbath, and see what they thought of their minister. When they came there they discovered, to their consternation, that it had been their minister himself who had allured them thither. And this condescending manner of gaining them procured such a constant attendance on public ordinances, as was at length accompanied by the fruits of righteousness, which are, through Jesus Christ, unto the praise of God.

There was also another person in the parish, who had a custom of going a-fowling on the Sabbath-day, and neglecting the church; in which practice he had continued for a considerable time. Mr

Guthrie asked him, what reason he had for so doing? He told him, that the Sabbath-day was the most fortunate day in the week for that sport. Guthrie asked, what he could make by that day's fowling? He replied, that he would make half-a-crown of money. Guthrie told him, if he would go to church on Sabbath, he would give him as much; and by that means got his promise. After sermon was over, Guthrie asked, if he would come back the next Sabbath-day, and he would give him the same? which he did, and from that time afterwards never failed to keep the church, and also freed Mr Guthrie of his promise. He afterwards became a member of his session.

He would frequently use innocent recreations, such as fishing, fowling, and playing on the ice, which contributed much to preserve a vigorous state of health; and while in frequent conversation with the neighbouring gentry, as these occasions gave him opportunity, he would bear in upon them reproofs and instructions, with an inoffensive familiarity. Mr Dunlop has observed of him "that he was animated by a flaming zeal for the glory of his blessed Master, and a tender compassion for the souls of men, and as it was the principal thing which made him desire life and health, that he might employ them in propagating the kingdom of God, and in turning transgressors from their ways, so the very hours of recreation were dedicated to this purpose; which was so endeared to him, that he knew how to make his diversions subservient to the nobler ends of his ministry. He made them the occasion of familiarising his people to him, and introducing himself to their affections; and, in the disguise of a sportsman, he gained some to a religious life, whom he could have little influence upon in a minister's gown; of which there happened several memorable examples."

His person was stately and well set; his features comely and handsome; he had a strong and clear voice, joined to a good ear, which gave him a great pleasure in music, and he failed not to employ that talent for the noblest use, the praising of his Maker and Saviour; in which part of divine worship his soul and body acted with united and unwearied vigour.

He was happily married in August 1645, to Agnes Campbell, daughter of David Campbell of Sheldon, in the shire of Ayr, a remote branch of the family of Loudon. His family affairs were both easy and comfortable. His wife was a gentlewoman endued with all the qualities that could render her a blessing to her husband, joined to handsome and comely features, good sense, and good breeding, sweetened by a modest cheerfulness of temper ; and, what was most comfortable to Mr Guthrie, she was sincerely pious, so that they lived a little more than twenty years in the most complete friendship, and with a constant mutual satisfaction, founded on the noblest principles ; one faith, one hope, one baptism, and a sovereign love to Jesus Christ, which zealously inspired them both. By her he had six children, two of whom only outlived himself, both of them daughters, who endeavoured to follow the example of their excellent parents. One of them was married to Miller of Glenlee, a gentleman in the shire of Ayr ; and the other to Mr Peter Warner, in 1681, who, after the Revolution, was settled at Irvine. The latter had two children, William, of Ardrie, in Ayrshire, and Margaret Warner, married to Mr Wodrow, minister of Eastwood, who wrote the History of the Sufferings of the Church of Scotland, betwixt the years 1660 and 1688 inclusive.

When William Guthrie was but young and newly married, he was appointed by the General Assembly to attend the army. When he was preparing for his departure, a violent fit of the gravel, to which he was often subject, reduced him to the greatest extremity of pain and danger. This made his religious spouse understand and improve the Divine chastisement. She then saw how easily God could put an end to his life, which she was too apprehensive about ; and brought herself to a resolution, never to oppose her inclination to his entering upon any employment, whereby he might honour his Master, though ever so much hazard should attend it.

While he was with the army, upon the defeat of a party he was then with, he was preserved in a very extraordinary manner, which made him ever after retain a greater sense of the Divine goodness, and, after his return to his parish, animated him to a more vigorous diligence in the work of the ministry, and propagating the kingdom of the Son of God, both among his people and all round about him ; his public preaching, especially at the administration of the Lord's Supper, and his private conversation, conspiring together for these noble purposes.

After this, William Guthrie had occasion again to be with the army, when the English sectaries prevailed, under Oliver Cromwell. After the defeat at Dunbar, Sept. 3, 1650, when the army was at Stirling, Samuel Rutherford wrote a letter to him, wherein, by way of caution, near the end, he says, " But let me obtest all the serious seekers of His face, His secret sealed ones, by the strongest consolations of the Spirit, by the gentleness of Jesus Christ, that Plant of Renown, by your last accounts, and appearing before God, when the white throne shall be set up, be not deceived with their fair words. Though my spirit be astonished at the cunning distinctions which are found out in the matters of the Covenant, that help may be had against these men, yet my heart trembleth to entertain the least thought of joining with these deceivers." Accordingly Guthrie joined the Protesters, and was chosen moderator at that synod at Edinburgh, after the public Resolutioners went out and left them.

The author of his memoirs saith, " His pleasant and facetious conversation procured him an universal respect from the English officers, and made them fond of his company ; while, at the same time, his courage and constancy did not fail him in the cause of his great Master, and was often useful to curb the extravagances of the sectaries, and maintain order and regularity." One instance of this happened at the sacrament of the Lord's Supper, at Glasgow, celebrated by Mr Andrew Gray. Several of the English officers had formed a design to put in execution the disorderly principle of a promiscuous admission to the Lord's table, by coming to it themselves, without acquainting the minister, or being in a due manner found worthy of that privilege. It being William Guthrie's turn to serve at that table, he spoke to them when they were leaving their pews in order to make the attempt, with such gravity, resolution, and zeal, that they were quite confounded, and sat down without making any further disturbance.

About this time that sect, called Quakers, endeavoured to sow their tares in Fenwick parish, when Mr Guthrie was some weeks absent about his own private affairs in Angus. He returned home before this infection had sunk deep, recovered some who were in hazard of being tainted by its fatal influence, and confounded the rest, that they despaired of any further attack upon his flock. This wild sect had made many proselytes to their demented delusions in Kilbride, Glasgow, and other neighbouring parishes; yea, they prospered so well in Glassford parish, that there is yet a churchyard in that place, where they buried their dead, with their heads to the east, contrary to the practice of all other Christians.

After this he had several calls to other parishes of more importance than Fenwick, such as Renfrew, Linlithgow, Stirling, Glasgow, and Edinburgh. But the air and recreation of a country life were useful to him in maintaining a healthful constitution; and, above all, the love his flock had to him caused him to put on an invincible obstinacy against all designs of separation from them; a relation which, when it is animated with this principle of spiritual life, and founded on so noble a bottom, enters most deeply into the soul. Indeed, a minister can scarcely miss to have peculiar tenderness and warmth of divine affections to those whose father he is after the Spirit, whom he hath been honoured of God in bringing to the kingdom of His Son, and begetting through the Gospel; whose heavenly birth is now the highest pleasure and brightest triumph of his life, and will be one day his crown of glory and rejoicing. Doubtless, when Mr Guthrie preferred Fenwick, a poor obscure parish, to the most considerable charges in the nation, it was also a proof of his mortification to the world, and that he was moved by views superior to temporal interests.

About the year 1656 or 1657, an unknown person somehow got a copy of a few imperfect notes of some sermons that Guthrie had preached from the 55th chapter of Isaiah, with relation to personal covenanting; and, without the least intimation made to him, printed them in a little pamphlet of sixty-one pages, under the title, "A Clear, Attractive, Warming Beam of Light, from Christ the Sun of Light, leading unto Himself." This book was indeed anonymous; but William Guthrie was reputed the author by the whole country, and was therefore obliged to take notice of it. He was equally displeased at the vanity of the title, and the defect of the work itself, which consisted of some broken notes of his sermons, confusedly huddled together by an injudicious hand. He saw that the only method to remedy this, was to review his own sermons; from which he soon composed that admirable treatise, "The Christian's Great Interest;" the only genuine work of Mr Guthrie, and one which hath been blessed by God with wonderful success in our own country; being published very seasonably, a little before the reintroduction of Prelacy into Scotland at the Restoration.

The author of his memoirs quotes the sentiments of Dr John Owen regarding it, who said, "You have truly men of great spirit in Scotland: there is, for a gentleman, Mr Baillie of Jerviswoode, a person of the greatest abilities I almost ever met with; and for a divine, said he (taking out of his pocket a little gilt copy of Mr Guthrie's treatise), *that* author I take to have been one of the greatest divines that ever wrote. It is my *vade mecum;* I carry it and the Sedan New Testament still about with me. I have written several folios, but there is more divinity in it than in them all." It was translated into Low Dutch by the reverend and pious Mr Koelman, and was highly esteemed in Holland; so that Mrs Guthrie and one of her daughters met there with uncommon civility and kindness, when their relation to its author was known. It was also translated into French and High Dutch; and we are informed that it was also translated into one of the Eastern languages, at the charge of that noble patron of religion, learning, and charity, the Hon. Robert Boyle.

At the Synod of Glasgow, held April 1661, after long reasoning about proper measures for the security of religion, the matter was referred to a committee; and William Guthrie prescribed the draft of an address to the Parliament, wherein a faithful testimony was given to the purity of our Reformation, in worship, doctrine, discipline, and government, in terms equally remarkable for their prudence and courage. All the committee approved of it, and it was transmitted to the Synod. But some, on the Resolution side, judging it not convenient, gave an opportunity to those who designed to comply with Prelacy to procure a delay, and, at that time, got it crushed. Yet it affords a proof of Guthrie's zealous honesty and firmness.

About this time, being the last time that he was with his cousin, James Guthrie, he happened to be very melancholy, which made Mr James say, "A penny for your thoughts, cousin!" Mr William answered, "There is a poor man at the door, give him the penny:" which being done, he proceeded, and said, "I'll tell you, cousin, what I am not only thinking upon, but am sure of, if I be not under a delusion. The malignants will be your death, and this gravel will be mine; but you will have the advantage of me, for you will die honourably before many witnesses, with a rope about your neck; and I will die whining upon a pickle straw, and will endure more pain before I rise from your table, than all the pain you will have in your death."

He took a resolution to wait on his worthy friend Mr James, at his execution on Saturday, June 1661, notwithstanding the apparent hazard at that time in so doing; but his session prevailed on him (although with much difficulty) by their earnest entreaties, to lay aside his design.

Through the interposition of the Earl of Eglinton and the Chancellor Glencairn (whom he had obliged before the Restoration, when he was imprisoned for his loyalty, and who now contributed what he could for his preservation), he had nearly four years further respite with his people at Fenwick, during which time his church, although a large country one, was overcrowded every Sabbath-day. Many came from distant parishes, such as Glasgow, Paisley, Hamilton, Lanark, Kilbride, Glassford, Strathaven, Newmilns, Eaglesham, and many other places, who hungered for the pure Gospel preached, and got a meal by the word of his ministry. It was their usual practice to come to Fenwick on Saturday, and after spending the greatest part of the night in prayer to God, and conversation about the great concerns of their souls, to attend the public worship on the Sabbath, dedicating the remainder of that holy day to religious exercises, and then to go home on Monday the length of ten, twelve, or twenty miles, without grudging in the least the long way, or the want of sleep and other refreshment; neither did they find themselves the less prepared for any other business through the week. These years, under the Divine influences of the Holy Spirit accompanying the ministry and ordinances dispensed by Mr Guthrie, were the most remarkable in all his life, and will still be had in remembrance. A blessing accompanied ordinances to people who came with such a disposition of soul; great numbers were converted unto the truth, and many built up in their most holy faith. In a word, he was honoured to be a means in the Lord's hand, of turning many to a religious life, who, after his being taken from them, could never, without exultation of soul, and emotion of revived affection, think upon their spiritual father, and the power of that victorious grace which, in those days, triumphed so gloriously. For many years afterwards they were considered, above many other parishes in the kingdom, as a civilised and religious people; he having, with a becoming boldness, fortified them in a zealous adherence to the purity of our Reformation, warned them of the defection that was then made by the introduction of Prelacy, and instructed them in the duty of such a difficult time; so that they never made any compliance with Prelatical schemes afterwards.

His extraordinary reputation, and the usefulness of his ministry, were admired and followed by all the country around; which provoked the jealous and angry Prelates against him, and was one of the causes of his being at last attacked by them. The Earl of Glencairn made a visit to the Archbishop of Glasgow, at his own house, and at parting asked as a favour, that William Guthrie might be overlooked, as knowing him to be an excellent man. The Archbishop not only refused, but with a disdainful, haughty air, told him, " That shall not be done—it cannot be—he is a ringleader and keeper up of schism in my diocese." Rowallan, and some other Presbyterian gentlemen, who were waiting on him, observing the Chancellor discomposed when the Archbishop left him, presumed to ask him what the matter was; to which the Earl answered, "We have set up these men, and they will tread us under their feet." In consequence of this resolution of Archbishop Burnet, Mr Guthrie was, by a commission from him, suspended; and the Archbishop dealt with several of his creatures, the curates, to intimate the sentence against him, but many refused; for, says Wodrow, "There was an awe upon their spirits, which scared them from meddling with this great man." At last he prevailed with the curate of Calder, and promised him five pounds sterling of reward. Guthrie being warned of this design of the Archbishop against him, advised his friends to make no resistance to his expulsion from the church and manse, since his enemy only wanted this as a handle to prosecute him criminally for his former zeal and faithfulness.

Accordingly, on Wednesday, July 20, he with his congregation kept the day with fasting and prayer. He preached to them from Hos. xiii. 9: "O Israel! thou hast destroyed thyself," and with great plainness and affection laid before them their own sins, and the sins of the land and age they lived in; and indeed the place was a *Bochim.* At the close of this day's work, he gave them intimation of sermon on the next Lord's day, very early; and accordingly his people and many others met him at the church of Fenwick, betwixt four and five in the morning, when he preached to them from the close of his last text: "But in Me is thine help." As usual on ordinary Sabbaths, he also now had two sermons, and a short interval betwixt them, and dismissed the people before nine in the morning. Upon this melancholy occasion, he directed them unto the great Fountain of help, when the Gospel and ministers were taken from them; and took his leave of them, commending them to God, who was able to build them up, and help them in time of need.

Upon the day appointed (the Sabbath-day), the curate came to Fenwick with a party of twelve soldiers, and by commission from the Archbishop discharged William Guthrie from preaching any more in Fenwick, declared the church vacant, and suspended him from the exercise of his ministry.

The curate, leaving the party without, came into the manse, and declared that the Archbishop and Committee, after much lenity showed to him for a long time, were constrained to pass the sentence of sus-

pension against him, for not keeping of presbyteries and synods with
the rest of his brethren, and for his unpeaceableness in the Church;
of which sentence he was appointed to make public intimation unto
him; and for that purpose he read his commission under the hand
of the Archbishop of Glasgow.

Mr Guthrie answered, "I judge it not convenient to say much in
answer to what you have spoken; only, whereas you allege there hath
been much lenity used towards me, be it known to you, that I take
the Lord for party in that, and thank Him first; yea, I look upon it
as a door which God opened to me for the preaching of the Gospel,
which neither you nor any man else was able to shut, till it was given
you of God. And as to that sentence passed against me, I declare
before these gentlemen (meaning the officers of the party), that I lay
no weight upon it, as it comes from you, or those that sent you,
though I do respect the civil authority, who, by their law, laid the
ground for this sentence passed against me. I declare I would not
surcease from the exercise of my ministry for all that sentence. And
as to the crimes I am charged with; I did keep presbyteries and
synods with the rest of my brethren; but I do not judge those who
do now sit in these to be my brethren, who have made defection from
the truth and cause of God; nor do I judge those to be free and
lawful courts of Christ that are now sitting. And as to my peaceable-
ness; I know that I am bidden follow peace with all men, but I know
also I am bidden follow it with holiness; and since I could not obtain
peace without prejudice to holiness, I thought myself obliged to let it
go. And as for your commission, sir, to intimate this sentence; I
here declare, I think myself called by the Lord to the work of the
ministry, and did forsake the nearest relation in the world, and gave
up myself to the service of the Gospel in this place, having received
an unanimous call from this parish, and was licensed and ordained
by the presbytery; and I bless the Lord he hath given me some
success and seals of my ministry, upon the souls and consciences of
not a few who are gone to heaven, and of some who are yet in the
way to it. And now, sir, if you will take it upon you to interrupt
my work among this people, I shall wish the Lord may forgive you
the guilt of it; and I cannot but leave all the bad consequences that
may fall out upon it betwixt God and your own consciences. And
here I do further declare, before these gentlemen, that I am suspended from my ministry for adhering to the Covenants and word of
God, from which you and others have apostatised."

Here the curate interrupting him, said, "That the Lord had a work before that Covenant had a being; and that he judged them apostates that adhered to that Covenant; and he wished that the Lord would not only forgive him (meaning Mr Guthrie), but if it were lawful to pray for the dead (at which expression the soldiers laughed), that the Lord might forgive the sins of this church these hundred years bypast." "It is true," said Guthrie, "the Lord had a work before that Covenant had a being; but it is as true, that it hath been more glorious since that Covenant; and it is a small thing for us to be judged of you, in adhering to this Covenant, who have so deeply corrupted your ways, and seem to reflect on the whole work of Reformation from Popery these hundred years bygone, by intimating that the Church had need of pardon for the same. As for you, gentlemen (added he to the soldiers), I wish the Lord may pardon your countenancing this man in his business." One of them scoffingly replied, "I wish we never do a greater fault." "Well," said Mr Guthrie, "a little sin may damn a man's soul."

After all this and more had passed, Mr Guthrie called for a glass of ale, and, craving a blessing himself, drank to the commander of the soldiers. After being civilly entertained, they left the house, and at parting with the curate Mr Guthrie signified so much to him, that he apprehended some evident mark of the Lord's displeasure was abiding him for what he was doing, and seriously warned him to prepare for some stroke coming upon him, and that very soon.

When the curate left the manse, he went to the church with the soldiers (now his hearers), preached to them not a quarter of an hour, and intimated to them from the pulpit the bishop's sentence against Mr Guthrie. Nobody came to hear him but his party, and a few children, who created some disturbance, till they were chased away by the soldiers. Indeed, the people were ready to have sacrificed their all, and resisted even unto blood, in Mr Guthrie's defence and the Gospel's, had they been permitted by him.

"As for the curate," says Mr Wodrow, "I am well assured he never preached any more after he left Fenwick. He reached Glasgow, but it is not certain if he reached Calder, though but four miles from Glasgow. In a few days he died in great torment, of an iliac passion, and his wife and children died all in a year or thereby, and none belonging to him were left. His reward of five pounds was dear bought; it was the price of blood, the blood of souls. Neither he nor his had any satisfaction in it. Such a dangerous thing it is to meddle with Christ's servants."

William Guthrie continued at Fenwick, until the year 1665. The brother to whom his paternal estate was made over dying in summer, his presence at home was necessary for ordering of his private affairs, which made him and his wife make a journey to Angus about the same time. He had not been long in that country until he was seized with a complication of distempers, the gravel, with which he had been formerly troubled, the gout, a violent heart-burning, and an ulcer in his kidneys; all which attacked him with great fury. Being thus tormented with violent pain, his friends were sometimes obliged to hold down his head, and lift up his feet, and yet he would say that the Lord had been kind to him, for all the ills he had done ; adding, "though I should die mad, yet I know I shall die in the Lord. Blessed are the dead that die in the Lord at all times, but more especially when a flood of errors, snares, and judgments, are beginning or coming on a nation, church, or people."

In the midst of all his heavy affliction, he still adored the measures of Divine Providence, though at the same time he longed for his dissolution, and expressed the satisfaction and joy with which he would make the grave his dwelling-place, when God should think fit to give him rest there. His compassionate Master did at last indulge the pious breathing of his soul; for, after eight or ten days illness, he was gathered to his fathers, in the house of his brother-in-law, Mr Lewis Skinner of Brechin, upon Wednesday forenoon, October 10, 1665, in the forty-fifth year of his age, and was buried in the church of Brechin, under Pitfrothy's desk.

During his sickness, he was visited by the Bishop of Brechin, and several Episcopal ministers and relations, who all had a high value for him ; notwithstanding that he expressed his sorrow with great freedom for their compliance with the corrupted establishment in ecclesiastical affairs. He died in the full assurance of faith as to his own interest in God's Covenant, and under the pleasing hope, that God would return in glory to the Church of Scotland.

John Livingstone, in his Memorable Characteristics, says : " Mr William Guthrie, minister at Fenwick, was a man of a most ready wit, fruitful invention, and apposite comparisons, qualified both to awaken and pacify conscience ; straight and zealous for the cause of Christ, and a great light in the west of Scotland." Elsewhere he says : " Mr Guthrie, in his doctrine, was as full and free as any man in Scotland had ever been ; which, together with the excellency of his preaching gift, did so recommend him to the affection of his people, that they turned the corn-field of his glebe into a little town, every one building a house for his family on it that they might live under the drop of his ministry."

Mr Crawford, in a MS. never published, says : " Mr Guthrie was a burning and a shining light, kept in after many others, by the favour of the old Earl of Eglinton, the Chancellor's father-in-law. He converted and confirmed many thousands of souls, and was esteemed the greatest preacher in Scotland."

And, indeed, he was accounted as singular a person for confirming those that were under soul exercise, as almost any in his age, or any age we have heard of. Many have made reflections on him, because he left off his ministry, on account of the Archbishop's suspension ; but his reasons may be taken from what hath been already related. It is true, indeed, the authority of the Stuarts was too much the idol of jealousy to many of our worthy Scots Reformers. For we may well think (as a late author, though no enemy unto these civil powers, says) that it was a wonder the nation did not rise up as one man, to cut off those who had razed the whole of the Presbyterian constitution. But the Lord, for holy and wise ends, saw meet to appoint it otherwise, and to cut off those in power by another arm, after they had all been brought to the furnace together; although they might well have all the while seen, as Mr Guthrie has observed, " That the civil power laid the foundation for the other."

As far as can be learned, William Guthrie never preached in Fenwick again, after the intimation of the Archbishop's sentence to him ; but it is well known, that he, with many of his people in Fenwick, upon a time went to Stewarton, to hear a young Presbyterian minister preach. When coming home, they said to him, that they were not pleased with that man's preaching, he being of a slow delivery. He said they were mistaken in the man ; he had a great sermon ; and if they pleased, at a convenient place, he should let them hear a good part thereof. And sitting all down on the ground, in a good summer night, about the sunsetting, he rehearsed the sermon, when they thought it a wonderfully great one, because of his good delivery, and their amazing love to him. After which they arose and set forward.

All allow that William Guthrie was a man of strong natural parts, notwithstanding his being a hard student at first. His voice was of the best sort, loud, and yet managed with a charming cadence and elevation ; his oratory was singular, and by it he was wholly master of the passions of his hearers. He was an eminent chirurgeon at the jointing of a broken soul, and at the stating of a doubtful conscience ; so that persons afflicted in spirit came far and near, and received much satisfaction and comfort by him. Those who were very rude, when he came first to the parish, at his departure were very sorrowful, and, at the curate's intimation of the Archbishop's commission, would have made resistance, if he would have permitted them, not fearing the hazards or hardships they might have endured on that account afterwards.

Besides his valuable treatise already mentioned, there are also a few very faithful sermons, bearing his name, said to be preached at Fenwick, from Matt. xiv. 24, and Hos. xiii. 9, etc. But because they are somewhat rude in expression, differing from the style of his treatise, some have thought them spurious, or at least not as they were at first delivered by him. And as for that treatise on Ruling Elders, which is now affixed to the last edition of his Works, it was written by his cousin, James Guthrie of Stirling. There are also some other discourses of his yet in manuscript, out of which I had occasion to transcribe seventeen sermons, published in the year 1779. There are a great variety of sermons, and notes of sermons, bearing his name, yet in manuscript, some of which seem to be written with his own hand.

Robert Blair.

OBERT BLAIR was born at Irvine in the year 1593. His father was John Blair of Windyedge, a younger brother of the ancient and honourable family of Blair of that ilk ; his mother was Beatrix Muir, of the ancient family of Rowallan. His father died when he was young, leaving his mother with six children, of whom Robert was the youngest. She continued nearly fifty years a widow, and lived till she was an hundred years old.

Robert entered the College of Glasgow, about the year 1608, where he studied hard, and made great progress ; but lest he should have been puffed up with his proficiency, as he himself observes, the Lord was pleased to visit him with a tertian fever, for full four months, to the great detriment of his studies.

Nothing remarkable occurred till the 20th year of his age, when he gave himself sometimes to the exercise of archery, and the like recreations ; but lest his studies should have been hindered, he resolved to be busy at them every other night, and, for that purpose, could find no place so proper as a room whereunto none were inclined to go, by reason of an apparition that was said to frequent it. Yea, it is said, that he himself had here seen the devil, in the likeness of one of his fellow-students, whom he took to be really his companion ; but chasing him to the corner of the room, and offering to pull him out, he found nothing ; at which, however, he was not at all troubled, studying the one part of the night without fear, and sleeping the other very sweetly, believing in Him who was still his great Preserver and Protector for ever.

Having now finished his course of philosophy, under the discipline of his own brother, Mr William Blair, who was afterwards minister at Dumbarton, he engaged for some time to be an assistant to an aged schoolmaster at Glasgow, who had above 300 scholars under his instruction, the half of whom were committed to the charge of Mr Blair. At this time he was called, by the ministry of the famous Mr Boyd of Trochrig, then principal of the College of Glasgow, into whose hand, as he himself observes in his Memoirs, the Lord did put the key of his heart so, that whenever he heard him in public or private, he profited much, Mr Boyd being, as it were, sent to him from God, to speak the words of eternal life.

Two years after, he was admitted in the room of his brother, Mr William, to be regent in the College of Glasgow, though not without the opposition of Archbishop Law, who had promised that place to another. But neither the principal nor regents giving place to the Archbishop's motion, Mr Blair was admitted. After his admission, his elder colleagues, perceiving what great skill and insight he had in Humanity, urged him to read the classical authors ; whereupon he began and read Plautus. But the Lord, being displeased with that design, diverted him from it, by his meeting with Augustine's Confession, wherein he inveighs sharply against the education of youth in heathen writings. Upon this he betook himself to the

THE COLLEGE KIRK, GLASGOW

reading of the Holy Scriptures, and the ancient fathers, especially Augustine, who had another relish ; and though he perceived that our divines were more sound than several of the ancients, yet, in his spare hours, he was wont to peruse the ancient authors, wherein he made considerable progress.

In summer 1616, he entered on trials for the ministry ; and it was laid upon him to preach in the College Kirk the first Sabbath after his license. Some years after, he was told by some of his hearers (who were better acquainted with religion than he was then) that in his sermon the Lord did speak to their hearts ; which not only surprised him, but also stirred him to follow after the Lord.

Upon an evening the same year, having been engaged with some irreligious company, when he returned to his chamber to his wonted devotion, he was threatened to be deserted of God. He had a restless night, and on the morrow resolved on a day of fasting, humiliation, and prayer. Towards the end of that day, he found access to God with sweet peace, through Jesus Christ, and turned to beware of such company ; but running into another extreme of rudeness and incivility to profane persons, he found it was very hard for shortsighted sinners to hold the right and the straight way.

While he was regent in the college, upon a report that some sinful oath was to be imposed upon the masters, he inquired at Mr Gavin Forsyth, one of his fellow-regents, what he would do in this? He answered, "By my faith, I must live!" Blair said, "Sir, I will not *swear* by my faith, as you do, but truly I intend to *live* by my faith; you may choose your own way, but I will adventure on the Lord." And so this man, to whom the matter of an oath was a small thing, did continue, after he was gone; but it is to be noticed, that he was many years in such poverty, as forced him to supplicate the General Assembly for some relief. Robert Blair (who was then moderator) upon his appearing in such a desperate case, could not shun observing that former passage of his, and upon meeting him in private, with great tenderness put him in mind, that he had been truly carried through by his faith, at which he had formerly scoffed.

Some time after Robert Blair was a regent in the college, he was under deep exercises of soul, wherein he attained unto much comfort. Among other things, that great saying, "the just shall live by faith," sounded loudly in his ears, which put him on a new search of the Scriptures, in which he went on till Mr Culverwell's Treatise on Faith came out; which being of the same nature with what is since published by the Westminster Assembly, he was thereby much satisfied and comforted. "By this study of the nature of faith," says he, "and especially of the text before mentioned, I learned—

"*First*, That nominal Christians, or common professors, were much deluded in their way of believing; and that not only Papists, who place faith in an implicit assent to the truth which they know not, and that it's better defined by ignorance than by knowledge, (a way of believing very suitable to Antichrist's slaves, who are led by the noses they know not which way), 'were hugely herein mistaken,' but also secure Protestants, abusing the description of old given of faith, that it is an assurance or assured knowledge, of the love of God in Christ. This assurance, indeed, no doubt is attainable, and many believers do attain and comfortably enjoy it, as our divines from the Holy Scriptures prove unanswerably against the Popish doctors, who maintain the necessity of perpetual doubting, and miscall that Christian comfortable assurance of the Protestants' presumption. But notwithstanding it is true of a high degree of faith, yet it agrees not to all the degrees of saving faith; so that hereby many gracious sound believers, who have received Jesus Christ, and rested on Him as He is offered to them in the Word, have been much puzzled, as if they were not believers at all. But, upon the other

hand, many secure, unhumbled misbelievers, who have not believed
in the Lord's holiness and hating of sin, who have not believed how
self-destroyed they are, out of self-love, without the warrant of the
Word, conceit themselves to be beloved of God; and that the
formerly mentioned description of faith agrees well to them.

"*Secondly*, I perceived that many who make right use of faith
in order to their justification, made not directly use thereof in order
to sanctification. But then I perceived that the living of the just by
faith reached further than I formerly conceived, and that the heart is
purified by faith. If any think, What! knew I not till then that
precious faith, being a grace, was not only a part of our holiness, but
did set forward other parts of holiness? I answer, I did indeed
know, and so accordingly made use of faith as a motive to stir up
to holiness, according to the apostle's exhortation: 'Having, therefore, these promises, dearly beloved, let us cleanse ourselves from
all filthiness of the flesh and spirit, perfecting holiness in the fear
of the Lord' (2 Cor. vii. 1). But I had not, before that, learned
to make use of faith as a mean and instrument to draw holiness out
of Christ, the well of salvation, though it may be I had both heard
that and spoken that by way of a transient notion; but then, I
learned to purpose that they who receive forgiveness of sins are sanc-
tified through faith in Christ, as our glorious Saviour taught Paul
(Acts xxvi. 18). Then I marvelled not that my progress met with
an obstruction for not making use of faith, as hath been said for sanctification. Then I perceived, that in making use of Christ for sanctification, without direct employing of faith to extract the same out of
Him, I was like one seeking water out of a deep well without a long
cord to let down the bucket and draw it up again. . . . .
Then was I like one that came to the storehouse, but got my provisions reached to me as it were by a window. I had come to the
right house, but not to the right door. But by this 'new' discovery I
did find a patent door made for provision and furniture in and
from Christ my Lord. So, blessed Lord, thou trainedst on thy poor
servant, step by step, suffering difficulties to arise, that greater clearing from thyself might flow in. . . . .

" I hoped then to make better progress with less stumbling; but
not long after, encountering difficulties, I wondered what discovery
would next clear the way. Then I found that the Spirit of holiness,
whose immediate and appropriate work was to sanctify, had been
slighted, and so grieved. For though the Holy Spirit had been teach-

ing, and I had been speaking of Him and to Him frequently, and seeking the pouring out of the same, and urging others to seek the same, yet that discovery appeared to me a new practical lesson; and so I laboured more to crave, cherish, and not grieve or quench the Holy Spirit, praying to be led into all truth, according to the Scriptures, by that blessed guide; and that by that heavenly Comforter, I might be comforted in all troubles, and sealed up thereby in strong assurance of my interest in God.

"About that time the Lord set me a work to stir up the students who were under my discipline earnestly to study piety, and to be diligent in secret seeking of the Lord; and my gracious Lord was pleased herein to bless my endeavours."

Dr John Cameron being brought from France, and settled principal of the college in Mr Boyd's place, and being wholly set on in promoting the cause of Episcopacy, urged Robert Blair to conform to the Perth Articles, but he utterly refused. And it being a thing usual in these days for the regents to meet to dispute some thesis, for their better improvement, Blair had the advantage of his opponent, who was a French student, and maintained that election did proceed upon foreseen faith. But the Doctor having stated himself in opposition to Blair in a way which tended to Arminianism, and Blair being urged to a second dispute by the Doctor himself, he did drive him to the mire of Arminianism so as did redound much to the Doctor's ignominy afterwards; and although he and Mr Blair were afterwards reconciled, yet, being nettled by that dispute, he improved all occasions against him. For that purpose, when Blair was on a visit to some of his godly friends and acquaintances, he caused one Gardner to search his Prelections on Aristotle's Ethics and Politics, who, finding some things capable of being wrested, brought them to the Doctor, who presented them to the Archbishop of Glasgow. This coming to Mr Blair's ears, he was so far from betraying innocence, being assured the Lord would clear his integrity, that he prepared a written apology, and desired a public hearing before the ministers and magistrates of the city, which being granted, he managed the point so properly, that all present professed their entire satisfaction with him; yea, one of the ministers of the city, who had been influenced against him formerly, said, in the face of that meeting, "Would to God King James had been present and heard what answers that man hath given." Such a powerful antagonist, however, rendered his life so uneasy, that he resolved to leave the college and go abroad, which resolution no sooner took air than the Doctor and the Archbishop, knowing his abilities, wrote letters to cause him stay. But he, finding that little trust was to be put in their fair promises, and being weary of teaching philosophy, demitted his charge, took his leave of the Doctor, wishing him well, although he was the cause of his going away, and left the college, to the great grief of his fellow-regents and students, and the people of Glasgow.

Though he had several charges in Scotland presented to him, and an invitation to go to France, yet, the day after he left Glasgow, being invited to go and be minister of Bangor, in the county of Down, in Ireland, he felt bound in spirit to set his face towards a voyage to that country. Although he met with a contrary wind, he had such recourse to God, upon the very first sight of that land, that he was made to exult with joy; and on coming near Bangor, he had a strong impression borne in upon him, that the dean thereof was sick. This he found to be true when he came thither; and being invited to preach there, he did so for three Sabbaths, to the good liking of the people of that parish. The dean, though formerly but a very naughty man, yet told Mr Blair that he was to succeed him in that place; and exhorted him, in the name of Christ, not to leave that good way wherein he had begun to walk, professing much sorrow that he had done so himself. He condemned Episcopacy more strongly than ever Mr Blair durst; and drawing his head towards his bosom, with both his arms, he blessed him; which conduct being so unlike himself, as also his speaking in a strain so different from his usual, made a gentlewoman standing by say, "An angel is speaking out of the dean's bed to Mr Blair," thinking it could not be such a man. Within a few days he died, and Robert Blair was settled minister there.

His ordination was on this manner. He went to Bishop Knox, and told him his opinions; and said, that a bishop's sole ordination did contradict his principles. But the Bishop being informed beforehand of his great parts and piety, answered him both wittily and submissively, saying, "Whatever you account of Episcopacy, yet I know you account Presbytery to have a Divine warrant. Will you not receive ordination from Mr Cunningham and the adjacent brethren, and let me come in among them in no other relation than a Presbyter?" for on no lower terms could he be answerable to law. This Mr Blair could not refuse. He was accordingly ordained about the year 1623.

Being thus settled, his charge was very great, having above 1200 persons come to age, besides children, who stood greatly in need of instruction ; and in this case he preached twice a week, besides the Lord's-day ; on all which occasions he found little difficulty either as to matter or method. He became the chief instrument of that great work which appeared shortly thereafter, at Six-mile Water, and other parts in the counties of Down and Antrim ; and that not only by his own ministry, wherein he was both diligent and faithful, but also in the great pains he took to stir up others unto the like duty.

While he was at Bangor, there was a man named Constable in the parish, who went to Scotland with horses to sell, and at a fair sold them all to a person who pretended he had not money at present, but gave him a bond till Martinmas. The poor man suspecting nothing, returned home ; and one night about that time, going homeward, near Bangor, his merchant (who was supposed to be the devil) met him : " Now (says he), you know my bargain, how I bought you at such a place, and now I am come, as I promised, to pay the price." " Bought me !" said the poor man trembling, " you bought but my horses." " Nay," said the devil, " I will let you know I bought yourself ;" and further said, that he must kill somebody, and the more excellent the person, the better it would be for him ; and particularly charged him to kill Mr Blair, else he would not free him. The man was so overcome with terror, through the violence of the temptation, that he determined the thing, and went to Mr Blair's house, with a dagger in his right hand, under his cloak, and though much confounded, was moving to get it out. But on Mr Blair speaking to him, he fell a trembling, and on inquiry declared the whole fact ; and withal said, he had laboured to draw out the dagger, but it would not come from the scabbard, though he knew not what hindered it ; for when he essayed to draw it forth again, it came out with ease. Mr Blair blessed the Lord, and exhorted him to choose him for his refuge, after which he departed. Two weeks afterwards, being confined to his bed, Constable sent for Mr Blair, and told him, that the night before, as he was returning home, the devil appeared to him, and challenged him for opening to Mr Blair what passed betwixt them, claiming him as his ; and putting the cap off his head, and the band from his neck, said, that on Hallow Evening he should have him soul and body, in spite of the minister and all others. He therefore begged Mr Blair, for Christ's sake, to be with him against that time. Mr Blair instructed him, prayed with him, and promised to be with him against the appointed time. Afterwards he had much hesitation in his own mind, whether to keep that appointment or not; yet, at last, he took one of his elders with him, and went according to promise, and spent the whole night in prayer, explaining the doctrine of Christ's temptation, and praising with short intermissions. In the morning they took courage, defying Satan and all his devices. The man seemed very penitent, and died in a little after.

It was during the first year of his ministry, that he resolved not to go through a whole book or chapter of the Bible, but to make choice of some passages which held forth important heads of religion, and to close the course with one sermon of heaven's glory, and another of hell's torments; but when he came to meditate on these subjects, he was held a whole day in great perplexity, and could fix upon neither method nor matter till night, when, after sorrowing for his disorder, the Lord, in great pity, brought both matter and method into his mind, which remained with him until he got the same delivered.

About this time he met with a most notable deliverance: for, staying in a high house at the end of the town until the manse should be built, and being late at his studies, the candle was burned out, and having called for another, as the landlady brought it from a room under which he lay, she saw to her astonishment, that a joist under his bed had taken fire. The consequence of this, had he been in bed as usual, in all probability had been dreadful to the whole town, as well as to him, the wind being strong: but, by the timeous alarm given, the danger was prevented, which made him give thanks to God for this great deliverance.

When he first celebrated the Lord's Supper, his heart was much lifted up in speaking of the New Covenant, which made him, under the view of a second administration of the ordinance, resolve to go back unto that inexhaustible fountain of consolation; and coming over to Scotland about that time, he received no small assistance from David Dickson, who was then restored unto his flock at Irvine, and was studying and preaching on the same subject.

But it was not many years that he could have liberty in the exercise of his office; for, in harvest of 1631, he and John Livingstone were, by Ecklim, Bishop of Down, suspended from their office. Upon recourse to Archbishop Usher, who sent a letter to the Bishop, their sentence was relaxed, and they went on in their ministry until May

1632, when they were, by the said Bishop, deposed from the office of the holy ministry.

After this no redress could be had; whereupon Mr Blair resolved on a journey to Court, to represent their petitions and grievances to King Charles I. On his arrival at London, he could have no access for some time to his Majesty, and so laboured under many difficulties with little hopes of redress, until one day, having gone to Greenwich Park, where, being wearied with waiting on the Court, and while at prayer, the Lord assured him that he would hunt the violent man to destroy him. And while thus in earnest with the Lord for a favourable return, he adventured to propose a sign, that, if the Lord would make the reeds growing hard by, (which were moved with the wind, as he was tossed in mind), to cease from shaking, he would take it as an assurance of the despatch of his business. To this the Lord condescended; for, in a little time it became so calm, that not one of them moved; and in a short time he got a despatch to his mind, wherein the King did not only sign his petition, but, with his own hand, wrote on the margin (directed to the depute), " Indulge these men, for they are Scotsmen."

It was while in England that he had, from Ezekiel xxiv. 16, a strange discovery of his wife's death, and the very bed whereon she was lying, and the particular acquaintances attending her; and

GREENWICH.

although she was in good health at his return home, yet in a little all this exactly came to pass.

After Blair's return, the King's letter being slighted by the depute, who was newly returned from England, he was forced to have recourse to Archbishop Usher, who wept that he could not help them. By the interposition of Lord Castlestuart with the King, they got six months' liberty. But upon the back of this, in November 1634, he was again summoned before the Bishop, and the sentence of excommunication pronounced against him by Ecklim, Bishop of Down. After the sentence was pronounced, Mr Blair rose up and publicly cited the Bishop to appear before the tribunal of Jesus Christ, to answer for that wicked deed. Whereupon he did appeal from the justice of God to his mercy; but Mr Blair replied: "Your appeal is like to be rejected, because you act against the light of your own conscience." In a few months after the Bishop fell sick; and the physician inquiring of his sickness, after some time's silence, he, with great difficulty, said: "It is my conscience, man." To which the doctor replied: "I have no cure for that;" and in a little after he died.

After Mr Blair's ejection, he preached often in his own, and in other houses, until the beginning of the year 1635, when he began to think of marriage with Catherine Montgomery, daughter to Hugh Montgomery, formerly of Busby in Ayrshire (then residing in Ireland). For this he came over to Scotland with his own and his wife's friends, and upon his return to Ireland, they were married in the month of May following.

Matters still continuing the same, he engaged with the rest of the ejected ministers in their resolution of building a ship, called the "Eaglewings," of about 115 tons, on purpose to go to New England. But about 300 or 400 leagues from Ireland, meeting with a terrible hurricane, they were forced back unto Carrickfergus, the same harbour from which they loosed; the Lord having work for them elsewhere, it was fit their purpose should be defeated. He continued four months after this in Ireland, until, upon information that he and Mr Livingstone were to be apprehended, they immediately went out of the way, took shipping, and landed in Scotland in the year 1637.

All that summer after Mr Blair's arrival, he was as much employed in public and private exercises as before, mostly at Irvine and the country around, and partly at Edinburgh. But things being then in a confusion, because the service-book was then urged upon the ministers, his old inclination to go to France revived; and upon an invitation to be chaplain of Colonel Hepburn's regiment (newly enlisted in Scotland for the French service), he embarked with them at Leith. Some of these recruits, who were mostly Highlanders, being desperately wicked, and threatening upon his reproofs to stab him, he resolved to quit that voyage. Calling to the shipmaster to set him on shore, without imparting his design, a boat was immediately ordered for his service; at which time he met with another deliverance, for, his foot sliding, he was in danger of going to the bottom; but the Lord so ordered, that he got hold of a rope, by which he hung till he was relieved.

Robert Blair's return gave great satisfaction to his friends at Edinburgh, and the Second Reformation being then in the ascendant, he got a call to be colleague to Mr Annan, at Ayr, in the spring of 1638; and upon May 2, at a meeting of the Presbytery, having preached from 2 Cor. iv. 5, he was, at the special desire of all the people thereof, admitted a minister. He stayed not long here; for having, before the General Assembly held at Glasgow in 1638, fully vindicated himself, both anent his affair with Dr Cameron while regent in the University, and his settlement in Ireland, he was, for his great parts and known abilities, ordered to be translated to St Andrews. But the Assembly's motives in this did prove his detriment for some time, and the burgh of Ayr, where the Lord had begun to bless his labours, had the favour for another year. But the Assembly held at Edinburgh, 1639, being offended at his disobeying, ordered him peremptorily to remove to St Andrews.

In the year 1640, when King Charles I., by the advice of the clergy, had caused burn the articles of the former treaty with the Scots, and again prepared to chastise them with a royal army, the Scots, resolving not always to play after-game, also raised an army, invaded England, routed about 4000 English at Newburn, had Newcastle surrendered to them, and within two days were masters of Durham. This produced a new treaty, more favourable to them than the former. With this army was Mr Blair, who went with Lord Lindsay's regiment; and when the treaty was on foot, the Committee of Estates and the army sent him up to assist the commissioners with his best advice.

Again, after the rebellion in Ireland, 1641, those who survived the storm supplicated the General Assembly, in the year 1642, for a supply of ministers, when several went over, and among the first Mr

Blair. During his stay there, he generally preached once every day, and twice on Sabbath, and frequently in the field, the auditories being so large ; and in some of these he also administered the Lord's Supper.

After his return the condition of the Church and State was various during the years 1643 and 1644. In August 1643, the Committee of the General Assembly, whereof Mr Blair was one, with John, Earl of Rutland, and other four Commissioners from the Parliament of England, and Messrs Stephen Marshall, and Philip Nye, ministers, agreed to a solemn league and covenant betwixt the two kingdoms of Scotland and England. And in the end of the same year, when the Scots assisted the English Parliament, Mr Blair was by the Commission of the General Assembly appointed minister to the Earl of Crawford's regiment ; with which he stayed until the King was routed at Marston Moor, July 1644, when he returned to his charge at St Andrews.

The Parliament and Commission of the Kirk sat at Perth in July 1645. The Parliament was opened with a sermon by Robert Blair ; and, after he had, upon the forenoon of the 27th (a day of solemn humiliation), preached again to the Parliament, he rode out to the army, then encamped at Forgandenny, and preached to Crawford's and Maitland's regiments, to the first of which he had been chaplain. He told the brigade that he was informed many of them were turned dissolute and profane ; and assured them, that though the Lord had covered their heads in the day of battle (few of them being killed at Marston Moor), they should not be able to stand before a less formidable foe, unless they repented. Though this freedom was taken in good part from one who wished them well, yet was it too little laid to heart ; and the most part of Crawford's regiment was cut off at Kilsyth, in three weeks afterwards. After the defeat at Kilsyth, several were for treating with the Marquis of Montrose, but Mr Blair opposed it ; so that nothing was concluded until the Lord began to look upon the affliction of His people. For the Committee of Estates recalled General David Leslie, with 4000 foot and 1000 dragoons, from England, to oppose whom Montrose marched southward, but was shamefully defeated at Philiphaugh, September 13, many of his forces being killed and taken prisoners, and he himself hardly escaping.

On the 26th, the Parliament and Commission of the General Assembly sat down at St Andrews (the plague being then in Edinburgh). Here Mr Blair preached before the Parliament, and also prayed before several sessions thereof; and when several prisoners, taken at Philip-haugh, were tried, and three of them, viz., Sir Robert Spottiswoode, Messrs Nathaniel Gordon and Andrew Guthrie, were condemned to be executed on the 17th of January thereafter, Mr Blair visited them often, and was at much pains with them. He prevailed so far with Gordon, that he desired to be released from the sentence of excom-munication under which he was; and accordingly Mr Blair did the same. The other two, who were bishops' sons, died impenitent— *Mali corvi malum ovum.*

In the year 1646, the General Assembly, sitting at Edinburgh, ordered Robert Blair (who was then Moderator), with Andrew Cant and Robert Douglas, to repair to King Charles I. at Newcastle, to concur with Alexander Henderson and others, who were labouring to convince him of the great bloodshed in these kingdoms, and recon-cile him to the Presbyterian Church government and the Covenants. When these three ministers got a hearing, the room was immediately filled with several sorts of people to see their reception. Andrew Cant, being oldest, began briskly to insinuate, with his wonted zeal and plainness, that the King favoured Popery; but Blair interrupted him, and modestly hinted, that it was not a fit time nor place for that. The King looking earnestly said, "That honest man speaks wisely and discreetly, therefore I appoint you three to attend me to-morrow at ten o'clock, in my bed-chamber." They attended accord-ing to appointment, but got little satisfaction; only Mr Blair asked his Majesty, if there were not abominations in Popery. The King, lifting his hat, said, "I take God to witness that there are abomina-tions in Popery, which I so much abhor, that ere I consent to them, I would rather lose my life and my crown." Yet after all this, Mr Blair and Mr Henderson (for these two he favoured most) having most earnestly desired him to satisfy the just desires of his subjects, he obstinately refused, though they besought him on their knees with tears. Renewed commissions for this end were sent from Scotland, but to no good purpose, and Mr Blair returned home to St Andrews.

Alexander Henderson died at Edinburgh, August 19, which the King no sooner heard, than he sent for Robert Blair to supply his place, as chaplain in Scotland. He, through fear of being ensnared, was at first averse to this, but having consulted with Mr David Dick-son, and reflecting that Mr Henderson had held his integrity fast unto the end, he applied himself to that employment with great diligence, every day praying before dinner and supper in the presence-chamber;

on the Lord's day lecturing once and preaching twice; besides preaching some week-days in St Nicholas's Church; conversing also much with the King, desiring him to condescend to the just desires of his Parliament; and at other times debating concerning Prelacy, liturgies, and ceremonies.

One day, after prayer, the King asked him, if it was warrantable in prayer to determine a controversy? Mr Blair taking the hint, said, he thought he had determined no controversy in that prayer. "Yes," said the King, "you have determined the Pope to be Antichrist, which is a controversy among orthodox divines." To this Mr Blair replied, "To me this is no controversy, and I am sorry that it should be accounted so by your Majesty: sure it was none to your father." This silenced the King, for he was a great defender of his father's opinions. King James' testimony, Mr Blair knew well, was of more authority with him than the testimony of any divine. After a few months' stay, Mr Blair was permitted to visit his flock and family.

After the sitting of the Scots Parliament, Mr Blair made another visit to the King at Newcastle, where he urged him, with all the arguments he was master of, to subscribe the Covenants, and abolish Episcopacy in England, and he was confident all honest Scotsmen would espouse his quarrel against his enemies. To this the King answered, that he was bound by his great oath to defend Episcopacy in that Church; and ere he wronged his conscience, by violating his coronation oath, he would lose his crown. Mr Blair asked the form of that oath. He said, it was to maintain it to the utmost of his power. "Then," said Mr Blair, "you have not only defended it to the utmost of your power, but so long, and so far, that now you have no power." But by nothing could he prevail upon the King, and so he left him with a sorrowful heart, and returned to St Andrews.

Again, in the year 1648, when Cromwell came to Edinburgh, the Commission of the Kirk sent Robert Blair, David Dickson and James Guthrie, to deal with him for an uniformity in England. When they came, he entertained them with smooth speeches, and solemn appeals to God as to the sincerity of his intentions. Blair being best acquainted with him, spoke for all the rest, and among other things, begged an answer to these three questions—(1.) What was his opinion of monarchical government? He answered, he was for monarchical government; (2.) What was his opinion anent toleration? He answered confidently, that he was altogether against toleration; (3.) What was his opinion concerning the government of the Church? "O, now," said Cromwell, "Mr Blair, you article me too severely; you must pardon me, that I give you not a present answer to this." This he evaded, because he had before, in conversation with Mr Blair, confessed he was for Independency. When they came out, Mr Dickson said, "I am glad to hear this man speak no worse;" whereunto Mr Blair replied, "If you knew him as well as I, you would not believe one word he says, for he is an egregious dissembler, and a great liar."

When the differences fell out betwixt the Resolutioners and Protesters, Mr Blair was at London, and afterwards for the most part remained neutral in that affair. For this he was subjected to some hardships, yet he never omitted any proper place or occasion for uniting and cementing these differences; none now in Scotland being more earnest in this than he, and the learned and pious Mr James Durham, minister at Glasgow. These two, meeting at St Andrews, had the influence to draw a meeting of the two sides to Edinburgh, where harmony was like to prevail; but the Lord's anger being still drawn out for the prevailing sins of that time, all promising beginnings were blasted, and all hopes of agreement did vanish. Thus affairs continued until the year 1660, when the kingdom being quite sick of distractions, restored Charles II.; the woeful consequences of which act are otherwise too well known. On this last occasion, Mr Blair again began to bestir himself to procure union betwixt the two foresaid parties, and for that end obtained a meeting; but his endeavours were frustrated, and no reconciliation could be made, till both sides were cast into the furnace of a sore and long persecution.

In September 1661, James Sharp came to St Andrews; and the Presbytery, having had assurance of his deceitful carriage at Court, and of the probability of his being made Archbishop of St Andrews, sent Mr Blair and another, to discharge their duty to him; which they did so faithfully, that Sharp was never at ease till Mr Blair was rooted out.

Mr Blair taking occasion, in a sermon from 1 Pet. iii. 13, etc., to enlarge on suffering for righteousness' sake, and giving his testimony to the Covenants and the work of Reformation, against the sinful and corrupt courses of the times, he was called before the council, November 5, when the Advocate and some noblemen were appointed to converse with him, where they posed him on the following points: (1.) Whether he had asserted Presbyterian government to be *jure divino?* (2.) Whether he had asserted that suffering for it was suffering for righteousness' sake? And (3.) Whether in his prayers against Popery, he had joined Prelacy with it?

Having answered all in the affirmative, professing his sorrow that they doubted his opinions in these points, he was first confined to his chamber in Edinburgh ; and afterwards, upon supplication, and the attestation of physicians on account of his health, he was permitted to retire to Inveresk, about the 12th of January 1662.

Mr Blair continued here till October following, enjoying much of God's presence amidst his outward trouble; but being again commanded before the council, by the way he took a sore fit of the gravel, and was for that time excused. Afterwards, through the Chancellor's favour, having got liberty to go where he pleased, except St Andrews, and the west country, he went to Kirkcaldy.

While at Kirkcaldy, he lectured and prayed often to some Christian friends in his own family ; and for his recreation taught his younger son the Greek language and logic. But the Archbishop, envying the repose Mr Blair and some others had in these circumstances, procured an act, that no outed minister should reside within twenty miles of an Archbishop's see ; upon which Mr Blair removed from Kirkcaldy, in February 1666, to Meikle Couston, in the parish of Aberdour, an obscure place, where he continued till his death, which was shortly after. For, upon the 10th of August, Mr Blair, being now worn out with old age, and his spirits sunk with sorrow and grief for the desolations of the Lord's sanctuary in Scotland, took his last sickness, and entertained most serious thoughts of his near approaching end, ever extolling the glorious and good Master whom he had served.

His sickness increasing, he was visited by many Christian friends and acquaintances, whom he strengthened by his many gracious and edifying words. At one time, when they told him of some severe acts of council newly made, at Archbishop Sharp's instigation, he prayed that the Lord would open his eyes, and give him repentance. At another time, to Mrs Rutherford, he said, he would not exchange conditions with that man (albeit he was now on the bed of languishing, and the other possessed of great riches and revenues) though all betwixt them were red gold, and given him to the bargain. When some ministers asked him, if he had any hopes of deliverance to the people of God, he said that he would not take upon him to determine the times and seasons which the Lord keeps in his own hand, but that it was to him a token for good, that the Lord was casting the prelates out of the affections of all ranks and degrees of people ; and even

RIPON CATHEDRAL.

some, who were most active in setting them up, were now beginning to loath them for their pride, falsehood, and covetousness.

To his wife and children he spake gravely and Christianly, and, after he had solemnly blessed them, he severally admonished them as he judged expedient. His son David said, " The best and worst of men have their thoughts and after-thoughts ; now, sir, God having given you time for after-thoughts on your way, we would hear what they are now." He answered, " I have again and again thought upon my former ways, and communed with mine heart; and as for my public actings and carriage, in reference to the Lord's work, if I were to begin again, I would just do as I have done." He often repeated the 16th and 23d psalms, and once the 71st, which he used to call his own psalm.

About two days before his death, his speech began to fail, and he could not be well heard or understood ; however, some things were not lost, for, speaking of some eminent saints then alive, he prayed earnestly that the Lord would bless them; and as an evidence of his love to them, he desired Mr George Hutchison, then president, to carry his Christian remembrance to them: When Mr Hutchison went from his bedside, he said to his wife and others who waited on him, that he rejoiced in suffering as a persecuted minister. " Is it not persecution," added he, " to thrust me from the work of the ministry, which was my delight, and hinder me from doing good to my people and flock, which was my joy and crown of rejoicing, and to chase me from place to place till I am wasted with heaviness and sorrow for the injuries done to the Lord's prerogative, interest, and cause ?" What he afterwards said was either forgotten or not understood, till at length, about four o'clock in the morning, he was gathered to his fathers by a blessed and happy death, the certain result of a holy life.

His body lies near the church wall in the burial place at Aberdour ; and upon the wall above his grave was erected a little monument with this inscription :—

> Hic reconditæ jacent mortuæ
> Exuviæ D. Roberti Blair, S. S.
> Evangelii apud Andreapolin
> Prœdicatoris fidelissimi.   Obiit
> Augusti 27, 1666.   Ætatis suæ 72.

Robert Blair was a man of a fine constitution both in body and mind, of a majestic but amiable countenance and carriage, thoroughly learned, and of a most public spirit for God.   He was of unremitting diligence and labour, in all the private as well as public duties of his station.   He did highly endear himself to the affection of his own

MONUMENT IN ABERDOUR CHURCHYARD.

people, and to the whole country wherein he lived, and their attachment to him was not a little strengthened by his conduct in the judicatories of the Church, which indeed constituted a distinguishing part of his character.

When the General Assembly resolved upon a new version of the Holy Bible, among others of the godly and learned in the ministry, Mr Blair had the books of Proverbs and Ecclesiastes assigned to him for his part; but he neglected that task till he was rendered useless for other purposes, and then set about and finished his Commentary on the Proverbs in 1666. He composed also some small poetical pieces; a poem in commendation of Jesus Christ, for the confutation of Popish errors; with some short epigrams on different subjects.

Hugh M'Kail.

HUGH M'KAIL was born about the year 1640, and was educated at the University of Edinburgh, under the inspection of his uncle, Mr Hugh M'Kail, in whose family he resided. In the winter of 1661, he offered himself for trials for the ministry, before the presbytery of Edinburgh, being then about twenty years old; and being by them licensed, he preached several times with great acceptance.

He preached his last public sermon, from Cant. i. 7, in the High Church of Edinburgh, upon the Sabbath immediately preceding the 8th of September 1662, the day fixed by Parliament for the removal of the ministers of Edinburgh. In this sermon, taking occasion to speak of the great and many persecutions to which the Church of God had been and was subjected, and amplifying the point from the persons and powers that had been instrumental therein, he said, that the Church and people of God had been persecuted by a Pharaoh upon the throne, a Haman in the State, and a Judas in the Church;

and these characters seemed so similar to those of the rulers of Church and State at the time, that though he made no particular application, he was reputed guilty. Whereupon, a few days after, a party of horse was sent to the place of his residence, near Edinburgh, to apprehend him; but upon little more than a moment's warning, he escaped out of bed into another chamber, where he was preserved from the search. After this, he was obliged to return to his father's house, near Liberton, and having lurked there for some time, he spent other four years in several other places before his death.

While he lived at his father's house, troubles arose in the west; and the news thereof having alarmed him, for such motives and considerations as he himself afterwards more fully declares, he joined himself, upon the 18th of November 1666, to those who rose in these parts for the assistance of that poor afflicted party. [The reference here is to what was afterwards known as the "Pentland Rising," which was regarded as formidable enough at the time, but which originated in the following very simple and unpremeditated manner. Sir James Turner, who had distinguished himself by his military exactions and cruelty, had sent some of his soldiers to a small village about twenty miles from Dumfries, to seize the property of an old man who had incurred his displeasure for some religious offence. While they were maltreating him in the most brutal manner, some of the villagers ventured to remonstrate; but the soldiers having resented the interference, a scuffle ensued, and the old man was set free. It was now impossible to stop here, without exposing themselves, and the inhabitants of the district, to summary vengeance. Accordingly, many of their friends having joined them, they marched to Dumfries, where they surprised Sir James Turner and his garrison, and made them prisoners. Up till this time the movement had been quite accidental and unpremeditated, but now there came a necessity for more deliberate and determined action. Having received considerable reinforcements, and having been joined by many of the ablest and most influential of the Presbyterians, among whom was Lieutenant-Colonel Wallace, a gallant and distinguished officer, they marched under his command to Lanark, where they arrived on the evening of the 25th; and where, on the following day, they renewed the Covenants in the most solemn manner. Their number at this time was about 1500, the horsemen being armed for the most part with sword and pistol, but many of the foot soldiers only with scythes and pitchforks. Unfortunately, however, and as so often happened, a difference of opinion sprang up among themselves, some wishing to give battle at once, and others urging the expediency of continuing their march eastwards, in the hope of receiving reinforcements in the Lothians. After deliberation, the second course was adopted as the best; but, in consequence, many left for their homes. And when, after a terrible march in extremely tempestuous weather, the army arrived in the neighbourhood of Edinburgh, it was reduced to a handful of about 900 men. To oppose them, General Dalziel had been sent out by the Government with a force of 3000 fully equipped and disciplined soldiers. The battle, which followed on the 28th, and which took place on Rullion Green, one of the slopes of the Pentlands, was nobly fought by the insurgents; although, with their disadvantages, the result could not be doubtful. The loss to the royal army was never known; but, on the side of the Presbyterians, about 50 were killed, and 100 surrendered on promise of quarter; which promise was, however, in many cases, shamefully violated. The killed were buried in trenches on the battle-field; and a monument, with the following inscription, still marks the spot where they fell:

> " A cloud of witnesses lie here,
>   Who, for Christ's interests, did appear;
>   For to restore true liberty,
>   O'erturned then by tyranny.
>   These heroes fought with great renown;
>   By falling got the Martyr's Crown!"

We shall not presume to say how far it was prudent, in their circumstances, to continue in arms, and brave the fury of the Government; but, in the words of De Foe, "we leave all those, who afterwards thought it lawful to join in the Revolution, and in taking arms against the oppressions and arbitrary government of King James, to judge whether these good men had not the same individual reasons and more for this Pentland expedition. And it is answer enough to all that shall read these sheets to say, that those men died for that lawful resisting of arbitrary power which has been justified as legal, and acknowledged to be justifiable by the practice and declaration of the respective Parliaments of both kingdoms."—ED.]

Being of a tender constitution, by the toil, fatigue, and continual marching in tempestuous weather, Hugh M'Kail was so disabled and weakened, that he could no longer endure; and upon the 27th, the day before the battle, he was obliged to leave his comrades near Cramond water. On his way to Liberton parish, passing through

Braid's Craigs, he was taken without any resistance (having only a small ordinary sword) by some of the countrymen who were sent out to view the fields. And here it is observable that his former escape was no more miraculous than his present taking was fatal; for the least caution might have prevented this misfortune; but God, who gave him the full experience of His turning all things to the good of them that love Him, did thus prepare the way for His own glory, and His servant's joy and victory.

He was brought to Edinburgh, first to the Town Council house, where he was searched for letters; but none being found, he was committed prisoner to the Tolbooth. Upon Wednesday the 28th, he was, by order of the Secret Council, brought before the Earl of Dumfries, Lord Sinclair, Sir Robert Murray of Priestfield, and others, in order to his examination. Being interrogated concerning his joining the westland forces, he, conceiving himself not obliged by any law or reason to be his own accuser, did decline the question. After some reasoning, he was desired to subscribe his name, but refused; and this fact, when reported to the Council, gave them great offence, and brought him under some suspicion of being a dissembler. On the 29th he was again called, when, to allay this prejudice, he gave in a declaration under his own hand, testifying that he had been with the westland forces. Though it was certainly known that he had both formed and subscribed this acknowledgment the night before, yet they still persisted in their jealousy. Suspecting him to have been privy to all the designs of that party, they dealt with him with the greater importunity to declare an account of the whole business; and upon December 3, the Boots (a most terrible instrument of torture) were laid on the council-house table before him, and he was certified, that, if he would not confess, he would be tortured next day. Accordingly he was called before them, and, being urged to confess, he solemnly declared, that he knew no more than what he had already confessed; whereupon they ordered the executioner to put his leg in the Boot, and to proceed to the torture, to the number of ten or eleven strokes, with considerable intervals; yet all did not move him to express any impatience or bitterness.

This torture was the cause of his not being indicted with the first ten, who were arraigned and sentenced on Wednesday, December 5, to be hanged on the Friday following. Many thought that his slight connection with the rising, and what he had suffered by torture, should have procured him some favour; but it was otherwise determined, for his former sermon was not forgotten, especially the words, "A Pharaoh upon the throne," etc.

Upon December 8, his brother went from Edinburgh to Glasgow, with a letter in his favour from the Marchioness of Douglas, and another from the Duchess of Hamilton, to the Lord Commissioner, but both proved ineffectual. His cousin, Mr Matthew M'Kail, carried another letter from the Marchioness of Douglas to the Archbishop of St Andrews for the same purpose, but with no better success.

On Monday the 10th, he and other seven received their indictment of treason, and were summoned to appear before the Justices on Wednesday, December 12; but his torture and close imprisonment (for so it was ordered) had cast him into a fever, whereby he was utterly unable to make his appearance. Therefore, upon Tuesday the 11th, he gave in to the Lords of the Council a supplication, declaring his weak and sickly condition, craving that they would surcease any legal procedure against him, and that they would discharge him of the foresaid appearance. Hereupon the Council ordered two physicians and two chirurgeons to visit him, and to return their attestations, upon soul and conscience, betwixt that time and the morrow at ten o'clock, to the Justices.

On December 16, he, being indifferently recovered, was with other three brought before the Justices, where the general indictment was read, founded both on old and recent Acts of Parliament, made against rising in arms, entering into leagues and covenants, and renewing the Solemn League and Covenant, without and against the King's authority. Hugh M'Kail was particularly charged with joining the rebels at Ayr, Ochiltree, Lanark, and other places, on horseback. Hereupon, being permitted to answer, he spoke in his own defence, both concerning the charge laid against him, and likewise of the ties and obligations that were upon this land to God; commending the institution, dignity, and blessing of Presbyterian government; and said, that the last words of the national Covenant had always a great weight upon his spirit. Here he was interrupted by the King's Advocate, who bade him forbear that discourse, and answer the question for the crime of rebellion. To this he answered, that the thing which moved him to declare as he had done, was that weighty important saying of our Lord Jesus: "Whosoever shall confess Me before men, him shall the Son of Man also confess before the angels of God." After the depositions of those examined anent him were read, with his replies to the same, the assize was inclosed; after which they gave their verdict unanimously, and by the mouth of Sir William Murray, their chancellor, reported him guilty. This being done, doom was pronounced, declaring and adjudging him and the rest to be taken on Saturday, December 20, to the market cross of Edinburgh, there to be hanged on a gibbet till dead, and their goods and lands to be escheated and forfeited for his Highness' use.

At the hearing of the sentence, he cheerfully said, " The Lord giveth, the Lord taketh away, blessed be the name of the Lord;" and he was then carried back to the Tolbooth through the guards, the people making lamentations for him by the way. After he came to his chamber, he immediately addressed himself to God in prayer, with great enlargement of heart, in behalf of himself and those who were condemned with him. Afterwards, he said to a friend, " O how good news; to be within four days' journey to enjoy the sight of Jesus Christ;" and protested that he was not so cumbered how to die as he had sometimes been to preach a sermon. To some women lamenting for him, he said, that his condition, though he was but young, and in the budding of his hopes and labours in the ministry, was not to be mourned; "for one drop of my blood," added he, "through the grace of God, may make more hearts contrite than many years' sermons might have done."

This afternoon he supplicated the Council for liberty to his father to visit him; which being granted, his father came next night, to whom he discoursed a little from the fifth commandment, concerning obedience to parents. After prayer, his father said to him, " Hugh, I have called thee a goodly olive-tree of fair fruit, and now a storm hath destroyed the tree and his fruit." He answered, that his too good thought had afflicted him. His father said, that he was persuaded God was visiting not his own sins, but his parents' sins, so that he might say, " Our fathers have sinned, and we have borne their inquity;" and added, " I have sinned; thou poor sheep, what hast thou done?." Hugh answered with many groans, that, through coming short of the fifth commandment, he had come short of the promise, that his days should be prolonged in the land of the living; and that God's controversy with his father was for overvaluing his children, especially himself.

Upon the 20th of December, through the importunity of friends, more than his own inclination, he gave in a petition to the Council,

EDINBURGH TOLBOOTH—SOUTH FRONT.

craving their clemency, after having declared his own innocence ; but it proved altogether ineffectual. During his abode in prison, the Lord was very graciously present with him, both to sustain him against the fears of death, and to expel the overcloudings of terror, unto which the best of men, through the frailty of flesh and blood, are sometimes subject. He was also wonderfully assisted in prayer and praise, to the admiration of all. On Thursday night, being at supper with his fellow-prisoners, his father, and one or two more, he said merrily to the former, "Eat to the full, and cherish your bodies, that we may be a fat Christmas-pie to the prelates." After supper, in thanksgiving, he broke forth into several expressions, both concerning himself and the Church of God, and at last used that exclamation in the book of Daniel, "What, Lord, shall be the end of these wonders ?"

The last night of his life he propounded and answered several questions for the strengthening of his fellow-prisoners, among others the following :

"How should I go from the Tolbooth through a multitude of gazing people, and guards of soldiers, to a scaffold and gibbet, and overcome the impression of all this ?"

The answer was, "By conceiving a deeper impression of a multi-

CROSS OF EDINBURGH.

tude of angels, who are on-lookers ; according to that saying, 'We are a gazing-stock to the world, angels, and men :' for the angels, rejoicing at our good confession, are present to convoy and carry our souls, as the soul of Lazarus, to Abraham's bosom ; not to receive them, for that is Jesus Christ's work alone, who will welcome them to heaven Himself, with the songs of angels and blessed spirits ; the angels are but ministering spirits, always ready to serve and strengthen dying believers."

"What is the way for us, who are hastening to it, to conceive of heaven, seeing the word saith, 'Eye hath not seen, nor ear heard ?'"

To this he answered, "that the Scripture helps us two ways to conceive of heaven : (1.) By way of similitude, as in Rev. xxi., where heaven is held forth by the representation of a glorious city, there described ; (2.) By holding forth the love of the saints to Jesus Christ, and teaching us to love Him in sincerity, which is the very joy and exultation of heaven (Rev. v. 12) ; and no other thing than the soul breathing forth love to Jesus Christ can rightly apprehend the joys of heaven."

The last words he spoke at supper were in commendation of love above knowledge. "Oh! notions of knowledge without love are of small worth, evanishing in nothing, and very dangerous " After supper, his father having given thanks, he read the 16th Psalm, and then said, " If there be anything in the world sadly and unwillingly to be left, it were the reading of the Scriptures. I said, that I shall not see the Lord in the land of the living ; but this needs not make us sad, for, where we go, the Lamb is the book of Scripture, and the light of the city ; and there is life ; even the River of the Water of Life, and living springs." He then called for a pen, saying, it was to write his testament, wherein he ordered some few books he had to be delivered to several persons. He went to bed about eleven o'clock, and slept till five in the morning, when he arose and called for his comrade John Wodrow, saying pleasantly, " Up, John, for you are too long in bed ; you and I look not like men going to be hanged this day, seeing we lie so long." Then he spake to him in the words of Isaiah xliii. 24 ; and after some short discourse, John said to him, " You and I shall be chambered shortly beside Mr Robertson." He answered, " John, I fear you bar me out, because you were more free before the Council than I was ; but I shall be as free as any of you upon the scaffold ;" adding, " I have got a clear ray of the majesty of the Lord after his awakening, but it was a little overclouded thereafter." He then prayed with great fervency, plead-ing his covenant relation with Him, and that they might be enabled that day to witness a good confession before many witnesses. His father, coming to him, bade him farewell ; to whom his last words were, that his sufferings would do more hurt to the prelates, and be more edifying to God's people, than if he were to continue in the ministry twenty years. Then he desired his father to go to his chamber, and pray earnestly to the Lord to be with him on the scaffold ; " for how to carry there," said he, " is my care ; even that I may be strengthened to endure to the end."

About two o'clock afternoon, he was brought to the scaffold, with other five who suffered with him ; where, to the conviction of all that formerly knew him, he had a fairer and more stayed countenance than ever they had before observed. Being come to the foot of the ladder, he directed his speech to the multitude northward, saying, that as his years in the world had been but few, his words then should not be many, and he then addressed to the people the speech and testimony which he had before written and subscribed.

Having done speaking, he sung a part of the 31st Psalm, and prayed with such power and fervency, as caused many to weep bitterly. Then he gave his hat and cloak from him ; and taking hold of the ladder to go up, he said with an audible voice, " I care no more to go up this ladder, and over it, than if I were going home to my father's house." Hearing a noise among the people, he called down to his fellow-sufferers, saying, " Friends and fellow-sufferers, be not afraid ; every step of this ladder is a degree nearer heaven :" and having seated himself thereon, he said, " I do partly believe that the noble counsellors and rulers of this land would have used some mitigation of this punishment, had they not been instigated by the prelates, so that our blood lies principally at the prelates' door; but this is my comfort, I know that my Redeemer liveth. And now I do willingly lay down my life for the truth and cause of God, the Covenants and work of Reformation, which were once counted the glory of this nation; and it is for endeavouring to defend this, and to extirpate that bitter root of Prelacy, that I embrace this rope "— the executioner then putting the rope about his neck.

Hearing the people weep, he said, " Your work is not to weep but to pray, that we may be honourably borne through ; and blessed be the Lord that supports me now. As I have been beholden to the prayers and kindness of many since my imprisonment and sentence, so I hope you will not be wanting to me now in the last step of my journey, that I may witness a good confession ; and that ye may know what the ground of my encouragement in this work is, I shall read to you in the last chapter of the Bible ;" which having read, he said, " Here you see the glory that is to be revealed on me ; a ' pure river of water of life ;' and here you see my access to the glory and reward ; ' Let him that is athirst, come ;' and here you see my welcome ; ' The Spirit and the Bride say, Come.' " Then he said, " I have one word more to say to my friends. Ye need neither to lament nor be ashamed of me in this condition, for I may make use of that expression of Christ's, ' I ascend to my Father and your Father, to my God and your God,'—to my King and your King, to the blessed apostles and martyrs, and to the city of the living God, the heavenly Jerusalem, to an innumerable company of angels, to the general assembly of the first-born, to God the Judge of all, to the spirits of just men made perfect, and to Jesus the Mediator of the new covenant; and I bid you all farewell, for God will be more comfortable to you than I could be, and He will be now more refreshing to me than you can be. Farewell, farewell in the Lord !"

The napkin being put on his face, he prayed a little, and putting it up with his hand, he said that he had a word more to say concerning what comfort he had in his death: " I hope you perceive no alteration or discouragement in my countenance and carriage, and as it may be your wonder, so I profess it is a wonder to myself: and I will tell you the reason of it. Besides the justice of my cause, my comfort is, what was said of Lazarus when he died, that the angels did carry his soul to Abraham's bosom; so that as there is a great solemnity here, a confluence of people, a scaffold, a gallows, a people looking out of windows; so there is a greater and more solemn preparation of angels to carry my soul to Christ's bosom. Again this is my comfort, that it is to come to Christ's hand; He will present it blameless and faultless to the Father, and then shall I be ever with the Lord. And now I leave off to speak any more to creatures, and begin my intercourse with God, which shall never be broken off. Farewell father and mother, friends and relations; farewell the world and all delights; farewell meat and drink; farewell sun, moon, and stars; welcome God and Father; welcome sweet Jesus Christ, the Mediator of the new covenant; welcome blessed Spirit of grace, and God of all consolation; welcome glory; welcome eternal life; and welcome death!"

Then he desired the executioner not to turn him over until he himself should put over his shoulders; which, after praying a little in private, he did, saying, "O Lord, into thy hands I commit my spirit, for thou hast redeemed me, O Lord God of truth." And thus, in the 26th year of his age, he died, as he lived, in the Lord.

His death was so much lamented by the onlookers and spectators, that there was scarcely a dry cheek seen in all the streets and windows about the Cross of Edinburgh, at the time of his execution. A late historian gives him this character, that " he was a youth of twenty-six years of age, universally beloved, singularly pious, and of very considerable learning. He had seen the world, and travelled some years abroad, and was of a very comely and graceful person. I am told," says he, " that he used to fast one day every week, and had frequently, before this, signified to his friends his impression of such a death as he now underwent. His share in the Pentland rising was known to be but small; and when he spoke of comfort and joy in his death, heavy were the groans of those present."

John Nevay.

OHN NEVAY was licensed and ordained a minister in the time of Scotland's purest Reformation, and settled in Newmilns in the parish of Loudon. Besides his soundness in the faith, shining piety in conversation, and great diligence in attending all the parts of his ministerial functions, particularly church-judicatories, he was one who was also very zealous in contending against several steps of defection, which were contrary to the work of reformation carried on in that period.

When the Earl of Callender and Major-General Middleton were cruelly harassing the Covenanters, and well affected people in the west of Scotland, because they would not join in the Duke of Hamilton's unlawful engagement in war against England (which was a manifest breach of the Solemn League and Covenant), John Nevay was one of those ministers who, with other well affected people, were assembled at the celebration of our Lord's Supper at Mauchline Muir, in the month of June 1648; where opposition (in their own defence) was made to the said Callender and Middleton's forces, who attacked them upon the last day of the solemnity.

When that pretended Assembly, held at Edinburgh and St Andrews in the year 1651, did approve and ratify the public resolutions for bringing the justly-excluded malignants into places of public power and trust, he was one of those who faithfully witnessed and protested against the sad course of covenant-breaking and land-defiling sin.

When that head of malignants, Charles II., was restored as king over these lands, in consequence of which the whole of our covenanted work of Reformation began to be defaced and overturned, it behoved the chief promoters thereof to be in the first place attacked. John Nevay, being the Earl of Loudon's chaplain, and very much valued by him, was included among the rest, and was, upon the 18th of November 1662, by order of the council, cited, with some others, to repair to Edinburgh, and appear before the council on the 9th of December after.

He did not compear until the 23d, when he was examined, and, upon his refusal of the oath of allegiance, he was banished, and executed a bond as follows :

" I John Nevay, minister of the Gospel at Newmilns, bind and oblige myself to remove forth of the king's dominions, and not to return under pain of death ; and that I shall remove before the first of February ; and that I shall not remain within the diocese of Glasgow and Edinburgh in the meantime. Subscribed at Edinburgh, December 23. " JOHN NEVAY."

Taking leave of his old parishioners (no doubt with a sorrowful heart) he prepared for his journey, and went over, among the rest of our banished ministers, to Holland, where, for some years, he preached to such as would come and hear him. Yet all the while he retained the affection of a most dear and loving pastor to his old parishioners of Loudon, sending them many sermons and several affectionate letters, wherein he not only exhorted them to steadfast-ness in the midst of manifold temptations, but also showed a longing desire to return to his own native land and parishioners. This is evident from that excellent letter, written some time before his death, dated at Rotterdam, October 22, 1669, in which, among many other things, he has these expressions : " I can do no more but pray for you ; and if I could do that well, I had done almost all that is required. I am not worthy of the esteem you have of me ; I have not whereof to glory, but much whereof I am ashamed, and which may make me go mourning to my grave ; but if you stand fast, I live ; you are all my crown and joy in this earth, next to the joy of Jerusalem and her King ; and I hope to have some of you my joy and crown in our Father's kingdom, besides those that are gone before us, and entered into the joy of the Lord. I have not been altogether ignorant of the changes and wars which have been amongst you ; deep calling unto deep ; nor how the Lord did sit on all your floods as King, and did give you many times more ease than others, and how you wanted not your share in the most honourable testi-mony that ever was given to the truth and kingdom of Christ in Scotland, since the days of Mr Patrick Hamilton, Mr George Wishart, and Mr Walter Mill, His martyrs."

That John Nevay was no mean divine in his day, either in part or learning, is fully evident, both from an act of the General Assembly in the year 1646, from which it appears that he was one of those four ministers who were appointed to revise and correct Rouse's paraphrase of David's Psalms in metre, lately sent from England (of which he had the last thirty for his share); and also from that elegant and handsome paraphrase of his upon the Song of Solomon, in Latin verse; both of which show him to have been of a profound judgment and rare abilities.

There are fifty-two sermons (or rather notes of sermons) of his published, upon the nature, properties, blessings, etc., of the Covenant of Grace; and thirty-nine sermons on Christ's Temptations, in manuscript, sent over from Holland for the benefit of his old parishioners of Newmilns, which might also have been published, if the former collection had met with that reception they deserved.

John Livingstone.

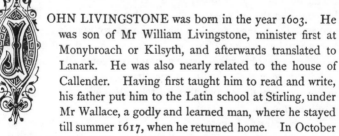 OHN LIVINGSTONE was born in the year 1603. He was son of Mr William Livingstone, minister first at Monybroach or Kilsyth, and afterwards translated to Lanark. He was also nearly related to the house of Callender. Having first taught him to read and write, his father put him to the Latin school at Stirling, under Mr Wallace, a godly and learned man, where he stayed till summer 1617, when he returned home. In October following he was sent to the College of Glasgow, where he stayed four years, until he passed his degree of Master of Arts in the year 1621.

After this he stayed with his father until he was ready to preach, during which time he began to observe the Lord's great goodness, in that he was born of such parents, who taught him the principles of religion as soon as he was capable of understanding anything. He

CARRICKFERGUS.

says, in his own account of his life, that he does not remember the time or means particularly whereby the Lord at first wrought upon his heart, only, when he was but very young, he would sometimes pray with some feeling, and read the Word with some delight; but thereafter he did often intermit such exercises, and then would have some challenges, and begin, and intermit again. He says he had no inclination to the ministry till a year or more after he had passed his course at the college; for he bent his desires to the knowledge and practice of medicine, and wished to go to France for that end, but when he proposed this to his father, he refused to comply. About this time his father, having purchased some land in the parish of Kilsyth, took the rights in his son's name, proposing that he should marry and live there; but this he refused, thinking it would divert him from his studies.

In the midst of these straits, John Livingstone resolved to set apart a day by himself before God, for more special direction; which he did near Cleghorn Wood, where, after much confusion anent the state of his soul, he at last thought it was made out to him, that he behoved to preach Jesus Christ, which, if he did not, he should have no assurance of salvation; upon which, laying aside all thoughts of other things, he betook himself to the study of divinity. He continued a year and a-half in his father's house, where he studied,

PORTRAIT OF CHARLES II.

and sometimes preached. During this time he wrote all his sermons before he preached them, until one day, being to preach after the communion of Quodquhan, and having in readiness a sermon which he had preached one day before, he perceived several there who had heard him at that time, and resolved to choose a new text, taking only some notes of the heads he was to deliver. Yet he says he found, at that time, more assistance in enlarging upon these points, and more motion in his own heart than ever he had found before, which made him never afterwards write any sermons, but only some notes for the help of his memory.

About April 1626, he was sent for by Lord Kenmuir to Galloway, in reference to a call to the parish of Anwoth; but some hindrance coming in the way, this design was laid aside. In the harvest following, he hearkened to another call to Torphichen; but this proved also unsuccessful.

After this he went to the Earl of Wigton's, where he stayed some time; and the most part of the summer he travelled from place to place, according as he got invitations to preach, which was especially at communions in Lanark, Irvine, Newmilns, Kinniel, etc. He was also sometimes invited to preach at Shotts; and in that place he says he used to find more liberty in preaching than elsewhere; yea, the day in all his life wherein he found most of the presence of God in preaching, he observes, was on a Monday after a communion at the Kirk of Shotts, June 21, 1630. The night before, he had been with some Christians, who spent the time in prayer and conference In the morning there came such a misgiving of spirit upon him, on con- sidering his own unworthiness and weakness, and the expectation of the people, that he thought to have stolen away somewhere, and declined that day's work ; but thinking he could not so distrust God, he went to preach, where he got remarkable assistance in speaking about one hour and a half, from Ezekiel xxxvi. 25. "Then will I sprinkle clean water upon you, and ye shall be clean : from all your filthiness, and from all your idols, will I cleanse you." Here he was led out in such a melting strain, that, by the down-pouring of the Spirit from on high, a most discernible change was wrought on about 500 of his hearers, who could date either their conversion, or some remarkable confirmation, from that day forward. Some little of that spirit, he says, remained on him the Thursday after, when he preached at Kilmarnock; but on the Monday following, preaching at Irvine, he was so deserted, that what he had meditated upon, written, and kept fully in memory, he could not get pronounced. This so discouraged him, that he resolved not to preach for some time, at least at Irvine ; but David Dickson would not suffer him to go till he preached next Sabbath ; which he did with some freedom.

This summer, being in Irvine, he got letters from Viscount Clanniboy, to come to Ireland, in reference to a call to Killinchie ; and, seeing no appearance of entering into the ministry in Scotland, he went thither, and got an unanimous call from that parish. Here he laboured with the utmost assiduity among the people, who were both rude and profane before, but now became the most experienced Christians in that country. But he was not above a year here, until the Bishop of Down suspended him and Robert Blair for nonconformity. They remained deposed until May 1632, when, by the intercession of Lord Castlestuart, a warrant was granted them from the King to be restored.

After this he married the eldest daughter of Bartholomew Fleming, merchant in Edinburgh, who was then in Ireland. In November 1635, he was again deposed by the Bishop of Down, and a little after, by his orders, excommunicated. This winter, seeing no ap- pearance of liberty, either to ministers or professors, from the bondage of the prelates, he, with others of the deposed ministers, formed a resolution to go to New England. Upon this, they built a ship for that purpose, and when all things were ready, they, about the 9th of September, loosed from Lochfergus. But a violent storm arising, they were driven near the banks of Newfoundland, where they were all in danger of being drowned; and, after prayer and consultation, they resolved to return. After this he stayed in Ireland, until he heard that he and Robert Blair were to be apprehended; when they went out of the way, and came over to Scotland. When he came to Irvine, David Dickson caused him to preach, for which he was called in question afterwards. Leaving Irvine, he passed by Loudon and Lanark to Edinburgh, where he continued some time.

About the beginning of March 1638, when the body of the nation was about to renew the national Covenant, he was sent post-haste to London with several copies of the Covenant, and letters to friends at Court. When he came there, Mr Borthwick delivered the letters for him; but he had been there only a few days when the Marquis of Hamilton informed him, that he had overheard King Charles I. say he was come, but he should put a pair of fetters about his feet. Whereupon, fearing he should be taken in the post-way, Livingstone bought a horse, and came home by St Alban's, and the western way, and was present at Lanark and other places when the Covenant was read and sworn unto. Excepting at the Kirk of Shotts already noticed, he says that he never saw such motions from the Spirit of God—all the people so generally and willingly concurring, yea, thousands of persons all at once lifting up their hands, and the tears falling from their eyes; so that, throughout the whole land, the people (a few Papists, and others who adhered to the prelates, excepted) universally entered into the Covenant of God, for the reformation of religion against Prelacy.

After this, in the year 1638, he got a call both from Stranraer in Galloway, and Straiton in Carrick. He referred the matter to Messrs Blair, Dickson, Cant, Henderson, Rutherford, and his father; who, having heard both parties, advised him to accept Stranraer, and he was received there by the presbytery upon the 5th of July, 1638. Here he remained in the faithful discharge of the ministry until harvest 1648, when he was, by the determination of the General Assembly, translated to Ancrum in Teviotdale. When he came to Ancrum, he found the people tractable, but very ignorant, and some of them very loose in their conduct, and it was a long time before any competent number of them were brought to such a condition, that he could venture to celebrate the Lord's Supper. However, by his diligence, some of them, through the grace of God, began to lay religion to heart.

In the year 1649, the Parliament and Church of Scotland had sent some commissioners to treat with King Charles II. at the Hague, in order to his restoration, but they returned without satisfaction. Yet the Parliament in summer 1650, sent other commissioners to prosecute the foresaid treaty at Breda; and the Commission of the Kirk chose Mr Livingstone and Mr Wood, and after that added Mr Hutchison to them, with the Lords Cassilis and Brodie as ruling elders, that in name of the Church they should present and prosecute their desires. Livingstone was very unwilling to go, and that for several reasons, the chief of which was that he suspected the King to be not right at heart in respect of the true Presbyterian religion. Notwithstanding this, seeing that many in the kingdom were ready to receive the King home upon any terms, he was prevailed on by Messrs Dickson, James Guthrie, and Patrick Gillespie, to go; but, after much conference and reasoning with the King at Breda, they were not like to come to any conclusion. Here Livingstone observed that the King still continued the use of the Service Book and his chaplains, and was many a night balling and dancing till near day. This, with many other things, made him conclude there would be no blessing on that treaty; but it was, to his unspeakable grief, at last concluded, and some time after, the King set sail for Scotland. Livingstone refused to go aboard with them, but when Brodie and Hutchison saw this, they desired him, before parting, to come into the ship, to speak of some matters in hand; and, on his doing so, the boat that should have waited his return made straight for shore without him. After this the King agreed with the commissioners to swear and subscribe the Covenants, and it was laid upon Livingstone to preach the next Sabbath, and tender the national solemn League and Covenant, and take his oath thereon. Judging that such a rash and precipitate swearing of the Covenants would not be for the honour of the cause they were embarked in, he did all he could to deter the King and commissioners from doing it until they came to Scotland; but when nothing would dissuade the King from his resolution, it was done. The King performed everything that could have been required of him, upon which Mr Livingstone observed, that it seems to have been the guilt, not only of commissioners, but of the whole kingdom; yea, and of the Church also, who knew the terms whereupon he was to be admitted to his government, and yet received him without any evidence of a real change upon his heart, and without his forsaking former principles, counsels, and company.

After they landed in Scotland, before he took his leave of the King at Dundee, John Livingstone used some freedom with him. After speaking somewhat to him anent his conduct, he advised him, that, as he saw the English army approaching in a most victorious manner, he should divert the stroke by a declaration (wherein he need not weaken his right to the crown of England), and refrain from prosecuting his title at present by fire and sword, until the storm blew over, when, perhaps, the nation would be in a better mood to be governed. But he did not relish this motion well, saying, he would not wish to sell his father's blood, which made Livingstone conclude, that he was not called to meddle in state-matters, for he should have little success. Another instance of this he gives us in the year 1654, when he and Mr Patrick Gillespie and Mr Menzies were called up by the Protector to London. On this occasion, he proposed that the heavy fines that were laid on many in Scotland, which they were unable to pay, should be taken off. Cromwell seemed to like the motion, but when he proposed it to the Council, they refused

While at London, preaching before the Protector, he mentioned the King in prayer, whereat some were greatly incensed; but Cromwell, knowing Livingstone's influence in Scotland, said, "Let him alone, he is a good man, and what are we poor men in comparison of the Kings of England."

The General Assembly appointed some ministers, and Livingstone among the rest, to wait upon the army, and the Committee of Estates then with it; but fear and apprehension kept him from going, and he went home until he got the sad news of the defeat at Dunbar. After this Cromwell wrote to him from Edinburgh, to come and speak to him, but he excused himself. That winter the unhappy difference falling out anent the public resolutions, his light carried him to join the Protesters against the Resolutioners, and the Assembly that followed thereafter. He was present at their first meeting in the west at Kilmarnock, and several other meetings of the protesting brethren afterwards; but not being satisfied with keeping these meetings so often, and continuing them so long, which he imagined made the breach wider, he declined them for some time.

After this he spent the rest of his time in the exercise of the ministry, both at Ancrum and other places, until summer 1660, when news was brought him that Charles II. was restored. Then he clearly foresaw that the overturning of the whole work of reformation would ensue, and a trial fall upon all who should adhere to the same. But, in the year 1662, when the Parliament and Council had, by proclamation, ordered all ministers who had come in since 1649, and had not kept the holiday of the 29th of May, either to acknowledge the prelates or remove, he then more clearly foresaw a storm approaching. At the last communion which he had at Ancrum, in the month of October, he says, that after sermon on Monday, it pleased the Lord to open his mouth, in a reasonably large discourse, anent the grounds and encouragements to suffer for the present controversy of the kingdom of Christ, in the appointing the government of His house. Then he took his leave of that place, although he knew nothing of what was shortly to follow after.

After he had, like Elijah, eaten before a great journey, having communicated before he entered upon suffering, he heard, in a little time, of the Council's procedure against him and about twelve or sixteen others who were to be brought before them. He went presently to Edinburgh, before the summons could reach him, and lurked there some time, until he got certain information of the Council's design, whether they were for their lives, like as was done with Mr Guthrie, or only for banishment, as was done with Mr M'Ward and Mr Simpson; when, finding that they intended only the last, he resolved to appear with his brethren. He appeared, December 11, and was examined before the Council. They required him to subscribe or take the oath of allegiance, which he, upon several solid grounds and reasons, refused; and sentence was pronounced, that in forty-eight hours he should depart from Edinburgh, and go to the north side of Tay, and within two months depart out of all the King's dominions. Accordingly, he went from Edinburgh to Leith; but thereafter, upon a petition in regard of his infirmity, he obtained leave to stay there until he should remove from the kingdom. He petitioned also for a few days to go home to see his wife and children, but was refused; as also for an extract of his sentence, but could not obtain it. In the year 1663 he left Leith (accompanied by several friends to the ship) and in eight days reached Rotterdam, where he found the rest of the banished ministers. He got frequent occasions of preaching to the Scots congregation at Rotterdam; and in December following, his wife, with two of his children, came over to him, and the other five were left in Scotland.

Here, upon a retrospective view of his life, he (in the foresaid Historical Account) observes, that the Lord had given him a body not very strong, and yet not weak, for he could hardly remember himself wearied in reading and studying, although he had continued seven or eight hours without rising; and also that there were but two recreations that he was in danger to be taken with. The first was hunting on horseback; this he had very little occasion of, yet he found it very enticing; the other was, singing in concerts of music, wherein he had some skill, and in which he took great delight. He says further, that he was always short-sighted, and could not discern any person or thing afar off; but hitherto he had found no occasion for spectacles, and could read small print as long, and with as little light, almost as any other. And, as to his inclination, he was generally soft and amorous, averse to debates, rather given to laziness than rashness, and too easily wrought upon. And although he could not say what Luther affirmed of himself concerning covetousness, yet he could say, he had been less troubled with covetousness and cares than many other evils, rather inclined to solitariness than company, and much troubled with wandering of mind and idle thoughts. As for outward things, he was never rich; and although, when in Killinchie, he had not above four pounds sterling of stipend a-year, yet he was never in want.

He further observes, that he could not remember any particular time of conversion, or that he was much cast down or lifted up. Only one night, in the Dean of Kilmarnock's, having been most of the day before in company with some people of Stewarton, who were under rare and sad exercise of mind, he lay down under heaviness that he never had such experience of, and, in the midst of his sleep, there came such a terror of the wrath of God upon him, that if it had but increased a little higher, or continued but a few minutes longer, he had been in a most dreadful condition. But it was instantly removed, and he thought it was said within his heart, "See what a fool thou art to desire the thing thou couldst not endure."

In his preaching he was sometimes much deserted and cast down, and again at other times greatly assisted. He himself declares, that he never preached a sermon, excepting two, that he would be earnest to see again in print. The first was at the Kirk of Shotts, as already noticed, and the other on a communion Mon-

ROTTERDAM.

day, at Holywood in Ireland; and both these times he had spent
the night before in conference and prayer with some Christians,
without more than ordinary preparation. For otherwise, says he,
his gift was rather suited to common people, than to learned, judicious auditors. He had a tolerable insight into the Hebrew,
Chaldee, and somewhat of the Syriac languages. Arabic he did
essay, but did not persevere in it. He had as much of the
French, Italian, Dutch, and Spanish, as enabled him to make use
of their books and Bibles. It was thrice laid upon him by the
General Assembly to write the history of the Church of Scotland
since the Reformation of 1638; but this, for certain reasons, he
altogether omitted. The greater part of his time in Holland he
spent in reducing the original text into a Latin translation of the
Bible; and for this purpose compared that by Pagninus with the
original text and with the later translations, such as the Munster,
the Tigurine, Junius, Diodati, the English, but especially the Dutch,
which he thought was the most accurate translation.

Whether by constant sitting at these studies, or from some other
reasons, such as the infirmities of old age creeping on, he could not
determine, but since the year 1664, there was such a continual pain
contracted in his bladder, that he could not walk abroad, and a shak-

ing of his hands, that he could scarcely write any. Otherwise, he blessed the Lord that hitherto he had found no great defection either in body or mind.

Thus he continued at Rotterdam until August 9, 1672, when he died. Some of his last words were, " Carry my commendation to Jesus Christ, till I come there myself." After a pause, he added, " I die in the faith, that the truths of God, which He hath helped the Church of Scotland to own, shall be owned by Him as truths as long as sun and moon endure, and that Independency, though there be good men and well-meaning professors of that way, will be found more to the prejudice of the work of God than many are aware of. I have had my own faults, as well as other men, but He made me always abhor show. I have, I know, given offence to many, through my slackness and negligence ; but I forgive, and desire to be forgiven." After a pause, for he was not able to speak much at a time, he said, " I would not have people to forecast the worst, but there is a dark cloud above the reformed Churches, which prognosticates a storm coming." His wife, fearing what shortly followed, desired him to take leave of his friends : " I dare not (replied he, with an affectionate tenderness), but it is likely our parting will only be for a short time." After this he fell asleep in the Lord.

Since our Reformation commenced in Scotland, there have been none whose labours in the Gospel have been more remarkably blessed with the downpouring of the Spirit in conversion work than John Livingstone. Yea, it is a question if any one, since the primitive times, can produce so many convincing and confirming seals of his ministry; as witness the Kirk of Shotts, and Holywood in Ireland, at which two places, it is said, about 1500 souls were either confirmed or converted and brought to Christ.

His works, besides his letter from Leith, 1663, to his parishioners at Ancrum, are, his Memorable Characteristics of Divine Providence, and a manuscript of his own life, of which this is an abbreviation. He also (while in his Patmos of Holland) wrote a new Latin translation of the Old Testament, which was revised and approved of by Vossius, Essenius, Nethnues, Luesden, and other eminent lights of that time. Before his death, it was put into the hands of the last named to be printed.

John Semple.

HIS extraordinary man was first employed as precentor to one of the ministers in Ireland, supposed to be Blair, Livingstone, or Cunningham. Having given evidence of very decided gifts and graces, he was set apart to the office of Scripture reader or catechist, and in this capacity became an eminent instrument of saving souls. Leaving Ireland, he came over to Kirkcudbright, where, after undergoing a searching examination for the ministry, he was appointed to the newly-constituted Church and parish of Carsphairn.—Ed.]

John Semple was, for his exemplary walk and singular piety, held in such esteem and veneration, that all ranks of people stood in awe of him ; and particularly the clergy, he being a great check upon the lazy and corrupt part of them, who oftentimes were much afraid of him. One time, coming from Carsphairn to Sanquhar, being twelve rough miles, on a Monday morning after the Sacrament, the ministers, being still in bed, got up in all haste, to prevent his reproof ; but he, perceiving them putting on their clothes, said, " What will become of the sheep, when the shepherds sleep so long ? In my way hither, I saw some shepherds on the hills looking after their flocks." This, considering his age, and early journey so many miles, after he had preached the day before at home, had much influence on them, and made them feel somewhat ashamed.

He was one who very carefully attended church-judicatories, from which he was seldom absent, and that from a principle of conscience; so that almost no impediment could hinder him in his purpose. One time going to the presbytery of Kirkcudbright, twenty miles distant from Carsphairn, when about to ford the water of Dee, he was told by some that it was impassable ; yet he persisted, saying, " I must go through, if the Lord will ; I am going about His work." He entered in, and the strength of the current carrying him and his horse beneath the ford, he fell, but immediately stood upright in the water, and, taking off his hat, he prayed a word; after which he and his horse got safely out, to the admiration of all the spectators.

He was also a man much given to secret prayer. He ordinarily prayed in the kirk before sacramental occasions, oftentimes setting apart Friday in wrestling with the Lord for his gracious presence on the Sabbath. He was often favoured with merciful returns, to the great comfort of ministers and people; and would appoint a week-day thereafter for thanksgiving to God.

As he was faithful and laborious in his Master's service, so he was also most courageous and bold, having no respect of persons, but sharply reproving all sorts of wickedness in the highest as well as in the lowest. And yet he was so convincingly a man of God, that the most wicked had a love for, and sometimes spoke very favourably of him, as one who wished their souls well; so much so that one time, some persons of quality calling him a varlet, another person of quality, whom he had often reproved for his wickedness, being present, said, he was sure, if he were, he was one of God's varlets. At another time, a gentleman, from whose house he was going home, sent one of the rudest of his servants, well furnished with a horse, broadsword, and loaded pistols, to attack him in a desert place in the night-time, and to do all that he could to frighten him. Accordingly he surprised him by holding a pistol to his breast, bidding him render up his purse, under pain of being shot; but Semple, with much presence of mind, although he knew nothing of the design, answered, " It seems you are a wicked man, who will either take my life or my purse, if God gives you leave. As for my purse, it will not do you much service, though you had it; and for my life, I am willing to lay it down when and where God pleaseth; however, if you will lay by your weapons, I will wrestle a fall with you for my life; which, if you be a man, you cannot refuse, seeing I have no weapons to fight with." After many threats (though all in vain), the servant revealed the plot, and asked him, if he was not at the first afraid? " Not in the least," answered he, " for although you had killed me, as I knew not but you might, I was sure to get the sooner to heaven;" and then they parted.

Mr Semple was a man who knew much of his Master's mind, as evidently appears by his discovering of several future events. When news came that Cromwell and those with him were engaged in the trial of Charles I., some persons asked him, what he thought would become of the king. He went to his closet a little, and coming back, he said to them, "the king is gone, he will neither do us good nor ill any more;" which of a truth came to pass. At another time, passing by the house at Kenmuir, as the masons were making some additions thereunto, he said, "Lads, ye are busy, enlarging and repairing the house, but it will be burnt like a crow's nest in a misty morning," which accordingly came to pass, for it was burnt in a dark misty morning by the English. Upon a certain time, when a neighbouring minister was distributing tokens before the Sacrament, and was reaching a token to a certain woman, Mr Semple (standing by) said, "Hold your hand, she hath gotten too many tokens already ; she is a witch ;" which, though none suspected her then, she herself confessed to be true, and was deservedly put to death for the same.

At another time, a minister in the shire of Galloway sent one of his elders to Mr Semple with a letter, earnestly desiring his help at the Sacrament, which was to be in three weeks after. He read the letter, went to his closet, and coming back, he said to the elder, "I am sorry you have come so far on a needless errand ; go home, and tell your minister, he hath had all the communions that ever he will have, for he is guilty of fornication, and God will bring it to light ere that time." This likewise came to pass. He often said to Lord Kenmuir, that he was a rough wicked man, for which God would shake him over hell before he died, and yet God would give him his soul for a prey; which had its accomplishment at last, to the no small comfort and satisfaction of all his near and dear relations.

When some Scots regiment, in the year 1648, was on its march through Carsphairn for Preston in England, to the Duke's engagement, (as it was commonly called), hearing that the Sacrament was to be dispensed next Lord's day, some of the soldiers put up their horses in the kirk, went to the manse, and destroyed the communion elements, in a most profane manner, Mr Semple being then from home. The next day he complained to the commanding officer in such a pathetic manner, representing the horrible vileness of such an action, that the officer not only regretted the action, but gave money for furnishing the elements again. He moreover told them, he was sorry for the errand they were going upon, for it would not prosper, and the profanity of that army would ruin them. About or after this, he went up to a hill and prayed ; and being interrogated by some acquaintances, What answer he got? He replied, That he had fought with neither small nor great, but with the Duke himself, whom he never left until he was beheaded. This also was sadly verified.

His painful endeavours were blessed with no small success, especially on sacramental occasions. This the devil envied very much, and particularly one time, among many, when Semple designed to administer the Lord's Supper ; before which he assured the people of a great communion, by a gracious and remarkable down-pouring of the Spirit, but that the devil would be envious about this good work, and that he was afraid he would be permitted to raise a storm or speat of rain, designing to drown some of them. "But," said he, "it shall not be in his power to drown any of you—no, not so much as a dog." Accordingly, it came to pass on Monday, that, when he was dismissing the people, they saw a man all in black entering the water a little above them, at which they were amazed, as the stream was very large. He lost his feet, as they apprehended, and came down on his back, waving his hand ; the people ran and got ropes, and threw them to him, and there were ten or twelve men upon the ropes, yet they were in danger of being all drawn into the water and drowned. Semple looking on, cried, "Quit the rope, and let him go ; I see who it is, it is the devil ; he will burn, but not drown ; and by drowning of you would have God dishonoured, because He hath got some glory to His free grace in being king to many of your souls at this time." All search was made in that country to find if any man was lost, but none was heard of, which made them to conclude it to be the devil.*

John Semple, being one of the faithful Protesters, in the year 1657, was apprehended with James Guthrie, at Edinburgh, in August 1660. After ten months' imprisonment in the Castle, he was brought before the bloody Council, who threatened him severely with death and banishment : but he answered with boldness, "My God will not let you either kill or banish me ; but I will go home

---

* I have been restrained from expunging several of these incidents, only by a strong desire to reproduce this work, as far as possible, in its original form. At the same time, before pronouncing very severe judgment on the author or subject of the memoir, we should remember the character of the age in which they lived, and the vast change which has passed over the opinions of men, even within a comparatively recent period. The belief in witches, for instance, was at one time almost universal, and every country has its melancholy stories of witch-trials and witch-burnings. Travellers also, who have visited the Wartburg, will not forget the ink marks on the wall, the standing witness to Luther's belief in the real personal appearances of the Evil One.—ED.

and die in peace, and my dust will lie among the bodies of my people." Accordingly he was dismissed, and on going home and entering his pulpit, he said, "I parted with thee too easily, but I shall hang by the wicks of thee now." Some time after the Restoration, while under hiding, being one night in bed with another minister, the back-side of the bed falling down to the ground, the enemy came and carried away the other minister, but got not him, which was a most remarkable deliverance.

He was so concerned for the salvation of his people, that when on his death-bed he sent for them, and preached to them with much fervency, showing them their miserable state by nature, and their need of a Saviour; expressing his sorrow to leave many of them as graceless as he got them. He spake with so much vehemency, as made many of them weep bitterly.

He died at Carsphairn about the year 1677, being upwards of seventy years of age, in much assurance of heaven, often longing to be there, rejoicing in the God of his salvation, and under great impressions of dreadful judgments to come on these covenanted sinning lands. When scarcely able to speak, he cried three times over, "A Popish sword for thee, O Scotland, England, and Ireland!"

James Mitchell.

AMES MITCHELL was educated at the University of Edinburgh, and was, with some other of his fellow-students, made Master of Arts in the year 1656. Mr Robert Leighton, afterwards archbishop, being then principal of that college, before the degree was conferred upon them, tendered to them the national and Solemn League and Covenant; which covenants, upon mature deliberation, he took, finding nothing in them but a short compend of the moral law, binding to our duty towards

God, and towards man, in their several stations, and taking the King's interest to be therein included. When others were taking the tender to Oliver Cromwell, he subscribed the oath of allegiance to King Charles II.; but how he was repaid for this after the Restoration, the following account will more fully discover.

James Mitchell, having received a license to preach the Gospel, very soon after the Restoration, was, with the rest of his faithful brethren, reduced to many hardships and difficulties. " I find," says an historian, "Mr Trail, minister at Edinburgh in the year 1661, recommending him to some ministers in Galloway as a good youth, that had not much to subsist upon, and as fit for a school, or teaching gentlemen's children ; there being no door of access then to the ministry for him, or any such, when Prelacy was on such an advance in Scotland."

But whether he employed himself in this manner, or if he preached on some occasions as he had opportunity, we have no certain account, only we find he joined with that faithful handful who rose in 1666. He was not at the engagement at Pentland, being sent in by Captain Arnot to Edinburgh the day before, upon some necessary business ; he was excepted, however, from the indemnity in the several lists for that purpose. About six weeks after this, Mitchell went abroad in the trading way to Flanders, and was for some time upon the borders of Germany, after which he, in the space of three quarters of a year, returned home with some Dutchmen of Amsterdam, having a cargo of different sorts of goods, which took some time to dispose of.

James Mitchell was now excluded from all mercy or favour from the Government. Having not yet laid down arms, and taking the Archbishop of St Andrews to be the main instigator of all the oppression and bloodshed of his faithful brethren, he took a resolution in 1668 to despatch him. For that purpose, upon the 11th of July, he waited his coming down in the afternoon to his coach, at the head of Blackfriars' Wynd in Edinburgh, upon which occasion Sharp was accompanied by Honeyman, Bishop of Orkney. When the Archbishop had entered, and taken his seat in the coach, Mitchell stepped straight to the north side and discharged a pistol, loaded with three balls, in at the door thereof. Honeyman, who was setting his foot in the boot of the coach, and reaching up his hand to step in, received the shot in the wrist, and the Primate escaped. Upon this, Mitchell crossed the street with much composure, till he came to

ARCHBISHOP SHARP'S RESIDENCE, EDINBURGH.

Niddry's Wynd-head, where a man offered to stop him, to whom he presented a pistol, upon which he let him go ; and stepping down the Wynd, and up Stevenlaw's Close, he went into a house, changed his clothes, and came straight to the street, as being the place where he would be least suspected. The cry arose, that a man was killed ; upon which some replied, it was only a bishop, and all was very soon calmed. Upon Monday the 13th, the Council issued a proclamation, offering a reward of five thousand merks to any one that would discover the perpetrator, with pardon to accessories ; but nothing more at that time ensued.

The Council, and those of the prelatical persuasion, made a mighty noise and handle of this against the Presbyterians ; whereas the deed was his only, without the knowledge or preconcert of any, as he himself in a letter declares. Yea, with a design to bespatter the Presbyterian Church of Scotland, a most scurrilous pamphlet was published at London, not only reflecting on our excellent reformers from Popery, publishing arrant lies anent Alexander Henderson, abusing David Dickson, and breaking jests upon the Remonstrants and Presbyterians, as they called them, but also in a most malicious and groundless kind of rhapsody, slandering James Mitchell.

After this, Mitchell shifted the best way he could, until the

PORTRAIT OF THE DUKE OF LAUDERDALE.

beginning of the year 1674, when he was discovered by Sir William Sharp, the Archbishop's brother, who, ere ever Mitchell was aware, caused a number of his servants, armed for that purpose, to lay hold on him, and commit him to prison. On the 10th of February he was examined by the Lord Chancellor, Lord Register, and Lord Halton. He denied the assassination of the Archbishop; but being taken apart by the Chancellor, he confessed that it was he who shot the Bishop of Orkney, while aiming at the Archbishop. This he did upon assurance of his life, given by the Chancellor in these words: "Upon my great oath and reputation, if I be Chancellor, I shall save your life." On the 12th he was examined before the Council, and said nothing but what he had said before the Committee. He was remitted to the Justice Court to receive his indictment and sentence, which was, to have his right hand struck off at the cross of Edinburgh, and his goods forfeited, which last part was not to be executed till his Majesty had got notice; "because," says Lord Halton, in a letter to Earl Kincardine, "assurance of his life was given him upon his confession."

However, he was on the 2d of March brought before the Lords of Justiciary, and indicted for being concerned at Pentland, and for the attempt on the Archbishop of St Andrews. He pleaded not guilty; and insisted that the things alleged against him should be proved. The Lords postponed the affair till the 25th. Meanwhile, the Council made an act (March 12) specifying, "that Mr James Mitchell confessed his firing the pistol at the Archbishop of St Andrews, upon assurance given him of life by one of the Committee, who had a warrant from the Lord Commissioner and Secret Council to give the same, and therefore did freely confess," etc. In the said act, it was declared, "that on account of his refusing to adhere to his confession, the promises made to him were void; and that the Lords of Justiciary and Jury ought to proceed against him without any regard to these." About the 25th, he was brought before the Justiciary again; but, as there was no proof against him, they, with consent of the Advocate, protracted the affair; and he was again remanded to prison.

Thus he continued until January 6, 1676, when he was ordered to be examined before the Council by torture, concerning his being in the rebellion, as they termed it, in the year 1666. Accordingly, he was brought before them upon the 18th about six o'clock at night. Linlithgow, being president, told him he was brought before them to see whether he would adhere to his former confession. He answered, "My Lord, it is not unknown to your Lordship, and others here present, that, by the Council's order, I was remitted to the Lords of Justiciary, before whom I received an indictment at my Lord Advocate's instance, to which indictment I answered at three several diets; and the last diet being deserted by my Lord Advocate, I humbly conceive, that, both by the law of the nation and the practice of this Court, I ought to have been set at liberty; yet notwithstanding, I was, contrary to law, equity, and justice, returned to prison, and upon what account I am this night before you, I am ignorant." The president told him he was only called to see if he would own his former confession. He replied, that he knew no crime he was guilty of, and therefore made no such confession as he alleged. Upon this the treasurer-depute said, that the panel was one of the most arrogant liars and rogues he had known. Mitchell replied, "My Lord, if there were fewer of these persons you have been speaking of in the nation, I should not be standing this night at the bar: but my Lord Advocate knoweth that what is alleged against me is not my confession." The president said, "Sir, we will cause a sharper thing make you confess." He answered, "My Lord, I hope you are Christians and not Pagans." Then he was returned to prison.

On the 22d, he was again called before them, to see if he would own his former confession, and a paper produced, alleged to be subscribed by him, but he would not acknowledge the same. The President said, "You see what is upon the table (meaning the Boots); I will see if that will make you do it." Mitchell answered, " My Lord, I confess, that by torture you may cause me to blaspheme God, as Saul did compel the saints; you may compel me to speak amiss of your Lordships, to call myself a thief, a murderer, and then panel me on it; but if you shall here put me to it, I protest before God and your Lordships, that nothing extorted from me by torture shall be made use of against me in judgment, nor have any force in law against me, or any other person. But to be plain with you, my Lords, I am so much of a Christian, that whatever your Lordships shall legally prove against me, if it be truth, I shall not deny it; but, on the contrary, I am so much of a man, and a Scotsman, that I never held myself obliged by the law of God, nature, and nations, to be my own accuser." The treasurer-depute said, " He hath the devil's logic, and sophisticates like him; ask him whether that be his subscription?" Mitchell replied, "I acknowledge no such thing;" and was then sent back to prison.

Upon the 24th, they assembled in their robes in the Inner Parliament House, and the Boots and executioner were presented. Mr Mitchell was again interrogated as above, but still persisting, he was ordered to the torture; and he knowing that, after the manner of the Spanish Inquisition, the more he confessed, either concerning himself or others, the more severe the torture would be to make him confess more, delivered himself in this manner: " My Lord, I have been now these two full years in prison, and more than one of them in bolts and fetters, which hath been more intolerable to me than many deaths, if I had been capable thereof; and it is well known that some, in a shorter time, have been tempted to make away with themselves; but respect and obedience to the express law and command of God hath made me to undergo all these hardships, and I hope this torture, with patience also, for the preservation of my own life, and the life of others, as far as lies in my power, and to keep innocent blood off your Lordships' persons and families, which, by the shedding of mine, you would doubtless bring upon yourselves and posterity, and wrath from the Lord to the consuming thereof, till there should be no escaping; and now again I protest. When you please, call for the man appointed for the work." The executioner being called, he was tied in a two-armed chair, and the Boot brought.

THE BOOTS.

The executioner asked which of the legs he should take; the Lords bade him take any of them. The executioner laying the left in the boot, Mitchell lifted it out again, saying, "Since the Judges have not determined, take the best of the two, for I freely bestow it in the cause," and so laid his right leg into the engine. After this the Advocate asked leave to speak but one word, but, notwithstanding, insisted at a great length; to which Mitchell answered: "The Advocate's word or two hath multiplied to so many, that my memory cannot serve, in the condition wherein I am (the torture being begun), to resume them in particular, but I shall essay to answer the scope of his discourse. Whereas he hath been speaking of the sovereignty of the magistrate, I shall go somewhat further than he hath done, and own that the magistrate whom God hath appointed is God's depute. Both the throne and the judgment are the Lord's, when he judgeth for God, and according to his law; and a part of his office is to deliver the poor oppressed out of the hand of the oppressor, and shed no innocent blood (Jer. xxii. 3). And whereas the Advocate has been hinting at the sinfulness of lying on any account; it is answered, that not only lying is sinful, but also a pernicious speaking of the truth is a horrid sin before the Lord, when it tendeth to the shedding of innocent blood; witness the case of

Doeg (Psalm lii. compared with 1 Sam. xxii. 18). But what my Lord Advocate has forged against me is false ; so that I am standing on my former ground, viz., the preservation of my own life, and the life of others, as far as lies in my power, the which I am expressly commanded by the Lord of Hosts."

Then the clerk's servant, being called, interrogated him during the torture in upwards of thirty questions, which were all in writing, of which the following are of the most importance :

Q. Are you that Mr James Mitchell who was excepted out of the King's grace and favour ?

A. I never committed any crime deserving to be excluded ?

Q. Were you at Pentland ?

A. No.

Q. Were you at Ayr ? and did you join with the rebels there ?

A. I never joined with any such.

Q. Where were you at the time of Pentland ?

A. In Edinburgh.

Q. When did you know of their rising in arms ?

A. When the rest of the city knew of it.

Q. Where did you meet with James Wallace ?*

A. I knew him not at that time.

Q. Did you go out of town with Captain Arnot ?

A. No.

The other questions were anent his going abroad, etc. He perceived that they intended to catch him in a contradiction, or to find any who would witness against him. At the beginning of the torture, he said, " My Lords, not knowing that I shall escape this torture with my life, I beseech you to remember what the apostle saith, ' He shall have judgment without mercy that hath shewed no mercy !' And now, my Lords, I do freely from my heart forgive you, who are sitting judges upon the bench, and the men who are appointed to be about this horrible piece of work, and also those who are vitiating their eyes in beholding the same ; and I entreat that God may never lay it to the charge of any of you, as I beg God may be pleased, for Christ's sake, to blot out my sins and iniquities, and never to lay them to my charge here or hereafter."

All this being over, the executioner took down his leg from a chest on which it was lying all the time in the Boot, and set both on

---

* This was Colonel Wallace, who commanded the Covenanters at Pentland.—
[ED.]

the ground ; and, thrusting in the shafts to drive the wedges, began his strokes—at every one of which, Mr Mitchell being asked if he had any more to say? answered No. Having, at the ninth stroke, fainted through the extremity of pain, the executioner cried, "Alas! my Lords, he is gone." Then they stopped the torture, and went off; and in a little time, when recovered, he was carried in the same chair to the Tolbooth.

It is indeed true, that James Mitchell made a confession, upon the promise of his life; but the Council having revoked their promise, because he would not adhere to his confession before the Justiciary (being advised by some friends not to trust too much to that promise), and be his own accuser, "the reader must determine," says a very impartial historian, "how far he was to blame now, in not owning his confession judicially, as they had judicially revoked the condition upon which the confession was made; and to put a man to torture for finding out things for which they had not the least proof, seems to be unprecedented and cruel; and to bring him to a farther trial, appears to be unjust." For as another author has well observed, "That when a confession or promise is made upon a condition, and that condition is judicially rescinded, the obligation of the promise or confession is taken away, and both parties are in *statu quo* (Jos. ii. 14); that in many cases it is lawful to conceal and obscure a necessary duty, and divert enemies from a pursuit of it for a time (1 Sam. xvi. 1, 2; Jer. xxxviii. 24); that when an open enemy perverts and overturns the very nature and matter of a discourse or confession, by leaving out the most material truths, and putting untruths and circumstances in their room, it no longer is the former discourse or confession; that when a person is brought before a limited judicatory, before whom nothing was ever confessed or proven, the person may justly stand to his defence, and put his enemies to bring in proof against him."

After this Mitchell continued in prison till the beginning of the following year, when he and Mr Fraser of Brea were, in charge of a party of twelve horse and thirty foot, sent to the Bass Rock, where he remained till about the 6th of December, at which time he was again brought to Edinburgh for his trial, which came on about the 7th of January 1678. On the 3d of that month, Sir George Lockhart and Mr John Ellis were appointed to plead for the panel; but Sharp would have his life, and Lauderdale gave way to him. Sir Archibald Primrose, lately turned out of the Register's place, took a copy of the

Council's act anent Mr Mitchell, and sent it to his counsel, and, a day or two before the trial, went to Lauderdale, who, together with Lord Rothes, Lord Halton, and Sharp were summoned as witnesses against the prisoner. Primrose told Lauderdale, that he thought a promise of life had been given; the latter denied it; the former wished that that act of the Council might be looked into; Lauderdale said he would not give himself the trouble to look over the books of Council.

When Mitchell's trial came on, the great proof was his confession, February 10, 1674; and many and long were the reasonings on the points of the indictment. Sir George Lockhart argued in behalf of the prisoner with great learning, to the admiration of the audience, that no extra-judicial confession could be allowed in Court, and that his confession was extorted from him by hopes and promises of life. The debates were so tedious that the Court adjourned to the 9th of January. The replies and duplies are too long to be inserted here, but the reader will find them at large in Wodrow's History.

The witnesses being examined, Lord Rothes (being shown Mr Mitchell's confession) swore that he was present, and saw him subscribe that paper, and heard him make that confession, but that he did not at all give any assurance to the prisoner for his life; nor did he remember that there was any warrant given by the Council to his Lordship for that effect. Halton and Lauderdale swore much to the same purpose; and the Archbishop swore, that he knew him, at the very first sight at the bar, to be the person who shot at him, but that he either gave him assurance, or a warrant to any to give it, was a false and malicious calumny. Nichol Sommerville, Mr Mitchell's brother-in-law, offered in Court to depone, that the Archbishop promised to him to secure his life, if he would prevail with him to confess. The Archbishop denied this, and called it a villainous lie. Several other depositions were taken; such as those of Sir William Paterson, Mr John Vanse, and the Bishop of Galloway, who all swore in Sharp's favour, it being dangerous for them, at this juncture, to do otherwise.

[On the records of the Privy Council it may yet be read, how, on the 12th of March 1674, Mitchell did "confess upon his knees he was the person, upon assurance given him by one of the committee as to his life, who had warrant from the Lord Commissioner and Council to give the same." In reference to the conduct of Sharp and the other witnesses on this occasion, Dr Burton, in his recently-published History, says that there was in it "that kind of crooked prevarication, that, in the eyes of some, is more offensive than a flat

THE BASS ROCK.

falsehood. It was by the committee that the promise was made, and the testimony of these witnesses was that none was given by the Council at large."—ED.]

After the witnesses were examined, the Advocate declared he had closed the probation; whereupon Mr Mitchell produced a copy of an act of Council, March 12, 1674, and prayed that the register might be produced, or the clerk obliged to give extracts; but this they refused to do. "Lockhart," says Burnet, "pleaded for this; but Lauderdale, who was only a witness, and had no right to speak, refused: and so it was neglected."

The assize was enclosed, and ordered to return their verdict to-morrow afternoon; which being done, the sentence was pronounced, "That the said Mr James Mitchell should be taken to the Grass-market of Edinburgh, upon Friday the 18th of January instant, between two and four o'clock in the afternoon, and there be hanged on a gibbet till he be dead, and all his moveables, goods, and gear be escheat, and in-brought to his Majesty's use." No sooner did the Court break up, than the Lords, being up-stairs, found the act recorded, and signed by Lord Rothes, the president of the Council.

"This action," says the last cited historian, "and all concerned in it, were looked on by the people with horror; and it was such a

THE GRASSMARKET OF EDINBURGH.

complication of treachery, perjury, and cruelty, as the like had not perhaps been known."

Two days after the sentence, orders came from Court for placing Mr Mitchell's head and hands on some public place of the city; but the sentence being passed, no alteration could be made; and, if Sharp had any hand in this, he missed his end and design. About the same time, Mitchell's wife petitioned the Council that her husband might be reprieved for some time, that she might see him and take her last farewell, especially as it was not above twelve days since she was delivered of a child, and was presently affected with a fever. But no regard was paid to this; the sentence must be executed.

While Mitchell was in prison, he emitted a large and most faithful testimony. In the first place he testifies against all profanity. Then he gives the cause of his suffering, in the words of Elijah, 1 Kings xix. 14, "I have been very jealous for the Lord God of hosts." He adheres to the covenanted work of Reformation and the Covenants; approves of *Lex Rex*, the Causes of God's Wrath, the Apological Relation, Naphtali, *Jus Populi*, etc. Afterwards he speaks of magistracy in these words :—" I believe magistracy to be an ordinance and appointment of God, as well under the New Testament as it was under the Old; and that whosoever resisteth the lawful magistrate in the exercise of his lawful power, resisteth the ordinance and appointment of God, Rom. xiii. 1, etc., 1 Pet. ii. 13, Deut. xvii. 15. The lawful magistrate must be a man qualified according to God's appointment, and not according to the people's lust and pleasure, lest in the end he should prove to them a prince of Sodom, and governor of Gomorrah, whom God in His righteousness should appoint for their judgment, and establish for their correction." Then he comes to be most explicit against the givers and receivers of the Indulgence, as an encroachment on Christ's crown and prerogative royal ; protests before God, angels, and men, against all acts in anywise derogatory to the work of God and Reformation ; likewise protests against all banishments, imprisoning, finings, and confinements, that the people of God have been put to for some years bypast, describing the woful state and condition of malignants, and all the enemies of Jesus Christ. And, in the last place, he speaks very fervently anent his own sufferings, state, and condition, which he begins to express in these words : " Now, if the Lord, in His wise and over-ruling providence, bring me to the close of my pilgrimage, to the full enjoyment of my long-looked-for and desired happiness, let Him take His own way and time in bringing me to it. And in the meantime, O thou my soul ! sing thou this song, Spring thou up, O well of thy happiness and salvation, of thy eternal hope and consolation : and whilst thou art burdened with this clog and tabernacle of clay, dig thou deep in it by faith, hope, and charity, and with all the instruments that God hath given thee ; dig in it by precepts and promises ; dig carefully, and dig continually ; ay, and until thou come to the Source and Head of the Fountain Himself, from whence the water of life floweth ; dig until thou come to the assembly of the first-born, where this song is most suitably sung, to the praise and glory of the rich grace and mercy of the Fountain of Life." And farther, when speaking of his mortification to the world, and other experiences, he says, " Although, O Lord, Thou shouldst send me, in the back tract and tenor of my life, to seek my soul's comfort and encouragement from them, yet I have no cause to complain of hard dealing from Thy hand, seeing it is Thy ordinary way with some of Thy people. 'O my God, my soul is cast down within me : therefore will I remember Thee from the land of Jordan and of the Hermonites ' (Psalm xlii. 6). Yea, the last time He brought me to the banqueting-house, and made love His banner over me, among the cold Highland hills beside Kippen, November 1673, He remembered his former loving-kindness towards me. But withal He spoke in mine ear, that there was a tempestuous storm to meet me in the face, which I behoved to go through in the strength of that provision." Then, after the reciting of several Scriptures, as comforting to him in his sufferings, he comes at last to conclude with these words : " And seeing I have not preferred nor sought after mine own things, but Thy honour and glory, the good, liberty, and safety of Thy Church and people (although it be now misconstrued by many), yet I hope at length that thou, Lord, wilt make my light to break forth as the morning, and my righteousness as the noon-day, and that shame and darkness shall cover all who are adversaries to my righteous cause ; for Thou, O Lord, art the shield of my head, and the sword of my excellency ; and mine enemies shall be found liars, and shall be subdued. Amen, yea, and amen."

Accordingly, upon the 18th of January, he was taken to the Grassmarket of Edinburgh, and the sentence put in execution. In the morning he delivered some copies of what he had to say, if permitted, at his death ; but not having liberty to deliver this part of his vindicatory speech to the people, he threw it over the scaffold, the substance of which was as follows :

" CHRISTIAN PEOPLE,

" It being rumoured abroad, immediately after I received my sentence, that I would not have liberty to speak in this place, I have not troubled myself to prepare any formal discourse, on account of the pretended crime for which I am accused and sentenced. Neither did I think it very necessary, the fame of the process having gone so much abroad, and that by a former indictment given me near four years ago, the diet of which was suffered to desert, in respect the late Advocate could not find a just way to reach me with the extra-judicial confession they opponed to me. All knew he was zealous in it, yet my charity to him is such, that he would not suffer that unwarrantable zeal so far to blind him, as to overstretch the laws of the land beyond their due limits, in prejudice of the life of a native subject : first, by an extreme inquiry of torture, and then by exiling me to the Bass, and then, after all, by giving me a new indictment at the instance of the new Advocate, who before was one of mine when I received the first indictment. To this new indictment, and debate in the process, I refer you ; and particularly to these two defences of an extra-judicial confession, and the promise of life given to me by the Chancellor, upon his own and the public faith of the kingdom; upon the verity whereof I am content to die, and ready to lay down my life, and hope your charity to me, a dying man, will be such as not to mistrust me therein; especially since this is notoriously proved by Act of Secret Council, although denied upon oath by the principal officers of State present in Council at the making of said Act, and whom the Act bears to have been present (the Duke of Lauderdale, his Majesty's Commissioner; being among the rest); which Act of Council was, by the Lords of Justiciary, most unjustly repelled. This much for a short account of the affair for which I am unjustly brought to this place. I acknowledge, however, that my private and particular sins have been such as deserved a worse death to me; but I hope in the merits of Jesus Christ, to be freed from the eternal punishment due to me for sin. I am confident that God doth not plead with me in this place for my private and particular sins, but I am brought here that the work of God may be made manifest for the trial of faith (John ix. 3, 1 Pet. i. 7); that I might be a witness for His despised truths and interests in this land, where I am called to seal the same with my blood; and I wish heartily that this my poor life may put an end to the persecu-tion of the true members of Christ in this place, so much urged by these perfidious prelates, in opposition to whom, and in testimony to the cause of Christ, I, at this time, lay down my life, and bless God that he hath thought me so much worthy as to do the same, for His glory and interest. Finally, concerning a Christian duty, in a singular and extraordinary case, and anent my particular judgment, concerning both Church and State, it is evidently declared and mani-fested elsewhere. Farewell all earthly enjoyments; and welcome Father, Son, and Holy Ghost, into whose hands I commit my spirit."

Here we have heard the end of the zealous and faithful James Mitchell, who, beyond all doubt, was a most pious man, notwith-standing the foul aspersions that have been, or will be, cast upon him, not only by malignant prelates, but even by the high-fliers or more corrupt part of the Presbyterian persuasion, on account of his firing at Archbishop Sharp; which, they think, is enough to explode, affront, or bespatter, all the faithful contendings of the true reformed and covenanted Church of Scotland. But in this Mitchell stands in need of little or no vindication; for by this time the reader may perceive, that he looked upon himself as in a state of war, and that, as Sharp was doubtless one of the chief instigators of the tyranny, bloodshed, and oppression in that dismal period, he no doubt thought that he had a right to take every opportunity of cutting him off, especially as all the ways of common justice were blocked up.

Yet all this opens no door for every private person at his own hand to execute justice on an open offender, where there is access to a lawful magistrate appointed for that end. Yea, what Mitchell himself saith anent this affair, in a letter dated Feb. 1674, is sufficient to stop the mouths of all that have, or may oppose the same, a few words of which may be quoted. After relating what passed betwixt him and the Chancellor, he says, that as to his design against Sharp, he looked on him to be the main instigator of all the oppression and bloodshed of his brethren that followed thereupon, and of the continual pursuing of his life; and he being a soldier, not having laid down arms, but being still upon his own defence, and having no other end or quarrel against any man, but what (according to his apprehension of him) may be understood by the many thousands of the faithful; besides the prosecution of the end of the same Covenant, which was, and is, in that point, the overthrow of prelates and prelacy; he being a declared enemy to him on that account, and he to him in like manner; and as he was always to take his advantage, he took of him also any opportunity that offered. "For," says he, "I, by his instigation, being excluded from all grace and favour, thought it my duty to pursue him on all occasions." A little farther on he instances Deut. xiii. 9, where the seducer or enticer to a false worship is to be put to death, and that by the hand of the witnesses, whereof he was one; he takes notice of Phinehas, Elijah, etc.; and then observing, that while the bishops would say that what they did was by law and authority, but what he did was contrary to both, he answers: "The King himself, and all the Estates of the land, both were and are obliged, by the oath of God upon them, to extirpate the perjured prelates and prelacy; and, in doing thereof, to defend one another with their lives and fortunes."

John Welwood.

OHN WELWOOD was born about the year 1649. He was son of Mr James Welwood, sometime minister in Tindergarth, in the county of Dumfries, and brother of Messrs Andrew Welwood and James Welwood, doctors of medicine at London. After having gone through the ordinary course of learning, he was licensed for the ministry, and afterwards preached in many places; but we do not hear that he was ever settled minister in any parish, it being then a time when all, who had any honesty or faithfulness in testifying against the sins and defections of the times, were thrust out of the Church, and prosecuted with the greatest severity. It is said that he preached five or six sermons in the parish where his father was minister, which were blessed with more discernible effects of good amongst that people than all the diligent painfulness his father had exercised.

Besides his singular piety and faithfulness in preaching, he was most fervent in pressing home all the duties of the Christian life, particularly the setting up and keeping of fellowship and society meetings for prayer and Christian conference, which he often frequented. One time, among several others, at Newhouse, in Livingstone parish, the night being far spent, he said: "Let one pray, and be short, that we may win to our apartments before it be light." It was the turn of one who exceeded many in gifts. But before he ended it was daylight within the house. After prayer, Welwood said: "James, James, your gifts have the start of your graces;" and to the rest he said: "Be advised, all of you, not to follow him at all times, and in all things; otherwise there will be many ins and many outs in your tract and walk."

In the year 1677, there was an Erastian meeting of the actually indulged and non-indulged, got up by the indulged and their favourites, in order, as they pretended, to promote a union between the parties; but rather, in reality, a conspiracy, without any honour or veracity, among these backsliders and false prophets. John Welwood, Richard Cameron, and another minister, were called before this meeting, in order to be deposed, or their license taken from them, for their faithfulness in preaching up separation from the actually indulged. But they declined their authority, as being no lawful judicatory of Jesus Christ, whilst thus made up of those who were indulged. Some of them went to Mr Hog, who was then in town, though not at this meeting, for his advice anent them: to whom he said, "His name is Welwood; but if ye take that unhappy course to depose him, he will perhaps turn out the Torwood at last."

John Welwood was a man of a lean and tender body. He slept, ate, and drank but little, as being under deep exercise about the defections and tyranny of that day, especially concerning the indulged, and the many who were pleading in their favour; and being of a sickly constitution before, he turned more melancholy and tender. Much about this time, he was informed against to the Council at Edinburgh, that he had intruded upon the kirk of Tarbolton, in the shire of Ayr. The Council appointed Glencairn and Lord Ross to see that he be turned out and apprehended; but nothing further can be learned anent this order.

One Sabbath, when he was going to preach, and the tent was set up for him, the laird, on whose ground it was, lifted it, and set it on that of another laird. But when Welwood saw it, he said, "in a short time he shall not have one furr of land." Some quarrelled him for saying so, this laird being then a great professor. He said, "Let alone a little, and he will turn out in his own colours." Shortly after this he was convicted of adultery, and became most miserable and contemptible, being, as was said, one of the Duke of York's four-pound Papists.

In the beginning of the year 1679, he said to William Nicholson, a Fifeshire man, "Ye shall have a brave summer of the Gospel this year; and for your further encouragement, an old man or woman, for very age, may live to see the bishops down, and yet the church not delivered; but ere all be done, we will get a few faithful ministers in Scotland to hear. But keep still amongst the faithful poor mourning remnant that is for God; for there is a cloud coming on the Church of Scotland, the like of which was never heard of, for the most part will turn to defection. But I see, on the other side of it, the Church's

OLD VIEW OF PERTH.

delivery, with ministers and Christians such as you would be ashamed
to open a mouth before."

Among his last public days of preaching, he preached at Boulterhall in Fife, upon that text, 1 Cor. i. 26 : " Not many noble are
called." Here he wished that all the Lord's people, whom He
had placed in stations of distinction, there and everywhere, would
express their thankfulness that the words, *not many*, were not, *not
any*, and that the whole of them were not excluded. In the end
of that sermon he said, pointing to St Andrews, " If that unhappy
Prelate Sharp die the natural death of men, God never spoke by
me." The Archbishop had a servant who, upon liberty from his
master on Saturday night, went to visit his brother, who was a
servant to a gentleman near Boulterhall, the Archbishop ordering
him to be home on Sabbath night. He went with the laird and his
brother on that day. Mr Welwood noticed him with the Archbishop's
livery on ; and when sermon was ended, he desired him to stand up,
for he had somewhat to say to him. " I desire you," said he, " before
all these witnesses, when thou goest home, to tell thy master, that his
treachery, tyranny, and wicked life, are near an end, and his death
shall be both sudden, surprising, and bloody, and as he had thirsted
after, and shed the blood of the saints, he shall not go to his grave in

peace." The youth went home, and at supper the Archbishop asked him if he had been at a conventicle? He said he had. He asked what the text was, and what he heard? The man told him several things, and particularly the above message from Mr Welwood. The Archbishop made sport of it, but his wife said, "I advise you to take more notice of that, for I hear that these men's words are not vain words."

Shortly after this he went to Perth, and there lodged in the house of John Barclay. His bodily weakness increasing, he was laid aside from serving his Master in public, and lingered under a consumptive distemper, until the beginning of April 1679, when he died. During the time of his sickness, while he was able to speak, he still laid himself out to do good to souls. None but such as were looked upon to be friends to the persecuted cause knew that he was in town, and his practice was to call them in, one family after another, at different times, and discourse to them about their spiritual state. His conversation was both convincing, edifying, and confirming. Many came to visit him, and among the rest, Mr Ayton, younger of Inchdarney, in Fife, a pious youth about eighteen years of age. On giving Mr Welwood an account of the great tyranny and wickedness of Prelate Sharp, Mr Welwood said, "You will shortly be quit of him; and he will get a sudden and *sharp* off-going; and you will be the first that will take the good news of his death to heaven." This literally came to pass the May following.

About the same time, he said to another who came to visit him, that many of the Lord's people would be in arms that summer for the defence of the Gospel; but he was fully persuaded that they would work no deliverance, and that, after the fall of that party, the public standard of the Gospel would fall for some time, so that there would not be a true faithful minister in Scotland, excepting two, unto whom they could resort, to hear or converse with anent the state of the Church; that they would also seal their testimony with their blood; and that after this there would be a dreadful defection and apostacy; but God would pour out His wrath upon the enemies of His church and people, whereby many of the Lord's people, who had made defection from His way, would fall among the rest in this common calamity. This stroke, he thought, would not be long, and upon the back thereof there would be the most glorious deliverance and Reformation that ever was in Britain, wherein the Church would never be troubled any more with Prelacy.

When drawing near his end, in conversation with some friends, Welwood used frequently to communicate his own exercise and experience, with the assurance he had obtained of his interest in Christ, saying, " I have no more doubt of my interest in Christ, than if I were in heaven already." And at another time he said, " Although I have been for some weeks without sensible comforting presence, yet I have not the least doubt of my interest in Christ ; I have oftentimes endeavoured to pick a hole in my interest, but cannot get it done." That morning ere he died, when he observed the light of the day, he said, " Now eternal light, and no more night and darkness to me :" and that night, he exchanged a weakly body, a wicked world, and a weary life, for an immortal crown of glory, in that heavenly inheritance which is prepared and reserved for such as him.

The night after his death, his corpse was removed from John Barclay's house into a private room, belonging to one Janet Hutton, till his friends might consult about his funeral, that so he might not be put to trouble for having concealed him. It was quickly spread abroad, however, that an intercommuned preacher was dead in town, upon which the magistrates ordered a messenger to go and arrest the corpse. It lay there that night ; and the next day, a considerable number of his friends in Fife, in good order, came to town to attend his burial. The magistrates, however, would not suffer him to be interred at Perth, but ordered the town militia to be raised, and imprisoned John Bryce, boxmaster or treasurer to the guildry, for refusing to give out the arms. However, they gave his friends leave to carry his corpse out of town, and bury it without the precincts, where they pleased ; but any of the town's people who were observed to accompany the funeral were imprisoned. After they were gone out of town, his friends sent two men before them to Drone, four miles from Perth, to prepare a grave in the churchyard. The men went to Mr Pitcairn, the minister there (one of the old Resolutioners) and desired the keys of the churchyard, that they might dig a grave for the corpse of Mr Welwood ; but he refused to give them. They went over the churchyard dyke, and digged a grave, and there the corpse was interred.

There appears to be only one of his sermons in print, said to be preached at Bogleshole, in Clydesdale, upon 1 Peter iv. 18: " And if the righteous scarcely be saved, where shall the ungodly and the sinner appear ? " There are also some of his religious letters written to his godly friends and acquaintances, yet extant in manuscript.

We are not to expect, however, to meet with anything considerable of the writings of John Welwood, or of the succeeding Worthies, seeing that, in such an afflicted state of the Church, they were constantly upon the watch, hunted and hurried from place to place, without the least time or convenience for writing; yea, and oftentimes what little fragments they had collected, fell into the hands of false friends and enemies, and were by them either destroyed or lost.

William Gordon of Earlstoun.

ILLIAM GORDON of Earlstoun was a son of that great reformer, Alexander Gordon of Earlstoun, and was lineally descended from that famous Alexander Gordon who entertained the followers of John Wickliffe, and who had a New Testament in the vulgar tongue, which they used to read in their meeting at the wood near Airds, beside Earlstoun. William Gordon, having thus the advantage of a religious education, began very early to follow Christ. As early as the year 1637, Samuel Rutherford, in a letter, admonished him thus: "Sir, lay the foundation thus, and ye shall not soon shrink nor be shaken; make tight work at the bottom, and your ship shall ride against all storms; if withal your anchor be fastened on good ground; I mean, within the vail." And, indeed, by the blessing of God, he began very early to distinguish himself for piety and religion, with a firm attachment to the Presbyterian interest, and the covenanted work of reformation, in which he continued steadfast and unmovable until he lost his life in the honourable cause.

What hand he had in the public affairs during Cromwell's usurpation I cannot so well say; we must suppose him, however, upon the Remonstrants' side. But the first public testimony he gave after the Restoration of Charles II., recorded in history, was about the year 1663, when commissioners were appointed by the Council to go south and inquire anent some opposition that was then made by the people to the settlement of curates at Kirkcudbright and Irongray. The said commissioners, knowing this worthy gentleman's firmness to Presbyterian principles, were resolved either to make him comply in settling an Episcopal incumbent in the parish of Dalry in Galloway, where, by the once Established laws, he had some right in presenting ; or, if he refused to concur with the bishop, which they had all reason imaginable to suspect he would, to bring him to further trouble. Accordingly, they wrote him a letter, in the following tenor :

"Finding the church of Dalry to be one of those to which the bishop hath presented an actual minister, Mr George Henry, fit and qualified for the charge, and that the gentleman is to come to your parish this Sabbath next to preach to that people, and that you are a person of special interest there, we do require you to cause this edict to be served, and the congregation to convene and countenance him, so as to be encouraged to prosecute his ministry in that place.— Your loving friends and servants,

"LINLITHGOW.
"GALLOWAY.
"ANNANDALE.
"DRUMLANARK."

To this letter Earlstoun gave a most respectful reply, showing, upon solid reasons, why he could not comply with their unjust demand, as the following excerpt from that letter evidences : "I ever judged it safest to obey God, and stand at a distance from whatsoever doth not tend to God's glory, and the edification of the souls of His scattered people, of which that congregation is a part. And besides, my Lords, it is known to many, that I pretend to lay claim to the right of patronage of that parish, and that I have already determined therein, with the consent of the people, to a truly worthy and qualified person, that he may be admitted to exercise his gifts amongst that people ; and for me to countenance the bearer of your Lordships' letter, were to procure me most impiously and dishonourably to wrong the majesty of God, and violently to take away the Christian liberty of His afflicted people, and enervate my own right." Though this worthy gentleman mentions the right of patronage, yet it is with this proviso or limitation—the choice or consent of the people ; otherwise, says he, it would wrong the majesty of God, take away the Christian liberty of the people, and invalidate his own right. How unlike is this to the species of patronage and claim of patrons at this time, when nothing but absolute power and arbitrary measures will satisfy them.

This was, without question, what the Government wanted, and so his trouble began ; for, on the 30th of July following, " The Lords of Council order letters to be directed to charge William Gordon of Earlstoun to compear before them, to answer for his seditious and factious carriage ; " that is, his refusing to comply with Prelacy, and hear the curates, and his favouring and hearing the outed ministers. And further, November 24, the same year, " The Council being informed that the Laird of Earlstoun kept conventicles and private meetings in his house, do order letters to be directed against him, to compear before this Council, to answer for his contempt, under pain of rebellion." But all this nowise dashed the courage of this faithful confessor of Christ in adhering to his persecuted and despised Gospel ; which made these malignant enemies yet pass a more severe and rigorous act against him : in which it was exhibited, that he had been at several conventicles (as they were pleased to call the preachings of the Gospel) where Mr Gabriel Semple, a deposed minister, did preach in the Corsock Wood and Wood of Airds, and heard texts of Scripture explained, both in his mother's and in his own house, by outed ministers ; and that being required to enact himself to abstain from all such meetings in time coming, and to live peaceably and orderly, conform to law, he refused to do the same. They did, therefore, order the said William Gordon of Earlstoun to be banished, and to depart forth of the kingdom within a month, and not to return under pain of death, and that he live peaceably during that time, under the penalty of £10,000, or otherwise to enter his person in prison.

It would appear, that he did not obey this sentence ; and, although we have little or no particular account of his sufferings, yet we are assured he endured a series of hardships. In the year 1667, he was turned out of his house and all, and the house made a garrison for Bannatyne, that wicked wretch, and his party ; after which, almost every year produced him new troubles, until the 22d or 23d of June 1679, when he emerged out of all his troubles, arrived at the haven of rest, and obtained his glorious reward.

[Three weeks before this the Covenanters had obtained a signal victory over Claverhouse and his dragoons. It was a Sabbath day, and a large number were assembled, for public worship, at a place called Drumclog, not far from Loudon Hill. When the minister, Mr Douglas, was beginning his sermon, one of the watchmen stationed on a neighbouring height fired his signal-gun, and soon afterwards Claverhouse was seen approaching from the east. "The armed men," to quote the words of Mr Dodds in his "Fifty Years' Struggle of the Scottish Covenanters," "drew out firmly and orderly from the rest of the meeting. Their aged parents, their wives, children, and kindred, and those of them who had no weapons, were left behind, and directed to retire slowly towards some security, in case their defenders should be overpowered. There they mustered on that hill-side, transformed at once from a peaceful assemblage of Christian worshippers into a body of stern and fearless warriors, ready to the last drop of their blood to protect their homes and the muirland temple of their God. They formed into a compact mass of fifty horse, fifty footmen with guns, and 150 on foot who were only equipped with halberts, pikes, and other rude and inefficient weapons. Hamilton took the command, and was supported by brave men and skilful soldiers, who acted as his officers—the veteran Henry Hall of Haughhead in Teviotdale, Hackston, and Burley, and the gallant young soldier-poet, the Körner of the Covenanting party, William Cleland of Douglas, now only in his eighteenth year. Being formed in battle array, a grand old tradition survives, which tells how this little host marched in solemn majesty down the brow of the hill, singing together, to the half-plaintive, half-triumphant 'Martyrs,' that sublime Psalm—

> 'In Judah's land God is well known,
> His name's in Israel great,' etc.

At the swamps of Drumclog they met face to face with Claverhouse and his dragoons, ranged on the opposite slope." The issue of the conflict which ensued is recorded by Claverhouse himself. "They pursued us," he says, "so hotly, that we got no time to rally. I saved the standards, but lost on the place about eight or ten men, besides wounded ; but the dragoons lost many more." The news of the victory at Drumclog spread like wild-fire throughout the land, and soon about 5000 persons from all quarters were assembled on the Muir of Hamilton, not far from Bothwell Bridge. These were ill-armed, ill-trained, and, worst of all, they were not united. Instead of attending to their drill and preparing for the impending conflict, they were too often engaged in hot disputes about the Indulgence and kindred subjects, and in hopeless attempts to state the grounds on which they continued in arms. Had the harmony which pervaded their ranks at Drumclog still continued, there might have been other and more signal victories. But alas! a very different spirit had seized upon them now, and the words of the Apostle James received a melancholy illustration—" Where envying and strife is, there is confusion and every evil work." At last on the morning of Sabbath the 22d June, the royal army, consisting of about 15,000 men, and commanded by the Duke of Monmouth, a natural son of the King, made its first attack upon the Bridge. This, which was the key of defence, was guarded by 300 men, under the command of Hackston, Hall, and Turnbull. " For three hours," to quote again the eloquent words of Mr Dodds, " they bore the brunt of attack, those three hundred wearied and over-tasked men. Well do they deserve the tribute of admiration and praise ; for theirs is the one bright act to irradiate the memory of this disastrous day. Overpowered by numbers, they sent for reinforcements ; but none came. Exhausted by long watching, fatigue, and the toils of the incessant contest, they begged to be relieved by some of the many troops that were standing idly on the muir ; but there was no commander, there was no order, every man was in hot dispute with his neighbour. If they were to stand alone and unsupported in the breach, 300 against the iron weight of 15,000, at least they required more ammunition, for their store was failing them. The answer returned was that the ammunition was exhausted. Who can imagine the despair of that gallant 300, and their three brave officers, who had watched that bridge night and day, and maintained their post against all odds and all comers? But madness ruled the hour. They were ordered to retire from the bridge and fall back to the main body on the muir." The rest is easily told. Monmouth did all in his power to prevent needless bloodshed, but the soldiers, led on by such men as Claverhouse and Dalziel, sprung like tigers upon the disordered and helpless multitude. Upwards of 400 were killed, and 1500 who surrendered as prisoners were dragged in triumph to Edinburgh, and, as the prisons were already full, they were put into the Greyfriars Churchyard, and kept there for several months without shelter or covering. At last, when their number, through various causes, was reduced to 250, they were shipped for the American plantations, but when off the coast of Orkney the vessel in which they were was wrecked, and all, with very few exceptions, were swallowed up in the

BATTLEFIELD OF DRUMCLOG.

raging deep. This was a merciful termination to their sufferings, for the captain had treated them in the most inhuman manner, and even refused to open the hatches and let them escape when the vessel was going to pieces. So true is the saying of Scripture, that "the tender mercies of the wicked are cruel."—Ed.]

Having some affairs to settle (perhaps with a view never to return) Gordon could not join the Covenanters who were then in arms near Bothwell; but sent his son, who was in the action. He himself hastening forward as soon as possible to their assistance, and not knowing of their disaster, was met near the place by a party of English dragoons who were in quest of the sufferers, and, like another valiant champion of Christ, he refused to surrender, or comply with their demand, and so they killed him upon the spot. His son being out of the way, and his friends not obtaining that his body should be burned amongst the bones of his ancestors, he was interred in the churchyard of Glassford; and though a pillar or monument was erected over his grave, yet no inscription was put on it, because of the severity of the times.

His son Alexander Gordon narrowly escaped being taken, by means of one of his tenants, who, knowing him as he rode through Hamilton, made him dismount, put on woman's clothes, and rock the cradle. After this, he went over to his brother-in-law, Mr Hamilton, to represent the low case of the united societies to the churches of the Netherlands. He was by them called home, and when returning back a second time, he was apprehended by the enemy, and put to the torture; but by means of his friend, the Duke of Gordon, his life was spared. However, he was sent to the Bass, and from thence I suppose, to Blackness, where, from the year 1683, he continued till he was liberated at the revolution. It is to be lamented, that after this, neither he, nor his son Sir Thomas, fully followed the steps of their ancestors.

Thus fell a renowned Gordon, one whose character at present I am in no capacity to describe; only I may venture to say, that he was a gentleman of good parts and endowments; a man devoted to religion and godliness; and a prime supporter of the Presbyterian interest in that part of the country where he lived. The Gordons have all along made no small figure in our Scottish history; but here was a patriot, a good Christian, a confessor, and, I may add, a martyr of Jesus Christ.

Messrs John Kid and John King.

OHN KID and JOHN KING suffered many hardships during the persecuting period, from the year 1670, to the time of their martyrdom, 1679. John King was some time chaplain to Lord Cardross; and it appears he was apprehended and imprisoned in the year 1674, but got out on a bond and surety for 5000 merks, to appear when called. Next year he was again apprehended by a party of the persecutors, in the said Lord Cardross's, but was immediately rescued from their hands by some country people, who had profited much by his ministry. After this he was taken a third time by bloody Claverhouse, near Hamilton, with about seventeen others, and brought to Evandale, where they were all rescued by their suffering brethren at Drumclog. After this he and John Kid were of great service, and preached often among the honest party of our sufferers, till their defeat at Bothwell, where Kid, among other prisoners, was taken and brought to Edinburgh. It would appear that King was apprehended also at the same time, and the circumstances of his capture are so interesting as to be worthy of being recorded.

John King having come to pay his respects to the Laird of Blair, in Dalry parish, near Kilwinning, to whom he had formerly been chaplain; Bryce Blair, a farmer, who had been groom at Blair House, getting notice, came and desired a visit also. Accordingly he went, and preached a short discourse on the Saturday night following. On the Sabbath morning a party of the enemy (said to be Crichton's dragoons) being in quest of him, and getting the scent, two of them in disguise came to an old man feeding cattle near Bryce Blair's house, and asked him, whether he knew where that godly minister Mr King was; for they were afraid he should be taken, as the enemy was in pursuit of him; and if they knew where he was they would secure him from them. The old man having more honesty than policy, cried out, "I'll run and tell him." Whereupon they rode full speed after him to the house. Finding a servant of the house waiting on the horses of Mr King and his servant, they immediately dismounted; and having driven their own horses into the standing corn, threatened him not to stir from the spot on pain of death. One of them took his own saddle, and putting it on Mr King's horse, said, "Many a mile have I rode after thee, but I shall ride upon thee now."

By this time the rest had surrounded the house; and Mr King and his servant being in bed, they immediately commanded them to rise and put on their clothes. While the servant was putting on his master's spurs, one of the soldiers swore at him, saying, was he putting a spur on a prisoner? He replied he would put on what he pleased: for which he received a blow from the soldier, who in his turn was reproved by another for striking a prisoner while making no resistance. Thus they were both carried off to Glasgow, attended by one David Cumming, of the same parish, as guide.

A party of English dragoons being there, one of them on horseback called for some ale, and drank to the confusion of the Covenants. Another of his companions asking him at the stable-green port where he was going, he answered, "To carry King to hell." But this poor wretch had not gone far, whistling and singing, till his carbine accidentally went off and killed him on the spot. "God shall shoot at them with an arrow; suddenly shall they be wounded" (Ps. lxiv. 7).

John King was taken to Edinburgh, where both he and Mr Kid were brought before the Council, July 9th. King confessed, when examined, that he was with those who rose at that time. Kid confessed that he had preached in the fields, but never where there were men in arms, except in two places. They signed their confession, which was afterwards produced in evidence against them before the Justiciary. On the 12th, Kid was again examined before the Council, and put to the torture. It seems he was more than once in the Boots, where he behaved with much meekness and patience. King was again examined on the 16th before the Justiciary, and Kid on the following day. On the 22d they received their indictments. The trial came on upon the 28th, when, upon their former petition on the 24th, advocates were allowed to plead for them; but no exculpation was allowed them. When their indictments were read, the Advocate produced their confessions before the Council as proof against them; and, accordingly, they were brought in guilty, and condemned to be hanged at the Market Cross of Edinburgh, on Thursday the 14th of August, and their heads and right arms to be cut off and disposed of at the Council's pleasure.

The same day in the forenoon the King's act of indemnity was published, and, to grace the solemnity, the two noble martyrs (who were denied a share therein) were in the afternoon brought forth to their execution. It was related by one there present, that, as they approached the place, walking together hand in hand, Mr Kid, looking about to Mr King, with a cheerful countenance, said, "I have often heard and read of a *Kid* sacrificed, but I seldom or never heard of a *King* made a sacrifice." Upon the scaffold they appeared with a great deal of courage and serenity of mind (as was usual with the martyrs in these times), and died in much peace and joy—even a joy that none of their persecutors could intermeddle with. Their heads were cut off on another scaffold prepared for the purpose.

Thus ended the lives of these two worthy ministers and martyrs of Jesus Christ, after having owned their allegiance to Zion's King and Lord, and given a faithful testimony against Popery, Prelacy, and Erastianism, and for the covenanted work of Reformation in its different parts and periods. The reader will find their dying testimonies in Naphtali, and the Western Martyrology. A few of their sermons I had occasion lately to publish.

John Brown.

OHN BROWN was ordained minister at Wamphray, in Annandale. There is no certain account how long he was there, only it was some time before the restoration of Charles II., as appears from his great faithfulness in opposing Prelacy, which was then about to be intruded upon the Church. Indeed, it was for his fortitude and freedom with some of his neighbouring ministers for their compliance with the prelates, contrary to the promise they had given him, that he was turned out of that place.

Upon the 6th of November 1662, he was brought before the Council; whether by letters to converse with the Council, or by a citation, it is not certain; but the same day, the Council's act against him runs thus:

"Mr John Brown of Wamphray, being convened before the Council, for abusing and reproaching some ministers for keeping the diocesan synod with the Archbishop of Glasgow, calling them perjured knaves and villains, did acknowledge that he called, them false knaves for so doing, because they had promised the contrary to him. The Council ordain him to be secured close prisoner in the Tolbooth, till further orders." He remained in prison till December 11, when, after Mr Livingstone and others had received their sentence, the Council came to this conclusion anent him: "Upon a petition presented by Mr John Brown, minister of Wamphray, now prisoner in Edinburgh, showing that he hath been kept close prisoner these five weeks by-past, and seeing that, by want of free air, and other necessaries for maintaining his crazy body, he is in hazard to lose his life, therefore humbly desiring warrant to be put at liberty, upon caution to enter his person when he should be commanded, as the petition bears; which being at length heard and considered, the Lords of Council ordain the supplicant to be put at liberty, forth of the Tolbooth, he first obliging himself to remove and depart off the King's dominions, and not to return without license from his Majesty and Council under pain of death."

Great were the hardships he underwent in prison, for (says Crookshank) "he was denied even the necessaries of life; and though, because of the ill treatment he met with, he was brought almost to the gates of death, yet he could not have the benefit of the free air, until he signed a bond, obliging himself to a voluntary banishment, and that without any just cause."

Upon the 23d of the same month, on presenting a petition to the Council, to prorogue the time of his removal from the kingdom, in regard he was not able to provide himself with necessaries, and the weather was so unseasonable that he could not have the opportunity of a ship, it was agreed to "grant him two months longer after the 11th of December by-past;—in the meantime, he being peaceable, acting nothing in the prejudice of the present Government." Next year he went over to Holland, then the asylum of the banished, where he lived many years, and he never, that we heard of, saw his native country any more.

How he employed himself mostly in Holland, we are at a loss to say, but his many elaborate papers, both practical, argumentative, and historical, which were either mostly written there, or published from thence, witness that. he was not idle; particularly those concerning the Indulgence, cess-paying, etc. These he sent for the support and strengthening of his persecuted brethren in the Church of Scotland, unto whom he and Mr M'Ward contributed all in their power, that they might be kept straight while labouring in the furnace of affliction, under a time of sore oppression and bloody tyranny. But hither did the malice of their enemies yet pursue them, for the King, by the instigation of Prelate Sharp, in the year 1676, wrote to the States-General to remove them from their province. And although the States neither did nor could reasonably grant this demand, seeing they had got the full stress of laws in Scotland many years before, yet it appears, that they persuaded rather than forced them to wander farther from the land of their nativity.

[They went first to Germany, but being soon permitted to re-cross the frontiers of Holland, they took up their abode for some time in the neighbourhood of Utrecht. After that they returned to Rotterdam. —Ed.]

Some time before his death, he was admitted minister of the Scots congregation at Rotterdam; where with great prudence and diligence he exercised his ministry; it being always his study and care to gain many souls to Christ. For as he was faithful in declaring the whole counsel of God to his people, in warning them against the evils of the time, so he was likewise a great textuarist, close in handling any truth he discoursed upon, and in the application most homely, warm, and searching, showing himself a most skilful casuist. His sermons were not so plain but the learned might admire them; nor so learned, but the plain understood them. His fellow-soldier and companion in tribulation (Mr M'Ward), in his "Earnest Contendings," gives him this testimony, that the whole of his sermons, without the intermixture of any other matter, had a speciality of pure Gospel tincture, breathing nothing but faith in Christ, and communion with Him.

The ordination of Richard Cameron seems to have been the last of his public employments, and his discourse (the last before his exit from this world, which appears to have been about the end of the year 1679) was from Jer. ii. 35: "Behold, I will plead with thee, because thou sayest, I have not sinned." Having finished his course with joy, he died in the Lord. "Blessed are the dead which die in the Lord, ... they rest from their labours, and their works do follow them."

No doubt Mr Brown was a man famous in his day, both for learning and faithfulness, warm zeal, and true piety. He was a notable writer, and a choice and pathetic preacher; in controversy he was acute, masculine, and strong; in history, plain and comprehensive; in divinity, substantial and divine. The first he discovers in his work printed in Latin against the Socinians, and his treatise *de Causa Dei contra Anti-Sabbatarios*, which the learned world know better than can be here described. There is also a large manuscript history, entitled, *Apologia pro Ecclesia*, A.D. 1660, consisting of 1600 pages in quarto, which he gave to Charles Gordon, some time minister at Dalmeny, to be by him presented to the first free General Assembly of the Church of Scotland, and which accordingly was presented to the General Assembly of 1692. Of this history, the Apologetical Relation seems to be an abridgement. His letters and other papers, particularly the "History of the Indulgence," written and sent home to his native country, manifest his great and fervent zeal for the cause of Christ: and his other practical pieces, such as that "on Justification;" "on the Romans;" "Quakerism the Way to Paganism;" "The Hope of Glory;" "Christ the Way, the Truth, and the Life;" the first and second parts of his "Life of Faith;" and "Enoch's Testament opened up," etc., all evidence his solid piety, and real acquaintance with God and godliness.

[The "History of the Indulgence," of which John Brown is here said to have been the author, treats of a subject to which frequent reference is made in the course of this volume, and which formed a real bone of contention among the Presbyterians. The Indulgence, as it was generally called, was nothing else than a royal license or permission to the outed ministers, to exercise the functions of their ministry under certain limitations. According to it power was given to the Privy Council, to nominate and appoint a certain number of them to vacant parishes. Those who would not receive collation from the bishops were not to have the stipends, but only the manse and glebe and a certain annuity; and those who refused to attend the diocesan synods of the bishops were to be confined in their ministry within the parishes to which they were appointed. But all who had lived "peaceably and orderly" in the places where they had resided were permitted to return to their churches, provided they were vacant. The opinion which Mr Brown and others entertained regarding this important decree, which was issued from White-hall in the month of June 1669, may be inferred from the following extract from his History: "This license or indulgence was a real clothing of the indulged and licensed (in the sense of the court) with authority to preach; as if all they had from Christ, conveyed to them by the ministry of church-officers, according to this appointment, had been null and altogether insignificant. Which one thing, in my apprehension, had been enough to have scared any that minded to stand unto their Presbyterian gospel and anti-erastian principles from accepting of licenses of this nature, so destructive to the very being of an ecclesiastical ministry, and to its dependence on and emanation from Christ Jesus the only King and Head of His Church. But the other thing here chiefly to be noticed is, that this device of the Indulgence was hatched and contrived of purpose to bear down these conventicles, and to give a more colourable show of justice in persecuting the zealous conventiclers." That Mr Brown was right in this latter opinion, may be inferred from these very significant words with which the royal proclamation concluded: "And seeing we have by these orders taken away all pretences for conventicles, and provided for the want of such as are and will be peaceable, if any shall be found hereafter to preach without authority, or keep conventicles, our express pleasure is, that you proceed with all severity against the

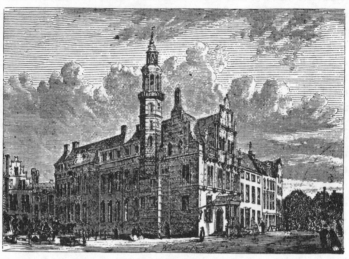

THE STADTHOUSE AT THE HAGUE.

preachers and hearers as seditious persons and contemners of our authority." Besides, this decree, which was from time to time revised and enlarged, was accompanied by other Acts, having for their object the thorough submission, and, if necessary, even the extermination of the poor, persecuted Covenanters. Every act of mercy and grace to those who accepted the Indulgence was, as Dr Burton, in his History, remarks, balanced "with additional machinery of repression and cruelty directed against recusants." We need not wonder, therefore, at the strong and even stern animosity which was manifested by the latter against all who accepted the Indulgence, or even refused to denounce it. This appeared most distinctly, and led to the most disastrous results, in connection with the battle of Bothwell Bridge, as has already in part been narrated.—Ed.]

OLD VIEW OF BERWICK.

Henry Hall of Haughhead.

ENRY HALL of Haughhead (in the parish of Eckford in Teviotdale), having had a religious education, began very early to mind a life of holiness, in all manner of godly conversation. In his younger years he was a most zealous opposer of the public resolutions that took place in the year 1651 ; insomuch that, when the minister of his parish complied with that course, he refused to hear him, and often went to Ancrum to hear John Livingstone. After the restoration of that wicked tyrant Charles II., being oppressed with the malicious persecutions of the curates and other malignants for his nonconformity, he was obliged, in the year 1665, to depart his native country, and go over to the border of England, where he was very much renowned for his singular zeal in propagating the Gospel, by instructing the ignorant, and procuring ministers to preach now and then among that people who, before his coming, were very rude and barbarous, though now many of them became famous for piety.

In the year 1666, he was taken prisoner on his way to Pentland, to the assistance of his covenanted brethren, and imprisoned with some others in Cessford Castle ; but by Divine providence, he soon escaped thence, through the favour of his friend the Earl of Roxburgh, who was a blood-relation of his, and to whom the castle then pertained. He retired again to Northumberland, where, from this time until the year 1679, he lived, being very much beloved by all who knew him, for his care and concern in propagating the Gospel of Christ in that country ; insomuch that his blameless and shining conversation drew love, reverence, and esteem, even from his very enemies. About the year 1678, the heat of the persecution in Scotland obliged many to wander about in Berwick and Northumberland, as Colonel Struthers was violently pursuing all Scots in those places. Haughhead was in that scuffle near Crookham, a village upon the English Border, where one of his nearest intimates, that gallant and religious gentleman, Thomas Kerr of Hayhop, fell. Upon this he was obliged to return to Scotland, where he wandered up and down in the hottest time of the persecution, mostly with Messrs Donald Cargill and Richard Cameron ; during which time, besides his many other Christian virtues, he sig- nalised himself by a real zeal, in defence of the persecuted Gospel in the fields. He was one of those four elders of the Church of Scot- land, who, at the council of war at Shawhead Muir, June 18, 1679, were chosen, with Messrs Cargill, Douglas, King, and Barclay, to draw up the " Causes of the Lord's Wrath against the Land," which were to be the subject of a fast on the day following. He had, indeed, an active hand in the most part of the transactions among the Cove- nanters at that time ; being one of the commanding officers in their army, from the skirmish at Drumclog, to their defeat at Bothwell Bridge.

After this, being outlawed, and diligently searched for and pursued after, he was forced to go over to Holland, the only refuge then of our Scots sufferers, to escape the violent hands of his indefatigable persecutors. But he had not stayed there long, until his zeal for the persecuted interest of Christ, and his tender sympathy for the afflicted remnant of his covenanted brethren, who were then wandering in Scotland amongst the desolate caves and dens of the earth, drew him home again ; choosing rather to undergo the utmost efforts of perse- cuting fury, than to live at ease in the time of Joseph's affliction ; making Moses' generous choice, rather to suffer affliction with the people of God, than to enjoy what momentary pleasures the ease of the world could afford. Nor was he very much concerned with the riches of this world ; for he hesitated not to give his ground to hold field preachings on, when few or none else would do it ; for he was still a true lover of the free and faithfully preached Gospel, and was always against the Indulgence.

About a quarter of a year after his return from Holland, he was mostly with Donald Cargill, lurking as privily as they could about Borrowstounness, and other places on both sides of the Frith of Forth. At last they were taken notice of by these two bloody hounds, the curates of Borrowstounness and Carriden, who soon smelled out Mr Cargill and his companion, and presently sent information to Middleton, Governor of Blackness Castle, who was a Papist. After consultation, he immediately took the scent after them, ordering his soldiers to follow him at a distance, by twos and threes together, at convenient intervals, to avoid suspicion, while he and his man rode on after them at some distance, till they came to Queensferry. Here, perceiving the house where they alighted, he sent his servant off in haste for his men, putting up his horse in another house ; and coming to them as a stranger, he pretended a great deal of kindness to them both, desiring that they might have a glass of wine together. When each had taken a glass, and were in some friendly conference, the Governor wearying that his men came not up, threw off the mask, and laid hands on them, saying, they were his prisoners, and commanded the people of the house in the King's name to assist. They all refused except one Thomas George, a waiter ; by whose assistance he got the gate shut.

In the meanwhile, Haughhead, being a bold and brisk man, struggled hard with the Governor, until Cargill got off ; but after the scuffle, as he was going off himself, having got clear of the Governor, Thomas George struck him on the head with a carbine, and wounded him mortally. However, he got out ; and by this time the women of the town, who were assembled at the gate to the rescue of the prisoners, convoyed him out of the town. He walked some time on foot, but was unable to speak much, save only to cast some little reflection upon a woman whose interposition hindered him from killing the Governor, and so making his escape more timeously. At last he fainted, and was carried to a country house near Echlin ; but although surgeons were speedily brought, yet he never recovered the use of his speech afterwards. Dalziel, living near by, was soon apprised of the occurrence, and came quickly with a party of the guards and seized him ; and although every one saw the gentleman just a-dying, yet such was his inhumanity, that he must carry him to Edinburgh. But he died in their hands on the way thither ; and made an end of this his earthly pilgrimage to receive his heavenly crown.

CANONGATE TOLBOOTH.

His corpse was carried to the Canongate Tolbooth, where it lay three days without burial; and even then, although his friends convened for that end, to do their last office to him, yet that could not be granted. At last they buried him clandestinely in the night; for such was the fury of these limbs of Antichrist, that after having slain the witnesses, they would not suffer them to be decently interred in the earth; which is another lasting evidence of the cruelty of those times.

Thus this worthy gentleman, after he had in an eminent manner served his day and generation, fell a victim to Prelatic fury. Upon him was found, when he was taken, a rude draft of an unsubscribed paper, afterwards called the Queensferry Paper; which the reader will find inserted at large in Wodrow's History, the substance of which is contained in Crookshank's History, and in the appendix to the "Cloud of Witnesses."

Richard Cameron.

RICHARD CAMERON was born in Falkland in the shire of Fife, his father being a merchant there. He was of the Episcopal persuasion at first; as, after he had passed his course of learning, he was for some time schoolmaster and precentor to the curate of Falkland. He sometimes attended the sermons of the Indulged, as he had opportunity; but at last it pleased the Lord to incline him to go out and hear the persecuted Gospel in the fields; which, when the curates understood, they set upon him, partly by flattery and partly by threats, and at last by more direct persecution, to make him forbear attending these meetings. But such was the wonderful working of the Lord by His powerful Spirit upon him, that having got a lively discovery of the sin and hazard of Prelacy, he deserted the curates altogether; and no sooner was he enlightened anent the evil of it, than he began more narrowly to search, that he might know what was his proper and necessary duty. The Lord was pleased to discover to him the sinfulness of the Indulgence, as flowing from the ecclesiastical supremacy usurped by the King; and, being zealously affected for the honour of Christ, wronged by that Erastian acknowledgment of the magistrate's usurped power over the church, he longed for an opportunity to give a testimony against it.

This made him leave Falkland, and go to Sir Walter Scott of Harden, who attended the Indulged meetings. Here he took the opportunity, notwithstanding many strong temptations to the contrary, to witness against the Indulged, particularly on Sabbath; for when called to attend the lady to church, he returned from the entry, refusing to go that day, and spent it in his chamber, where he met with much of the Lord's presence, as he himself afterwards testified, and got very evident discoveries of the nature of these temptations and suggestions of Satan, which were likely to prevail with him before. Upon Monday, giving a reason to the said Sir Walter and his lady why he went not to church with them, he took occasion to be plain and express in testifying against the Indulgence in the original rise, spring, and complex nature thereof; and finding his service would be no longer acceptable to them, he went to the south, where he met with John Welch, minister of Irongray. He stayed some time in his company, who, finding him a man every way qualified for the ministry, pressed him to accept a license to preach, which he for some time refused, chiefly upon the account that having such clear discoveries of the sinfulness of the Indulgence, he could not but testify against it explicitly as soon as he should have an opportunity to preach the Gospel in public. But the force of his objections being answered by Mr Welch's serious solicitations, he was prevailed on to accept of a license from the outed ministers, who were then preaching in the fields, and had not complied with the Indulgence. Accordingly he was licensed by Mr Welch and Mr Semple, at Haughhead in Teviotdale, at the house of Henry Hall. Here he told them, he should be a bone of contention among them; for if he preached against a national sin among them, it should be against the Indulgences, and for the duty of separation from the Indulged.

After he was licensed, they sent him at first to preach in Annandale. He said, how could he go there? He knew not what sort of people they were. But Mr Welch said, "Go your way, Ritchie, and set the fire of hell to their tail." He went, and the first day he preached upon the text Jer. iii. 19, "How shall I put thee among the children?" In the application he said, "Put you amongst the children! the offspring of robbers and thieves." Many have heard of Annandale thieves. Some of them got a merciful cast that day, and told afterwards, that it was the first field-meeting ever they attended; and that they went out of curiosity to see how a minister could preach in a tent, and people sit on the ground. After this, he preached several times with Mr Welch, Mr Semple, and others, until the year 1679, when he and Mr Welwood were called before that Erastian meeting at Edinburgh, in order to be deposed for their freedom and faithfulness in preaching against the sinful compliance of that time.

After this he preached at Maybole, where many thousands of people were assembled together, it being the first time that the sacrament of the Lord's supper was then dispensed in the open fields. At this time he used yet more freedom in testifying against the sinfulness of the Indulgence, for which he was also called before another meeting of the indulged in Galloway; and a little after that, he was again called before a presbytery of them, at Sundewall, in Dunscore, in Nithsdale. This was the third time they had designed to take his license from him. Here it was that Robert Gray, a Northumberland man (who suffered afterwards in the Grassmarket in the year 1682), Robert Nelson, and others, protested against them for such conduct. At this meeting they prevailed with him to give his promise, that for some short time he should forbear such an explicit way of preaching against the Indulgence, and separation from them who were indulged. This promise lay heavy on him afterwards, as will appear in its own proper place.

After the giving of this promise, finding himself by virtue thereof bound up from declaring the whole counsel of God, he turned a little melancholy; and, to get the definite time of that unhappy promise exhausted, he went over to Holland, in the end of the year 1678, not knowing what work the Lord had for him there; where he conversed with Mr M'Ward and others of our banished Worthies. In his private conversation and exercise in families, but especially by his public sermon in the Scots Kirk at Rotterdam, he was most refreshing unto many souls. He dwelt mostly upon conversion work, from that text, Matt. xi. 28: "Come unto me, all ye that labour and are heavy laden, and I will give you rest;" which was most satisfying and agreeable to Mr M'Ward, Mr Brown, and others, who had been informed by the Indulged, and those of their persuasion, that he could preach nothing but babble against the Indulgence, cess-paying, etc. Here he touched upon none of these things, except in prayer, when lamenting over the deplorable case of Scotland by means of defection and tyranny.

About this time Mr M'Ward said to him, "Richard, the public standard is now fallen in Scotland; and, if I know anything of the mind of the Lord, ye are called to undergo your trials before us, to go home, and lift the fallen standard, and display it publicly before the world. But before ye put your hand to it, ye shall go to as many of the field ministers as ye can find, and give them your hearty invitation to go with you; and if they will not go, go alone, and the Lord will go with you."

Accordingly he was ordained by Mr M'Ward, Mr Brown, and Roleman, a famous Dutch divine. When their hands were lifted up from his head, Mr M'Ward continued his still, and cried out, "Behold, all ye beholders, here is the head of a faithful minister and servant of

THE CASTLE OF MAYBOLE.

Jesus Christ, who shall lose the same for his Master's interest, and it shall be set up before sun and moon, in the view of the world."

In the beginning of the year 1680, he returned to Scotland, where he spent some time in going from minister to minister, of those who formerly kept up the public standard of the Gospel in the fields. But all in vain: for the persecution after Bothwell Bridge being then so hot against all who had not accepted the Indulgence and Indemnity, none of them would adventure upon that hazard, except Donald Cargill and Thomas Douglas, who came together, and kept a public fast-day in Darmeid Muir, betwixt Clydesdale and Lothian; one of the chief causes of which was the reception of the Duke of York, that sworn vassal of antichrist, in Scotland, after he had been excluded from England and several other places. After several meetings among themselves, for forming the declaration and testimony which they were about to publish to the world, at last they agreed upon one, which they published at the market-cross of Sanquhar, June 22, 1680, from which place it is commonly called the Sanquhar Declaration. After this they were obliged, for some time, to separate one from another, and go to different corners of the land; and that not only upon account of the urgent call and necessity of the people, who were then in a most starving condition with respect to the free

MONUMENT AT AIRSMOSS.

and faithfully preached Gospel, but also on account of the indefatigable scrutiny of the enemy, who, for their better encouragement, had, by proclamation, offered 5000 merks for apprehending Cameron, 3000 for Cargill and Douglas, and 100 for each of the rest who were concerned in the publication of the foresaid declaration.

After parting, Richard Cameron went to Swine Knowe, in New Monkland, where he had a most confirming and comforting day upon that soul-refreshing text, Isa. xxxii. 2 : "And a man shall be as an hiding-place from the wind, and a covert from the tempest." In his preface that day, he said he was fully assured that the Lord, in mercy unto this Church and nation, would sweep the throne of Britain of that unhappy race of the name of Stuart, for their treachery, tyranny and lechery, but especially their usurping the royal prerogatives of Christ, and this he was as sure of as his hands were upon that cloth, yea, and more sure, for he had that by sense, but the other by faith. . . . Mr H. E. (probably Henry Erskine), who suffered much by imprisonment and otherwise in this period, and who, although otherwise a worthy good man, was so misled, that he had one time premeditated a sermon, wherein he intended to speak somewhat against Mr Cameron and Mr Cargill (so far was he from taking part with them), heard on the Saturday night an audible voice, which said twice unto him,

Audi (hear) ! He answered, *Audio* (I hear) ! The voice spoke again, and said, " Beware of calling Cameron's words vain." This stopped him from his intended purpose ; which he told himself unto an old reverend minister, who afterwards related the matter as above stated.

When Richard Cameron came to preach in and about Cumnock, he was much opposed by the lairds of Logan and Horsecleugh, who represented him as a Jesuit, and a vile, naughty person. But yet some of the Lord's people, who had retained their former faithfulness, gave him a call to preach in that parish. When he began, he exhorted the people to mind that they were in the sight and presence of a holy God, and that all of them were hastening to an endless state of either weal or woe. Andrew Dalziel, a debauchee (a cocker or fowler), who was in the house, it being a stormy day, cried out, " Sir, we neither know you nor your God." Mr Cameron, musing a little, said, " You, and all who do not know my God in mercy, shall know Him in His judgments, which shall be sudden and surprising in a few days upon you ; and I, as a sent servant of Jesus Christ, whose commission I bear, and whose badge I wear upon my breast, give you warning, and leave you to the justice of God." Accordingly, in a few days after, the said Andrew, being in perfect health, took his breakfast plentifully, but before he rose he fell a-vomiting, and died in a most frightful manner. This admonishing passage, together with the power and presence of the Lord going along with the Gospel, as dispensed by him during the little time he was there, made the foresaid two lairds desire a conference with him, to which he readily assented ; after which they were obliged to acknowledge that they had been in the wrong, and desired his forgiveness. He said, from his heart he forgave them what wrongs they had done to him ; but for what wrongs they had done to the interest of Christ, it was not his part to forgive them ; but he was persuaded that they would be remarkably punished for it. To the laird of Logan he said, that he should be written childless ; and to Horsecleugh, that he should suffer by burning—both of which afterwards came to pass.

Upon the 4th of July following, being eighteen days before his death, he preached at the Grass Waterside near Cumnock. In his preface that day, he said, " There are three or four things I have to tell you this day which I must not omit, because I will be but a breakfast or four-hours to the enemy, some day or other shortly ; and then my work and my time will both be finished. And the *First* is this : As for the King who is now upon the throne of Britain, after him there shall not be a crowned King of the name of Stuart in Scotland. *Secondly*, There shall not be an old Covenanter's head above ground, that swore these Covenants with uplifted hands, ere ye get a right Reformation set up in Scotland. *Thirdly*, A man shall ride a day's journey in the shires of Galloway, Ayr, and Clydesdale, and not see a reeking house nor hear a cock crow, ere ye get a right Reformation; and several other shires shall be little better. And *Fourthly*, The rod that the Lord will make instrumental in this, will be the French and other foreigners, together with a party in this land joining them; but ye, that stand to the testimony in that day, be not discouraged at the fewness of your number; for when Christ comes to raise up His own work in Scotland, He will not want men enough to work for him."

In the week following, he preached in the parish of Carluke, upon these words, Is. xlix. 24: "Shall the prey be taken from the mighty, or the lawful captive delivered?" The Sabbath following, at Hind Bottom, near Crawfordjohn, he preached on these words, John v. 40: "And ye will not come to me, that ye might have life." In the time of this sermon he fell a-weeping, and the greater part of the multitude also, so that few dry cheeks were to be seen among them. After this, to the day of his death, he mostly kept his chamber door shut until night; for the mistress of the house where he stayed, having been several times at the door, got no access. At last she forced it up, and finding him very melancholy, earnestly desired to know how it was with him. He said, "That weary promise I gave to these ministers has lain heavy upon me, and for it my carcass shall dung the wilderness, and that ere it be long." Being now near his end, he had such a large earnest of the Spirit, and such a longing desire for full possession of the heavenly inheritance, that he seldom prayed in a family, asked a blessing, or gave thanks, but he prayed for patience to wait until the Lord's appointed time came.

The last Sabbath he preached was with Donald Cargill in Clydesdale, on Psalm xlvi. 10: "Be still, and know that I am God." That day he said he was sure that the Lord would lift up a standard against antichrist which would go to the gates of Rome, and burn it with fire, and that "blood" should be their sign and "no quarter" their word; and earnestly he wished that it might begin in Scotland. At their parting, they concluded to meet the second Sabbath after this at Craigmead, but he was killed on the Thursday thereafter. The Sabbath following, Cargill preached in the parish of Shotts, upon that text 2 Sam. iii. 38 : " Know ye not that there is a prince and a great man fallen this day in Israel ? "

The last night of his life, he was in the house of William Mitchell of Meadowhead, at the Water of Ayr, where about twenty-three horse and forty foot had continued with him that week. That morning a woman gave him water to wash his face and hands ; and having washed and dried them with a towel, he looked to his hands, and laid them on his face, saying, " This is their last washing. I have need to make them clean, for there are many to see them." At this the woman's mother wept, but he said, " Weep not for me, but for yourself and yours, and for the sins of a sinful land, for ye have many melancholy, sorrowful, and weary days before you."

The people who remained with him were in some hesitation whether they should abide together for their own defence, or disperse and shift for themselves. But that day, being the 22d of July, they were surprised by Bruce of Earlshall ; who, having got command of Airley's troop and Strachan's dragoons, upon notice given him by Sir John Cochrane of Ochiltree, came furiously upon them, about four o'clock in the afternoon, when lying on the east end of Airsmoss. When they saw the enemy approaching, and no possibility of escaping, they all gathered round Cameron, while he prayed a short word ; wherein he repeated this expression thrice over, " Lord, spare the green, and take the ripe." When ended, he said to his brother, with great intrepidity, " Come, let us fight it out to the last ; for this is the day that I have longed for, and the day that I have prayed for, to die fighting against our Lord's avowed enemies ! This is the day that we will get the crown ! " And to the rest he said, " Be encouraged all of you to fight it out valiantly ; for all of you that shall fall this day, I see heaven's gates open to receive you." But the enemy approaching, they immediately drew up ; eight horse with Cameron on the right, the rest with valiant Hackston on the left, and the foot in the middle ; where they all behaved with much bravery, until overpowered by a superior number. At last Hackston was taken a prisoner, as will afterwards be more fully narrated ; Cameron was killed on the spot, and his head and hands cut off, and taken to Edinburgh.

His father being in prison for the same cause, they carried them to him, to add grief unto his former sorrow, and inquired at him if he knew them. Taking his son's head and hands, which were very fair— being a man of a fair complexion like himself—he kissed them, and said, " I know—I know them ; they are my son's—my own dear son's.

It is the Lord—good is the will of the Lord, who cannot wrong me nor mine, but hath made goodness and mercy to follow us all our days." After which, by order of the Council, his head was fixed upon the Netherbow Port, and his hands beside it, with the fingers upward.

Thus this valiant soldier and minister of Jesus Christ came to his end, after he had been not only highly instrumental in turning many souls unto God, but also in lifting up a faithful standard for his royal Lord and Master, against all His enemies, and the defections and sinful compliances of that time. One of his and Christ's declared enemies, when he looked at his head at Edinburgh, give him this testimony, saying, " There's the head and hands of a man who lived praying and preaching, and died praying and fighting." And wherever the faithful contendings of the Covenanted Church of Scotland are made mention of, this, to his honour, shall be recorded of him.

When he was slain, there was found upon him a short paper, or bond of mutual defence, which the reader will find inserted in Wodrow's History, and in the Appendix to the " Cloud of Witnesses." There are a few of his Letters now published along with Mr Renwick's Collection of Letters. But the only sermon of his that appeared in print formerly, is that preached at Carluke, entitled, " Good news to Scotland," published in 1733. He wrote also a defence of the Sanquhar Declaration, but we can give no account of its ever being published. Some more of his sermons were lately published.

AN ACROSTIC ON HIS NAME.

Most noble Cameron of renown,
A fame of thee shall ne'er go down ;
Since truth with zeal thou didst pursue,
To Zion's King loyal and true.
Ev'n when the dragon spu'd his flood,
Resist thou didst unto the blood ;
Ran swiftly, in thy Christian race,
In faith and patience, to that place
Christ did prepare for such as thee
He knew would not his standard flee ;
A pattern of valour and zeal,
Rather to suffer than to fail,
Didst show thyself with might and main,
Counting that dross others thought gain ;
A faithful witness 'gainst all those,
Men of all sorts did truth oppose ;
Even thou with Moses didst esteem
Reproaches for the God of Heaven ;
On Him alone thou didst rely,
Not sparing for His cause to die.

David Hackston of Rathillet.

AVID HACKSTON of Rathillet, in the shire of Fife, is said in his younger years to have been without the least sense of anything religious, until it pleased the Lord, in His infinite goodness, to incline him to go out and attend the Gospel then preached in the fields, where he was caught in the Gospel net, and became such a true convert, that after a most mature deliberation upon the controverted points of the principles of religion in that period, he embarked in the noble cause, for which he afterwards suffered, with a full resolution to stand and fall with the despised persecuted people, cause, and interest of Jesus Christ.

There is no account of any public appearances that this worthy gentleman made until the 3d of May 1679, when we find him, with other eight gentlemen, going in quest of one Carmichael, who, by means of Archbishop Sharp, had got commission to harass and persecute all he could find in the shire of Fife, for nonconformity; but not finding him, when they were ready to drop the search, they providentially met with their arch-enemy himself. Whenever they descried his coach, one of them said, "It seems that the Lord hath delivered him into our hand;" and proposed that they should choose one for their leader, whose orders the rest were to obey. Upon this they chose David Hackston for their commander, but he absolutely refused, upon account of a difference subsisting betwixt Sharp and him in a civil process, wherein he judged himself to have been wronged by the Primate; which deed he thought would give the world ground to think it was rather out of personal pique and revenge, which he professed he was free of. They then chose another, and came up with the coach; and having got the Archbishop out, and given him some wounds, he fell on the ground. They ordered him to pray; but instead of that, seeing Rathillet at some distance (who had never alighted from his horse), he crept towards him on his hands and his feet, and said, "Sir, I know you are a gentleman, you will protect me." To this he answered, "I shall never lay a hand on you." At last Sharp was killed; after which every one judged of the action as their inclination moved them. However, the deed was wholly charged upon Hackston and his brother-in-law, Balfour of Kinloch, although he had no active hand in this action.

About the latter end of the same month of May, that he might not be found wanting to the Lord's cause, interest, and people, upon any emergent occasion, he, with some friends from Fife, joined that suffering handful of Covenanters at Evandale, where, after Mr Hamilton and others had drawn up a declaration, he and Mr Douglas went to the marketcross of Rutherglen, and, upon the anniversary day, the 29th of May, they extinguished the bonfires, and published the said testimony. They returned back to Evandale, where they were attacked by Claverhouse, upon the 1st of June, near Drumclog. Here Hackston was appointed one of the commanding officers (under Robert Hamilton, who commanded in chief) where he behaved with much valour and gallantry during that skirmish. After this he was a very useful instrument among that faithful remnant: as witness his repeated protests against the corrupt and Erastian party; and had an active hand in the most part of the public transactions among them, until that fatal day, the 22d of June, when he and his troop of horse were the last upon the field of battle at Bothwell Bridge.

But this worthy and religious gentleman, being now declared a rebel to the king (though no rebel to Zion's King) and a proclamation issued, wherein a reward of 10,000 merks was offered to any who could inform of or apprehend him, or any of those concerned in the death of Archbishop Sharp, was obliged to retire out of the way for about a year's space; in which time he did not neglect to attend the Gospel in the fields, wherever he could have it faithfully dispensed. But having run fast and done much in a little time, it could not be expected he should continue long; and upon the 22d of July 1680, having for a few days been with that little party who attended Richard Cameron at Airsmoss, they were surprised by Bruce of Earlshall, with Airley's troop and Strachan's dragoons.

Here, being commander-in-chief of that little band, and seeing the enemy approaching fast, he rode off to seek some strength of ground for their better advantage, and the rest followed; but seeing they could go no farther, they turned back, and drew up quickly;

PORTRAIT OF GENERAL DALZIEL.

eight horse being on the right, fifteen on the left; and the foot, who
were but ill armed, in the middle. He then asked, if they were all
willing to fight? They all answered, they were. Both bodies advanced, and a strong party of the enemy's horse coming hard upon
them, their horse fired, killing and wounding several of them, both
horse and foot. After this they advanced to the enemy's very faces,
when, after giving and receiving fire, valiant Hackston being in the
front, and finding the horse behind him broke, rode in among them,
and out again without any damage. But being assaulted by several,
with whom he fought a long time, they following him, and he them
by turns, he at length stuck in a bog, and the foremost of them, one
Ramsay, an old acquaintance, followed him in, and they being on
foot fought with small swords, without much advantage on either
side. At length closing, he was struck down by three on horseback
who came behind him, and falling, after he had received three sore
wounds on the head, they saved his life.

He was, with the rest of the prisoners, carried to the rear, where
they gave them all a testimony of being brave resolute men. After
this he was brought to Douglas, and from thence to Lanark, where
Dalziel threatened to roast him for not satisfying him with answers.
After this, he and other three prisoners were taken to Edinburgh,
whare, by order of the Council, they were received by the magistrates

at the Watergate. Sitting on a horse's bare back, with his face backward, and the other three being laid on a goad of iron, they were carried up the street, with Mr Cameron's head on a halbert before them, to the Parliament Close, where Hackston was taken down, and the rest loosed by the hands of the hangman.

He was immediately brought before the Council, where his indictment was read by the Chancellor, and himself examined ; which examination, and his answers thereunto, being elsewhere inserted at large, it may suffice here to observe, that being asked if he thought the Archbishop's death murder? he told them, that he was not obliged to answer such questions ; yet he would not call it so, but rather say, it was not murder. Being further asked, if he owned the King's authority, he replied, that though he was not obliged to answer that question, yet, as he was permitted to speak, he would say something to it. There could be no lawful authority, but what was of God ; and no authority, stated in a direct opposition to God, could be of God ; and he knew of no authority nor justiciary this day in these nations, but what was in direct opposition to God, and so could neither be of God, nor lawful ; and that their fruits were proving it, in that they were setting murderers, sorcerers, and such others, at liberty from justice, and employing them in their service, and were making it their whole work to oppress, kill, and destroy the Lord's people. Bishop Paterson asked, if ever Pilate, and that judicature who were direct enemies to Christ, were disowned by Him as judges ? He said, that he would answer no perjured prelate in the nation. Paterson replied, that he could not be called perjured, since he never took that sacrilegious Covenant. Hackston said, that God would own that Covenant when there were none of them to oppose it. Notwithstanding these bold, free, and open answers, they threatened him with torture ; but this he nowise regarded.

Upon the 26th, he was again brought before the Council, where he answered much to the same purpose as before. The Chancellor said, he was a vicious man. He answered, that while he was so, he had been acceptable to him ; but now when otherwise, it was not so. He asked him, if he would yet own that cause with his blood, if at liberty? He answered, that, before him, both their fathers had owned it with the hazard of their blood. Then he was called by all a murderer. He answered, that God, to whom he referred it, should decide betwixt them, who were most murderers in His sight, he or they. Bishop Paterson's brother in conference told him, that the whole Council found that he was a man of great parts, and also of good birth. He said, that for his birth he was related to the best in the kingdom, which he thought little of; and as for his parts, they were very small; yet he trusted so much to the goodness of that cause for which he was a prisoner, that if they would give God that justice, as to let His cause be disputed, he doubted not to plead it against all that could speak against it.

Upon the 27th, he was taken before the Justiciary, where he declined the King's authority as a usurper of the prerogative of the Son of God, whereby he had involved the land in idolatry, perjury, and other wickedness; and declined them as exercising under him the supreme power over the Church, usurped from Jesus Christ, and therefore durst not with his own consent sustain them as competent judges, regarding them as open and declared enemies to the living God, and competitors for the throne and power belonging to Him only.

On the 29th, he was brought to his trial, when the Council, in a most unprecedented way, appointed the manner of his execution; for they well knew his judges would find him guilty. Upon Friday the 30th, being brought again before them, they asked, if he had any more to say. He answered, " What I have said I will seal." Then they told him, they had something to say to him; and commanded him to sit down and receive his sentence. This he did, but told them, that they were all murderers, for all the power they had was derived from tyranny, and that, these years bygone, they had not only tyrannised over the church of God, but also ground the faces of the poor; so that oppression, perjury, and bloodshed, were to be found in their skirts.

Upon this he was carried from the bar, and drawn backwards on a hurdle to the place of execution at the Cross of Edinburgh. None were suffered to be with him but two bailies, the executioner, and his servants. He was permitted to pray to God Almighty, but not to speak to the people. Being come upon the scaffold, his right hand was struck off, and, a little after, his left; which he endured with great firmness and constancy. The hangman being long in cutting off the right hand, he desired him to strike on the joint of the left; which being done, he was drawn up to the top of the gallows with a pulley, and suffered to fall down a considerable way upon the lower scaffold, three times with his whole weight, and then fixed at the top of the gallows. Then the executioner, with a large knife, cut open his breast, and pulled out his heart, before he was dead, for it moved when it fell on the scaffold. He then stuck his knife in it, and showed it on all sides to the people, crying, " Here is the heart of a traitor." At last he threw it into a fire prepared for that purpose ; and having quartered his body, his head was fixed on the Nether Bow, one of his quarters, with his hands, at St Andrews, another at Glasgow, a third at Leith, and the fourth at Burntisland.

Thus fell this champion for the cause of Christ, a sacrifice unto Prelatic fury, to gratify the lust and ambition of wicked and bloody men. Whether his courage, constancy, or faithfulness had the pre-eminence, it is hard to determine ; but his memory is still alive, and it is better not to say any more of him, than either too much or too little.

Robert Ker of Kersland.

OBERT KER of Kersland, being born and educated in a very religious family, began early to discover more than an ordinary zeal for religion. But the first public appea rance that we find he made for the cause and inte rest of true religion was in the year 1666, about November 26, when he, Caldwell and some others of the Renfrew gentlemen gathered themselves together, and marched eastward to join Colonel Wallace and the little handful who renewed the Covenants at Lanark. Having heard that General Dalziel was by that time got betwixt them and their friends, they were obliged to disperse ; but this could not escape the knowledge of the Council; for the laird of Blackstoun, one of their own number, upon a promise of pardon, informed against the rest, and so redeemed his own neck by accusing his neighbour; but of this he had nothing to boast of afterwards.

Kersland was after this obliged to retire out of the way ; and the next year he was forfeited in his life and fortune, and his estate given to Lieutenant-General Drummond, of Cromlie, and his lands in Beith to William Blair of that Ilk; which estates they unjustly held till the Revolution.

After this, to elude the storm, he thought fit to retire, and go over to Holland, and there chose to live with his family at Utrecht; where he had the advantage of hearing the Gospel, and other excellent conversation. In that place he continued nearly three years. But his friends thinking it necessary that he should come home to settle some of his affairs, if possible, his lady returned in the end of 1669, and himself soon followed. To his unspeakable grief, he found, when he came to Edinburgh, that she was ill of a fever in the house of a woman who was a favourer of the sufferers. And though he lodged in a more private place, and only used to come in the evenings to visit his sick lady, yet Cannon of Mardrogate, who had not altogether cast off the mask (at least his treachery and apostacy were not then discovered), having got notice of it, he soon gave information to the Chancellor, and orders were procured from Lauderdale, then in town, to search that house, on pretence that John Welch was keeping conventicles in the Lady Kersland's chamber; but the design was for Kersland himself, as the sequel will declare.

Accordingly a party came; and finding no conventicle, were just going to retire, when one Murray, having particular notice from Mardrogate, that when any company came to the room in the evening, Kersland used to retire behind a bed, and having a torch in his hand, provided for that end, said, he behoved to search the room; and so went straight behind the bed and brought him out, charging him to render his arms. Kersland told him he had none but the Bible, which he had then in his hand; and that was enough to condemn him in these times. At parting with his lady she showed much calmness and composure, exhorting him to do nothing that might wound his conscience out of regard to her or her children, and repeated that text of Scripture, " No man having put his hand to the plough, and looking back, is fit for the kingdom of heaven."

He was forthwith taken to the guard-house and then to the Abbey, where a committee of the Council, that same night, was gathered for his examination. When he was brought before them, they examined him concerning the lawfulness of the gathering at Pentland; which he, in plain terms, owned to be lawful and what he thought duty: upon which he was immediately imprisoned. When going away, the Chancellor upbraided him with what had passed betwixt him and his lady; which he suffered with much patience.

THE TOLBOOTH AND TRONGATE OF GLASGOW

He was nearly three months prisoner in Edinburgh; and from thence was sent to Dumbarton Castle, where he continued near a year and a half. Then, he was ordered to Aberdeen, where he was kept close prisoner, without fire, for three months space in the cold winter season. From Aberdeen he was brought south to Stirling Castle, where he continued some years; and then was a second time returned to Dumbarton, where he continued till October 1677. The Council then confined him to Irvine, and allowed him some time to transport himself and his family, then at Glasgow, to that place.

Coming to his family at Glasgow, he was visited by many friends and acquaintances; and the same night, convoying the Lady Caldwell and her daughter, he was taken by some of the guards, and kept in the guard-house till next day; when the commanding officer would have dismissed him, but first he behoved to know the Archbishop's pleasure, who immediately ordered him a close prisoner in the Tolbooth. The Archbishop took horse immediately for Edinburgh; Lady Kersland followed after, if possible, to prevent misinformation. In the meantime, a fire breaking out in Glasgow, the Tolbooth was in danger, and the magistrates refusing to let out the prisoners, the well-affected people of the town got long ladders and set the prisoners free, and Kersland among the rest, after he had been eight years prisoner. After the hurry was over, he inclined to surrender himself again prisoner; but hearing from his lady of the Archbishop's design against him, he retired all that winter. In the spring and summer following he kept company with the persecuted ministers, heard the Gospel preached in the fields, and was at communions, particularly that at Maybole. About the beginning of harvest 1678, he returned to Utrecht, where he continued until the day of his death.

When near his departure, his dear acquaintance, Sir Robert Hamilton, being with him, and signifying to him that he might be spared as another Caleb to see the good land when the storm was over, he, among his last words, said to him, "What is man before the Lord? yea, what is a nation? As a drop of a bucket, or as the small dust of the balance; yea, less than nothing and vanity. But this much I can say in humility, that through free grace, I have endeavoured to keep the post that God hath set me at. These fourteen years I have not desired to lift the one foot, till the Lord showed me where to set down the other." And so, in a few minutes he finished his course with joy, and fell asleep in Jesus, November 14, 1680, leaving his wife and five children in a strange land.

It were superfluous to insist here upon the character of the thrice renowned Ker. It is evident to all, he was a man of a great mind, far above a servile and mercenary disposition. He was, for a number of years, hurried from place to place, and guarded from prison to prison, but he endured all this with undaunted courage. He lost a good estate for the cause of Christ; and though he got not the martyr's crown, yet he, beyond all doubt, obtained the sufferer's reward.

DUMBARTON CASTLE, FROM THE NORTH.

Donald Cargill.

ONALD CARGILL seems to have been born about the year 1610. He was the eldest son of a most respected family in the parish of Rattray. After he had been some time in the schools of Aberdeen, he went to St Andrews, where, having perfected his course of philosophy, his father pressed upon him much to study divinity, in order for the ministry. But he, through tenderness of spirit, constantly refused, telling his father, that the work of the ministry was too great a burden for his weak shoulders; and requested him to command to any other employment he pleased. His father still continuing to urge him, he resolved to set apart a day of private fasting, to seek the Lord's mind therein; and after much wrestling with the Lord by prayer, the third chapter of Ezekiel, and chiefly these words, in the first verse, "Son of man, eat this roll, and go speak unto the house of Israel," made a strong impression upon his mind, so that he durst no longer refuse his father's desire, but dedicated himself wholly to the ministry.

After being licensed, he got a call to the Barony Church of Glasgow. It was so ordered by Divine Providence, that the very first text the presbytery ordered him to preach from, were these words in the third of Ezekiel, already mentioned, by which he was more confirmed that he had God's call to this parish. It had been long vacant, by reason that two ministers of the Resolution party, Messrs Young and Blair, had still opposed the settlement of such godly men as had been called by the people. But in reference to Mr Cargill's call, they were, in God's providence, much deterred from their wonted opposition. Cargill, perceiving the lightness and unconcerned behaviour of the people under the Word, was much discouraged thereat, so that he resolved to return home, and not accept the call, which when he was urged by some godly ministers not to do, and his reason asked, he answered, "they are a rebellious people." The ministers solicited him to stay, but in vain. But when his horse was

GLASGOW CATHEDRAL, SHOWING THE CRYPT, OR BARONY CHURCH.

ready, and he just going to begin his journey, being in the house of Mr Durham, where he had saluted several of his Christian friends that came to see him take horse, as he was taking farewell of a certain godly woman, she said to him, "Sir, you have promised to preach on Thursday; have you appointed a meal for poor starving people, and will you go away and not give it? If you do, the curse of God will go with you." This so moved him, that he durst not go away as he intended; but sitting down, he desired her and others to pray for him. So he remained and was settled in that parish, where he continued to exercise his ministry with great success, to the unspeakable satisfaction both of his own parish, and of all the godly that heard and knew him, until, by the unhappy restoration of Charles II., Prelacy was again restored.

Upon the 29th of May following, the day consecrated in commemoration of the said Restoration, he had occasion to preach in his own church, it being his ordinary week-day's preaching. Seeing an unusual throng of people who came to hear him, who thought he had preached in compliance with that solemnity, upon entering the pulpit, he said, "We are not come here to keep this day upon the account for which others keep it. We thought once to have blessed the day wherein the King came home again, but now we think we shall have reason to curse it; and if any of you come here in order to the solemnising of this day, we desire you to remove." And enlarging upon these words in Hosea ix. 1 : "Rejoice not, O Israel, for joy, as other people : for thou hast gone a-whoring from thy God; thou hast loved a reward upon every corn-floor," he said, "This is the first step of our going a-whoring from God ; and whoever of the Lord's people this day are rejoicing, their joy will be like the crackling of thorns under a pot; it will soon be turned to mourning. He (meaning the King) will be the wofullest sight that ever the poor Church of Scotland saw. Wo, wo, wo unto him ! His name shall stink while the world stands, for treachery, tyranny, and lechery."

This did extremely enrage the malignant party against him ; so that, being hotly pursued, he was obliged to abscond, remaining sometimes in private houses, and sometimes lying all night among broom near the city, yet never omitting any proper occasion of private preaching, catechising, visiting of families, and other ministerial duties. At length, when the churches were all vacated of Presbyterians by an act of Council 1662, Middleton sent a band of soldiers to apprehend him, who, coming to the church, found him not, he having providentially just stepped out of one door a minute before they came in at the other; whereupon they took the keys of the church door with them, and departed. In the meanwhile the Council passed an act of confinement, banishing him to the north side of the Tay, under penalty of being imprisoned and prosecuted as a seditious person; but this sentence he no way regarded.

During this time, partly by grief for the ruin of God's work in the land, and partly by the toils and inconveniences of his labours and accommodation, his voice became so broken, that he could not be heard by many together. This was a sore trial to him, and discouraged him from preaching in the fields ; but one day, Mr Blackader coming to preach near Glasgow, he essayed to preach with him, and standing on a chair, as his custom was, he lectured on Isa. xliv. 3, "I will pour water on him that is thirsty." The people were much afraid, knowing his voice to be sore broken, lest they should not hear, by reason of the great concourse. But it pleased the Lord to loose his tongue, and restore his voice to such a distinct clearness, that none could easily exceed him ; and not only his voice, but his spirit was so enlarged, and such a door of utterance given him, that Mr Blackader, succeeding him, said to the people, "Ye, that have such preaching, have no need to invite strangers to preach to you ; make good use of your mercy." After this he continued to preach without the city, a great multitude attending and profiting by his ministry, being wonderfully preserved in the midst of dangers, the enemy several times sending out to watch him, and catch something from his mouth whereof they might accuse him.

In the month of October 1665, they made a public search for him in the city: but he, being informed, took horse, and rode out of town. At a narrow pass of the way, he met a good number of musketeers. As he passed them, turning to another way on the right hand, one of them asked him, "Sir, what o'clock is it?" He answered, "It is six." Another of them knowing his voice, said, "There is the man we are seeking!" Upon hearing this, he put spurs to his horse, and so escaped.

For about three years he usually resided in the house of Margare Craig, a very godly woman, where he lectured morning and evening to such as came to hear him. And though they searched strictly for him here, yet Providence so ordered it, that he was either casually or purposely absent; for the Lord was often so gracious to him, that He left him not without some notice of approaching hazard. Thus, one Sabbath, going to Woodside to preach, as he was about to mount his horse, having one foot in the stirrup, he turned about to his man, and said, "I must not go yonder to-day." A party of the enemy came there at that time in quest of him; but missing the mark they aimed at, they fell upon the people, apprehending and imprisoning several of them.

Another of his remarkable escapes was on a search made for him in the city, where they came to his chamber, but found him not, he being providentially in another house that night. But what is most remarkable, being one day preaching privately in the house of one Mr Callender, they came and beset the house, and the people put him and another into a window, closing the window up with books. The search was so strict that they searched the very ceiling of the house, until one of the searchers fell through the lower loft. Had they removed but one of the books, they would certainly have found him. But the Lord so ordered that they did not; for as one of the soldiers was about to take up one of them, the maid cried to the commander that he was going to take her master's books, and he was ordered to let them be. So narrowly did Cargill escape this danger.

Thus he continued until the 23d of November 1668, when the Council, upon information of a breach of his confinement, cited him to appear before them on the 11th of January thereafter. But though he was apprehended and brought before the Council and strictly examined, wherein he was most singularly strengthened to bear faith ful testimony to his Master's honour, and His persecuted cause and truths, yet, by the interposition of some persons of quality, his own friends, and his wife's relations, he was dismissed, and presently returned to Glasgow, where he performed all the ministerial duties as when in his own church, notwithstanding the diligence of his persecutors in searching for him.

Some time before Bothwell, notwithstanding all the searches that were made for him by the enemy, which were both strict and frequent, he preached publicly for eighteen Sabbath-days to multitudes, consisting of several thousands, within little more than a quarter of a mile of the city of Glasgow; yea, so near it, that the Psalms, when sung, were heard in several parts of it; and yet all this time he was uninterrupted.

At Bothwell, being taken by the enemy, and struck down to the ground with a sword, and seeing nothing but present death for him, having received several dangerous wounds in the head, one of the soldiers asked his name; he told him it was Donald Cargill; another asked him if he was a minister; he answered he was; whereupon they let him go. When his wounds were examined, he feared to ask if they were mortal, desiring, in submission to God, to live, judging that the Lord had yet further work for him to accomplish.

Some time after the battle at Bothwell, he was pursued from his own chamber out of town, and forced to go through several thorn hedges. But he was no sooner out than he saw a troop of dragoons just opposite to him. Back he could not go, soldiers being posted everywhere to catch him; upon which he went forward, near by the troop, who looked to him, and he to them, until he got past. On coming to the place of the water at which he intended to go over, he saw another troop standing on the other side, who called to him, but he made them no answer; and going about a mile up the water, he escaped, and preached at Langside next Sabbath without interruption. At another time, being in a house beset with soldiers, he went through the midst of them, they thinking it was the goodman of the house, and escaped. It appears that it was about this time he resolved to go over to Holland, but we have no certain account where or what time he stayed there; but from the following account, it could not be long.

After Bothwell he fell into deep exercise anent his call to the ministry; but, by the grace and goodness of God, he soon emerged out of it, and also got much light anent the duty of the day, being a faithful contender against the enemy's usurped power, and against the sinful compliance of ministers, in accepting the Indulgence, with indemnities, oaths, bonds, and all other corruptions.

There was a certain woman in Rutherglen, about two miles from Glasgow, who, by the instigation of some, both ministers and professors, was persuaded to advise her husband to go but once to hear the curate, to prevent the family being reduced But going the next day after to milk her cows, two or three of them dropped down dead at her feet, and Satan, as she conceived, appeared unto her, which cast her under sad and sore exercise and desertion, so that she was brought to question her interest in Christ, and all that had formerly passed betwixt God and her soul, and was often tempted to destroy herself, and sundry times attempted it. Being before known to be an eminent Christian, she was visited by many Christians, but without success, crying out that she was undone; she had denied Christ, and He had denied her. After continuing a long time in this state she cried for Mr Cargill, who came to her, but found her distemper so strong, that for several visits he was obliged to leave her as he found her, to his no small grief. However, after setting some days apart on her behalf, he at last came again to her, and finding her no better, but still rejecting all comfort, still crying out that she had no interest in the mercy of God or merits of Christ, and had sinned the unpardonable sin, he, looking in her face for a considerable time, took out his Bible, and naming her, said, 'I have this day a commission from my Lord and Master to renew the marriage contract betwixt you and Him; and if ye will not consent, I am to require your subscription on this Bible, that you are willing to quit all right, interest in, or pretence unto Him." Then he offered her pen and ink for that purpose. She was silent for some time, but at last cried out, "O! salvation is come unto this house. I take Him—I take Him on His own terms, as He is offered unto me by His faithful ambassador." From that time her bonds were loosed.

One time Donald Cargill, Walter Smith, and some other Christian friends being met in a friend's house in Edinburgh, one of the company told him of the general bonding of the Western gentlemen for suppressing field-meetings, and putting all out of their grounds who frequented them. After sitting silent for some time, he answered, with several heavy sighs and groans, "The enemy have been filling up their cup; and ministers and professors must have time to fill up theirs also; and it shall not be full till their enemies and they be clasped in one another's arms; and then, as the Lord lives, He will bring the wheel of His wrath and justice over them altogether."

Some time after the beginning of the year 1680, he retired toward the Firth of Forth, where he continued until that scuffle at Queensferry in which worthy Haughhead was killed, and he himself sorely wounded. But escaping, a certain woman found him in a private place on the south side of the town, and tying up his wounds with her head-cloths, conducted him to the house of Robert Puntens, in Carlowrie, where a surgeon dressed them, and Mrs Puntens gave him some warm milk, and he lay in their barn all night. From thence he went to the south, and next Sabbath preached at Cairnhill, somewhere adjacent to Loudon, in his blood and wounds (for no danger could stop him from going about doing good). His text was in Heb. xi. 32: "And what shall I more say, for time would fail me to tell of Gideon," etc. At night, some persons said to him, "We think, sir, preaching and praying go best with you when your danger and distress are greatest." He said, it had been so, and he hoped it would still be so, that the more his enemies and others did thrust at him that he might fall, the more sensibly the Lord had helped him; and then (as it had been to himself) he repeated these words from the 118th Psalm, "The Lord is my strength and song, and is become my salvation," which was the Psalm he sung upon the scaffold.

After this, he and Ricnard Cameron met and preached together in Darmeidmuir, and other places, until Cameron was slain at Airsmoss. Then he went north, where, in the month of September following, he had a most numerous meeting in the Torwood near Stirling, at which he pronounced the sentence of excommunication against some of the most violent persecutors of that day, as formally as the present state of things would permit. Some time before this, it is said, he was very distant, and spoke little in company; only to some he said, he had a blast to give with the trumpet, that the Lord had put in his hand, which would sound in the ears of many in Britain, and other places in Europe also. It is said that nobody knew what he was to do that morning, except Mr Walter Smith, to whom he imparted the thoughts of his heart.

When he began, some friends feared he would be shot. His landlord, in whose house he had been that night, cast his coat and ran for it. In the forenoon, he lectured on Ezek. xxi. 25, etc., and preached on 1 Cor. v. 13, and then having discoursed some time on the nature of excommunication, he proceeded to the sentence; [a sentence which, De Foe says, "was expressly founded upon the same grounds as was afterwards the renouncing of the King by the Revolution, and was abundantly justified by the practice of the whole nation in the Revolution."—ED.]. After this, in the afternoon, he preached from Lam. iii. 31, 32 : " For the Lord will not cast off for ever."

The next Lord's day, he preached at Fallow-hill, in the parish of Livingstone. In the preface, he said, " I know I am, and will be condemned by many for excommunicating those wicked men, but, condemn me who will, I know I am approven of by God, and am persuaded, that what I have done on earth, is ratified in heaven ; for, if ever I knew the mind of God, and was clear in my call to any piece of my generation work, it was that. And I shall give you two signs, that ye may know I am in no delusion. If some of these men do not find that sentence binding upon them ere they go off the stage, and be obliged to confess it, and if these men die the ordinary death of men, then God hath not spoken by me."

About the 22d of October following, a long and severe proclamation was issued against him and his followers, wherein a reward of 5000 merks was offered for apprehending him. Next month Middleton, Governor of Blackness, having been frustrated in his design at Queensferry, laid another plot for him, by consulting one James Henderson there, who by forging and signing letters, in the name of Bailie Adam in Culross, and some other serious Christians in Fife, invited Mr Cargill to come over, and preach to them at the Hill of Beath. Accordingly, Henderson went to Edinburgh with the letters, and, after a most diligent search, found Mr Cargill in the West Bow. Being willing to answer the call, Henderson proposed to go before, and have a boat ready at the ferry when they came ; and that he might know him, he desired to see Mr Cargill's clothes, Mr Skeen and Mr Boig being in the same room. In the meantime, he had Middleton's soldiers lying at Muttonhole, about three miles from Edinburgh. Mr Skeen, Archibald Stuart, Mrs Muir, and Marion Hervey, took the way before, on foot ; Mr Cargill and Mr Boig being to follow on horseback. Whenever they came to the place, the soldiers spied them; but Mrs Muir having escaped, went and stopped Mr Cargill and Mr Boig, who fled back to Edinburgh.

After this remarkable escape, Cargill, seeing nothing but the violent flames of treachery and tyranny against him above all others, retired for about three months to England, where the Lord blessed his labours, to the conviction and edification of many. In the time of his absence the delusion of the Gibbites arose, from one John Gibb, a sailor in Borrowstounness, who, with other three men, and twenty-six women, vented and maintained the most strange delusions. Some time after, Mr Cargill returned from England, and was at no small pains to reclaim them, but with little success. After his last conference with them at Darngavel, in Cambusnethan parish, he came next Sabbath and preached at the Underbank Wood, below Lanark, whence he went to Loudon Hill, where he preached upon a fast-day, being the 5th of May. Here he intended only to have preached once, and to have baptized some children. His text was Matt. xix. 28, "Ye which have followed me, in the regeneration when the Son of man shall sit in the throne of His glory, ye also shall sit upon twelve thrones, judging the twelve tribes of Israel." When sermon was over, and the children baptized, more children were brought, whereupon friends pressed him to preach in the afternoon; which he did from these words, Luke xxiii. 28, "Weep not for me, but weep for yourselves, and for your children." In the meanwhile the enemy at Glasgow, getting notice of this meeting, seized all the horses in and about the town that they could come by, and mounted in quest of him; yea, such was their haste and fury, that one of the soldiers, who happened to be behind the rest, riding furiously down the street called the Stockwell at mid-day, rode over a child, and killed her on the spot. Just as Mr Cargill was praying at the close, a lad alarmed them of the enemy's approach. They (having no sentinels that day, which was not their ordinary) were so surprised, that many of them who had been at Pentland, Bothwell, Airsmoss, and other dangers, were seized with fear, some of the women throwing their children from them. In this confusion, Mr Cargill was running straight on the enemy; but Gavin Wotherspoon and others hailed him to the moss, to which the people fled. The dragoons fired hard upon them; but there were none either killed or taken that day.

About this time, some spoke to Mr Cargill of his preaching and praying short. They said, "O Sir, it is long betwixt meals, and we are in a starving condition ; all is good, sweet, and wholesome, that you deliver, but why do you so straighten us ?" He said, " Ever since I bowed a knee in good earnest to pray, I never durst preach and pray with my gifts ; and when my heart is not affected, and comes not up with my mouth, I always think it time to quit it. What comes not from the heart I have little hope will go to the hearts of others." Then he repeated these words in the 51st Psalm, " Then will I teach transgressors thy ways."

From Loudon Hill he took a tour through Ayrshire to Carrick and Galloway, preaching, baptizing, and marrying some people, but stayed not long until he returned to Clydesdale. He designed, after his return, to have preached one day at Tinto Hill, but the Lady of St John's Kirk gave it out to be at Home Common. He being in the house of John Liddel, near Tinto, went out to spend the Sabbath morning by himself, and seeing the people all passing by, he inquired the reason, which being told, he rose and followed them five miles off. The morning being warm (about the 1st of June), and the heights steep, he was very much fatigued before he got to the place, where a man gave him a drink of water out of his bonnet, and another between sermons, this being the only entertainment he got that day, for he had tasted nothing in the morning. Here he lectured on the 6th of Isaiah, and preached on these words, Rom. xl. 20, " Be not high-minded, but fear." From thence he went to Fife, and baptized many children, and preached one day at Daven Common, and then returned to the Benty Ridge in Cambusnethan, where he received a call from the hands of two men to go back to Galloway, but got it not answered. To these two men he said, " If I be not under a delusion (for that was his ordinary way of speaking of things to come), the French and other foreigners, with some unhappy men in this land, will be your stroke. It will come at such a nick of time, when one of these nations will not be in a capacity to help another. For me I am to die shortly by the hand of those murderers, and shall not see it. I know not how the Lord's people that have to meet with it, will endure it ; but the foresight and forethought of it make me tremble." And then, as if it had been to himself, he said, " Short, but very sharp ! "

Mr Cargill, in that short time, had run very fast towards his end, which now hastened apace. Having left the Benty Ridge, he preached one day at Auchingilloch, and then came to Dunsyre Common, betwixt Clydesdale and Lothian, where he preached his

QUEENSFERRY.

last sermon upon that text, Isa. xxii. 20, " Come, my people, and enter into your chambers."

Some time that night, through the persuasion of Mr Smith and Mr Boig, he went with the lady of St John's Kirk as far as Covington Mill, to the house of one Andrew Fisher. In the mean-time, James Irvine of Bonshaw, having got a general commission, marched with a party of dragoons from Kilbride, and next morning, by sun-rising, came to St John's Kirk, and having searched it, he searched also the house of one Thomson, and going to Covington Mill, he there apprehended Mr Cargill, Mr Smith, and Mr Boig. Bonshaw, when he found them, cried out, " O blessed Bonshaw— and blessed day that ever I was born—that has found such a prize! A prize of 5000 merks for apprehending of him this morning!" They marched hard to Lanark, and put them in jail, until they got some refreshment, and then bringing them out in haste, got horses and set the prisoners on their bare backs. Bonshaw tied Mr Car-gill's feet below the horse's belly, with his own hand, very hard; at which he looked down to him, and said, " Why do you tie me. so hard? Your wickedness is great : you will not long escape the just judgment of God; and, if I be not mistaken, it will seize you in this very place." This accordingly came next year to pass; for having got this price of blood, one of his comrades, in a rage, ran him through with a sword at Lanark, and his last words were, "G—d d—n my soul eternally, for I am gone!" "Evil shall hunt the violent man."

They came to Glasgow in haste, fearing a rescue of the prisoners; and while waiting at the tolbooth till the magistrates came to receive him, John Nisbet, the Archbishop's factor, said to Mr Cargill in ridicule three times over, "Will you give us one word more?" (alluding to an expression he used sometimes when preaching). To whom Mr Cargill said with regret, "Mock not, lest your bands be made strong. The day is coming, when you shall not have one word to say, though you would." This also came quickly to pass: for, not many days after, he fell suddenly ill, and for three days his tongue swelled, and though he was most earnest to speak, yet he could not command one word, and died in great torment and seeming terror.

From Glasgow they were taken to Edinburgh, and on July 15th were brought before the Council. Chancellor Rothes (being one of those whom Cargill had excommunicated at Torwood) raged against him, threatening him with torture and violent death; to whom he said, "My Lord Rothes, forbear to threaten me, for die what death I will, your eyes shall not see it." This accordingly came to pass; for he died the morning of that day, in the afternoon of which Mr Cargill was executed.

When before the Council, he was asked if he acknowledged the King's authority, etc. He answered, that as the magistrate's authority is now established by the act of Parliament and explanatory act, he denied the same. Being also examined anent the excommunication at Torwood, he declined to answer, as being an ecclesiastical matter, and they a civil judicatory. He owned the lawfulness of defensive arms in cases of necessity, and denied that those who rose at Bothwell were rebels; and being interrogated anent the Sanquhar declaration, he declined to give his judgment until he had more time to peruse the contents thereof. He further declared, he could not give his sense of the killing of the Archbishop; but that the Scriptures say, upon the Lord's giving a call to a private man to kill, he might do it lawfully, and gave the instances of Jael and Phinehas. These were the most material points on which he was examined.

While he was in prison, a gentlewoman, who came to visit him, told him, weeping, "That these Heaven-daring enemies were contriving a most violent death for him—some, a barrel, with many pikes, to roll him in; others, an iron-chair, red-hot, to roast him in." But he said, " Let you nor none of the Lord's people be troubled for these things, for all that they will get leave to do to me will be to knit me up, cut me down, and chop off my old head, and then fare them well: they have done with me, and I with them for ever!"

He was again before the Council on the 19th, but refused to answer their questions, except anent the excommunications. There was some motion made to spare him, as he was an old man, and send him a prisoner to the Bass during life; which motion being put to a vote, was, by the casting vote of the Earl of Rothes, rejected; who doomed him to the gallows, there to die like a traitor.

Upon the 26th he was brought before the Justiciary, and indicted in common form. His confession being produced in evidence against him, he was brought in guilty of high treason, and condemned, with the rest, to be hanged at the cross of Edinburgh, and his head placed on the Nether Bow. When they came to these words in his indictment, viz., *having cast off all fear of God*, etc. he caused the clerk to stop, and, pointing to the Advocate, Sir George M'Kenzie, said, "The man that hath caused that paper to be drawn up, hath done it contrary to the light of his own conscience, for he knoweth that I have been a fearer of God from mine infancy; but that man, I say, who took the Holy Bible in his hand, and said, it would never be well with the land, until that book was destroyed, he is the man that hath cast off all fear of God." The Advocate stormed at this, but could not deny the truth thereof.

When they got their sentence announced by sound of trumpet, he said, " This is a weary sound, but the sound of the last trumpet will be a joyful sound to me, and all that will be found leaning on Christ's righteousness."

Being come to the scaffold, he stood with his back to the ladder, and desired the attention of the numerous spectators. After singing from the 16th verse of the 118th Psalm, he began to speak to three sorts of people, but being interrupted by the drum, he said, with a smiling countenance, " Ye see we have no liberty to speak what we would, but God knoweth our hearts." As he proceeded he was again interrupted. Then, after a little pause of silence, he began to exhort the people; and to show his own comfort in laying down his life, in the assurance of a blessed eternity, expressed himself in these words, "Now, I am as sure of my interest in Christ and peace with God, as all within this Bible and the Spirit of God can make me; and I am fully persuaded that this is the very way for which I suffer, and that He will return gloriously to Scotland; but it will be terrifying to many. Therefore I entreat you, be not discouraged at the way of Christ, and the cause for which I am to lay down my life, and step into eternity, where my soul shall be as full of Him as it can desire to be. And now this is the sweetest and most glorious day that ever mine eyes did see. Enemies are now enraged against the way and people of God, but ere long they shall be enraged one against another, to their own confusion." Here the drums did beat a third time. Then, setting his foot on the ladder, he said, "The Lord knows I go on this ladder with less fear and perturbation of mind, than ever I entered the pulpit to preach." When up, he sat down and said, "Now, I am near the getting of the crown which shall be sure, for which I bless the Lord, and desire all of you to bless Him that He hath brought me here, and made me triumph over devils, men, and sin. They shall wound me no more. I forgive all men the wrongs they have done me; and I pray the sufferers may be kept from sin, and helped to know their duty." Then, having prayed a little within himself, he lifted up the napkin, and said, "Farewell, all relations and friends in Christ; farewell acquaintances and earthly enjoyment; farewell reading and preaching, praying and believing, wanderings, reproach, and sufferings. Welcome Father, Son, and Holy Ghost; into thy hands I commit my spirit." Then he prayed a little, and the executioner turned him over as he was praying; and so he finished his course, and the ministry that he had received of the Lord.

Take his character from Sir Robert Hamilton of Preston, who was his contemporary. "He was affectionate, affable, and tender hearted, to all such as he thought had anything of the image of God in them; sober and temperate in his diet, saying commonly, it was well won that was won off the flesh; generous, liberal, and most charitable to the poor; a great hater of covetousness; a frequent visiter of the sick; much alone, loving to be retired; and when about his Master's public work, laying hold of every opportunity to edify; in conversation, still dropping what might minister grace to the hearers; his countenance was edifying to beholders; often sighing with deep groans; preaching in season and out of season, upon all hazards; ever the same in judgment and practice. From his youth he was much given to the duty of secret prayer, for whole nights together; wherein it was observed, that, both in secret and in families, he always sat straight upon his knees, with his hands lifted up; and in this posture (as some took notice) he died with the rope about his neck."

Besides his last speech and testimony, and several other religious letters, with the lecture, sermon, and sentence of excommunication at Torwood, which are all published, there are several other sermons, and notes of sermons, interspersed among various hands, some of which have been published. Yet, if we may believe one, who heard several of them preached, they are nothing to what they were when delivered; and however pathetic, yet they are doubtless far inferior to what they would have been, had they been corrected and published by the worthy author himself.

AN ACROSTIC ON HIS NAME.

Most sweet and savoury is thy fame,
And more renowned is thy name,
Surely, than any can record,
Thou highly favoured of the Lord!
Exalted thou on earth didst live;
Rich grace to thee the Lord did give.

During the time thou dwelt'st below,
On in a course to heaven didst go.
Not casten down with doubts and fears,
Assured of heaven near thirty years,
Labour thou didst in Christ's vineyard;
Diligent wast, no time thou spar'd.

Christ's standard thou didst bear alone,
After others from it were gone,
Right zeal for truth was found in thee,
Great sinners censur'd'st faithfully.
In holding truth didst constant prove,
Laidst down thy life out of true love.

Walter Smith.

WALTER SMITH was son of Walter Smith, in the parish of St Ninians, near Airth, in Stirlingshire. He was an eminent Christian, and a good scholar. He went over to Holland, where he studied some time under the famous Leusden, who had a great esteem and value for him, as being one both of high attainments and great experience in the serious exercise and solid practice of Christianity.

In 1679, we find that he made no mean figure among that little handful of the Lord's suffering remnant, who rose in their own defence at Bothwell Bridge. For he was both chosen clerk to the council of war, and also a commanding officer among the honest party; and had the honour not only to witness and protest against the sinful compliance of that corrupt Erastian party who then foisted themselves in amongst them, but was also one of three who were appointed to draw up the " Causes of the Lord's Wrath against the Land " (of which the Hamilton Declaration was to form the last cause), together with a new Declaration which they intended to have published at that time. Although both of these were undertaken, yet the Lord did not honour them to publish the same, as some of them, with great regret, unto their dying day, did acknowledge.

After the overthrow and dispersion of the Covenanters at Bothwell (in which the Erastian party among them had no little hand), it appears that Walter Smith went over for some time to Holland, but did not stay long, for we meet with him again with Donald Cargill at Torwood, in September 1680 ; after which, he was very helpful to him in his conversation, and advice in difficult cases, and praying in families (when Cargill was fatigued with sore travel, being an old man, and going then often on foot), and many times in public preaching days precenting for him.

He had a longing desire to preach Christ and Him crucified unto the world, and the word of salvation through His name. Mr Cargill had the same desire ; and for that end, it is said, had written to two ministers to meet him at Cummerhead, in Lesmahagow, in Clydesdale. But ere that day came, the door was closed, for they were in the enemy's hands. However, Walter Smith followed the example of our blessed Lord and Saviour, by going about doing good in many places and to many persons, in spiritual edifying conversation, and was a singular example of true piety and zeal; which had more influence upon many, than most part of the ministers of that day.

A little before his death, he drew up twenty-two rules for fellowship or society meetings, which at that time, partly by his instrumentality, greatly increased from the river Tay to Newcastle. These afterwards settled into a general and quarterly correspondence, that so they might speak one with another, when they wanted the public preaching of the Gospel, and appoint general fasting days through the whole community, wherein their own sins, and the prevailing sins and defections of the times, were confessed—each society to meet and spend some time of the Lord's day together, when deprived of the public ordinances. Mr Cargill said that these society meetings would increase more and more for a time; but when the judgments came upon these sinful lands, there would be few society meetings when there would be most need—few mourners, prayers, and pleaders, because of carnality, security, darkness, deadness, and divisions.

But Walter Smith was now well nigh the evening of his life, and his labours both. For having been with Mr Cargill when he preached his last sermon in Dunsyre Common, betwixt Clydesdale and Lothian, he was, next morning, by wicked Bonshaw (who had formerly traded in fine horses betwixt the two kingdoms), apprehended at Covington Mill. He was, with the rest of the prisoners, carried from Lanark to Glasgow, and from thence taken to Edinburgh, where, upon the 14th of July, he was brought before the Council, and there asked, if he owned the King and his authority as lawful? He answered: " I could not acknowledge the present authority the King is now invested with, and the exercise thereof, being now clothed with a supremacy over the Church." Being interrogated, if the King's falling from the Covenant looses him from his obedience, and if the King thereby loses his authority? he answered, " I think he is obliged to perform all the duties of the Covenant, conform to the Word of God; the king is only to be obeyed in terms of the Covenant." Being further interrogated anent the Torwood excommunication, he declared that he thought " their reasons were just."

On the 19th of July he was again brought before them, and interrogated, If he owned the Sanquhar Declaration? It was then read to him, and he owned the same in all its articles, except that he looked not upon these persons as the formal representatives of the Presbyterian Church, as they called themselves. And as to that ex-pression, "The King should have been denuded many years ago," he did not like the word *denuded*, but said, "what the King has done, justifies the people revolting against him." As to these words, where the King is called an usurper and a tyrant, he said, "Certainly the King is an usurper," and wished he was not a tyrant.

Upon the 26th, he was with the rest brought before the Justiciary, where being indicted in common form, their confessions were pro-duced as evidence against them. They were all brought in guilty of high treason, and condemned to be hanged at the cross of Edinburgh, upon the 27th, and their heads to be severed from their bodies, and those of Messrs Cargill, Smith, and Boig, to be placed on the Nether Bow, and the heads of the others on the West Port; all which was done accordingly.

After Cargill was executed, Walter Smith was brought upon the scaffold, where he adhered to the very same cause with Mr Cargill, and declared the same usurpation of Christ's crown and dignity, and died with great assurance of his interest in Christ, declaring his abhorrence of Popery, Prelacy, Erastianism, and all other steps of defection. He went up the ladder with all signs of cheerfulness; and when the executioner was to untie his cravat, he would not suffer him, but untied it himself, and, calling to his brother, he threw it down, saying, "This is the last token you shall get from me." After the napkin was drawn over his face, he uncovered it again, and said, "I have one word more to say, and that is, to all who have any love to God and His righteous cause, that they would set time apart, and sing a song of praise to the Lord, for what He has done for my soul; and my soul saith, To Him be praise." Then the napkin being let down, he was turned over praying, and died in the Lord, with his face bend-ing upon Mr Cargill's breast. These two clave to one another in love and unity in their life; and between them, in their death, there was little difference. "Saul and Jonathan were lovely and pleasant in their lives, and in their death they were not divided."

The now glorified Walter Smith was a man no less learned than pious, faithful, and religious. His old master, the professor of divinity at Utrecht in Holland, when he heard of his public violent bloody death of martyrdom, gave him this testimony, weeping and saying in broken English, "O Smith! the great, brave Smith! who exceeded all that ever I taught; he was capable to teach many, but few to instruct him." Besides some letters, and the forementioned twenty-two rules for fellowship-meetings, he wrote also Twenty Steps of National Defection; all which are now published; and if these, with his last testimony, be rightly considered, it will appear that his writings were inferior to few of the contendings of that time.

Robert Garnock.

ROBERT GARNOCK was born in Stirling, and baptized by the faithful Mr James Guthrie. In his younger years, his parents took much pains to train him up in the way of duty; but soon after the Restoration, the faithful Presbyterian ministers being turned out, curates were put in their place, and with them came ignorance, profanity, and persecution. Some time after this, Mr Law preached at his own house in Monteith, and Mr Hutchison sometimes at Kippen. Having one Saturday evening gone out to his grandmother's house in the country, and having an uncle who frequented these meetings, he went along with him to a place called Shield Brae. Next Sabbath he went with him through great difficulty, being then but young, through frost and snow, and heard Mr Law at Monteith: which sermon, through the Divine blessing, wrought much upon his mind. Thus he continued for a considerable time to go out in the end of the week for an opportunity of hearing the Gospel, and to return in the beginning of next week to Stirling; but he did not let his parents know anything of the matter.

At one time he heard a proclamation read at the Cross announcing that all who did not hear or receive privileges from the curates were to be severely punished; which much troubled his mind, making him hesitate whether to go to a field preaching which was to take place on the next Sabbath. At last he resolved to go, in reference to which he says, "The Lord inclined my heart to go, and put that word to me, Go for once, go for all, if they take thee for that which is to come. So I went there, and the Lord did me good; for I got at that sermon that which, although they had rent me in a thousand pieces, I would not have said what I had said before. So the Lord made me follow the Gospel for a long time ; and though I knew little then what I meant, yet He put it in my heart still to keep by the honest side, and not to comply or join with enemies of one kind or another ; yea, not to watch, ward, or strengthen their hands any manner of way. When I was asked, why I would not keep watch (or stand sentry) on the town, as it was commanded duty? I told them, I would not lift arms against the work of God. If I ever carried arms, it should be for the defence of the Gospel."

Garnock now became a persecuted man, and was obliged to leave the town. His father being a blacksmith, he had learned the same trade, and went for some time to Glasgow, to follow his occupation. From Glasgow he returned home, and from thence to Borrowstounness, where he had great debate, as he himself expresses it, "about that woful Indulgence." "I did not know," he says, "the dreadful hazard of hearing them (that is, the Indulged), until I saw they preached at the hazard of men's lives. This made me examine the matter, until I found out that they were directly wrong, and contrary to Scripture, had changed their head, had quitted Jesus Christ as their head, and had taken their commission from men, owning that perjured adulterous wretch Charles II. as head of the Church ; receiving their commission to preach in such and such places from him, and those bloody thieves under him."

From Borrowstounness he proceeded to Falkirk, and thence home to Stirling, where he remained some time under a series of difficulties. For after he got off when taken with others at the Shield Brae, while he was making bold to visit Mr Skeen, he was arrested in the castle, and kept all night, and used very barbarously by the soldiers ; and at eight o'clock next morning was taken before the provost, who not being then at leisure, he was imprisoned till the afternoon. But, by the intercession of one Colin M'Kenzie, to whom his father was smith, he was got out, and without so much as paying the jailor's fee. "I had much of the Lord's kindness at that time (says he) although I did not then know what it meant: and so I was thrust forth into my wandering again."

About this time Garnock intended to go to Ireland ; but being disappointed, he returned to Stirling, where he was tossed to and fro for some time ; and yet he remarks, he had some sweet times in this condition; particularly one night when he was down in the Carse with one Baron Hendry. After this, heavy trials ensued unto him from professors of religion, because he testified against their compliance with the current of the times, upon which account, he and the Society meeting which he attended could not agree. This made him leave them, and go to one in the country ; which, he says, "was more sound in judgment, and of an undaunted courage and zeal for God and His cause ; for the life of religion was in that Society."

At this time he fell into such a degree of temptation, by the devices of the enemy of man's salvation, that he was made to supplicate the Lord several times, that he might not be permitted to affright him in visible shape : which he then apprehended he was attempting to do. But from these dreadful oppressions he was at last, through the goodness of God, happily delivered; although, as yet, he knew but little of experimental religion. And, says he, " The world thought I had religion ; but to know the hidden things of godliness was yet a mystery to me. I did not know anything as yet of the new birth, or what it was spiritually to take the kingdom of heaven by violence." This serves to show, that one may do and suffer many things for Christ and religion, and yet at the same time be a stranger to the life and power thereof.

But anon he falls into another difficulty, for a proclamation being issued, that all betwixt thirteen and sixteen were to pay poll-money, word was sent his father, that if he would pay it, he should have his liberty; which was no small temptation. But this he absolutely refused, and also told his father plainly, when urged by him to do it, that if one plack (or four pennies) would do it, he would not give it. His father said, he would give it for him ; to whom he answered, if he did, he need never expect it, or any consideration for it, from him. For the result of the matter, hear his own words: "And oh! but the Lord was kind to me then, and His love was better than life. I was tossed in my wanderings and banishment with many ups and downs, till I came to Edinburgh, where I heard of a communion to be on the borders of England, and then I went to it. Oh! let me bless the Lord, that ever trysted me with such a lot as that was: for the 20th, 21st, and 22nd of April 1677, were the three most wonderful days with the Lord's presence that ever I saw on earth. Oh! but His power was wonderfully seen, and great to all the assembly, especially to me. Oh!

the three wonderful days of the Lord's presence at East Nisbet in the Merse; that was the greatest communion, I suppose, these twenty years; I got there what I will never forget while I live. Glory to His sweet name that ever there was such a day in Scotland; His work was wonderful to me, both in spirituals and temporals. Oh! that I could get Him praised and magnified for it. He was seen that day sitting at the head of His table, and His spikenard 'sending forth a pleasant smell.' Both good and bad were made to cry out, and some to say, with the disciples, 'It is good for us to be here.' They would have been content to have stayed there; and I thought it was a heaven begun to be in that place."

After this Garnock returned to Stirling, and got liberty to follow his employment for some time. But lo! another difficulty occurred; for while the Highland host was ordered west, in the beginning of 1678, the town was called to arms, and all, excepting a very few, obeyed. He refused, and went out of town with these few, and kept a meeting. When he returned, his father told him he was passed for the first time, but it behoved him to mount guard to-morrow. He refused; his father was angry, and urged him with the practices of others. He told his father, he would hang his faith upon no man's belt. On the morrow, when the drums beat to mount the guard, being the day of his social meeting, he went out of the town under a heavy load of reproach even from professors, who did not scruple to say, that it was not principle of conscience he hesitated upon, but that he might have liberty to stroll through the country; which was no easy matter to bear. Orders were given to apprehend him; but at that time he escaped their hand, and wandered from one place to another, until the beginning of August 1678, when he came to Carrick communion at Maybole; and what his exercise was there, himself thus expresses: "I was wonderfully trysted there, but not so as at the other. I went to the first table, and then went and heard worthy Messrs Kid and Cameron, who never left the fields till they sealed and crowned it with their blood, preach at a little distance from the meeting. I cannot say but the Lord was kind to me there, on the day after, and on the fast day in the middle of the week after that, near the borders of Kilmarnock parish, where a division arose about the Indulgence, which to this day is never yet done away. After my return home, I was made to enter into covenant with Him, upon His own terms, against the Indulgence and all other compliances; and because, through the Lord's strength, I had resolved to keep my bargain, and

not join with them, it was said, I had got new light, and I was much
reproached ; yet I got much of the Lord's kindness when attending
the preached Gospel in the fields, to which I would sometimes go
twenty miles."

Having thus wandered to and fro for some time, Garnock went
to Edinburgh to see the prisoners, and returned to Stirling in the
end of the week. Late on Saturday night he heard of a field-preach-
ing; and seeing the soldiers and troopers marching out of the town
to attack the people at that meeting, he made himself ready, and,
with a few others, went towards it. They soon arrived near the place ;
but the soldiers coming forward, the people, seeing the enemy, turned
off. He, with a few armed men and the minister, took to a hill above
Fintry, beside the Craigs of Ballglass. This little handful drew up in
the best posture the time and place would allow, and sung a psalm,
at which the soldiers were so affrighted, that they afterwards said the
very matches had almost fallen out of their hands. At last a trooper
coming on commanded them to dismiss, but this they refused. This
was repeated several times, till the captain of the foot came forward
and gave them the same charge; which they also refused. Upon
this, he commanded a party of his men to advance and fire upon
them ; which they did once or twice ; which was by this little company returned with much courage and agility, until the whole party,
and the commanding officer, consisting of forty-eight men and sixteen
horsemen, fired upon this little handful, which he thinks amounted to
not above eighteen that had arms, with a few women. After several
volleys were returned on both sides, one of the sufferers stepped forward and shot one side of the captain's periwig off, at which the foot
fled ; but the horsemen, taking advantage of the rising ground, surrounded the small party. They then fired on a young man, but
missed him. However, they took him and some others prisoners.
The rest fled. Garnock was hindermost, being the last on the place
of action, and says, he intended not to have been taken, but rather
killed. At last one of the enemy came after him, on which he resolved either to kill or be killed before he surrendered, catching a
pistol from one for that purpose. But another coming to his assistance, the trooper fled, and so they escaped unto the other side of a
precipice, where they stayed until the enemy were gone, who marched
directly with their prisoners to Stirling.

After the fray was over, Garnock stayed till evening, and spoke
with some friends and the minister, who strongly dissuaded him from

going into Stirling. But as he was now approaching the eve of his pilgrimage, with Paul in another case when going up to Jerusalem, he could not be prevailed upon, and so went to town. Having entered it about one in the morning, he went into a house at the foot of the Castlehill, and there got his arms left with much difficulty; but, as he was near the head of the Castlehill, he was, by two soldiers, who were lying in wait for those who had been at that meeting, apprehended and brought to the guard. He was then brought before Lord Linlithgow's son, who asked him if he was at that preaching? He told him he was at no preaching. Linlithgow's son said he was a liar. Garnock said he was no liar; "And seeing ye will not believe me," he said, "I will tell no more, prove the rest." Linlithgow said he would make him do it. But he answered he should not. Then he asked his name, trade, and his father's name, and where they dwelt? all which he answered. Then he bade keep him fast. At night he was much abused by the soldiers; some of them who had been wounded in the skirmish, threatening him with torture, gagging in the mouth, etc., all which he bore with much patience. In the morning, a sergeant came to examine him; but he refused to answer him. At last, the commanding officer came and asked him, if he was at that skirmish? He answered, that for being there he was taken; "and whether," he said, "I was there or not, I am not bound to give you an account." So he went out, and in a little returned with the Provost, who thought to surprise him by asking, "Who of Stirling folk were there?" He answered, "they were both your neighbours and mine;" and further, that though he had been there, he might account him very imprudent to tell; for though he thought it his duty to ask, yet it was not his to answer, and he should rather commend him for so doing. After several other things anent that affair, he was commanded to be kept a close prisoner, and none, not so much as his father, allowed to speak to him; but he did not want company at that time; for, says he, "Oh! but I had a sweet time of it! The Lord's countenance was better unto me than all the company in the world."

The forementioned skirmish occurred May 8, 1679. Upon the 19th of the same month, he was put into the common prison, amongst malefactors; where he got more liberty, having some others of the sufferers with him. However, they were very much disturbed by a notorious murderer, who, being drunk one time, thought to have killed him with a large plank or form. But happily the stroke did not hurt him, though he struck with all his force twice, whereby another was almost killed. This made him and other five to lie sometimes upon the stairs, for they could have no other place; though they desired the thieves' hole, they could not obtain it. And thus they passed the time with much pain and trouble until June 10, that the Fife men were defeated at Bewly, and numbers taken, who were brought in prisoners on the 11th; whereby they were very much thronged. Here he continued till the battle at Bothwell on the 22d, after which there was no small confusion by tendering and pressing of a bond of conformity against offensive arms, wherein he got his share during that time.

Upon the 13th of July, he was brought forth, and in company with about 100 more prisoners, under a strong guard of red-coats, taken from Stirling to Edinburgh, and put into the Greyfriars churchyard, amongst the Bothwell prisoners. There he was more vexed—both by the enemy and his fellow-sufferers—than ever ; a specimen of which is here given in his own words :

"Some of my neighbours desired the Bond, so they put it to me, but I refused. However, the most part of them took it; nay, some of them supplicated for any bond. This made some of us conclude it was our duty to testify against it; which piece of employment was put upon me, against which some of the prisoners obtested. So I was rendered odious; but many a day the Lord was kind to me in that yard, and kept me from many a fear and snare ; His love was sweet unto me. The men complained of us to the commanders, who sent and examined me on the Bond and other things. They said I should be gagged, and every day I was vexed with them, until almost the whole prisoners petitioned for it. There was as good as seventy ministers sent into the yard to take it; and they said it was not a head to suffer upon. When they had done, they sent in two gentle-women with the commission ; and they set upon me. I told them, if every one of them had as much of it as I had, they would not be so busy to press it ; for before this the bloody crew came to the yard, and called on me, and asked if I would take the Bond. I said, No. They said, I would get no other sentence ; so I was sore put to it. I would often have been at the doing of something ; but the Lord would not suffer me. So, in His strength, I fought on against my own heart and them all, and overcame. But oh ! the cross was sweet and easy unto me ; none need fear to venture on suffering in His way and strength. Oh ! happy days, that ever I was trysted with such a thing ! My bargaining with lovely Jesus was sweet unto me. It is true,

OLD VIEW OF STIRLING CASTLE.

'affliction for the present seemeth not joyous but grievous; but after-wards it yieldeth the peaceable fruits of righteousness to those who are exercised thereby.' I never knew the treachery of ministers, and their dreadful hypocrisy and double dealing in the matters of God, before that time, and I could never love them after that; for they made many a one rack his conscience in taking that Bond. I was brought out of the yard, October 25, with a guard of soldiers. When coming out, one Mr White asked, if I would take the Bond? I, smiling, said, No. He, in way of jeer, said I had a face to glorify God in the Grassmarket. So I bade farewell to all my neighbours, who were sorry; and White bade me take good night with them, for I should never see them more. But I said, Lads, take good heart, for we may meet again for all this. So I was brought before their Council Court. They asked, if I would take the Bond? I said, No. Some of them said, 'Maybe he does not know it;' but Hatton said, 'He knows it well enough.' So one of them read it. I asked, if they would have me subscribe a lie to take away my life; for I never was in rebellion, nor intended to be so. They said, they would make another bond for me. I answered, they needed not trouble them-selves; for I was not designed to subscribe any bond at this time.

Q. "'Will you rise in rebellion against the King?'

A. "'I was not rising in rebellion against the King.'

GREYFRIARS' CHURCHYARD.

Q. " ' Will you take the Bond, never to rise against the King and his authority ?'

A. " ' What is the thing you call authority ?   They said, if they, the soldiers, or any other subject, should kill me, I was bound not to resist.   I answered, that I would never do.'

Q. " ' Is the Archbishop's death murder ?'

A. " ' I am a prisoner, and so no judge.'

Q. " ' Is Bothwell Bridge rebellion ?'

A. " ' I am not bound to give my judgment in that.'

" Then one of them said, ' I told you what the rebel rascal would say ; you will be hanged.'   ' Sir,' I answered, ' you must first convict me of a crime.'   They said, ' You did excommunicate prisoners for taking the Bond.'   I said, ' That was not in my power ; and, moreover, I was not before them for that, and that they should prove it if they were able.'   They said, ' They would hang me for rebellion.' I said ' You cannot : for if you walk according to your own laws, I should have my liberty.   They said, ' Should we give a rebellious knave, like you, your liberty ?   You should be hanged immediately.' I answered, ' That lies not yet in your power.'   So they caused quickly to take me away, and put me in the iron-house Tolbooth.   Much more passed that I must not spend time to notice.

" So they brought me to the iron-house, to fifteen of my dear companions in tribulation; and there we were a sweet company, being all of one judgment. There, serving the Lord, day and night, in singleness of heart, His blessedness was seen amongst us; for His love was better than life. We were all with one accord trysted sweetly together: and oh! it was sweet to be in this company, and pleasant to those who came in to see us, until the indictments came in amongst us. There were ten got their indictments. Six came off, and four got their sentence, to die at Magus Muir. There were fifteen brought out of the yard, and some of them got their liberty offered, if they would witness against me. But they refused; so they got all their indictments; but all complied, save one, who was sentenced to die with the other four at Magus Muir."

In this situation, Garnock continued till November 13th, when he was, by the intercession of some friends, brought to the west galleries on the other side of the Tolbooth, where he continued some time, till called again before some of the Council: after which he was again committed to close prison for a time, till one night, being called again forth by one of the keepers, Mr John Blair, being present, accosted him thus: "Wherefore do you refuse the Bond?" He answered, "I have no time now for that matter!" "But out of that place," said Blair, "you shall not go, for the Covenants and the 13th of the Romans bind you to it." I answered, "No; they just bound me to the contrary. What if Popery should come to the land, should we bind ourselves never to defend the true religion?" He said, "We were loosed then." I said, "No; Presbyterians are taken by their word, and they abide by it; and ere all were done, it should be a dear bond unto them; as for my part, I would rather go to the Grassmarket, and seal it with my blood." After Garnock came down, the keeper of the Tolbooth abused him in a very indiscreet manner, saying, that if there were no more men, he should be hanged; that he was an ignorant fool; ministers nor men could not convince him; and bade take him off again to close prison, where he was again as much vexed with a company of bonders as ever; for they were not only become lax in principle, but in duty also. So he roundly told them, "You are far from what you were in the iron-house, before you took the Bond; then you would have been up at duty by two or three in the morning; now you lie in bed till eight or nine in the day." They said, It was true enough; but said no more.

After these got their liberty, Garnock was associated with other prisoners, some of whom were kept in for debt. And then, he says, he would have been up by four in the morning, and made exercise amongst them three times a-day; and the Lord was kind to him during that time; he resolved never to make any compliance, and in this he was made to eat meat out of the eater, and sweet out of the strong. But some gentlemen, prisoners for religion, where he was before, prevailed with the keeper of the Tolbooth to have him back to them about the beginning of 1680. Here the old temptation to compliance, and tampering with the enemy, was afresh renewed; for the ministers coming in to visit these, when they could do no more, they brought them to the rooms to preach, and made him hear them; which he positively refused. At last, they brought a minister, one of his acquaintance, who was to have preached in the field on the day he was taken. But hearing that he had made some compliance with the enemy, he would not go to the next room to hear him make exercise, till he knew the certainty of the matter; after which he came to another room, where they had some conference. " He asked after my welfare; and if I was going out of prison? I told him, I blessed the Lord for it, I was well, and was not going out yet. After some conversation anent field-preachings, particularly one by Richard Cameron at Monkland, which he condemned, he asked, Why I did not hear ministers? I answered, I desire to hear none but what are faithful; for I am a prisoner, and would gladly be in the right way, not to wrong myself. He said, Wherein are they unfaithful? I said, In changing their Head, quitting the Lord's way, and taking on with covenant breakers, and murderers of His people. He said, How could you prove that? I said, Their practice proves it. He said, These were but failings, and these would not perjure a man; and it is not for you to cast off ministers : you know not what you are doing. I said, I do not cast them off; they cast off themselves, by quitting the holding of the ministry of Christ. He asked, How prove you that? I said, The 10th of John proves it; for they come not in by the door. You may put me wrong; but I think, that also in Gal. i. 6, proves it : " I marvel that ye are so soon removed from him that called you." You may read that at your leisure, how Paul had not his Gospel from men, nor by the will of men. He said, Lay by these; but what is the reason you will not hear others? I said, I desire to hear none of these gaping for the Indulgence, and not faithful in preaching against it."

They had then some conference anent Cameron and Cargill, in which he said, Mr Cameron was no minister, and Mr Cargill was once one, and had quitted it; that they received their doctrines from men, their hearers, who said, you must preach such and such doctrines, and we will hear you. To all this Garnock gave pertinent answers.

"He then said, 'Robert, do not think I am angry that you come not to hear me ; for I desire not you, nor any of your faction, to come and hear me, for I cannot preach to all your humours.' I said, it was all the worse for that. He said that none of these faults would cast off a minister ; they were but failings, not principles. I said, I could not debate, but I should let any Christian judge, whether it was no principle for a minister to hold Christ head of the Church. I told him, that there was once a day I would have ventured my life at his back for the defence of Christ's Gospel, but not now ; and I was more willing to lay down my life now, for His sweet and dear truths, than ever I was. He said, the Lord pity and help me. I said, I had much need of it ; and so he went away, and rendered me odious. This, amongst other things, made me to go to God, and engage in covenant with His Son never to hear any of those who betrayed His cause, till I saw evidences of their repentance. And I would have been willing to have quitted all for that ' Chiefest among ten thousand.' "

Thus he continued, till, he says, he got bad counsel from some of his friends to supplicate for his liberty ; and they prevailed so far as to draw up a supplication, and brought it to him to subscribe. But when taking the pen in his hand, "The Lord bade me hold," says he, "and one came and bade me take heed. So I did it not, for which I bless His holy name. But this lets me see, there is no standing in me ; had it not been His free love, I had gone the blackest way ever one did."

The night before Hackston of Rathillet was put to death, being down stairs, and hearing of the way and manner in which he was to be executed, Garnock went up (though it was treason to speak to him) and told him of it ; which he could scarcely believe. But the keepers hearing, came up and assured him to the contrary, and threatened to put Garnock in the irons. Also, they got eight grey-coats to watch Mr Hackston all night, so that he might not know till at the place of execution.

It would appear that Garnock was not put in irons until some time after, that a young woman, who was taken at Queensferry, when Haughhead was killed, having liberty to come into the Lady Gilkercleugh, then in prison, was conveyed out in a gentleman's habit. Of this he and another got the blame, though entirely innocent, and were laid in irons. The other got his liberty, but Robert continued alone, as they intended to send him off with some soldiers to Tangiers. But the Lord having otherwise determined, they could not get as many of the Council convened as to get an order made out; and so he was continued in prison; during which time he endured a sore conflict with those of his fellow-prisoners who still complied and got off. Others came in their place, who set upon him afresh; so that he, and any one who was of his judgment, could scarcely get liberty to worship God in the room without disturbance. Those who were faithful, and a comfort to him, were taken from him and executed, while he was still retained in prison.

To relate all the trials and difficulties he underwent, during the time of his imprisonment, near the space of two years and a half, with his various exercises, and the remarkable goodness of God towards him all that time, would be more than can conveniently be accomplished at present. I shall only notice one or two very strange occurrences of Divine Providence towards him, and his condition towards the end of his narrative and life, which he thus records:

" I have no reason but to go through with cheerfulness, whatever He puts me to for owning of His cause; for if it had not been His sweet love to me, I might have been a sufferer for the worst of crimes. For there is in me what is in the worst of creatures; a remarkable instance of which I was trysted with long since, which, while I live, I will not forget. Being at home working with my father, and having mended a chest-lock to an honest woman, I went with it to put it on. The woman not being at leisure, there was a gun standing beside me; and having ofttimes guns amongst my hands to dress, I took it up, and, not observing that it was loaded, thinking the gun not good, tried to fire it, whereupon it went off, and the ball went up through a loft above, and almost killed a woman and a child. Had not Providence directed that shot, I had suffered as a murderer: and am I not obliged to follow and suffer for the ' Chiefest among ten thousand,' who has so honoured me a poor wretch? Many other things have escaped me; for I may not stay to mention what the Lord has done for me, both at field-preachings and other places. I have had a continued warfare, and my predominants grew mightily on my hand, which made my life sometimes heavy; but among the many sweet nights and days I have had, was the 23d in the evening, and 24th in the morning, of August 1681. The Lord was kind to me. That was the beginning of mornings indeed, wherein I got some of the Lord's love, found an open door, and got a little within the court, and there was allowed to give in what I had to say, either as to my own soul's case, or the case of the Church, which is low at this day. I have indeed had some sweet days since; but I have misguided them, and could not keep in with Him: for my corruptions are so mighty, that sometimes I have been made to cry out, Woe is me that ever I was born, a man of strife and contention to many! 'O wretched man that I am! who shall deliver me from the body of this death?' But the Lord maketh up all again with His love, so that I may have ups and downs in my case. I have forgotten some things particularly worthy of remark; such as, one night I was set upon by a French captain, when out of town; but the Lord remarkably delivered me, and brought me back again. So the Lord has let me see I might have suffered for worse actions. So that I have no ground but to be for God while I live, and bless His name that ever honoured me with this dignity of suffering for His name and honourable cause.

"What will become of me is yet uncertain; but, considering what the land was doing in bringing in of Popery, the love I bear to the Lord and His righteous cause made me give in my protestation against the Parliament, which this present year, 1681, has made laws for the strengthening of Popery. I could do no less; for the glory of God was dearer to me than my life.

"And now, for anything I know, I will be tortured and my life taken, and so will get no more written. As to any that read it, I beg of them to shun all that is evil in my life, as they wish to shun hell; and if there be anything in it that is for use, I request the Lord that He may bring it home upon them when I am gone, and make it useful for them that read it. So I bid you all farewell, desiring none of you may slight your time or duty as I have done; but shun the appearance of evil, cleave to that which is good, and spend much of your time with God. Be not idle night nor day, and give not over much sleep unto yourselves. O sirs! if you would be prevailed with to spend time for God, it would be the sweetest and most desirable service ever you took in hand. Oh! be persuaded to fall in love with Him, who is, without compare, 'the chiefest among ten thousand, yea, altogether lovely.' Take Him for your all, and bind yourselves hand and foot to His obedience. Let your ears be nailed to the posts of His doors, and be His servants for ever.

"And now, seeing I get no more time allowed me here on earth, I close with my hearty farewell to all friends ; and pray the Lord may guide them in all truth, and keep them from the dreadful snares that are coming on this covenanted land of Scotland. So I bid you all farewell; be faithful to the death. I know not certainly what may become of me after this, but I look and expect, that my time in this world is now near an end, and so desire to welcome all that the Lord sends. Thinking presently to be called in before God's enemies, I subscribe this

  "Sep. 28, 1681.   "ROBERT GARNOCK."

Having now seen a little of the life and exercises of Robert Garnock, we come to notice somewhat anent his trial, death, or martyrdom, which now hastens apace. According to his own expectation above narrated, he was brought before the Council, October 1, where he disowned the King's authority, refused them as his judges, and on the 7th was brought before the Justiciary, and indicted, " That he did, before the Council, on the 1st of October, decline the authority of the King and Council, and called the King and Council tyrants, murderers, perjured, and mansworn, declaring it was lawful to rise in arms against them ; and gave in a most treasonable paper, termed ' A Protestation and Testimony against Parliamenters ;' wherein he terms the members of Parliament idolaters, usurpers of the Lord's inheritance ; and protests against their procedure in their hell-hatched acts : which paper is signed by his hand, whereby he is guilty of treason. He further gave in a declaration to the Council, wherein the said Robert Garnock disowns the King's authority and government, and protests against the Council as tyrants. Therefore," etc. By such an explicit confession, his own papers being turned to an indictment, without any matters of fact against him, there was no difficulty of probation, his own protest and declinature being produced before the Justiciary and assize to which he was remitted.

Before the assize was inclosed, Robert Garnock, and other five who were indicted with him, delivered a paper to the judges, containing a protestation and warning, wherein they advise them to consider what they are doing, and upon what grounds they pass a sentence upon them. They declare they are not rebels ; they disown no authority that is according to the Word of God, and the Covenants the land is bound by. They charge them to consider how

THE TOLBOOTH—NORTH VIEW.

deep a sin covenant-breaking is; and put them in mind that they are to be answerable to the great Judge of all for what they do in this matter; and say they do this, since they are in hazard of their lives. It is a dangerous thing, they add, to pass a sentence on men merely because of their conscience and judgment, only because they cannot in conscience yield to the iniquitous laws of men; that they are free subjects, never taken in any action contrary to the present laws; that those, whom they once thought should or would rule for God, have turned their authority for tyranny and inhumanity, and employ it both in destroying the laws of God, and murdering His people against and without law, as they themselves can prove and witness; for after two years' imprisonment, one of them most cruelly and tyrant-like rose from the place of judgment, and drew a sword, and would have killed one of them, but Providence ordered it otherwise; however, the wound was yet to be shown. After reminding them of David Finlay, murdered at New-mills, James Mitchell's case, and James Lermond, who was murdered after he was three times freed by the assize, they add, that, after such murders as deserve death, they cannot see how they can own them as judges; imploring them to notice what they do; assuring them their blood will be heavy upon them: concluding with Jer.

xxvi. 15; and charging them not to take innocent blood on their heads. This was subscribed at Edinburgh, October 7, 1681, by ROBERT GARNOCK, D. FARRIE, J. STEWART, ALEX. RUSSELL, P. FORMAN, and C. LAPSLAY.

Notwithstanding all this, they were brought in guilty, and sentenced to be executed at the Gallow Lea, betwixt Leith and Edinburgh, upon the 10th October—Forman's hand to be cut off before, and the heads and hands of the rest after, death, and to be set upon the Pleasance Port.

What Garnock's deportment and exercises were at the place of execution, we are at a loss to describe; but, from what is already related, we may safely conclude, that, through Divine grace, his demeanour was truly noble and Christian. But that the reader may guess somewhat of his temper and disposition about that time, I shall extract a few sentences from his last speech and dying testimony.

" I bless the Lord that ever He honoured the like of me with a bloody gibbet and bloody winding-sheet for His noble, honourable, and sweet cause. Oh! will ye love Him, sirs? Oh! He is well worth the loving and quitting all for. Oh! for many lives to seal the sweet cause with! If I had as many lives as there are hairs on my head, I would think them all too little to be martyrs for truth. I bless the Lord I do not suffer unwillingly nor by constraint, but heartily and cheerfully. I have been a long time prisoner, and have been altered of my prison. I was amongst and in the company of the most part who suffered since Bothwell, and was in company with many ensnaring persons (though I do not question their being godly folk), and yet the Lord kept me from hearkening to their counsel. Glory, glory to His sweet name! It is many times my wonder how I have done such and such things; but it is He that has done them: He hath done all things in me and for me; holy is His name. I bless the Lord I am this day to step out of time into eternity, and I am no more troubled than if I were to take a match by marriage on earth, and not so much. I bless the Lord I have much peace of conscience in what I have done. Oh! but I think it a very weighty piece of business to be within twelve hours of eternity, and not troubled. Indeed, the Lord is kind, and has trained me up for this day, and now I can want Him no longer. I shall be filled with His love this night; for I will be with Him in paradise, and get a new song put in my mouth, the song of Moses and the Lamb: I will be in amongst the general assembly of the first-born, and enjoy the sweet presence of God and His Son Jesus Christ, and the spirits of just men made perfect—I am sure of it.

" Now, my Lord is bringing me to conformity with Himself, and honouring me with my worthy pastor, Mr James Guthrie. Although I knew nothing when he was alive, yet the Lord hath honoured me to protest against Popery, and to seal it with my blood; and He hath honoured me to protest against Prelacy, and to seal it with my blood. The Lord has kept me in prison to this day for that end: Mr Guthrie's head is on one port of Edinburgh, and mine must go on another. Glory, glory to the Lord's sweet name for what He hath done for me!

" Now I bless the Lord, I am not, as many suspect me, thinking to win heaven by my suffering. No; there is no attaining of it but through the precious blood of the Son of God. Now, ye that are the true seekers of God, and the butt of the world's malice, oh! be diligent and run fast. Time is precious. Oh! make use of it, and act for God, contend for truth, stand for God against all His enemies, fear not the wrath of men, love one another, wrestle with God mutually in societies. Confess your faults one to another, pray with one another, reprove, exhort, and rebuke one another in love. Slight no commanded duty; be faithful in your stations, as you will be answerable at the great day; seek not counsel from men; follow none farther than they hold by truth.

" Now, farewell sweet reproaches for my lovely Lord Jesus; though once they were not joyous but grievous, yet now they are sweet. And I bless the Lord for it, I heartily forgive all men for anything they have said of me; I pray it may not be laid unto their charge in the day of accounts; and for what they have done to God and His cause, I leave that to God and their own conscience! Farewell to all Christian acquaintance, father and mother! Farewell sweet prison for my royal Lord Jesus Christ, now at an end! Farewell all crosses of one sort or another, and everything in time, reading, praising, and believing! Welcome eternal life, and the spirits of just men made perfect! Welcome Father, Son, and Holy Ghost, into thy hands I commit my spirit."

The foregoing sentence in all its parts, was executed upon them all, except Lapslay, who got off. And so they had their passage from the valley of misery into the celestial country above, to inhabit the land where "the inhabitants say not, I am sick, and the people that dwell therein are forgiven their iniquities."

The faithful and pious James Renwick was present and was much affected at this execution; after which he assembled some friends, lifted the bodies in the night, and buried them in the West Kirk. They also got their heads down; but day approaching, they could not make the same place, and were obliged to turn aside to Laurieston's Yards (where one Alexander Tweedie, then in company with them, was gardener), where they in a box interred them. The gardener, it is said, planted a white rose bush above them, and a red one a little below them, which proved more fruitful than any bushes in all the garden. This place being uncultivated for a considerable time, they lay till October 7th, 1728, when another gardener, trenching the ground, found them. They were lifted, and by direction were laid on a table in the summer-house of the proprietor, and a fair linen cloth being cut out and laid upon them, all had access to come and see them; where they beheld a hole in each head, which the hangman made with his hammer, when he drove them on the pikes. On the 19th they were put into a coffin, covered with black, and by some friends carried to Greyfriars Churchyard, and interred near the Martyrs' Tomb, it being nearly forty-five years since their separation from their bodies. They were reburied on the same day, Wednesday, and about four o'clock afternoon, the same time that at first they went to their resting place, and attended, says one present, " by the greatest multitude of people, old and young, men and women, ministers and others, that ever I saw together." And there they lie, awaiting a glorious resurrection on the morning of the last day, when they shall be raised up with more honour than at their death they were treated with reproach and ignominy.

Thus died Robert Garnock, in the flower of his youth, a young man, but old in experimental religion. His faithfulness was as remarkable as his piety, and his courage and constancy as both. He was inured to tribulations almost from his youth, and was so far from being discouraged at the cross of Christ, that, in imitation of the primitive martyrs, he seemed rather ambitious of suffering. He always aimed at honesty; and notwithstanding opposition from pretended friends and professed foes, he was, by the Lord's strength, enabled to remain unshaken to the last; for, though he well-nigh tripped, yet he was seldom foiled, never vanquished. May the Lord enable many to emulate him who now inherits the promise, " Be thou faithful unto death, and I will give thee a crown of life."

PORTRAIT OF ROBERT M'WARD.

Robert M'Ward.

ROBERT M'WARD was born in Glenluce, in Galloway,
[The year of his birth is unknown. In 1643 he was
enrolled as a student of divinity at St Andrews, under
Samuel Rutherford, and soon afterwards accompanied
that eminent divine to the Westminster Assembly in
the capacity of private secretary. In 1650 he was
appointed to the Chair of Humanity at St Andrews,
and in 1656, he succeeded Andrew Gray as minister of the outer
High Church, Glasgow.—ED.] There he continued in the faithful
discharge of his duty until the year 1661, when this good man
and affectionate preacher began to observe the design of the
Government to overturn the whole covenanted work of Reformation. In the month of February that year, he gave a most faithful
and seasonable testimony against the glaring defections of that time,
in an excellent sermon in the Tron Church of Glasgow, which was
afterwards the ground of a most severe prosecution. His text was
in Amos iii. 2 : "You only have I known of all the families of the
earth." He had preached upon it for some time upon the week-
days ; and after he had run over personal abounding sins, and those
of the city, he came to the general and national sins, that were then
abounding. Having enlarged upon these things with Scriptural

eloquence, in a most moving way, he used a good many pertinent directions to his hearers to mourn, consider, repent, and return, to wrestle and pour out their souls before the Lord, and encouraged them to these duties from this : That God would look upon these duties as their dissent from what is done prejudicial to His work and interest, and would mark them among the mourners in Zion. But what was most noticed, was that with which he closed the sermon referred to : " For my part, as a poor member of the Church of Scotland, and an unworthy minister in it, I do this day call you who are the people of God to witness, that I humbly offer my dissent from all acts which are or shall be passed against the Covenants and the work of Reformation in Scotland : and I protest that I am desirous to be free of the guilt thereof, and pray that God may put it upon record in heaven."

The noise of this quickly flew abroad, and Mr M'Ward was brought to Edinburgh under a guard, and imprisoned. Very soon after, he had an indictment given him by the King's Advocate for treasonable preaching and sedition. What its nature was, we may easily guess from the scope of his excellent sermon. He was allowed lawyers, whereby his process became pretty long and tedious ; but upon the 6th of June, he was brought before the Parliament, where he had a public opportunity of giving proof of his eminent parts and solid judgment. His charming eloquence was owned by his very adversaries ; and he defended, by Scripture and reason, the expressions in his sermon before the bar of the House. His excellent speech had not the influence that might have been expected; yet doubtless it had some, for the House delayed coming to an issue. He indeed expected a sentence of death, which no way damped him, but his Master had more work for him elsewhere.

Whether by orders from Court to shed no more blood, or for some other reason, his affair was delayed for a time ; and, upon some encouragement given him of success, he, upon the Monday following, gave in a supplication to the Parliament, wherein he exchanges the words " protest " and " dissent," which he had used in his sermon, for those of " testifying, solemnly declaring, and bearing witness ; " and yet at the same time declares, he is not brought to this alteration so much for fear of his person, as from an earnest desire to remove out of the way any or the least occasion of stumbling, that there may be the more ready and easy access, without prejudice of words, to ponder and give judgment of the matter ; and withal, humbly prostrates himself at their honours' feet, to be disposed of as they shall think meet.

This supplication, with what went before, might have softened the persecutors (as the historian observes), and yet it had no effect; for Archbishop Sharp and his friends resolved now to be rid, as much as they could, of the most eminent Presbyterian ministers, and therefore he behoved to be banished, which was the highest thing they could go to, unless they had taken his life. Upon the 5th or 6th of July, the Parliament gave him for answer: "That they pass sentence of banishment upon the supplicant, allowing him six months to tarry in the nation—one of which only in Glasgow—with power to receive the following year's stipend at departure."

His Master having work for him elsewhere, he submitted to the sentence, and transported himself and his family to Rotterdam, where for a while, upon the death of Mr Alexander Petrie (author of the Compendious Church History), he was employed as minister of the Scots congregation, to the no small edification of many; and that not only to such as were fled hither from the rage and fury of the bloody persecutors, but also to those who resorted to him and Mr Brown for their advice in difficult cases, in carrying on and bearing up a faithful testimony against both right and left hand extremes, with every other prevailing corruption and defection in that day; it being a day of "treading down in the valley of vision."

The rage of his persecutors followed him, even in a strange land; for about the end of the year 1676, the King, by the influence of Sharp, wrote to the States General to remove James Wallace, Robert M'Ward, and John Brown out of their provinces. But the States, considering that Messrs M'Ward and Brown had already submitted to the Scots law, and that, having received the sentence of banishment during life out of the King's dominion, they had come under their protection, could not be prevailed on to remove them out of these provinces, or cause them to be any further disquieted; and for this end, sent a letter to their ambassador at the Court of England, to signify the same to His Majesty. [They persuaded them, however, to retire for a little to Germany.—ED.]

Afterwards this famous man was concerned in ordaining Richard Cameron, when in Holland, in the year 1679; and sent him home, with positive instructions to lift up and bear a free and faithful standard against every defection and encroachment made upon the Church of Christ in Scotland, particularly the Indulgences, against which Mr

M'Ward never failed to give a free and faithful testimony, as is evident from several of his writings, particularly that in answer to Mr Fleming.

He remained at Rotterdam until the year 1681 or 1682. It is said, that when in his last sickness, he desired Mr Shield and some other friends to carry him out to see a comet or blazing star that then appeared ; and when he saw it, he blessed the Lord that now he was about to close his eyes, and was not to see the woful days that were coming on Britain and Ireland, but especially upon sinful Scotland. After this he died, and entered into his Master's joy, after he had been for twenty years absent from his native country.

It were altogether superfluous here to insist upon the character of this faithful minister and witness of Jesus Christ, seeing that his own writings do fully evidence him to have been a man of admirable eloquence, learning, and singular zeal and faithfulness. While remaining in Holland he wrote several works, which are said to be the following : " The Poor Man's Cup of Cold Water, ministered to the Saints and Sufferers for Christ in Scotland," published about 1679 ; " Earnest Contendings," etc., published in 1723 ; " Banders Disbanded ;" with several prefatory epistles to some of Mr Brown's works. He wrote also many other papers and letters, but especially a " History of the Defections of the Church of Scotland," which has never hitherto been published. Some accounts bear that " Naphtali " was written by him, but Wodrow says otherwise.

Captain John Paton.

OHN PATON was born at Meadowhead, in the parish of Fenwick, and shire of Ayr. He was brought up in the art and occupation of husbandry till near the state of manhood ; but of the way and manner in which he first entered upon a military life, there are various accounts. Some say he enlisted as a volunteer, and went abroad to the wars in Germany, where, for some heroic achievement, at the taking of a certain city (probably by

Gustavus Adolphus, King of Sweden) he was advanced to a captain's post, and that when he returned home, he was so much changed that his parents scarcely knew him. Other accounts bear, that he was with the Scots army who went to Edinburgh in January, 1643-4, and was at the battle of Marston Moor; at which place, it is said, that by some bad drink an asthmatical disorder was contracted in his breast, which continued ever after. But in either case he must have returned home very suddenly; for it is said, that in 1645, when the ministers in the western shires called upon their own parish militia to oppose Montrose's insurrection, he was appointed by Mr William Guthrie to the post of captain, and behaved with much gallantry among the Covenanters, particularly upon their defeat by Montrose at Kilsyth.

Montrose having, upon July 2d, obtained a victory over the Covenanters, advanced over the Forth; upon the 14th he encamped at Kilsyth, near Stirling, and upon the 15th, encountered the Covenanters' army, commanded by Lieutenant-General Baillie. At the first onset, some of Montrose's Highlanders going too far up the hill, were surrounded by the Covenanters, and were likely to have been worsted; but the old Lord Airly being sent from Montrose with fresh supplies of men, the Covenanters were obliged to give way, and were by the enemy driven back into a standing marsh or bog, where there was no probability either of fighting or escaping. In this emergency one of the Captain's acquaintance, when sinking, cried out to him, for God's sake to help; but when he got time to look that way, he could not see him, for he was gone through the surface of the marsh, and could never be found afterwards. After this disaster, the swiftest of the Covenanters' horse got to Stirling, but the foot were mostly killed on the spot; and in the chase, which, according to some historians, continued for the space of fourteen miles, the greater part of the Covenanters' army was either drowned, or cut off and killed by these cruel savages.

In this extremity, the Captain, as soon as he could get free of the bog, made the best of his way sword in hand through the enemy, till he had got safe to Colonels Hacket and Strachan, when all three rode off together. They had not gone far till they were encountered by about fifteen of the enemy, all of whom they killed, except two who escaped. When they had gone a little farther, they were again attacked by about thirteen more, and of these they killed ten. But, upon the approach of about eleven Highlanders more, one of the

PORTRAIT OF THE MARQUIS OF MONTROSE.

Colonels said, in a familiar dialect, " Johnny, if thou dost not some-what now, we are all dead men ; " to whom the Captain answered, " Fear not ; for we will do what we can before we either yield or flee before them." They killed nine of them, and put the rest to flight.

About this time the Lord began to look upon the affliction of His people. For Montrose having defeated the Covenanters at five or six different times, the Committee of Estates began to bethink them-selves, and for that end saw cause to recall General David Leslie, with 4000 foot and 1000 dragoons, from England. To oppose him, Montrose marched southward ; but was shamefully routed by Leslie at Philiphaugh, upon the 13th of September. Many of his forces were killed and taken prisoners, and he himself escaped with much difficulty. After this, Mr William Guthrie and Captain Paton returned home to Fenwick.

Thus matters went on till 1646, when there arose two factions in Scotland, headed by the Duke of Hamilton and the Marquis of Argyle ; the one of which aimed at bringing down King Charles I. to Scotland, the other opposed it. However, the levies went on, whereby the Duke, with a potent army, marched to England.

In the meanwhile, Major-General Middleton came upon a handful of the Covenanters, assembled at the celebration of the Lord's Supper at Mauchline, a small village in Ayrshire. At this place were William Adair, William Guthrie, and John Nevay, ministers, and the Earl of Loudon, who solicited Middleton to let the people dismiss in a peaceable manner, which he promised to do. But, in a most perfidious way, he fell upon them on the Monday after, which occasioned some bloodshed on both sides; for Captain Paton (being still suspicious of these malignants, notwithstanding all their fair promises) caused his people from Fenwick to take arms with them; and although they only acted on the defensive, still it is said that the captain that day killed eighteen of the enemy with his own hand.

The Duke of Hamilton and his army being defeated, and he himself afterwards beheaded, the English following up the victory, Cromwell and his men entered Scotland, and by them the Engagers were not only made to yield, but quite dispersed. Whereupon some of the stragglers came to the West for plunder, and took up their residence for some time in the muirs of Loudon, Eaglesham, and Fenwick, which made the Captain again bestir himself. Taking a party of Fenwick men, he went in quest of them, and found some of them at a certain house in that parish called Lochgoin, and there gave them such a fright, though without any bloodshed, as made them give their promise never to molest or trouble that house, or any other place in the bounds again, under pain of death. And they went off without any further molestation.

Charles I. having been beheaded, January 30, 1649, and Charles II. called home from Breda 1650, the Scotch Parliament, upon notice of an invasion from the English, appointed a levy of 10,000 foot and 3000 horse, to be instantly raised for the defence of the King and kingdom; among whom the Captain again took the field, for he was now become too popular to be hid in obscurity.

Accordingly, Cromwell and his army having entered Scotland in July 1650, several skirmishes ensued betwixt the English and the Scots, when the latter were, upon the 3d of September, totally routed at Dunbar. After this, the Act of Classes being repealed, both Church and State began to act in different capacities, and to look as suspiciously on one another as on the common enemy. There were in the army, on the Protesters' side, Colonels Ker, Hacket, and Strachan; and of inferior officers, Major Stuart, Captain Arnot, brother to the laird of Lochridge, Captain Paton, and others. The contention came to such a crisis, that Colonels Ker and Strachan threw up their commissions, and came to the West with some other officers, many of whom were esteemed the most religious and best affected in the army. They proceeded so far as to give battle to the English at Hamilton, but were worsted; the Lord's wrath having gone forth against the whole land, because Achan was in the camp of our Scottish Israel.

The King and the Scotch army being no longer able to hold out against the English, shifted about, and went for England; and about the end of August 1651, Worcester surrendered to them. But the Parliamentary army following hard upon their heels, totally routed them upon the 3d of September, which made the King flee out of the kingdom. After this the Captain returned home, when he saw how fruitless and unsuccessful this expedition had been.

About this time, he took the farm of Meadowhead, where he was born, and married Janet Lindsay, who only lived a very short time. Here he no less excelled in the duties of the Christian life, in a private station, than he did while a soldier in the camp. Being under the ministry of Mr William Guthrie, he was made a member of his session, and continued so till that bright and shining light in the Church was extinguished by Charles II. That King having been restored, and the yoke of supremacy and tyranny wreathed by him about the neck of both Church and State, matters grew even worse till the year 1666, when, upon the excesses committed in the South and West by Sir James Turner, some people rose, under the command of Barscob and other gentlemen from Galloway, for their own defence. Several parties from the shire of Ayr joined them, commanded by Colonel James Wallace from Auchens. Captain Arnot came with a party from Mauchline; Lockhart of Wicketshaw, with a party from Carluke; Major Lermont, with a party from above Galston; Neilson of Corsock, with a party from Galloway; and Captain Paton, who now behoved to take the field again, commanded a party of horse from Loudon, Fenwick, and other places.

Being assembled, they went eastward, and renewed the Covenants at Lanark; from thence they went to Bathgate, then to Colinton, and so on till they came to Rullion, near Pentland Hills, where they were, upon that fatal day, November 28, attacked by General Dalziel and the King's forces. At their first onset, Captain Arnot, with a party of horse, fought a party of Dalziel's men with good success; and after him, another party made the General's men flee; but upon their last encounter, about sunset, Dalziel, being repulsed so often, advanced the whole left wing of his army upon Colonel Wallace's right, where he had scarcely three weak horse to receive them, and they were obliged to give way. Here Captain Paton, who was all along with Captain Arnot in the first encounter, behaved with great courage and gallantry. Dalziel, knowing him in the former wars, advanced upon him himself, thinking to take him prisoner. Upon his approach, each presented their pistols. At their first discharge, Captain Paton, perceiving the pistol-ball to hop down upon Dalziel's boots, and knowing what was the cause (he having proof armour), put his hand to his pocket for some small pieces of silver he had there for the purpose, and put one of them into his other pistol. But Dalziel, having his eye on him in the meanwhile, retreated behind his own man, who by that means was slain. The Colonel's men, being flanked on all hands by Dalziel's men, were broken and overpowered; so that the Captain and other two horsemen from Fenwick were surrounded five men deep, through whom he and the two men at his back had to make their way, when there was almost no other on the field of battle; having, in this last rencounter, stood almost an hour.

Whenever Dalziel perceived him go off, he commanded three of his men to follow hard after him, giving them marks whereby they should know him. Immediately they came up with the Captain, before whom was a great slough, out of which three Galloway men had just drawn their horses. They cried to the Captain, what would they do now? He answered them, "What was the fray? he saw but three men coming upon them;" and having caused his horse to jump the ditch, he faced about, and with his sword drawn in his hand, stood still, till the first, coming up, endeavoured to make his horse jump over also. Upon this, he with his sword clave the trooper's head in two; and the horse, being injured, fell into the bog, with the other two men and horses. The Captain then told them to take his compliments to their master, and tell him he was not coming that night; and so came off, and got safe home at last. This sword, or short shabble, yet remains. It was then, by his progenitors, counted to have twenty-eight gaps, which made them afterwards observe, that there were just as many years of the persecution as there were steps or broken pieces in its edge.

After this, Christ's followers and witnesses were reduced to many hardships, particularly such as had been any way accessory to the rising at Pentland, so that they were obliged to resort to the wilderness, and other desolate and solitary places. The winter following, he and about twenty persons had a very remarkable deliverance from the enemy. Being assembled at Lochgoin, upon a certain night, for fellowship and godly conversation, they were warned (through a repeated dream of the enemy's approach) by the old man of the house, who had gone to bed for some rest on account of his infirmity ; and that, just within as much time as enabled then to make their escape, the enemy being within a short distance of the house. After they got off, the old man rose up quickly, and met the soldiers with an apology for the state the house was then in (it being but a little after day-break), and nothing at that time was discovered.

About this time, the Captain sometimes remained at home, and sometimes in those remote places wherein he could best be concealed from the fury of his persecutors. He married a second wife, Janet Millar from Eaglesham (whose father fell at Bothwell Bridge) ; by whom he had six children, who continued to possess the farms of Meadowhead and Artnock in tack, until the day of his death.

He frequented the pure preached Gospel wherever he could obtain it, and was a great encourager of the practice of carrying arms for the defence thereof, which he took to be a proper mean in part to restrain the enemy from violence. But things growing still worse and worse, new troops of horse and companies of foot being poured in upon the western shires, on purpose to suppress and search out these field-meetings (which occasioned the rising in 1679), by these unparalleled severities, they were, with those of whom the apostle speaks, " destitute, afflicted, tormented ; (of whom the world was not worthy :) they wandered in deserts, and in mountains, and in dens and caves of the earth " (Heb. xi. 37, 38).

The persecuted Covenanters, under the command of Mr Robert Hamilton, having got the victory over Claverhouse on the 1st of June 1679, at Drumclog in Evandale, in which skirmish there were about thirty-six or forty of that bloody crew killed, went on the next day towards Glasgow in pursuit of the enemy; but that proving unsuccessful, they returned, and on June 3, formed themselves into a camp, and held a council of war. On the 4th they rendezvoused at Kyperidge, and on the 5th they went to Commissary Fleming's park, in the parish of Kilbride ; by which time, Captain Paton, who all this time had not been idle, came to them with a body of horsemen from Fenwick and Galston ; and many others joined them, so that they were greatly increased.

They had hitherto been of one heart and one mind ; but a certain party of horse from Carrick came to them, with whom were Mr Welch and some other ministers who favoured the Indulgence; after which they never had a day to do well, until they were defeated at Bothwell Bridge, upon the 22d of June following.

The protesting party would not join with those of the Erastian side, till they should declare themselves for God and His cause, against all and every defection whatever; but Mr Welch and his party found out a way to get rid of such officers as they feared most opposition from; for orders were given to Rathillet, Haughhead, Carmichael, and Smith, to go to Glasgow, to meet with Mr King and Captain Paton; and they obeyed. When at Glasgow, King and Paton led them out of the town, as they apprehended for the purpose of preaching, but upon inquiry where they were going, it was answered that according to orders sent privately to Mr King and Captain Paton, they were to go and disperse a meeting of the enemy at Campsie: Upon going there they found no such thing; which made them believe it was only a stratagem to get free of Mr King and the rest of the faithful officers.

The faithful officers were Robert Hamilton, David Hackston of Rathillet, Hall of Haughhead, Captain Paton in Meadowhead, John Balfour of Kinloch, Walter Smith, William Carmichael, William Cleland, James Henderson, and Robert Fleming. Their ministers were Donald Cargill, Thomas Douglas, John Kid, and John King. Richard Cameron was then in Holland. Henry Hall of Haughhead, John Paton in Meadowhead, William Carmichael, and Andrew Turnbull, were ruling elders of the Church of Scotland.

Thus the Protesting party continued to struggle with the Erastian party, in which contendings Captain Paton had no small share, until that fatal day, June 22, when they were routed, and made to flee before the enemy. The Captain at this time was made a Major; and some accounts bear, that the day preceding he was made a Colonel. Wilson, in his History of Bothwell Bridge, says, that he supposes John Paton, Robert Fleming, James Henderson, and William Cleland, were chosen to be Colonels of regiments. However, as he did not enjoy this place long, we find him still afterwards called by the name of Captain John Paton.

After the defeat at Bothwell Bridge, Captain Paton made the best of his way homeward; and having had a fine horse, with all manner of furnishings, from the sheriff of Ayr, he gave it to one to take home to his master. However, it was robbed of all its fine mounting by an old intelligencer (of the same name as was supposed), which very much surprised the sheriff when he received the horse, and the Captain when he got notice thereof. This was a most base and shameful action, designing to stain the character of this honest and good man.

The sufferers were now exposed to new hardships, and none more so than Captain Paton, who was not only declared rebel by order of proclamation, but also a round sum was offered for his head, which made him be more hotly pursued, and that even in his most secret lurking places. In this time, a little after Bothwell, he had another most remarkable escape and deliverance from his bloodthirsty enemies, which fell out in this manner.

The Captain, with a few more, was one night quartered in the forementioned house of Lochgoin,* with James Howie, who was one of his fellow-sufferers. At the same hour a party, being out in quest of some of the sufferers, came to Meadowhead, and from thence went to another remote place in the muirs of Fenwick, called Croilburn, but finding nothing, they went next to Lochgoin, as apprehending they would not miss their design there ; and that they might come upon this place more securely, they sent about five men with one Sergeant Rae, by another way, by which the main body could not come so well up undiscovered.

The sufferers had watched all night, which was very stormy, by turns, and about day-break the Captain, on account of his asthmatical disorder, went to the far end of the house for some rest. In the meanwhile George Woodburn went out to make observations, from which he was but a little time returned, when on a sudden, ere they were aware, Sergeant Rae came to the inner door of the house and cried out, "Dogs! I have found you now." The four men took to

---

* This house was always a harbour to our late sufferers, both gentlemen, ministers, and private Christians, for which, and for their non-conformity to Prelacy, the family were not only harassed, pillaged, and plundered ten or twelve times during that period, but also both James Howie the possessor, and John Howie, his son, were, by virtue of a proclamation, May 5, 1679, declared rebels, and their names inserted in the fugitives' roll. They were so happy as to survive the Revolution, yet they never acceded to the Revolution Church. The said James Howie, when dying, November 1691, emitted a latter will or testament, wherein he not only gave good and satisfying evidence of his own wellbeing and saving interest in Jesus Christ, but also gave a most faithful testimony to Scotland's covenanted work of reformation, and that in all the parts and periods thereof.

FENWICK CHURCH—(EXTERIOR).

the spence—James and John Howie happening to be then in the byre among the cattle. The wife of the house, Isabel Howie, seeing none but the sergeant, cried to take to the hills, and not be killed in the house. She took hold of Rae, as he was coming boldly forward to the door of the place in which they were, and ran him backward out of the outer door of the house, giving him such a hasty turn as made him fall on the ground. In the meanwhile, the Captain being alarmed, got up, put on his shoes, though not very hastily, and they all got out, by which time the rest of the party was up. The sergeant fired his gun at them, which John Kirkland answered with his. The bullet passed so near the sergeant that it took off the knot of hair on the side of his head. The alarm being now general, the Captain and the rest took the way for Eaglesham muirs, and the soldiers followed. Two of the men ran with the Captain, and other two stayed by turns, and fired back on the enemy, the enemy fired on them likewise; but by reason of some wetness their guns had got in coming through the water, they were not so ready to fire, which helped the others to escape.

After they had pursued them some time, John Kirkland turned about, and, stooping down on his knee, aimed so well that he shot a Highland sergeant through the thigh, which made the foremost

FENWICK CHURCH—(INTERIOR).

stop as they came forward, till they were again commanded to run. By this time the sufferers had gained some ground, and being come to the muirs of Eaglesham, the four men went to the heights, in view of the enemy, and caused the Captain, who was old and not able to run, take another way by himself. At last he got a mare upon the field, and took the liberty to mount her a little, that he might be more suddenly out of their reach. But ere he was aware, a party of dragoons going from Newmills was at hand; and what was more observable, he wanted his shoes, having cast them off before, and was riding on the beast's bare back: but he passed by them very slowly and got off undiscovered. At length he gave the mare her liberty, and went into another of his lurking places. All this happened on a Monday morning; and on the morrow these persecutors returned, and, plundering the house, drove off the cattle, and left almost nothing remaining.

About this time the Captain met with another deliverance, for, having a child removed by death, the incumbent of the parish, knowing the time when the corpse was to be interred, gave notice to a party of soldiers at Kilmarnock, to come up and take him at the burial of his child. But some persons present at the burial persuaded him to return back, in case the enemy should come upon them at the churchyard; which he accordingly did, when he was but a little distance from the Church.

He was also a great succourer of those sufferers himself, in so far as his circumstances could admit, several of his fellow-companions in the tribulation and patience of Jesus Christ resorting at certain times to him; such as David Hackston of Rathillet, Balfour of Kinloch, and Donald Cargill. It is said, that Mr Cargill dispensed the sacrament of baptism to twenty-two children in his barn at Meadowhead, some time after the engagement at Bothwell Bridge.

Being now near the end of his race and weary pilgrimage, about the beginning of August 1684, he came to the house of Robert Howie in Floack, in the parish of Mearns (formerly one of his hiding places), where he was, by five soldiers, apprehended before ever he or any in the house were aware. He had no arms, yet the indwellers there offered him their assistance, if he wanted it. Indeed they were in a condition to have rescued him; yea, he himself, once in a day, could have extricated himself from double that number. But he said, it would bring them to further trouble, and as for himself, he was now become weary of his life; being so hunted from place to place, and being well stricken in years, his hidings became the more irksome. He was not afraid to die, for he knew well, that whenever he fell into their hands, this would be the case, and he had got time to think thereon for many years; and for his interest in Christ, of that he was sure. They took him to Kilmarnock, but knew not who he was (taking him for some old minister or other), till they came to a place on the highway, called Moor Yeat, where the good man of that place, seeing him in these circumstances, said, "Alas! Captain Paton, are you there!" Then to their joy, they knew whom they had got into their hands. He was carried to Kilmarnock (where his eldest daughter, being about fourteen years of age, got access to see him) then to Ayr, then back to Glasgow, and soon after to Edinburgh.

It is reported as a fact, that General Dalziel met him here, and took him in his arms, saying, "John, I am both glad and sorry to see you. If I had met you on the way, before you came hither, I should have set you at liberty; but now it is too late. But be not afraid, I will write to his Majesty for your life." The Captain replied, "You will not be heard." Dalziel said, "Will I not? If he does not grant me the life of one man, I shall never draw a sword for him again." And it is said that, having spoken some time together, a man came and said to the Captain, "You are a rebel to the King;" to whom he replied, " Friend, I have done more for the King than perhaps thou hast done." Dalziel said, " Yes, John, that is true " (perhaps meaning at Worcester) ; and struck the man on the head with his cane till he staggered, saying, he would teach him better manners than to use such a prisoner so. After this and more reasoning, the Captain thanked him for his courtesy, and they parted.

His trial was not long delayed. Wodrow says, that in April 16, the Council ordered a reward of £20 sterling to Cornet Lewis Lauder, for apprehending John Paton, who had been a notorious rebel these eighteen years. He was brought before the Justiciary, and indicted for being with the rebels at Glasgow, Bothwell, etc. The Advocate passed his being at Pentland, and insisted on his being at Bothwell. The Lords found his libel relevant, and for probation they referred to his own confession before the Council, that he, John Paton, of Meadowhead in Fenwick, was taken in the parish of Mearns, in the house of Robert Howie, in Floack ; that he haunted ordinarily in the fields and muirs ; that he was moved by the country people to go out in the year 1666, and commanded a party at Pentland ; that he joined with the rebels at Glasgow, about eight days before the engagement at Bothwell, and commanded a party there, etc. The assize had no more to cognise upon but his own confession, yet brought him in guilty, and the Lords condemned him to be hanged at the Grassmarket of Edinburgh, on the 23rd of April. But, by other accounts, he was charged before the Council for being a rebel since the year 1640 ; for being an opposer of Montrose ; for being at Mauchline Muir, etc.

He was prevailed on to petition the Council, upon which he was respited to the 30th, and from that to May 9, when he suffered according to his sentence. No doubt Dalziel was as good as his word ; for it is said, that he obtained a reprieve for him from the King ; but that, coming to the hands of Bishop Paterson, was kept up by him till he was executed ; which enraged the General not a little. It seems that they had a mind to spare him ; but, as he observed in his last speech, the prelates put an effectual stop to that. In the last eight days that he lived, he got a room by himself, that he might more conveniently prepare for death ; which was a favour at that time granted him above many others.

What Captain Paton's conduct or deportment at the place of execution was, we are now at a loss to know, only it is believed it was such as well became such a valiant servant and soldier of Jesus Christ,

MONUMENT IN FENWICK CHURCHYARD (NOW REMOVED).

an evidence of which we have in his last speech and dying testimony, wherein among other things he said, "You are come here to look on me a dying man, and you need not expect that I shall say much, for I was never a great orator, or eloquent of tongue, though I may say as much to the commendation of God in Christ Jesus, as ever a poor sinner had to say. I bless the Lord I am not come here as a thief or murderer, and I am free of the blood of all men, and hate bloodshed, directly or indirectly; and now I am a poor sinner, and never could merit anything but wrath; and I have no righteousness of my own; all is Jesus Christ's, and His alone. Now, as to my interrogations, I was not clear to deny Pentland or Bothwell. The Council asked me if I acknowledged authority? I said, all authority according to the word of God. They charged me with many things as if I had been a rebel since the year 1640, at Montrose's taking, and at Mauchline Muir. Lord, forgive them, for they know not what they do!" Then after intimating his adherence to the Scriptures, the Covenants, and the whole work of Reformation; he said, "Now I leave my testimony as a dying man against that horrid usurpation of our Lord's prerogative and crown-right; I mean that supremacy established by law in these lands, which is a manifest usurpation of His crown, for He is given by the Father to be Head of the Church" (Col. i. 18).

NEW MONUMENT IN FENWICK CHURCHYARD.

Further, he addressed himself in a few words to two or three sorts of people, exhorting them to be diligent in the exercise of duty ; and then, in the last place, saluted all his friends in Christ, whether prisoned, banished, widows, fatherless, wandering and cast out for Christ's sake and the Gospel's. He forgave all his enemies, in the following words ; "Now, as to my persecutors, I forgive all of them ; instigators, reproachers, soldiers, private council, justiciaries, appre-henders, in what they have done to me ; but what they have done in despite against the image of God in me, who am a poor thing without that, it is not mine to forgive them ; but I wish they may seek forgive-ness of Him who hath it to give, and would do no more wickedly." Then he left his wife and six small children on the Lord, took his leave of worldly enjoyments, and concluded saying, "Farewell, sweet Scriptures, preaching, praying, reading, singing, and all duties. Wel-come. Father, Son, and Holy Spirit ! I desire to commit my soul to thee in well-doing ! Lord, receive my spirit ! "

Thus another gallant soldier of Jesus Christ came to his end, the actions of whose life, and demeanour at death, do fully indicate that he was of no rugged disposition, as has been by some asserted of these our late sufferers ; but rather of a meek, judicious, and Christian con-versation, tempered with true zeal and faithfulness for the cause and interest of Zion's King and Lord. He was of a middle stature (as accounts bear), strong and robust, somewhat fair of complexion, with large eye-brows. But what enhanced him more, was courage and magnanimity of mind, which accompanied him upon every emergent occasion ; and though his extraction was but mean, it might be truly said of him, that he lived a hero, and died a martyr.

John Nisbet of Hardhill.

OHN NISBET, born about the year 1627, was son to James Nisbet, and lineally descended from Murdoch Nisbet in Hardhill, who, about 1500, joined those called the Lollards of Kyle. They, on persecution being raised against them, fled over the seas, and took a copy of the New Testament in writing. Some time after, he returned home, digged a vault in the bottom of his own house, unto which he retired, serving God, reading his new book, and instructing such as had access to him.

John Nisbet, having the advantage of a tall, strong, well-built body, and of a bold, daring, public spirit, went abroad and joined the army, which was of great use to him afterwards. Having spent some time in foreign countries, he returned to Scotland, and swore the Covenants, when King Charles, at his coronation, swore them at Scone, in the year 1650.

Having left the army, he married Margaret Law, who proved an equal, true, and kind yoke-fellow to him all the days of her life. By her he had several children, three of whom survived himself, viz., Hugh, James, and Alexander. In the month of December 1683, she died, on the eighth day of her sickness, and was buried in Stonehouse churchyard. This behoved to be done in the night, that it might not be known ; neither would any do it, but such as might not appear in the day time. The curate, having knowledge of it, threatened to take the corpse up, burn it, or cast it to the dogs; but some of the persecuted party sent him a letter, assuring him, that if he touched the grave, they would burn him and his family, and all he had; so he forbare.

John Nisbet early applied himself to the study of the holy Scriptures, which, through the grace of God, was so effectual, that he not only became well acquainted with the most interesting parts of practical religion, but also attained no small degree of knowledge in points of principle. This proved of unspeakable advantage in all that occurred to him in the after part of his life while maintaining the testimony of that day. He took the Hardhill in the parish of Loudon, in which station he behaved with much discretion and prudence. No sooner did Prelacy and Erastianism appear, at the restoration of Charles II., in opposition to our ancient and laudable form of Church government, than he took part with the Presbyterian side. Having got a child baptized by one of the ejected ministers (as they were then called), the incumbent or curate of the parish was so enraged, that he declared his resolution from the pulpit, to excommunicate him the next Lord's day. But, behold, the Lord's hand interposed, for before that day came the curate was in eternity.

John Nisbet, being always active for religion, and a great encourager of field-meetings, was, with the rest of Christ's faithful witnesses, obliged to go without the camp bearing His reproach. When that faithful remnant assembled together, and renewed the Covenant at Lanark, 1666, his conscience led him to join them, which being known, and he being threatened for doing so, he resolved to follow these persecuted people, and so kept with them in arms till their defeat, upon the 28th of November, at Pentland hills, at which fight he behaved with great courage and resolution. He fought till he was so wounded, that he was stripped for dead among the slain; and yet such was the providence of God, that, having more work for him to accomplish, he was preserved.

He had espoused Christ's cause by deliberate choice, and was indeed of an excellent spirit; and, as Solomon says, more excellent than his neighbour; his natural temper was likewise noble and generous. As he was travelling through a muir, on a snowy day, one of his old neighbours, who was seeking sheep, met him, and cried out, "O Hardhill, are you yet alive? I was told you were going in a pilgrim's habit, and that your bairns were begging, and yet I see you look as well as ever." Then taking out a rixdollar, he offered it to him. John seeing this, took out a ducat, and offered it to him, saying, "I will have none of yours, but will give you if you please, that you may see that nothing is wanting to him that fears the Lord. I never thought that you would have gone so far with the enemies of God, as to sell your conscience to save your gear. Take warning, H——, go home and mourn for that, and all your other sins, before God; for, if mercy do not prevent, you will certainly perish." The poor man thanked him, put up his money, and went home.

After his remarkable escape at Pentland, John Nisbet returned home, where probably he continued (not without enduring many hardships) till the year 1679. His fame for courage, wisdom, and resolution among the sufferers, was such that, when those who were assembled near Loudon Hill to hear the Gospel, came in view of an engagement with Claverhouse, who attacked them that day at Drumclog, he was sent for by a man named Woodburn, in the Mains of Loudon, to come with all haste to their assistance. But before he and his friends got half-way, they heard the platoons of the engagement, and yet they rode with such alacrity, that they just came up as the firing was over. Upon their approach, Hardhill (for so he was commonly called) cried to them to jump the ditch, and get over upon the enemy, sword in hand, which they did with so great resolution and success, that in a little they obtained a complete victory over the enemy, wherein Hardhill had a share by his vigorous activity in the latter end of the skirmish.

The suffering party, knowing now that they were fully exposed to the rage and resentment of their bloody persecuting foes, resolved to abide together: and for that purpose sent a party to Glasgow in pursuit of the enemy, of which Hardhill was one. After this, he continued with them, and was of no small advantage to the honest party, till that fatal day, June 22d, when they fled and fell before the enemy at Bothwell Bridge. "Here," says Wodrow, "he was a captain, if I mistake not; and being sent with his party along with those who defended the bridge, he fought with great gallantry, and stood as long as any man would stand by him, and then making his retreat just in time, through the goodness of God he escaped from their hands at this time also."

After Bothwell he was denounced a rebel, and a large reward offered to such as would apprehend him; at which time the enemy seized all that he had, stripped his wife and four children, turning them out of doors, whereby he was reduced to the condition of those

BOTHWELL BRIDGE.

mentioned in Heb. xi. 38, "They wandered in deserts, and in mountains, and in dens and caves of the earth." Thus he lived for near the space of five years, suffering all manner of hardships, not accepting deliverance, that he might preserve to himself the free enjoyment of the Gospel faithfully preached in the fields. Being a man of a public spirit, a great observer of fellowship meetings (alas! a duty too much neglected), and very staunch upon points of testimony, he became very popular among the more faithful part of our sufferers, and was by them often employed as one of their commissioners to the general meeting, which they had erected some years before this, that they might the better understand the mind of one another in carrying on a testimony in their broken state.

One thing very remarkable occurred. On Sabbath night (being that day eight days before he was taken), as he and four more were travelling, it being very dark, no wind, but a thick, small rain; no moon, for that was not her season; behold, suddenly the clouds clave asunder, toward east and west, over their heads, and a light sprang out beyond that of the sun, which lasted about the space of two minutes. They heard a noise, and were much amazed, saying one to another, What may that mean? But Hardhill did not speak, uttering only three deep groans. One of them asked him, What it might mean? He said, "We know not well at present, but within a a little we shall know better: yet we have a more sure word of prophecy, unto which we would do well to take heed." Then he groaned again, saying, "As for me, I am ready to live or to die for Him, as He in His providence shall call me to it, and bear me through in it: and although I have suffered much from prelates and false friends these twenty-one years, yet now I would not for a thousand worlds I had done otherwise. If the Lord spare me, I will be more zealous for His precious truths; if not, I am ready to seal His cause with my blood; for I have longed for it these sixteen years, and it may be I will ere long get it to do. Welcome be His will, and if He help me through with it, I shall praise Him to all eternity." This made them all wonder, he being a very reserved man; for although he was a strict observer of the Sabbath, a great examiner of Scripture, and a great wrestler in prayer, yet he was so reserved as to his own case and soul's concernment, that few knew how it was with him as to that until he came to prison.

All this and more could not escape the knowledge of the Government, as is evident from Alexander Gordon of Earlston's answers before the Council, 1683; and we find that one of the articles that John Richmond suffered for at the Cross of Glasgow, March 19, 1684, was his being in company with John Nisbet. This made the search after him and other sufferers more determined. In the month of November 1683, having retired, amongst other of his lurking-places, unto a certain house called the Midland, in the parish of Fenwick, where other three of his faithful brethren were assembled for prayer and other religious exercises on a Saturday night, viz., Peter Gemmel, a younger brother of the house of Horsehill in the same parish, George Woodburn, a brother of the Woodburns in the Mains of Loudon, and John Fergus-hill from Tarbolton, they hearing that Lieutenant Nisbet and a party of Colonel Buchan's dragoons were out in quest of the wanderers (as they were sometimes called), resolved on the Sabbath morning to depart. But old John Fergushill not being able to go by reason of infirmity, they were obliged to return with him after they had got a little way from the house, and were the same day apprehended. The way and manner of this, with his answers both at Ayr and before the Council at Edinburgh, as they stand in an old manuscript, given under his own hand, while he saw their prisoner, was as follows:

" First when the enemy came within sight of the house, we seeing no way of escape, John Fergushill went to the far end of the house, and the other two and I followed ; and ere we were well at the far end, some of the enemy were in the house. And then, in a little after, they came and put up their horses, and went to and fro in the house for more than an hour ; and we four still at the far end of the house ; and we resolved with one another to keep close till they should just come on us, and if it should have pleased the Lord to have hid us there, we resolved not to have owned them, but if they found us out, we thought to fight, saying one to another, it was death at length. They got all out of the house, and had their horses drawn forth, but in a little time came back, tittling one to another, and at last called for a candle to search the house with, and came within a yard of us with the light burning. According to our former resolution, we did resist them, having only three shot, and one of them misgiving, and they fired about twenty-four shot at us ; and when we had nothing else, we clubbed our guns, till two of them were quite broke, and then went in grips with some of them ; and when they saw they could not prevail, they all cried to go out and fire the house. Upon this we went out after them, and I received six wounds in the going out ; after which, they getting notice what I was, some of themselves cried out to spare my life, for the Council had offered 3000 merks for me. So they brought me towards the end of the yard, and tied my hands behind my back, having shot the other three to death. He that commanded them scoffingly asked me what I thought of myself now ? I smiled, and said, I had full contentment with my lot, but thought that I was at a loss that I was in time, and my brethren in eternity. At this he swore he had reserved my life for a farther judgment to me. When we were going towards Kilmarnock, the Lieutenant (who was a cousin of his own), called for me, and he and I went before the rest, and discoursed soberly about several things. I was free in telling him what I held to be sin, and what I held to be duty ; and when he came to Kilmarnock Tolbooth, he caused slack my arms a little, and inquired if I desired my wounds dressed ; and, at the desire of some friends in the town, he caused bring in straw and some clothes for my brother, John Gemmel, and me to lie upon, but would not suffer us to cast off our clothes. On Monday, on the way to Ayr, he raged against me, and said that I had the blood of the three men on my head that were killed yesterday ; and that I was guilty of all, and the cause of all the troubles that were come on the poor barony of Cunningham, first and last. But when we came near the town, he called me out from the rest, and soberly asked 'me what he should say to the superior officers in my behalf? I told him, that if the Lord would keep me from wronging truth, I was at a point already in what he put me to as to suffering. When we first entered the Tolbooth of Ayr, there came two, and asked some things at me, but they were to little purpose. Then I was taken out with a guard, and brought before Buchan. He asked me: 1st, If I was at that conventicle? I told him, I looked upon it as my duty. 2d, How many armed men were there? I told him, I went to hear the Gospel preached, and not to take up the account of what men were there. 3d, Where away went they? I told him, it was more than I could tell. 4th, Do you own the King? I told him, while the King owned the way and work of God, I thought myself bound both to own and fight for him ; and when he quitted the way of God, I thought I was obliged to quit him. 5th, Will you own the Duke of York as King? I told him, I would not, for it was both against my principles and the laws of the nation. 6th, Were you clear to join with Argyle ? I said, No. He held me long, and spake of many things. We had the musters through hands, Popery, Prelacy, Presbyterianism, malignants, defensive and offensive arms, there being none in the room but ourselves. I thought it remarkable, that all the time from Sabbath and to this present, I had and have as much peace and quietness of my mind as ever in my life. Oh! help me to praise Him! for He alone did it. Now, my dear friends and acquaintances, cease not to pray for me while I am in the body, for I may say I fear nothing but that through weakness I wrong truth. And my last advice is, that ye be more diligent in following Christian duties. Alas ! that I was not more sincere, zealous, and forward for His work and cause in my day. Cease to be jealous one of another, and only let self-examination be more studied ; and this, through His blessing, shall open a door to more of a Christian soul exercise ; and more of a soul-exercise, through His blessing, would keep away vain jangling, that does no way profit, but gives way to Satan and his temptations.

"When I came to Edinburgh, I was the first night kept in the guard. The next night I was brought into their council-house, where were present Drummond (Earl of Perth), Linlithgow, and one Paterson, together with some others. They first said to me, that they looked upon me as one acquainted with all that was done amongst

these rebellious persons; therefore the Lords of his Majesty's Privy
Council would take it as a great favour that I would be free in
telling them what I knew that might most conduce to the peace and
security of the nation. I told them, that when I came to particulars,
I would speak nothing but truth, for I was more afraid to lie than to
die; but I hoped they would be so much Christians as not to bid
me tell anything that would burden my conscience. Then they
began thus. (1.) What did ye in your meetings? I told them, we
only sung a part of a Psalm, read a part of the Scripture, and prayed
time about. (2.) Why call ye them fellowship and society meetings?
A. I wonder why you ask such questions, for these meetings were
called so when our Church was in her power. (3.) Were there any
such meetings at that time? *A.* There were in some places of the
land. (4.) Did the ministers of the place meet with them in these?
A. Sometimes they did, and sometimes they did not. (5.) What
mean you by your general meetings, and what do you do at them?
While I was thinking what to answer, one of themselves told them
more distinctly than I could have done, and jeeringly said, looking
to me, 'When they have done, then they distribute their collections.'
I held my peace all the time. (6.) Where keep ye these meetings?
A. In the wildest muirs we can think of. (7.) Will you own the
King's authority? *A.* No. (8.) What is your reason; you own the
Scriptures, and your own Confession of Faith? *A.* That I do with
all my heart. (9.) Why do you not own the King's authority?
(naming several passages of Scripture, and that in the 23d chapter of
the Confession.) *A.* There is a vast difference—he being a Roman
Catholic, and I being not only brought up in the Presbyterian
principles from my youth, but also sworn against Popery. (10.)
What is that to you; though he be Popish, he is not bidding you
be a Papist, nor hindering you to live in your own religion? *A.*
The contrary does appear; for we have not liberty to hear a Gospel
preaching, but we are taken, killed, and put to the hardest of
sufferings. They said, it was not so, for we might have the Gospel
if our wild principles would suffer us to hear it. I said, they might
say so, but the contrary was well known through the land; for
they banished our faithful ministers, and thrust in such as live rather
like profligates than like ministers, so that poor things neither can
nor dare join with them. (11.) Are ye clear to join with Argyle?
A. No. Then one of them said, Ye will have no king but Mr
James Renwick; and asked if I conversed with any other minister

upon the field than Mr Renwick. I told them I conversed with no other. A number of other things passed that were to little purpose.

"Sirs, this is a true hint of any material thing that passed betwixt them and me. As for their drinking of healths, never one of them spoke of it to me; neither did ever any of them bid me pray for their king; but they said, that they knew I was that much of a Christian that I would pray for all men. I told them I was bound to pray for all, but prayer being instituted by a holy God, who was the hearer of prayer, no Christian could pray when every profligate did bid him; and it was no advantage to their cause to suffer such a thing.

"How it may be afterwards with me, I cannot positively say; for God is a free Sovereign, and may come and go as He pleaseth. But this I say, and can affirm, that He has not quarrelled with me since I was prisoner, but has always waited on to supply me with all consolation and strength, as my necessity required; and now, when I cannot lay down my own head, nor lift it without help, yet of all the cases I ever was in, I had never more contentment. I can now give the cross of Christ a noble commendation. It was always sweet and pleasant, but never so sweet and pleasant as now. Under all my wanderings, and all my toilings, a prison was still so terrifying to me, that I could never have been so sure as I would have been. But immediately at my taking, He so shined on me, and ever since, that He and His cross are to me far beyond whatever He was before. Therefore let none scare or stand at a distance from their duty for fear of the cross; for now I can say from experience, that it is as easy, yea, and more sweet, to lie in prison in irons, than it is to be at liberty. But I must forbear at present."

Upon the 26th, he was ordered by the Council to be prosecuted. Accordingly, on the 30th, he was before the Justiciary, and arraigned, his own confession being the only proof against him, which runs thus: "John Nisbet of Hardhill, prisoner, confesses, when examined before the Council, that he was at Drumclog, had arms, and made use of them against the King's forces, and that he was at Glasgow, and that he was at a field-meeting within these two months, betwixt Eaglesham and Kilbride," etc. This being read, he adhered to, but refused to subscribe it. The assize brought him in guilty, and the Lords sentenced him to be hanged at the Grassmarket, December 4, betwixt two and four in the afternoon, and his lands, goods, and gear, to be forfeited to the King's use.

It was inserted by the Council in his confession, that the reason why he could not join with Argyle was, that Colonel Cleland told him Argyle and his party were against all kingly government. Wodrow thinks this false, and that it was only foisted in by the clerk of the Council, it not being the first time that things of this nature had been done by them. But he must have been in a mistake here; for, in one of Hardhill's papers, in manuscript, left behind him in way of testimony, he gives this as the first reason for his not joining with Argyle, and the second was to the same purpose with what Wodrow has observed, viz., because the societies could not espouse his declaration, as the state of the quarrel was not concerted according to the ancient plea of the Scottish Covenanters, and because it opened a door to a sinful confederacy.

His sentence was accordingly executed. He appeared upon the scaffold with a great deal of courage and Christian composure, and died in much assurance, and with a joy which none of his persecutors could intermeddle with. It was affirmed by some who were present at his execution, that the scaffold or gibbet gave way and came down, which made some present flatter themselves, that, by some laws in being, he had won his life, as they used to say in such cases. But they were disappointed, for he was not to escape so : " to this end he was born." Immediately all was reared up, and the martyr executed.

In his last testimony, which is inserted in the "Cloud of Witnesses," after a recital of many choice Scripture texts, which had been comforting and strengthening to him in the house of his pilgrimage, he comes, among other things in point of testimony, to say, ' Now, my dear friends in Christ, since the public Resolutioners were for bringing in the Malignants and their interest, I have always thought it my duty to join with the Lord's people in witnessing against these sinful courses, and now we see clearly, that it has ended in nothing less than the making us captains, that we may return to Egypt by the open doors that are made wide to bring in popery, and set up idolatry in the Lord's covenanted land to defile it. Wherefore it is the unquestionable and indispensable duty of all who have any love to God, and to his Son Jesus Christ, to witness faithfully, constantly, and conscientiously, against all that the enemies have done or are doing to the overthrow of the glorious work of reformation, and banishing Christ out of these lands, by robbing him of his crown-rights. And however it be, that many, both ministers and professors, are turning their backs upon Christ and His cause, reproaching and casting dirt upon you and the testimony of the day ; yet let not this weaken your hands, for I assure you it will not be long to the fourth watch, and then He will come in garments dyed in blood, to raise up saviours upon the Mount Zion, to judge the mount of Esau ; and then the cause of Jacob and Joseph shall be for fire, and the Malignants, Prelates, and Papists, shall be for stubble, the flame whereof shall be great. But my generation work being done with my time, I go to Him who loved me, and washed me from all my sin."

Then he goes on declaring that he adheres to the Scriptures, Confession of Faith, Catechisms Larger and Shorter, and all the acts of reformation attained to in Scotland from 1638 to 1649, with all the protestations, declarations, etc., given by the faithful since that time ; owns all their appearances in arms, at Pentland, Drumclog, Bothwell, Airsmoss, etc., against God's stated enemies, and the enemies of the Gospel, and kingly government, as appointed and emitted in the word of God, they entering covenant-ways, and with covenant qualifications ; and withal adds, " But I am persuaded Scotland's covenanted God will cut off the name of Stuart, because they have stated themselves against religion, reformation, and the thriving of Christ's kingdom and kingly government in these lands ; and although men idolise them so much now, yet ere long, there shall be none of them to tyrannise in covenanted Britain any more."

Then he proceeds in protesting against Popery, Prelacy, the granters and acceptors of the Indulgence, and exhorting the people of God to forbear contention and censuring one another, to keep up their sweet fellowship and society meetings, with which he had been much comforted. He concludes by bidding farewell to all his dear fellow sufferers, to his children, Christian friends, sweet Bible, and to his wanderings and contendings for truth ; and by welcoming death, the city of his God, the blessed company of angels, and the spirits of just men ; but above all, the Father, Son, and Holy Ghost, into whose hands he commits his spirit.

After he wrote his last speech, he was taken out immediately to the Council, and from that to the place of execution. All the way thither he had his eyes lifted up to heaven. He seemed to rejoice, and his face shone visibly. He spoke but little till he came to the scaffold, but when he came there, he stepped upon it, and cried out, " My soul doth magnify the Lord, my soul doth magnify the Lord. I have longed these sixteen years to seal the precious cause and interest of precious Christ with my blood, who hath answered and granted my request, and has left me no more to do but to come here and pour out my last prayer, sing forth my last praises of Him in time on this

PORTRAIT OF JAMES II.

sweet and desirable scaffold, mount that ladder, and then I shall get home to my Father's house, see, enjoy, serve, and sing forth the praises of my glorious Redeemer for ever, world without end." Then he resumed the heads of his last testimony to the truth, and enlarged on what he owned and disowned ; but the drums being beat, little could be heard ; only with difficulty he was heard to say, "The covenanted God of Scotland hath a dreadful storm of wrath provided, which he will surely pour out suddenly and unexpectedly, like a thunderbolt, upon these covenanted lands, for their perfidy, treachery, and apostacy : and then men shall say, they have got well away that got a scaffold for Christ." He exhorted all to make use of Christ for a hiding place ; "for blood shall be the judgment of these lands." He sang the first six verses of the 34th Psalm, and read the 8th chapter of the Romans, and prayed divinely with great presence of mind, and very loud. Then he went up the ladder, rejoicing and praising the Lord, as all evidently saw ; and so he ended the race which he had run with faith and patience, upon the 4th of December 1685, in the fifty-eighth year of his age.

He was a man of strong memory, good judgment, and much given to self-denial. It is said of him, that during his hidings in a cave, near or about his own house, he wrote out all the New Testament, which probably, according to some accounts, might be a transcription of an old copy, which one of his ancestors is said to have copied out in the time of Popery, when the Scriptures were not permitted to be read in the vulgar language.

Hardhill was always a man very particular upon the testimony of the day, which made some compliers censure him as one too harsh and rugged in point of principle. But this must be altogether groundless; for in one of the forementioned manuscripts he lets fall these words : " Now, as for misreports, that were so much spread of me, I declare, as a dying person going out of time to eternity, that the Lord never suffered me in the least to incline to follow any one of those persons who were drawn away to follow erroneous principles. Only I thought it still my duty to be tender of them, as they had souls, wondering always wherefore I was right in any measure, and they got leave to fall in such a manner. I could never endure to hear one creature rail and cry out against another, knowing we are all alike by nature." And afterwards, when speaking of Argyle's declaration, he further says : " Let all beware of refusing to join with ministers or professors upon account of personal infirmities, which is ready to raise prejudice among persons. But it shall be found a walking contrary to the Word of God, and so contrary to God Himself, to join either with ministers or professors, that hold it lawful to meddle with sinful things ; for the Holy Scriptures allow of no such thing. He is a holy God : and all that name the name of God must depart from evil."

There were also twenty-six steps of defection drawn up by him (yet in manuscript), wherein he is most explicit in proving from clear Scripture proofs the sinfulness of the land's apostasy from God, both nationally and personally, from the public resolutions to the time of his death in 1685. He was by some thought too severe in his design of killing the prisoners at Drumclog. But in this he was not altogether to blame ; for the enemy's word was " No quarter," and the sufferers' was the same ; and we find it grieved Robert Hamilton very much, when he beheld some of them spared, after the Lord had delivered them into their hand. " Happy shall he be that rewardeth thee as thou hast served us " (Ps. cxxxvii. 8). Yea, Hardhill himself seems to have had clear grounds and motives for this, in one of the above-mentioned steps of defection, with which we shall conclude this narrative.

15*thly*, As there has been rash, envious, and carnal executing of justice on His and the Church's enemies, so He has also been provoked to reject, cast off, and take the power out of His people's hand, for being sparing of them, when He brought forth and gave a commission to execute on them that vengeance due unto them (Ps. cxlix. 9). For as justice ought to be executed in such and such a way and manner as aforesaid, so it ought to be fully executed without sparing, as is clear from Joshua vii. 24. For sparing the life of the enemy and fleeing upon the spoil, 1 Sam. xv. 19, Saul is sharply rebuked ; and though he excused himself, yet for that very thing he is rejected from being king. Let the practice of Drumclog be remembered and mourned for. If there was not a deep ignorance, reason might teach this ; for what master, having servants, and putting them to do his work, would take such a slight at his servants' hands as to do a part of his work, and come and say to the master, that it is not necessary to do the rest ; when the not doing of it would be dishonourable to the master, and hurtful to the whole family. Therefore was the wrath of God against His people, insomuch that He abhorred His inheritance, and hid His face from His people, making them afraid at the shaking of a leaf, and to flee when none pursueth, being a scorn and hissing to enemies, and fear to some who desire to befriend His cause. And, O ! lay to heart and mourn for what has been done to provoke Him to anger, in not seeking the truth to execute judgment ; therefore He has not pardoned. " Behold, for your iniquities have ye sold yourselves, and for your transgressions is your mother put away " (Isa. l. 1).

Alexander Peden.

LEXANDER PEDEN was born in the parish of Sorn, in the shire of Ayr. After he had passed his courses of learning at the University, he was for some time employed as schoolmaster, precentor, and session-clerk, to Mr John Guthrie, minister of the Gospel, then at Tarbolton. When he was about to enter into the ministry, he was accused by a young woman, as being the father of her child ; but of this aspersion he was fully cleared by the confession of the real father. The woman, after suffering many calamities, put an end to her life, in the very same place where Mr Peden had spent twenty-four hours, seeking the Divine direction, while he was embarrassed with that affair.

A little before the Restoration he was settled minister at New Glenluce in Galloway, where he continued for about the space of three years, until he was, among others, thrust out by the violence and tyranny of these times. When he was about to depart from that parish, he lectured upon Acts xx. from the seventh verse to the end, and preached in the forenoon from these words, in the 31st verse, "Therefore watch, and remember, that, by the space of three years, I ceased not to warn every one," etc. : asserting that he had declared unto them the whole counsel of God, and had kept back nothing, professing he was free from the blood of all souls. In the afternoon he preached from the 32d verse, "And now, brethren, I commend you to God, and to the word of His grace," which occasioned a weeping day in that church. He many times requested them to be silent; but they sorrowed most of all, when he told them, they should never see his face in that pulpit again. He continued till night, and when he closed the pulpit door, he knocked three times very hard on it, with his Bible, saying three times over, "I arrest thee in my Master's name, that none ever enter thee but such as come in by the door as I have done." Accordingly, never did any one enter that pulpit until the Revolution, when one of the Presbyterian persuasion opened it.

About the beginning of the year 1666, a proclamation was emitted by the Council against him, and several of the ejected ministers, wherein he was charged with holding conventicles, preaching, and baptising children at Ralstoun in Kilmarnock parish, and at Castlehill in Craigie parish, where he baptized twenty-five children. Upon his non-appearance at this citation, he was next year declared a rebel, and forfeited in both life and fortune.

After this he joined with that faithful party, which, in the same year, was defeated at Pentland ; and with them he came the length of Clyde, where he had a melancholy view of their end, and parted with them there. Afterwards, when one of his friends said to him, "Sir, you did well that left them, seeing you were persuaded that they would fall and flee before the enemy," he was offended, and said, "Glory, glory to God, that He sent me not to hell immediately, for I should have stayed with them though I should have been all cut to pieces."

In the same year he met with a very remarkable deliverance; for he, Mr Welch, and the laird of Glerover, riding together, they met a party of the enemy's horse, whom there was no escaping. The laird fainted, fearing they should be taken. Peden, seeing this, said, " Keep up your courage and confidence, for God hath laid an arrest on these men, that they shall do us no harm." When they met they were courteous, and asked the way. Peden went off the way, and showed them the ford of the water of Titt. When he returned, the laird said, "Why did you go? you might have let the lad go with them." " No," said he, " they might have asked questions of the lad, which might have discovered us; but as for me, I knew they would be like Egyptian dogs; they could not move a tongue against me, my time being not yet come."

He passed his time sometimes in Scotland and sometimes in Ireland, until June 1673, when he was, by Major Cockburn, taken in the house of Hugh Ferguson of Knockdew, in Carrick, who constrained him to stay all night. Peden told them that it would be a dear night's quarters to them both: accordingly they were both carried prisoners to Edinburgh. There the said Hugh was fined in 1000 merks for reset, harbour, and converse with him.

Some time after his examination he was sent prisoner to the Bass. One Sabbath morning, being about the public worship of God, a young girl, about the age of fourteen years, came to the chamber door, mocking with loud laughter. He said, " Poor thing, thou laughest and mockest at the worship of God, but ere long God shall write such a sudden and surprising judgment on thee, that shall stay thy laughing." Very shortly after that, as she was walking on the rock, a blast of wind swept her off to the sea, where she was lost. Another day, as he was walking on the rock, some soldiers were passing by, and one of them cried, " The devil take him." He said, " Fy, fy! poor man, thou knowest not what thou art saying; but thou shalt repent that." At this he stood astonished, and went to the guard distracted, crying out for Mr Peden, saying, the devil would immediately come and take him away. Peden came, and spoke to and prayed for him, and next morning came to him again, and found him in his right mind, under deep convictions of great guilt. The guard being to change, they commanded him to his arms, but he refused, and said, he would lift no arms against Jesus Christ, His cause, and people, adding, "I have done that too long." The Governor threatened him with death next day by ten o'clock. He confidently said, three times over, that, though he should tear him in pieces, he should never lift arms in that way. About three days after, the Governor put him forth of the garrison, setting him ashore; and he having a wife and children, took a house in East Lothian, where he became a singular Christian.

Alexander Peden was brought from the Bass to Edinburgh, and sentence of banishment passed upon him in December 1678, along with other sixty prisoners for the same cause, to go to America, never to be seen again in Scotland, under pain of death. After this sentence was passed, he often said the ship was not yet built which should take him and these prisoners to Virginia, or any other of the English plantations in America. When they were on shipboard in the roads of Leith, there was a report that the enemy was to send down thumbkins to keep them in order, at which they were much discouraged. He went on deck, and said, "Why are you so discouraged? You need not fear; there will neither thumbkins nor bootkins come here; lift up your hearts, for the day of your redemption draweth near. If we were once at London, we will all be set at liberty." In their voyage thither, they had the opportunity of commanding the ship, and escaping, but would not adventure upon it without his advice. He said, "Let all alone, for the Lord will set all at liberty, in a way more conducive to His own glory, and our own safety." Accordingly, when they arrived, the skipper, who received them at Leith, being to carry them no farther, delivered them to another, to carry them to Virginia, to whom they were represented as thieves and robbers. But when he came to see them, and found they were all grave, sober Christians, banished for Presbyterian principles, he would sail the sea with none such. In this confusion, as the one skipper would not receive them, and the other would keep them no longer at his own expense, they were set at liberty. Some say the skipper got compliments from friends in London; others assure us, that they got off through the means of the Lord Shaftesbury, who was always friendly to the Presbyterians. However, it is certain they were all liberated at Gravesend, without any bond or imposition whatever; and in their way homeward, the English showed them no small degree of kindness.

After they were set at liberty, Mr Peden stayed in London, and other places in England, until June 1679, when he came to Scotland. On that dismal day, the 22nd of that month, when the Lord's people fell and fled before their enemies at Bothwell Bridge, he was forty miles distant, being near the Border, where he kept himself retired until the middle of the day, when some friends said to him, " Sir, the people are waiting for sermon "—it being the Lord's day. To whom he said, " Let the people go to their prayers ; for me, I neither can nor will preach any this day ; for our friends are fallen and fled before the enemy at Hamilton, and they are hashing and hagging them down, and their blood is running down like water."

Shortly after Bothwell Bridge, he went to Ireland, but did not stay long ; for in the year 1680, being near Mauchline, in the shire of Ayr, Robert Brown, at Corsehouse, in Loudon parish, and Hugh Pinaneve, factor to the Earl of Loudon, stabling their horses in the house where he was, went to a fair at Mauchline. In the afternoon, when they came to take their horses, they got some drink ; in the taking of which, the said Hugh broke out into railing against our sufferers, particularly against Richard Cameron, who was lately before that slain at Airsmoss. Peden, being in another room, overhearing all, was so grieved, that he came to the chamber door, and said to him, " Sir, hold your peace ; ere twelve o'clock you shall know what a man Richard Cameron was ; God shall punish that blasphemous mouth of yours in such a manner, that you shall be set up for a beacon to all such railing Rabshakehs." Robert Brown, knowing Mr Peden, hastened to his horse, being persuaded that his word would not fall to the ground ; and, fearing also that some mischief might befall him in Hugh's company, he hastened home to his own house, and the said Hugh to the Earl's ; where, casting off his boots, he was struck with a sudden sickness and pain through his body, with his mouth wide open, and his tongue hanging out in a fearful manner. They sent for Brown to take some blood from him, but all in vain, for he died before midnight.

After this, in the year 1682, Mr Peden married that singular Christian, John Brown, at his house in Priesthill, in the parish of Muirkirk, in Kyle, to Isabel Weir. After marriage, he said to the bride, Isabel, " You have got a good man to be your husband, but you will not enjoy him long ; prize his company, and keep linen by you to be his winding sheet, for you will need it when ye are not looking for it, and it will be a bloody one." This sadly came to pass in the beginning of May 1685.

In the same year, 1682, he went to Ireland again, and coming to the house of William Steel in Glenwhary, in the county of Antrim, he inquired at Mrs Steel, if she wanted a servant for threshing of victual.

She said they did, and asked what his wages were a-day and a-week. He said the common rate was a common rule : to which she assented. At night he was put to bed in the barn with the servant lad, and that night he spent in prayer and groaning, Next day, he threshed with the lad, and the next night he spent in the same way. The second day, the lad said to his mistress, " This man sleeps none, but groans and prays all night; I can get no sleep with him; he threshes very well, and not sparing himself, though I think he hath not been used to it; and when I put the barn in order, he goes to such a place, and prays for the afflicted Church of Scotland, and names so many people in the furnace." He wrought the second day. His mistress watched and overheard him praying, as the lad had said. At night she desired her husband to inquire if he was a minister ; which he did, and desired him to be free with him, and he should not only be no enemy to him, but a friend. Mr Peden said, he was not ashamed of his office, and gave an account of his circumstances; and he was no more set to work, or to lie with the lad. He stayed some considerable time in that place, and was a blessed instrument in the conversion of some, and the civilising of others. There was a servant lass in that house, whom he could not look upon but with frowns ; and at last he said to William Steel and his wife, " Put her away, for she will be a stain to your family; she is with child and will murder it, and will be punished for the same." This accordingly came to pass ; for which she was burned at Carrickfergus—the usual punishment of malefactors in that country.

In the year 1684, being in the house of John Slowan, in the parish of Connor, in the same county of Antrim, about ten o'clock at night, sitting by the fire side, discoursing with some honest people, he started to his feet and said, " Flee off, Sandy, and hide yourself, for Colonel —— is coming to this house to apprehend you, and I advise you all to do the like, for they will be here within an hour;" which came to pass. When they had made a most inquisitive search, without and within the house, and gone round the thorn-bush, where he was lying praying, they went off without their prey. He came in, and said, " And has this gentleman given poor Sandy and thir poor things such a fright? For this night's work, God shall give him such a blow within a few days, as all the physicians on earth shall not be able to cure ;" This likewise came to pass, for he soon died in great misery, vermin issuing from all the pores of his body, with such a nauseous smell that none could enter the room where he lay.

LARNE, CO. ANTRIM, IRELAND.

At another time, when he was in the same parish, David Cunningham, minister in the meeting-house there, one Sabbath-day broke out into very bitter reflections against Mr Peden. Mr Vernon, one of Mr Cunningham's elders, being much offended thereat, told Peden on Monday what he had said. Peden, taking a turn in his garden, came back, and charged him to go tell Mr Cunningham from him, that before Saturday night, he should be as free of a meeting-house as he was. This accordingly came to pass; for he got a charge that same week, not to enter his meeting-house under pain of death.

One time, travelling alone in Ireland, it being a dark mist, and night approaching, he was obliged to go to a house belonging to a Quaker, where he begged the shelter of his roof all night. The Quaker said, " Thou art a stranger; thou art very welcome, and shalt be kindly entertained; but I cannot wait upon thee, for I am going to the meeting." Peden said, " I will along with you." The Quaker said, " Thou mayest if thou pleasest, but thou must not trouble us." He said, " I shall be civil." When they came to the meeting, as their custom was, they sat for some time silent, some with their faces to the wall, and some covered; and, there being a void in the loft above, there came down the appearance of a raven, and sat on one man's head, who rose up and spoke with such vehemence, that the foam flew from his mouth. It went to a second, and he did so likewise. Peden, sitting next the landlord, said, "Do you not see? You will not deny yon afterwards." He answered, "Thou promised to be silent." From a second it went to a third man's head, who did as the former two. When they dismissed, on the way home, Peden said to his landlord, "I always thought there was devilry amongst you, but I never thought that he had appeared visibly, till now I have seen it. Oh! for the Lord's sake, quit this way, and flee to the Lord Jesus, in whom there is redemption through His blood, even the forgiveness of all your iniquities." The poor man fell a-weeping, and said, "I perceive that God hath sent thee to my house, and put it in thy heart to go along with me, and permitted the devil to appear visibly amongst us this night. I never saw the like before; let me have the help of thy prayers, for I resolve, through the Lord's grace, to follow this way no longer." After this, he became a singular Christian; and when dying blessed the Lord that in mercy he sent the man of God to his house.

Before he left Ireland, he preached in several places, particularly one time near the forementioned Mr Vernon's house, in the year 1685, where he made a most clear discovery of the many hardships his fellow-sufferers were then undergoing in Scotland; and of the death of Charles II., the news of which came not to Ireland till twenty-four hours thereafter.

After this he longed to be out of Ireland, partly through a fearful apprehension of the dismal rebellion that broke out there about four years after, and partly from a desire he had to take part with the sufferings of Scotland. And before his departure from thence, he baptized a child of John Maxwell, a Glasgow man, who had fled over from the persecution; which was all the drink money (as he expressed it) that he had to leave in Ireland.

After he and twenty Scots sufferers came aboard ship, he went on deck, and prayed (there not being then the least wind), where he made a rehearsal of times and places when and where the Lord had heard and helped them in the day of their distress, and now they were in a great strait. Waving his hand to the west, from whence he desired the wind, he said, "Lord, give us a loof-ful of wind; fill the sails, Lord, and give us a fresh gale, and let us have a swift and safe passage over to the bloody land, come of us what will." When he began to pray, the sails were hanging all straight down, but ere he ended, they were all blown full, and they got a very swift and safe passage over. In the morning after they landed, he lectured, ere they parted, on a brae-side ; where he had some awful threatenings against Scotland, saying, " The time was coming, that they might travel many miles in Galloway, Nithsdale, Ayr, and Clydesdale, and not see a reeking house, or hear a cock crow." He further added, " My soul trembles to think what will become of the indulged, backslidden, and upsitting ministers of Scotland ; as the Lord lives, none of them shall ever be honoured to put a right pin in the Lord's tabernacle, nor assert Christ's kingly prerogative as Head and King of His Church."

After his arrival in Scotland, in the beginning of the year 1685, he met with several remarkable deliverances from the enemy. One time, fleeing from them on horseback, he was obliged to cross a water, where he was in imminent danger. After he got out, he cried, " Lads, do not follow, for I assure you, ye want my boat, and so will drown ; and consider where your landing will be," which affrighted them from entering the water. At another time, being also hard pursued, he was forced to take a bog and moss before him. One of the dragoons, being more forward than the rest, ran himself into that dangerous bog, where he and the horse were never seen more.

About this time, he preached one Sabbath night in a sheep-house, the hazard of the time affording no better. That night he lectured upon Amos vii. 8 : " Behold, I will set a plumb-line in the midst of my people Israel." In this lecture, he said, " I'll tell you good news. Our Lord will take a feather out of Antichrist's wing, which shall bring down the Duke of York, and banish him out of these kingdoms. And there shall never a man of the house of Stuart sit upon the throne of Britain after the Duke of York, whose reign is now short; for their lechery, treachery, tyranny, and shedding the precious blood of the Lord's people. But, oh! black, black will the days be that will come upon Ireland! so that they shall travel forty miles and not see a reeking house, or hear a cock crow." When ended, he and those with him lay down in the sheep-house, and got some sleep ; and early next morning he went up a burnside, and stayed long. When he came back, he sung the 32d Psalm, from the seventh verse to the end, and then repeated that verse,

> " Thou art my hiding-place, thou shalt
> From trouble keep me free ;
> Thou with songs of deliverance
> About shalt compass me."

"These and the following," he said, "are sweet lines, which I got at the burnside this morning, and I will get more to-morrow ; and so will get daily provision. He is never behind with any who put their trust in Him, and we will go on in His strength, making mention of His righteousness and of His only." He met with another remarkable deliverance, for the enemy coming upon him, and some others, they were pursued by both horse and foot a considerable way. At last, getting some little height between them and the enemy, he stood still, and said, "Let us pray here, for if the Lord hear not our prayers, and save us, we are all dead men." Then he began, saying, "Lord, it is Thy enemy's day, hour, and power ; they may not be idle. But hast Thou no other work for them, but to send them after us ? Send them after them to whom Thou wilt give strength to flee, for our strength is gone. Twine them about the hill, Lord, and cast the lap of Thy cloak over Old Sandy, and thir poor things, and save us this one time ; and we'll keep it in remembrance, and tell it to the commendation of Thy goodness, pity, and compassion, what Thou didst for us at such a time." And in this he was heard, for a cloud of mist intervened immediately betwixt them ; and in the meantime, a post came to the enemy to go in quest of Renwick, and a great company with him.

At this time it was seldom that Mr Peden could be prevailed on to preach ; frequently answering and advising people to pray much, saying, "It was praying folk that would get through the storm ; they would yet get preaching, both meikle and good ; but not much of it, until judgment was poured out to lay the land desolate."

In the same year, 1685, being in Carrick, John Clark of Moorbrook, being with him, said, "Sir, what think you of this time? Is it not a dark and melancholy day? Can there be a more discouraging time than this?" He said, "Yes, John, this is a dark, discouraging time, but there will be a darker time than this ; these silly, graceless creatures, the curates, shall go down ; and after them shall arise a party called Presbyterians, but having little more than the name, and these shall, as really as Christ was crucified without the gates of Jerusalem on Mount Calvary bodily,—I say they shall as really crucify Christ in His cause and interest in Scotland ; and shall lay Him in His grave, and His friends shall give Him His winding sheet, and He shall lie as one buried for a considerable time. Oh ! then, John, there shall be darkness and dark days, such as the poor Church of Scotland never saw the like, nor shall ever see, if once they were over ; yea, John, they shall be so dark, that if a poor thing would go between the east sea-bank and the west sea-bank, seeking a minister to whom he would communicate his case, or tell him the mind of the Lord concerning the time, he shall not find one." John asked "where the Testimony should be then ?" He answered, " In the hands of a few, who will be despised and undervalued of all, but especially by these ministers who buried Christ ; but after that He shall get up upon them ; and at the crack of His winding-sheet, as many of them as are alive, who were at His burial, shall be distracted and mad with fear, not knowing what to do. Then, John, there shall be brave days, such as the Church of Scotland never saw the like ; but I shall not see them, though you may."

About this time, as Peden was preaching in the day-time in the parish of Girvan, and being in the fields, David Mason, then a professor, came in haste, trampling upon the people to be near him. At this he said, " There comes the devil's rattle-bag ; we do not want him here." After this, the said David became officer and informer of that district, running through, rattling, and summoning the people to their unhappy courts for nonconformity ; at which he and his got the name of " the devil's rattle-bag." After the Revolution he complained to his minister, that he and his family got that name. The minister said, " You well deserve it ; and he was an honest man that gave you it ; you and yours must enjoy it ; there is no help for that."

It is very remarkable, that being sick, and the landlord where Peden stayed being afraid to keep him in his house (the enemy being then in search of hiding people), he made him a bed among the standing corn ; at which time a great rain fell out, insomuch that the waters were raised, and yet not one drop was to be observed within ten feet of his bed, while he lay in that field.

Much about the same time, he came to Garfield, in the parish of Mauchline, to the house of Matthew Hogg, a smith by trade. He went to the barn, but thought himself not safe there, foot and horse of the enemy searching for wanderers, as they were then called, and he desired the favour of his loft, being an old waste house two storeys high. Hogg refused. Peden then said, " Weel, weel, poor man, you will not let me have the shelter of your roof ; but that same house will be your judgment and ruin yet." Some time after this, the gable of that house fell, and killed both him and his son.

Peden's last sermon was preached in the Collimwood, at the

Water of Ayr, a short time before his death. In the preface, he said,
" There are four or five things I have to tell you this night, and the
first is, A bloody sword, a bloody sword, a bloody sword for thee, O
Scotland, that shall pierce the hearts of many. *2dly*, Many miles
shall ye travel and see nothing but desolation and ruinous wastes in
thee, O Scotland. *3dly*, The most fertile places in thee shall be as
waste as the mountains. *4thly*, The woman with child shall be
ripped up and dashed in pieces. And *5thly*, Many a conventicle
has God had in thee, O Scotland ; but, ere long, God will hold a
conventicle that will make Scotland tremble. Many a preaching has
God bestowed on thee ; but ere long, God's judgment shall be as
frequent as these precious meetings were, wherein He sent forth
His servants to give faithful warning of the hazard of thy apostacy
from God, in breaking, burning, and burying His covenant, persecuting, slighting, and contemning the Gospel, shedding the precious
blood of His saints and servants. God sent forth a Welwood, a Kid,
a King, a Cameron, a Cargill, and others to preach to thee : but ere
long, God shall preach to thee by fire and a bloody sword. God will
let none of these men's words fall to the ground, whom He sent forth
with a commission to preach these things in His name." In the
sermon, he further said, that a few years after his death, there would
be a wonderful alteration of affairs in Britain and Ireland, and Scotland's persecution should cease ; upon which every one would
believe the deliverance was come, and consequently would be fatally
secure ; but they would be very far mistaken, for both Scotland and
England would be scourged by foreigners (a set of unhappy men in
these lands taking part with them), before any of them could pretend
to be happy, or get a thorough deliverance ; which would be more
severe chastisement than any other they had met with, or could come
under, if once that were over.

    After much wandering from place to place, through Kyle, Carrick,
and Galloway (his death drawing near), Peden came to his brother's
house, in the parish of Sorn, where he was born, where he caused dig
a cave, with a willow bush covering the mouth thereof, near to his
brother's house. The enemy got notice, and searched the house narrowly several times, but found him not. While in this cave, he said
to some friends—1. That God would make Scotland a desolation ;
2. That there would be a remnant in the land whom God would
spare and hide; 3. They would be in holes and caves of the earth,
and be supplied with meat and drink ; and when they came out of

their holes, they would not have freedom to walk for stumbling on dead corpses; and 4. A stone cut out of the mountain would come down, and God would be avenged on the great ones of the earth, and the inhabitants of the land, for their wickedness; and then the Church would come forth with a bonny bairn-time at her back of young ones. And he wished that the Lord's people might be hid in their caves, as if they were not in the world; for nothing would do until God appeared with His judgments. He also gave them a sign, That if he were but once buried, they might be in doubt; but if oftener than once, they might be persuaded that all he had said would come to pass; and earnestly desired them to take his corpse out to Airsmoss, and bury him beside Ritchie (meaning Richard Cameron), that he might have rest in his grave, for he had got little during his life. But he said, bury him where they would, he would be lifted again; but the man who would first put hands to his corpse, four things would befall him: 1. He would get a great fall from a house; 2. He would fall in adultery; 3. In theft, and for that he should leave the land; 4. He would make a melancholy end abroad for murder; all which came to pass. This man was one Murdoch, a mason by trade, but then in the military service, being the first man who put hands to his corpse.

Peden had for some time been too credulous in believing the misrepresentations of some false brethren concerning James Renwick, whereby he was much alienated from him. This exceedingly grieved Renwick, stumbled some of his followers, and confirmed some of his adversaries, who boasted that Peden was turned his enemy. But now, when dying, he sent for Renwick, who came to him in all haste, and found him lying in very low circumstances. When he came in, he raised himself upon his elbow, with his head on his hand, and said, "Are you the James Renwick there is so much noise about?" He answered, "Father, my name is James Renwick, but I have given the world no ground to make any noise about me, for I have espoused no new principles or practices, but what our reformers and covenanters maintained." He caused him to sit down, and give him an account of his conversion, principles, and call to the ministry; all which Renwick did, in a most distinct manner. When ended, Peden said, "Sir, you have answered me to my soul's satisfaction; I am very sorry that I should have believed any such evil reports of you, which not only quenched my love to, and marred my sympathy with you, but led me to express myself so bitterly against you, for which I have sadly smarted. But, sir, ere you go, you must pray for me, for I am old, and going to leave the world." This Renwick did with more than ordinary enlargement. When he ended, Peden took him by the hand, and drew him to him, and kissed him, saying, "Sir, I find you a faithful servant to your Master ; go on in a single dependence upon the Lord, and ye will get honestly through and clear off the stage, when many others who hold their heads high will lie in the mire, and make foul hands and garments." And then he prayed that the Lord might spirit, strengthen, support, and comfort him in all duties and difficulties.

A little before his death, Peden said, "Ye will all be displeased at the place where I shall be buried at last, but I discharge you all to lift my corpse again." At last, one morning early he left the cave, and came to his brother's door. His brother's wife said, " Where are you going? The enemy will be here." He said, " I know that." "Alas ! sir," said she, "what will become of you ; you must go back to the cave again." He said, " I have done with that, for it is discovered ; but there is no matter, for within forty-eight hours, I will be beyond the reach of all the devil's temptations, and his instruments in hell and on earth, and they shall trouble me no more." About three hours after he entered the house, the enemy came, and having found him not in the cave, searched the barn narrowly, casting the unthreshed corn, searched the house, stabbing the beds, but entered not into the place where he lay. Within forty-eight hours after this, after a weary pilgrimage, he became an inhabitant of that land, where the weary are at rest, being then past sixty years of age.

He was buried in the laird of Auchinleck's isle, but a troop of dragoons came and lifted his corpse, and carried it two miles to Cumnock gallows-foot (after he had been forty days in the grave), where he lies buried beside other martyrs.

Thus died Alexander Peden, so much famed for his singular piety, zeal, and faithfulness, and indefatigableness in the duty of prayer, but especially exceeding all we have heard of in latter times for that gift of foreseeing and foretelling future events, both with respect to the Church and nation of Scotland and Ireland, and particular persons and families, several of which are already accomplished. A gentleman of late, when speaking in his writings of Mr Peden, says, "Abundance of this good man's predictions are well-known to be already come to pass." And although these things are now made to stoop or yield to the force of ridicule, the sarcasms of the profane, and the fashions of an atheistical age and generation ; yet we must believe and conclude with the Spirit of God, that the secrets of the Lord both have been, are, and will be, with them who fear His name.

There are some few of Peden's sermons in print, especially two preached at Glenluce, in 1682, the one from Matt. xxi. 38, and the other from Luke xxiv. 21 ; which prophetical sermons, though in a homely style, are of a most zealous and spiritual strain, now reprinted in a late collection of sermons. As for those papers handed about under his name, anent James Renwick and his followers, they are, with good reason, looked upon as altogether spurious.

John Blackader.

OHN BLACKADER was a lineal descendant, and the only representative, of the house of Tulliallan. After having undergone his course of classical learning, he was ordained minister of the Gospel at Troqueer, near Dumfries, where he continued faithfully to discharge the trust committed to his care, until he was, with many others of his faithful brethren, thrust out by that act commonly called the drunken act of Glasgow, in the year 1662. At that time a party came from Dumfries to seize him ; but he was gone out of the way. His wife and children, to whom the soldiers were extremely rude, were forced to retire to the parish of Glencairn. In the year 1665, a party of Sir James Turner's men came thither in quest of him ; but happily he and his wife were at Edinburgh. With great fury, and terrible oaths and execrations, they turned out the children from their beds, in the middle of the night, caused one of them to hold the candle till they searched Blackader's books and papers, and took what they listed. They stabbed the beds with their swords, threatened to roast the children on the fire, and caused one of them to run near half a mile in a dark night in his shirt.

After this, Blackader went and preached in the fields, where he had numerous meetings, particularly at the Hill of Beath, in Fife, in the year 1670. He had before been by the Council's letter put to the horn; and after this he came west, about the year 1675, and preached in the parish of Kilbride and other places. The same year, being at the Cow Hill, in Livingstone parish, he went out one evening in the month of August, to a retired place. When he came in again, he seemed somewhat melancholy. Being asked by some friends what was the reason, he said that he was afraid of a contagious mist that should go through the land in many places that night, which might have sad effects, and death to follow; and, as a precaution, he desired them to keep doors and windows as close as possible, and to notice where it stood thickest and longest. This they did: and it was upon a little town called the Craigs, wherein were but a few families; within four months after, thirty corpses went out of that place, and great dearth and scarcity followed for three years space after.

Blackader stood out against the Indulgence, and preached sometimes with Mr John Dickson, they being both of one sentiment. He continued under several hardships until the year 1678, when he went over to Mr M'Ward in Holland. He continued some time there, and having returned home, he was about Edinburgh at the time of Bothwell Bridge; after that battle, he was of no small use to the prisoners, in dissuading them from taking the Bond, and other compliances; which he did by letters.

After he had endured a series of hardships, and surmounted a number of difficulties, Blackader came to discharge his last public work at a muir side, at Newhouse, in the parish of Livingstone, March 28, 1681. He lectured upon Micah iv. 9, where he asserted, that the nearer the delivery, rains and showers would come thicker and sorer, and that they had been in the fields; but ere they were delivered, they would go down to Babylon; that either Popery would overspread the land, or else would be at the breaking in upon it, like an inundation of water. In preaching upon 1 Thess. iii. 3, amongst other things, he desired people to take good heed what ministers they heard, and what advice they followed; and praying, he said that he was as clear and willing to hold up the blessed standard of the Gospel as ever; and blessed the Lord he was free of every bond and imposition. "The Lord rebuke, give repentance and forgiveness," said he, "to these ministers who persuaded the poor prisoners to take the Bond; for their perishing at sea is more shocking to me than the thousands of them that have been slain in the fields."

He went to Edinburgh, and was apprehended by Major Johnston upon the 6th of April following, and brought first to General
Dalziel, then to the guard, and then before a Committee of Council,
consisting of the Chancellor, General, Advocate, and Bishop Paterson.
The Chancellor asked, if he had excommunicated the King, or was at
Torwood? He answered, he was not there these four years. *Chan.*
But do ye approve of what was done there? *Ans.* I am not free to
declare my inward sentiments of things and persons; and therefore I
humbly beg to be excused. You may form a libel against me, and I
shall endeavour to answer it as I can. *Chan.* But we hear you
keep conventicles since the indemnity. *Ans.* I am a minister of the
Gospel, though unworthy, and under the strictest obligation to exercise my ministry, as I shall be answerable at the great day. I did,
and so do still, count it my duty to exercise my ministry, as I am
called thereunto. *Chan.* But you have preached in the fields; that
is to say, on muirs and hillsides; I shall not ask you if you have
preached in houses, though there is no liberty even for that. *Ans.* I
place no case of conscience, nor make any difference, between preaching in houses and in the fields, but as it may best serve the con-
veniency of the hearers; nor know I any restriction as to either in the
Word. My commission reaches to houses and fields, within and without doors. *Chan.* We doubt not but you know and have seen the laws
discharging such preaching. *Ans.* I have; and I am sorry that ever any
laws were made against preaching fhe Gospel. *Chan.* Not against the
Gospel, but against rebellion. The Chancellor asked if he kept conventicles in Fife? which he did not deny. He was then carried to the guard.

The Council sat in the afternoon, but he was not again called
before them; but, without a further hearing, was sentenced to go to
the Bass. Accordingly, April 7, he was carried thither. On the
way, at Fisherrow, there happened to be a gathering of the people;
when the captain, apprehending it might be for his rescue, told Mr
Blackader that if they attempted anything of this kind, he would
instantly shoot him through the head. He told the captain that he
knew nothing of any such design.

He continued at the Bass till the end of the year 1685, when he
contracted a rheumatism from the air of the place. A motion was
made for his liberation on bail, on this account, but it never took
effect; and so he entered into the joy of his Lord, about the beginning of the year 1686. As the interest of Christ always lay near his
heart through his life, so amongst his last words he said that the

Lord would yet arise and defend His own cause, in spite of all His enemies.

Thus died John Blackader, a pious man, and a powerful preacher. There are several well-vouched instances of the Lord's countenancing his ministry, while in the fields, and of the remarkable success of his sermons, which were not so low and flat, but the pious learned might admire them ; nor so learned, but the plainest capacity might understand them. In a word, he was possessed of many singular virtues. His going through so many imminent dangers with such undaunted courage was remarkable, and his love to God and His Church exemplary

I have only seen two of his many pathetic sermons, which are very extensive, upon the sufferings of Christ, from Isa. liii. 11—" He shall see of the travail of his soul, and shall be satisfied." The reader will find them in a small collection of sermons lately published. [He was buried in the churchyard of North Berwick, where a handsome tombstone still marks his grave, bearing the following epitaph :— " Here lies the body of Mr John Blackader, minister of the Gospel at Troqueer, in Galloway, who died on the Bass after five years' imprisonment, anno dom. 1685, and of his age sixty-three years."—Ed.]

MONUMENT AT NORTH BERWICK.

James Renwick.

AMES RENWICK was born in the parish of Glencairn, in Dumfriesshire, February 15, 1662. His parents, though not rich, were exemplary for piety. His father, Andrew Renwick, a weaver by trade, and his mother, Elizabeth Corsan, had several children, who died young; for which, when the latter was pouring forth her motherly grief, her husband used to comfort her with declaring that he was well satisfied to have children, whether they lived or died young or old, provided they might be heirs of glory. With this she could not attain to be satisfied; but she had it for her exercise to seek a child from the Lord, that might not only be an heir of glory, but might live to serve Him in his generation. Whereupon, when James was born, she took it as an answer of prayer, and reputed herself under manifold engagements to dedicate him to the Lord, who satisfied her with very early evidences of His accepting that return of His own gift, and confirmed the same by very remarkable appearances of His gracious dealings with the child. For, by the time he was two years of age, he was observed to be aiming at prayer, even in the cradle, wherewith his mother conceived such expectations and hopes, that the Lord would be with him and do good by him, as that all the reproaches he sustained, the difficulties and dangers that he underwent to his dying day, never moved her in the least from the confidence that the Lord would carry him through and off the stage, in some honourable way for His own glory. His father also, before his death in February 1, 1679, obtained the same persuasion, that James' time in the world would be but short, but that the Lord would make some eminent use of him.

After James Renwick had learned to read the Bible, when about six years old, the Lord gave him some sproutings of gracious preparation, training him in his way, exercising him with doubts and debates as to the Maker of all things, how all things were made, and for what end, and with strange suppositions of so many invisible worlds, above and beneath; with which he was transported into a train of musing, and continued in this exercise for about the space of two years, until, by prayer and meditation on the history of the creation, he came to a thorough belief that God made all things, and that all which He made was very good. And yet, after he came to more maturity, he relapsed into a deeper labyrinth of darkness about these foundation truths, and was so assaulted with temptations of atheism, that, being in the fields, and looking to the mountains, he said that if these were all devouring furnaces of burning brimstone, he would be content to go through them all, if so be he could be assured there was a God. Out of this, however, he emerged, through grace, into the sweet serenity of a settled persuasion of the being of a God, and of his interest in Him.

From his younger years, he made much conscience of obeying his parents, whose order (if they had spoken of putting him to any trade) he would no way decline; yet his inclination was constant for his book, until Providence propitiously furnished him with means of greater proficiency at Edinburgh; for many were so enamoured of his hopeful disposition, that they earnestly promoted his education. When he was ready for the university, they encouraged him in attending gentlemen's sons, for the improvement both of their studies and his own; but this association of youths, as it is usually accompanied with temptations to vanity, enticed him, with some others, to spend too much of his time in gaming and recreations. It was then (for no other part of his life can be instanced), that some who knew him not, took occasion from this extravagance to reproach him with profanity and flagitiousness, which he ever abhorred, and disdained the very suspicion thereof. When his time at the college drew near an end, he evinced such a fear of offending God, that upon his refusal of the oath of allegiance then tendered, he was denied his share of the public solemnity of laureation with the rest of the candidates but received it privately at Edinburgh. After this he continued his studies, attending for a time on private and persecuted meetings for Gospel ordinances.

But upon a deplorable discovery of the unfaithfulness even of nonconformist ministers, he was again for some time plunged into the depths of darkness, doubting what should be the end of such backsliding courses, until, upon a more inquisitive search after such ministers as were most free from these defections, he found more light; his knowledge of the iniquity of these courses was augmented, and his zeal increased. And being more confirmed, when he beheld how signally the faithful ministers were owned of the Lord, and carried off the stage with great steadfastness, faith, and patience (especially that faithful minister and martyr, Donald Cargill, at whose execution he was present, July 27, 1681), he was so moved, that he determined to embark with these witnesses in the cause for which they suffered. He was afterwards so strengthened and established in this resolution, getting instruction about these things in and from the Word, so sealed with a strong hand upon his soul, that the temptations, tribulations, oppositions, and contradictions he met with from all hands to the day of his death, could never shake his mind to doubt the least concerning them.

Accordingly, in this persuasion, formed upon grounds of Scripture and reason, he, in October 1681, came to a meeting with some of these faithful witnesses of Christ, and, conferring about the testimonies of some other martyrs lately executed (which he was very earnest always to gather and keep on record), he refreshed them greatly by a discourse, showing how much he was grieved and offended with those who heard the curates, pleaded for cess-paying, and defended the owning of the tyrants' authority, etc., and how sad it was to him that none were giving a formal testimony against these things; and in the end added, that he would think it a great ease to his mind to know and be engaged with a remnant that would prosecute and propagate their testimony against the corruptions of the times to the succeeding generations, and would desire nothing more than to be helped to be serviceable to them.

At his first coming among them he could not but be taken notice of; for, while some were speaking of removing the bodies of the martyrs, lately executed at the Gallowlea, Renwick was very froward to promote it, and active to assist therein. Also, when the sincere seekers of God, who were scattered up and down the land, and adhered to the Testimony, as Cameron and Cargill left it towards the end of 1681, began to settle a correspondence in general, for preserving union, understanding one another's minds, and preventing declension to right and left hand extremes, and had agreed upon emitting that declaration published at Lanark, Jan. 12, 1682, Renwick was employed in proclaiming it, but had no hand in the penning thereof, otherwise it might have been more considerately worded than what it was; for though he approved of the matter of it, yet he always

UTRECHT.

acknowledged there were some expressions therein rather unadvised.

After the publishing of this declaration, the next general meeting, finding themselves reproached and informed against, both at home and abroad, as if they had fallen from the principles of the Church of Scotland, thought it expedient to send Alexander Gordon of Earlstoun to Holland to vindicate themselves, and to crave that sympathy which they could not obtain from their own countrymen. This at length, through mercy, proved so encouraging, that a door was opened to provide for a succession of faithful ministers, by sending some there to be fitted for the work of the ministry. Accordingly, Renwick, with some others, went to Holland. His comrades were ready, and sailed before, which made him impatiently haste to follow; yet, at his departure, he affirmed to a comrade that, as they did not depart together, he saw something should fall out, which should obstruct their coming home together also. This was verified by the falling off of Mr Flint (however forward at that time), to a contrary course of defection.

When he went over, he was settled at the University of Groningen, where he plied his studies so hard, and with such proficiency, that from the necessities of his friends in Scotland, who were longing for his labours, and his own ardent desire to be at the work, in a short

MONTALBAN'S TOWER, AMSTERDAM.

time he was ready for ordination. To hasten this, his dear friend
Robert Hamilton, who merited so much of those who reaped the
benefit of Renwick's labours afterwards, applied to Mr Brakel, a godly
Dutch minister, who was much delighted at first with the motion,
and advised that it should be done at Emden; but this could not
be obtained, because the principal man there who was to have the
management of the affair, was Cocceian in his judgment. Whereupon Hamilton solicited the Classes of Gröningen to undertake it,
which they willingly promised to do : and calling for the testimonials
of Mr Renwick, and two others who went over at that time, Renwick's
was produced (being providentially in readiness when the others were
a-wanting), and though in a rude dress, were sustained. The Classes
being convened, they were called in and had an open harangue,
wherein open testimony was given against all the forms and corruptions of their Church ; whereat they were so far from being offended,
that after a solemn and serious consideration, they declared it was
the Lord's cause, and, cost what it would, though all the kings of
the earth were against it, they would go through with it. They all
three should have passed together, but upon some differences arising,
the other two were retarded. It was the custom of the place, that every
but one that passes must pay twenty guilders for the use of the church ;
the Classes declared, that they would be at all the charges themselves.

The next difficulty was, that being told it was impossible for any to pass without subscribing their Catechism, and observing that their forms and corruptions were therein justified, Mr Renwick resolutely answered that he would do no such thing, being engaged by a solemn covenant to the contrary. This was like to spoil all ; but at length they condescended that he should subscribe the Confession and Catechism of the Church of Scotland, a practice never before heard of in that land ; which was accepted. The day of ordination being come, Mr Renwick was called in a very respectful way. After spending some time in prayer, the examination began, which lasted from ten in the morning to two o'clock in the afternoon. Then his friends, who were attending in the church, were called in (amongst whom was his honoured friend Mr Hamilton, and another elder of the Church of Scotland), to witness the laying on of hands, which, after the exhortation, they performed with prayer, the whole meeting melting in tears ; and thereafter he had a discourse to the Classes. With this solemnity they were so much affected, that at dinner, to which he and his friends were invited, the president declared the great satisfaction all the brethren had in Mr Renwick ; that they thought the whole time he was before them, he was so filled with the Spirit of God, that his face seemed to shine, and that they had never seen or found so much of the Lord's spirit accompanying any work as that ordination.

But no sooner were these difficulties over, than others of a more disagreeable aspect began to arise, which, if they had appeared but one day sooner, might have stopped the ordination, at least for a time. On the very next day, Mr Brakel told them that a formal libel was coming from the Scottish ministers at Rotterdam, containing heavy accusations against the poor society-people in Scotland, which they behoved either to vindicate, or else the ordination must be stopped ; but this being too late as to Renwick, it came to nothing at last.

After Renwick's ordination, he had a most longing desire to improve his talents for the poor persecuted people in Scotland, who were his brethren ; and having received large testimonials of his ordination and learning (particularly in the Hebrew and Greek tongues) from the Classes, and finding a ship ready to sail, he embarked at the Brill ; but waiting some days for a wind, he was so discouraged by some profane passengers pressing the King's health, etc., that he was forced to leave that vessel, and take another bound for Ireland. A storm compelled them to put into Rye harbour, in England, about the time when there was so much noise of the Ryehouse plot, which created him no small danger; but, after many perils at sea, he arrived safe at Dublin, where he had many conflicts with the ministers there, anent their defections and indifference; and yet in such a gaining and Gospel way, that he left conviction on their spirits of his being a pious and zealous youth, which procured him a speedy passage to Scotland. In this passage Renwick had considerable dangers, and a prospect of more, as not knowing how or where he should come to land, all ports being then so strictly observed, and the skipper refusing to let him go till his name should be given up. But at last he was prevailed on to give him a cast to the shore, where he began his weary and uncertain wanderings through an unknown wilderness, amongst unknown people, it being some time before he could meet with any of the societies.

In September 1683 Renwick commenced his ministerial work in Scotland, taking up the testimony of the standard of Christ where it was fixed, and had fallen at the removal of the former witnesses, Cameron and Cargill, which, in the strength of his Master, he undertook to prosecute and maintain against the opposition from all hands, that seemed unsupportable to sense and reason. In the midst of these difficulties, he was received by a poor persecuted people, who had lost all the worldly enjoyment they had for the sake of the Gospel. His first public meeting was in the moss at Darmeid, where, for their information and his own vindication, he thought it expedient not only to let them know how he was called to the ministry, and what he adhered to, but, besides, to unbosom himself about the then puzzling questions of the time, particularly concerning ministers, defections, etc.; showing whom he could not join with, and his reasons for so doing; and in the end telling them on what grounds he stood, and resolved to stand upon, even to the length of (the Lord assisting him) sealing them with his blood.

After this the father of lies began to spue out a flood of reproaches, to swallow up and bury his name and work in contempt, which were very credulously entertained and industriously spread, not only by the profane, but even by many professors. Some said he had excommunicated all the ministers in Scotland, and some after they were dead; whereas he only gave reasons why he could not keep communion with them in the present circumstances. Others said that he was no Presbyterian, and that his design was only to propagate schism; but the truth was, he was a professed witness against all the defections of Presbyterians from any part of their covenanted work of reformation. Again, other ministers alleged he was a Sectarian, Independent, or Anabaptist, or they knew not what. But when he had sometimes occasion to be among these in and about Newcastle, and Northumberland, they were as much offended as any at his faithful freedom in discovering the evils of their way, and declared that they never met with such severe dealing from any Presbyterian before.

But the general outcry was, that he had no mission at all. Some slandered him, saying that he came only by chance, at a throw of the dice; with many other calumnies, refuted by the foregoing relation. Others gave out that he and his followers maintained the murdering principles, and the delirious and detestable blasphemies of Gibb, all which shameless and senseless fictions he ever opposed and abhorred. Yea, some ministers, more seemingly serious in their essays to prejudice the people against him, said, that they had sought and got the mind of the Lord in it, that his labours should never profit the Church of Scotland, nor any soul in it, assuring themselves that, ere it were long, he would break, and bring to nothing, him and them that followed him; comparing them to Jannes and Jambres who withstood Moses. Under all these reproaches he was remarkably supported, and went on in his Master's business, while He had any work for him to do.

In the meanwhile, from the noise that went through the country concerning him, the Council got notice: and thereupon, being enraged at the report of his preaching in the fields, they raised a hotter and more cruel persecution against him than can be instanced ever to have been against any one man in the nation; nay, than ever the most notorious murderer was pursued with. For, having publicly proclaimed him as a traitor, rebel, etc., they proceeded to pursue his followers with all the rigour that hellish fury and malice could suggest or invent; and yet the more they opposed, the more his followers grew and increased.

In 1684, his difficulties from enemies, and discouragements from friends opposed to him, and manifold vexations from all hands, began to increase more and more; yet all the while he would not intermit one day's preaching, but was still incessant and undaunted in his work. This made the ministers inform against him, as if he had intruded upon other men's labours; alleging that, when another minister had appointed to preach in a place, he unexpectedly came and preached in the same parish; and for that purpose, instanced one time near

Paisley; whereas he went upon a call from several in the district, without knowing then whether there was such a minister in that country. It is confessed that he had sometimes taken the churches to preach in, when either the weather, instant hazard at the time, or respect to secrecy and safety, did exclude from every other place. But, could this be called intrusion, to creep into the church for one night, when they could not stand, nor durst they be seen, without?

The same year, in prosecution of a cruel information against him, the soldiers became more vigilant in their endeavours to seek and hunt after him; and from them he had many remarkable deliverances. Particularly in the month of July, as he was going to a meeting, a country man, seeing him wearied, gave him a horse for some miles to ride on, when they were surprised by Lieutenant Dundas and a party of dragoons. The two men with him were taken and pitifully wounded. He escaped their hands, and went up Dungavel Hill; but was so closely pursued (they being so near that they fired at him all the time), that he was forced to leave the horse, losing thereby his cloak-bag, with many papers. Seeing no other refuge, he was fain to run towards a heap of stones, where, for a little moment, getting out of their sight, he found a hollow place into which he crept. Committing himself by earnest ejaculation to God, in submission to live or die, and, believing that he should be reserved for greater work, that part of Scripture often came into his mind, "Depart from me, all ye workers of iniquity" (Ps. vi. 8), together with these words, "For He shall give His angels charge over thee, to keep thee in all thy ways" (Ps. xci. 11). In the meantime the enemy searched up and down the hill, yet were restrained from looking into that place where he was. Many such sore and desperate chases he and those with him met with; often continuing whole nights and days without intermission, in the wildest places of the country, for many miles together, without so much as a possibility of escaping the rage of those who pursued them.

The same year, on the 4th of September, letters of intercommuning were issued against him, commanding all to give him no reset or supply, nor furnish him with meat, drink, house, harbour, or anything useful to him; and requiring all sheriffs to apprehend and commit to prison his person wherever they could find him; by virtue of which, the sufferers were reduced to incredible straits, not only in being murdered, but also from hunger, cold, harassings, etc. In this perplexity, being neither able to flee nor fight, they were forced to publish an apologetical representation, showing how far they might, according to the approven principles and practices, and covenant engagements of our reformers, restrict and reduce to practice that privilege of extraordinary executing of judgment on the murdering beasts of prey, who professed and prosecuted a daily trade of destroying innocents. When this declaration was first proposed, Renwick was somewhat averse to it, fearing the sad effects it might produce ; but, considering that the necessity of the case would admit of no delay, he consented, and concurred in the publication thereof. Accordingly it was fixed upon several market crosses and parish church doors, November 8, 1684.

After the publication of this declaration, rage and reproach seemed to strive which should show the greatest violence against the publishers and owners of it. The Council issued a proclamation for discovering such as owned, or would not disown it ; requiring that none above the age of sixteen travel without a pass, and that any who would apprehend any of them should have 500 merks for each person ; and that every one should take the oath of abjuration ; whereby the temptation and hazard became so dreadful, that many were shot instantly in the fields ; others, refusing the oath, were brought in, sentenced, and executed in one day; yea, spectators at executions were required to say, whether these men suffered justly or not. When Renwick, with a sad and troubled heart, observed all these dolorous effects, and more, he was often heard to say, that though he had peace in his end and aim by it, yet he wished from his heart that the declaration had never been published.

Neither was the year 1685 anything better. For it became now the enemy's greatest ambition and emulation who could destroy most of these poor wandering mountain men, as they were called ; and when they had spent all their balls, they were nothing nearer their purpose than when they began ; for the more they were afflicted, the more they grew. "The bush did burn, but was not consumed, because the Lord was in the bush."

Charles II. being dead, and the Duke of York, a professed papist, being proclaimed in February 1685, Renwick could not let go this opportunity of witnessing against the usurpation by a Papist of the government of the nation, and his design of overturning the covenanted work of Reformation, and introducing Popery. Accordingly, he and about 200 men went to Sanquhar, May 28, 1685, and published that declaration, afterwards called the Sanquhar Declaration.

In the meantime, the Earl of Argyle's expedition taking place, Renwick was much solicited to join with them. He expressed the esteem he had for Argyle's honest and laudable intention, and spoke very favourably of him, declaring his willingness to concur, if the quarrel and declaration were rightly stated ; but because it was not concerted according to the ancient plea of our Scottish Covenants, he could not agree with them, which created unto him a new series of trouble and reproach, and that from all hands, and from none more than the indulged.

In the year 1686, Renwick was constrained to be more public and explicit in his testimony against the designs and defections of the time, wherein he met with more contradictions and opposition from all sides, and more discouraging and distracting treatment, even from some who once followed him: and was much troubled with letters of accusation against him from many hands. One of the ministers that came over with Argyle, wrote a very vindictive letter against him ; which letter he answered at large. He also was traduced, both at home and abroad, by Alexander Gordon, who sometime joined with that suffering party ; but by none more than Robert Cathcart, in Carrick, who wrote a most scurrilous libel against him, and from which Renwick vindicated himself in the plainest terms. But this not satisfying the said Robert Cathcart, he, in the name of his friends in Carrick, and the shire of Wigtown, though without the knowledge of the half of them, took a protest against Renwick's preaching or conversing within their jurisdiction, giving him occasion, with David, to complain, " They speak vanity, their heart gathereth iniquity ; yea, mine own familiar friend, in whom I trusted, hath lifted up his heel against me."

Notwithstanding the obloquy he sustained from all sorts of opposers, he had one faithful and fervent wrestler on his side, Alexander Peden ; and yet a little before his death, these reproachers so far prevailed as to instigate Peden to a declared opposition against Renwick, which not only contributed to grieve him much, but was also an occasion of stumbling to many others of the well affected, and to the confirmation of his opposers.* Yet, nevertheless, he proceeded in his progress through the country, preaching, catechising, and baptising. In travelling through Galloway, he encountered a most insolent protestation given in against him by the professors

* *See* Peden's Life, page 519 in this volume, for an account of the interview between these good men.

DUBLIN BAY.

between the rivers Dee and Cree, subscribed by one Hutchison ; which paper he read over at a public meeting in that district (after a lecture upon Psalm xv., and a sermon from Song ii. 2), giving the people to know what was done in their name, with some animad-versions thereon, as having a tendency to overturn several pieces of our valuable reformation ; exhorting them, if there were any there who concurred therein, that they would speedily retract their hand from such an iniquity.

Shortly after this, while his work was increasing daily on his hand, and his difficulties multiplying, the Lord made his burden lighter, by the help of David Houston from Ireland, and Alexander Shields, who joined with him in witnessing against the sins of the time, which, as it was very refreshing to him, and satisfied his longing desires and endeavours, so it enabled him withal to answer those who said, that he neither desired to join with another minister, nor so much as desire to meet with any other. The first charge was now confuted, and as for the other, it is well known how far he travelled, both in Scotland and England, to meet with ministers who would unite with him, but was superciliously refused. He once sent a friend for that purpose, to a minister of great note in Glendale, in Northumberland, but in vain. At another time, happening to be in a much respected gentlewoman's house in the same country, where providentially Dr Rule came to visit, Renwick overheard him, in another room, discharging her by many arguments, from entertaining or countenancing Renwick, if he should come that way; whereupon he sent for the Doctor, letting him know, that the same person was in the house, and that he desired to discourse with him on that head, but this he refused.

After this, one informed against him to the Holland ministers, who returned back with Mr Brakel's advice to Renwick and others; but as it savoured of a Gospel spirit, not like that of his informer, it was no way offensive to him. Mr Roleman, another famous Dutch divine, and a great sympathiser once with Renwick, and that afflicted party, by false information turned also his enemy. It was more grievous that such a great man should be so credulous, but all these things never moved him, being fully resolved to suffer this and more for the cause of Christ.

In 1687, a proclamation was issued, February 12, tolerating the moderate Presbyterians to meet in their private houses to hear the Indulged ministers, while the field-meetings were to be prosecuted with the utmost rigour of law. A second proclamation was given, June 28, allowing all to serve God in their own way, in any house. A third was emitted, October 5, declaring that all preachers and hearers, at any meeting in the open fields, should be prosecuted with the utmost severity that law would allow, that all dissenting ministers who preach in houses should teach nothing that might alienate the hearts of the people from the Government; and that the privy councillors, sheriffs, etc., should be acquainted with the places set apart for their preaching. This proclamation, it seems, was granted as an answer to an address for toleration given in, in name of all the Presbyterian ministers, July 21, 1687.

Renwick now found it his duty, not only to declare against the granters, but also against the accepters of this Toleration; warning the people of the hazard of their accession to it. At this the Indulged were so incensed, that no sooner was their meeting well settled, than they began to show their teeth at him, calling him an intruder, a Jesuit, a white devil, going through the land carrying the devil's white flag, and saying that he had done more hurt to the Church of Scotland than its enemies had done these twenty years. They also spread papers through the country, as given under his hand, to render him odious; which in truth were nothing else than forgeries, wherein they only revealed their own treachery.

Yet all this could not move Renwick, even when his enemies were shooting their arrows at him. Being not only the butt of the wicked, but the scorn of professors, who were at their ease, and a man much wondered at every way, yet he still continued at his work, his inward man growing more and more, when his outward man was much decayed; and his zeal for fulfilling his ministry and finishing his testimony still increasing the more, the less peace and accommodation he could find in the world. At the same time, he became so weak, that he could not mount or sit on horseback; so that he behoved to be carried to the place of preaching, but never in the least complained of any distemper in the time thereof.

In the meanwhile, the persecution against him was so furious, that in less than five months after the Toleration, fifteen most desperate searches were made for him; to encourage which, a proclamation was made, October 18, wherein a reward of £100 sterling was offered to any who could bring in the persons of him and some others, either dead or alive.

In the beginning of the year 1688, being now near the end of his course, he ran very fast, and wrought very hard, both as a Christian and as a minister. And having for some time had a design to emit something in the way of testimony against both the granters and the accepters of the Toleration, which might afterwards stand on record, he went towards Edinburgh, and on his way, at Peebles, he escaped very narrowly being apprehended. When at Edinburgh, he longed and could have no rest till he got that delivered, which he, with the concurrence of some others, had drawn up in form; and upon inquiry, hearing that there was to be no presbytery or synod of tolerated ministers for some time, he went to Mr Hugh Kennedy, a minister of great note among them, who, he heard, was moderator, and delivered a protestation into his hands; and then, upon some reasons, emitted it in public as his testimony against the Toleration.

From thence he went to Fife, and preached some Sabbaths; and upon the 29th of January, he preached his last sermon at Borrowstounness. Then he returned to Edinburgh, and lodged in a friend's house on the Castlehill, who dealt in uncustomed goods; and, wanting his wonted circumspection (his time being come), John Justice, a custom officer, discovered the house that very night. Hearing him praying in the family, he suspected who it was, attacked the house next morning, February 1, and pretending to search for uncustomed goods, they got entrance. When Mr Renwick came to the door,

Justice challenged him in these words, " My life for it, this is Renwick." After which he went to the street, crying for assistance to carry the dog Renwick to the guard.

In the meantime, Renwick and other two friends essayed to make their escape at another door, but were repelled by the officers. Thereupon he discharged a pistol, which made the assailants give way ; but as he passed through them, one with a long staff hit him on the breast, which doubtless disabled him from running. Going down the Castle Wynd, towards the head of the Cowgate, having lost his hat, he was taken notice of, and seized by a fellow on the street, while the other two escaped.

He was taken to the guard, and there kept for some time ; and Graham, captain of the guard, seeing him of a little stature and comely youthful countenance, cried, "What ! is this the boy Renwick that the nation hath been so much troubled with ?" At the same time, Bailie Charters coming in, with great insolency accused him of licentious practices, to which he replied with deserved disdain. He was then carried before a quorum of the Council, and when Graham delivered him off his hand he was heard to say, " Now I have given Renwick up to the Presbyterians, let them do with him what they please." What passed before the Council could not be learned.

He was committed close prisoner, and laid in irons ; where, as soon as he was left alone, he betook himself in prayer to his God, making a free offer of his life to Him, requesting through-bearing grace, and that his enemies might be restrained from torturing his body ; all which requests were signally granted, and by him thankfully acknowledged before his execution.

Before he received his indictment, he was taken before the Chancellor, in the Viscount of Tarbet's lodging, and there examined concerning his owning the authority of James II., the cess, and carrying arms at field-meetings, when he delivered himself with such freedom and boldness as astonished all present. The reason why he was interrogated anent the cess was, that a pocket-book was found upon him, which he owned, in which were the notes of two sermons he had preached on these points. There were also some capitals in the same book ; and because the committee was urgent to know the names, he, partly to avoid torture, and knowing they could render the persons no more obnoxious, ingenuously declared the truth of the matter ; which ingenuousness did much allay their rage against him. Being asked by the Chancellor, what persuasion he was of ? He answered, of the Protestant Presbyterian persuasion. Again, how it came to pass that he differed so much from other Presbyterians, who had accepted of the Toleration, and owned the king's authority, and what he thought of them? He answered, that he was a Presbyterian, and adhered to the old Presbyterian principles, principles which all were obliged by the Covenants to maintain, and which were once generally professed and maintained by the nation, from 1640 to 1660; from which they had apostatized for a little liberty, they knew not how long, as they themselves had done for a little honour. The Chancellor replied, and the rest applauded, that they believed these were the Presbyterian principles, and that all Presbyterians would own them as well as he, if they had but the courage. However, on February 3, he received his indictment upon the three foresaid heads, viz., disowning the king's authority, the unlawfulness of paying the cess, and the unlawfulness of defensive arms; all which he was to answer to on the 8th of February. To the indictment was added a list of forty-five persons, out of which the jury was to be chosen, and a list of the witnesses to be brought against him.

After receiving his indictment, his mother got access to see him, to whom he spoke many savoury words. On Sabbath, February 5, he regretted that now he must leave his poor flock, and declared, that if it were his choice, he could not think of it without terror, to enter again into and venture upon that conflict with a body of sin and death; yet, if he were again to go and preach in the field, he durst not vary in the least, nor flinch one hair-breadth from the testimony, but would look on himself as obliged to use the same freedom and faithfulness as he had done before. In a letter, on February 6, he desired that the persons, whose names were deciphered, might be acquainted with it; and concluded, " I desire none may be troubled on my behalf, but that they rather rejoice with him, who, with hope and joy, is waiting for his coronation-hour." Another time his mother having asked him how he was, he answered, he was well, but that since his last examination he could scarcely pray. At which she looked on him with an affrighted countenance, and he told her that he could hardly pray, being so taken up with praising, and ravished with the joy of the Lord. When his mother was expressing her fear of fainting, saying, " How shall I look upon that head and those hands set up among the rest on the port of the city?" He smiled, telling her she should not see that; for, said he, " I have offered my life unto the Lord, and have sought that He may bind them up; and I am persuaded that they shall not be permitted to torture my body, nor touch one hair of my head farther." He was at first much afraid of the tortures, but now, having obtained a persuasion that these were not to be his trials, through grace he was helped to say, the terror of them was so removed, that he would rather choose to be cast into a cauldron of burning oil, than do anything that might wrong truth. When some other friends were permitted to see him, he exhorted them to make sure of their peace with God, and to study steadfastness in His ways; and when they regretted their loss of him, he said they had more need to thank the Lord, that he should now be taken away from these reproaches, which had broken his heart, and which could not be otherwise wiped off, even though he should get his life, without yielding in the least.

Monday, February 8, he appeared before the Justiciary, and when his indictment was read, the Justice Clerk asked him, if he adhered to his former confession, and acknowledged all that was in the libel? He answered, " All, except where it is said I have cast off all fear of God: that I deny, for it is because I fear to offend God, and violate His law, that I am here standing ready to be condemned." Then he was interrogated, if he owned authority, and James II. to be his lawful sovereign? He answered, "I own all authority that hath its prescriptions and limitations from the Word of God, but I cannot own this usurper as lawful king, seeing both by the Word of God, and likewise by the ancient laws of the kingdom, which admit none to the crown of Scotland until he swear to defend the Protestant religion (which a man of his profession could not do), such an one is incapable to bear rule." They urged, Could he deny him to be King? Was he not the late King's brother? Had the late King any children lawfully begotten? Was he not declared to be his successor by Act of Parliament? He answered, that he was no doubt King *de facto*, but not *de jure;* that he was brother to the other King, he knew nothing to the contrary; what children the other had he knew not; but from the Word of God, which ought to be the rule of all laws, or from the ancient laws of the kingdom, it could not be shown that he had, or ever could have any right. The next question was, If he owned, and had taught it to be unlawful to pay cesses and taxations to his Majesty? He answered, " For the present cess, enacted for the present usurper, I hold it unlawful to pay it, both in regard it is oppressive to the subject, it is for the maintenance of tyranny, and it is imposed for suppressing the Gospel. Would it have been thought lawful for the Jews, in the days of Nebuchadnezzar, to have brought every one a coal to augment the flame of the furnace to devour the three children, if so they had been required by that tyrant?"

Next they moved the question, If he owned he had taught his hearers to come armed to their meetings, and in case of opposition, to resist? He answered, "It were inconsistent with reason and religion both, to do otherwise: you yourselves would do it in the like circumstances. I own that I taught them to carry arms to defend themselves, and resist your unjust violence." Further, they asked, If he owned the note-book, and the two sermons written therein, and that he had preached them? He said, "If ye have added nothing, I will own it; and am ready to seal all the truths contained therein with my blood." All his confession being read over, he was required to subscribe it. He said, "I will not do it, since I look on it as a partial owning of your authority." After refusing several times, he said, "With protestation, I will subscribe the paper, as it is my testimony, but not in obedience to you."

Then the assizers were called in by fives, and sworn, against whom he objected nothing, but protested that none might sit on his assize who professed Protestant or Presbyterian principles, or an adherence to the Covenanted work of Reformation. He was brought in guilty, and sentence passed, that he should be executed in the Grassmarket on the Friday following. Lord Linlithgow, Justice-General, asked, If he desired longer time? He answered, that it was all one to him; if it was protracted, it was welcome; if it was shortened, it was welcome; his Master's time was the best. He was then returned to prison. Without his knowledge, and against his will, yea, after openly refusing the Advocate to desire it, he was reprieved to the 17th day, which gave occasion to several to renew their reproaches.

Though none who suffered in the former part of this dismal period spoke with more fortitude, freedom, and boldness than Mr Renwick, yet none were treated with so much moderation. The lenity of the Justiciary was much admired beyond their ordinary; for they allowed him to say what he pleased, without threatening and interruption, even though he gave none of them the title of Lord, except Linlithgow, who was a nobleman by birth. And though his friends (which was not usual after sentence), were denied access, yet both Papists and Episcopals were permitted to see him. Bishop Paterson often visited him; nay, besought another reprieve for him, which would easily have been granted, had he only petitioned for it.

The Bishop asked him, "Think you none can be saved but those of your principles?" He answered, "I never said nor thought that none could be saved except they were of these principles ; but these are truths which I suffer for, and which I have not rashly concluded on, but deliberately, and for a long time have been confirmed that they are sufficient points to suffer for." The Bishop took his leave, declaring his sorrow for his being so tenacious, and said, " It was a great loss he had been of such principles, for he was a pretty lad." Again, the night before he suffered, he sent to him to signify his readiness to serve him to the utmost of his power. Renwick thanked him for his courtesy, but knew nothing he could do, or that *he* could desire.

Mr M'Naught, one of the curates, paid him a visit in his canonical habit, which Mr Renwick did not like. The curate, among other things, asked his opinion concerning the Toleration, and those that accepted it. Renwick declared that he was against the Toleration ; but as for them that embraced it, he judged them to be godly men. The curate leaving him, commended him for one of great gravity and ingenuity. Dalrymple, the King's Advocate, came also to visit him, and declared that he was sorry for his death, and that it should fall out in his short time. Several Popish priests and gentlemen of the guard, with some of the tolerated ministers, were permitted to converse with him. A priest, at leaving him, was overheard saying, he was a most obstinate heretic ; for he had used such freedom with him, that it became a proverb in the Tolbooth at the time, " Begone, as Renwick said to the priests."

Several petitions were written from several hands, of the most favourable strain that could be invented, and sent him to subscribe, but all in vain ; yea, it was offered to him, if he would but let a drop of ink fall on a bit of paper, it would satisfy, but he would not. In the meantime, he was kept so close that he could get nothing written. His own testimony which he was writing was taken from him, and pen and ink removed. However, he got a short paper written the night before, which is to be found in the Cloud of Witnesses, as his last speech and testimony.

On Tuesday the 14th, he was brought before the Council on account of The Informatory Vindication ; but what passed there cannot be learned, farther than their signifying how much kindness they had shown him, in that they had reprieved him without his application, a thing never done before. He answered with extraordinary cheerful-

ness, rejoicing that he was counted worthy to suffer shame for the
name of his Master. A friend asking him how he was? he said,
"Very well; and he would be better within three days." He told
his mother, that the last execution he was witness to, was Robert
Gray's; and that he had a strong impression in his mind that his
should be the next. He often said that he saw need for his suffering
at this time; and that he was persuaded his death would do more
good than his life for many years could have done. Being asked,
What he thought God would do with the remnant behind him? He
answered, "It would be well with them; for God would not forsake
nor cast off His inheritance."

On the day of his execution, the chief jailor begged that, at the
place of execution, he would not mention the causes of his death,
and would forbear all reflections. Renwick told him, that what God
would give him to speak, he would speak, and nothing less. The
jailor told him, that he might still have his life, if he would but sign
that petition which he offered him. He answered, he never read in
Scripture or in history, that martyrs petitioned for their lives, when
called to suffer for truth, though they might require them not to take
their life, and remonstrate against the wickedness of murdering them;
but in the present circumstance he judged it would be found a reced-
ing from truth, and a declining from a testimony for Christ.

His mother and sisters having obtained leave to see him, after
some refreshment, in returning thanks, he said, "O Lord, Thou hast
brought me within two hours of eternity, and this is no matter of
terror to me, more than if I were to lie down in a bed of roses; nay,
through grace to Thy praise, I may say I never had the fear of death
since I came to this prison; but from the place where I was taken,
I could have gone very composedly to the scaffold. O! how can I
contain this, to be within two hours of the crown of glory!" He
exhorted them much to prepare for death; "for it is," said he, "the
king of terrors, though not to me now, as it was sometimes in my hidings; but now let us be glad and rejoice, for the marriage of the
Lamb is come, and His wife hath made herself ready. Would ever I
have thought that the fear of suffering and of death could be so taken
from me? But what shall I say to it? 'It is the doing of the Lord,
and marvellous in our eyes.' I have many times counted the cost of
following Christ, but never thought it would be so easy; and now,
who knows the honour and happiness of that? 'He that confesseth
me before men, him will I confess before my Father.'" He said

CASTLEHILL, EDINBURGH.

many times, " Now I am near the end of time, I desire to bless the Lord ; it is an inexpressibly sweet and satisfying peace to me, that He hath kept me from complying with enemies in the least." Perceiving his mother weep, he exhorted her to remember, that they who loved anything better than Christ were not worthy of Him. " If ye love me, rejoice that I am going to my Father, to obtain the enjoyment of what eye hath not seen, nor ear heard, nor heart conceived." Then he went to prayer ; wherein he ran out much in praise, and pleaded much in behalf of the suffering remnant, that the Lord would raise up witnesses that might transmit the Testimony to succeeding generations, and that He would not leave Scotland, asserting, with great confidence of hope, that He was strengthened in the hope of it, that the Lord would be gracious to Scotland.

At length, hearing the drums beat for the guard, he fell into a transport, saying, " Yonder is the welcome warning to my marriage ; the bridegroom is coming ; I am ready ; I am ready." Then taking his leave of his mother and sisters, he entreated them not to be discouraged, for, ere all were done, they should see matter of praise in that day's work. He was taken to the low Council-house, as was usual, where after his sentence was read, they desired him there to speak what he had to say. He said, " I have nothing to say to you, but that which is written in Jer. xxvi. 14, 15, 'As for me, behold I am in your hand.'" He was told that the drums would beat at the scaffold all the time, and therefore they desired him to pray there ; but he refused, and declared, he would not be limited in what he would say, and that he had premeditated nothing, but would speak what was given him. They offered him any minister to be with him, but he answered, " If I would have had any of them for my counsellors or comforters, I should not have been here this day. I require none with me but this one man," meaning the friend that was waiting upon him.

He went from thence to the scaffold with great cheerfulness, as one in a transport of triumphant joy, and had the greatest crowd of spectators that has perhaps been seen at any execution ; but little was heard, on account of the beating of the drums all the time without in-termission, from his first ascending the scaffold until he was cast over. Yet, from the friends and others permitted to attend him, some of his last words were collected.

When he first went on to the scaffold, some forbade him to speak anything, because the people could not hear ; which he took no notice of. There was a curate standing at the side of the scaffold, who, tempting him, said, " Own our King, and we shall pray for you." He answered, " I will have none of your prayers ; I am come here to bear my testimony against you, and such as you are." The curate said, " Own our King and pray for him, whatever you say against us." He replied, " I will discourse no more with you : I am within a little to appear before Him who is King of kings, and Lord of lords, who shall pour shame, contempt, and confusion upon all the kings of the earth who have not ruled for Him."

Then he sang Psalm ciii., read Rev. xix.; then prayed, commend-ing his soul to God through the Redeemer, and his cause to be vindicated in His own time, and appealed to the Lord if this was not the most joyful day he ever saw in the world, a day that he had much longed for. He insisted much in blessing the Lord for honour-ing him with the crown of martyrdom, an honour which the angels were not privileged with, being incapable of laying down their lives for their princely Master. He complained of being disturbed in worshipping God, but, said he, " I shall soon be above these clouds ; then shall I enjoy Thee, and glorify Thee, without interruption, or intermission, for ever." Prayer being ended, he spoke thus to the people, much to the purpose of his written testimony :

" Spectators, I am come here this day to lay down my life for adhering to the truths of Christ, for which I am neither afraid nor ashamed to suffer. Nay, I bless the Lord that ever He counted me worthy, or enabled me to suffer anything for Him; and I desire to praise His grace that He hath not only kept me from the gross pollutions of the time, but also from the many ordinary pollutions of children; and for such as I have been stained with, He hath washed and cleansed me from them in His own blood. I am this day to lay down my life for these three things: 1. For disowning the usurpation and tyranny of James Duke of York. 2. For preaching that it was unlawful to pay the cess expressly exacted for bearing down the Gospel. 3. For teaching that it was lawful for people to carry arms for defending themselves in their meeting for the persecuted Gospel ordinances. I think a testimony for these is worth many lives; and if I had ten thousand, I would think it little enough to lay them all down for the same.

"Dear friends, I die a Presbyterian Protestant; I own the word of God as the rule of faith and manners; I own the Confession of Faith, Larger and Shorter Catechisms, Sum of Saving Knowledge, Directory for Public and Family Worship, Covenants, National and Solemn League, Acts of General Assemblies, and all the faithful contendings that have been for the Covenanted Reformation. I leave my testimony approving the preaching in the fields, and defending the same by arms. I adjoin my testimony to all these truths that have been sealed by bloodshed, either on scaffold, field, or seas, for the cause of Christ. I leave my testimony against Popery, Prelacy, Erastianism, against all profanity, and everything contrary to sound doctrine and the power of godliness; particularly against all usurpations and encroachments made upon Christ's right, the Prince of the kings of the earth, who alone must bear the glory of ruling in His own kingdom the Church; and in particular against the absolute power affected by this usurper, that belongs to no mortal, but is the incommunicable prerogative of Jehovah, and against his Toleration flowing from this absolute power."

Here he was ordered to have done. He answered, "I have near done;" and then said, "Ye that are the people of God, do not weary to maintain the testimony of the day in your stations and places; and, whatever ye do, make sure of an interest in Christ; for there is a storm coming that shall try your foundation. Scotland must be rid of Scotland before the delivery come: and you that are strangers to God, break off your sins by repentance, else I will be a sad witness against you in the day of the Lord."

Here they made him desist, and go up the ladder, where he prayed, and said, " Lord, I die in the faith that Thou wilt not leave Scotland, but that Thou wilt make the blood of thy witnesses the seed of Thy Church, and return again and be glorious in our land. And now, Lord, I am ready. The bride, the Lamb's wife, hath made herself ready." The napkin being tied about his face, he said to his friend attending, " Farewell, be diligent in duty, make your peace with God through Christ ; there is a great trial coming. As to the remnant I leave, I have committed them to God. Tell them from me, not to weary nor be discouraged in maintaining the Testimony, and the Lord will provide you teachers and ministers, and when He comes, He will make these despised truths glorious in the earth." He was turned over, with these words in his mouth, " Lord, into Thy hands I commend my spirit, for Thou hast redeemed me, Lord God of truth."

Thus died the faithful, pious, and zealous James Renwick, on the third day over the 26th year of his age ; a young man, and a young minister, but a ripe Christian, and renowned martyr of Christ, for whose sake he loved not his life unto the death ; by whose blood, and the word of whose testimony, he overcame, and thus got above all snares and sorrow, and, to the conviction of many that formerly reproached him, was as signally vindicated (as he was in his life shamefully reproached), from all the aspersions, obloquies, and calumnies that were cast upon him, for prosecuting that Testimony for truth ; which now he sealed with his blood, in such a treasure of patience, meekness, humility, constancy, courage, burning love, and blazing zeal, as did very much confound enemies, convince neutrals, confirm halters, comfort friends, and astonish all.

He was of stature somewhat low, of a fair complexion, and like another young David, of a ruddy and beautiful countenance. Most men spoke well of him after he was dead ; even his murderers as well as others said that they thought he went to heaven. Malignants generally said, he died a Presbyterian. The Viscount of Tarbet, one of the councillors, one day in company, when speaking of him, said, " He was one of the stiffest maintainers of his principles that ever came before us. Others we used always to cause one time or other to waver, but him we could never move. Where we left him, there we found him ; we could never make him yield or vary in the least. He was the man we have seen most plainly and pertinaciously adhering to the old way of Presbyterian government, who, if he had lived in Knox's days would not have died by any laws then in being." He was the last that on a scaffold sealed his testimony for religion, liberty, and the Covenanted work of Reformation in Scotland.

Besides what hand Renwick had in the Informatory Vindication, and the forementioned Testimony against the Toleration, both of which have long ago been published, a collection of very valuable prefaces, lectures, and sermons of his, in two volumes, by some well-wishers to the same cause and testimony, has also been of late published; as also another collection of very choice letters, written by him, from July 8, 1682, to the day of his death, February 17, 1688. There is also a treatise of his upon the admission of ruling-elders, which the reader will find affixed to his Life and Vindication of his Testimony, written by Mr Shields.

[Renwick was the last of the "Worthies" who suffered martyrdom in Scotland. Within a year after his death, the Stuarts were exiles in another land, William of Orange was proclaimed king of England, and the despised and persecuted Cameronians had the distinguished honour of being called to Edinburgh to protect the Parliament whilst deliberating on the transfer of the Scottish crown. Those, whose lives follow, undoubtedly shared in the sufferings of the persecuting period, but were privileged to survive the Revolution, and to die in more peaceful times.—ED.]

Alexander Moncrieff.

N virtue of an Act of the General Assembly, 1642, appointing a list of six able men for the planting of vacant churches, Alexander Moncrieff was pitched upon for the church of Scoonie in Fife ; and upon September 26, 1643, was received there with great contentment.

After this he had an active hand in carrying on the work of reformation at that time ; and was nominated in the commission for the affairs of the Kirk. In the years 1650 and 1651, he made no small appearance among those called Protesters; and had a particular hand in the "Western Remonstrance," and the "Causes of God's Wrath," which were drawn up about that time.

During Cromwell's usurpation he suffered much for his loyalty in praying for the King, upon account of which his house was often searched, and rifled by the English, and he himself obliged to hide. Upon the Sabbath he had spies set upon him, and was closely watched whither he went after preaching. He was frequently pursued, and one time a party of horse came after him ; yet by a special providence (though attacked once and again by them), he escaped. A little after, however, he was seized by them in a neighbouring congregation and imprisoned some time.

After he was liberated he was pitched upon as a person of great courage and magnanimity, to present the Protestation and Testimony against the Toleration, and the errors and sectaries that then prevailed in Church and State, given in October 1658, to General Monck, drawn up and signed by himself, Samuel Rutherford, James Guthrie, and many others. This he did with great firmness, for which he was exposed to new extremities ; but what return he had for all his faithfulness and loyalty to the king, comes immediately to be discovered. For no sooner was King Charles II. restored and settled in his dominions, than this worthy and good man was involved in a new series of sufferings. Being assembled at Edinburgh, with James Guthrie, and eight others of his brethren, in August 1660, where they drew up that humble supplication and address to the king, commonly called, "The Paper of the 23d of August," they were all imprisoned in the Castle of Edinburgh, except Mr Hay of Craignethan, who escaped.

He continued under confinement until July 12, 1661, when, much about the same time with James Guthrie, he had his indictment and charge, which runs much upon his having a share in the "Remonstrance," and in forming the "Causes of God's Wrath." Refusing to retract anything in them, he was brought before the Parliament several times ; and their prosecution for his life was so hot, that the Earl of Athol, and others in Parliament, particularly interested and concerned in this good man and his wife, being importuned by her to appear for him in Parliament, dealt with her to endeavour to prevail with him to recede from some of his principles, otherwise they told her it was impossible to save his life. This excellent woman answered, that they all knew she was happy in a good

husband, and she had a great affection for him, and had many children; yet she knew him to be so steadfast to his principles, where his
conscience was concerned, that nobody needed deal with him on that
head; for her part, before she would contribute anything that would
break his peace with his Master, she would rather choose to receive
his head at the Cross. About the same time, two ladies of the first
quality were pleased so far to concern themselves in his case, as to
provide a compliment in plate (which was not unusual at that time),
and send it to the Advocate's lady. Afterwards they went and visited
her on his behalf, but were told by her it was impossible to save his
life, and the compliment was returned.

Yet it was so over-ruled in Providence, that Moncrieff being
much respected, and his hardships almost universally regretted, upon
account of his eminent piety, integrity and uprightness, several of all
ranks and of different persuasions, unknown to him, began to make
application and interpose in his favour, so that the spirit of some of
his most violent persecutors began to abate. His process lingered, till,
after a tedious imprisonment, he fell sick, and obtained the favour of
confinement in Edinburgh. The Parliament passed this sentence
upon him, " That he, the said Alexander Moncrieff, be for ever incapable of exercising any public trust, civil or ecclesiastic, within the
kingdom, until, in the next session of Parliament, further orders be
taken concerning him, and discharge him in the meantime to go to
his parish." And all this was for owning before them his accession
to the " Remonstrance " and " Causes of God's Wrath."

After this sentence, when living peaceably about eight or nine
miles from his own parish, people began to resort to him, and hear
him preach; whereupon, by virtue of an act made against him, he was
charged to remove twenty miles from his house and charge, and seven
or eight from a bishop's seat or royal burgh. He was then with his
family forced from his house, and obliged to wander in a great storm;
and yet when he had removed to a place at a competent distance,
even then he got a second charge to remove farther, till he was
obliged to go to a remote place in the Highlands, where his God,
who had all along countenanced and supported him wonderfully in
his troubles, honoured him to be instrumental in the conversion of
many.

The persecution somewhat abating, he removed to Perth, for the
education of his children, where he continued preaching the Gospel.
A few at first, but afterwards a great many, attended his ministry.

Being again informed against, a party of the horse-guards were sent to apprehend him, but he escaped, though his house was narrowly searched. This forced him from his family, and he was obliged to lurk a good while after this.

At length he came with his family to Edinburgh, where he preached the Gospel many years, under a series of persecutions. He was intercommuned in the year 1675, and his house, and many other places in and about the city, were narrowly searched for him ; yet he was always marvellously hid, of which many instances might be given. When he went to the country, many a time parties of the guard were sent in quest of him, and sometimes he would meet them in his return, and pass through the midst of them unknown. When he was one time lodged in a remote part of the suburbs of Edinburgh, a captain, with a party, searched every house and chamber of the close, but never entered the house in which he was, though the door was open.

Again, when he was lurking in a private house without the walls of Edinburgh, a party was sent to apprehend him. Providentially he had gone out to walk. The party, observing him by his gravity to be a minister, said one to another, " That may be the man we are seeking." " Nay," said another, " he would not be walking there." On another occasion, when he was advertised that the soldiers were coming to search for him in his own house, he lingered till another minister came to him, who said, " Sir, you must surely have a protection from heaven, that you are so secure here, when the town is in such disorder, and a general search being made." Immediately he departed, and in a little after Moncrieff went out, and was not well down stairs before the guard came up and searched his house. He took a short turn in the street, and came back just as the guard went off.

But the persecution growing still worse, he was obliged to disperse his family for some time. He was solicited, when in these circumstances, to leave the kingdom, and had an ample call to Londonderry in Ireland ; yet he always declined to leave his native country, and in his pleasant way used to say that he would suffer where he had sinned, and essay to keep possession of his Master's house, till He should come again. He had a sore sickness about the beginning of June 1680, in which time he uttered many heavenly expressions. But he recovered, and continued in this the house of his pilgrimage until harvest 1688, when he died, and got above all sin and sorrow, after he had endured a great fight of affliction to obtain a crown of eternal life.

LONDONDERRY.

He was mighty in prayer, and had some very remarkable and strange returns thereof. His memory was savoury a long time after his death. Many could bear witness that God was with him of a truth. He left many seals of his ministry in Fife, and was a most faithful and painful minister. His sufferings are a little hinted at in Mr Robert Fleming's "Fulfilling of the Scriptures," though neither he nor his persecutors are named. The story runs thus :

" The first relates to a considerable family in this country, who made it their business to trouble and persecute the minister of that parish, an eminently holy and faithful man. Yea, upon account of his faithfulness, the old laird of that house did pursue him out of malice, with a false libel, before the synod, either to get him broken and put out of the parish, or at least to crush his spirit, and weaken him in the exercise of his ministry ; but in this he was disappointed, the Lord clearing the innocence of His servant and the malice of the other. For that gentleman, while he went to the stable where his horses were, being then at the synod on that account, was in the place stricken with sickness, forced to hasten home and take his bed, and was there seized with horror of conscience, which made him often cry, entreating most earnestly for his minister whom he had thus persecuted, and often said, " Oh ! to see his face," telling his friends, that if he would not come to him, they should carry him to his house. But his lady did, out of malice, in a most rude and violent way, hinder the minister's access to him; and thus that poor gentleman died in great horror and anguish.

"After his death his lady still pursued the quarrel with no less malice, until she also fell sick, and had much terror upon her conscience, crying out for the minister, who was providentially absent, so that she was denied in that which she kept back from her husband. But he came to her before her death, and she confessed, with much bitterness, her wrong to him. After this, a young man, who had been their chaplain, and engaged by them to appear as a witness against that godly man, was so terrified in his conscience, that he could get no rest till he went to the next synod, to acknowledge that horrid sin, in bearing false witness against his minister; but being by some kept from a public appearance, he went to another part of the country, where it is reported he died distracted.

"Last of all, the young laird, who succeeded in that estate, would needs pursue the quarrel; and finding more access through the change of the times, he did so endeavour, with some who were in power, that an order was passed for banishing him out of that parish; and although he was then otherwise accused upon account of the public cause, yet it was known the violent persecution of that gentleman was the main cause of that sentence, as those who had a hand in passing it did confess; for he had solemnly sworn, that if he lived there that minister should not be in that place. Returning to his house a few days after, and boasting how he had kept his word, and got his minister cast out of his parish, he was suddenly struck by the Lord with a high fever, which plucked him away in the very strength of his years."

Angus Macbean.

NGUS MACBEAN was born about the year 1656. After he had spent some time at the grammar-school with great proficiency, he went to the University of Aberdeen; where he began to distinguish himself, no less for his great regard to practical religion, although he was yet of the episcopal persuasion, than for his extraordinary parts and abilities in learning.

About this time the bishops, having found their mistake in sending men of little learning and less religion to the south and west of Scotland, where the people were much disaffected towards them, applied to the professors of divinity to name some of the greatest abilities to be sent to these parts. Accordingly Professor Menzies singled out Angus Macbean from amongst all his students, to be sent to the town of Ayr; but he did not continue long there, having got a call to be minister of Inverness, which he accepted of, and was there admitted, December 29, 1683. Here he proved a very pathetic and zealous preacher, and one of the most esteemed of that way. He usually once a week lectured on a large portion of Scripture, which was not the custom in that apostate and degenerate age.

But notwithstanding of his being in the highest esteem among the prevailing party, the constancy shown by the sufferers for the cause of truth, and the cruelty used towards them, made such deep impression on his mind, as could never afterwards be rooted out or effaced. As a natural consequence of the Toleration granted by the Duke of York, the mass was openly set up in the castle of Inverness, against which Macbean preached publicly, and warned the people of the imminent danger the nation was then in. At this the priest was so incensed, that he sent Macbean a letter, challenging him to a public dispute. This letter he received in a crowd on the weekly market, where he usually walked with some constables to prevent common swearing. He went to a shop, and there wrote such an answer to the priest as

INVERNESS.

determined him to send him no more challenges. The report of this having spread, some of King James's officers, being there, entered into a resolution to go to church next Lord's day, and take him out of the pulpit in case he uttered aught against that way. Of this he was informed late on Saturday, and was importuned by some friends to abstain from saying anything that might exasperate them. But he preached next day on Col. i. 18, and proved that Christ was the sole King and Head of His Church, in opposition to the usurpation of both Popery and Erastianism; whereupon the officers got all up to execute their design, which the good man did not observe till he turned himself about, for they sat in a loft on the left side of the pulpit. Upon this he said, with an authority that put them out of countenance, "for these things I am become the song of drunkards:" on which they all sat down, for it was when drinking that they had formed that wicked design.

From the Popish controversy he was led to a more serious inquiry into the merits of what was then the real controversy; and after serious wrestling with God, and earnest prayer for light and direction from Him, in which he spent several nights in his garden, he at length determined fully to declare for the truth, whatever might be the consequence. Accordingly, in June 1867, he declined to sit in the Presbytery, but continued to preach. In August the Presbytery were informed, not only that he absented himself wilfully, but that he disowned the government of the Church by archbishops, bishops, etc., and appointed a committee to converse with him. They reported, at a subsequent diet, that Macbean declared plainly to them, that he had no freedom to meet them in their judicatories any more ; that it was over the belly of convictions that he had entered into the ministry under bishops ; and that these convictions were returning with greater force upon his conscience, so that he could not overcome them ; that he was convinced Presbytery was the only government God owned in these nations ; that he was fully determined to make all the satisfaction he could to the Presbyterians ; to preach for them and in their favours ; and that though he should be dispensed with by bishop and presbytery from keeping their meetings, he could not promise that in his preaching he would not give ground of misconstruction to those that owned Prelacy. At the same time, his colleague, Gilbert Marshall, farther reported, that Macbean, both in his public lectures and sermons, did so reflect upon the government of the Church, as was like to make a schism at Inverness : and therefore he had caused cite him to that meeting, to answer for his reproachful doctrine that could not be endured. Macbean did not appear before them ; nevertheless the magistrates prevailed with the presbytery to desist from proceeding against him at that time ; but shortly thereafter the presbytery referred him to the Synod of Moray, who appointed a committee to join with the Presbytery of Inverness to deal with him.

In the meantime, Macbean went to church without his canonical habit, publicly renounced Prelacy, declared himself a Presbyterian, and, as he found not freedom in the exercise of his charge in that place, he demitted it. He preached his farewell sermon on Job xxxiv. 31, 32. The Scriptures he advanced and insisted on, as warrants for his conduct, were Isa. viii. 11-14, Jer. xv. 18-21, 2 Cor. vi. 17, 18; and to prove that Christ was sole Head of the Church, Eph. v. 23, Col. i. 18, 1 Pet. ii. 7. Next Lord's-day he went to Ross, and there, in Mr Macgilligen's meeting-house, preached the truths he formerly opposed ; and sometimes thereafter he preached at Inverness.

On this surprising change, a great opposition among the prevailing party soon appeared against him, which was the less to be wondered at, as he embraced every opportunity of declaring for the cause of truth which they were so violent against, and the Presbytery of Inverness sent one of their number to inform the Bishop of Moray, then at Glasgow, of the whole affair. But the Bishop dying at that time, the Archbishop of St Andrews took the affair into his cognisance, and procured an order from the Council to bring him to Edinburgh. In consequence of this he was carried south in January 1688, in very tempestuous weather, and was called before the Council, where he made a noble and bold stand in defence of the truths he had so solemnly professed. One of the questions asked of him was, If he thought the king's power was limited? To which he answered, that he knew no power but the Almighty's to be unlimited. And though the Council could not then find wherewith to attack him anent the State, yet, to please the bishops, he must be imprisoned; and upon the 27th of February thereafter, the Archbishop of St Andrews convened him before himself, the Bishop of Moray, and five doctors and ministers in Edinburgh, where, in virtue of his metropolitan capacity, he deposed him from the exercise of his pastoral office, and deprived him of all benefits that might accrue to him, since the time of his wilful desertion; with certification that if he should transgress therein, the sentence of excommunication should pass against him.

Macbean was thereupon remanded back to prison, and though the inhabitants of Inverness wrote, earnestly soliciting him to make some compliance, that they might be favoured with his return, yet he valiantly withstood their entreaties; and by his answer, dated July 1688, he dissuaded them from insisting on it, as what he assured them would never happen, and condemned himself in the strongest manner for his adherence to Prelacy, declaring against it in the most express way, as anti-scriptural as well as tyrannical. His confinement, and the fatigue of his journey, having given such a shock to his constitution that his life was in danger, Sir Robert Gordon of Gordonstoun, and Duncan Forbes of Culloden, offered a bail bond for 10,000 merks to the Earl of Perth, then Chancellor, that they would present him when called upon, providing he was set at liberty; but this was refused, though he was in a very languishing condition in the Tolbooth. Here he remained till the Earl of Perth ran away, when the Edinburgh mob set the prisoners at liberty. After this he continued about Edinburgh till February 1689, when he joyfully finished his course in the Lord, in the thirty-third year of his age. Some days before, news came that the Parliament of England had settled the crown on King William III., who put an end to those bloody times, and that tyrannical Government.

Angus Macbean, without all doubt, was a man both pious and learned, although at first brought up in the Prelatical persuasion. When near his death, he frequently compared himself in this particular to Moses, who from Mount Pisgah saw the land of promise, but for his sinful compliance, as he always called it, would not be allowed to enter therein. He had some time before his death a firm belief of the amazing deliverance which the Church and nation was soon to meet with, and left this mortal life, rejoicing in hope of the glory of God.

Thomas Hog.

HOMAS HOG was born in the beginning of the year 1628, in the burgh of Tain, in the county of Ross. His parents were careful to give their son a liberal education, for which purpose he was early sent to school. From his commencement of the study of letters he discovered an uncommon genius, and soon made such proficiency as rendered him respected during his youth. He was much addicted to the harmless diversions of that age, yet they did never abate his progress in study, nor his detestation of anything immoral, or unbecoming the character of a scholar. He was put to the University in the New Town of Aberdeen, where he made great proficiency, and at last was admitted Master of Arts, with the universal approbation of the regents of the college.

About this time a very remarkable incident occurred, which confirmed Hog's aversion to drunkenness, and his belief in an overruling Providence. Having accompanied a merchant of Aberdeen, who was going on a voyage, to a ship at the mouth of the Dee, upon his return with two burgesses who had gone on the same errand, and through the importunity of one of them, they all turned aside to take a bottle in an inn by the way. There he tarried till he thought they had

ST DUTHACH'S CHURCH, TAIN.

drunk sufficiently, when, finding they were not disposed to go home, he laid down his share of the reckoning, and was going away. They, however, being averse to part with him, and resolute in their cups, laid hold on him; but he being full six feet high, and proportionably strong and vigorous, soon twisted himself out of their grips, and went off. Having come home to his chamber, he went to bed at his usual hour; but, though in good health, he could get no rest till the clock struck one, when he fell asleep, and rested quietly till the morning, when he arose. On coming forth to his class, one met him, weeping, and told him, that the two men he had left last night, after continuing a while at their cups, fell a contending, and then a fighting, in which the one killed the other. He asked, "At what time?" and being told "just at one," he adored that Providence which had both seasonably disposed him to leave them, and made him uneasy whilst the sin was thus being committed.

But though Mr Hog was adorned with these natural and acquired accomplishments which constitute a truly amiable person, heightened with the lustre of an unblameable life; yet, as he himself acknowledged, he remained a stranger to the saving operations of the Spirit of God, till the arm of the Lord was gloriously revealed in the revival of the work of Reformation during 1638 and following years, when the

OLD MACHAR CATHEDRAL, ABERDEEN.

influences of His grace were poured out upon many through the nation. Still his conversation was strictly moral, he frequented societies, conversed and prayed with them, and was diligent in the use of means; and in reference to the public state of religion and reformation, he was sound, bold, and resolute, in his straits acknowledging the Lord, bringing these his difficulties before Him, to which he thought that he got some notable returns. Yet upon all these he himself declared, that if he were then in a state of grace and salvation, he was not in that state afterwards; for the whole of the following work, which by the Spirit and word of God was wrought on his heart, was founded on a strong and clear conviction of his having been at that time out of Christ, notwithstanding all the forementioned attainments.

What the manner and means of his saving conversion were, we are at a loss to describe; only we find he was under a very deep and severe law-work, and that his convictions were very close, particular, and pointed, setting his sin before him. During this work, which was of long continuance, whole clouds of sin were charged home upon him, without end or measure, so that he was brought well nigh to despair. He was then chaplain to the Earl of Sutherland, and the work of God flourished in several souls about that house. The butler was at the same time under the same law exercise, and yet the one did not know of the other's call; but the Countess, an eminent Christian, wanted not some discerning of what was working with them both, and particularly with Mr Hog, as will appear by what follows.

One time when Mr Hog was sitting alone in his chamber in extreme anguish, nothing but wrath in his view, a horrible temptation was thrown in like a thunderbolt. It seemed as if some one were saying, " Why do you continue under such intolerable extremity of distress? Put rather an end to a miserable life immediately." Upon this suggestion, he resented the temptation and tempter with indignation; his penknife, at which the enemy pointed, lying well sharpened upon the table. Lest the assault should have been renewed, he rose up, and threw it over the window, after which he sat down, and fell a musing upon the intricacies of his distress. While in the midst of this terrible whirlpool, the Countess, contrary to her custom (though she had been ever affable at table), knocked gently at the door, and invited him to go and partake with her of a present of summer fruit. He went with her, and behaved so, that nothing could be known concerning his former troubles. She discovered by her kind speech and behaviour, that she was either impressed with his danger, or that she suspected somewhat of the matter with him. After this entertainment he returned to his room, and found the temptation mercifully removed.

As to the manner of his relief, we learn in general, that, from a conviction of actual sin, he was carried up to the fountain-head, original sin, and to a conviction of unbelief as the seat of this fountain, according to Rom. xi. 32, John iii. 18, 36. The Lord having in this manner laid a solid, clear, and excellent foundation, Mr Hog was at length blessed with faith's views of the glory of Christ in His offices and person; which did so ravish his soul as to render him most willing, through grace, to forego, endure, and, in the strength of Jesus, to adventure upon anything in His cause, and for His sake.

But the most considerable adventure, while in this family, was his being the instrument in converting a young gentleman, of the name of Munro, who frequented the house, and who, though of a sober deportment, was void of real religion. He took great pleasure in Mr Hog's company, but wasted his time with idle, frothy, and useless discourse. Mr Hog bore with him for some time, but, pitying his case, used all means possible with him, till by Divine grace he was wholly brought over from a state of nature into a state of grace. If he had visited Mr Hog often before, he made many more visits to him after this; but never gave him occasion to impeach him, for the gentleman became eminently gracious; and, as an evidence that this free dealing was blest, the good man, in his after conduct, did so excel in the virtues opposite to his former blemishes, that he was esteemed for accommodating differences; and several gentlemen did submit their contests to him, and acquiesced in his sole determination.

After Mr Hog was settled at Kiltearn, this gentleman paid him a visit; when, after mutual salutations, he addressed Mr Hog as follows: "Sir, my course is well-nigh finished, and I am upon my entrance into a state of eternal rest. The Lord hath His own way of giving the watchful Christian previous warning concerning the end of the warfare (2 Peter i. 14); and I, being so privileged, have been seriously pondering where it may be most convenient to breathe out my last, and quietly lay down this tabernacle; and seeing, after deliberation, I can find no place so fit as with you, I have adventured to come and die with you." At this time the gentleman was in good health, and ate his meat as well as ever; whereupon Mr Hog endeavoured to divert him from these thoughts; but he firmly persisted in his persuasion; and, accordingly, in a few days he was seized with a fever, whereof he died.

Mr Hog was licensed to preach the Gospel in the 26th year of his age, and ere one year elapsed several parishes were competing for him, some of which could have yielded him a greater living than what he ever had. But he preferred Kiltearn to the rest, because he understood that sovereign grace was pursuing some elect vessels there; and he knew that several gentlemen in the neighbourhood, especially the Baron of Fowlis, were friends to religion. Accordingly, he was ordained minister there in 1654 or 1655, with the unanimous consent and approbation of all concerned.

Mr Hog, being thus settled, heartily applied himself to his work, taking heed to himself and his doctrine, that he might both save himself and them that heard him. He exhibited a good example before them in all manner of temperance and Christian virtues, but was more especially remarkable in his public character. His concern and sympathy for the ignorant was great. The bulk of the people of that parish, through the long infirmity of their former pastor, and the intervening vacation, being neglected in their examination, became very ignorant, but he was at great pains in distributing catechisms and other elementary books among them; and, going from house to house, he prayed with, exhorted, and instructed them in the things pertaining to the kingdom of God. His deportment was attended with as much dignity, proper to that function, as had been observed in any; and no wonder, for few were favoured with so many testimonies of the Divine presence in the discharge of their ministry; as witness, the judicious and famous John Munro of Ross, Thomas Taylor, Angus Macbean, minister at Inverness, William Bulloch, his own servant, Christian Mackintosh, a poor woman in the depths of soul distress, John Welwood, and others, who were either converted or confirmed by him while in this parish, or after his ejection, while he was settled at Knockgoudy, in Moray. There was no instance more remarkable than that of Monro of Lumlair, a heritor in that parish, who was at first dreadfully offended at some reprehensory expressions of Mr Hog, which yet were made the means of his thorough conversion, so that he ever looked on Mr Hog after as his best friend, and laid himself out to promote the success of his ministry.

So soon as it pleased the Lord thus to bless his parochial labours with a gracious change wrought upon a considerable number of the people, he took care to unite the more judicious in societies for prayer and conference. These he kept under his own inspection, and did heartily concur with them; for he himself was much in the exercise of that duty, and had several notable returns to prayer, of which we have several instances.

1. A good woman having come with this sore lamentation, that her daughter was distracted, Mr Hog charged one or two devout persons (for he frequently employed such on extraordinary occasions) to set apart a day and a night for fasting and prayer, and join with him in prayer for the maid next day. Accordingly, when this appointment was performed, she recovered her senses as well as before.

2. A daughter of the laird of Park, his brother-in-law, who lodged with him, was seized with a high fever, which left little hope of life. Mr Hog loved the child dearly, and while he and his wife were jointly supplicating the Lord in prayer, acknowledging their own and the child's iniquity, the fever instantly left her. This passage was found in his own diary, which he concludes with admiration upon the goodness of God, to whom he ascribes the praise of all.

3. In like manner, a child of the Rev. Mr Urquhart having been at the point of death, those present pressed Mr Hog to pray, for he was now become so esteemed that none other would in such case do it, while he was present; upon which he solemnly charged them to join with him, and having fervently wrestled in prayer and supplica-

tion for some time, the child was restored to health. A like instance
is found of a child of Kinmundy's in his own diary.

4. David Dunbar, who lived at a distance, being in a frenzy, came
to Mr Hog's house in one of his fits. Mr Hog caused him to sit
down, and advised with Mr Fraser of Brea, and some others present,
what could be done for the lad. Some were for letting blood, but
Mr Hog said, " The prelates have deprived us of money, wherewith
to pay physicians, therefore let us employ Him who cures freely,"
and then laid it on Mr Fraser to pray ; who put it back on himself.
So after commanding the distracted person to be still, he prayed
fervently for the poor man ; who was immediately restored to his right
mind. This is faithfully attested by those who were eye and ear
witnesses.

5. Mr Hog having once gone to see a gracious woman in great
extremity of distress, both of body and mind, he prayed with her and
for her, using this remarkable expression among many others, " O
Lord, rebuke this temptation, and we in Thy name rebuke the same :"
and immediately the woman was restored both in body and mind.
And yet, notwithstanding the Lord had honoured him in such a manner, it is doubtful if any in his day more carefully guarded against
delusions than he did, it being his custom, whenever he bowed a knee,
to request to be saved from delusions.

But as Mr Hog was sent of God to be an ambassador of peace to
some, so he was also a messenger of wrath to others. Of this we
have several instances, but none more particular than the following,
of a certain gentleman in the parish, who had one dead in his family,
whom he intended to bury in the kirk. On account of the vulgar
superstition, the General Assembly had by an act prohibited the
same ; and Mr Hog being a strenuous defender of the act of the
Church, the gentleman was nonplussed what to do. But William
Munro, a strong, hectoring fellow, engaged to make his way good
against all opposition, and succeeded so far, that the people with
the corpse were entering the churchyard when Mr Hog got notice.
He went out and set his back to the door through which the corpse
was to pass, and began to reason with the people to convince them
of their error in breaking through good order. This had not the
desired effect, for the fellow laid violent hands on Mr Hog to pull
him from the door ; but he, having the spirit of a man, as well as of
a Christian, turned on his adversary, wrested the key out of his hand,
told the assailant, were he to repel force with force, probably he

would be no gainer; and then said to the people, "This man hath grieved the Spirit of the Lord, and you shall see either his sudden repentance, or a singular judgment befall him." Accordingly the poor wretch continued in his wicked courses, and met with the foretold judgment in a few months after that. Having made a violent attack upon some one, the person assaulted drew out the wretch's sword and dagger, and thrust him through the belly, so that his bowels burst out, and he died most miserably.

Another instance of this kind occurred while Mr Hog was lecturing in the laird of Letham's house, in the county of Moray. During the time of worship he observed a servant laugh once and again, and, after an admonition, the third time; at which Mr Hog paused a little, and then with an air of severity said, " The Spirit of God is grieved by one in the company, for mocking at these great truths; therefore I am bold to say, such offers of grace shall be visibly and more suddenly punished than any here could wish." After they had supped and retired to their apartments, a message came to his chamber, telling him, that the forementioned mocker was seized with a sudden sickness, and cried bitterly for him. Upon this Mr Hog arose, quickly cast on his gown, and came downstairs to see him, without losing a minute's time; but ere he got to him, the poor creature was dead.

Mr Hog adhered to the side of the Protesters, and was in 1661 deposed by the synod of Ross, because he would not decline that party judicially. Afterwards, when he knew he was to be put out of the charge at Kiltearn in 1662, he had a farewell sermon to his congregation, in which, with the apostle Paul, he took God and their own consciences to witness that he had not shunned to declare the whole counsel of God to them; and added, that the storm would be of a long continuance; but, after all, the sky would clear, and he would live to see it, and be called to his own charge again as minister of Kiltearn, and die with them. He further said, "If any of you shall decline from the good way, and these truths wherein ye have been taught, and shall comply with the wicked designs now carried on, I take heaven and earth to witness against you; I take the stones of these walls I preached within, every word that was spoken, and every one of you, to be witnesses against another." With many other words he exhorted them; and his labours were not altogether in vain; for there was not a parish in Scotland that complied less with the corruptions of the times.

After Mr Hog's ejection, John Card, who was converted by his ministry, told him, that he should go to Moray. Of this he had no thoughts then, but in a little the laird of Park offered him Knockgoudy, near Auldearn, to labour and dwell in. This he accepted, and went thither, where he was a very useful instrument in the hand of the Lord, in turning many souls to Him, as has been already said. Finding his private ministry so blessed with success, he adventured to give the sacrament in this place ; which was a bold attempt, considering the severity of the laws at that time. But this solemnity being remarkably blessed with the Divine presence and glory, the communicants returned to their habitations with unspeakable joy, and, among the rest, one Macleod, who came from Ross-shire, and understood nothing of the English language. But Mr Hog understanding the Gaelic language, Macleod told him, that he came hither obeying the command of his exalted Redeemer, and understood what was preached there in the English, as well as if every word had been spoken in his own tongue. When Mr Hog interpreted this to the rest, they were filled with wonder, and the good man was allowed to communicate, which he did with joy.

In 1668, he was imprisoned for the truth at Forres, upon a complaint for keeping conventicles, etc. ; and there he was wonderfully strengthened and comforted, having great joy in his sufferings. Upon his account many prayers were put up by many in Moray ; and their prayers, as one saith of the Church's prayers for Peter while in the like case, set God a-working. The effect was, that Mr Hog, contrary to his own knowledge or expectation, was set at liberty, without any concession on his part.

He was again apprehended about the year 1676, for the same cause, and sent to Edinburgh. He said to some in company, " I thank my God, this messenger was most welcome to me ; " and giving a scratch with his nails on the wall, he said, " I trust in the living God, that before my conscience shall get that much of a scratch, this neck shall go for it." Accordingly, when tried, he submitted himself joyfully to a prison, rather than bind himself from preaching ; and was sent to the Bass, where, by the air of the place and his close confinement, he fell into a bloody flux, whereof he was in great danger. A physician being called, he gave his opinion, unless he was liberated from that place, there was no hope of life ; but Mr Hog, hesitating, would not address that mongrel court at any rate. However, the doctor, of his own accord, did it without his knowledge, and gave in a petition to the Council, in the strongest terms he could devise. The petition being read, some of the Lords interceded for Mr Hog, and said, that he lived more quietly, and travelled not the country so much as other Presbyterians did. Upon this Archbishop Sharp, taking up the argument, said, that the prisoner did, and was in a capacity to do, more hurt to their interests, sitting in his elbow-chair, than twenty others could do by travelling from this corner of the land to the other : and if the justice of God was pursuing him, to take him off the stage, the clemency of the government should not interpose to hinder it ; and it was his opinion, that if there was any place in the prison worse than another, he should be put there. This motion, being seconded by the pre-lates, was put to vote, and carried, " to the closest prison in the Bass ;" which was speedily put in execution. When the keeper inti-mated this to Mr Hog, he said, it was as severe as if Satan himself had penned it. His servant, William Bulloch, being with him when he carried him down to that low nasty dungeon in the Bass, fell a-weeping, and cried, " Now master, your death is unavoidable." But the good man, directing his eyes up, said, " Now that men have no mercy, the Lord will show Himself merciful ; from the moment of my entering this dungeon, I date my recovery." And so it fell out, for the very next day he recovered surprisingly, and in a short time was as well as ever. Yet afterwards, when speaking of the arch-prelate, he never showed any resentment, but merrily said, " com-mend him to me for a good physician."

In the end of 1679, being brought to Edinburgh before the Council, and refusing to take the Bond to live peaceably, he was remanded back to prison, and afterwards liberated ; but on what con-ditions we do not learn.

About the year 1683, falling again under the displeasure of the Government, for holding private conventicles, he was banished by the Privy Council, and ordained to depart the kingdom in forty-eight hours, unless he gave caution not to exercise any part of his ministry, under the penalty of 5000 merks, over and above performance. These conditions he would by no means submit to, and therefore re-tired to Berwick, and from thence to London, with the design, on the first opportunity, of going from thence to Carolina ; but the pretended plot, called the Presbyterian plot, then falling out, he was thrown into prison, where he continued some time. His money being near spent (for, besides his own and servant's maintenance, he paid ten shillings sterling weekly to the keeper for a place by himself, and not to be put down among thieves and felons), he said to his servant, "William, I'll set to-morrow apart for prayer, and see that no person be allowed to come in to interrupt me." Accordingly he rose early, and continued close at meditation and prayer till twelve o'clock, when a person in the habit of a gentleman desired to speak with him. William Bulloch told him, that his master was retired : but he still interceded to see him : upon which William, seeing the man of a grave aspect, reported his desire to his master, who invited him to his room. Mr Hog received him courteously. The other entertained him with a discourse about suffering for a good God, and a good cause, and showed that " our light afflictions, which are but for a moment, are not to be compared with the glory that shall be revealed." After this he rose and embraced Mr Hog most lovingly, exhorted him to continue in well doing, and then took out of his pocket a white paper, and gave it to him. Mr Hog, finding its weight, understood it was money, and said to the stranger, " Upon what account, sir, do you give me this money?" The other answered, "Because I am appointed by your great and exalted Master to do so." Mr Hog asked his name, and upon his refusing to tell it, said, "Sir, it is not curiosity that prompts me to ask, but I hope to be enlarged, and then I shall account it my duty to call for you at your dwelling in this city, for I suppose you are a citizen of London." The other replied, "You must ask no more questions, but ' be faithful to the death, and thou shalt have a crown of life.' " Then he retired, and Mr Hog never saw nor heard of him any more. On opening the paper, there were five pounds sterling in it, which to the good man was sweeter than if he had got £1000 settled on him yearly.

After he was set at liberty, being at London in 1685, when the Duke of Monmouth landed in England, and Argyle in Scotland, he plainly told some of his acquaintances, that God would never honour either of these men to be instruments of deliverance. And much about the same time, some Protestants at Court, knowing he was in the city, and that he was endued with a prophetic spirit, drew King James II's. attention so far, that he wanted Mr Hog to be consulted concerning affairs at that juncture. This being communicated to him, he concealed his mind, till he consulted the Lord by prayer. In the meantime he made ready for his departure, and then told them, what he charged them to report faithfully, that if King James had

seriously adhered to the principles of our reformed religion, his
throne should have been established in righteousness, and if he would
yet turn from Popery, matters might be well with him, but if otherwise, the land would spue him out. When this was reported, the
King ordered that he should be speedily apprehended, but he, having
foreseen this, escaped by a speedy flight to Holland.

When in Holland, he was soon introduced to the Prince of Orange,
who had him in great esteem, and let him into the secret of his resolution to deliver these nations from Popery and tyranny. As to the Indulgence, Mr Hog agreed with worthy Mr M'Ward and Mr Brown, but
was far from clearness to withdraw from all Presbyterian ministers,
who either had not taken the benefit of the Indulgence, or were exposed to suffering notwithstanding the same.

Mr Hog returned to Scotland in 1688, where he stayed till 1691 ;
when his old parishioners, finding the way cleared, sent commissioners
to accompany him back to his parish of Kiltearn, where he was received with great joy in June or July that year. But his constitution
being broken, he was unable to discharge his function much in public
after that ; however, his conversation became still more heavenly.
King William III. as a reward to his merit, resolving to have this
good man near him, sent him a commission to be one of his chaplains, which was no mean evidence of his esteem for him, and the
truth of his prediction concerning him. But before ever that honour
was bestowed upon him, he was seized with the trouble, or rather the
complication of troubles, whereof he died.

His sickness was considerably long, and accompanied with great
pain. One time his judicious servant, hearing the heavy moans he
made, asked whether it was soul or bodily pain, that extorted such
heavy groans from him? To this he composedly replied, " No
soul-trouble, man, for a hundred and a hundred times my Lord hath
assured me that I shall be with Him for ever ; but I am making moan
for my body ;" and thereupon entertained him agreeably concerning
the Lord's purging away sin from His own children (Isa. xxvii. 9). At
another time he said, " Pity me, O ye my friends, and do not pray
for my life ; you see I have a complication of diseases upon me ;
allow me to go to my eternal rest ;" and then, with deep concern of
soul, he cried, " Look, O my God, upon mine affliction, and forgive
all my sins." "And yet," says his servant, " never was his conversation more heavenly and spiritual, than when thus chastised." Towards
his end, he was much feasted with our Saviour's comfortable message

to His disciples, "I ascend unto my Father, and your Father; and to my God, and your God" (John xx. 17). To the writer of some remarkable passages of his life, he said, that he could not give a look to the Lord, but he was persuaded of His everlasting love. And to Mr Stuart, who succeeded him in that place, at another time he said, "Never did the sun in the firmament shine more brightly to the eyes of my body, than Christ the Sun of Righteousness hath shined on my soul." "And some time after," continues the same writer, "when I understood he was very low, I made him my last visit, and when I asked him how he did, he answered, 'The unchangeableness of my God is my rock.' Upon Sabbath evening (for I stayed with him that week), when I came from the church, his speech was unintelligible to me, but his servant desired me to pray, and commit his soul and body to God. After prayer I retired a little, and when I returned, I found all present in tears at his dissolution, especially his wife and his faithful servant William Bulloch." Mr James Hog and the forementioned writer of these remarkable passages add, that as he had many times foretold that his Lord and Saviour was coming, so in the end he cried out, "Now He is come! My Lord is come! Praise, praises to Him for evermore! Amen." And with these words death closed his eyes, upon the 4th day of January 1692, being about sixty years old.

Mr Hog was of a tall stature, and remarkable for his courage and fortitude of mind. He was most temperate in his diet and sleep; gluttony, he said, was a great incentive to lust, and rising betimes is not only good for the health, but best adapted for study, wherein he took great pleasure. His more serious work, his necessary diversions, as visiting of friends, and even meaner things, were all gone about by the rule of duty. He was sought unto by many for his good and faithful advices, and in prayer he was most solemn and fervent; the profoundest reverence, the lowest submission, and yet a marvellous boldness and intimacy with God, attended his engagements in this exercise. It might be truly said of him, as of Luther, when he prayed, "It was with so much reverence as if he was praying to God, and with so much boldness as if he had been speaking to his friend." Though the Lord did not bless him with children, he gave him the powerful assurance of that promise, Isa. lvi. 5, I will give thee "a name better than of sons and of daughters;" which He signally fulfilled to him in making him the instrument of begetting many sons and daughters to the Lord.

Robert Fleming.

OBERT FLEMING was born at Bathans in East-Lothian, in the year 1630. He was son to Mr James Fleming, minister of the Gospel there, who being a very godly and religious man, took great care of his education, and for that purpose sent him first to the College of Edinburgh, where he completed the course of philosophy with great applause, and made great progress in the learned languages. Being removed to St Andrews, he passed his course of theology in that University, under the conduct of Samuel Rutherford.

His natural parts being very great, his understanding quick and penetrative, his judgment clear and profound, his fancy rich, his memory strong, and his expressions masculine, they did with much grace take with them who were not acquainted with his accents and idioms. To all these his acquired learning was answerable, the culture of which he, through the Divine blessing, improved with great diligence. History, the eye of learning, he singularly affected, especially sacred history, the right eye. But to him all history was sacred, seeing he considered God's actions more than man's therein. Nor did he value any man, but for the knowledge of God, wherewith he himself was much acquainted, for his conversion to God was very early.

Before he was fully twenty-three years old he was called to a pastoral charge, and was settled at Cambuslang, in Clydesdale, where he served the Lord in the ministry till after the Restoration of Charles II., when that storm arose which drove out so many, and particularly that Act, commonly called the Glasgow Act, whereby nearly 400 faithful ministers were ejected, of whom the world was not worthy.

He had taken to wife Christina Hamilton, justly famed for her person, gifts, and graces. By her he had seven children, and, with them and himself sweetly committed unto his God's provision, he humbly received the honour of his ejection. Of the children, the Lord received three of them to Himself before their mother; two of them died after her, and the other two survived their father for some time. As for his worldly substance, his share seemed according to Agur's desire, and with Luther he said, to his knowledge he never desired much of it, or was very careful for or about it; for during the most tragical days his table was spread and his cup filled, and his head anointed with fresh oil, his children were liberally educated, and in his work he was profusely rich; but of his own laying up he had no treasure but in heaven. His own testimony of his life was this, that it was made up of seeming contrarieties, great outward trouble, and great inward comfort; "and I never found," said he, "more comfort than when under most affliction."

For some time after his ejection, he lived at Edinburgh, Fife, and other places, until September 1673, when all the ministers in and about Edinburgh were called to appear before the Council to hear their sentence, and repair to the places of their confinement. He and some others not appearing, were ordered to be apprehended, wherever they could be found. This made him shift as well as he could for some time, till he was at last apprehended and imprisoned in the Tolbooth of Edinburgh, where he was during the time of Bothwell battle. A little after he was, with some others, called before the Council, and though they were willing to find bail for their appearance when called, yet because they refused to live peaceably, and not to rise against the King, or any authorised by him, they were remanded to prison. However, he was liberated, and went to Holland, where, after the death of that famous and faithful Mr Brown, he was admitted minister of the Scots congregation at Rotterdam.

And here again his activity in the ministry was such as was to be expected from such a large soul, comprehensive of the interest of God and His church. What a writer he was need not here be told; but in preaching he might be called a Boanerges, and a Barnabas also, for converse, and for all things useful. What might Cambuslang testify of him? What might Edinburgh and adjacent places, where, after his ejection, he lived and laboured? What might Rotterdam say, where, from the year 1679 till towards his end, he was a most bright and shining light? There was no time wherein we may suppose that he had no good design going on. It is well known that the sun of his life did set on an excellent design, which was that of sending forth a treatise concerning the ways of the Holy Ghost's working upon the souls of men.

As he was religious, so he was said to be of a peaceable and friendly disposition, not affecting controversy much. When speaking of the differences amongst some brethren, he would say, " I am amazed to see good men thus tear one another in the dark ; nor can I understand how they should have grace in a lively exercise, who value their own particular designs above the interest of the catholic Church." Nor is it to be forgot what he said to one of his own begotten sons in the faith, " I bless God," said he, " that in fifteen years' time I have never given any man's credit a thrust behind his back ; but when I had grounds to speak well of any man, I did so with faithfulness, and when I wanted a subject that way, I kept silence."

And, according to his practice, his life was a life of worship extraordinary. His solemn dedication of himself to his God was frequent ; his soliloquies with Him almost perpetual. Spending his days and years after this manner, we find it was his custom, from the fifteenth or sixteenth year of his age, to set apart the first day of every year for renewing his covenant with God ; and if interrupted that day, to take the next day following. For the first years of his life we cannot give any particular account of the manner of his doing this ; but we may guess what it was from the few instances following :

" 1691. In the entry of this new year, as I have now done for many years most solemnly, I desire again to renew my personal engaging of myself to the Lord my God, and for Him, and with my whole heart and desire to enter myself into His service, and take on His blessed yoke, and humbly to lay claim, take, and embrace Him (O Him !) to be my God, my all, my light, and my salvation, my shield, and exceeding great reward. ' Whom have I in heaven but Thee, O Lord, or in the earth whom I desire besides Thee ?' And now, under Thy blessed hand, my soul desires, and does here testify my trusting myself, and securing my whole interest, my credit, my conduct, my comfort, my assistance, and my poor children, and to leave myself herein on Thy gracious hand, on my dearest Lord, whilst in time. As I write this, the 2d day of January 1691.'

" 1692. In the entry and first day of this new year, I desire, as formerly, to enter in this hidden record a new surrender and offering of myself to my dear Lord and Master, who hath been wonderfully tender and gracious to me, and hath brought me by His immediate conduct through the days and years of my pilgrimage past ; hath still cared for his poor servant, and given more singular mercies and evidences of respect than to many else ; and now, as still formerly, hath taken me through this last year with singular evidences of His presence and assistance; and as I trusted myself to my Lord, so He hath graciously answered ; for which, and His special grace hitherto, I desire to insert this witness of my soul's blessing the Lord my God.

" And now I do here, with my full and joyful consent, testify my giving up myself again to the Lord, and to His work and service here, and wherever He shall call me, with desire to consecrate my old age to my God and the guide of my youth. I love my Master and His services, and let my ears be nailed to the posts of His door, as one who would not go free from that blessed yoke and service ; and lay in hope the whole assistance hereof on His grace and help. To Him I commit myself, my ways, my works, and services, which with my whole desire I offer to my Lord, in whose hand I desire to secure my credit for the Gospel's sake, my comfort and enlargement in this day of deep trouble and anguish, together with my poor children, and the whole interest of my family and concerns, desiring to put myself with humble confidence, and all that is dear to me, under His care and conduct. O my soul, bless thou the Lord ! This I write the 1st of January 1692. ' My Lord and my God.' "

" 1694. In the first day and Monday of this new year, 1694, as I have done formerly, through most of my life past, so now I desire to renew my dedication and engagement to the Lord my God, and to join in the same witness with what herein hath been formerly, with my whole heart and desire, and to offer to my dearest Lord praise, in remembrance of what He hath been through the year past, and in the whole of my life, whose gracious tender conduct hath been so wonderful (and well hast Thou, Lord, dealt with thy servant, according to thy word) in all that hath befallen me.

" And now I do again, by a surrender, witness my entire commitment of myself, my poor children, my credit for the Gospel, my conduct and comfort in so extraordinary a juncture, to my dearest Lord, to His gracious and compassionate care and providence ; together with my works, and any small design to serve Him and my generation ; and I do entreat new supplies of His grace and strength, to secure and make His poor servant, if it were His blessed will, yet

SCOTS CHURCH, ROTTERDAM.

more abundantly forthcoming to Him. And with hopes of acceptance, I write this, 1st January 1694. *Post tenebras spero lucem.*"

But now, drawing near his end, in the same year, 1694, upon the
17th of July, Robert Fleming took sickness, and on the 25th died.
On his first arrest, he said to sueh as were about him, "Oh! friends,
sickness and death are serious things." But till the spark of his fever
was risen to a flame, he was not aware his sickness was to be fatal;
for he told a relation, that if it should be so, it was strange, seeing
the Lord did not hide from him the things that He did with him
and his; yet before his death, he was apprehensive of its approach.
Calling to him a friend, he asked, "What freedom find you in prayer
for me? Seems God to beckon to your petitions, or does He bring
you up, and leave dark impressions on your mind? This way," said
he, "I have often known the mind of the Lord." His friend telling
him he was under darkness in the case, he replied, "I know your
mind, trouble not yourself for me; I think I may say, I have been
long above the fear of death."

All the while his groans and struggling showed him to be under
no small pain: but his answers to inquiring friends certified, that
the distress did not enter his soul. Always he would say, "I am
very well," or, "I was never better," or, "I feel no sickness;" while

THE STADTHOUSE, AMSTERDAM.

he seemed to be sensible of everything besides pain. But the malignant distemper wasting his natural spirits, he could speak but little, though what he spoke was all of it like himself. Having felt indisposed for his wonted meditation and prayer, he said to some near him, "I have not been able in a manner to form one serious thought since I was sick, or to apply myself unto God; He has applied Himself unto me, and one of His manifestations was such as I could have borne no more." Opening his eyes after a long sleep, one of his sons asked how he did? He answered, "never better." "Do you know me?" said his son. To this, with a sweet smile, he answered, "Yes, yes, dear son, I know you." This was about two hours before he died. About an hour afterwards he cried earnestly, "Help, help, for the Lord's sake;" and then breathed weaker and weaker, till he gave up the ghost, and, after he had seen the salvation of God, he departed in peace, in the sixty-fourth year of his age.

Thus died Robert Fleming, after he had served his day and generation. His works yet declare what sort of a man he was. Besides the forenamed treatise, the "Confirming Work of Religion," his "Epistolary Discourse," and his well-known book, the "Fulfilling of the Scriptures," he left a writing behind him, under this title, "A Short Index of some of the Great Appearances of the Lord in the

Dispensations of His Providence to His Poor Servant." And although the obscurity of the hints leaves us somewhat in the dark, yet, as they serve to show forth his Master's particular care over His servant, who was most industrious in observing the Lord's special providences over others, and as they may perhaps give some further light into the different transactions of his life, they are here inserted.

" 1. How near I was brought to death in my infancy, given over and esteemed a burden to my friends, so as my death was made desirable to them, I being the refuse of my father's children ; yet even I was then God's choice, and in a most singular way restored.

" 2. That remarkable deliverance, in receiving a blow by a club when a child which was so near my eye as endangered both my sight and life.

" 3. The strange and extraordinary impression I had of an audible voice in the church at night, when, being a child, I had got up to the pulpit, calling me to make haste.

" 4. That I of all my father's sons should be spared, when other three were so promising, and should thus come to be the only male heir surviving of such a stock.

" 5. That solemn and memorable day of communion at Greyfriars, in the entry of the year 1643, where I had so extraordinary a sense of the Lord's presence, yea, whence I can date the first sealing evidence of my conversion, now forty years past.

" 6. The Lord's gracious and signal preservation and deliverance given me at Dunbar fight.

" 7. The solemn times and near approaches of the Lord to my soul; the first at Elve, when I went there ; and the other a little after my father's death, in the high study.

" 8. The Scripture, Acts xii., was given me to be my first text, and how I was unexpectedly and by surprise engaged therein.

" 9. The great deliverances at sea going to Dundee, the first time in company with the Duke of Lauderdale, the other in company with Mr Gray of Glasgow.

" 10. The extraordinary dream and marvellous vision I had, twice repeated, with the inexpressible joy after the same.

" 11. These memorable impressions and passages about my health, when it seemed hopeless, at my first entry upon the ministry, and the strange expression of Mr Simpson of Newmills.

" 12. The Lord's immediate and wonderful appearance for me in my first entry to the ministry, with that extraordinary storm on the day of my ordination, and the amazing assault which followed the same, wherein Satan's immediate appearance against me was so visible.

" 13. The great and conspicuous seal given to my ministry from the Lord, in the conversion of several persons, with that marvellous power which then accompanied the Word on the hearts of the people.

" 14. That signal appearance of the Lord, and His marvellous condescension in my marriage-lot, and in the whole conduct of the same.

" 15. My deliverance from so imminent hazard of my life, in the fall from my horse at Kilmarnock.

" 16. The Lord's marvellous assistance at the two communions of Cathcart and Dunlop, with the great enlargement I had in the last of these two places, at the last table.

" 17. That as the entry to my charge was with such a bright sunshine, so no less did the Lord appear at my parting from that place.

" 18. The Lord's special providence as to my outward lot after my removal thence, in many circumstances that way.

" 19. The gracious sparing my wife so long, when her life was in such hazard in 1665 and 1672.

" 20. The preservation I had in going over to Fife in 1672, and the settlement I got there.

" 21. The dream at Boussay, wherein I got such express warning as to my wife's removal, with the Lord's marvellous appearance and presence the Thursday after, at St Johnston's.

" 22. That extraordinary warning I got again of my dear wife's death, and the manner of it, at London, in 1674.

" 23. These two remarkable Scripture places given me at West Nisbet, on my return from London, 1674, viz., that in Romans iv. in the forenoon, and that in Psalm cxv. in the afternoon.

" 24. Those great and signal confirmations given me at my wife's death, and that great extraordinary voice, so distinct and clear, which I heard a few nights after her death.

" 25. These special confirmations given me at my leaving my country at West Nisbet, Redesdale, Stanton, and the first day at sea from Shields.

" 26. These solemn passages to confirm my faith, from Hebrews xi. and Exodus xxxiii., and at other times at London, and the last night there before I went away.

" 27. These extraordinary and signal times I had at my first entering at Rotterdam.

"28. These two marvellous providences that did occur to me at Worden, and about the business of William Mader.

"29. The marvellous sign given me of the state of my family, in what happened as to the sudden withering of the tree, and its extraordinary reviving again, at the first entry to my house at Rotterdam.

"30. The great deliverance from fire in the High Street.

"31. The good providence in returning my diary after it had been long lost.

"32. The special providence in preserving my son from perishing in water.

"33. The surprising relief when cited by the Council of Scotland to appear, with that sweet resignation to the Lord which I had then under such a pungent trial.

"34. The remarkable warning I was forced to give, that some present should be taken away by death before next Lord's-day.

"35. The Lord's immediate supporting under a long series of wonders (I may truly say), for which I am obliged in a singular way to set up my Ebenezer, that hitherto hath the Lord helped.

"36. The remarkable appearance of the Lord with me (which I omitted in its place) in the strange providence relating to Mr Monypenny's death in Prestonpans.

"37. The solemn providence and wonder in my life ; my fall under the York coach in August 1654, when the great wheel went over my leg, so as I could feel it passing me without hurting, far less breaking my leg, as if it had been thus carried over in a just poise, to let me see how Providence watched over me.

"38. The comfort God gave me in my children, and those extraordinary confirmations I got from God upon the death of those sweet children whom God removed from me to Himself."

Now, reader, go and do thou likewise, for "blessed is that servant whom his Lord, when He cometh, shall find so doing " (Matt. xxiv.).

Alexander Shields.

LEXANDER SHIELDS, son of James Shields of Haugh-head, in the Merse, was born in 1660 or 1661. Being sent to school, when capable of instruction, he made such proficiency, that in a short time he entered upon the study of philosophy, under Sir William Paterson, then regent of the college of Edinburgh (afterwards clerk to the bloody Council), where his progress was no less remarkable. Having received the degree of Master of Arts, and that with no small applause; and having furnished his mind with no small degree of the auxiliary branches of learning, he began to think upon the study of divinity in view for the ministry. But finding little encouragement this way for any who could not in conscience join with Prelacy, or the prevailing defections of those called the Indulged, he took a resolution, and went over among others to Holland, shortly before or after Bothwell, for the further improvement of his studies, where he continued for a short time, and then returned to his native country.

Upon his going to London, to be an amanuensis to Dr Owen, or some one of the English divines who was writing books for the press, he had a letter of recommendation to Mr Blackie, a Scots minister, who, appointing him to speak with him at a certain season, had several ministers convened unknown to him, and did press and enjoin him to take license. Being carried into it, in that sudden and surprising way, he accepted of it from the Scots dissenting ministers at London, but without any imposition or sinful restriction. However, the oath of allegiance becoming in a little time the trial of that place, Shields studied, as he had occasion, to show its sinfulness; which these ministers took so ill that they threatened to stop his mouth; but he refused to submit himself thereunto.

It was not long, however, that he could have liberty here to exercise his office; for, upon the 11th January 1685, he was, with some others, apprehended by the city-marischal, at a private meeting in Gutter Lane, who came upon them at unawares, and commanded them to surrender in the King's name. Shields, being first in his way, replied, "What King do you mean? by whose authority do you disturb the peaceable ordinances of Jesus Christ? Sir, you dishonour your King in making him an enemy to the worship of God." To this the marischal said, he had other business to do than to stand prating with him. Shields made an attempt to escape, but was not able, and he and his companions were brought before the Lord Mayor, who threatened to send him to Bridewell. However, bail was offered and admitted for him, to answer at Guildhall upon the 14th. Upon that day he attended, with a firm resolution to answer; but, while he went out for a refreshment, he was called for, and none answering, his bail-bond was forfeited, which afterwards gave him no small uneasiness when his bail's wife said to him, "Alas! why have you ruined our family?" However, to prevent further damage, he appeared on the 20th, when he was arraigned in common form and examined, Whether he was at Bothwell, and if he approved of Archbishop Sharp's death? with several other questions. To these he replied, that he was not obliged to give an account of his thoughts, and that he came there to answer to his indictment, and not to such questions. Upon this he was taken to Newgate by a single officer, without any *mittimus*, or any express order unto what prison he should be committed. By the way, he says, he could have escaped, had he not been led or betrayed there by flattery. It was some days before his *mittimus* came, by which he was ordered to be kept in custody till the next quarter-session, which was to be at Guildhall on the 23d of February following.

But Charles the II. dying in this interval, he was, March 5, with other seven who were apprehended with him, put on board the "Kitchen" yacht for Scotland, and landed at Leith on the 13th, and the next day was examined before the Council, where he pled liberty of thought, telling them to prove the accusation, and waiving a direct answer anent owning the King's authority. This led to his slip afterwards, as he, in his Impartial Relation of his sufferings, observes among other reflections: "In this I cannot but adore the wisdom of the Lord's conduct, but with blushing at the folly of mine. I was indeed determined, I think, by a sovereign hand, and led upon this not usually trodden path by truth's confessors beyond my ordinary genius or inclination, to fence with these long weapons, declining

direct answers, which is the most difficult road, and most liable to
snares; and wherein it is more hard to avoid wronging truth than in
the plain and open-hearted way." However, he was remanded back
to prison till the 23d, when he was brought before the Justiciary, and
interrogated, Whether he would abjure the Apologetical Declaration,
and own the authority of James VII.? Being still reserved, he was
sent back till the 25th, and from thence continued till the day following, which he calls the day of his fatal fall, the just desert of his
former blind and bold approaches to the brink of these precipices
over which he had looked, and was now left to fall. Here he was
again examined to the effect aforesaid, and withal threatened with the
most severe usage if he did not satisfy them. On this he gave in a
minute in writing, wherein, after a short preamble, he says, "The
result of my thoughts is: in the sincerity of an unfeigned conscience,
and in the fear of God, I do renounce and disown that and all other
declarations, in so far as that they declare war against the King expressly, purposely, or designedly, and assert that it is lawful to kill
all employed by his Majesty, or any, because so employed in Church,
State, army, or country." When they read this, they said, it was
satisfactory, and required him to hold up his hand. This he still
refused, till allowed to dictate to the clerk what words he should
swear; which being done, he protested, that it might not be con-
strued in any other sense than the genuine words he delivered in the
minute he did subscribe and swear. What induced him to this,
he says, was, "They gave it in his own meaning; and so far was his
mind deceived, that by a quibble and nice distinction, he thought
the word might bear, that this was not a disowning of that nor any
declaration that ever he saw, save one of their pretending; nor that
either, but 'in so far,' or 'if so be;' which different expressions he
was taught to confound by scholastic notions infused into him by the
Court, and some of the Indulged ministers while in prison." Having
so done, the Justiciary dismissed him, but, on pretence he was the
Council's prisoner, he was sent back to his now more weary prison
than ever. For he had no sooner made this foolish and unfaithful
step of compliance (as he himself expresses it), than his conscience
smote him, and, continuing so to do, he aggravated his fall in such a
sort as he wanted words to express.

Yet after all this his dangers were not over; for having written
a letter to John Balfour, to be by him transmitted to some friends
in Holland, declaring his grief and sorrow, and his mind anent his

THE DARIEN HOUSE, EDINBURGH.

former compliances, it fell into the enemies' hands ; whereupon he was again brought before the Lords of Council ; and though much threatening ensued, yet he owned the letter, and declared his sorrow for what he had formerly done. After this they appointed him to confer with the Archbishops of Glasgow and St Andrews, and the Bishop of Dunkeld. With them he had a long reasoning, and, among other things, they objected that all powers were ordained of God, be they what they will. He answered, " All power is ordained of God, by His provident will, but every power assumed by man is not so by His approbative and perceptive will." One of the prelates said, that even His provident will is not to be resisted. He answered, that the holy product of it cannot, and may not, but the instrument He made use of sometimes might be resisted. It was urged that Nero was then reigning when this command of non-resistance was given. He answered, that the command was given in general for our instruction how to carry in our duty under lawful magistrates. Then they asked him, how he would reconcile his principles with that article in the " Confession of Faith," " That difference in religion," etc. He answered, " Very easily : for though difference in religion did not make void his power, yet it might stop his admission to that power where that religion he differed from was established by law."

DUNNOTTAR CASTLE.

He was continued till August 6, when he was again before the Justiciary, and indicted ; which made him write two letters, one to the Advocate, and the other to his old regent, Sir William Paterson ; which he thought somewhat mitigated their fury. Whereupon he drew up a declaration of his sentiments, and gave it in to the Lords of Council, upon which much reasoning between them ensued. After two conferences, wherein he was asked many questions, in the third he condescended to sign the oath of abjuration, which they had so much insisted he should again take, as he had at their command torn his name from the first ; only it was worded thus, " If so be such things are there inserted ;" which he told them, he was sure was not the case. This with difficulty was granted. As he subscribed, he protested before them, " That none were to think by this he justified the Act of Succession, or the abrogation of the ancient laws about it, or the want of security for religion and liberty, or that he acknowledged the Divine approbation of it." When all was over he was detained till next day, when he was sent to the Bass, and doubtless would have suffered there, had he not got out in women's clothes and escaped.

[The seven who were apprehended along with him in London, and were sent with him in the " Kitchen " yacht to Leith, did not escape so easily. They were among the prisoners, who, on the alarm occasioned by Argyle's invasion, were suddenly hurried off, on the 18th of May, to Dunnottar Castle, whose ruins are now among the most majestic in Scotland, and which stands on a stupendous rock about 160 feet above the level of the sea, not far from Stonehaven. It had been purchased from the Earl Marischal for a State prison, and to it the prisoners were now sent for greater security. On their arrival after a long and exhausting march, during which they had been subjected to the most painful and humiliating treatment, they were, 167 in number, thrust into one small apartment, which is now known as the Whigs' Vault, and which has been compared to the Black Hole of Calcutta. After some days, forty-two of them were removed to the dungeon below, which is only about 15 feet by 9, and has no window, but only a small horizontal chink close to the floor for the admission of light and air. From a petition, presented to the Council by the wives of two of the prisoners, we extract the following passage, which speaks for itself: "That the petitioners' said husbands, who are under no sentence, with many others, having been sent prisoners to the said Castle, they are in a most lamentable condition, there being a hundred and ten of them in one vault where there is little or no daylight at all, and, contrary to all modesty, men and women promiscuously together ; and forty-two more in another room in the same condition, and no person allowed to come near them with meat or drink, but such meat and drink as scarce any rational creature can live upon, and yet at extraordinary rates." Need we wonder that, after enduring such sufferings for several months, when they were brought back to Leith and re-examined, several of them purchased their liberty by taking the prescribed oaths ; and that of eighty, who were sent off to the plantations, a large number died on the voyage? —Ed.]

After his escape, without seeking after any other party whatsoever, Shields went straight to James Renwick, and the faithful contending remnant then in the fields; and upon the 5th of December 1686 he attended a meeting for preaching at the wood of Earlstoun in Galloway, after which he continued with Renwick for some time. During this time he ceased not, both in public and private, to give full proof and evidence of his hearty grief and sorrow for his former apostacy and compliances. Upon the 22d he came to their general meeting, where he gave them full satisfaction in espousing all and every part of their testimony, and likewise made a public confession of his own guilt; wherein he acknowledged that he had involved himself in the guilt of owning the so-called authority of James VII., showing the sinfulness thereof, and taking shame to himself; his guilt in taking the oath of abjuration, and his relapsing into the same iniquity, the sinfulness of which he held forth at great length; and spoke so largely to these particulars, as discovering the heinousness of that sin, as made Renwick say, " I think none could have done it, unless they had known the terrors of the Lord ;" and again, " I thought it both singular and promising to see a clergyman come forth with such a confession of his own defections, when so few of that set are seen in our age to be honoured with the like."

After this, when Renwick and the united societies were necessitated to publish their Informatory Vindication, Shields went over to Holland to have the same printed, about the beginning of the year 1687 ; but it appears he was necessitated to return home before the work was finished.

After Renwick's death he continued for some time in the fields, preaching in Crawford Muir, at Disinkorn Hill in Galston parish, and many other places. About the end of the same year, 1688, when Kersland and the united societies, who had during the interregnum of the Government thrust out some of the curates, and demolished some of the Popish monuments of idolatry, were obliged to publish a vindication of themselves in these proceedings (which they did at the Cross of Douglas), Mr Shields being present, did sing some verses in the beginning of the 76th Psalm; and while expatiating on the same, said, that this psalm was sweetly sung by famous Mr Robert Bruce, at the Cross of Edinburgh, on the dispersion of the Spanish Armada a hundred years before.

Upon the 3d of March, 1689, when he, Mr Linning, and Mr Boyd renewed the Covenants at Borland Hill in Lesmahagow, Mr Shields stood up again before a vast confluence of people, and declared his unfeigned sorrow for his former sin of compliances, to the affecting of all the multitude, and the abundant satisfaction of the godly there present, who had been grieved therewith.

At and after the Revolution, he was of much service to the army, and greatly esteemed by William III. On his return home, he, with the foresaid Messrs Linning and Boyd, presented a large paper of proposals to the first General Assembly after the Revolution, craving a redress of their grievances, and likewise showing on what terms they and their people could and would join with them. But this paper being judged by the Committee of this Assembly to contain "peremptory and gross mistakes, unseasonable and impracticable proposals, and uncharitable and injurious reflections, tending rather to kindle contention than compose divisions," it never once got a hearing, but was thrown over the bar of that Assembly. Yet, notwithstanding all this, the three foresaid brethren, being resolved to unite with them at any rate, gave in another, called the shorter paper, importing their submission, casting down all their former proposals and desires at the Assembly's feet, "to be disposed of as their wisdom should think fit;" which paper he, through their insinuation, was brought to subscribe. Of this, it is said, he sadly repented afterwards; for having dropped his former testimony at their feet, who trampled on it, though they did not rend him, yet they soon found out a way to get rid of him. Soon after the Revolution, he was settled minister at St Andrews, where he continued in the discharge of his office until the year 1699, when he, with Messrs Borland, Stobo, and Dalgleish, were pitched upon to go over with their countrymen to the national settlement at Darien in America. There, by letters under his own hand, he gave a particular account of matters, from which it is evident that his spirit was quite sunk with the divisions, impiety, and unrighteousness of too many of that handful, and at last was sadly crushed with the fatal disappointment of the undertaking, through the conduct of the existing Government; which, had it been faithfully and well managed, might have been of great advantage to this nation, as well as to the Christian religion. While in Caledonia he preached mostly on Acts xvii. 26, 27: God "hath determined the times before appointed, and the bounds of their habitation; that they should seek the Lord, if haply they might feel after Him, and find Him, though He be not far from every one of us."

One time, as he and the rest of the ministers made a tour up the country, upon their return they were bewildered in the woods. Hearing the noise of the sea, they got at last to the shore, and being obliged to pass through various windings and bendings of the coast, under lash of the swelling surges, they were sometimes compelled to climb upon their hands and feet over the steep and hard rocks, until at last Mr Shields was like to faint; which troubled them much. Their provisions and cordials being spent, at length they came to a welcome spring of fresh water gushing out of the rock by the seaside. "This well (says Mr Borland) was to us as the well was to Hagar in the wilderness. By this well we rested a little; and Mr Shields having drank of it, was refreshed and strengthened, and, with the help of the Lord, we were enabled to proceed on our journey." After this Mr Shields and Mr Borland escaped death very narrowly, the ship sinking in the harbour of Kingston a very little after they were gone out of it.

Shields died of a malignant fever, June 14, 1700, in a Scotswoman's house at Port Royal, in Jamaica, not long after he left Caledonia. A kind countrywoman, Isabel Murray, paid the expense of his funeral. His last sermon was from the last words of Hosea: "Who is wise, and he shall understand these things? prudent, and he shall know them? for the ways of the Lord are right, and the just shall walk in them : but the transgressors shall fall therein."

Thus the so much famed Alexander Shields, after he had tasted somewhat of the various vicissitudes of life and fortune, was obliged to die in a strange land. He was a man of low stature, ruddy complexion, quick and piercing wit, full of zeal, whatever way he intended, of a public spirit, and firm in the cause he espoused ; pretty well skilled in most branches of learning, in arguing very ready, only somewhat fiery ; but in writing on controversy he exceeded most men in that age.

His works are—The Hind let Loose; Mr Renwick's Life, and the Vindication of his Dying Testimony ; his own Impartial Relation ; the Renovation of the Covenant at Borland Hill. There are also some lectures and sermons of his in print; a "Vindication of our Solemn Covenants ;" and several of his Religious Letters, both before and after the Revolution. After his death, Mr Linning published an essay of his on Church Communion. But how far this agrees with his conduct at the Revolution, or what coherency it hath with his other writings, or if Mr Linning had any hand therein, is not our province to determine at present. There are also three pocket volumes of his Journals yet in manuscript, which were, among other valuable papers, redeemed from destruction after Mr Linning's death.

John Dickson.

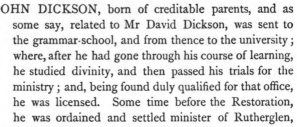OHN DICKSON, born of creditable parents, and as some say, related to Mr David Dickson, was sent to the grammar-school, and from thence to the university; where, after he had gone through his course of learning, he studied divinity, and then passed his trials for the ministry; and, being found duly qualified for that office, he was licensed. Some time before the Restoration, he was ordained and settled minister of Rutherglen, where he continued for some time a most faithful, diligent, and painful preacher of the Gospel.

Very soon after the restoration of Charles II., Prelacy beginning to advance in Scotland, he was, upon the 13th of October 1660, brought before the Committee of Estates, and by them imprisoned in the Tolbooth of Edinburgh, information having been given in against him by Sir James Hamilton of Elistoun, and some of his parishioners, of some expressions he had used in a sermon, reflecting upon the government and Committee of Estates, and tending to sedition and division. For this he was kept in prison till the Parliament met, and his church declared vacant; and though he got out at this time, yet he was exposed to much trouble and suffering afterwards.

After this, John Dickson was obliged to wander from place to place, with the rest of those who could not in conscience comply with the current of defection and apostacy at that time; preaching to such as employed him; wherein he ceased not to show the sinfulness of bonding, cess-paying, and the Indulgence. He likewise wrote a faithful warning to the shire of Fife, showing, in the most affecting and striking manner, the hazard and evil of such compliances.

In 1670, he preached at Glenvail, and in June that year, he and Mr Blackader preached to a numerous congregation at Beath Hill, in Dunfermline parish, Fifeshire. While they were at public worship there, upon the Lord's day, a lieutenant of militia came up on horseback to the people, and made a great deal of disturbance, intending to fright, and if possible, to scatter them ; whereupon one, more courageous than the rest, stepped forward to him, and after entreating him to remove peaceably, took his horse by the bridle, pulled out a pistol, and told him he would shoot him dead, if he were not silent; and he was there compelled to sit on horseback till public worship was over, after which he had his liberty to go where he pleased. For this horrid insult (as the persecutors were pleased to call it), a decreet was obtained by the King's Advocate, on the 11th of August, against Mr Dickson, Mr Blackader, and several other ministers, wherein they were charged with holding conventicles in houses and in fields; and, not compearing, they were, in absence, denounced and put to the horn, which obliged them to wander up and down the country, sometimes preaching in the fields where they had opportunity.

John Dickson thus continued in the midst of imminent hazards. For by virtue of a new modelled Council, June 4, 1674, there were orders to send out parties in quest of all conventicle-preachers (as those were called who accepted not of the Indulgence), amongst whom were Messrs Dickson, Welch, and Blackader. For Mr Welch 400 pounds sterling were offered, and 1000 merks for Mr Dickson and each of the rest; nay, the soldiers and their assistants were indemnified, in the case of resistance, if any slaughter was committed in apprehending them. By this Mr Dickson was exposed to new dangers, but he escaped their fury for some time.

After Bothwell battle, the persecution becoming still hotter, and the searches more frequent, he was apprehended in the year 1680, and brought prisoner to Edinburgh by some of the guards, under caution to answer before the Council, September 1, who ordered him to be sent to the Bass, where he continued prisoner near the space of seven years.

While prisoner in the Bass, he wrote a most excellent letter to some friends, wherein he not only bewails and laments the apostacy of these lands from God, demanding what our noble forefathers would think or say, were they then alive to behold it, but also gives many practical and suitable directions how to behave in following Christ and owning His cause under the cross, and walking in the furnace of affliction and tribulation.

On getting out of the Bass, he returned very soon after the Revolution to his flock at Rutherglen, where he again exercised his ministerial function, and that upon all hazards. In 1698, October 4, at the sitting down of the synod at Ayr, he preached a very free and faithful sermon, upon the duty and qualification of a faithful watchman, from these words, "I have set watchmen upon thy walls, O Jerusalem" (Isa. lxii. 6).

Although Mr Dickson acceded to the Revolution Church, yet he was much grieved when he beheld how far inferior the glory of the second temple was to the first; which does most evidently appear from his own words, in a letter written a little before his death in 1700, and which may stand here for his dying testimony:

"The conception you have of the dispensation of the Lord towards this poor plagued Church, and the temper of the spirits of professors under this dispensation, is not different from what many of the Lord's people are groaning under. There is palpably a sensible difference betwixt what the Church now is, and what it was many years ago; yea, what it hath been within these few years. The Church hath lost much ground, and is still upon the losing hand, and it seems will continue so until it pleaseth the Lord to pour down His spirit from on high, or else, by some sharp awakening dispensation, rouse up drowsy souls out of the lethargy wherein they are fallen. It is many years since the sun fell low upon Scotland; many a dismal day hath it seen since 1649. At that time our Reformation mounted towards its highest horizon, and since we left off building on that excellent foundation laid by our honoured forefathers, we have still moved from ill to worse, and are like to do so still more, unless our gracious God prevent it, until we slide ourselves out of sight and sense of a reformation. We have been lately trysted with a wonderful deliverance from the slavery of a heaven-daring enemy, but not one line of reformation is pencilled upon our deliverance. We have the shell of ordinances and church government, but want the kernel, the great things of Christ's law; as to contend for His interest is wrapt under a cloud. It is a long time since our Covenant and solemn engagements looked pale. They have lost colour and verdure since the rescinding of our vows to God. These covenants are turned skeletons, fearsome and affrighting, and former respect to them is like gradually to dwine away under a consumption. There are some few things that made them the glory of nations that are turned to a shadow.

"(1.) They were the fruits of many prayers, fasting, tears, wrestling, and indefatigable labours of the greatest and best men that ever

RUTHERGLEN CHURCH.

breathed in our nation, recovering a people, sunk into antichristian darkness, to enjoy liberty due to them by Christ's purchase.

"(2.) The renewing them so many times in old King James's reign spoke out the fervency of these worthy spirits in ardour and affection to them, as so many jewels of so great value, that they were set as gems and pearls in Christ's crown, to wear so long as His interest remained in the Church.

"(3.) The blessings accompanying the entering unto and renewing these Covenants were so fluent in all church-ordinances, both secret, private, and public, that whatever was planted in so fruitful a soil of such blessing and influence of the Spirit, could not but grow up as calves in the stall, fat and full of sap.

"(4). These Covenants were to our forefathers like the rending of their own clothes, as Elisha did, and taking up Elijah's mantle, and clothing themselves with it (2 Kings ii. 12, 13); enjoying of Moses's spirit (Deut. xxiv.); and like Joshua (chap. xxiv.) when dying, leaving a testimony of remembrance to posterity, by engaging them in these Covenants.

"(5.) So long as our Church cleaved to these our Covenants, it fell out with them as it did with King Asa (2 Chron. xv. 2); the Lord was with them while they were with Him. But our fathers' offspring forsaking God, he forsook them; from that day that our Covenants were so ignominiously treated, unto this day, all calamities as to our religious concerns have fallen upon us.

" (6.) The late sufferings of all who shed their heart's blood upon the fields and scaffolds, their imprisonments, and banishments, were all dyed with the crimson blood of the Covenant. From that day of the force and fury of enemies, the giddy Church, straying in the wilderness, is much fallen out of sight either of pillar of cloud or fire. Our intermixtures are turned pernicious to the glory and honour of Christ's house, which should not be a den of buyers and sellers. Although the sufferings of our late brethren seemed to be heavy to bear, yet two prime truths were sealed with their blood (and that of the best, as of our honourable nobles, faithful ministers, gentry, burghers, and commons of all sorts), which were never before sealed, either by the blood of our primitive martyrs, or our late martyrs in the dawning of our Reformation. The two truths were, Christ's Headship in the Church in despite of supremacy and bold Erastianism; and our Covenants; which two truths were in the mouths of all our Worthies, when mounting their bloody theatres and scaffolds; ascending, as it were, up unto God, in a perfumed cloud of transporting joy, that they were honoured to suffer upon such clear grounds. That supremacy was so aghasted by our Covenants, that no rest could it have till it got the gravestone laid upon them, and so conjured all who tasted the liquor of that supremacy, that the thoughts of getting the buried Covenants out of the grave were more terrible to them than the devils, who are now in the place of our vows to God, managing their diabolical games in these places where the Covenants were most in honour and request, the one burned, and the other rising in its room. Much blood and treasure have been spent to set the flourishing crown upon Christ's head in Scotland; Declarations, Acts of councils and parliament, Remonstrances, Engagements, Vows, and Covenants; but the sealing blood of the late martyrs was the copestone of all. The primitive martyrs sealed the prophetic office of Christ with their heart's blood; the reforming martyrs sealed His priestly office with theirs; and last of all, our martyrs have again so sealed His kingly office. They indeed have cemented it upon His royal head, so that to the end of the world it shall not drop off again.

" Let us never dream of a reviving spirit among us, till there be a reviving respect to these solemn vows to God. If there was but a little appearance of that spirit which actuated our worthy forefathers in our public assemblies and preachings, ye would see a wonderful alteration in the face of affairs : the fields, I assure you, would look white, near to harvest. If you would trace our defections, from the breach of the Act of classes in 1650, all along to this day of our being bound in the grave of neutrality, and all to edge up the spirit of the people to a due sense of our woful and irrevocable-like backsliding from God (who had acted many wonders for Scotland), would you not find a perfumed smoke of incense springing from our altar in savoury and soul-refreshing blessings ? But, ah ! when shall this day dawn ? So long as the common enemy are gaining their long wished for hopes, ministers in their public preaching must confine themselves to their nick-named faith and repentance, without noticing any encroachments upon Christ's proper rights to His Church in the glorious work of Reformation ; test-constructed fire-brands and seditions, which, in running the full career, may gradually drop into superstition through neutrality, and thence plunge into an abyss of the shadow of Popery.

"But to sum up shortly all my present thoughts of the time in this one : I cannot see an escape of the Church, in its present circumstance, from a sharp and more trying furnace than ever it has yet met with. Come the trial from what airt it will, it fears me ; our principles are so slippery, and the truths of God so superficially rooted in us, that when we are thrown into the furnace, many of us shall melt into dross. It is many years since I heard one of the greatest seers in our nation, in horror and with fear, dreading the heavy judgments of God upon the biased professors of the west of Scotland. But all this I say (not diminishing my hopes of the Lord's reserving His purchased inheritance in His own covenanted land), though Malachi be affrighted at the day of His coming, and be made to cry out, Who may abide it, when He sits refiner and purifier of the sons of Levi (Mal. iii. 1, 2, 3), a remnant shall be left, that shall be as the teil tree or the oak, whose seed is in them when they cast their leaves ; so the holy seed shall be the substance thereof.

" To revive a reflection upon two stupendous passages of Providence, I know would have an embittering relish to many professors in our country side. The one is upon the last Indulgence, wherein professors, by bond and penalty, obliged themselves to produce their minister before the Council, when called. For this was a restriction so narrow, that all the freedom and faithfulness of ministers in their office was so blocked up, that either conscience towards God in discharging of necessary duties behoved utterly to be buried, or else the life of their minister exposed to sacrifice. And if this be not an universal evil to be mourned over, let conscience and reason judge; yet this is looked upon to be but a snare, in these gloomy times, of inconsiderable moment, though it was the brat clecked by that supremacy, which not only hath wounded our solemn vows to death, but bound the freedom and faithfulness of the Church seers, as to the public interest of Christ, in their graves.

"The other stupendous providence is the obliterating the rich blessing of the Gospel in our late suffering times; when blessings not only accompanied those solemn field meetings, but extraordinary influences, in gifts of freedom and faithfulness, were poured down upon these ministers, who went out with their lives in their hands, setting their faces as flints against the heaven-daring violence done to the Mediator. I call to mind a circumstance with perpetuated remembrance, that in one shire of this kingdom there were about thirty ministers who cheerfully offered up their services to Christ, all by turns, out of Edinburgh. Each of these, when they returned to Edinburgh, being questioned what pleasure, what delight, and what liberty they had in managing that hazardous task? They answered, that so soon as they set foot on these bounds, another spirit came upon them; and no other reason could they give for it, but that God wrought so mightily, they looked upon it as *genius loci*, that God sensibly at that time was in that county working wonders. But the most part of all these are in their places, resting in their graves, and their works do follow them.

"Thus, in answer to yours, I have given you some of my confused thoughts of the present times, wishing you God's blessing in sucking honey out of the eater."

Thus lived and died worthy John Dickson, in a good old age, in the year 1700, after he had, by his longevity, seen somewhat of the glory both of the first and second temples, and emerged out of all his troubles, having got a most perspicuous view of our national apostasy, our breach of Covenant, and other defections, past, present, and to come, with the Lord's goodness and mercy towards His own remnant; and all this from the top of Mount Pisgah, when he was about to enter upon the confines of Immanuel's land in glory.

Of his works we have only seen his Synod Sermon, and the foresaid letters, in print. If there be any other, it is more than is known at present, except the foresaid Warning to the Indulged in the shire of Fife, which was some time ago also published. These, however, show him to be a most pathetic writer, and one who makes as striking and lively impression upon the mind, as any man of his time.

Sir Robert Hamilton of Preston.

OBERT HAMILTON (afterwards Sir Robert Hamilton), brother to Sir William Hamilton of Preston, was born about the year 1650. He was probably a son of Sir Walter Hamilton the reformer, and was lineally descended from the famous Sir John Hamilton of Preston, who was Commissioner for East Lothian at the black Parliament held in Edinburgh, 1621, where he most boldly voted against the ratification of the five articles of Perth. For this, and because he would not recall his vote, the King's Commissioner, the Marquis of Hamilton, and the Secretary, thought to have disgraced him, but found themselves utterly disappointed. Although they sent the Bishop of Dunblane, and after him Lord Scone, for that purpose, he would not yield, and when desired by the Secretary to absent himself, he told him that he would stay and bear witness to the truth, and would render his life and all he had, before he would recall one word he had spoken ; and that they should find him as true to his word as any Hamilton in Scotland.

Robert Hamilton having received a liberal education (as is usual for men in such circumstances), the Lord in His free and sovereign mercy, and by the efficacious working of the Holy Spirit, inclined his heart, before he was twenty-six years of age, to fall in love with His service ; and for that purpose He made him attend the free and faithful, though persecuted Gospel, at that time preached in the fields, whereby in a short time he came to espouse the true covenanted testimony of the Church of Christ in Scotland, for which he was, through divine grace, enabled to be a true and faithful witness to his life's end.

The first of his public appearances, in defence of that noble cause wherein he had embarked, was in 1679, when, after consulting with Donald Cargill, he, with Thomas Douglas, and Hackston of Rathillet, drew up that declaration, afterwards called the Rutherglen Declaration, which they published upon May 27, at the market-cross of that burgh, after they had extinguished the bonfires; that day being kept as a holy anniversary-day for the restoration of Charles II. After this he returned with that little handful to Evandale, where he was by them appointed to command in chief, June 1st, at the skirmish of Drumclog; and wherein he showed much bravery, in putting Claverhouse and that bloody crew to flight, killing thirty-six or forty of them, Claverhouse himself narrowly escaping. But the Erastian party coming up shortly after this, occasioned them and Mr Hamilton their general no small disturbance, they being to them " a snare upon Mispah, and a net spread upon Tabor." And although he most strenuously opposed them in all their sinful course of defection and compliances, yet he was treacherously betrayed into giving his consent to publishing the Hamilton Declaration. For they promised that they would be faithful in all time coming, in preaching against the Indulgence and all the land's defections; that what was ambiguous in that declaration should be, at the honest party's desire, explained; what was wrong should be left out, and what was wanting should be supplied before it was printed, or otherwise published (save the reading of it that day); but one word of this they never fulfilled or kept.

But it were a task too tedious here to enumerate all the struggles and contendings among them at that time; only it is to be remarked that it was through his great, I may say deserved, confidence in Cargill's faithfulness, who was the principal minister among those called the protesting party, that Mr Hamilton was again so pitifully ensnared by the corrupt party in subscribing the declaration to the Duke of Monmouth, when they were about to engage with the enemy. For they being intent upon supplicating, the honest party consented only that an information should be drawn up by Mr Cargill and Mr Morton, and sent to the Duke, of his own and his father's rebellion against God by their blasphemy, persecution, and usurpation in Church and State; but the corrupt party drawing up their own supplication, sent one of their party with it in the one hand, and pen and ink in the other, to Mr Hamilton to subscribe, just as they were going to engage the enemy. Mr Hamilton asked, if it was Mr Cargill's work? He answered yes; whereas Cargill knew nothing of it. Being in haste, and having no doubt of Cargill's veracity, he did that which was matter of great grief to him afterwards, as he himself, in a letter from Holland, dated 1685, doth fully testify.

After the defeat at Bothwell Bridge, Mr Hamilton was, by the Erastian party and their accomplices, most horridly stigmatised and reproached, as that he had betrayed them to the enemy, sold them for money, swept the priming off the cannon at the bridge, etc. But from all these reproaches he has been sufficiently vindicated by Wilson, in his Impartial Relation of Bothwell Bridge.

Shortly after the battle he went over to Holland; his estate was forfeited in 1684, and he was sentenced to be executed, whenever apprehended. During his stay, he was of great service and use to his countrymen, and had the honour to be employed by them as commissioner of the persecuted true Presbyterian Church of Christ in Scotland, having received commission to represent their case, and crave the sympathy of foreign churches. It was by his skill, industry, and faithfulness that he prevailed with the Presbytery of Gröningen, in 1683, to ordain the famous and faithful James Renwick a minister of the Gospel for the persecuted Church in Scotland: and afterwards with the Presbytery of Emden, to ordain Mr Thomas Linning a minister of the Gospel for the same church.

Mr Hamilton, by virtue of his commissions, which about that time he had received from the united societies, went through several places of Germany in the end of 1686. An old manuscript, given under his own hand, dated March 10, 1687, bears, that through many hazards and difficulties, he arrived about October 10, at Basel, in Switzerland, from whence he went to Geneva, about November 16; and so into Berne, Zurich, and other places in Holland and the Helvetian Cantons, not without many imminent hazards and dangers. In these places he conferred with most of their professors, and other learned men, craving their judgment and sympathy towards his mother Church, and the poor persecuted people in the kingdom of Scotland.

Mr Hamilton returned home at the Revolution in 1688, about which time his brother, Sir William Hamilton of Preston, died, and he fell heir to his estate and honours. And although after that he was designated by the name of Sir Robert Hamilton of Preston, yet because he could not in conscience enter into, possess, or

PRESTON TOWER.

enjoy that estate, unless he had owned the title of the Prince and Princess of Orange as King and Queen of these three covenanted nations, and, in consequence of that, the Prelatical government as then established upon the ruins of the cause and work of God in these nations, he never entered or intermeddled with his brother's estate in any manner of way. With Moses he made that noble choice, rather to suffer affliction with the people of God, than enjoy the pleasures of sin for a season ; and did esteem a steadfast adherence to the cause of Christ, with all the reproaches that followed thereon, greater riches than all his brother's estate. Out of true love to Jesus Christ, His covenanted cause, interest, and people, he laid his worldly honour in the dust, continuing still a companion in the faith, patience, affliction and tribulation, of that poor, mean, and despised handful of the Lord's witnesses in these lands, who still owned and adhered to the state of the Lord's covenanted cause in Scotland.

A little after his return from Holland, when Messrs Linning, Shields, and Boyd were drawing and enticing those who had formerly been faithful to, and owning and suffering for the Lord's covenanted cause, into a conformity and compliance with the defection of that time, at a general meeting held at Douglas, 6th November 1689, Sir Robert Hamilton gave a faithful protestation against these pro-

HADDINGTON CHURCH.

ceedings, and particularly their owning the government, while sworn to Prelacy, in opposition to our laudable establishment and covenanted work of reformation. He also protested against the raising of the Angus regiment, which he took to be a sinful association with malignants : and likewise, against joining with Erastian ministers at that time (from whom they had formerly most justly withdrawn) without any evidence of repentance for the many gross sins and defections they were guilty of. And after these three ministers aforesaid had yielded up the noble cause, and drawn many of the owners thereof into the same state of compliance with themselves, he had the honour to be the chief instrument, in the Lord's hand, of gathering together out of their dispersion such of the old sufferers as had escaped these defections, and in bringing them again into a united party and general correspondence, upon the former laudable and honest state of the Testimony.

Sir Robert Hamilton had also a principal hand in drawing up and publishing a faithful Declaration at Sanquhar, August 10, 1692, for which he was apprehended by some of the old persecuting soldiers at Earlstoun, upon the 10th of September following, and by them carried to Edinburgh, and there and elsewhere kept prisoner till the 5th of May 1693. When he was brought before the Council, September 15th, 1692, there were present the Viscount of Tarbet, president Lothian, Ker, General Livingston, Lord Linlithgow, Lord Breadalbane, and Sir William Lockhart, solicitor. He was examined concerning the Declaration, but he declined them, and all upon whom they depended, as incompetent judges, because they were not qualified according to the word of God and our solemn Covenants. Being interrogated, if he would take the oath of allegiance? he answered, "No, it being an unlimited oath, not founded upon our covenants." If he would own the authority of King William and Queen Mary? he answered, "I wish them well." But being asked again, if he would own them and their government, live peaceably, and not rise against them? he replied, "When they are admitted according to the laws of the Crown, and the Acts of Parliament 1648 and 1649, founded upon our sacred Covenants, then I shall give my answer;" whereupon some of them turned hot, and Lothian said, that they were pursuing the ends of the Covenant. Sir Robert replied, "How can that be, when joining with, and exalting the greatest of its enemies, whom by covenant we are bound to extirpate?" Another answered that the King had taken the coronation-oath. Sir Robert asked, "What religion was established when that oath was taken?" They said Prelacy was abolished; but he returned, "Presbytery was not established, so that the King is not bound in religion, save to Prelacy, in Scotland." Being urged to the last question, he adhered to his former answers: at which some of them raged and said, that he would give no security for obedience and peaceable living. To this he made answer, "I marvel why such questions are asked at me, who have lived so retired hitherto, neither plotting with York, France, or Monmouth, or any such, as the rumour was; nor acting anything contrary to the laws of the nation enacted in the time of the purity of Presbytery." Lothian said, "We are ashamed of you." He replied, "Better you be ashamed of me, than I be ashamed of the laws of the Church and nation, whereof you seem to be ashamed." Lothian said, "You desire to be involved in troubles." Sir Robert answered, "I am not so lavish of either life or liberty; but if the asserting of truth is an evidence thereof, it might be thought more strange."

He was remanded back to prison, where he continued until the 5th of May 1693, when he was liberated. The day before his liberation, he gave in a most faithful protestation and declinature to the Privy Council and Parliament of Scotland, with another letter of the same nature to Sir James Stuart, the Advocate. Upon his coming forth, he was so far from yielding one jot, that he left another protestation in the hands of the keepers of the Tolbooth, showing that, for his adhering to, and appearing for the fun-

damental laws and laudable constitution of our Church and covenanted nation, he had been unjustly apprehended and kept for
eight months close prisoner; and that for his own exoneration
and truth's vindication, he left this protestation, disdaining all engagements to live peaceably, which were a condemning himself of
former unpeaceableness, which he positively denies. In coming to
any terms respecting oaths or bonds with those who had broken covenants, overturned the Reformation, and destroyed the people of God,
or engaging unto a sinful peace with them, or any in confederacy
with them, he declared that he came out of prison merely because
of finding open doors, and desired his protestation to be inserted in
the ordinary register.

From his liberation to the day of his death, he continued most faithful in contending earnestly for "the faith which was once delivered
unto the saints" (Jude 3); and did greatly strengthen and encourage
the rest of the suffering remnant, with whom he continued in Christian
communion, both by his pious and godly example, and seasonable
counsel and advice, with respect to principles, and what concerned the
salvation of their souls, for the right carrying on of the Testimony for
the cause that they were owning. Some years before his death he
was taken ill with the stone, by which he endured a very sharp and
sore affliction, with a great deal of Christian patience and holy submission to the will of God; and when drawing near his journey's
end, he gave a faithful testimony to the Lord's noble and honourable
cause, which he had so long owned and suffered for. Sir Robert
having been most unjustly branded for running to some extremes in
principles, both before and after the Revolution, a copy of his own
dying testimony may perhaps be the best vindication that can be
produced. It is as follows:

"Though I have many things that might discourage me from
showing myself this way at such a time, when the Lord's controverted
truths, His covenanted reformation, and the wrestlings of His faithful
and slain witnesses, are things so much flouted at, despised and
buried, not only by the profane, but, alas! even by the ministers and
professors of this generation; yet I could not but leave this short line
to you, who of all interests in the world have been my greatest comfort. Being now come to the utmost period of my time, and looking
in upon my eternal state, it cannot be readily apprehended by
rational men, that I should dare to write anything, but according to
what I expect shortly to be judged, having had such a long time to

consider on my ways, under a sharp affliction. As for my case, I
bless God it is many years since my interest in Him was secured, and
under my afflictions from all airts, He hath been a present help in
time of my greatest need. I have been a man of reproach, a man of
contention; but praise to Him, it was not for my own things, but for
the things of my Lord Jesus Christ. Whatever were my infirmities,
yet His glory, the rising and flourishing of His kingdom, was still the
mark I laboured to shoot at. Nor is it now my design to vindicate
myself from the calumnies that have been cast upon my name; for
when His slain witnesses shall be vindicated, and His own glory and
buried truths raised up, in that day He will assuredly take away the
reproaches of His servants, and will raise and beautify the name of
His living and dead witnesses. Only this I must add; though I cannot but say that reproaches have broken my heart, yet with what I
have met with before, and at the time of Bothwell battle, and also
since, I had often more difficulty to carry myself humbly under the
glory of His cross, than to bear the burden of it. Oh! peace with
God, and peace of conscience, is a sweet feast!

"Now, as to His public cause, that He hath honoured you in some
measure to side with, stand fast therein. Let no man take your
crown, for it is the road He will take in coming to this poor land; and
praise Him for honouring such poor things as you are, as to make you
wish well to His cause, when Church, and State, and all ranks have
turned their backs upon it. My humble advice to you as a dying
brother, is, to stand still, and beware of all tampering with these
betrayers of the royal interest and concerns of Christ's kingdom, and
listen to no conferences with the ministers and professors of this
generation, till the public defections of this land, the doleful source
of all our ruin and misery, that sin of the public Resolutions, the compliance with Prelacy, the Church-ruining and dividing Indulgences
and Toleration, the present sinful course of vindicating all these
defections, and burying all the testimonies against the same; I say,
until these be acknowledged, and publicly rejected and disowned
both by Church and State.

"I die a true Protestant, and, to my knowledge, a Reformed
Presbyterian, in opposition to Popery, Prelacy, and malignancy, and
whatever is contrary to truth, and the power of godliness, as well
against flattering pretenders to unwarrantable zeal on the right hand,
as against lukewarmness on the left; adhering with my soul to the
holy sweet Scriptures, which have often comforted me in the house of

my pilgrimage, our Confession of Faith, our Catechisms, the Directory for Worship, Covenants, National and Solemn League and Covenant, Acknowledgment of Sins, and Engagement to Duties, with the Causes of God's Wrath, and to all the faithful public testimonies given against defections of old or late, particularly those contained in the Informatory Vindication, and that against the Toleration, and the two last Declarations emitted since that fatal Revolution; which testimonies I ever looked upon as a door of hope of the Lord's returning again to these poor backsliding lands.

"And now, my dear friends, let nothing discourage you in that way. The Lord will maintain His own cause, and make it yet to triumph. The nearer to the day, it may be the darker, but yet "in the evening time it shall be light;" and the farther distant ye keep from all the courses and interests of this generation, the greater will your peace and security be. Oh! labour to be in Christ, for Him, and like Him. Be much in reading of the Holy Scriptures, much in prayer and holy unity among yourselves. Be zealous and tender in keeping up your private fellowship for prayer and Christian conference, as also your public correspondence and general meetings. Go to them and come from them as those intrusted, really concerned and weighted, with Christ's precious controverted truths in Scotland ; and labour still to take Christ along with you to all your meetings, and to behave yourselves as under His holy and all-seeing eye when at them, that ye may always return with a blessing from His rich hand.

"Now, farewell, my dear Christian friends; the Lord send us a joyful meeting at His own right hand, after time ; which shall be the earnest desire, while in time, of your dying friend,

"R. HAMILTON.

"BORROWSTOUNNESS, *Sept.* 5, 1701."

And so, after he had come through many tribulations, and at last endured a series of sore bodily afflictions, in all which he was still kept faithful in testifying for the word of Christ's patience, he yielded up his life to that God who gave him his being, at Borrowstounness, October 21, being then fifty-one years of age. " Because thou hast kept the word of my patience, I also will keep thee from the hour of temptation, which shall come upon all the world, to try them hat dwell upon the earth."

Thus died another of Christ's faithful witnesses, Sir Robert Hamilton, who, for soundness in the faith, true piety, the real exercise of godliness, a conversation becoming the Gospel, and a true understanding of the right state of the Lord's cause, in every part thereof, accompanied with a true love and affection to, and zeal according to knowledge for the same, with steadfastness and stability to the last, maintained His cause against every opposition. He was equally superior to the influence of fear or flattery, and was preferable to most of the same rank in that age ; and without flattery it may be said, he was an honour to the name of Hamilton, and to his nation. The faithful Mr Renwick called him *Mi pater*, "my father," and ever had a high esteem and regard for him, as the contents of most part of his letters bear. Yea, in the very last letter he wrote, he accosts him thus : "If I had lived, and been qualified for writing a book, and if it had been dedicated to any, you would have been the man ; for I have loved you, and I have peace before God in that ; and I bless His name that ever I have been acquainted with you." And indeed he was not mistaken in him, for he was one who both professed and practised truth, was bold in Christ's cause, and had ventured life, wealth, reputation, and all, in defence thereof. He was of such constancy of life and manners, that it might be truly said of him, as was said of the Emperor Marcus Antoninus, *In omni vita sui similis, nec ulla unquam in re mutatus fuit : Itaque vere fuit vir bonus, nec fictum aut simulatum quicquam habuit.* "In every part of his life he was consistent, showing no tendency to fickleness in anything ; so that he was truly a good man, free from all falsehood or dissimulation."

AN ACROSTIC ON HIS NAME.

Sin wrought our death, death strikes, and none doth spare ;
It levels sceptres with the ploughing-share :
Raging among poor mortals everywhere.
Religion's lovers death must also own,
Or this brave soul his life had not laid down.
But weep not : Why ? Death challenges but dross ;
Eternal gain compensates temporal loss ;
Rest from his labour, sickness, grief, and pain,
This makes him happy, and our mourning vain.
Had he not reason rather to be glad
At death's approach, that life he never had
Must meet him there ? He enters now that land,
In view of which, believing, he did stand,
Longing for ling'ring death, still crying, Come,
Take me, Lord, hence, unto my Father's home.
O, faithless age ! of glory take a sight ;
Nor death nor grave shall then so much affright.

[At his death, the title became extinct for more than a hundred years. The next heir-male was Robert Hamilton of Airdrie, who belonged to a collateral branch of the family, but for some unknown reason he never assumed the baronetcy. In 1816, William Hamilton, afterwards known as Sir William Hamilton, the eminent Professor of Logic and Metaphysics in the University of Edinburgh, claimed and obtained the family honours ; and, a few years later, he succeeded in purchasing the old tower of Preston, or Prestonpans, the ancient seat of the family. He died on the 6th of May 1865, aged 68 years. —ED.]

William Veitch.

WILLIAM VEITCH was born at Roberton, in the shire of Lanark, in the year 1640. He was the youngest son of Mr John Veitch, who was minister of that place for about the space of forty-five years. His brothers were, John Veitch, who was minister of Westruther, in the shire of Berwick, fifty-four years ; James Veitch, who was ordained minister in Mauchline, in the shire of Ayr, in 1656 ; and David Veitch, the most eminent of them all, who was sometime minister at Govan, near Glasgow, and was contemporary and co-presbyter with the famous James Durham, and to whom Samuel Rutherford gave this testimony at his trials : "That the like of Mr David Veitch, in his age, for learning and piety, he had never known."

William, being laureate at Glasgow, in the year 1650, resolved to follow the study and practice of physic, as having so many brethren in the function of the ministry, and Episcopacy being apparently settled in the kingdom. But being then in the family of Sir Andrew Kerr of Greenhead, John Livingstone, minister of Ancrum (who frequented that house, as did other godly ministers), by many arguments dissuaded him from his intended design, and exhorted him

LANARK.

to follow the footsteps of his brothers, who were then much esteemed in the Church.

About the beginning of 1663, he went to Moray, where he was some time chaplain to Sir Hugh Campbell of Cawdor; but at the instigation of M'Kenzie, then Bishop of Moray, he was obliged, about September 1664, to leave this family. He returned to his father, then dwelling at Lanark, having been ejected from his own parish by the prelates: at which time he became acquainted with Marion Fairlie, whom he married; and who, being a woman eminent for religion, proved a great blessing to him afterwards.

In the year 1666, he was solicited, and prevailed upon, by Mr John Welch of Irongray, to join the honest party, who were so oppressed by the inhuman cruelties of Sir James Turner and his forces then lying at Dumfries. Accordingly, after the Galloway forces had taken Sir James prisoner, William Veitch and Major Lermont went west and joined them on a hill above Galston. Next day they sent him with forty or fifty horse to take up quarters in the town of Ayr.

After some respite, they marched up the Water of Ayr towards Douglas, and from thence to Lanark, Dalziel and his forces having come as far as Strathaven in quest of them; but hearing they were at Lanark, he turned his march after them. In the meantime, the

COMMUNION STONES OF IRONGRAY.

honest party being above 1500 horse and foot, it was thought proper that the National and Solemn League and Covenant should be renewed, which they did with great solemnity. Hearing that Dalziel approached, they concluded it would be best to abide some time there, as the heavy rains had made the Clyde impassable for him, except by boat, which was broken, and as fifty of their number might be able to stop his passage at the river ; which might serve as a dash upon the enemy, and an encouragement for friends to join them at that place. But unhappily a letter came from Sir James Stuart (Advocate, after the Revolution), to Messrs Welch and Semple, to come as near Edinburgh as possible, where they would get men and other necessaries. This made them break their resolution, and march for Bathgate, where, both night and snow coming on, they concluded to go forward to Colinton.

Having taken up their quarters, they consulted how they should do in answer to Sir James Stuart's letter, and at last voted Mr Veitch to go to Edinburgh, and converse with him anent the promised supply. This, against his own mind, he undertook, at the importunity of Colonel Wallace, and, having disguised himself with an old hat and cloak, and a baggage horse, Mr M'Cormick convoyed him on his road, minding him of several things to communicate to Sir James Stuart. He had gone but a little way, when he met a brisk young fellow, riding with a drawn sword in his hand, who asked, which way he came? He said, " Biggar way." " But," says he, " Did you not see all Colinton on fire ; I fear my house be burnt, for I hear the Whigs are come." Mr Veitch declared his ignorance of this ; and so they parted. Near Greenhill Park he met three women, who told him, that if he went by Greenhill House he was a dead man, for there Lord Kingston was placed with a party to intercept all the Whigs coming to the city. This made him take a by-road to Liberton Wynd. A little farther, he espied a sentinel on horseback, which obliged him to take Dalkeith way. But coming thither, some colliers told him, there was no getting to the city, all the ports being shut, and guards set upon them. This put him to a stand. Reason said, "You must turn back ;" Credit cried, " You must go forward, or lose your reputation." And so he proceeded till he was taken by two sentinels, and carried to the Potterrow Port, where he was examined by the captain of the guard, and, instead of being let into the city, was sent with a file of musketeers back to Lord Kingston. Mr Veitch, in this sad dilemma, had no other comfort but to put up his desires to God, that he would direct him what to do or say, if He had a mind to spare him any longer. He was examined by Kingston, to whom he gave soft answers. In the meantime, an alarm arising that the Whigs, as they called them, were approaching, Kingston called them to their arms ; whereupon Mr Veitch asked for arms, saying, he would go against them in the first rank. This made Kingston say he was a brave fellow.

After the hurry was over, with great difficulty he got off into the city ; but finding nothing could be done there, the next morning, hearing that the western forces marched toward Pentland Hills, he ventured to return by Liberton way toward the House o' Muir. When passing through Roslin Muir, on his way to Glencross Water, a party of Dalziel's horse had almost taken him. But being within cry of Captain Paton, now lieutenant of the rear guard of the western army, he beat back Dalziel's horse, and delivered him, saying, " Oh! sir, we took you for a dead man, and repented sore we sent you on such an unreasonable undertaking." As they rode toward Pentland Hills, they perceived their friends leaving the highway, marching their main body towards the hill, and a select body to the top. General Dalziel's coming from Currie through the hills occasioned this.

It was now about twelve o'clock, the 28th of November 1666. It having been snow and frost the night before, the day was pretty clear, and sunshine. In half-an-hour, Dalziel's select party, under Drummond, fell upon their select party, but was beaten back, to the great consternation of their army, hundreds of whom, as they were marching through the hills, threw down their arms and ran away; Drummond himself afterwards acknowledging, that if they had pursued this advantage, they had utterly ruined Dalziel's army. M'Lelland of Barmaguhen, and Mr Crookshanks commanded the first party, who took some prisoners; Major Lermont commanded the second party, who beat the enemy again. The Duke of Hamilton narrowly escaped by the Dean of Hamilton laying his sword upon the Duke's back, which warded off the countryman's blow. Dalziel sending up a party to rescue him, Major Lermont's horse was shot under him, but he, starting back to a dike, killed one of the four pursuers, mounted his horse, and came off in spite of the other three. The last encounter was just as daylight was going, when the Covenanters were broken, and Mr Veitch fell in amongst a whole troop of the enemy, who turned his horse in the dark, and violently carried him along with them, not knowing but he was one of their own. But they falling down the hill in the pursuit, and he wearing upwards, and the moon rising clear, for fear of being discovered, he was obliged to steer off; which they perceiving, cried out, and pursued, discharging several shots at him. But their horses sinking, they could not make the hill, and so he escaped, and came that night to a herd's house in Dunsyre Common, within a mile of his own habitation.

A little after this, William Veitch met with another remarkable deliverance at the laird of Auston's, when the enemy were there in pursuit of his son-in-law, Major Lermont. After this, he was obliged to abscond, and went to Newcastle, where he continued some time. Here he took the name of William Johnstone, his mother being of that family. After a considerable time of trouble, for he had the flux through the fatigue and cold he had got in the winter, he went home to visit his wife, where he again narrowly escaped, and returned to Newcastle. From thence he was invited to London, where he preached sometimes for Mr Blackie, particularly one Sabbath, on these words, " If thou hadst known, even thou, at least in this thy day, the things which belong unto thy peace ! but now they are hid from thine eyes " (Luke xix. 42). After the blessing was pronounced, some of the auditors cried, " Treason, treason ! " which surprised Mr

Blackie and the people, till one Colonel Blood stood up and said, " Good people, we have nothing but reason, reason :" and so he took off Mr Veitch, which ended the business.

Thus William Veitch travelled from place to place ; sometimes at London, sometimes at Nottingham, Chester, Lancaster, sometimes in Northumberland, especially in Redesdale, till the year 1671 ; when he was persuaded to bring his wife and family to that county, which he did, and settled for some time within the parish of Rothbury. But no sooner was he settled here, though in a moorish place, than the Popish gang stirred up enemies against him on account of his little meeting ; which obliged him to remove five miles farther up the country, to a place called Alnham-hall, where many out of curiosity frequented his preaching. Anabaptists also, who kept seventh-day Sabbaths, were punctual attenders.

Here he had no small success in the reformation of people's morals, several instances of which, for brevity's sake, must here be omitted. But the devil, envying these small beginnings, again stirred him up enemies, particularly one Justice Lorrain, who, at the instigation of the clergy, issued warrants to apprehend him. This failing, Lorrain in one of his drinking fits, promised to go in person next Sabbath, and put an end to these meetings. But not many hours after, he, by an unusual and strange accident, got his leg broken, so that he could not travel for many weeks.

This design being frustrated, Parson Ward of Kirk Harle went to the Bishop of Durham, and returned well armed, as he thought, against William Veitch, having orders to excommunicate him. But being detained by another curate, they drank all night together ; and that he might be home against Sabbath, he so tired his horse, that he was not able to get him on alone. He hired the herdman of Alnham to lead him, taking his club to drive him on ; but while he was unmercifully beating the poor beast, it, without regard to his coat, canon, or the orders he carried, kicked him on the cheek, till the blood gushed out. The boy that led the horse, seeing him fall, ran to a gentlewoman's house hard by, who sent out two servants with a barrow, and carried him in, where he had his wounds dressed. He lay there several weeks under cure, so they were again disappointed

Having continued there four years, Veitch removed to Stantonhall, where he found the country filled with Papists, and the parish-church of Long Horsley with a violent persecutor, Mr Thomas Bell. This man, though he was his own countryman, and had received many favours from Mr Veitch's brother, yet was so maliciously set against him, that he vowed to some professed Papists, who were urging him on against those meetings, that he should either ruin Mr Veitch or he him. And, as the event proved, he was no false prophet ; for he never gave over till he got Major Oglethorpe to apprehend him, which he did, on January 17, 1679.

After various changes, he was brought to Edinburgh, and taken before a committee of the Council, February 22, where Sharp was president. Sharp put many questions to him, to see if he could ensnare him. One of them was, " Have you taken the Covenant ?" He answered, " This honourable Board may easily perceive, I was not capable to take the Covenant when you and other ministers tendered it :" at which the whole company gave a laugh, which somewhat nettled the bishops. They asked, " Did you never take it since ?" He answered, " I judge myself obliged to covenant myself away to God, and frequently to renew it :" at which Bishop Paterson stood up and said, " You will get no good of this man ; he is all evasion." After other questions, he was required to subscribe his own confession, to which he assented, if without their additions, which at last, through Lundy's influence, they granted. And though they could prove nothing criminal against him, he was remanded to prison, and, by a letter from the King, turned over to the Criminal Court, which was to meet on March 18, but was adjourned to two different terms after, till the month of July, when sentence of death was to have been passed upon him, upon the old sentence in 1666. William Veitch, seeing his danger, prevailed with his friend, Mr Gilbert Elliot, to ride post to London ; where, not having access to the Duke of Lauderdale, he applied to Lord Shaftesbury, and got his case printed, and a copy given to each member of Parliament. The King being applied to, and threatened with a Parliamentary inquiry, wrote a letter and sent an express to stop all criminal process against him ; by which (procured by Lauderdale out of antipathy to Monmouth), who was minded to have interceded to the King for him, he was liberated, under a sentence of banishment to retire to England ; which he did in a short time after.

Whilst these affairs were transacting, Sharp was cut off at Magus Muir, the account of which it were needless to relate here. We may mention, however, a circumstance or two, in addition to what has been already stated :

After they had fired several pistols at Sharp in the coach, he was pulled out, and Balfour of Kinloch, having a brazen blunderbuss charged with several bullets, fired it so near his breast, that his gown, clothes, and shirt were burnt, and he fell flat on his face. They, thinking a window was made through his body, went off; but one of them, staying to tighten his horse's girth, heard Sharp's daughter call to the coachman for help, for her father was yet alive; which made him call back the rest, knowing, if he was not dead, their case would be worse than ever. Balfour coming to him while yet lying on his face, and putting his hat off with his foot, struck him on the head till his brains were seen; when, with a cry, he expired. Having searched his pockets, he found the King's letter for executing more cruelties, as also a little purse with two pistol bullets, a little ball made up of all colours of silk, like an ordinary plumb, and a bit of parchment, a finger breadth in length, with two long words written upon it which none could read, though the characters were like Hebrew or Chaldaic. These they took, but meddled with neither money nor watch. After Sharp was, by the Council's order, examined by two surgeons, the blue marks of the bullets were seen about his neck, back, and breast, where the clothes were burnt; but in all these places the skin was not broken; so that the wound in his head had alone killed him. This occasioned a universal talk, that he had got proof against shot from the devil, and that the forementioned purse contained the sorcery or charm. However, his brother got liberty to erect a marble monument to him, which, instead of honour—the usual object of such sumptuous structures—stands in St Andrews as an ensign of his infamy to this day.

The rising of Bothwell immediately followed this; but the Covenanters being defeated, an indemnity was granted to those concerned therein, one of the conditions being, that no minister should preach without liberty given, which no faithful minister could assent to. Monmouth, upon Shaftesbury's recommendation, inserted William Veitch's name in the roll with the rest; but, by Bishop Paterson's means, his name was excluded. This made Monmouth say that he should get the matter done another way, as soon as he came to London; which coming to Lauderdale's ears at Court, by means of Lord Stair, the King signed a warrant, turning the sentence of death to banishment from Scotland; and so he was liberated, and returned back to his old habitation in England.

Not long after his return, hearing they intended in these parts to apprehend him again, he retired westward to the English borders, where he frequently preached at Keelderhead, Wheeler, Causeway, Deadwater, and other places.   The wonderful success which the preaching of the Gospel, by ministers retiring thither under the persecuting period, had to the repressing, yea, almost extinguishing the feuds, thefts, and robberies, so natural to these places and people about the borders, is worthy of serious observation.   Before William Veitch's apprehension, he had preached with much success at Blewcairn, in Lauder Muir, and several places in the Merse and Teviotdale ; especially at Fogo Muir, upon these words, " Thou shalt arise, and have mercy upon Zion : for the time to favour her, yea, the set time, is come" (Psalm cii. 13).

After this Veitch had a very remarkable escape from his enemies. He went to Berwick upon a line from Mr Temple, but the news coming in the meantime, that the Earl of Argyle had escaped from Edinburgh, caused no small confusion in Berwick, so that he left the town ; and having surmounted several difficulties, by means of his good friends and acquaintances, he got to the house of Mr Ogle, the outed minister of Berwick, now six miles from the place.   He desired him to stay till Sabbath was over, and perform an old promise, of giving a sermon to a Mr Hall and his lady, to which he assented.   But going to bed at Mr Ogle's, he, being weary, fell asleep, and dreamed that his house at Stanton Hall, more than thirty miles distant, was on fire ; which made him awake in no small consternation.   He resolved to take journey home ; but it not being time to rise, he fell asleep, and dreamed the same thing over again, awaking all in a sweat.   The doubling of the dream he took for a clear call to go home ; and telling the dream to Mr Ogle, who called it a mere fancy, he excused himself the best way he could to the laird and lady, before whom he was to preach, and went off.   About a mile and a half from his own house, he met Pringle of Torwoodlee's man, who said, " O Sir, you are long looked for at your house ;" which made him ask what was the matter ? and if his family were all well !   He answered, " Yes ; but," says he, " there is a stranger (viz. Argyle), and your wife longs to see you, and we have been for two days sending about the country to find you."   After some converse with the Earl, he undertook, with his wife's consent, to do his best for bringing him safe to London ; and, under the name of Mr Hope, he took him along with him to Midburn Grange, where he was to preach that Sabbath.   On Monday he took

ST NICHOLAS' CHURCH, NEWCASTLE.

him to a friend's house between Newcastle and Newburn, where he
left him, and going to Newcastle, bought three horses at his own
expense, the Earl being then scarce of money. After this they came
to Leeds, and then to Rotherham, where they stayed one night.
From thence they set off, and at last arrived safe at London. After
staying some time in London, Argyle went to join Monmouth in Holland, and Mr Veitch returned to his house in Stanton Hall. But the
thing becoming known, he narrowly escaped being taken; and after
lurking sometimes in one place, and sometimes in another, he was
obliged to go over secretly to Holland, where he met with old friends
and acquaintances, the Duke of Monmouth, the Earl of Argyle, the Earl
of Melvill, Hume of Polwarth, Pringle of Torwoodlee, and Sir James
Stuart. Monmouth and Argyle having agreed to make a simultaneous
descent, the one on England, and the other on Scotland, several o
their friends were sent over *incognito*, to warn their friends in both
kingdoms to make ready. It was Veitch's part to give notice to
Northumberland and the Scottish Borders. He had a verbal commission from Argyle to procure money for buying arms, drums,
colours, horses, and recruiting men, especially Parliamentarian
officers; somewhat of all which he did. But the matter taking air,
he was obliged to hide himself near Redesdale Head, even from his

PORTRAIT OF WILLIAM III.

very friends, till the season of appearing came, when he narrowly escaped being taken, while hid on Carter Fell, covered with only heather, Colonel Struthers and Meldrum's troop being out in quest of him and others.

This enterprise having failed, Argyle being defeated and taken in Scotland, and Monmouth in England, the design came to nothing. Mr Veitch, besides his time and trouble, lost about £120 sterling, and interest; and although Argyle's son, the late Duke, made repeated promises to reimburse him, yet never was there anything of this kind done, his kindness being soon forgotten.

Prior to this affair of Monmouth and Argyle, one tyrant was cut off to make way for another. As the death of King Charles II. is related by so many historians, it were needless to relate it here : only the following circumstances seem more full, and somewhat different from the accounts of most writers in that period. The Duchess of Portsmouth, the King's harlot (for so we may call her), being, by the Duke of York's direction, to give the King a treat on Sabbath night, was well supplied by him with wines, especially claret, which the King loved. After he was drunk, they bribed his servant to put a dose of poison in his coffee, and advised the Duchess to keep him all night ; and knowing that, when he first awaked in the morning, he usually called for his snuff, they hired the Duchess's chamber-maid to put poisoned snuff into his box. Accordingly, having drunk the coffee at night, in the morning he awoke, and cried out he was deadly sick, and called for his snuff-box, and took a deal of it. Then growing worse, he called for his servant to put on his clothes; which being done, he staggered and got to the window, and leaning on it, cried, "I am gone, I am poisoned, get me to my chamber." The Duke of York, getting notice, came running undressed to lament his fate; saying, "Alas! Sir, what is the matter?" To whom he answered, "Oh! you know too well;" and was in a passion at him. In the meantime, he called for an antidote against poison which he had got from a German mountebank; but that could not be found, being taken out of the way; neither was his physician to be got, being, as was thought, out of town. All things failing, he, being so enraged, made at his brother. But all entries being secured, in the meantime the Duke seeing him so mad, and that the poison was not likely soon to do his turn, set four ruffians on him, which made him cry out; but they soon choked him with his cravat, and beat him instantly on the head, so that he died. It is said his head swelled bigger than two heads, and his body stank, so that they were obliged to take him out in the night, and bury him privately. The most judicious historians that I have read on this subject, grant that Charles II. was poisoned by the direction of the Papists; but Bishop Burnet in his History, and Dr Welwood in his Memoirs, say the King had no suspicion that he was poisoned. Burnet insinuates, that his harlot, the Duchess of Portsmouth, and her confessor, were the instruments, and that the King died in good terms with his brother. Dr Welwood, who gives both sides, relates the following story: some time the King, having drunk more liberally than usual, retired to the next room, in the castle of Windsor, wrapped himself in his cloak, and fell asleep on a couch. He was but a little time returned to the company, when a servant belonging to one of them lay down on the same couch, and was found stabbed dead with a poignard; nor was it ever known who did it. The matter was hushed up, and no inquiry made   But, as to the circumstance of his death, Mr Veitch no doubt had the advantages to know, as well as many others, being often at London, and acquainted with some who frequented the Court.

After the defeat of Monmouth and Argyle, William Veitch was obliged to lurk for some time in a wood near Newcastle, until the storm was a little calmed; then he ventured to Newcastle, to see his wife and family, where he met with some of his Scots relations and some other good people of the town who were also there. They spent a part of the night in prayer and mourning over the sad case that the Church and nation were now in, the most part fearing they were never like to see good days again.

After this Mr Veitch, being wearied with such toil and confinement, went with a Nottingham merchant to Yorkshire, and stayed some time in a town called South Cave. From thence he was invited to preach to the people of Beverley. Here he met with another remarkable deliverance; for the mayor and aldermen compassed the house where he was preaching, and caused the clerk to mark down all their names. Mr Veitch, by means of his landlord, got off under the name of William Robertson; and so he escaped and hid himself some time among bushes, and then went to a man's house two miles from town, where he preached out the rest of his sermon to some of the people that followed, and then went home with his landlord.

Mr Veitch, while in Yorkshire, met with another deliverance; for a Scots Jesuit Priest procured a warrant to apprehend him; but, by a divine providence, he escaped their hands, and so went toward Newcastle. From Newcastle he went to Nottingham. While there, King James's indemnity and liberty were proclaimed, and then he had a call from the people of Beverley to be their minister, which he complied with. At this place he had a numerous congregation, and several times he was invited to preach at Hull, six miles from thence. The people declared there was never such a reformation. Some of the justices of the peace, being Papists, were greatly incensed against it, and used all means to stop his preaching there, but were opposed by the people. Mr Veitch never had more satisfaction in his ministerial work, as he himself says, than in that place.

Having preached six or seven months, and having wrought a great reformation at Beverley among the people, he was strongly invited to his native country, by those who had accepted of the Toleration then granted. His wife being anxious for his return, he took his leave of Beverley, a pleasant city, after having preached his farewell sermon, when there were many tears shed. In his way home, he visited his friends at Dartoun, who persuaded him to stay some time, where he settled a congregation, and left Mr Long as his successor to that people. After all impediments were removed, he returned to his native land; where the people in the parishes of Oxnam, Crailing, Eckford, Linton, Morebattle, and Hownam, gave him a call to preach to them at Whitton Hall; to which charge he entered in April 1688. Here he continued that summer, and sometimes was invited to preach at Redesdale, on the English side. But the Prince of Orange having landed in England, November 4, 1688, the ministers of Scotland who had been outed, thought it expedient to meet at Edinburgh, and called all their brethren to attend there and deliberate.

It fell out unexpectedly to William Veitch, that the meeting voted him to preach the next day after he came, in the new meeting-house over against Liberton Wynd. This he was most averse to, being a stranger to the transactions, for the most part, in Scotland for upwards of thirty years. But his reasons not being heard, he was so perplexed what to do, that till eight o'clock, he could not find a text. At length falling upon Psalm cxix. 118, "Thou hast trodden down all them that err from Thy statutes: for their deceit is falsehood," he was taken up the whole night in thinking on it, without going to bed. When he came to the pulpit, seeing sixteen of the old ministers sitting, and the congregation greatly increasing, his fear increased also. However, he delivered his thoughts upon the subject, with respect to the present circumstances, with such freedom and plainness, as offended the prelates, who afterwards sent him a message, that ere long they resolved to be even with him. All the answer he returned them was, to put on their spurs. Upon the other hand, he seemed to give some offence to the godly party, by some free expressions he used with respect to the present government, if Presbytery was erected.

When the Presbyterian Church was restored, he had calls to several parishes—viz., one to Crailing, another to Melrose, and a third to Peebles, which he was persuaded, by the Earl of Crawford and others, to embrace. Yet he met with such opposition there, from the old Duke of Queensberry, that the Church was so overawed as to loose him from that charge. Having now received a call from Edinburgh, one from Paisley, and another from Dumfries, the Assembly, hearing his aversion to Edinburgh, after he had been minister of Peebles full four years from September 1690, voted him to Dumfries in 1694. He left Peebles with great reluctance, not only with respect to the parish, but the country round about; and, upon a new call, struggled to be back; but lost it only by four voices. However, he lost all his legal stipend the four years, which, with the expense of suit, amounted to 10,000 merks.

Mr Veitch's hard usage from the Assembly, with their illegal re-

DUMFRIES.

moving him merely to please the Duke, and their sending him to Dumfries, made him resolve to leave the nation, and refuse to submit to their sentence. In the meantime, his old friends in England, hearing this, sent a gentleman to bring him back to them. Mr Veitch went with him; but he refused to settle with them, till he had handsomely ended with the Commission of the Church, to which the matter had been referred. Upon his return, they persuaded him to submit; which at last he did, and continued minister in Dumfries until the day of his death, which occurred about the year 1720, being then about eighty years of age.

From the foregoing account two things are conspicuous: 1. That the whole of William Veitch's life, at least during the persecuting period, was attended with a train of remarkable occurrences of Divine providence; 2. That he must have been a most powerful and awakening preacher, from the influence he had upon the manners or morals of those who attended his sermons. Nor is it any disparagement to him that a certain black-mouthed calumniator, in his "Presbyterian Eloquence Displayed," has published to the world, that he murdered the bodies as well as the souls of two or three persons with one sermon, because, says he, "preaching in the town of Jedburgh, he declared, 'There are two thousand of you here, but I am sure eighty of you will not be saved;' upon which three of his ignorant hearers despatched themselves soon after." Indeed, it must be granted that, after the Revolution, in the latter end of his life, he became somewhat inimical and unfriendly to some of those who professed to own and adhere to the same cause and testimony which he himself had contended and suffered for. Whether this proceeded from the dotage of old age (as some would have it), or from mistaken principles, or anything else, we cannot, and shall not at present determine.

John Balfour of Kinloch.

OHN BALFOUR of Kinloch, sometimes called Burley, was a gentleman in the north of Fife. He joined with the more faithful part of our late sufferers; and although he was by some reckoned none of the most religious, yet he was always zealous and honest-hearted, courageous in every enterprise, and a brave soldier, seldom any escaping that came into his hands. He was the principal actor in killing that arch-traitor to the Lord and his Christ, Prelate James Sharp. After this, his goods and gear were inventoried by the Sheriff, and he was forfeited in life and fortune, and a reward of 10,000 merks offered to any who could apprehend him.

He was a commanding officer at Bothwell and Drumclog. At Drumclog he was the first who, with his party, got over the ditch upon Claverhouse and his dragoons. At Bothwell he was still among the more faithful part, and at the fight behaved with great gallantry. At the meeting at Loudon Hill, dispersed May 5, 1681, it is said that he disarmed one of the Duke of Hamilton's men with his own hand, taking a pair of fine pistols belonging to the Duke from his saddle, and telling him to inform his master that he would keep them till

PORTRAIT OF JOHN GRAHAM OF CLAVERHOUSE.

they met. Afterwards, when the Duke asked his man, what he was like? he told him that he was a little man, squint-eyed, and of a very fierce aspect. The Duke said, he knew who it was, and withal prayed, that he might never see his face, for, if he should, he was sure he would not live long.

After this Balfour lurked mostly amongst his suffering brethren, till a little before the Revolution, when he went over to Holland, where he joined the Prince of Orange, afterwards King William III. Here, having still a desire to be avenged upon those who persecuted the Lord's cause and people in Scotland, it is said that he obtained liberty from the Prince for that purpose, but died at sea before the arrival of the ship in Scotland, whereby that design was never accomplished, and so the land was never purged by the blood of them who had shed innocent blood, according to the law of the Lord, "Whoso sheddeth man's blood, by man shall his blood be shed" (Gen. ix. 6).

Messrs Robert Traill.

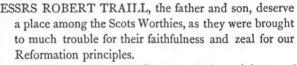

ESSRS ROBERT TRAILL, the father and son, deserve a place among the Scots Worthies, as they were brought to much trouble for their faithfulness and zeal for our Reformation principles.

Old Mr Robert Traill, one of the ministers of Edinburgh, along with Mr James Guthrie and others, met in a private house in Edinburgh, and assisted in drawing up an humble address and supplication to the King; but before it was finished, they were apprehended by the Government, and committed prisoners to the Castle of Edinburgh, without a hearing. Matters went so high at that time, that a simple proposal of petitioning the King for a redress of grievances was reckoned criminal.

He was brought, August 1661, before the Lords of Articles, and afterwards before the Parliament, where he delivered an excellent speech in his own defence, and pointed out the cruelty and injustice then exercised, and the many false accusations that were exhibited against him and his reverend brethren at that time; which may be found in Wodrow's History. After seven months' imprisonment, he wrote to Mr Thomas Wylie, minister at Kirkcudbright, and says, "I need not write to you how matters go here. This I must say, your imprisoned brethren are kindly dealt with by our good Lord, for whose cause and interest we suffer; and if any of us be straitened, it is not in Him, for we have large allowance from Him, could we take it. We know it fares the better with us, that you, and such as you, remember us at the throne. We are waiting from day to day to see what men will do with us; at best we are expecting banishment; but our sentence must proceed from the Lord; and whatsoever it shall be, it is good from Him; and whithersoever He is willing to send us, we know that He shall be with us, and shall let us know, that the earth is His, and the fulness thereof." Such was the resigned Christian temper of these Worthies. He was afterwards banished, and took refuge in Holland.

On the 19th of July 1677, their persecuting fury also broke out against his son Robert. Being accused of holding field-conventicles, he was brought before the Council, where he acknowledged that he had kept house-conventicles. But being asked, if he had preached at field-conventicles, he referred that to proof, because the law made it criminal. He owned that he had conversed with John Welch when on the English Border, and that he was ordained to the ministry by Presbyterian ministers at London in the year 1660. But, refusing to clear himself by oath, he was sent to the Bass; Major Johnstone getting £1000 Scots for apprehending him.

We have no account at what time he was released; but he was afterwards a useful minister to a congregation of dissenters in London; where he continued many years, and laboured with great diligence, zeal, and success. Here he published his Vindication of the Protestant Doctrine of Justification (prompted thereto by his zeal for that distinguishing doctrine of the Reformation) and his Sermons on the Throne of Grace and the Lord's Prayer, at the earnest desire of those who heard them. His sermons on Heb. x. 20-24, entitled, "A Steadfast Adherence to the Profession of our Faith," were published after his death, at the request of many of his hearers.

The simplicity and evangelical strain of the works of Mr Traill have been savoury to many, and will ever be so, while religion and Scripture doctrine are in request.

MARTYRS' MONUMENT, GREYFRIARS CHURCHYARD.

Conclusion.

DURING the twenty-eight years of persecution in Scotland, above 18,000 people, according to calculation, suffered death, or the utmost hardships and extremities. Of these 1700 were shipped to the plantations, besides 750 who were banished to the northern islands, of whom 200 were wilfully murdered. Those who suffered by imprisonment, confinement, and other cruelties of this nature, were computed at or about 3600, including 800 who were outlawed, and 55 who were sentenced to be executed when apprehended. Those killed in several skirmishes or on surprise, and those who died of their wounds on such occasions, were reckoned to be 680. Those who went into voluntary banishment to other countries were calculated at 7000. About 498 were murdered in cold blood, without process of law, besides 362 who were by form of law executed. The number of those who perished through cold, hunger, and other distresses, contracted in their flight to the mountains, and who sometimes even when on the point of death were murdered by the bloody soldiers, cannot well be calculated, but will certainly make up the number above specified.

Yet, like the Lord's Church and people of old, while in Egypt, the more they were oppressed, the more they grew, the blood of the martyrs being always the seed of the Church. Yea, to the honour of truth, and the praise of that God whom they served, they were so far from being spent, wasted, or eradicated, that at the Revolution they could raise a regiment in one day, without beat of drum, the ancient motto of the Church of Scotland, *Nec tamen Consumebatur*, being verified now as evidently as ever : " Behold the bush burned with fire, and the bush was not consumed."

" Wherefore, seeing we also are compassed about with so great a cloud of witnesses, let us lay aside every weight, and the sin which doth so easily beset us, and let us run with patience the race that is set before us " (Heb. xii. 1).

" These are they which came out of great tribulation, and have washed their robes, and made them white in the blood of the Lamb " (Rev. vii. 14).

" I saw, under the altar, the souls of them that were slain for the word of God, and for the testimony which they held : and they cried with a loud voice, saying, How long, O Lord, holy and true, dost Thou not judge and avenge our blood on them that dwell upon the earth ?" (Rev. vi. 9, 10).

" Here is the patience of the saints : here are they that keep the commandments of God, and the faith of Jesus" (Rev. xiv. 12).

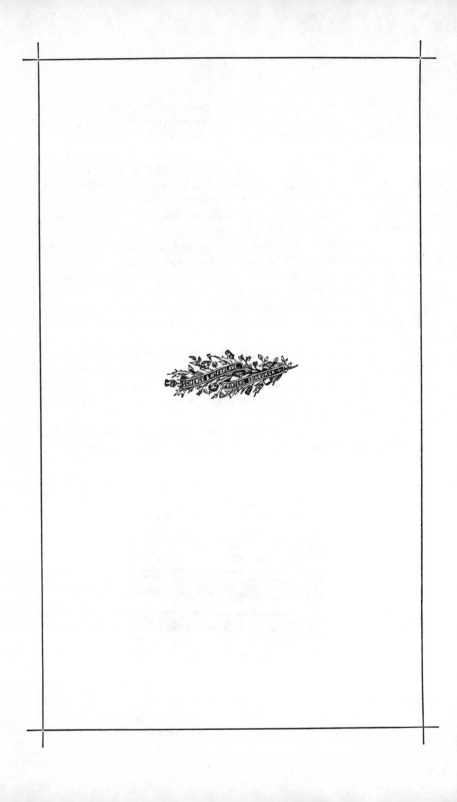

SCHENCK & McFARLANE, PRINTERS, EDINBURGH.